AMERICAN SECRET PROJECTS 3

AMERICAN SECRET PROJECTS 3

US Airlifters since 1962

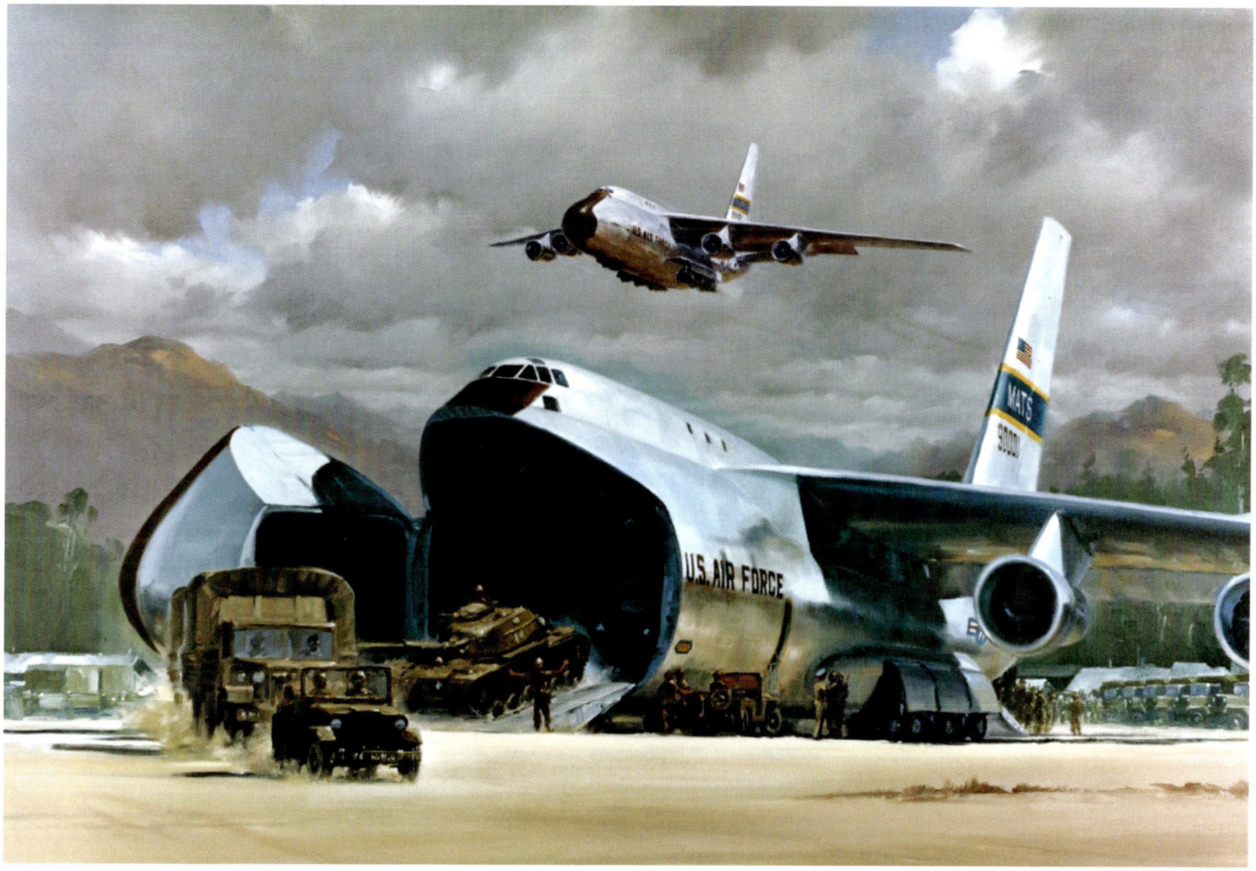

GEORGE COX AND CRAIG KASTON

Crécy Publishing Ltd

American Secret Projects
U S Airlifters since 1962
George Cox and Craig Kaston

This book is dedicated to the design and industrial genius of the American aviation industry, which has developed an amazing panoply of aircraft, changing the whole course of air transportation, both passenger and freight, military and civil.

First published in 2020 by Crécy Publishing

A CIP record for this book is available from the British Library

Printed in Turkey by Pelikan Print

ISBN 9781910809334

Crécy Publishing Ltd
1a Ringway Trading Estate, Shadowmoss Rd
Manchester M22 5LH
Tel (0044) 161 499 0024

www.crecy.co.uk

FRONT COVER
This specially commissioned artwork depicts the Boeing C-XX airlifter concept from 1976 as it might have appeared in service in the early 1980s. Illustrating MAC's around the clock operations, these aircraft of the 63rd MAW are in action at Norton Air Force Base with an Army CH-47C being loaded in the foreground. *Artwork by Daniel Uhr*

TITLE PAGE
The frontispiece to *American Secret Projects 2* featured art by Douglas's R. G. Smith. Painted in 1948, it depicted the loading of outsized equipment in a C-124 airlifter.

Scarcely fifteen years later, the advances in technology and size are unmistakable as the proposed Douglas C-5 (Model D-916) is depicted disgorging combat equipment at a forward operating location. No less remarkable is the advancement in R. G. Smith's technique as his gouache paintings became the public face of the Douglas Aircraft Company in the 1960s. *Boeing*

REAR COVER
TOP: A model of Boeing's Model 1050 (named internally by Boeing as the C-16); the trijet entry into the 1980 C-X competition. McDonnell Douglas's D-9000 design won and was built as the C-17 Globemaster III. *Boeing*

MIDDLE Top view of the Northrop SOFTA (Special Operations Forces Transport Aircraft), designed at the company's Advanced technology Design Center at the B-2 Division in the early-1990s. *Courtesy of Northrop Grumman Corporation*

BOTTOM Douglas's full-scale D-902/3 fuselage mockup, built in 1963. Built to demonstrate the loading of various pieces of cargo such as tanks, bridging equipment, fuel trucks and helicopters, the mock-up did not attempt to represent the wings and engines. *Boeing*

REAR FLAP
TOP Sir George Cox *Author*
BOTTOM Craig Kaston *Chad Slattery*

Contents

Introduction

The effectiveness of military strategy has always been dependent on the ability to move armies and their equipment rapidly and to support them thereafter. Over the centuries the horse, the wagon, the ship, the railway and the truck have all played their part in transforming the nature of military strategy. Experience during the Second World War made it clear that air transportation represented a similar advance.

Not only was the USA called upon simultaneously to fight battles in Europe, Africa, Asia and the Pacific, but it was also clear in the aftermath of the war that to enable it to project power and maintain global peace America would have to maintain permanent bases in many parts of the world. It also needed to be able to deploy large forces at short notice.

This growing need for enhanced deployment/support capability led to a new requirement: an aircraft designed from the outset to transport fully equipped troops or to carry large, heavy and irregularly shaped cargo that could be easily loaded and unloaded. The aircraft also had to be robust enough to operate in near-battlefield conditions. It heralded the birth of the airlifter.

Over the following decades, aerospace technology would keep advancing and military requirements would keep changing. This would result in an endless stream of aircraft designs, surprisingly few of which would ever see the light of day. For every aircraft that made it into production and reached operational service, many others would only make it as far as an experimental prototype or a non-flying mock-up. But behind these there were scores more: imaginative designs that would never be seen outside the aircraft manufacturers' advanced design offices. Even the successful designs were usually the outcome of earlier, unrevealed proposals that had been progressively refined.

Unlike proposals for new fighters or bombers, the military could not afford, or perhaps saw no reason, to order the construction of prototypes of several competing designs for airlifters. The choice therefore had often to be made off the drawing board. However, the decision as to which aircraft should be ordered was made not just made on the basis of estimated (or claimed) performance, but on issues such as confidence in meeting the specification, the perceived ability of the prime contractor to fulfil a large production order, cost, available funding and competition with other military programmes, as well as political considerations such as to where the work should be placed.

As a consequence, many of the failed designs described in this book were only 'failures' in the sense that the military was never persuaded to buy them. They inevitably include many proposals that would have turned into fine aircraft – and perhaps a few embarrassing failures.

Together all these designs chart the history of both aeronautical progress and military strategy over a fascinating seventy-year period.

Scope and structure

Our previous volume, *American Secret Projects 2*, dealt with developments from the emergence of the airlifter at the start of the Second World War up until 1961. This companion second volume, *American Secret Projects 3*, continues the story from 1962 to the present day. Together they give a complete history of American military airlifter design, including those projects that led to successful aircraft and those proposals that never saw the light of day.

The book covers strategic and tactical fixed-wing transports – the former concerned with moving troops and materiel around the globe, the latter with delivering them to the areas of conflict – but makes no attempt to cover all types of aircraft used for military transportation. Space alone forces the exclusion of the many unmodified civil airliners and business-class aircraft drafted into military service (such as the C-21 Learjet), small, special-task aircraft, non-US designs (such as the Shorts C-23 Sherpa), surface and ground-effects transports, flying boats, and rotary-winged aircraft. Any of these would justify a volume in their own right.

The projects and proposals are covered, as far as possible, in chronological order, looking at the historical context of each period and how this defined the capabilities that were sought. Events such as the Second World War, the Berlin Airlift, the Korean War, the Cold War, and the Vietnam War all had a big influence on military requirements. Some projects were the initiative of a particular aircraft manufacturing company, while others were prepared in response to an official invitation to tender.

Within each era, designs are grouped according to either their intended purpose or the official specification against which they were being submitted, enabling the reader to contrast the competing propositions. The individual projects are described and are illustrated exclusively with original factory drawings, company artwork and promotional models. All figures and dimensions are therefore given in their original form, with metric conversions provided in every case, and a Glossary is provided as an appendix.

To cater for the international nature and breadth of reader backgrounds, a 'primer' chapter is included to summarise the history of US military air transportation, setting it within the framework of its evolving command structure. Further chapters are devoted to three specialised categories of airlifter, where developments span several decades. One of these covers the adaptation of large-scale airlifter airframes for special purposes; another looks at the specialised demands of delivering cargo and personnel to ships at sea; and a third looks at how airlifters were planned to be used to explore the potential for nuclear propulsion.

It should be stressed that neither book makes any pretence at being complete. Despite extensive research and unprecedented access to aircraft company records, there are undoubtedly many proposals for which no records have survived or, if they have, they have yet to be uncovered.

While the book confines itself to its specific subject – the design of the military airlifter in the United States – it must be remembered that this progression did not take place in isolation. The development of military airlifters has had a significant influence on the advance of aviation more generally. Not only is freight increasingly transported around the world by air, but the advances in military airframe design and engine technology have both influenced and benefitted from the parallel advances in commercial aviation.

The history of airlifter design is, therefore, a fascinating reflection of the advance of aviation more generally and of its influence on our lives and world events. This book and its companion second volume record for the first time the depth of creative thinking behind that history.

Sir George Cox
Buckinghamshire UK

Craig Kaston
Oxnard, California

Acknowledgements

This book has been made possible only by the generous and widespread support of many contributors, keen to see this hitherto under-explored subject accorded its proper place in aviation history. Special thanks must go to the Boeing Company for making available heritage materials for Boeing, Douglas and North American Aviation and to Northrop Grumman Aerospace Systems for the Northrop and Grumman archive information.

The authors are indebted to the following who so generously contributed their knowledge and insights:

Aerospace Projects Review and Scott Lowther

Air Force Historical Research Agency; Archie DiFante

Air Force Material Command (AFMC) History Office; Yancy Mailes (Director, History & Museum Program) and Ray Ortensie (Historian)

American Aviation Historical Society (AAHS); Hayden Hamilton

The Boeing Company and Mike Lombardi, Tom Lubbesmeyer and Pat McGinnis, Corporate Historians

Grumman History Center; John Eagan

Glenn L. Martin Maryland Aviation Museum; Stan Piet (Archivist)

The Greater St Louis Air & Space Museum; Nankivil (President)

Northrop Grumman Aerospace Systems (for heritage Northrop and Grumman materials); Tony Chong, Aerospace Systems Sector Historian

San Diego Air and Space Museum; Katrina Pescador (Director of Library & Archives), Debbie Seracini (Archivist) and Pam Gay (Librarian)

The Secret Projects Forum and Paul Martell-Mead (along with the many dedicated contributors to the website across the world)

Wright State University Libraries, Special Collections; Bill Stolz (Archivist for Reference and Outreach)

Individuals include: Mark Aldrich; Allen Arata; G. H. 'Gerry' Balzer; Bob Bradley; Tony Buttler; Tom Culbert (special thanks); Dennis R. Jenkins; the late Harry Gann (for early inspiration); Al Huber; Tony Landis; Ray Leader (Flight Leader); Mike Machat (special thanks); Paul Minert (special thanks); Terry Panopalis; Mick Roth; Caroline Sheen; Chad Slattery (special thanks); Bill Spidle; Dave Stern; Steve Thomas, Tommy H. Thomason; Jim Ueda; Tim White; Kane Wickham and Chris Yasaki.

Special thanks are due to the late John Aldaz, without whose encouragement the project would never have started, and without whose support it would never have been finished.

Thanks and appreciation are also due to Jeremy Pratt, Gillian Richardson and Charlotte Stear; and their production team at Crécy for all their patience and help.

Craig Kaston would also express his appreciation and gratitude to his late wife, Telka Marie who patiently and enthusiastically endured the process of the creation of these two books.

Chapter One

The Evolution of American Military Airlift

A brief overview

ABOVE Carrying the nose art 'the Roc VIII', this was the first of twenty-five Berlin Airlift missions for the C-74. Arriving on 19 August 1948, the C-74 showed the promise and drawbacks of the large airlifter: it carried 23 tons of flour but could fly only into the largest airport, Gatow, whose runway had just been extended to 6,000ft/1,829m. Even so, landings were described as 'precarious'. *Author collection*

Before looking at the many proposals described in the following pages, it is useful to recap the history of US military air transportation, enabling the various designs to be seen in context.

The origins of American military air transportation

By the time the Second World War broke out the US Army already possessed a limited number of passenger aircraft. These were assigned to individual Army bases and used mainly for high-level communications, much like winged staff cars. There was no 'transport command' as such, and little serious thought was given to using aircraft for the wholesale movement of troops, let alone military cargo. Indeed, there was no real reason to do so. There was no demand to deploy or to support forces in remote locations with great urgency. Accordingly, there were no purpose-designed military transports.

The start of the war changed this reality. With little advance warning, the US was faced with having to supply and support armed forces virtually around the globe. Fortunately, there was a solution to this sudden and urgent requirement. During the 1930s several aircraft companies developed passenger aircraft to serve the expanding civil market. These aircraft, such as the Douglas DC-3 and DC-4 and the Curtiss CW-20, represented the very forefront of aeronautical design. Pressed into military service, as the C-47, C-54 and C-46 respectively, more than 14,000 of these adapted airliners were produced over the next four years.

Despite their invaluable contribution to the war effort, these aircraft were not ideally suited to their military role. Designed to carry limited numbers of privileged passengers in luxury and operate from well-serviced airfields, they were never intended to be packed with troops or military equipment using hastily constructed airstrips with limited handling facilities. Of more significance, their cabins were restricted in height, and when the aircraft were parked their cargo decks were either sloped or 14ft (around 4.3m) above the ground. It rapidly became clear that a key requirement for a military transport was the ease with which the aircraft could be loaded and unloaded. Speed of turnaround proved to be a far more important performance criterion than flying speed. This lesson was further underlined shortly after the war during the Berlin Airlift, when in 1948/49 the same aircraft had to be used to supply everything required to keep a city running for nearly a year. With an aeroplane landing every thirty seconds, turnaround was everything.

Because of these shortcomings the post-war years gave rise to the birth of the true airlifter: an aircraft designed from the outset to meet a set of military requirements. However, in common with other categories of military aircraft these requirements were to prove both diverse and subject to continual change.

The result was a plethora of imaginative designs, covering everything from tactical assault aircraft to strategic logistic transports. This early design history is fully described in *American Secret Projects 2: Airlifters from the Second World War to 1961*.

The 1950s: The emergence of the purpose-designed military transport

The development of specialised military transports brought about substantial advances in the Air Force's airlift capabilities. Despite that, the Air Force struggled throughout this decade to keep pace with the growing and changing demands being put upon it. Having fought a further war in Korea, the United States was now supporting numerous bases around the globe while engaged in the Cold War and an arms race with the Soviet Union.

While these demands brought about a huge increase in military expenditure, and undoubtedly accelerated research and development, it also meant that airlifter proposals competed for funding with many other requirements. Compared with bombers and missiles, which were needed to provide a nuclear deterrent, and with interceptors to counter the potential Soviet threat, transport projects were up against tough competition within the Air Force's priorities, let alone the demands of the other services.

It is significant that the first swept-wing jet transport (the KC-135) was ordered into production not as an airlifter but as a high-speed tanker for air-to-air refuelling of nuclear bombers.

Nevertheless, several significant transport aircraft emerged from this period. Three stand out, and had an influence of the future of airlifter design as described in this book. The first was the Fairchild (earlier Chase) C-123. Having started life as an assault glider, it became the first rugged assault aircraft, setting a pattern for future aircraft in this category. The second was the Lockheed C-130, which emerged as the winner of a formal USAF competition for a tactical transport and would arguably go on to be the most successful military transport of all time. The third was the Lockheed C-141, which emerged from a further competition, this time for a high-speed, long-range transport. When it was ordered into production at the start of the 1960s, it had the distinction of being the Air Force's first purpose-designed jet-airlifter. Of more significance, its configuration – high-mounted swept wings, podded engines and T-tail – set the pattern for future generations of military transports, both in the USA and elsewhere.

How these aircraft emerged, and the many competing designs that fell by the wayside, are also described in *American Secret Projects 2: Airlifters from the Second World War to 1961*.

Despite all the advances of the 1950s and the substantial increase in airlift capability, the Air Force struggled throughout this era to keep pace with the demands put upon it. By the end of the decade the service was under great pressure. It also had to fend off strong lobbying in Washington on behalf of the airlines, which were pushing for all air transportation (other than close Army support) to be handed over to the private sector (which in the shape of the Civil Reserve Air Fleet was already carrying out much of this task). The Air Force managed to fend off this attack but was still faced with the challenge of urgently modernising its fleet.

It is against this background that the developments described in this book progressively built up today's airlift capability, although along a path that took many twists and turns.

The 1960s: New requirements, new solutions

The order for the C-141 promised to fill an important gap in the Air Force's capability. Even so, there were two important requirements that still needed fulfilling, and these would dominate design thinking during the coming decade. The first was the quest for size; the other was the perceived need (and opportunity) to introduce vertical take-off and landing (VTOL) capability.

Despite the fact that the C-141 weighed in at over five times that of the wartime C 54 and nearly twice the maximum take-off weight of the C-124, the aircraft was developed to serve the Air Force's heavy-lift needs in the 1950s – it still did not meet all of the Army's requirements. It was not simply a matter of payload, it was also the need for access to a much bigger cargo bay. The feasibility of building such an aircraft was facilitated by an important advance in propulsion technology in the form of the high-bypass-ratio turbofan, which enabled the construction of much larger and more efficient jet engines.

The competition to build the new giant aircraft proved both long and tortuous, with repeated rewriting of the competition's rules. It was to lead

ABOVE The Lockheed C-141 Starlifter proved to be a long-lived workhorse, serving the Air Force for five decades. A stretched C-141 is pictured here. *Mike Wilson collection*

eventually to an aircraft that would serve the Air Force's heavy-lift strategic needs for the following seventy years, albeit almost bankrupting the winner in the process. Ironically, the loser, Boeing, was to turn its attention to the commercial market, using its experience – and, importantly, the same engines – to build an airliner on a scale never seen before. Betting the company on the outcome, the Model 747 was to change the whole future of passenger air travel.

At the same time the quest for VTOL, which had seemed so promising at the start of the 1960s, was proving an elusive goal. A formal competition produced six different submissions fully meeting the specified requirements, together with several other 'non-compliant' proposals. They covered a wide range of ideas for attaining vertical capability, some already tried with experimental aircraft, others completely novel. A winner was chosen, the XC-142, but got no further than five prototypes. VTOL – as a practical operational prospect, using the technology of the time, proved to be feasible but not worth the complexities and the associated performance penalties in conventional flight. However, the effort was not wasted as it revealed that short take-off and landing (STOL) was a more readily attainable, and in many ways a much more worthwhile, goal. VTOL would eventually come, but not yet.

The 1970s: Exploiting the potential for STOL and other opportunities

With the Air Force's attention re-focussed on STOL, a further competition was initiated. This led to orders for two pairs of flying prototypes. Both performed impressively, but once again events overtook earlier plans. Neither resulted in a production order, but the experience from one was put to good use, leading eventually to the C-17, which together with the much-developed C-130 and the C-5, provides the basis of today's Air Force transportation capability.

The availability of large high-performance airlifters created possibilities for their wider adaptation and their consideration for potential new uses. Proposals were submitted for such purposes as airborne missile launchers, nuclear test beds and space-vehicle transporters. These proposals produced some of the largest and most bizarre aircraft concepts ever put forward.

Attention also turned to the possibility of utilising the greatly improved capability of transport aircraft for a further military role, namely supplying the Navy on the high seas. Given the much improved performance in terms range and landing/take-off performance, several proposals were put forward for operating large passenger/freight aircraft from aircraft carriers. Incredibly, this involved the kind of aircraft normally seen operating out of the world's major airports. While none of these advanced beyond the proposal stage, studies and some land-based flight tests demonstrated that this was not due to lack of feasibility.

1990s onwards: Potential futures and a new requirement

With the introduction of the C-17 in 1995, operating alongside the C-5 and much-developed versions of the C-130, the Air Force's basic transportation needs were at last fulfilled across the whole strategic and tactical range. Nonetheless, studies continued into the kind of aircraft that might eventually replace this fleet. These included aircraft of a size that would dwarf the C-5, together with completely new configurations made possible by advances in aerodynamics, computational capability and materials.

In the interim a new military requirement has arisen, not replacing any of the established capabilities but adding to them. Modern conflicts increasingly involve a need to insert and extract troops from within hostile territory, if possible remaining undetected throughout. This requires the application of low-observable (or 'stealth') technology to transport aircraft and the introduction of VTOL capability. Much of the work on such proposals remains shrouded in secrecy. This book describes some of the latest projects to be revealed, giving an indication of what the future might look like.

Between this volume and its earlier companion, *American Secret Projects 2: Airlifters from the Second World War to 1961*, the complete history of American airlifter design has been mapped out and illustrated by the hundreds of proposals put forward. The progress has been remarkable. The first military transport ordered into large-scale production, the C-47, carried a payload of 6,000lb/2,722kg; today's C-5M carries up to 460,000lb/208,652kg. The proposals and aircraft described demonstrate not just the remarkable progress that has been achieved but also the huge imagination of the engineers involved. It is a story that is far from ended.

ABOVE Although primarily regarded as a tanker, the McDonnell Douglas (now Boeing) KC-10A Extender (adapted from the commercial DC-10) has a very respectable cargo capacity for non-tactical applications. Every purpose-built tanker that the Air Force bought has a secondary cargo airlift capability. *Boeing*

BELOW Fifteen years in the making, the McDonnell Douglas/Boeing C-17 Globemaster III evolved from the 1970s YC-15 and replaced the C-141 as the jet airlifter used in the greatest numbers in the Air Force. *US Air Force photo by Staff Sgt Jacob N. Bailey*

Chapter Two
A Quest for Size

1960 to 1970, The way to the C-5

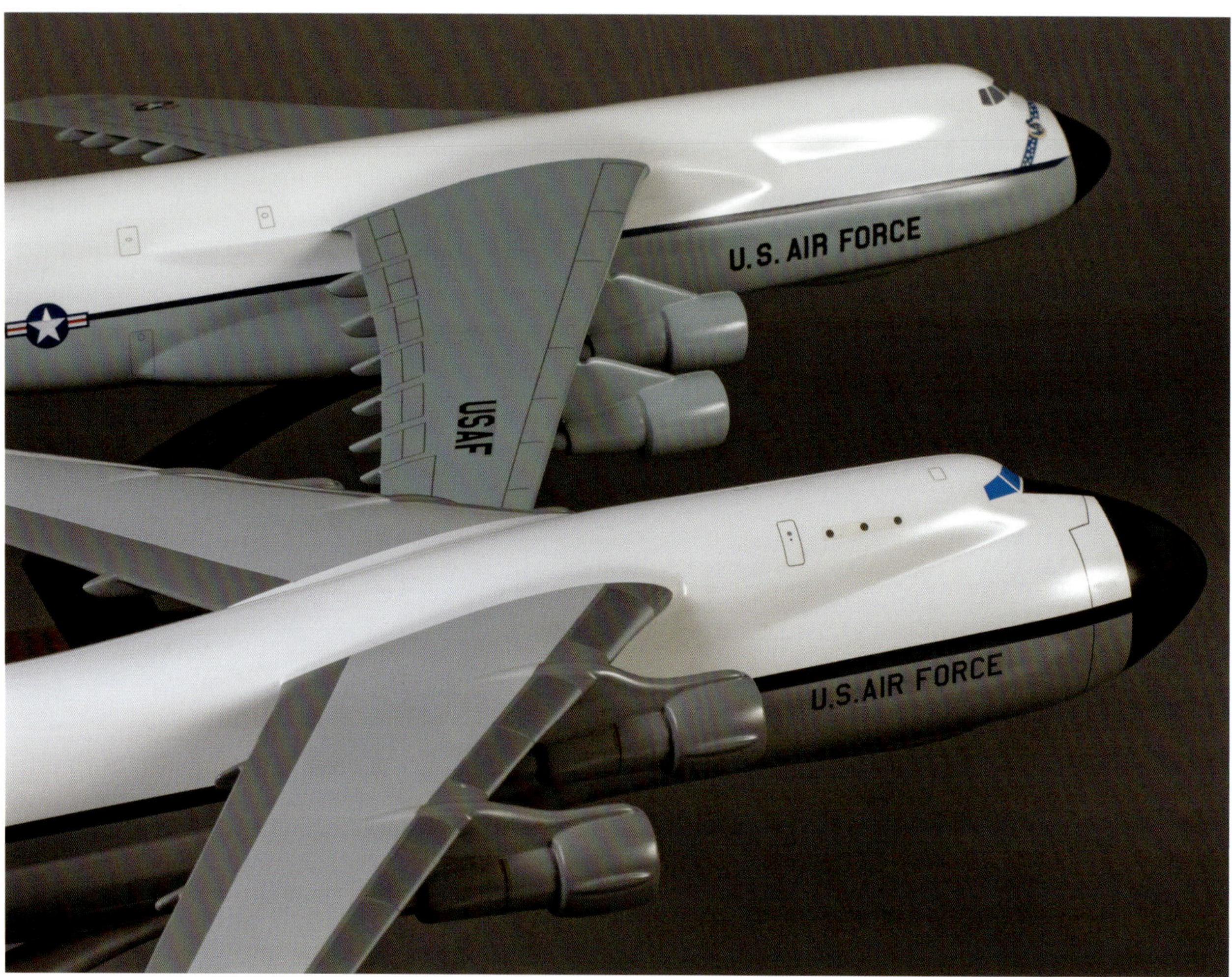

ABOVE Designed to the common C-5A specification, the finalist Boeing Model 750 (front) and Lockheed L-500 (rear) show many differences in fuselage and wing design. *John Aldaz collection*

Even while competing to meet what some considered the relatively modest Specific Operational Requirements of SOR 182 for the C-141, the major aircraft companies were already working on proposals for a new heavy lifter, which they believed the Air Force would have to acquire sooner or later. Moreover, by the early 1960s a general consensus had formed within the Air Force that the C-141 did not fully satisfy the requirements of MATS (Military Air Transport Service).

This marked the start of a path that eventually led to the C-5A, the airlifter that would provide the Air Force's strategic heavy-lift capability for the following seventy years. It was, however, a very torturous journey. It would start with attempts to find a straightforward replacement for the C-133 before leading to a series of increasingly complex specifications and competitions. These would absorb huge resources from – and put substantial strains on – leading US aircraft manufacturers. The competitions would also have a major bearing on engine development, ushering in the era of the very large, high-bypass-ratio jet engine. The path to the C-5A was also punctuated by scores of abandoned or rejected – albeit highly impressive – airlifter designs.

Initial designs to replace the C-133

Arguably, the industry's awareness of the looming problem of a deficiency in heavy-lift capability was ahead of that of either the Department of Defense (DoD) or the Air Force. The industry's response was a twofold approach. One element was to mount a campaign to educate the Army and the DoD that the C-141, although representing a big step up in performance from the C-124, was still limited. The C-141 could not handle the outsized cargo that was being carried by the C-133, which in any case was out of production and subject to continuing structural and powerplant problems. The second element of the two-prong effort was to design prospective aircraft which could overcome the combined C-141/C-133 limitations.

Both Boeing and Douglas had the advantage of already having successful long-range jet airliners in production; they naturally looked at how these might form a basis for the large heavy lifter that the Air Force needed. It was not a case of adapting an airliner for military use, as had been the norm in the past, but rather marrying a totally different, greatly enlarged fuselage to as much of the existing aerodynamic surfaces and engines as possible. Such a move, theoretically, would dramatically cut development time and costs.

In late 1961 both Boeing and Douglas put forward proposals along these lines. Boeing's was based on the C-135A Stratolifter, which it termed the 'Advanced C-135'; the Douglas proposal was based on the DC-8F, and designated the Model 2234C.

The 'Advanced C-135'

The Boeing 'Advanced C-135', known internally as the Model 738-21H, was based on the C-135A with a greatly enlarged upper fuselage, and made extensive use of elements of the existing aircraft.

In promoting the Advanced C-135, Boeing emphasised its ability to accommodate outsize loads, particularly when compared to the C-133. Although it was virtually the same length as the earlier aircraft, the volume of its cargo hold and its accessibility for loading and unloading were both much greater. A full-width loading ramp in the rear fuselage could be lowered to ground level for drive-in access. The ramp could also be partially lowered in flight to allow air-dropping.

The total volume of the main cargo hold was 17,070cu ft (485m^3) with another 1,420cu ft (40m^3) of under-deck space. The main deck was 12ft wide by 13ft high (3.36m by 3.66m), and had an unobstructed length of 84ft 2 in (25.67m), sufficient to load eleven standard 463L cargo pallets. Two additional pallets could be locked down on the loading ramp.

ABOVE **The Boeing Advanced C-135 airdropping heavy equipment.** *Boeing*

BELOW **A cutaway of the Boeing Advanced C-135 showing loading options.** *Boeing*

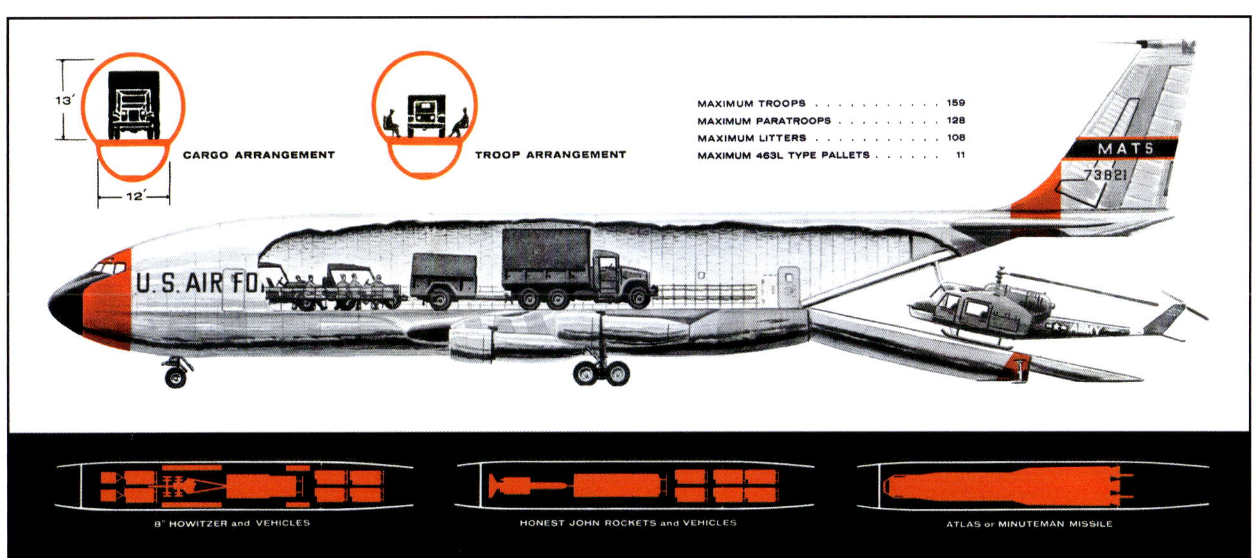

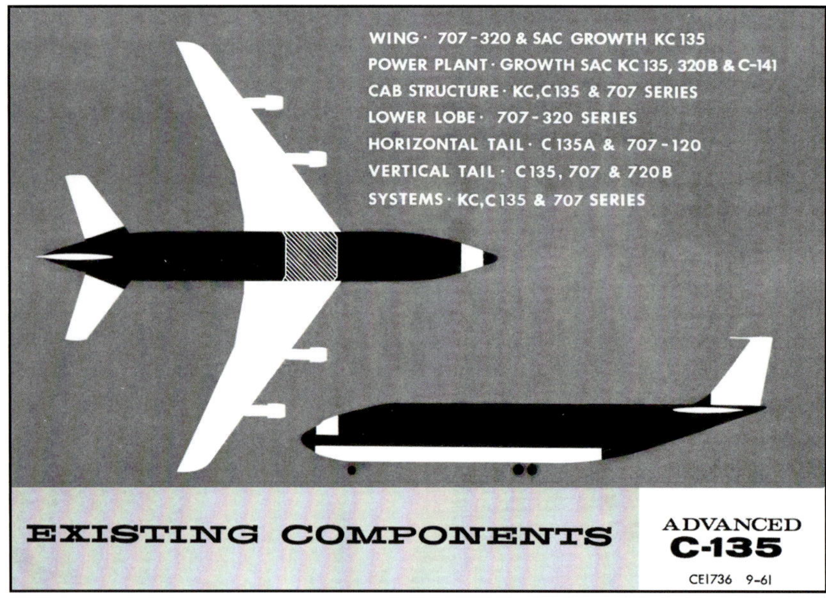

ABOVE The Advanced C-135's use of existing components (shown in white). *Boeing*

Boeing Model 738-21H 'Advanced C-135'	
Powerplant	4 x P&W TF-33-P-7 turbofans @ 21,000lb (93.5kN) thrust
Span	145ft 7in (44.40m)
Length	161ft 5in (49.23m)
Height	48ft 4in (14.74m)
Design TOW	336,000lb (152,544kg)
Overload TOW	371,000lb (168,434kg) limited to 2G
Payload	100,000lb (45,359kg)
Cargo volume	18,490cu ft (517.7m³)
Range	2,300mi (3,700km) with 100,000lb (45,359kg) payload 4,000mi (6,436km) with 60,000lb (27,240kg) payload

Compared to the C-133, the Advanced C-135 was also over 70% faster. As a consequence, Boeing promotional literature claimed that it could transport a whole infantry division with 35% fewer sorties than its predecessor.

Douglas Model 2234C

Like its Boeing equivalent, the corresponding Douglas approach to replacing the C-133 was to take a proven aircraft and modify the design of the basic fuselage to accommodate outsized loads. As the company put it: 'The Douglas Model 2234C is a direct growth from the DC-8F in all aspects except the enlarged fuselage and the method of loading. It offers great potential as a C-133 replacement if such replacement is to be accomplished on an interim, or off the shelf, basis.'

The design marked the first appearance of a full 'swing nose' on a Douglas heavy jet airlifter. A smaller tail ramp was also included to allow the air-dropping of cargo. The wing was essentially that of the D-1920/DC-8 but with increased leading-edge sweep, slightly greater span and a forward extension near the fuselage to accommodate extra fuel tanks. Powered by Pratt & Whitney JT3D-8A turbofan engines, the D-2243C's cruising speed was projected to be more than 470kt (867km/h). At 350,000lb (158,900kg), the gross weight was around 11% higher than the contemporary freight version of the DC-8.

Douglas Model 2234C	
Powerplant	4 x P&W JT3D-3B turbofans @ 18,000lb (80.6kN) thrust
Span	142ft 4in (43.40m)
Length	155ft (47.28m)
Height	48ft 3in (14.72m)
Gross weight	350,000lb (158,900kg)
Cruising speed	470kt (867km/h) plus
Cruising altitude	30,000ft (9,150m)
T/O distance	8,200ft (2,500m)

BELOW The Douglas Model 2243C. *Boeing*

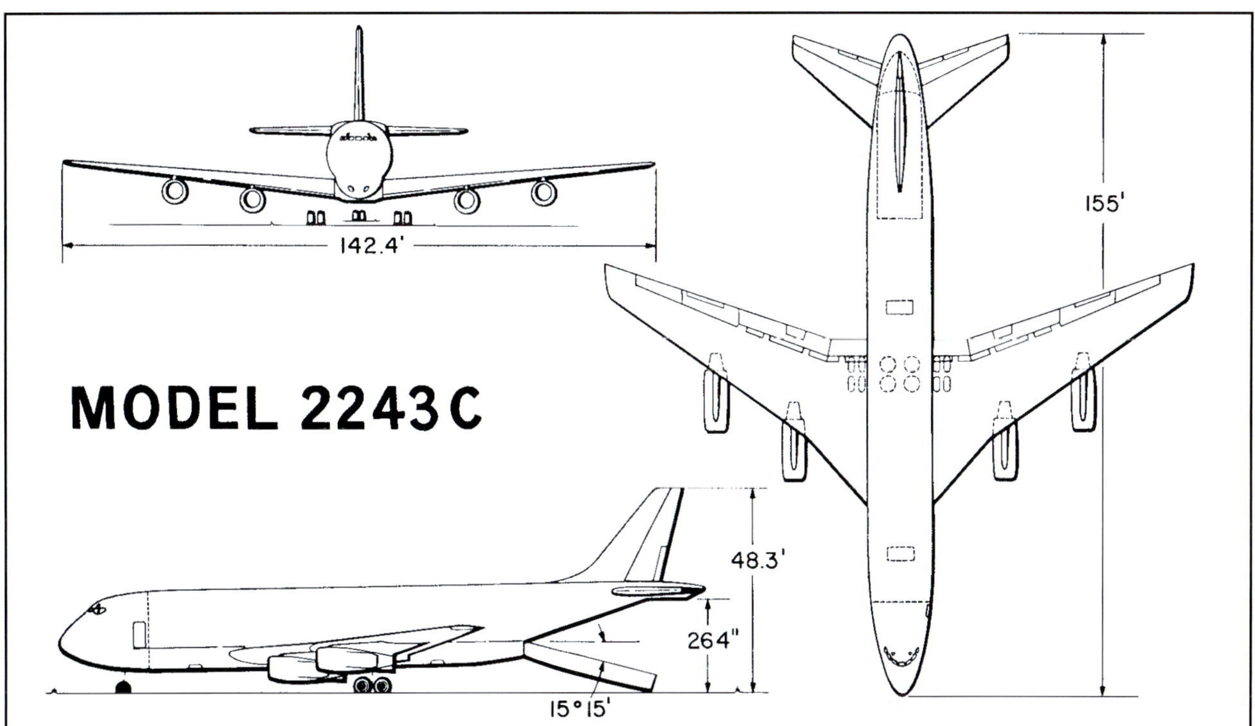

ABOVE **Douglas Model 2234C general arrangement; the reuse of DC-8's lower fuselage lobe, tail and slightly modified wings is apparent.** *Boeing*

BELOW **On the other hand, the airframe suggested by the Douglas 'C-133 Replacement' was an 'clean sheet design' that presaged the eventual C-5 configuration.** *Boeing*

Douglas 'C-133 Replacement' study

A Douglas study dated 28 December 1961 pointed out that the Model 2243C had reached the limits in terms of enlarging the upper lobe of the DC-8 fuselage, since retaining the existing lower lobe would limit the deck width to 132in (335cm). Further increases in the upper lobe diameter would result in large amounts of the fuselage volume extending outside the usable limit of the floor.

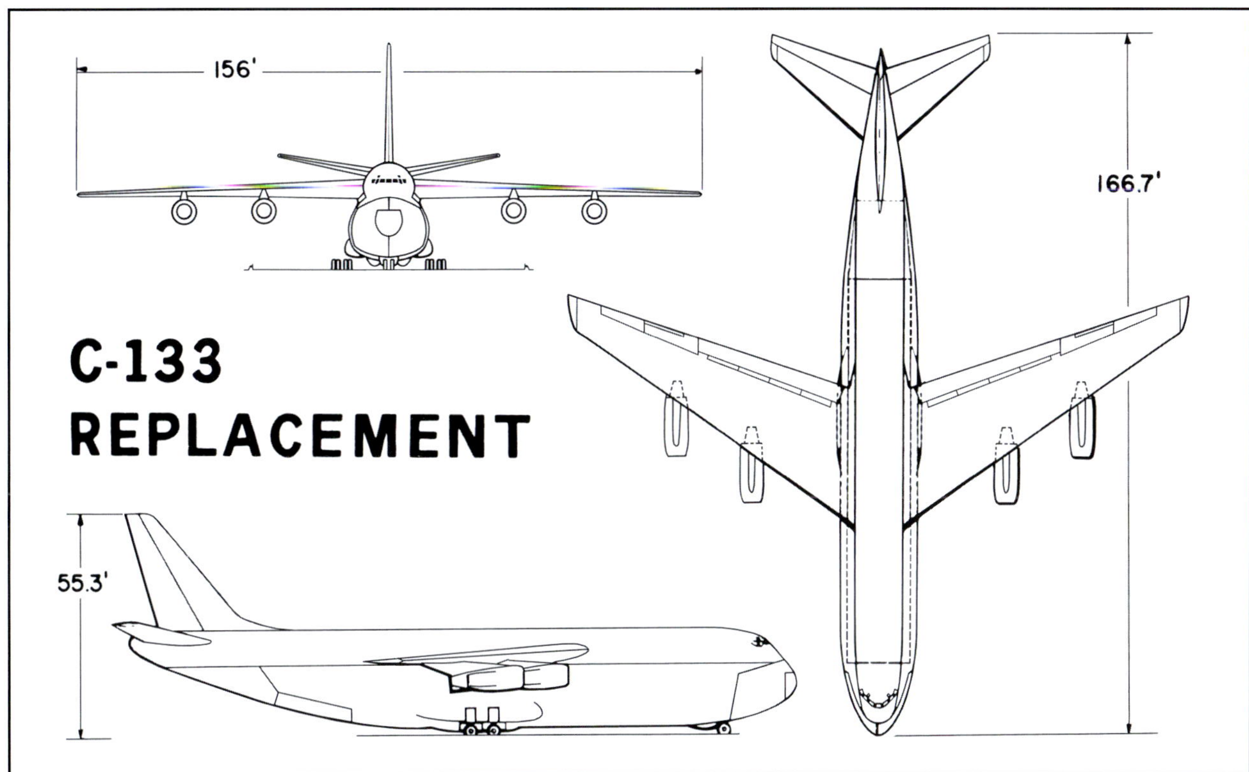

Douglas 'C-133 Replacement' study proposal

Powerplant	4 x P&W JT3D-3B turbofans @ 18,000lb (80.6kN) thrust (later growth version TF33s @ 24,000lb (106.8kN) thrust)
Span	156ft (47.58m)
Length	166.7ft (50.81m)
Height	55.3ft (16.85m)

Widening the cargo deck required a new approach, switching the larger lobe to become the bottom part of the fuselage. This then required moving the wing, to allow a straight-through unobstructed cargo deck, which in turn necessitated a much deeper fuselage. With a cross section resembling an enlarged YC-132 (the aborted proposal described in *American Secret Projects 2*), this design study featured a main cargo deck 100ft (30.5m) long and 16ft (4.88m) wide, with an aft compartment in the upper lobe accommodating 100 troops. Aircraft gross weight was estimated at 400,000 to 450,000lb (181,600 to 204,300kg).

The aircraft was likely to use growth versions of the TF-33 powerplants currently being installed in the C-141. With a projected thrust of about 24,000lb (107kN), these uprated engines were anticipated to be available by 1965 or 1966. Wing area would depend on the take-off performance required, ranging from approximately 3,300sq ft (307m^2) for field lengths consistent with current commercial jet transports, to about 4,000sq ft (372m^2) if improved performance was sought.

'C-133 Replacement' – request for information

After due consideration, the Air Force elected not to pursue any of the proposals for an interim replacement for the C-133, tempting as these might have seemed in terms of cost and early availability. Instead, it embarked on a path that would eventually lead to the C-5. In May 1962 the Air Force prepared, then revised, a new draft SOR. Although this had not yet been formally issued, it had been circulated to industry and by the middle of June five companies were already working on studies to satisfy it: Boeing, Convair, Douglas, Lockheed and North American Aviation.

On 28 June 1962 the Air Force held a briefing to issue a request to industry for cost estimates for a C-133 replacement aircraft, on the basis of the 29 May 1962 SOR draft requirements. Quantities of either fifty or one hundred aircraft were contemplated. Both Boeing and Douglas responded to this request. Boeing submitted four different aircraft configurations 'based on Advanced C-135 technology' and utilising 707-320B and B-52 components, each one separately costed. For its part, Douglas presented three different designs, reflecting the customer's uncertainty in interpreting exactly what was wanted. These were the Models D-890, D-895 and the D-900. Respectively, these represented a low-wing, low-cost option, a lowest-cost option, and a higher-capability, higher-cost option.

Douglas proposals for a C-133 replacement

The Douglas Model D-890 was the end-point of the Model 2243 evolutionary process that used the existing DC-8 lower lobe and wing structure. The lower aft fuselage ramp of the Model 2243 was replaced by a 'swing nose', whereby the forward fuselage including the cockpit could swing to one side to allow straight-in loading of cargo. This allowed loads to span the full width of the cargo compartment, whereas the tapering of the aft fuselage limited the width of rear cargo doors.

The DC-8 wings and tail surfaces were mated to a new circular fuselage. However, this would still have suffered the disadvantage of having a high-bed cargo compartment. The engines were to be Pratt & Whitney JT3D-8As in C-141 nacelles as an off-the-shelf arrangement.

The second Douglas proposal was the D-895, which the company also referred to as the 'C-133X'. This was an

Douglas model numbers

It should be noted that a subtle change had taken place in the usage of Douglas model numbers at the Long Beach Division somewhere around 1960 to 1961. Previously the term 'Model 1875' (for instance) had been used formally where a design number was referenced. This changed with the addition of the 'D-' prefix, such as 'Model D-890', at about this time.

In addition, there was some duplication between the design numbers assigned to CX-4/C-5A designs (running from D-900 to D-918, skipping the D-905 Skyhawk International) and certain other Douglas projects. The reason for this is unknown but may be due to the fact that the C-5A engineering activities were separated from the Long Beach Division into the new 'C-5 Division' in 1964 and coordination was lost. When the C-5 Division was dissolved after the contract loss, the C-5 project numbers were apparently not 'backed' into the master project/specification logs.

Specification/model number duplications include:

- DS-911 — DC-8 Procedure Trainer
- D-912 — Advanced Jet Trainer VT-AT(X)
- DTS-914 — Training Device for the A-3B Skywarrior
- D-915 to D-919 — Advanced Tactical Transport Studies (numbers assigned 15 December 1966) – the YC-15 AMST evolved under a succession of 'D-915' designations.

In addition, the model number D-920 was reserved on 1 November 1963 for the [A-4] Skyhawk International proposed for Norway. No contemporary evidence could be found for its use on the C-5 programme.

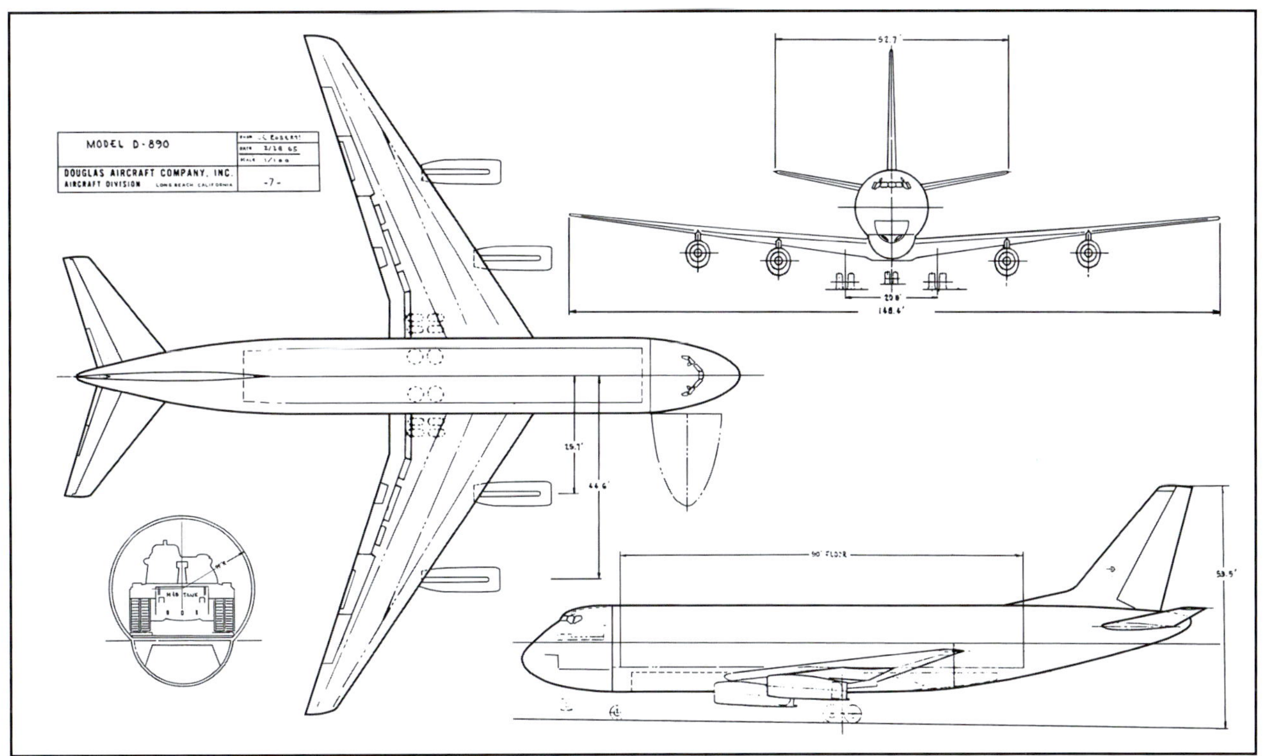

ABOVE **Douglas Model D-890 general arrangement.** *Boeing*

BELOW **The Model D-890 was Douglas' last attempt to retain a low wing in a heavy airlifter design.** *Boeing*

imaginative approach to rework the surviving C-133 fleet by mating the fuselages to new wings and tail surfaces. This was the lowest-cost option, though the availability of C-133s barely provided for the minimum quantity of required aircraft.

All the fuselages would be inspected and repaired as necessary, and brought up to a common C-133B standard. The original wing would be replaced by a modified DC-8 wing using C-141A engines (JT3D-8As) and nacelles. The tail group would also be replaced with DC-8 components, although the horizontal stabiliser was moved higher to eliminate the aerodynamic interactions with the fuselage that had plagued the C-133.

The resulting design's appearance, with its unusual combination of high-mounted wings and pronounced dihedral, reflected its mixed ancestry. A later version eliminated the dihedral and likely improved flight handling, although at the cost of redesigned engine pylon mounts and a modified wing centre section.

In contrast to the two previous designs, the D-900 represented the preferred Douglas concept for an outsized cargo carrier, one that was to be capable of simple loading and unloading techniques and also capable of carrying all the items in the inventory of the Army Airborne and Infantry Divisions.

A completely new nose-loading fuselage was married to a high wing, which enabled the aircraft to have a low cargo deck. The ultimate cargo load was 130,000lb (59,000kg), dropping to 100,000lb (45,359kg) at an unrefuelled range of 4,055 nautical miles (7,500km).

The basic cargo compartment was 13ft wide by 13ft tall and 100ft long (3.97m by 3.97m and 30.5m); the swing nose allowed unrestricted use of the full width and height. Douglas also

Douglas C-133 replacements

	D-890	D-895	D-900
Powerplant	4 x P&W TF-33-P-7 turbofans @ 20,250lb (90.1kN) thrust	4 x P&W JT3D-8A turbofans @ 21,000lb (93kN) thrust	4 x P&W JT3D-8A turbofans @ 21,000lb (93kN) thrust
Wingspan	142ft 4in (43.41m)	146.1ft (44.56m) original, 142ft 4in (43.41m) later	175ft 6in (53.53m)
Length	149ft 6in (45.60m)	164.7ft (50.23m)	175ft (53.34 m)
Wing area	2,930sq ft (272.5m²)	n/a	n/a
Max TOW	350,000lb (158,900kg)	n/a	n/a
Max payload	100,000lb (45,359kg)	n/a	130,000lb (59,020kg)
Range	2,750nmi (5,088km) with 100,000lb (45,359kg) payload 100,000lb (45,359kg) payload	n/a	4,055nmi (1,841km) with
	4,500nmi (8,325km) with50,000lb (22,700kg) payload 50,000lb (22,700kg) payload	n/a	5,805nmi (10,740km) with

BELOW The Douglas Model D-895 adaptation of the C-133. *Boeing*

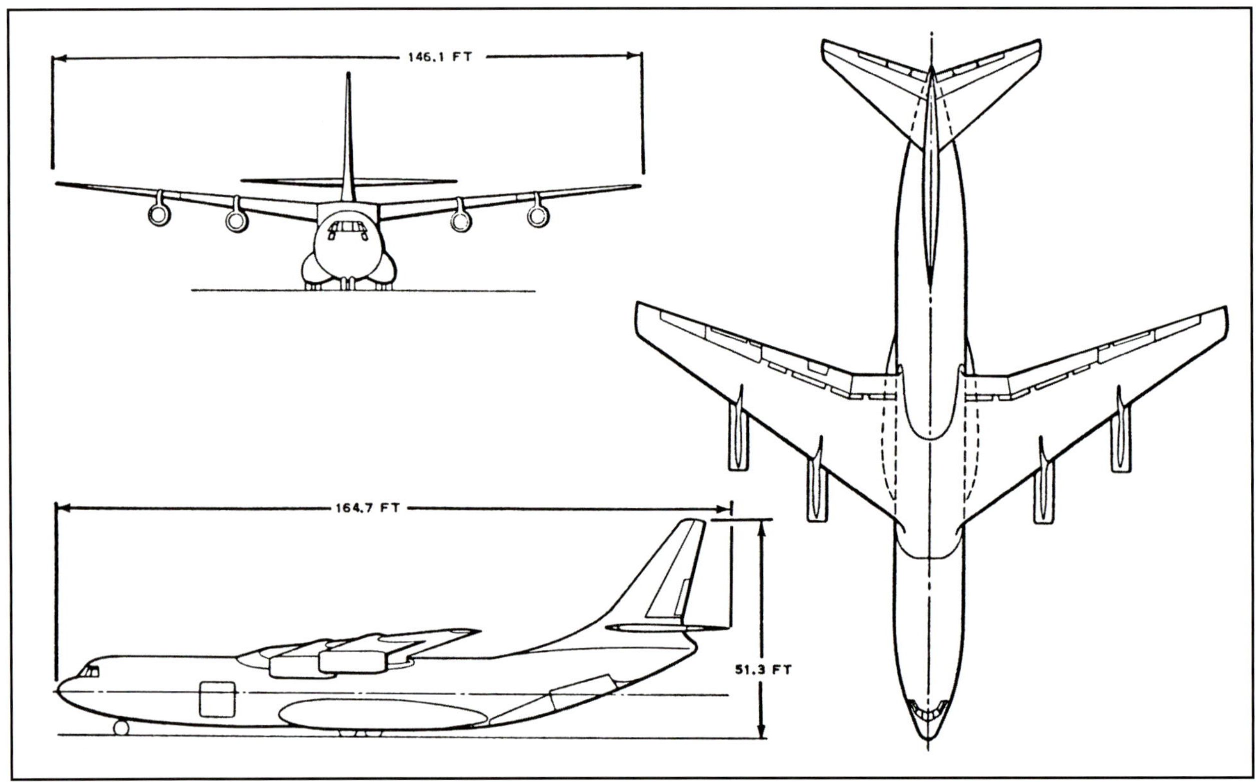

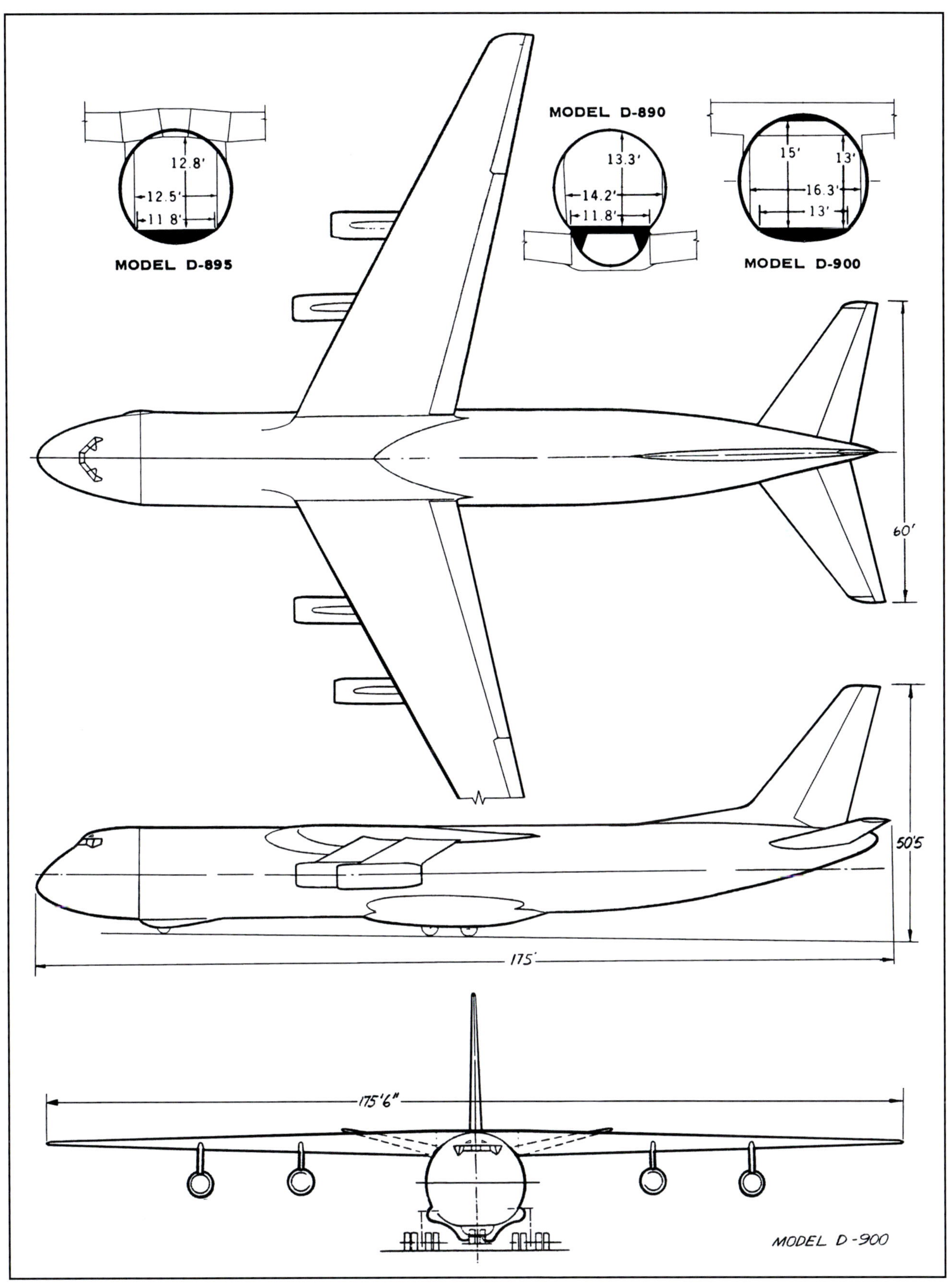

ABOVE **Douglas Model D-900 general arrangement.** *Boeing*

ABOVE A manufacturer's model of the Douglas D-900. *John Aldaz collection*

BELOW A comparison of the Douglas D-890 (lower) and D-900 (upper) models. The larger D-900's high wing and circular fuselage cross section required storage of the landing gear in external belly fairings. *John Aldaz collection*

investigated an alternative nose-loading arrangement, but the clamshell doors and revised cockpit incurred severe penalties in weight, drag and cost when compared to the swing-nose concept. To enable air-dropping of supplies and equipment, the design included a smaller tail ramp.

The Heavy Lifter Programme: CX-4

The request for cost estimates for a C-133 Replacement had been issued on 28 June 1962, and Boeing submitted its data on 3 July. This extremely short interval indicates that it was primarily a costing exercise by the Air Force rather than a full technical evaluation of competing designs. As a consequence, none of the above proposals was carried forward in its existing form. Nonetheless, this provided a useful baseline of what industry thought was feasible. The process of defining a clear set of requirements took a large step forward on 6 July, when Air Force Secretary Zuckert formally requested the Army's advice on its airlift requirements. The analysis was forwarded to the Air Force Chief of Staff on 17 August 1962.

Subsequently, the USAF submitted a QOR (Qualitative Operating Requirement) to the Army for what would become known as the CX-4 programme. However, CX-4 was very short-lived; the Army quickly realised that the QOR was still inadequate for its requirements, and that it really needed an aircraft that was both larger and capable of operating from semi-prepared airstrips. After negotiation, SOR 214 was released on 25 March 1964 for what had now become the CX-HLS programme, and which would eventually become the C-5A. Before going on to examine the competing designs, it is probably useful to summarise this somewhat complex path, as shown in the accompanying table.

As called for by the Air Force, many of the early studies were based on six TF33 turbofan engines: these were the most powerful engines then available suited to large transport aircraft. Boeing, Convair, Douglas, Lockheed and Martin all responded to this CX-4 requirement, though no details could be found for the Martin submission.

C-5 development milestones

1962	
May	Initial SOR drafted
June	Companies known to be working on draft requirements: Boeing, Convair, Douglas, Lockheed and North American Aviation
June	RFI issued for replacement of C-133
July	CX-4 programme formalised by DoD
Sept	SOR 214 reaches its third draft
1963	
Nov	CX-4 redesignated as CX-HLC (Heavy Logistics Carrier)
Nov	CX-X designation given to a technologically advanced version of CX-HLC
1964	
Jan	CX-HLC redesignated as GT (Global Transport)
Jan	GT redesignated as CX-HLS (Cargo Experimental – Heavy Logistics System)
Mar	SOR 214 formally released
May	Revised SOR 214-1 released
Aug	North American Aviation joins Douglas team
Sept	Martin joins Douglas team
Dec	RFP issued for 'Long-Range Transport Support System C-5A (CX-HLS) Weapon System 410-A'
1965	
April	Final proposals submitted by Boeing, Douglas and Lockheed
Sept	Contract awarded to Lockheed

Boeing CX-4 submissions: Models 748 and 749

Formal Boeing design efforts on the CX-4 began on 27 September 1962 with the 'Baseline 1' aircraft. This design, which featured a high wing and nose loading, was assigned the Boeing Model Number 748A. Working from this base, Boeing explored a diverse range of options:

Model 748A-1 to -4
Baseline aircraft with variations in floor area

Model 748A-5 and -6
Tail loaders versus nose loaders

Model 748A-10 to -12A
Exhibition purposes to stimulate customer interest

Model 748A-13
Wider body cross section, low wing

Model 748A-15
Larger wing

These were succeeded by the Model 748B, which incorporated a major design change to the wing. Further studies were carried out, running from the Model 748B-1 to the Model 748B-52, in a period lasting from January to November 1963.

The Model 748B-15 was an example at the heavier end of the range, with a gross weight of 630,000lb (286,000kg). Dual (tandem) nose wheels were planned as well as a main gear

Pre-Concept Formulation Phase (PCFP), 1963 to April 1964

The major requirements of the draft SOR (as issued in June 1963) were as follows:

Basic Design Mission:	Payload 100,000-130,000lb (45,359-59,020kg) over 4,000nmi (7,400km)
Alternative Mission:	Payload 50,000lb (22,700kg) for 5,500nmi (10,180km)
Structural Capability:	130,000-150,000lb (59,000-68,000kg) payload at a shorter range
Cruise Performance:	Not less than 440kt (814km/h) at 30,000ft (9,150m)
Take-off/landing:	8,000ft (2,440m) at sea-level at max gross weight at 89.5°F (32°C), to clear 50ft (15.25m) 4,000ft (1,220m) on standard day with 4,000nmi (7,400km) fuel, to clear 50ft (15.25m)
Cargo compartment:	Length 100-110ft (30.50-33.55m) Width 16-17.5ft (4.88-5.38m) Height 13.5ft (4.18m) Two palletised rows Airfield requirement: Rear or support airfields
Loading:	Straight-through – nose with 9ft by 10ft (2.75m by 3.05m) secondary aft door
Power:	Six turbofans

Boeing Model 748

	Baseline aircraft	Model 748B-15	Model 748B-33
Powerplant	6 x JT3D-8B turbofans @ 23,000lb (102kN) thrust	6 x JT3D-8B turbofans 23,000lb (102.31kN) thrust	6 x JT3D-8A turbofans @ 21,000lb (93.41kN) thrust
Wingspan	210ft 10in (64.30m)	205ft 10in (62.74m)	203ft (61.92m)
Body width	17.5ft (5.34m)	17.5ft (5.34m)	17.5ft (5.34m)
Wing area	4,468sq ft (415m²)	5,000sq ft (465m²)	4,900sq ft (456m²)
Payload	150,000lb (68,100kg)	n/a	n/a
Max TOW	540,000lb (245,160kg)	630,000lb (286,000kg)	518,000lb (335,200kg)
Range	4,000nmi (7,400km)	n/a	n/a
Cargo deck	n/a	17.5ft (5.38m) width 110ft (33.55m) length	16ft (4.88m) width 100ft (30.50m) length

employing eight four-wheel bogies. The low end of the range was represented by the Model 748B-33 with a gross weight of 518,000lb (335,200kg), which allowed the use of a single nose gear and only four main landing gears. Both designs used an upward-opening nose.

At this point in the trade-off studies (or 'trade studies' as they are often termed within the industry), the fuselage was not fully optimised aerodynamically. It had a roughly

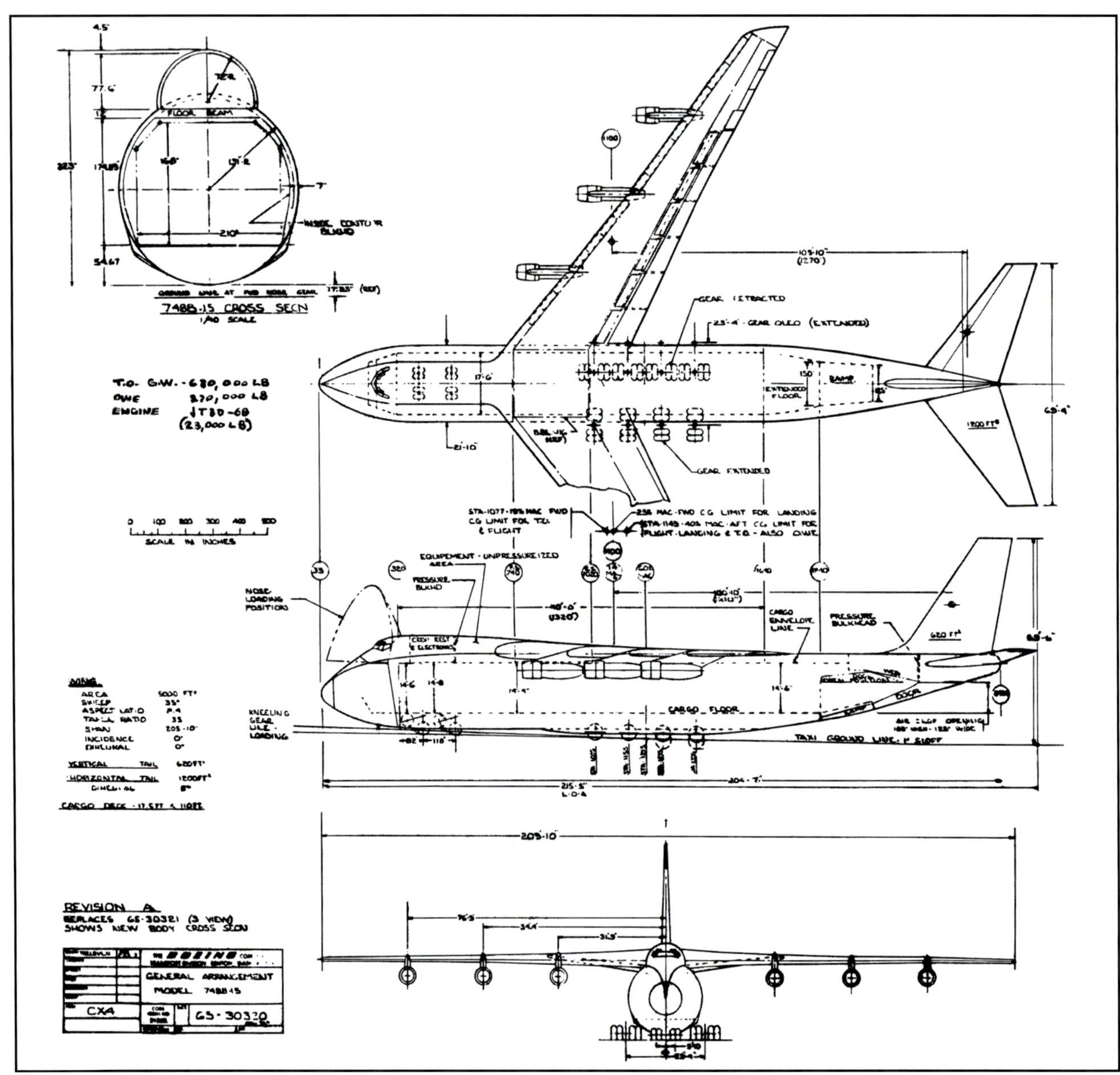

ABOVE General arrangement of the Boeing Model 748B-15, which was at the high end of the size/payload range. *Boeing*

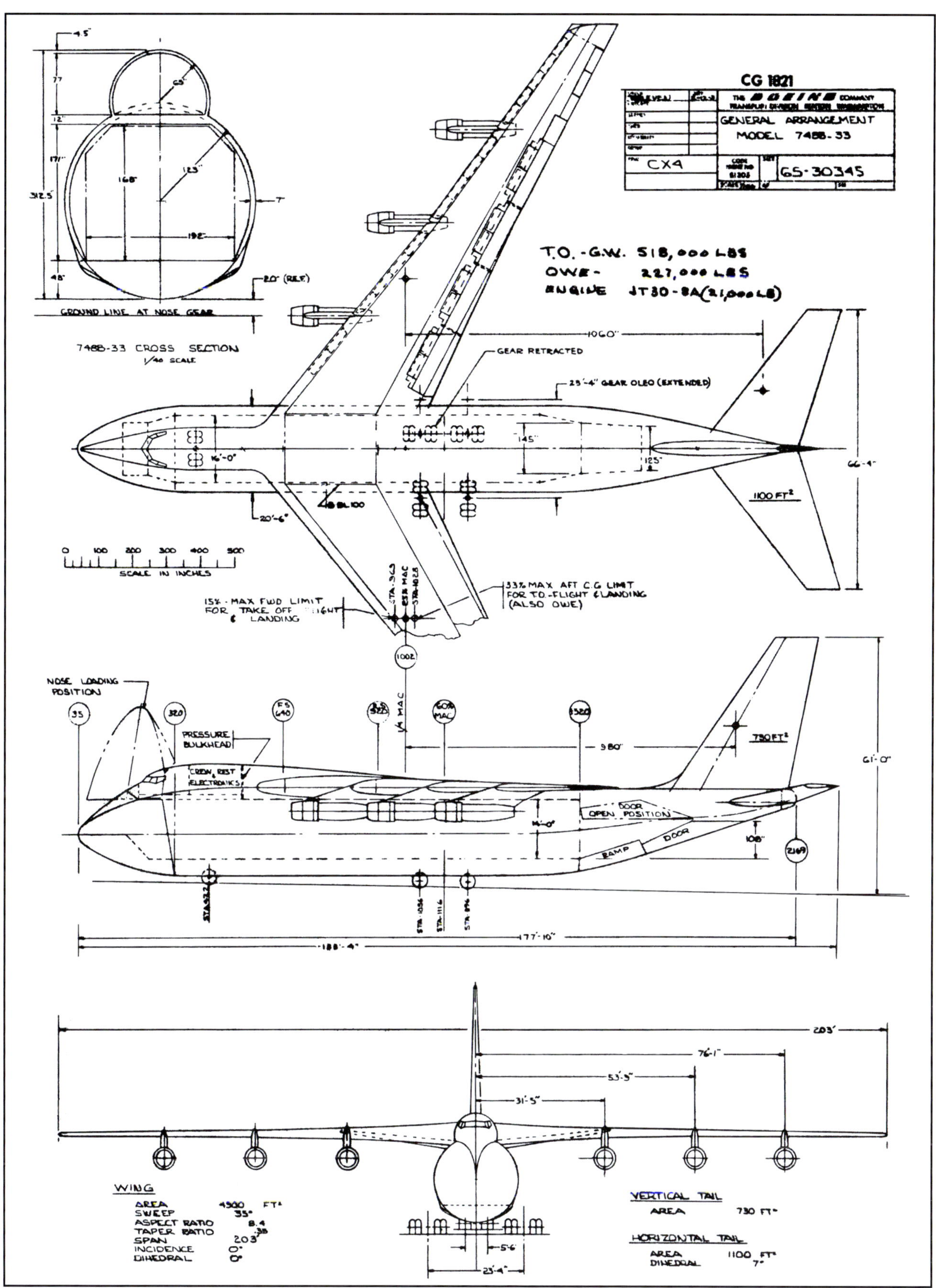

ABOVE General arrangement of the 'lightweight' Boeing Model 748B-33 with shortened fuselage and only four main landing gear. *Boeing*

ABOVE An early illustration of a four-engine Boeing Model 748 configuration emphasising its size. *Boeing*

circular cross section, with the cockpit in a 'cab-over' configuration adapted from the KC-135/707. Interestingly, a surviving display model of one of the six-engine designs shows that the aircraft was also considered for an air-refuelling tanker role. By November 1963 new baselines had been selected, with the 748B-53 as the baseline aircraft with the 748B-54 as an alternative with larger engines and increased gross weight (reflecting the promised availability of engines of 30,000lb/133.5kN thrust).

The Model 748 studies led to a further series collectively grouped under the designation Model 749. It was an intense but prolific period for the Boeing team: during just sixteen months ending in January 1964, designs progressed from the Model 749-1 to the 749-62.

Working against the draft SOR, these trade-off studies revealed some interesting relationships between size and weight. Engineers calculated that the take-off gross weight would increase by 6,000lb (2,724kg) per additional 1ft (30.5cm) of body width (at constant floor area). Thus, for a given cargo area, a short, wide airplane would weigh more than its longer, more slender equivalent – in addition to incurring higher drag.

Boeing also studied the effect of increasing the payload while holding the floor loading constant (resulting in an increase in fuselage size). Calculations showed that an increase in payload from 100,000lb (45,359kg) to 120,000lb (54,480kg) resulted in an 110,000lb (49,940kg) increase in take-off weight. Furthermore, take-off distance (assuming the same wing and engines were employed) increased by 2,000ft (610m). The multiple trade-offs would clearly have to be a matter of customer choice: balancing cargo size, shape, loading requirements and take-off performance.

Convair CX-4 studies

Convair went through a series of advanced design concept trade-off studies before arriving at the company's preferred option. These examined three turboprop and six turbofan options.

One set of designs focussed on an aircraft powered by six Pratt & Whitney YT57 turboprops fitted with variable-camber propellers. While this offered highly attractive fuel efficiency, it suffered from the disadvantage that the propellers extended over the whole span of the wing and had very little ground clearance. The fact that the T57 project had been cancelled six years earlier indicates that this design was part of a trade-off study where various concepts were evaluated rather than being a fully developed design proposal. Gross weight was set at 560,000lb (254,200kg).

LEFT Humorous artwork produced to commemorate a demonstration held at Boeing's CX-4 loading mock-up at McChord AFB, where re-enactors portraying the Army's 7th Cavalry thundered out of the cargo hold. It was intended to demonstrate the aircraft's ability to deliver soldiers, fully equipped and ready for combat, anywhere in the world, but Boeing senior management was reportedly not amused. *Boeing*

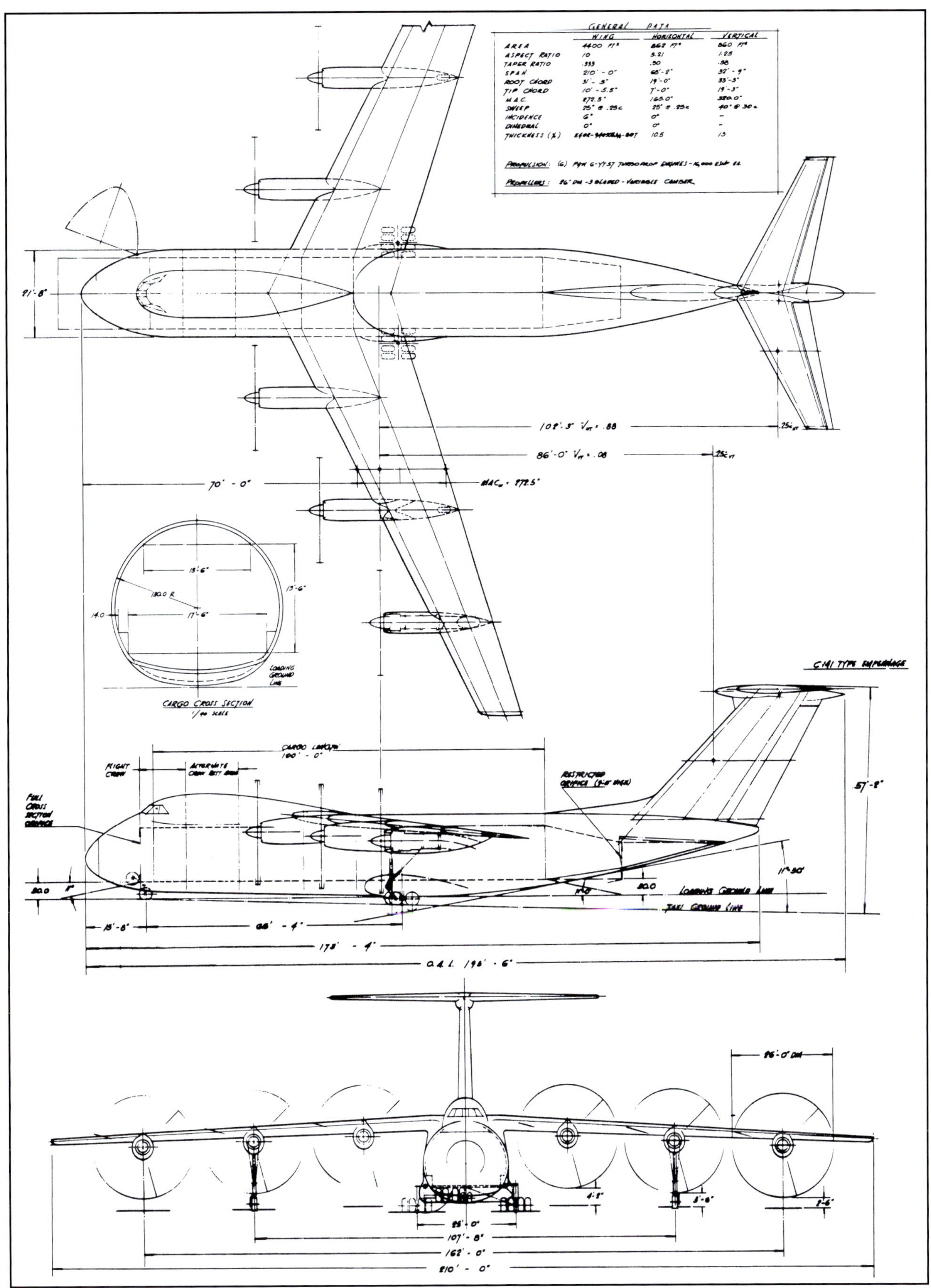

ABOVE **The General Dynamics/Convair CX-4 study explored the use of six T57 turboprops.** *San Diego Air and Space Museum*

General Dynamics/Convair CX-4 studies

	T57 turboprop	Amphibian	Preferred concept
Powerplant	6x P&W YT57 turboprop, 16,000eshp (11,940kW)	4 x P&W STF-200-D2	4 x P&W STF-200-D2
Span	210ft (64m)	234ft (71.3m)	230ft (71.3m)
Length	195ft 6in (59.6m)	204ft 6in (62.3m)	204ft 6in (62.3m)
Height	57ft 2in (17.4m)	63ft 6 in (19.6m)	62ft 1in (18.9m)
Wing area	4,400sq ft (408.8m²)	7,020sq ft (652.2m²)	7,020sq ft (652.2m²)
Max payload	165,000lb (74,842.7kg)	165,000lb (74,842.7kg)	165,000lb (74,842.7kg)
Cruise speed	440kt (814.9kph)	440kt (814.9kph)	440kt (814.9kph)
Range	4,000nmi (7408km)	4,000nmi (7408km)	4,000nmi (7408km)

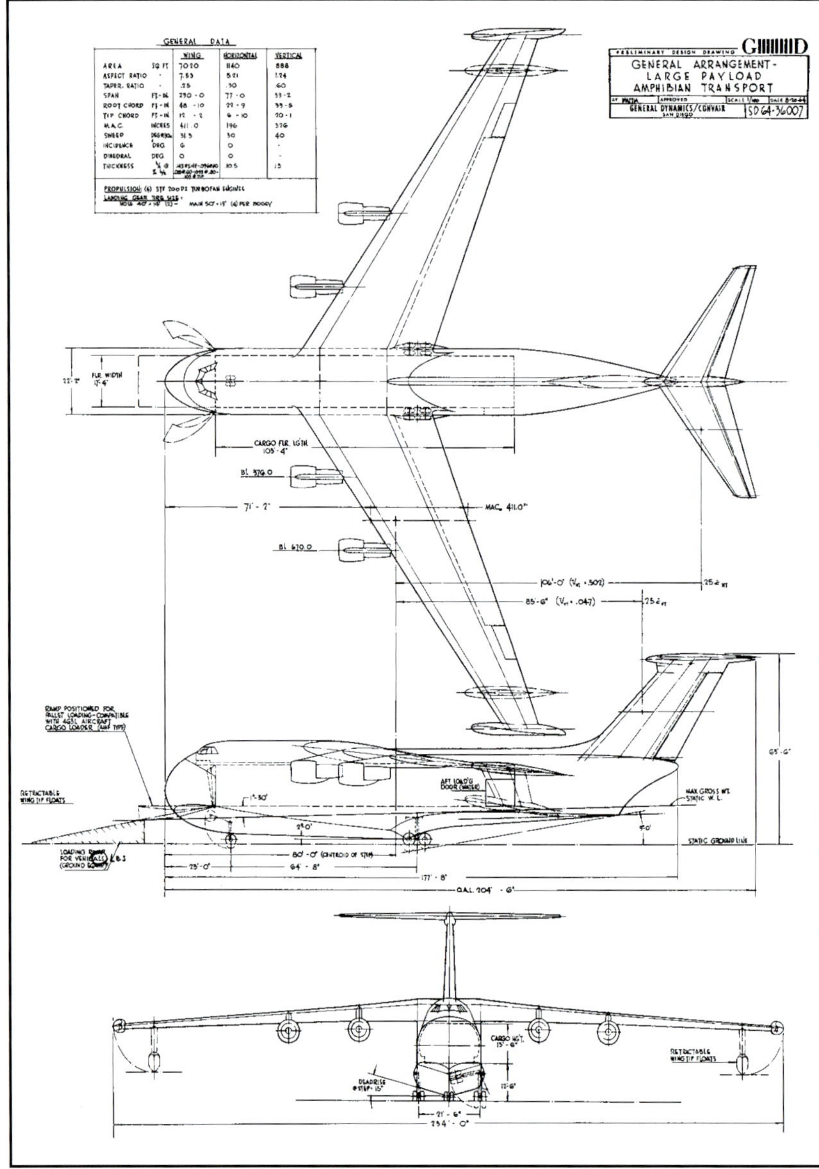

ABOVE General Dynamics/Convair also researched the potential for an amphibious CX-4 concept. *San Diego Air and Space Museum*

Convair also evaluated an amphibious version. The concept called for cargo to be loaded at a land base and delivered to a 'seadrome'. This addressed the possibility that a destination airbase – requiring a runway almost 2 miles (3.22km) long and a large ramp area – might not be widely available, and certainly not at every brushfire war location.

The baseline land version used the specified six Pratt & Whitney TF33 engines. As advanced studies continued, the engine manufacturers revealed details of their higher-bypass turbofan engines. These were then explored, before focusing on the highest-powered version of the Pratt & Whitney STF-200 family, STF-200-D2 high-bypass turbofans with a bypass ratio of four. Pratt had also been developing a geared turbofan called the STF-210. It promised high thrust at very low fuel consumption with a bypass ratio of ten, but the engine was in an early stage of development and Pratt was reluctant to offer it. This preferred version of the aircraft had a maximum take-off weight of 546,600lb (248,200kg), though it was suggested that this could be reduced to 531,700lb (242,000kg) if part of the aluminium structure was replaced by 50,000lb (22,700kg) of titanium.

The various iterations included both high and low tailplanes. All had a side-hinged nose positioned ahead of the cockpit, and in the final version the flight deck was raised in a bulge over the cargo area, similar to the Boeing proposal. All configurations had a tail ramp to allow both drive-through loading and air-dropping as required by the Air Force, with the exception of the amphibian, which had a side-loading door in the aft fuselage.

A Convair illustrator emphasised the design's huge size by superimposing silhouettes of the proposed C-5A on those of the proposed Convair Model 61 (C-141) and B-36. This is an interesting reflection on the advance in aviation during this era; just twenty years earlier the B-36 had been thought of as a massive aeroplane.

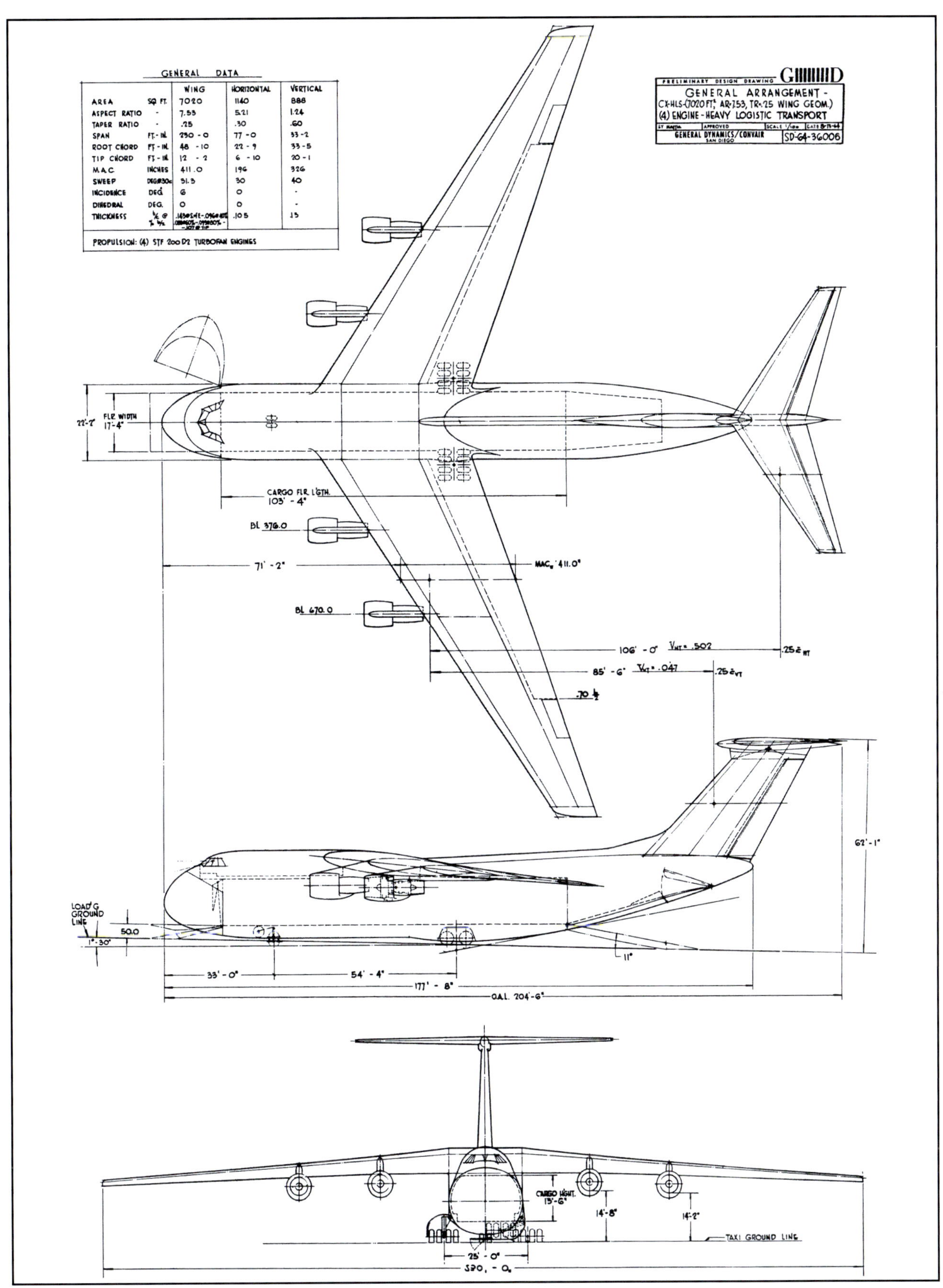

ABOVE General Dynamics/Convair's preferred CX-4 design showed a high-wing, T-tail configuration that would become familiar. *San Diego Air and Space Museum*

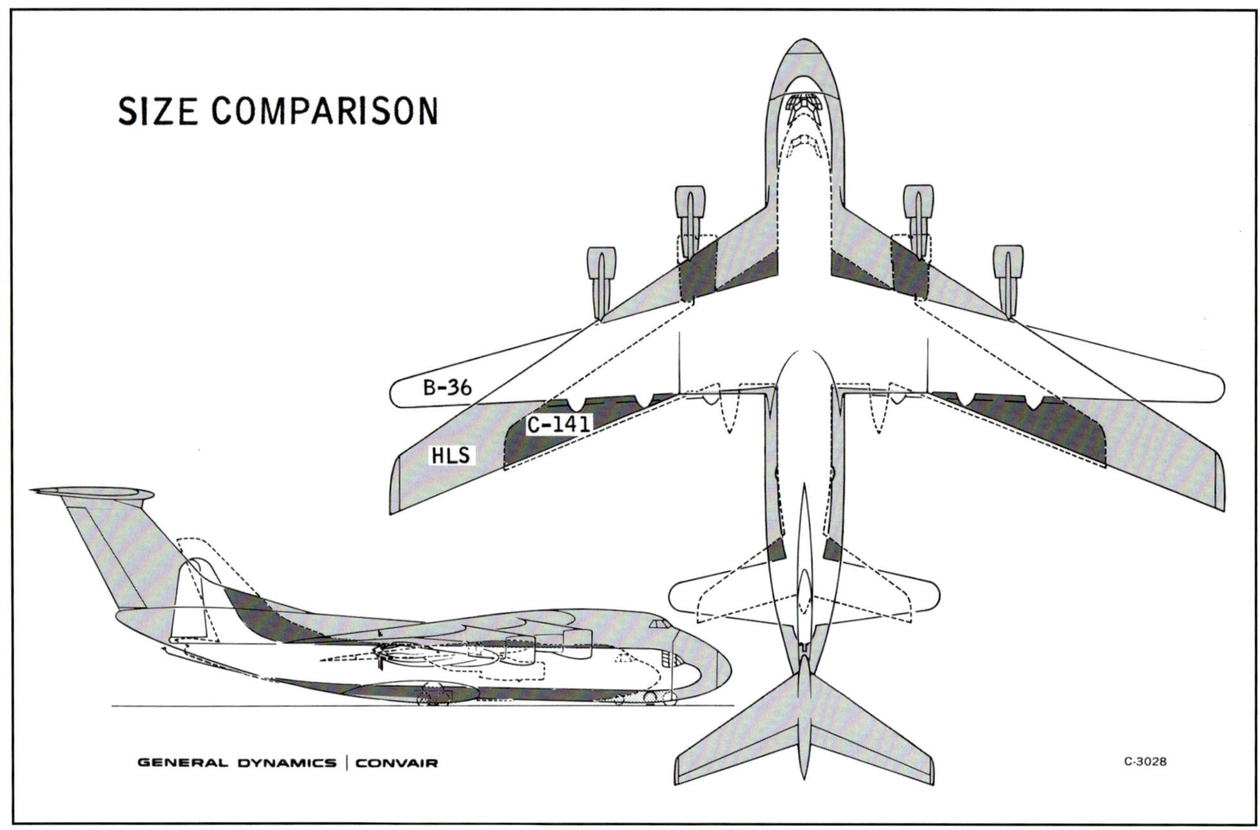

ABOVE Convair size overlays show the size differentials between the B-36, Model 61 (Convair's proposed C-141) and the preferred CX-4 design. *San Diego Air and Space Museum*

Douglas CX-4 studies

As did other contractors, Douglas evaluated numerous configurations before settling on a final proposal. The company began by examining options to modify existing designs, starting with the high-wing D-895 and the low-wing D-890, discussed earlier as C-133 replacements, before concluding that a wholly new design, the D-900 with a cargo floor 13ft (3.97m) wide, would serve as the best basis for further development.

The early versions, the D-902 and D-903, had nearly identical fuselages, but the choice of engines starkly illustrated the need for the development of the high-bypass turbofan engine. The D-902's use of the six proven Pratt & Whitney JT3D-8A turbojets housed in C-141 nacelles imposed a structural weight penalty of 20,500lb (9,300kg), resulting in the need for an additional 420sq ft (39.06m^2) of wing area compared to the D-903.

Douglas CX-4 design variations

Floor width	Six-engine models	Four-engine models
11.8ft (3.60m)	-	D-890, D-895
13ft (3.97m)	-	D-900
15ft (4.58m)	D-901	-
16ft (4.88m)	D-902	D-903
17.8ft (5.43m)	D-906*, D-906B, D-906C**	D-906C**, D-906F-1, D-908-1, D-911-1
19.5ft (5.95m)	-	D-904
19.3ft (5.85m)	-	D-908-3, D-909, D-910, D-911, D-914, D-916, D-917 (final C-5A proposed designs), D-918 'Commercial C-5'

* 6 x TF33 or 6 x 'New' 30,000lb (133.5kN) thrust (STF-200)
** D-906C had both four- and six-engine versions

In contrast, the D-903 was to use four of Pratt & Whitney's projected STF-200A-1 turbofans. This combination had less drag and a maximum take-off weight advantage of 467,000lb (212,00kg) as opposed to the D-902's 506,000lb (230,000kg). This was clearly the preferred option, although the Air Force had also directed evaluation of a six-engine aircraft.

The common fuselage cargo box was sized at 16ft (4.88m) wide by 100ft (30.5m) long (not including space on the rear loading ramp), yielding an area of 1,606sq ft (149.40m^2). The cockpit, crew relief facilities and avionics were located on the nose section, which was 26.7ft (8.14m) long. Douglas examined designs with raised cockpits and clamshell doors, but chose a swing-nose loading arrangement for its lesser drag, weight and cost advantages. The aircraft also had double-hinged,

ABOVE **The swing-nose Douglas Model D-902 is depicted in flight.** *Boeing*

BELOW **The Douglas Model D-902/3 cargo loading mock-up, built in 1963.** *Boeing*

upward-folding doors in the rear fuselage to facilitate air-dropping. The internal ramp could be partially lowered for this purpose, or fully lowered to provide ground loading with access 9.3ft (2.84m) high by 10ft (3.05m) wide. This ramp also acted as the rear pressurised bulkhead, which meant that the hinged doors could be left unpressurised, thereby eliminating sealing problems.

Douglas built a full-scale fuselage mock-up of the D-902 in early 1963. Loading demonstrations were carried out for USAF, Army, Navy, Marine Corps and DoD personnel on 2 and 3 May 1963. The mock-up was located in the southern end of Douglas Long Beach's Building 13, where the first C-133A had undergone the formal pre-flight inspection in 1955, and where all C-74s, C-124s and C-133s had been assembled.

During the presentation, Douglas demonstrated seventeen representative loads, including an Army medium-tank company, an Air Force Minuteman ICBM transporter/erector, and NASA Apollo modules.

ABOVE Mock-ups for the unsuccessful Douglas Apollo spacecraft proposal were also used in the loading demonstrations. Pictured are the Command Module (top left), Lunar Excursion Module (LEM) Descent stage (top right), Service Module (bottom left) and LEM Ascent stage (bottom right). *Boeing*

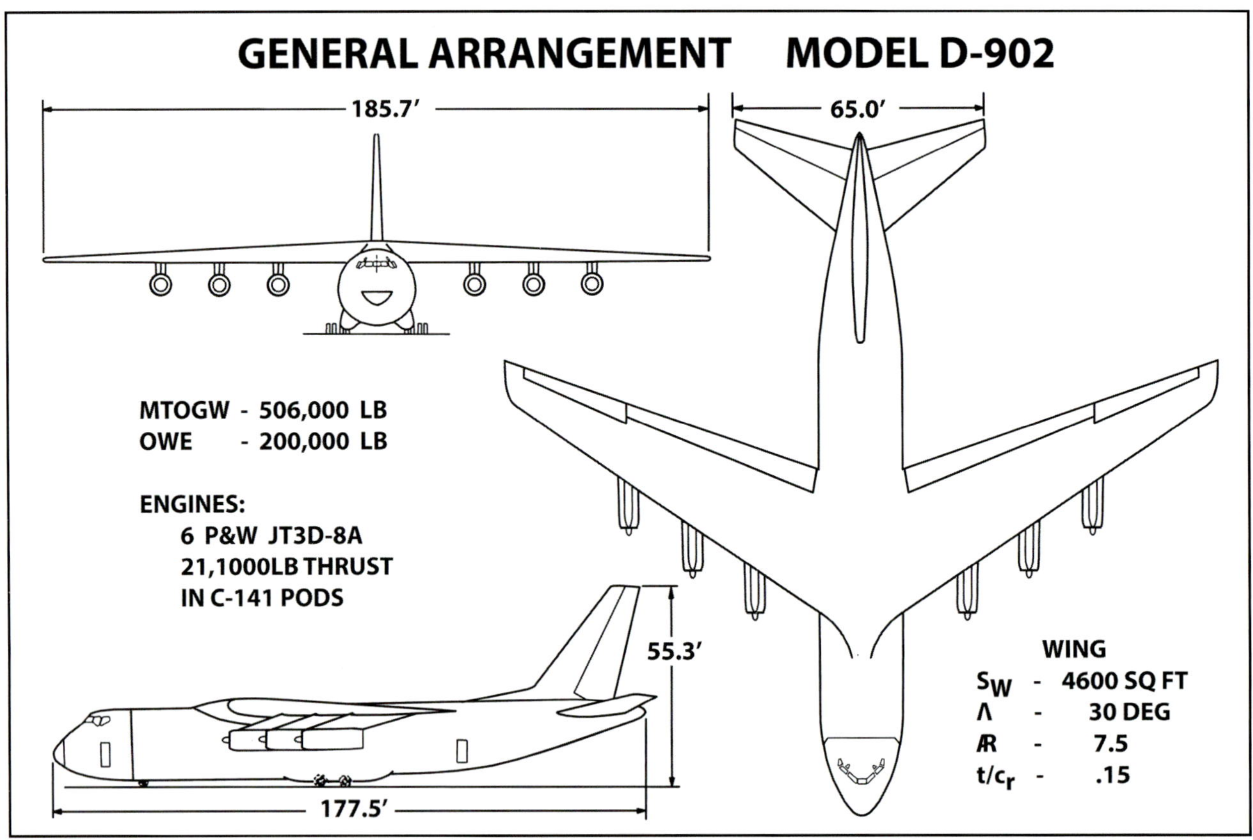

BELOW Douglas Model D-902 general arrangement. The D-902 and D-903 represented Douglas' best thinking in response to the preliminary Air Force and Army requirements in 1962. The lighter D-903 was to have an identical fuselage, with a smaller wing of 4,380sq ft (388.33m²) spanning 177.2ft (54.01m), a shorter tail of 52.3ft (54.01m) and a maximum gross weight of 467,000lb (211,828kg). The D-903 was to be powered by four 'new design' turbofans of 30,000lb (133.45kN) thrust. *Boeing*

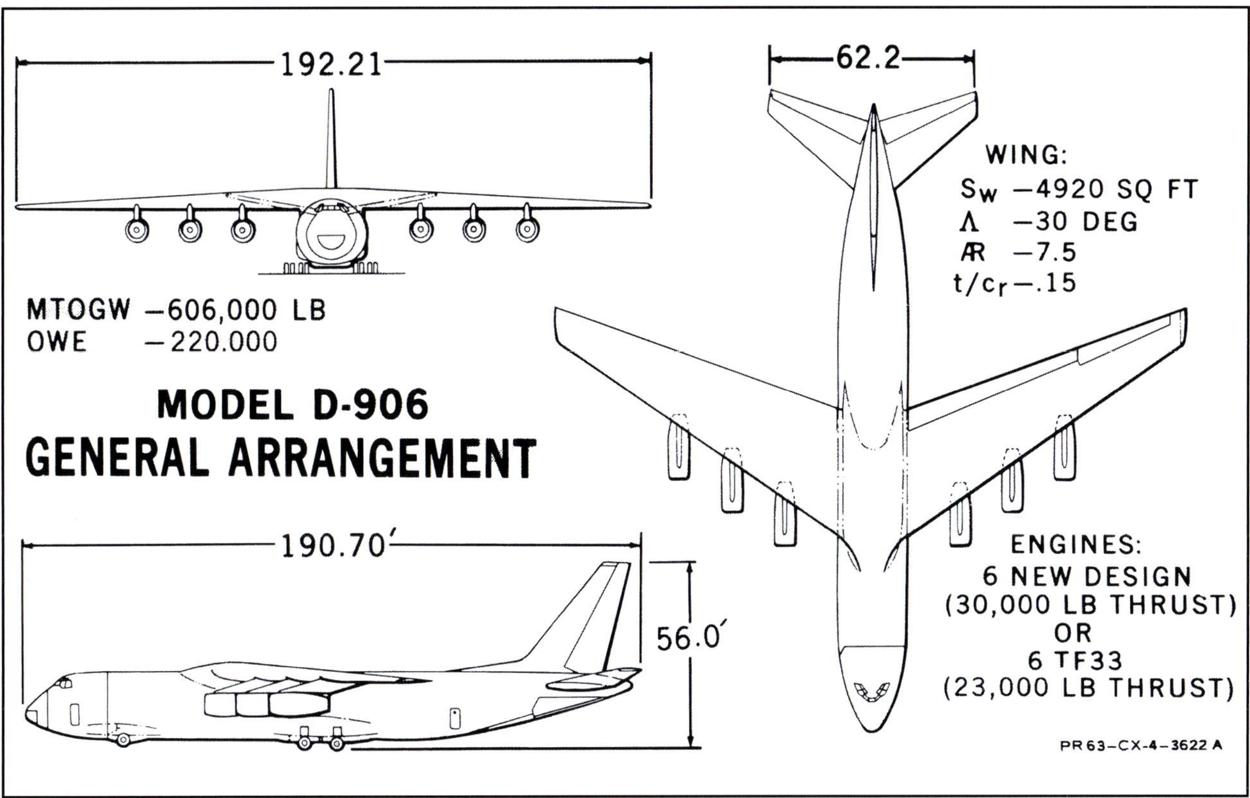

ABOVE The Model D-906 (later D-906A) was larger and heavier than the D-902, and served as the basis for the four-engined follow-on D-906C and D-909 designs. *Boeing*

Douglas Models D-902 and D-906A

	D-902	D-906A
Powerplant	6 x P&W JT3D-8A @ 21,000lb (93.5kN) thrust	6 x 30,000lb (133.5kN) thrust turbofans
Span	185ft 8in (56.64m)	192ft 2.5in (58.59m)
Length	177ft 6in (54.14m)	190ft 8.5in (58.13m)
Wing area	4,600sq ft (428m²)	4,920sq ft (457m²)
Payload	n/a	195,000lb (88,451kg)
Max TOW	506,000lb (230,000kg)	606,000lb (274,900kg)
Range	n/a	3,260nmi (6,040 km)

Lockheed CX-4 studies

Lockheed's early trade studies generally employed the same high-wing, pylon-mounted engine configuration used on the C-141. However, the company also considered proposing a totally new and much larger aircraft, and was exploring trade-offs between turboprop and turbofan engines. The family of concepts was based on a common fixed fuselage with a cargo compartment 17.5ft (5.30m) wide, 13.5ft (4.09m) high, and 100ft (30.5m) long. The aft opening was 10ft (3.05m) high and 13.5ft (4.12m) wide. All designs featured a raised crew compartment perched above a hinged nose that swung sideways to reveal the full cargo compartment cross section, and high wings with single-slotted Fowler flaps.

Lockheed's GL-194-12 exemplified the company's early design direction. It used six JT3D-1 (TF33) turbofan engines and had a design payload of 100,000lb (45,359kg). Lockheed proposed it for cargo, personnel, tanker and ICBM transport missions, in that order.

By the end of the pre-CFP phase in April 1964, Lockheed's recommended configuration had evolved substantially, although looking superficially similar to the earlier studies. It retained the high wing and the number of engines remained at six, but the powerplant choice was now Pratt & Whitney's proposed STF-200C, rated at 26,000lbst (118kN) thrust. Gross weight had increased to 579,000lb (263,000kg), mandating an increased wing area of 5,000sq ft (465m²), spanning 199ft (60.70m). The uprated design would enable it to transport a 155,000lb (70,400kg) cargo load at a 4,000nmi (7,400km) range.

Lockheed Model GL-194-12

Powerplant	6 x P&W JT3D-1 (TF33) turbofans @ 23,000lb (102kN) thrust
Span	165ft 1in (50.3m)
Length	170ft 5in (51.9m)
Height	47ft 1in (14.6m)
Wing area	4,700sq ft (436.6m²)
Payload	100,000lb (45,359kg)
Max TOW	411,090lb to 422,600lb (187,000kg to 191,860kg)

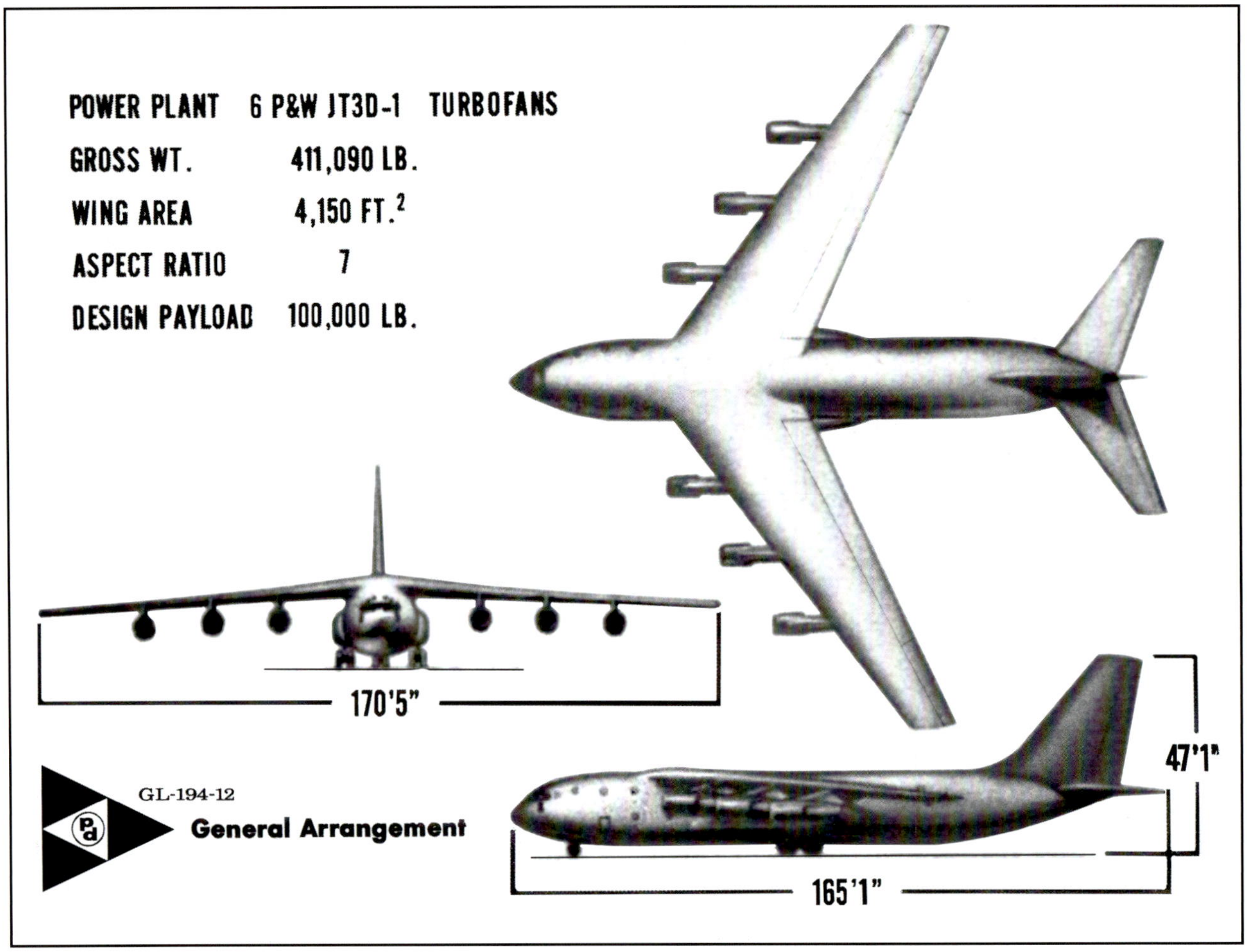

POWER PLANT 6 P&W JT3D-1 TURBOFANS
GROSS WT. 411,090 LB.
WING AREA 4,150 FT.²
ASPECT RATIO 7
DESIGN PAYLOAD 100,000 LB.
170'5"
47'1"
165'1"
GL-194-12
General Arrangement

ABOVE Lockheed Model GL-194-12 general arrangement. *Lockheed*

BELOW The Lockheed CX-HLS 1963 Pre-CFP configuration with six engines. *Lockheed*

LOCKHEED-GEORGIA
199'
202'
50'
Pre-CFP
Recommended
Configuration-
1963

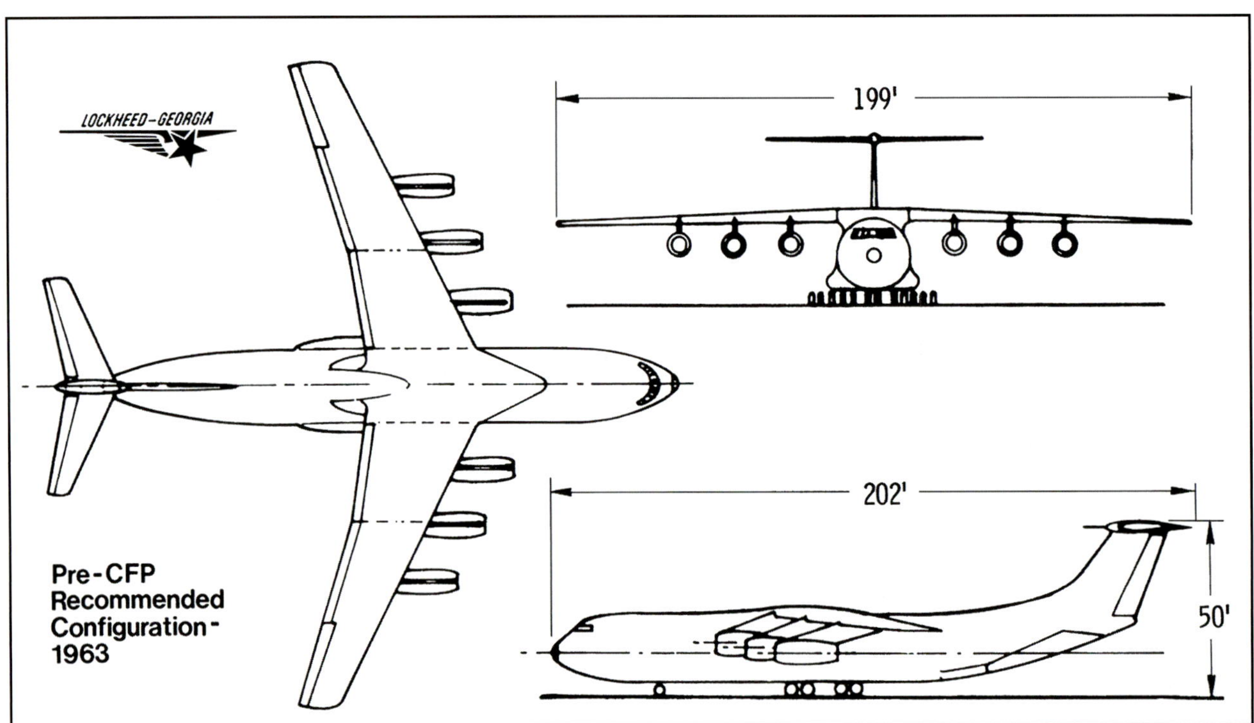

CX-X: An alternative Heavy Cargo Lifter

All three manufacturers were making good progress in refining their CX-4 studies when a further element of confusion was introduced. On 1 November 1963 the Air Force Systems Command (AFSC) Aeronautical Systems Division (ASD) proposed that the 'global airlifter' role be fulfilled by an alternative concept that it called 'CX-X'. Requirements for CX-X had been outlined under the just-completed 'Project Forecast', a wide-ranging study that looked at how newly developing technologies could fulfil future Air Force needs and missions. Project Forecast had been chaired by General Bernard Schriever, head of AFSC, who championed this new transport requirement.

The CX-X, as broadly specified by an Advanced Development Objective (ADO), would weigh less than the CX-4 but be capable of carrying a much larger payload over a 5,000-mile (8,045km) route segment. Planners anticipated that the CX-X would air-drop its cargo on most missions, rather than landing and unloading. However, this was not the end of the rethink. CX-X was subsequently redefined as a much heavier aircraft with several additional performance criteria. These new specifications would require leading-edge technology in any proposed new design.

In a history of the C-5A programme, Marcelle Size-Knaacke outlined the problem that CX-X created:

> 'Lt Gen Joe W. Kelly, Commander of the Military Air Transport Service which would operate the new transport, found the CX-X ADO far too ambitious. MATS had not requested so advanced a transport in its SOR, and, though Kelly recognised that Schriever's mandate was to advance technology, he pointed out that his own obligation was to obtain for MATS the most reliable airplane possible. From Kelly's viewpoint, the characteristics of the CX-4, revised and then abandoned, had been well defined. Only "minor technical problems" remained with the CX-4, and these could be solved with "current state-of-the art technology", enabling MATS to meet the requirement, now being emphasised, that a new transport attain an early initial operational capability.
>
> 'Intent upon advancing the limits of technology at Systems Command, Schriever could not have disagreed more. He believed that the revised specific operational requirement for the CX-4 envisaged an interim aircraft only, and an inadequate one at that. What MATS needed, in the AFSC Commander's adamant opinion, was the best CX-X, and technological advances proposed for such an aircraft could not be sacrificed for the sake of expediency. This seemed especially important because the future new transport was due to stay in the operational inventory for several decades.'

	CX-X (original ADO)	CX-X (later definition)
Max TOW	375,000-500,000lb (170,097-226,796kg)	499,000lb (152,000kg)
Max payload	180,000lb (81,700kg)	163,200lb (74,100kg)
Range	5,000mi (8,045km) with max payload	6,000mi (9,650km) with 123,200lb (55,930kg) payload 12,000mi (19,000km) with no payload, unrefuelled
Cargo box	-	77.5ft (23.64m) x 13.5ft (4.12m) x 10.5ft (3.20m)
Take-off distance	-	5,400ft (1,650m)
Max speed	-	Mach 0.75

Technological advances required to satisfy CX-X

To understand why it was felt possible to specify such high performance requirements for the CX-X aircraft, it is necessary to recognise that in 1962 two technologies that promised to greatly extend aircraft range appeared to be close to realisation, one in the engine field and one in aerodynamics.

Engine technologies

The first factor, in engine technologies, was the application of 'regenerative/recuperative' technology to turboprop engines. This involved adding a large heat exchanger to the engine to extract waste heat energy from the exhaust flow and heat the intake air after the compressor prior to combustion. Whether the energy (and hence fuel) saving was worth the extra weight and complexity was yet to be determined.

While this technology was seen as ideally suited for a very-long-range turboprop multi-purpose aircraft (a subject of separate studies), it languished because no approved mission requirement actually existed to exploit it. Exacerbating the problem of a niche application was the fact that large American turboprop development had stalled with the cancellation of the T57 (together with the XC-132) in March 1957, and had been completely eclipsed by turbojet and turbofan developments. In any case, initial studies showed that the speeds requested by the aircraft users were beyond those comfortably attained by turboprop propulsion.

The high-bypass turbofan was the key engine technology. The basic theory proposed that turbojet efficiency could be improved if a wide-diameter auxiliary stage was added to the compressor, with part of the accelerated airflow diverted around the core of the engine. A large volume of air would thus bypass the combustion and turbine system. The overall engine would be handling a much greater mass of air, albeit accelerating most of it to a far more modest exhaust speed (V jet).

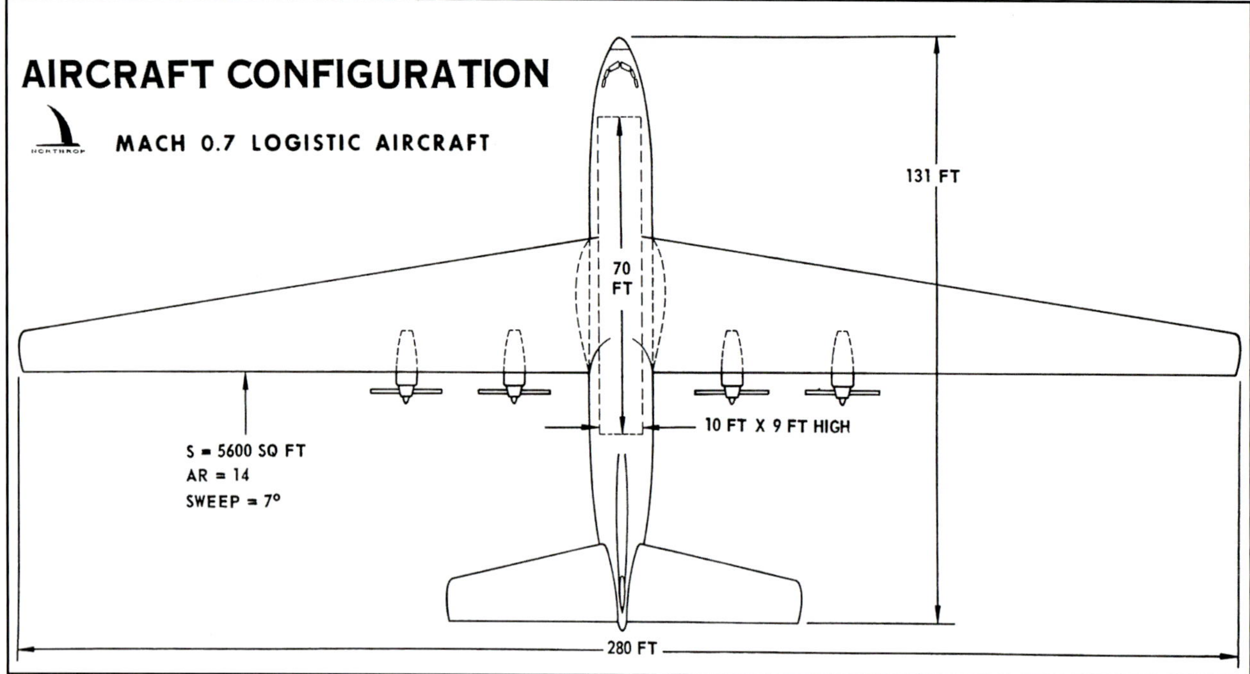

ABOVE **A Northrop example of a regenerative-turboprop-powered logistic transport design with an ultimate range of more than 7,000 miles.** *Courtesy of Northrop Grumman Corporation*

BELOW **Although unidentified, this model displays several characteristics of the Multi-Purpose Long Endurance (MPLE) airlifter configurations studied in the early 1960s. The very high aspect ratio wing coupled with the pusher turboprop engines (which eliminate propwash over the airfoil) would have been designed for high-efficiency cruise. The lower fuselage has both nose and tail clamshell doors for cargo loading, and the inverted gull wing would have permitted shorter and lighter main landing gear struts. From the dimensions and appearance of the model, the span would have been around 170ft (51.9m). Assuming the use of Allison Model 550-B7 turboprop engines and a reasonable power to weight ratio, a gross weight of 235,000 to 275,000 pounds (106,594 to 124,738kg) could be estimated. Use of regenerative/ recuperative features on the engines could also serve to extend range.** *Author collection*

However, while thrust is proportional to V jet, fuel consumption is proportional to V^2 jet. The result is that at normal operating speeds the turbofan gives approximately twice as much thrust for the same rate of fuel consumption as a turbojet of similar core size.

The theory had been understood since the advent of the jet engine; however, its successful application had to wait for advances in engineering technology and new high-temperature materials for the core.

TF33 (JT3D) variants had a bypass ratio of about 1.4 to 1. However, the JT3D was limited by the technology of the JT3C (J57 turbojet) from which it had been modified; the 'drop-in' modification did not optimise the engine hot section to provide the power for greater fan bypass ratios. Only a completely new engine, designed with the hot section optimised for greater power extraction to drive larger fans, could yield bypass ratios of 3 or even greater.

Two further engine technologies were on the distant horizon. One was the tip-driven remote fan championed by GE. Dubbed a 'Cruise Fan', the design was an enlarged version of the tip-driven fans used on the Ryan XV-5A and projected for use on the V/STOL CX-6. GE rig-tested an 80in (203cm) tip-driven fan driven by the entire exhaust flow from a J79 turbojet, and bypass ratios of up to 10 were promised. Pratt & Whitney on the other hand never pursued the tip-driven fan but rather cautiously eyed the geared turbofan, which also promised a bypass ratio of 10, but would need years of gearbox development.

Boundary Layer Control (BLC) investigations

The aerodynamic technology was Boundary Layer Control (BLC), which promised up to a 40% range extension by greatly reducing airflow turbulence, and hence drag. The primary proponent of the technology was Dr Werner Pfenninger, who began investigating laminar flow phenomenon in Switzerland in 1936. He was brought to the US in 1949 by Jack Northrop, and at Northrop Aircraft he continued his studies and basic tests with a small group under an Air Force contract. These progressed to flight hardware with an F-94 fighter fitted with a partial wing 'glove'. Similar research was also being carried out in the UK using the de Havilland Vampire as the test vehicle.

The concept centred on smoothing the airflow around the wing, which could be done in two ways. The first, called Natural Laminar Flow, coupled airfoil design with careful manufacturing techniques to ensure a smooth wing surface. The second technique used active measures, sucking turbulent air through holes or slots in the wing surface and exhausting it at the trailing edge.

BELOW **As part of its LFC studies, Northrop envisaged a large airlifter as an application for the technology.**
Courtesy of Northrop Grumman Corporation

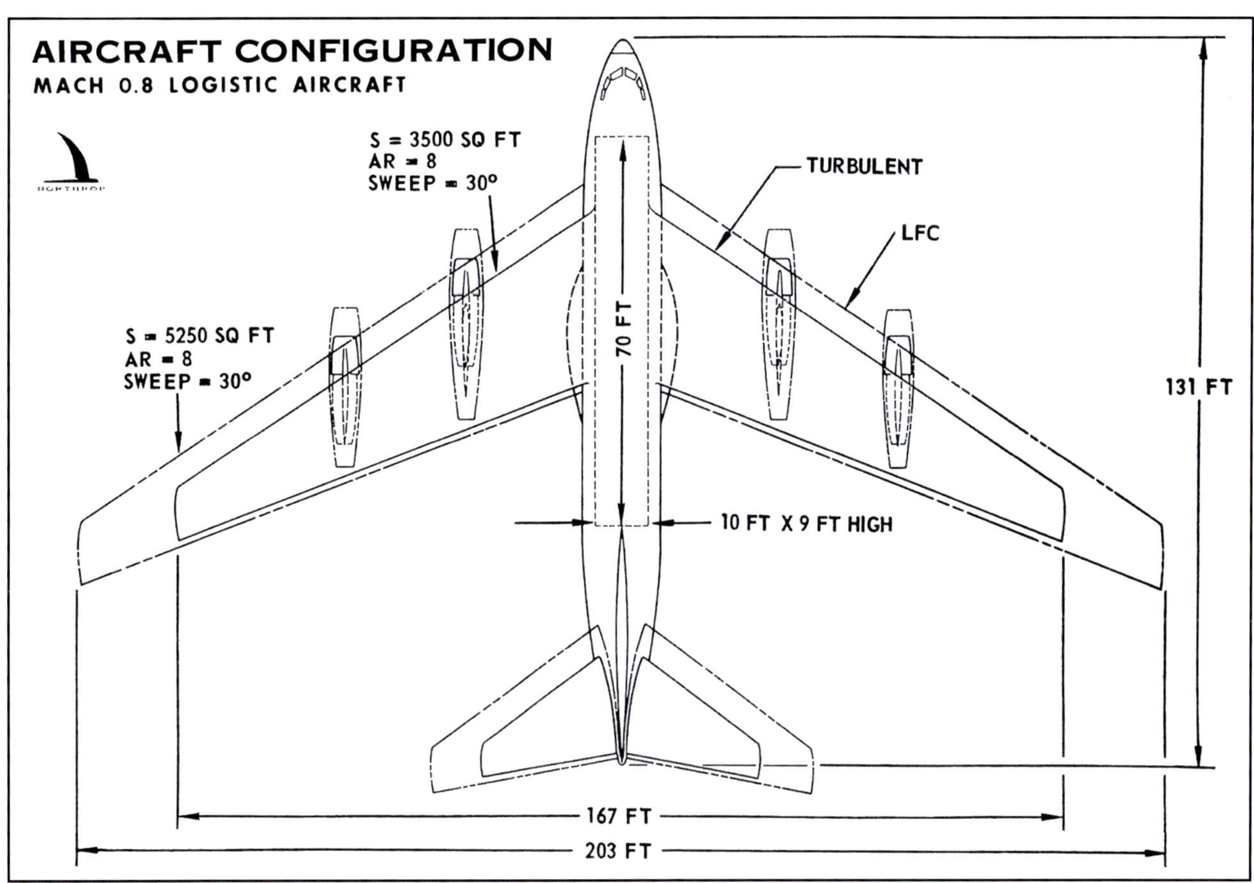

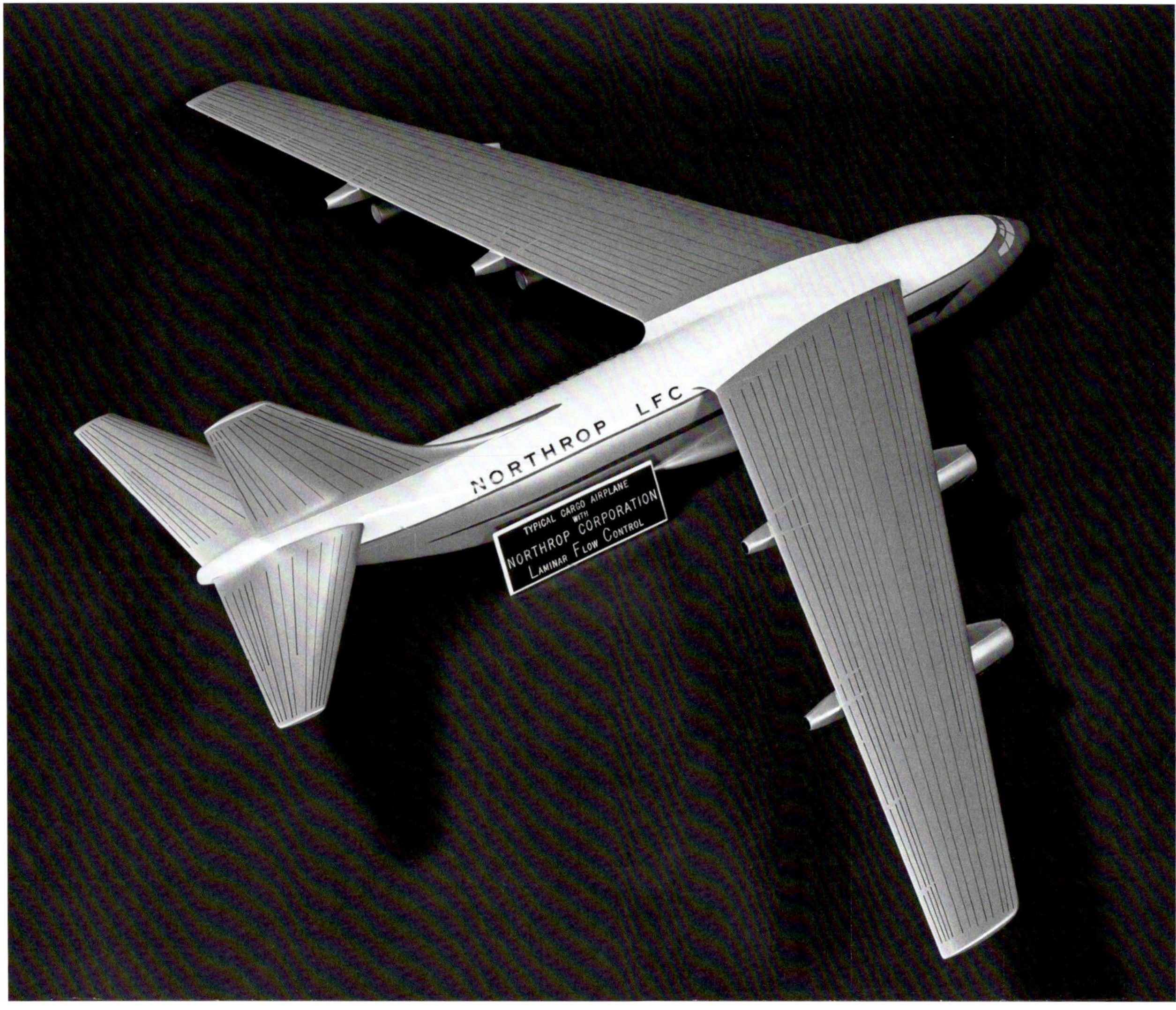

ABOVE The Northrop LFC concept airlifter had slotted wings and tail surfaces. *Courtesy of Northrop Grumman Corporation*

BLC was promising enough that the Air Force awarded Northrop a $34 million research and development contract on 23 August 1960 to modify two Douglas WB-66D bombers as test beds. At this time Northrop coined the term 'Laminar Flow Control' (LFC). The term 'Boundary Layer Control' (BLC) had come to be used to describe the use of high-pressure air expelled through leading or trailing edge flaps to maintain airflow attachment, as with the F-4 Phantom and the British Blackburn Buccaneer.

Boeing Model 741-6 LFC test bed

While Northrop was carrying out its research, Boeing indicated its own intense interest in LFC by submitting a proposal to the Air Force to construct a test bed. Known as the Model 741-6, it was based on converting a KC-135 aircraft by rebuilding the wing and relocating the engines, at a price of $16.4 million for a single-aircraft test programme or $21 million for a two-aircraft programme.

The objective was to remove 90% of the boundary layer air from the wings by means of suction through a series of span-wise slots. The extraction was to be accomplished by four air compressors driven by Lycoming T55 turboshaft engines, with two sets per wing. The aircraft propulsion system consisted of four J57-P-43W engines mounted in pairs on the mid-aft fuselage, in specially modified B-52 engine pods.

Boeing Model 741-6	
Powerplant	4 x P&W J57-P-43W turbojets @ 13,750lb (61.16kN) thrust
Wingspan	134ft 5.5in (41.0m)
Length	128ft 10in (39.3m)
Height	38ft 4in (11.70m)
Max TOW	297,000lb (134,800kg)
Max payload	82,000lb (37,230kg)
Range	5,400nmi (10,000km) with 80,000lb (36,320kg) payload 6,600nmi (12,210km) with 40,000lb (18,160kg) payload 7,300nmi (13,500km) with 20,000lb (9,080kg) payload

RIGHT **The Boeing Model 741-6 test-bed had fuselage-mounted engines to avoid disturbing the laminar air flow on the new wing.** *Boeing*

Boeing forecast major improvements in both range and endurance. Assuming a common maximum GTOW of 297,000lb (134,800kg) and a payload of 40,000lb (18,160kg), the 741-6 could fly 1,300nmi (2,400km) further than the KC-135, a range extension of 25%. Trading 20,000lb (9,080kg) payload for fuel, the 741-6 had a projected endurance of nearly fifteen hours at a TOW of 243,000lb (109,900kg).

Boeing's proposal was submitted on 10 October 1960 but was not accepted. Instead, the Air Force opted for the Northrop proposal for the WB-66D-based test bed, two examples of which flew under the X-21A designation.

BELOW **The Boeing Model 741-6 Laminar Flow Control test aircraft.** *Boeing*

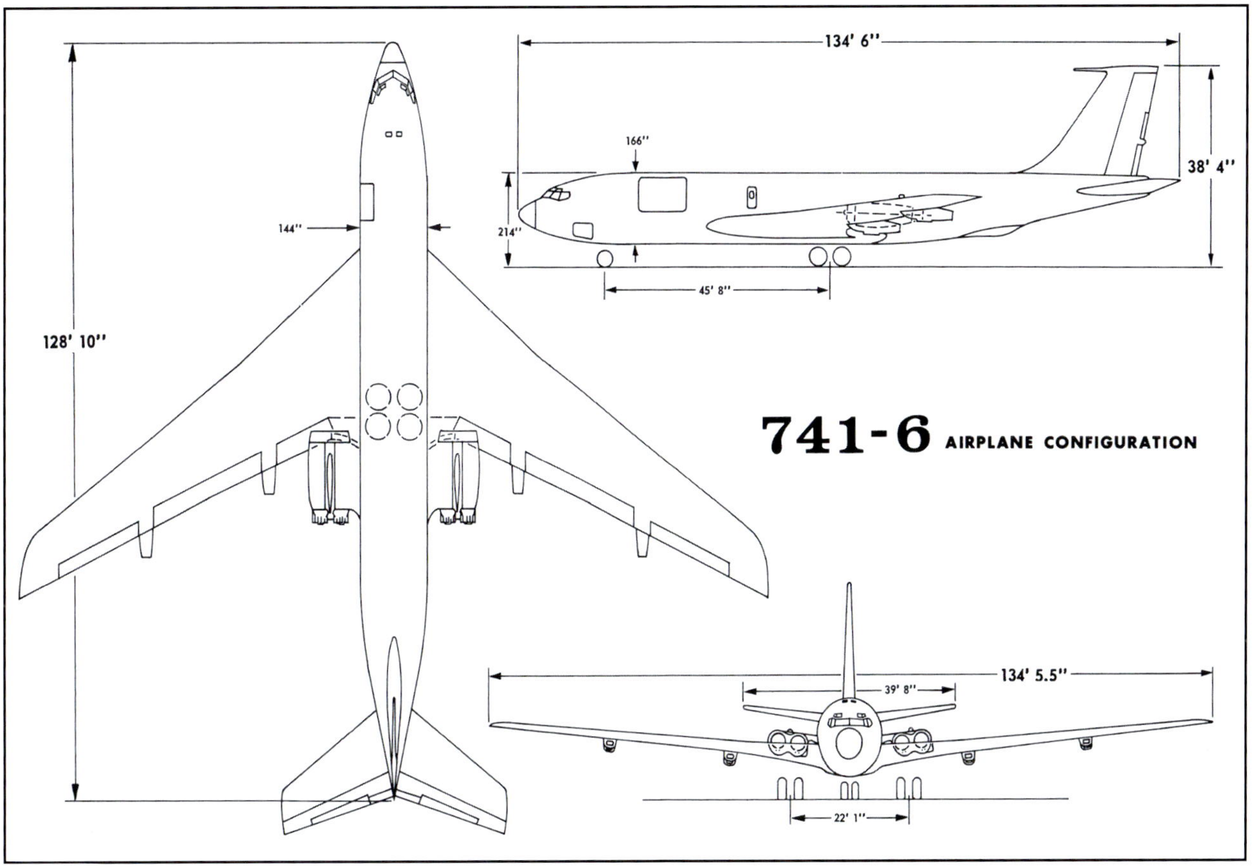

128' 10''

144''

134' 6''

166''

214''

38' 4''

45' 8''

741-6 AIRPLANE CONFIGURATION

134' 5.5''

39' 8''

22' 1''

Boeing Model 748B-28A LFC

Boeing continued to pursue its interest in LFC and in February 1963 proposed a further concept aircraft, the Model 748B-28A. This combined an LFC wing with the 748B fuselage. Suction for the LFC slots on the wing, which had a 206ft (62.83m) span and an area of 5,000sq ft (465m²), was to be provided by two 'bleed and burn' turbine engines mounted in the wing trailing edge structure near the fuselage. The wing was to be swept to 30°, and have a slightly higher than average aspect ratio of 8.5 for cruise efficiency. Both the wing (including flaps and ailerons) and the horizontal stabiliser were to have full-chord LFC suction slots, although this was not applied to the vertical stabiliser.

The engines were mounted on the sides of the fuselage, leaving the entire wing clear for the LFC slots, ducting and fuel. With four JT3D-8B engines rated at 17,000lb (76kN) thrust, the aircraft was thrust-limited and only met the minimum requirements of the SOR regarding payload. The thrust contribution of the LFC engines was not detailed. A rear ramp allowed for an air-drop capability; however, the opening was less than that of the C-130. To save weight, a lightweight landing gear was planned, but this ruled out any 'rough field' capability.

Boeing Model 748B-28A LFC	
Powerplant	4 x JT3D-8B turbofans @ 23,000lb (102kN) thrust
Span	206ft (62.83m)
Length	187ft (57m)
Height	55ft (16.8m)
Max TOW	438,000lb (198,673kg)
Cargo bay	100ft (30.5m) long x 16ft (4.88m) wide x 14ft (4.27m) high

Douglas Model D-906C LFC studies

Douglas also studied LFC integration with its CX-4 variants. The engineering study effort ran from January to April 1964. All studies retained the D-906C nose and centre-body sections, and modified the aft section as necessitated by empennage revision or engine installations. The effort was intended to define the most promising basic configurations for employing LFC rather than being a detailed engineering exercise.

A total of eight configurations were created for evaluation:

1. Minimum configuration change (engine nacelles under the wing)

BELOW Boeing Model 748B-28A general arrangement. *Boeing*

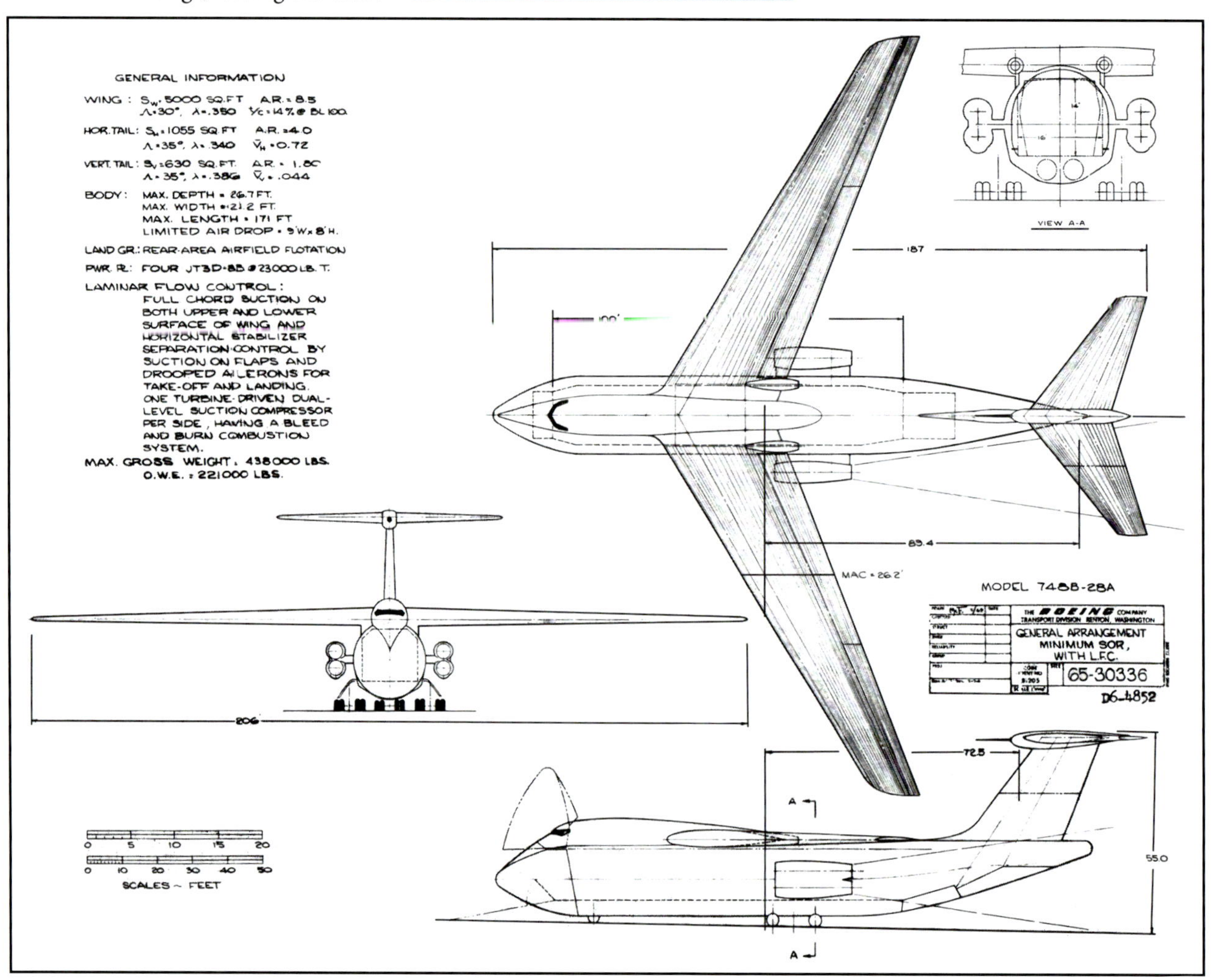

2 Aft fuselage clustered engines (at the base of the vertical tail)
3 Dual engine pods attached to the fuselage sides
4 Wing trailing edge, pylon-mounted engine pods
5 Engines buried in the wing root (similar to the Vickers Valiant)
6 Buried engines – forward swept wing
7 Tandem wings – dual engine pods
8 Canard wing

Two of the most interesting – and certainly least conventional – configurations were the sixth and seventh, with the forward-swept wing and tandem wing respectively.

The forward-sweep wing was employed for the purpose of reducing empty weight. The wing carry-through structure, the landing gear and empennage were all attached to common fuselage frames, and a common fuselage bulkhead served the front spar of the wing and the aft landing gear strut. Similarly, a single bulkhead served the wing rear spar and vertical tail front spar. Thus the length or the highly stressed part of the fuselage structure was reduced by 40%, resulting in a substantial reduction in weight. A further feature was the aft sweep of the wingtip; this aerodynamically counteracted the natural divergence associated with a forward-swept wing.

The tandem-wing configuration of the seventh option – the most radical of the configurations – offered the advantages of a clean wing, less airfoil surface area, less induced drag, and drastically reduced span. The latter meant that modified DC-8 wings could be employed, which was attractive cost-wise. The elimination of the horizontal stabiliser also reduced the empennage area by 67%, reducing weight and drag.

However, the tandem wing configuration had a serious flaw. Quoting Douglas's own report:

> 'By nature, the tandem wing creates unfavourable interference between the forward and aft surfaces due to downwash from the forward wing. Because of the inherent high induced drag of a tandem wing arrangement, application to a long-range cargo airplane does not appear attractive.'

Douglas CX-HLS Laminar Flow Control studies

	LFC Concept 'Six'	LFC Concept 'Seven'
Powerplant	4 x P&W JT3D-8B turbofans @ 23,000lb (102kN) thrust	x P&W JT3D-8B turbofans 4 @ 23,000lb (102kN) thrust
Wingspan	213ft (64.9m)	135ft (41.1m)
Length	208ft (63.4m)	180ft (54.9m)
Height	63.2ft (19.3m)	64.6ft (19.7m)
Wing area	6,500sq ft (603.9m²)	6,600sq ft (613.25m²)

BELOW Douglas LFC 'Study Configuration 6 – Forward Swept Wing'. *Boeing*

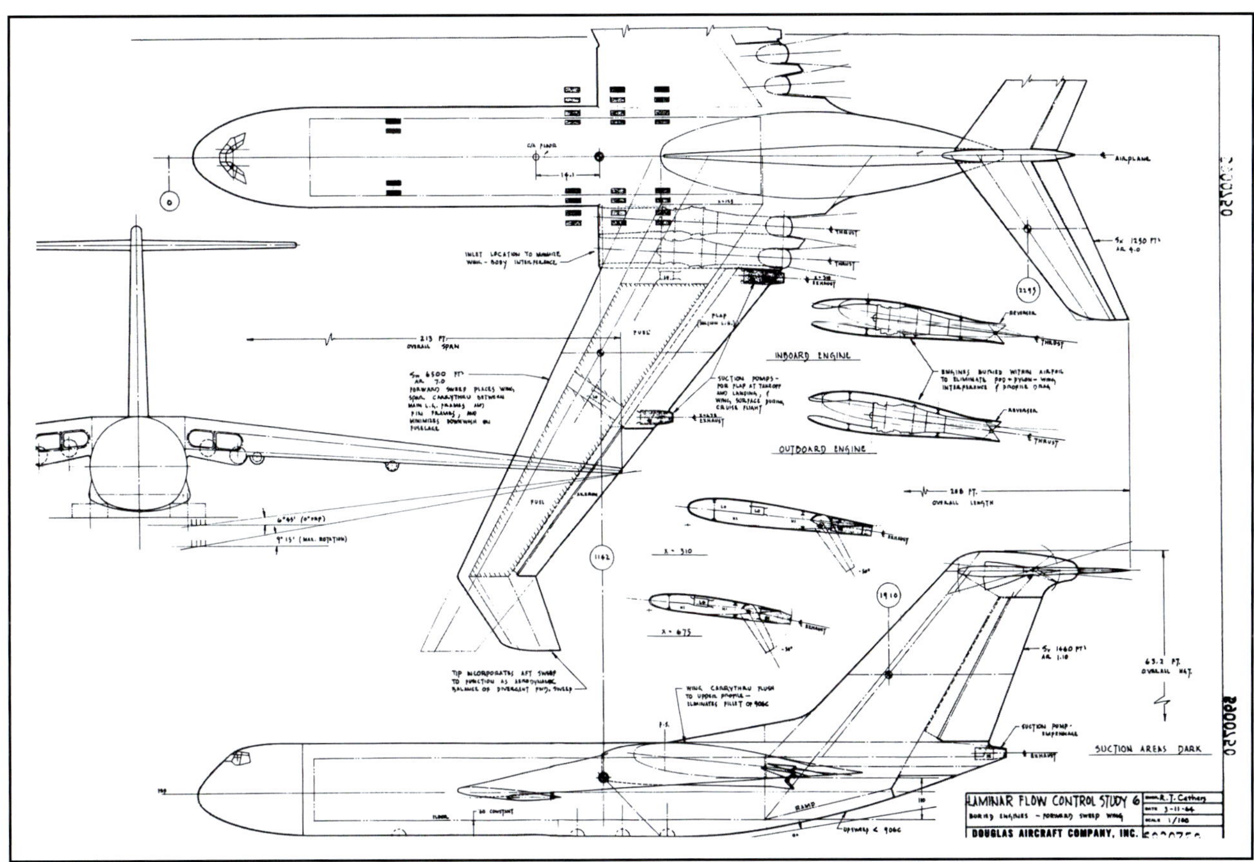

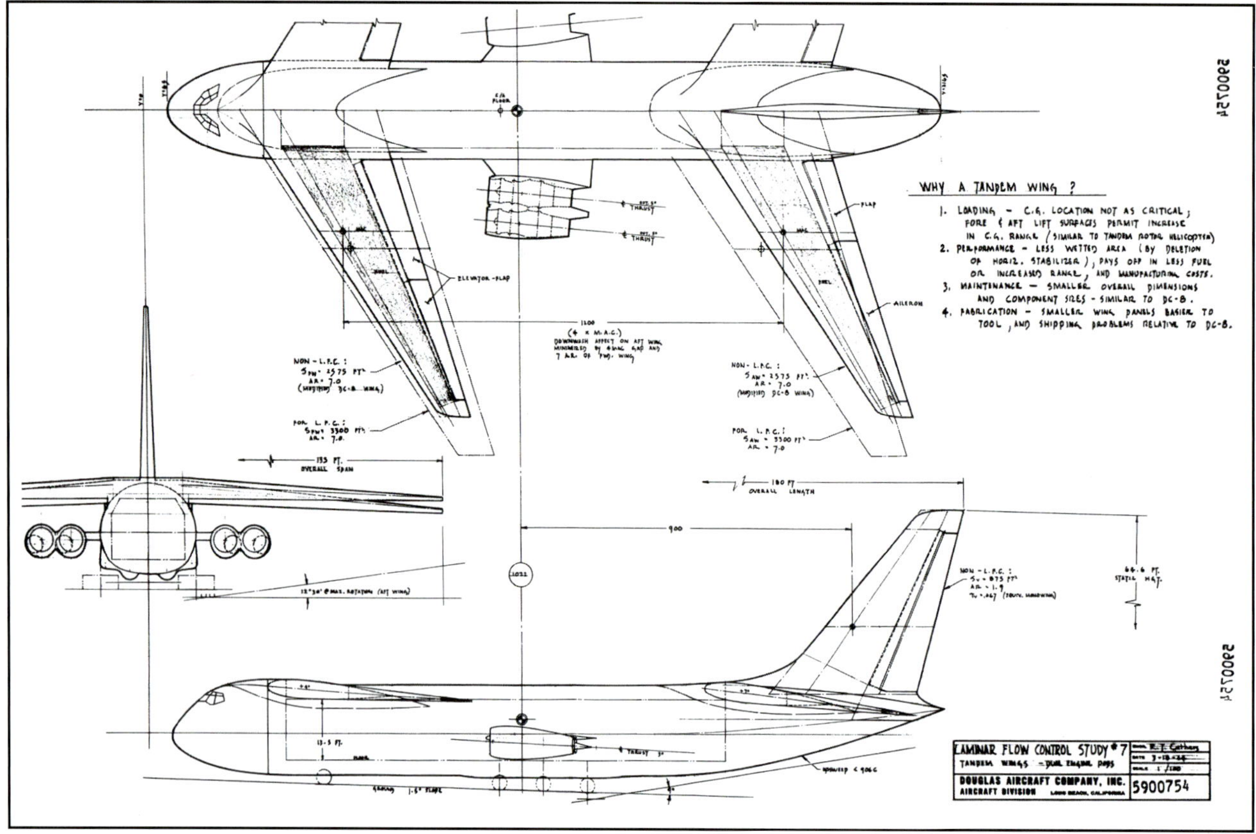

ABOVE Douglas LFC 'Study Configuration 7 – Tandem Wing'. *Boeing*

The outcome of the CX-X studies

Ultimately, the CX-X initiative proved an interruption to the process of developing a new airlifter, rather than a useful step along the way. Of the new technologies investigated, only one – the high-bypass turbofan – would eventually fulfil the anticipated promise and have any influence on the design and operation of the C-5.

Regenerative/recuperative turboprops proved incapable of providing either the power needed, or the speed desired, for the intended cargo aircraft.

The X-21 test programme found that the LFC concept was fraught with practical difficulties in both fabrication and operation. Minute differences in surface contour were enough to trip the laminar flow into turbulence. Any build-up of dirt, dust or insects degraded performance. Even very small, invisible ice crystals near clouds had an effect. It was found that, at least as far as the X-21 was concerned, LFC worked best in level flight in clear, clean air with little turbulence – rendering it incapable of widespread practical application.

Clearly, with the different goals of the CX-4 and CX-X initiatives, the Air Force was not speaking with one voice when it came to meeting the needs of the Army. However, a compromise was achieved: the CX-4 was dead, replaced in November 1963 by CX-HLC (Cargo Experimental – Heavy Logistics Carrier). That in turn was renamed in January 1964 as GT (Global Transport) and, later that month, as CX-HLS (Cargo Experimental – Heavy Logistics System). The separate CX-X initiative continued for some months under AFSC leadership, but withered as unresponsive to the requirements of the CX-HLS stakeholders.

CX-HLS: Concept Formulation Phase (CFP), May to September 1964

After the diversion of the CX-X initiative, on 27 April 1964 the Air Force issued Requests for Proposal for parametric CX-HLS studies for the next phase of the effort, with responses due on 18 May. The DoD had authorised some $17 million in December 1963 for studies, the first that the Air Force directly funded. A significant amount was directed to the engine manufacturers for advanced engine development and component testing.

On 5 June 1964 the Air Force selected three manufacturers for the Concept Formulation Phase. Not surprisingly, these were Boeing, Douglas and Lockheed. General Dynamics (Convair) and Martin Marietta were eliminated. Of the engine-makers, General Electric and

Pratt & Whitney were to continue work, with Curtiss-Wright leaving the competition. The detailed recommendations and submissions for the next programme phase were required by December 1964.

A memorandum distributed to Douglas engineers during the CFP effort clearly laid out the purpose of the study effort and provides an insight into Douglas's goals in undertaking it:

'Objectives of the Final Report:

1 To provide the Air Force with essential data which provides the basis for definition of the system characteristics and requirements that best satisfy the military objectives for the CX-HLS.
2 To provide the Air Force with essential prerequisite information necessary for requesting authorisation to proceed to the Project Definition Phase.
3 To present this data and information in a manner which positively convinces the Air Force that Douglas is the best qualified contractor to carry on this program through the Definition and Acquisition Phase.

'Meeting the Objectives:
In order to meet these objectives, the report must be responsive to the requirements in the "Statement of Work" and the subsequent requests for information. Remember that Douglas is providing a technical service for the Air Force. The data and information we submit must be useful to the Air Force in meeting their primary objective – to define CX-HLS system characteristics and requirements which best satisfy the military objectives.'

Boeing Model 750 development

Boeing changed the Model 748 designation to Model 750 in anticipation of receipt of the CFP contract, in order to separate the work effort prior to, and after receipt of, the contract in June 1964. These were assigned to match the contract tasks to be performed as follows:

750-100 series
Task II aircraft with GE-1/6 engines

750-200 series
Task II aircraft with P&W STF 200-D2 engines

750-1000 series
Task III aircraft with GE-1/6 engines

750-2000 series
Task III aircraft with P&W STF-200-D2 engines

750-3000 series
Task III aircraft with six P&W TF-33 engines, blown trailing edge flaps and reduced maximum design payloads. (Studies on this variant ended early on.)

BELOW **A model of a Boeing Model 750 design near the end of the CX-HLS Project Definition Phase. The constant section aft of the cockpit, pointed nose and wing anhedral would all later be modified.** *Boeing*

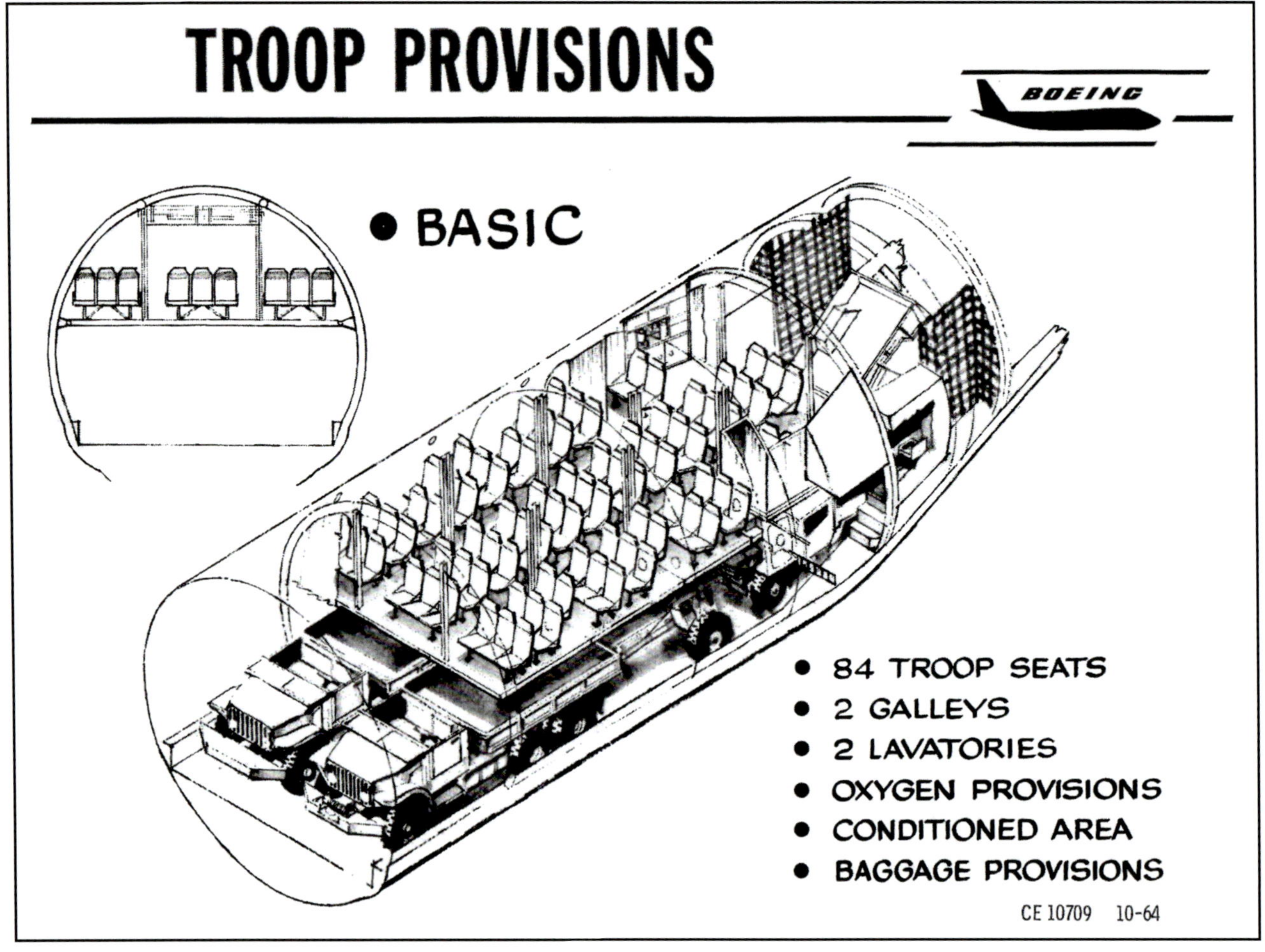

ABOVE Boeing offered troop seating in a 'mezzanine deck' in the aft fuselage that was removable to accommodate outsized (tall) cargo. *Boeing*

Per DoD request, Boeing also explored the feasibility of utilising the CX-HLS Transport aircraft for commercial purposes. By October 1964 engineers had investigated eight derivatives of the Model 750, with five in the 750-2100 to 2104 sequence. However, per a 14 October 1964 Boeing memo, further work was done under new model numbers 757-2105 to 2107 explicitly to segregate the commercial studies from the military airlifter.

By 1 October 1964 Boeing noted that the aircraft studies conducted on the Model 750 had reached the following totals:

750-1001 to 750-1054	54
750-2001 to 750-2050	50
750-3001 to 750-3060	60

Douglas Model D-909/910/911

As Douglas continued its engineering effort with the D-909, it also expanded its industrial team by adding North American Aviation and Martin Marietta as major subcontractors, on 3 August and 8 September 1964 respectively.

The D-909 had the largest fuselage cross section yet, at 18.5ft (5.64m), with an increased length of 206ft (62.79m). While it retained the swing nose of the designs going back to the D-900, Douglas began studying upward-opening visor concepts when several concerns were raised about the arrangement:

- Aircraft systems could not be operated with the nose/cockpit open
- It gave rise to possible structural issues with fuselage twisting when the nose was open
- It needed powerful cargo restraints (which added weight) to prevent the cargo being catapulted through the cockpit in the event of a crash

The D-909 was designed with the P&W STF-200-D engines, and the D-910 was an identical design with the GE 1/6 engine. The D-911 was similar to the D-909, but with uprated P&W engines.

Lockheed Model L-500

By the end of the study period, Lockheed parametric studies had led the company to propose a design to the Air Force that reflected differing priorities. By selecting a 25° wing sweep (Boeing and Douglas having selected 35°), Lockheed settled for a

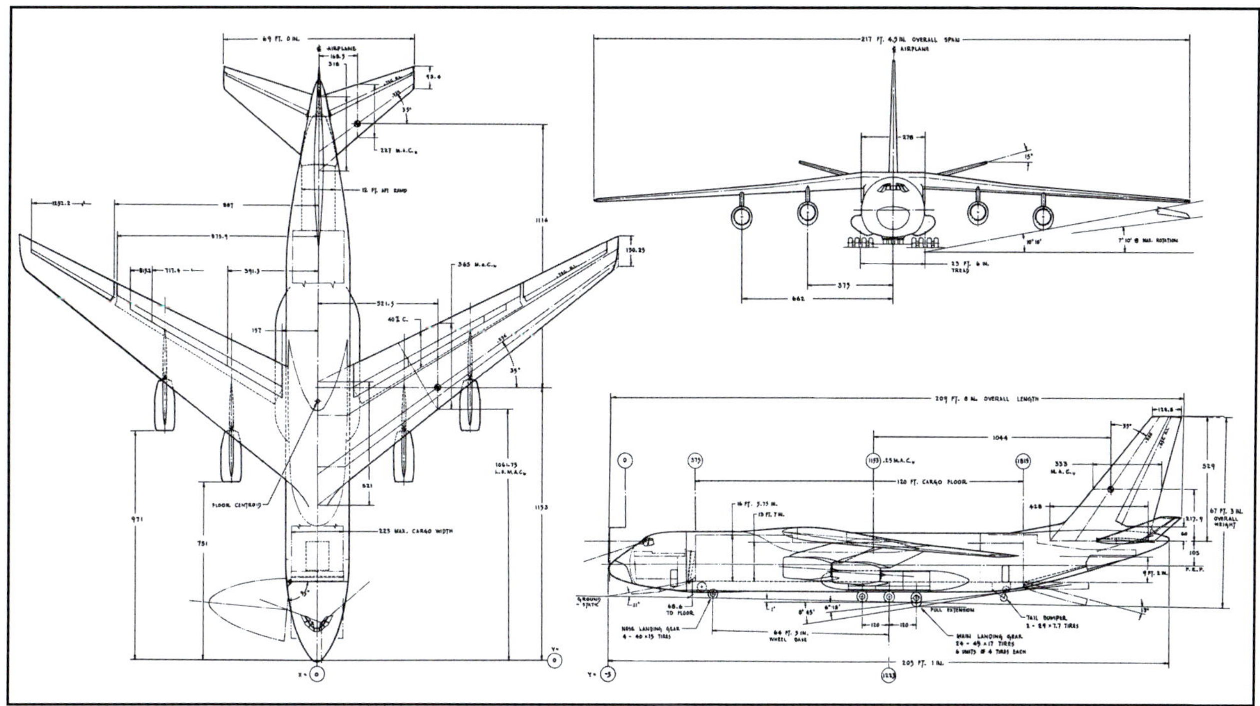

ABOVE **Douglas Model D-909 general arrangement.** *Boeing*

BELOW **The swing-nose Douglas Model D-909 as envisaged in a remote, unimproved location.** *Boeing*

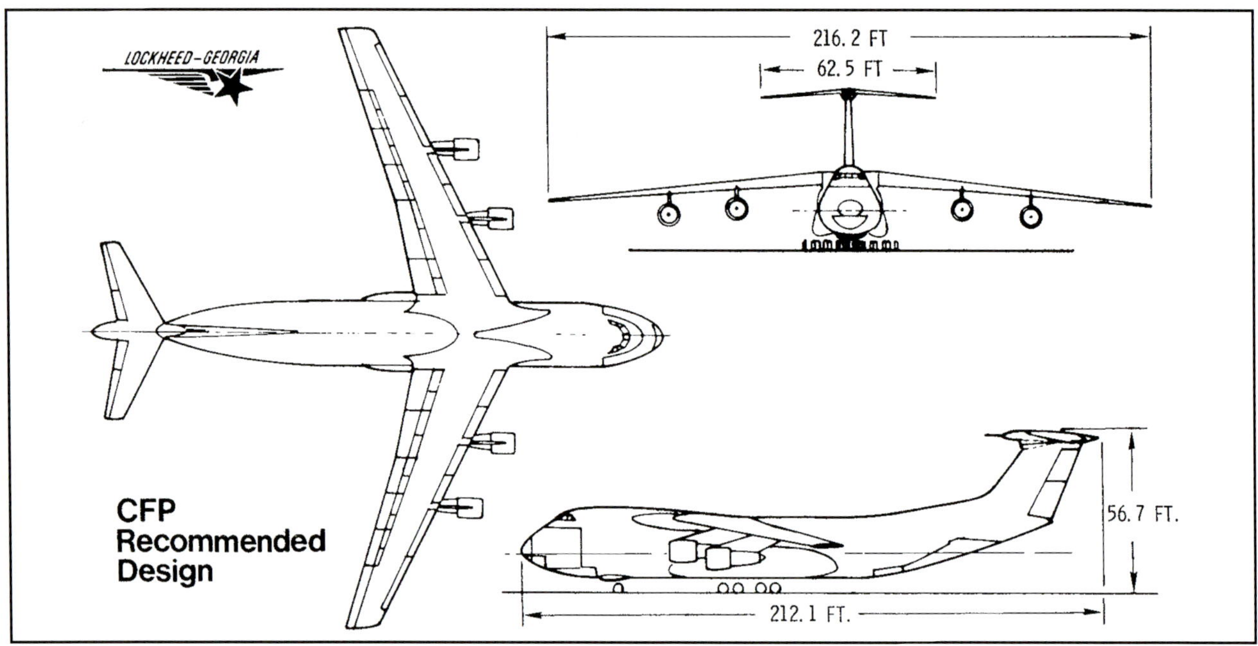

LOCKHEED-GEORGIA CFP TRADE STUDY **Nose Loading Comparison**	△OWE	△TOGW	RELATIVE SYSTEM COST	RAMP AREA FT^2
13.5' X 17.5' - FULL SWING - CONV. SHAPE	-7,730	-14,630	1.044	0
13.5' X 17.5' - SIDE SWING - RAISED CAB	0	0	1.000	210
13.5' X 17.5' - KNIGHT'S VISOR - RAISED CAB	-717	-1,155	0.994	242
13.5' X 17.5' - SPLIT - RAISED CAB	+350	+562	0.980	282
9' X 13.5' - CLAMSHELL - RAISED CAB	-717	-1,155	1.000	194
13.5' X 17.5' - SIDE SWING - MINIMUM RAISED COCKPIT	-5,320	-9,490	1.051	0
NO OPENING - CONVENTIONAL SHAPE	-19,540	-33,650	1.022	0

ABOVE General arrangement of the Lockheed recommended design at the end of the Concept Formulation Phase. *Lockheed*

LEFT The Lockheed-recommended C-5A design with simple Fowler flaps as of August 1964. *Lockheed*

cruise speed that just met the minimum specified by the RFP. However, the benefits of a lower cruise speed included lower fuel consumption and a wing better suited for lower take-off and landing speeds. Lockheed had taken the same approach with the 25° wing sweep of the C-141, which avoided the need for leading edge flaps and slats for low-speed lift generation.

The cargo compartment size was set at 100ft (30.48m) long by 17.5ft (5.34m) wide by 13.5ft (4.12m) high. Compartments as large as 140ft (42.7m) long by 19.5ft (5.95m) wide were studied but rejected as being too big (penalising performance and weight). At the same time, the cockpit was relocated to a position over the cargo compartment, but the fuselage retained its circular cross section aft of the wing. Lockheed submitted mid-term reports on 27 July, and final reports for Air Force evaluation on 14 September 1964.

LEFT Lockheed evaluated nose-loading options in a series of trade studies, concluding that the 'knight's visor' was the best option. *Lockheed*

CX-HLS: Project Definition Phase, December 1964 to October 1965

September 1964 saw the completion of the Concept Formulation Phase as each contractor's parametric studies converged on its preferred solutions. The upcoming Project Definition Phase (PDP) would see optimisation and 'fine tuning' of the designs. This phase led to yet another programme name change: the CX-HLS designation was changed by the Air Force to C-5A on 22 February 1965.

At this time one of the Air Force's major concerns was the progressive growth in weight of the proposals – a common occurrence, since the design of almost any aircraft increases from initial concept to final version. However, it was a particular concern for such a large aircraft, with every additional pound both increasing cost and reducing performance (in range or payload – or both). Pressure from the Air Force forced continual redesign and the adoption of more exotic and expensive manufacturing processes.

Contracts were awarded in January 1965 for the PDP (also known as the Phase 1B effort), with expectations for a selection and development contract award some time in August 1965.

Boeing Models 750-1050/2050 and 750-1101/2101

	Model 750-1050/2050	Model 750-1101/2101
Powerplant	GE or PW turbofans	GE or PW turbofans @ 40,000lb (178kN) thrust
Wing area	5,500sq ft (512m²)	6,000sq ft (558m²)
Vertical fin area	800sq ft (74.3m²)	830sq ft (77.1m²)
Horizontal stabiliser area	1,260sq ft (117.1m²)	1,440sq ft (133.8m²)
Payload	n/a	200,000lb (90,800kg) or 591 troops

Boeing Model 750

Boeing started this phase of project development by redesignating Models 750-1050 and 750-2050 as Models 750-1101 (GE) and 750-2101 (P&W) on 8 January 1965, to reflect the requirements of the Request for Proposal dated 10 December 1964. Differences included increased wing area and tail surface areas, moving the main landing gear forward, and increasing the tyre sizes. These changes were accompanied by an anticipated increase in engine thrust. As a result the aircraft could now carry a payload of 200,000lb (90,800kg) and the upper deck above the cargo bay could accommodate eighty-four troops. Fully configured as a troop transport, it could potentially carry 591 troops.

By 12 February 1965 further design changes became necessary when Boeing's initial response to the RFP was judged by the Air Force System Program Office (SPO) to have too high a gross take-off weight. Coordination between the SPO and Boeing resulted in a redesign – the Model 750-1105 (GE) – with a reduction in gross weight from 692,000lb (314,200kg) to 665,000lb (301,900kg). Engineers accomplished this by reducing the wing area from 6,000sq ft (558m²) to 5,500sq ft (511.5m²), shortening the fuselage by 80in (203cm), and introducing a host of detail changes.

BELOW **The Boeing Model 750 is depicted making a rough field landing.** *Boeing*

Boeing Model 750-GE and Model 750-PW

Designation	Engine	Thrust	Bypass ratio
Model 750-GE* (750-1124)	GE 1/6-F4C	40,000lb (178kN)	8.0 BPR
Model 750-PW* (750-2124)	P&W JTF14E-2B	40,000lb (178kN)	3.8 BPR

* As a practical matter, the Boeing model numbers were truncated to '750 (GE)' and '750 (PW)' for the 20 April 1965 proposal submission, obscuring the previous engineering design designations from public view.

The Model 750-2105 (with P&W engines) was reduced in size proportionately – from 707,000lb (321,000kg) to 693,000lb (314,600kg) – with the same wing and body changes. Continued effort by the SPO and Boeing to reduce the aircraft size resulted in reducing the operating weight empty (OWE) from 321,000lb (110,700kg) to 314,000lb (142,600kg) gross weight, leaving the wing and tail unchanged.

On 20 April 1965 Boeing submitted its firm proposals for the 'C-5A Long Range Heavy Logistic Transport Support System' – the Models 750-1124 (GE) and 750-2124 (P&W). These differed only in their engines and had the same potential maximum gross weight of 725,000lb (329,200kg) and maximum useful load of 415,000lb (188,400kg).

Douglas Models D-916 and D-917

Douglas intensified its focus on the project by establishing the 'C-5 Division' within the Douglas Aircraft Group at Long Beach on 15 December 1964. This was widely announced. However, what was unknown outside the company was the fact that the new D-912 configuration had abandoned the swing cockpit/nose in favour of a fixed 'cab-over' cockpit and a swing nose. Once this decision had been made, Douglas immediately began the construction of a new fuselage 'loading mock-up'. Meanwhile, continuing changes resulted in a further design iteration, the D-913. This, in turn, was superseded by a further point design, offered with different engines, designated the D-914 (GE) and D-915 (P&W) respectively. By March 1965 Douglas finalised its submittal designs, again differentiated by engine option, as shown in the accompanying table.

The D-916 and the D-917 aircraft were identical with the exception of engines, nacelles and pylons. The corresponding maximum gross take-off weights had grown to 663,000lb (301,000kg) and 699,000lb (303,700kg). Accordingly, the wingspan had increased from the 185.7ft (56.64m) of the D-902 to 222.7ft (67.92m) on the D-916/17.

Douglas Models D-916 and D-917

Designation	Engine	Thrust	Bypass ratio
Model D-916	GE 1/6-F4C	40,000lb (178kN)	8.0 BPR
Model D-917	P&W JTF14-(2D)*	40,200lb (178.9kN)	3.8 BPR

*The formal P&W 'in-house' JTF-14 model designation superseded the 'study' STF-200 designation when engine test rigs were built.

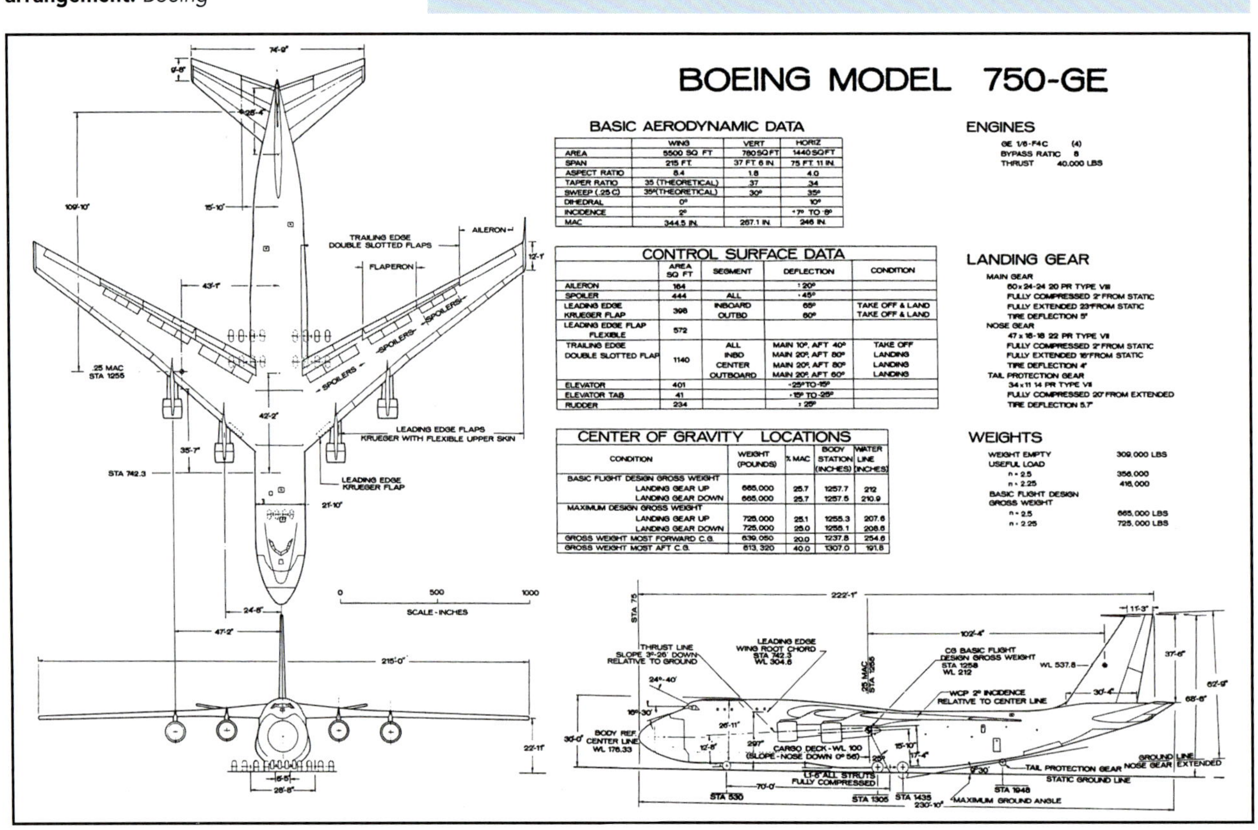

BELOW Boeing Model 750-GE general arrangement. *Boeing*

Douglas reported that the D916/917 could meet or beat all of the stipulated requirements and carry 50,000lb (22,670kg) over 5,805 miles, 100,000lb (45,359kg) over 4,055 miles (6,525km), or an ultimate 130,000lb (59,020kg) payload. At its maximum take-off weight it could clear a 50ft (15.24m) obstacle after a ground run of 7,900ft (2,410m) and land with a 100,000lb (45,359kg) payload within a distance of 3,260ft (994m).

Douglas had chosen a fuselage 25ft (7.63m) in diameter and a large cargo deck 19.3ft (5.88m) wide. In a major change, the cockpit was moved to a fixed 'cab-over' position so that only the nose cone swung to the right. Further, the cockpit was raised 2ft (61cm) to allow a taller forward compartment. The government requirement for carrying troops led to a 'mezzanine' troop deck aft of the wing. The trade-off was a reduction in the main cargo compartment height in this area. A second nose landing gear (in tandem behind the first) was added for improved weight distribution.

In its proposal summary, Douglas re-emphasised its commitment to the program with the following statement: 'The C-5A is the only new aircraft system under development at Douglas. Douglas management's decision not to pursue the SST, AMPSS, CX-6, or ADO-12 programs and to confine commercial programs to DC-8 and DC-9 model improvements was made so that the full engineering and development talents of the Douglas Aircraft Group could be devoted to the C-5A Program.'

RIGHT Built in early 1965, the Douglas mock-up was frozen at the Model D-912B configuration. Continuing design refinement resulted in wing, landing gear and engine changes, but the fuselage mock-up was close to the D-916/917 designs as submitted in April 1965. *Boeing*

BELOW A Douglas Model D-916 display model with cargo inserts. Passengers would be carried on an upper deck (light blue) fore and aft of the wing carry-through structure. *Boeing*

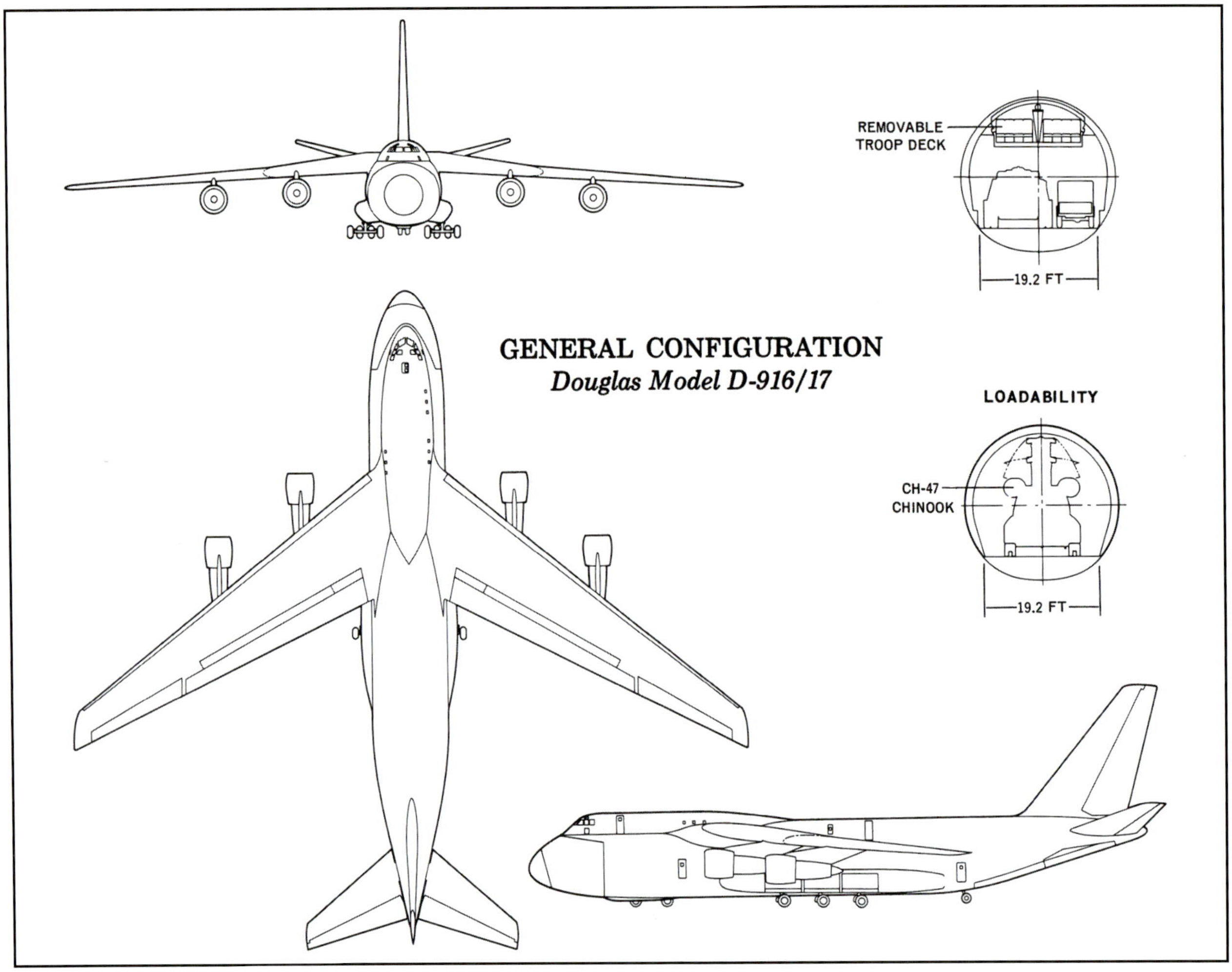

REMOVABLE TROOP DECK
19.2 FT
GENERAL CONFIGURATION
Douglas Model D-916/17
LOADABILITY
CH-47 CHINOOK
19.2 FT

ABOVE **Douglas Model D-916/917 general arrangement with GE engines.** *Boeing*

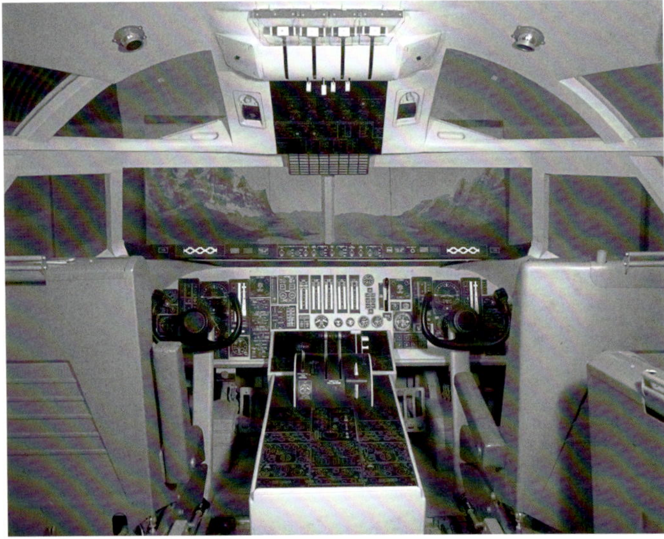

BELOW **Douglas's reasoning for the wider deck is illustrated here – the extra 20.5in (52.1cm) allowed the side-by-side carriage of many vehicle types in what would otherwise be wasted space. However, the larger cross section caused added airframe drag, which reduced range and speed.** *Boeing*

17.5 FOOT FLOOR
19.2 FOOT FLOOR
AVL
158 IN.
AVL
63
M-60
143 IN.
74
74
74
74
74
74

BELOW **The Douglas C-5A cockpit mock-up, with the vertical 'tape' instruments that came into vogue in the early 1960s. The flight engineer was to be seated in the right foreground.** *Boeing*

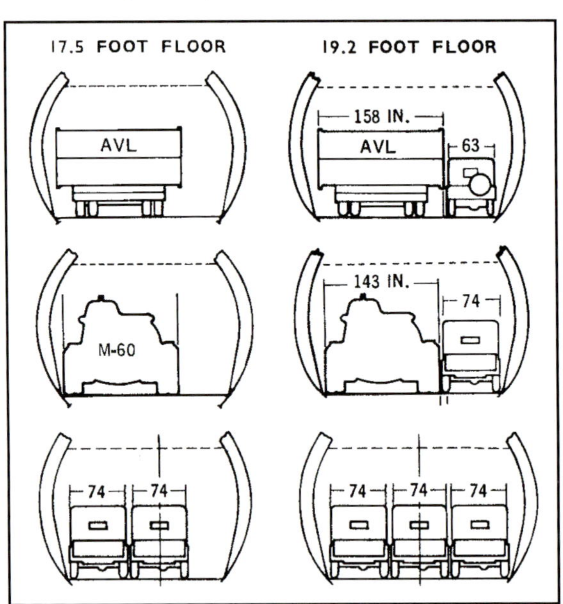

Lockheed Model L-500

Lockheed's L-500 of April 1965 had evolved considerably from the design recommended at the end of the Concept Formulation Phase in August of the previous year. The overall design had been enlarged in size by about 5% to 10%, with the length increasing from 212.1ft to 231ft (64.6m to 70.4m). Conversely, wingspan decreased from 216.2ft (65.94m) to 211.8ft (64.60m) as the Lockheed designers were forced to reduce the aspect ratio of the wing to cope with recalculated bending moments and to maintain structural margins. Lockheed maintained a wing sweep (at quarter chord) of 25°, which was less than that of its competitors. Payload was set at 100,000lb (45,359kg) at a range of 5,500nmi (10,180km) at a GTOW of 685,000lb (311,000kg). The maximum gross TOW was now set at 749,000lb (340,000kg). Payload could be increased with corresponding range reductions.

The aircraft was also subtly reshaped, with the cargo deck widened from 17.5ft (5.34m) to 19.3ft (5.89m). The wing-to-body fairing and landing gear fairings received particular wind tunnel attention to seek drag reduction. The most visible change since 1964 was the extension of the upper fuselage bubble aft of the wing. The added volume allowed Lockheed to create a dedicated aft passenger compartment housing seventy-five passengers. A kneeling landing gear was chosen, allowing the use of shorter and lighter integral loading ramps. Rough field capability (flotation) was to be improved by in-flight tyre deflation prior to landing.

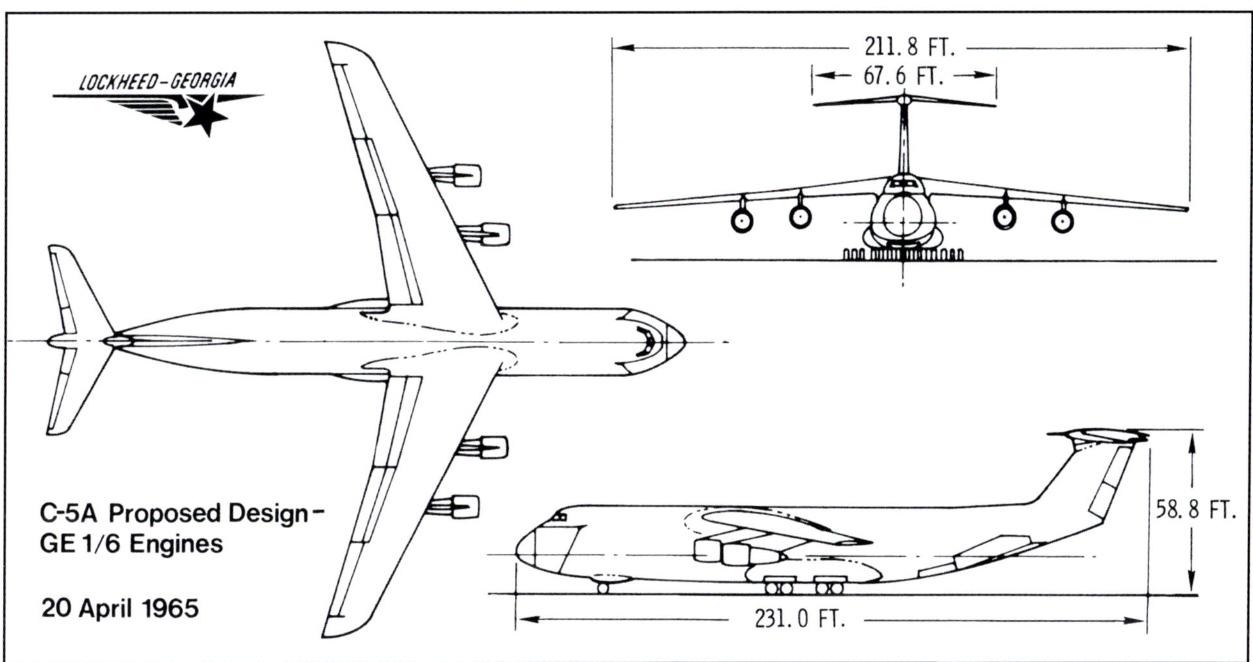

ABOVE **The Lockheed recommended C-5A design as of April 1965.** *Lockheed*

BELOW **The Lockheed Model L-500 loading mock-up. The wing fillet and landing gear sponson fairings would see continuing revisions to reduce drag.** *Lockheed*

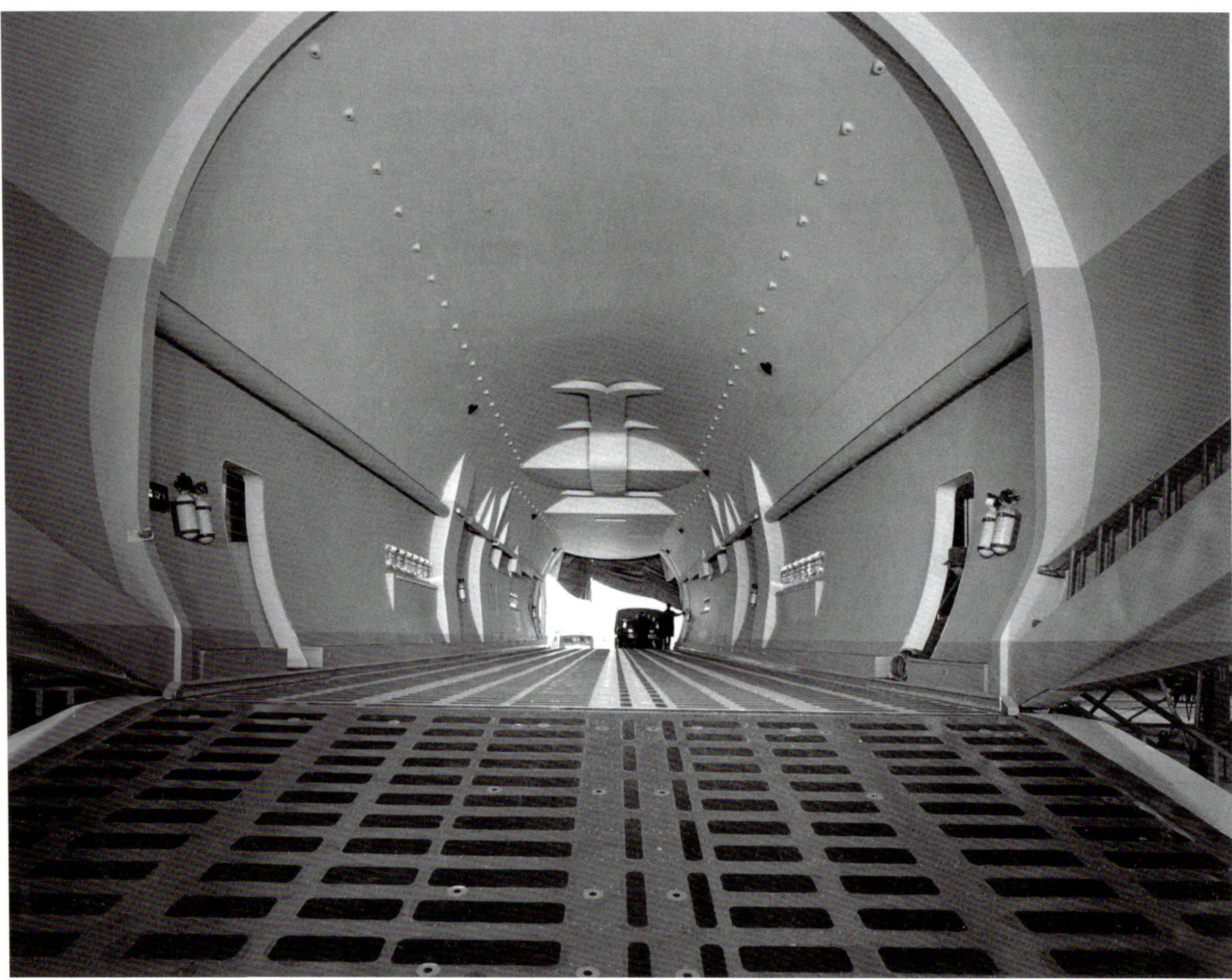

ABOVE The view (looking forward) of the Lockheed Model L-500 cargo compartment mock-up. The upper aft passenger deck had not been added at this point. *NARA II via Dennis R. Jenkins*

Companies submitted their final proposals on 20 April 1965 to the USAF's Aeronautical Systems Division (ASD) at Wright-Patterson AFB, Dayton. In summary, the proposals all featured a high wing with four pylon-mounted high-bypass turbofans, together with front and rear loading/unloading, with the facility for troop seating on the upper deck. The main differences related to the mounting of the horizontal stabiliser (conventionally on two designs, with the Lockheed aircraft employing a T-tail, as on its C-141) and in the arrangement for front loading. For the latter, Boeing and Douglas opted for a side-swinging nose with a fixed flight deck, while Lockheed chose an upward-opening arrangement. The last had the unique advantage of allowing the aircraft to taxi (albeit slowly) with the nose 'visor' open. Interestingly, Boeing had started with an upward-lifting nose and Douglas with a side-swinging forward fuselage and flight deck.

Post-submittal changes and engine selection

Even after the proposals had been submitted in April 1965, development work continued on a month-by-month basis, funded by the Air Force. Under the concept of 'technical transfusion', the Air Force negotiated with each contractor to incorporate selected features from their competitors' designs in order to assure that the final proposals would have all of the best features from three proposals. Lockheed, for instance, received 1,456 plan and specification change requests.

Boeing added 'A' designations to the in-house model numbers as a result of the Air Force's requested revisions. The primary change was to move from the two-row/four-tyres-per-axle main landing gear to a three-row/two-tyres-per-axle gear to improve rough field capability. A series of weight-saving measures were also incorporated. To address Air Force concerns about the length of the take-off and landing runs, Lockheed had to increase the L-500 wing area by a further 200sq ft (18.6m^2), bringing the span to 222ft 8.5in (67.93m), and increase the flap area.

In the meantime, the issue of engine selection was settled in a separate competition in early August 1965 when the Air Force selected General Electric over Pratt & Whitney. Although both engines were rated at a nominal 40,000lbst (178kN) at sea level, the GE

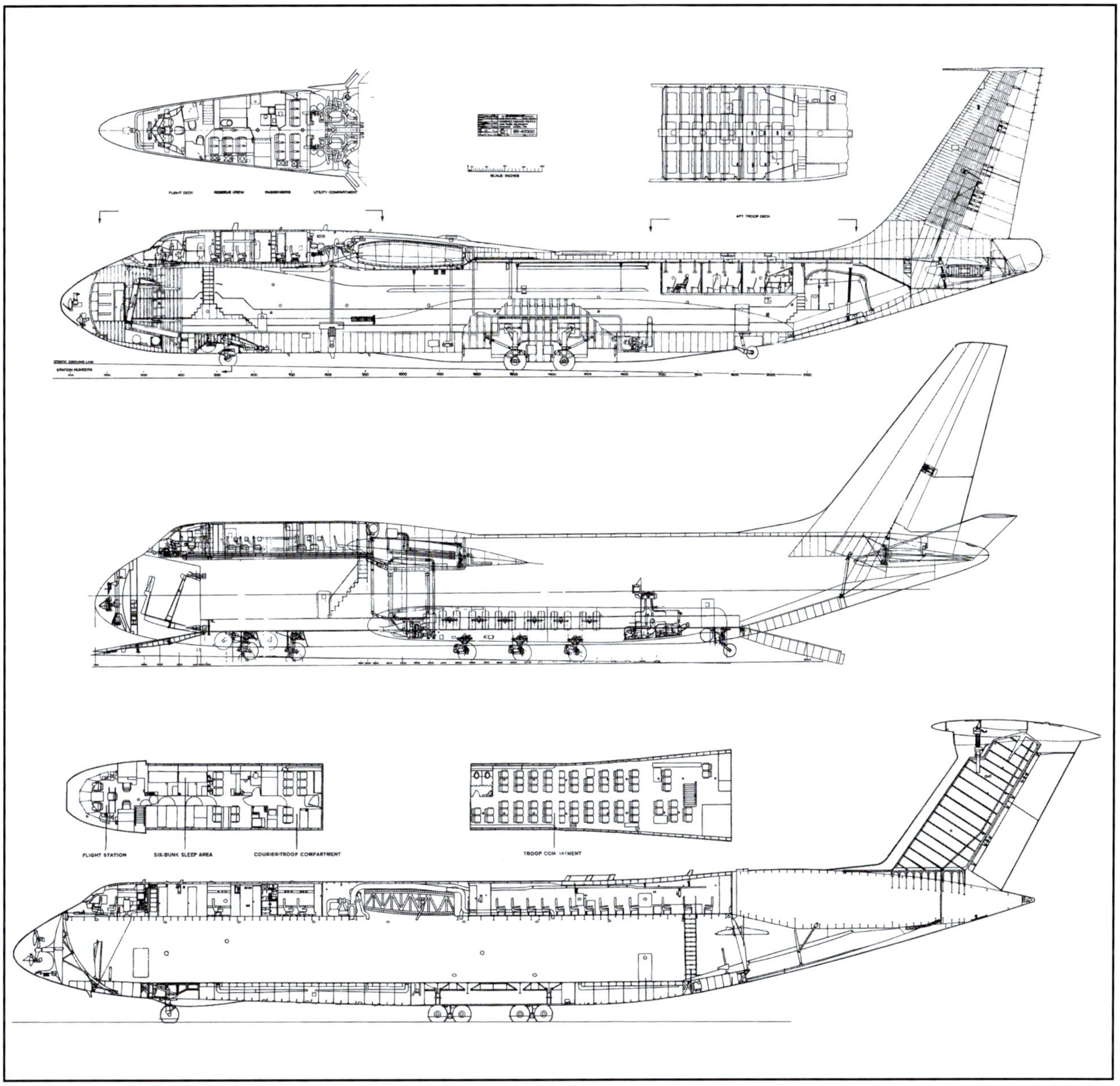

ABOVE **Inboard profiles (to the same scale) for the Boeing Model 750-GE (top), Douglas Model D-916 (middle) – April 1965 submissions – and Lockheed C-5A (bottom, as built).** *Authors, based on Boeing, Douglas and Lockheed drawings*

BELOW **The cross sections of the Boeing Model 750, Douglas Model D-916 and Lockheed Model L-500 illustrate landing gear stowage and cargo deck height differences. Some cargo (in this case a jeep) could be hoisted up under the Boeing wing to open up deck space. The Lockheed L-500 shows the different elevation capabilities of the 'kneeling' landing gear.** *Authors, based on Boeing, Douglas and Lockheed drawings*

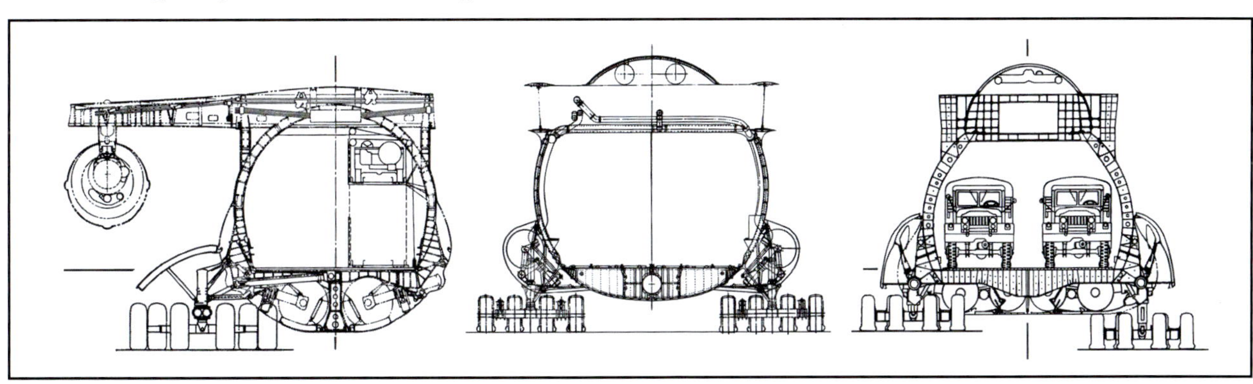

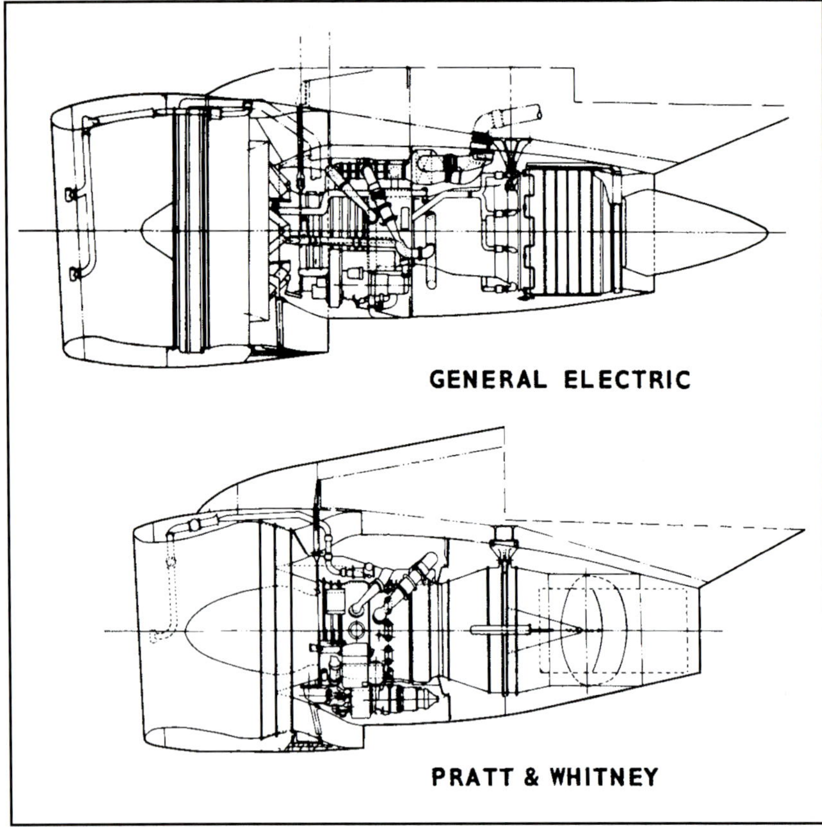

ABOVE A comparison of the more fuel-efficient GE 1/6 and the smaller, lighter and less complex P&W STF-200 engines proposed for the C-5A. *Boeing*

engine (receiving the 'TF39' Air Force designation) had a higher bypass ratio and lower fuel consumption (but with poorer performance at high altitudes). The P&W offering was smaller and lighter with better performance at altitude, but had a lower bypass ratio with higher fuel consumption.

Evaluation of the Three C-5A Proposals

The main characteristics of the three C-5A proposals (in their final form) were as shown in the accompanying table.

A unique insight into the evaluation of the three submissions is found in a letter from Air Force Secretary Eugene Zuckert to Defense Secretary McNamara dated 23 September 1965, which summarised the technical and cost evaluations of the three proposals.

According to this document, the Boeing submission was judged at the outset as meeting the RFP mission performance requirements with two relatively minor exceptions. The first related to the necessity to reduce the cruise speed slightly to meet the range requirement in the event of an engine-out take-off, something that Boeing proposed to overcome by using a blown-flap arrangement to improve three-engine climb rate. The second was a small shortfall in range (120nmi or 222km) when undertaking a maximum weight mission while cruising at 470kt (870km); however, this could be easily overcome simply by cruising at 440kt (815km/h), which was still within the RFP requirements. As a result it was judged 'that there was no redesign risk involved in meeting the mission performance requirements of the RFP or the IOC date.'

The proposal drew praise both for both its high cruise speed and – thanks to its external blown-flap system – its low-speed handling and short-field capability.

Boeing was assessed as using the total loadable area more efficiently than its two competitors, but the cargo compartment was seen as likely to create loading problems since it had the least uniform floor plan and ceiling height. Moreover, the width of 17.5ft (5.34m) – the minimum specified in the RFP – required asymmetric positioning of the 463L pallets in order to accommodate the two-abreast layout. This meant that careful preplanning was required to make full use of the space – something not always possible under emergency conditions. On other hand, for air-drop missions Boeing's loadable floor length of 136ft (41.48m) enabled it to exceed the air-drop capability of the shorter 120ft (36.6m) floor length designs of Douglas and Lockheed.

Overall, the Boeing proposal was judged as having 'provided the best technically balanced design for meeting the various performance requirements of the RFP.'

Proposed C-5A characteristics (revised submissions of 4 September 1965)

	Boeing Model 750	Douglas Model D-916D	Lockheed Model L-500
Wing area	5,500sq ft (511.5m²)	6,200sq ft (576.6m²)	6,200sq ft (576.6m²)
Wingspan	215ft (65.58m)	222.8ft (69.95m)	222.7ft (67.92m)
Length	222ft (67.71m)	208.1ft (63.47m)	236.2ft (72.04m)
Height	68.6ft (20.92m)	70.2ft (21.41m)	58.6ft (17.87m)
Useable cargo area	2,804sq ft (260.8m²)	2,807sq ft (261.1m²)	2,747sq ft (255.57m²)
Useable cargo volume	39,106cu ft (1,095m³)	43,900cu ft (1,247m³)	37,837cu ft (1,075m³)
Operating weight empty	318,768lb (144,721kg)	318,529lb (144,612kg)	323,718lb (146,968kg)
Basic gross weight	665,000lb (301,910kg)	666,700lb (302,681kg)	732,500lb (332,555kg)
Maximum gross weight	725,000lb (329,150kg)	716,700lb (325,382kg)	769,000lb (349,126kg)

ABOVE The final configuration of the Boeing Model 750 with the additional set of main landing gear. *John Aldaz photo*

The Douglas design provided the largest cargo compartment, with a usable cargo volume of 43,900cu ft (1,247m^3) compared to 36,218cu ft (1,029m^3) and 37,837cu ft (1,075m^3) for the Boeing and Lockheed aircraft, excluding the space provided for troops. As such, it offered the best outsize cargo envelope and was the only design that permitted the loading of a Chinook helicopter without major disassembly.

Several other aspects of the submission drew praise, particularly with regard to internal facilities, and it was evaluated as the most easily maintained of the three designs. The in-flight refuelling capability was also considered the best, offering maximum clearance between tanker and receiver and the best possible pilot visibility during refuelling operations.

However, evaluators judged that the Douglas proposal fell short on much more significant considerations:

> 'The Douglas aircraft did not meet the RFP mission performance requirements in range/payload and it could not land within a 4,000ft (1,220m) restriction at the mid-point of a 5,000nmi (9,255kg) unrefuelled mission without a reduction in required payload. Additionally, Douglas did not propose to meet the desired 265,000lb (120,310kg) maximum payload, and offered a 250,000lb (113,500kg) payload instead.'

Douglas received the performance assessment on 1 September and quickly responded with a series of drag-reducing design changes that included lowering the nose profile, revising the engine nacelles, changing the incidence of the wing and stretching the aft fuselage. Additionally, the main landing gear, which had retracted upward and rotated 180° into large sponsons, was revised to retract downward and inward into the fuselage under the cargo deck to reduce drag. This complicated the fuselage pressure vessel design and increased weight, which had led Douglas to reject this option in prior trade-off studies.

The Air Force was not convinced, and concluded:

> 'The Douglas aircraft is still estimated to be deficient in range/payload even with all aerodynamic design changes proposed. The Air Force concludes that a re-sizing of the aircraft to a higher gross weight would be required in order for it to perform the specified missions. There is, therefore, a high risk to the government in assuming that the aircraft would be able to perform the required mission within a reasonable date of the desired IOC, despite the fact that the contractor would be contractually bound to do so.'

This effectively ruled out Douglas.

The Lockheed proposal was the heaviest of the three, and also the slowest, with a cruise speed of 440kt (814km/h) – the minimum stipulated by the RFP – as opposed to the 470kt (870km/h) that could be achieved by the Boeing and Douglas designs. It was initially evaluated as having superior payload/range capability but also having poor take-off and landing performance, although the latter was partly due to different assumptions as to how it should be calculated.

When informed of these deficiencies, Lockheed responded with a series of design changes, increasing the wing area by 600sq ft (55.8m^2), increasing the flap span, and improving the engine inlet and thrust reverser installation. Although these changes added around 8,300lb (3,768kg) to the aircraft's weight, Lockheed's design was still assessed as exceeding the range and/or payload of the other two competitors.

Lockheed also scored well in terms of the aircraft's cargo-loading capability. The selection of a cargo compartment with a constant width of 19ft (5.80m) and a uniform height 18.5ft (5.64m) resulted in the easiest

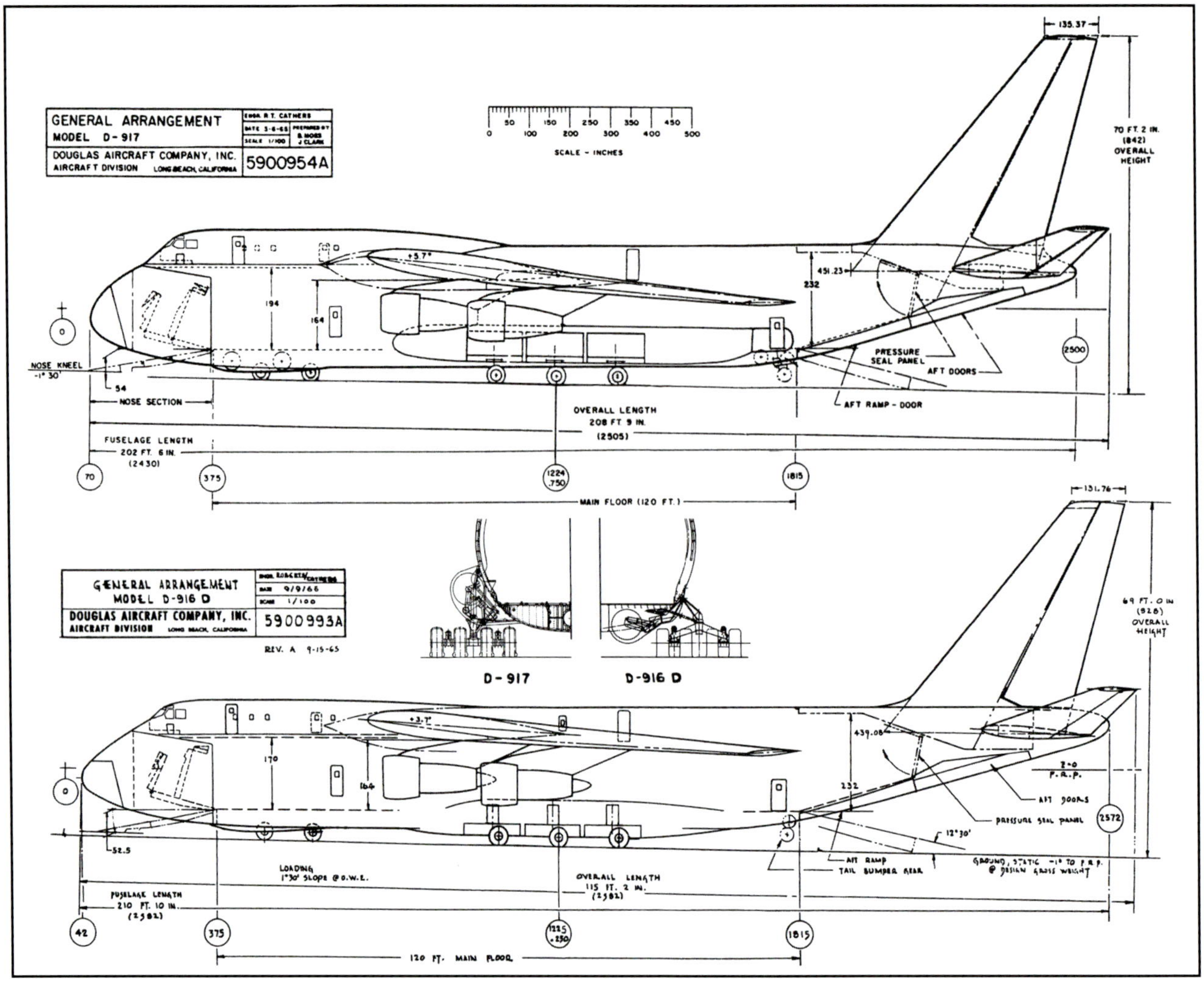

GENERAL ARRANGEMENT
MODEL D-917
DOUGLAS AIRCRAFT COMPANY, INC.
AIRCRAFT DIVISION LONG BEACH, CALIFORNIA
5900954A

SCALE - INCHES

OVERALL LENGTH 208 FT 9 IN. (2505)

FUSELAGE LENGTH 202 FT. 6 IN. (2430)

NOSE SECTION

NOSE KNEEL

MAIN FLOOR (120 FT.)

PRESSURE SEAL PANEL

AFT DOORS

AFT RAMP - DOOR

70 FT. 2 IN. (842) OVERALL HEIGHT

D-917

D-916 D

GENERAL ARRANGEMENT
MODEL D-916 D
DOUGLAS AIRCRAFT COMPANY, INC.
AIRCRAFT DIVISION LONG BEACH, CALIFORNIA
5900993A
REV. A 9-15-65

69 FT. 0 IN (828) OVERALL HEIGHT

LOADING 1°30' SLOPE @ O.W.E.

OVERALL LENGTH 115 FT. 2 IN. (2582)

FUSELAGE LENGTH 210 FT. 10 IN. (2582)

AFT RAMP

TAIL BUMPER REAR

AFT DOORS

PRESSURE SEAL PANEL

120 FT. MAIN FLOOR

ABOVE A comparison between the Douglas Model D-917 (upper) and the last-minute Model D-916D (lower), with a revised down-and-inward retracting main landing gear and a lower drag fuselage, which was submitted to the Air Force. *Boeing*

BELOW A Lockheed cutaway model displays the full-length L-500 'double bubble' fuselage with a long and narrow permanent passenger compartment aft of the wing. The main compartment ceiling was a single height, limiting outsized cargo, but simplifying loading. *NARA II via Dennis R. Jenkins*

configuration to load of any of the three designs, and it provided the flexibility to load vehicles, or cargo pallets two and three abreast, or combinations of mixed loads. The design of the forward and aft loading ramps provided a unique full-width loading capability with minimum manoeuvring requirements for vehicle loading. The facilities for air-dropping were also well planned, drawing on Lockheed's extensive experience with the C-130.

With two competitive designs, both meeting the RFP requirements (with different strengths), the decision came down largely to a matter of cost, or rather assessed cost-effectiveness. As can be imagined, the cost estimate submitted by the bidders for the development and build of the first fifty-seven (Run 'A') aircraft was difficult to pin down to a single number. The accompanying table presents each contractor's Target Price together with a Ceiling Price.

Contractor's proposed C-5A costs ($ million)	Boeing	Douglas	Lockheed
Contractor proposed cost			
Target Price	2,216	1,972	1,886
Ceiling Price (130 per cent)	2,619	2,331	2,229
Most probable cost (government independent estimate)			
Proposed Target Cost	2,014	1,793	1,714
Bottom of range (low)	1,911	1,793	1,714
Most Probable Cost	2,055	2,019	1,860
Top of range (high)	2,198	2,156	1,986

The Air Force evaluated the cost proposals, then produced its own adjusted estimates of Low, Likely and High Costs. Further adjustments included projections of future cost and rate increases. Despite the spread in the numbers, it was clear that Lockheed had the lowest cost and Boeing the highest. However, given the high technical assessment of the Boeing submission, the decision was not clear-cut.

The Source Selection Board (SSB), which was made up of four Air Force Generals, recommended Boeing, whereas MATS and the Air Force Systems Command preferred Lockheed. The matter went to the Air Force Air Council, comprising twelve four-star Generals, and it selected the Lockheed proposal by an eight to four vote. Defense Secretary McNamara ratified the decision, personally announcing on 30 September 1965 that Lockheed had won the competition.

Almost certainly other considerations would have come into play in the decision, one being pressure to spread work across different suppliers. This was not a matter of fairness but rather a wish to maintain competitive supplier capability, enforced by political pressures from the representatives of different states. Of the three short-listed CX-HLS competitors, Boeing was in Washington, Douglas in California, and Lockheed in Georgia; the SST contenders were Boeing in Washington and Lockheed in California; and the Manned Orbiting Laboratory (MOL) space station was being worked on by Boeing in Washington as well as both Douglas and Lockheed in California. On 25 August 1965 Douglas won the Air Force MOL contract and Boeing appeared to be the front runner for the SST funding. This would leave only Lockheed-Georgia with no major new aerospace contract, at a time when the end of C-141 manufacturing was in sight. How far these considerations played a part one can only surmise but, together with Lockheed's lowest-price bid, it certainly did nothing to impede that company's selection as the winner of the CX-HLS competition.

The question of cost also has to be viewed against the socio-economic environment at the time. In addition to expanding the Vietnam War and supporting the Apollo moon project (which at its peak was consuming 0.4% of US GDP), the Lyndon Johnson administration was pursuing a domestic agenda that would require some heavy spending, as well as endeavouring to fund three expensive aerospace programmes: the CX-HLS, the Manned Orbital Laboratory and the SST.

In terms of these three major aerospace programmes, Lockheed would in fact end up being the only winner: Douglas (now merged with McDonnell) was informed of the MOL programme cancellation in June 1968, while the US Congress terminated the SST programme in May 1971.

Boeing's own assessment of the competition was summed up in a speech by Boeing's Chief Engineer Ed Wells to the company's senior management. It was based on an internal review of the C-5A programme carried out in June 1966. He stated:

> 'On Monday, November 1, T. Wilson and I met with Secretaries Brown, Charles, Flax, and Paul, in Secretary Brown's office to receive an informal debriefing on the C-5A decision with particular reference to what we might learn and what guidance they might give us which would be of value in our future efforts for the military services. The secretaries answered our questions quite directly, and we received all of the information which we could have considered proper to receive…
>
> 'They were complimentary concerning our proposal on C-5A, and said that the excellence of our proposal made it most difficult for them to make their decision, but that they finally had to make it on the price difference alone because it overrode our other advantages.'

He further summarised:

> 'Our system had the advantage of lower operating costs by reason of its employing a smaller, more efficient airplane. Lockheed

proposed a larger airplane which although less efficient at long ranges could carry a somewhat larger payload at short ranges. At equal prices, our system would have a clear cost-effectiveness advantage; in fact, we would probably have had such an advantage even at a price disadvantage of many millions of dollars. However, when the difference turned out to be in the order of 300 million dollars, our superior effectiveness was not considered sufficient to overcome the price differential. In the final analysis, Boeing was superior on effectiveness, Lockheed was superior on cost to government, and in the combination Lockheed was judged to offer superior cost-effectiveness.'

Wells cited two lessons for Boeing's management to learn from the competition:

'Lesson one is that price will tend to become more, rather than less significant in future competitions of this type and we must develop our capability to meet strong price competition without taking potentially dangerous risks. We must set a competitive price and develop both an attractive design and an effective management plan which will insure a profit at that price.

'Lesson number two is "never underestimate the capability of your competitor". In the C-5A competition we did not fully allow for the determination of our competitor to quote as low a price as he quoted, and we did not properly assess what he was prepared to guarantee in system performance. In the particular case of the C-5A, our underestimation of our competitor was probably not a deciding factor, but the fact remains that it is always risky to underestimate his capability, and in the next round this could be a determining factor.'

Commercial developments stemming from CX-HLS and C-5

Given the substantial investment that the three big aircraft companies made in the CX-HLS design programme, it is not surprising that they looked at the possibilities for further exploiting their efforts in the commercial market – boosted by the availability of the new high-bypass turbofans. The work started while the competitive proposals were still being evaluated, with the added benefit of keeping the design teams intact and ready to respond to any requests for changes or hopefully

BELOW Boeing's technical and performance advantages were greatly overshadowed by Lockheed's lower price.
John Aldaz collection

develop the winning bid. Inevitably their first proposals were simply to offer straightforward commercial versions of the three C-5A designs as they stood. However, while a high-wing configuration is ideally suited to military requirements, operating out of poorly equipped, ill-prepared airstrips, it is not well suited to passenger-carrying. Nor is it even well suited to using commercial freight terminals.

Once the company had been awarded the C-5A contract, Lockheed was in no position to develop a new design aimed purely at the commercial market. In time it did offer both a passenger-carrying and a freighter version of the aircraft, under the designation L-500. As an airliner it had the potential to carry up to a thousand passengers, but there were no takers for either version. Meanwhile, Douglas worked initially on commercial derivatives of its D-916 and later D-918, before offering its low-wing, full-fuselage-length double-deck D-956, which was tailored to the airlines. However, the latter represented too big a step up in scale for the airlines; they opted instead for the Boeing offering, its Model 747.

Just how much the Boeing 747 benefitted from the design work that went into CX-HLS competition is a matter of conjecture. Boeing's Joe Sutter is quoted as saying, 'We started with a blank sheet of paper. The high-bypass turbofan is the only thing that survived the USAF competition.' Nonetheless, it is hard to imagine that all the experience of working on the design of an unprecedentedly large transport aircraft could have been of no relevance. Whatever the truth, the 747 was nonetheless a bold initiative by Boeing. Until then every new generation of aircraft had rendered the current fleet obsolete by being one thing: faster. Speed was deemed the only real advantage of air travel, which at that time was still the province of the relatively wealthy.

Boeing's big new aeroplane was no faster than the 707s and DC-8s that it was designed to replace on the major long-haul routes. Furthermore, industry observers noted that few of

BELOW **An early Douglas Model D-916C commercial airliner seating concept based on the proposed D-916 airframe.** *Boeing*

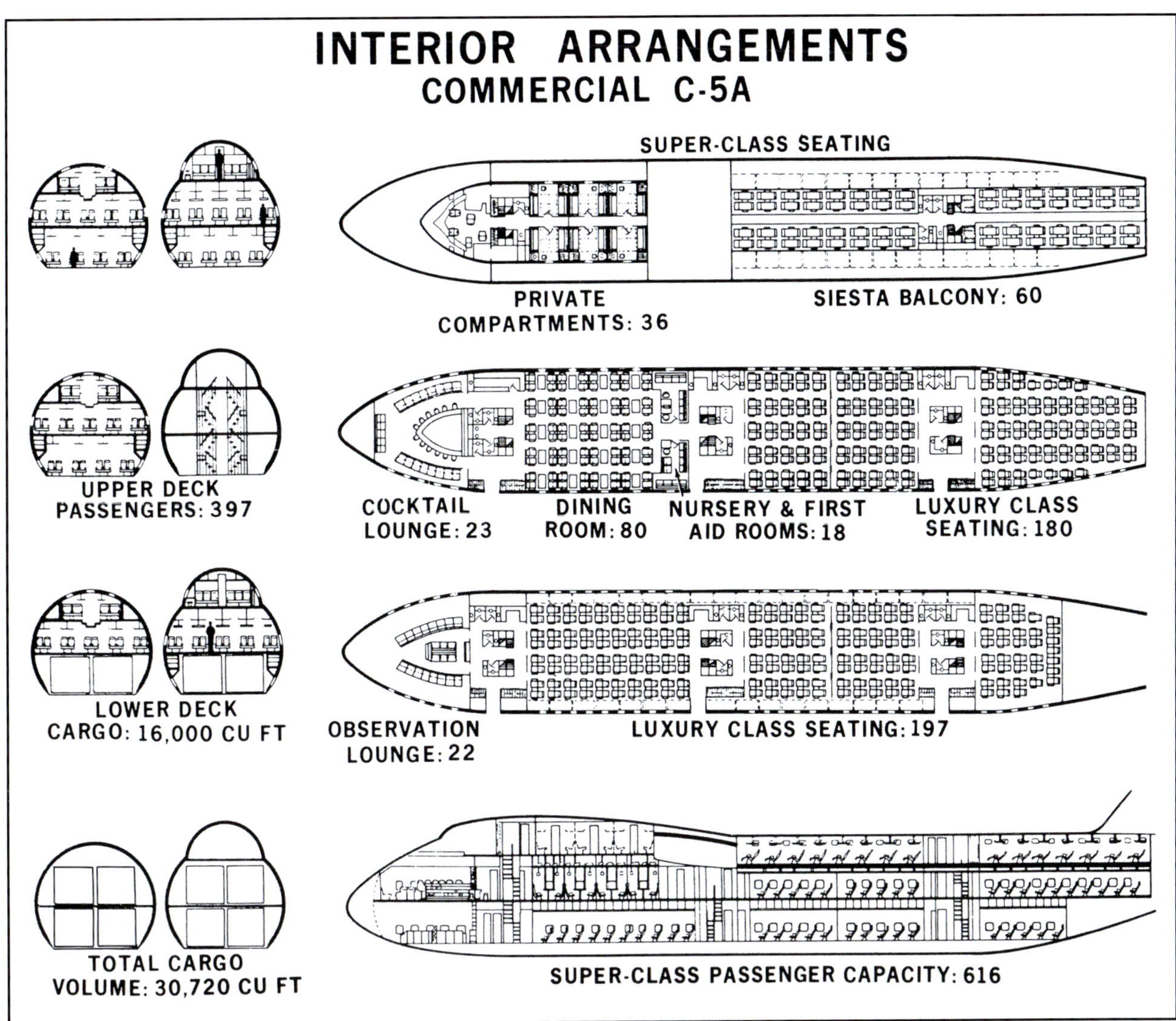

the world's airports were equipped to handle such a large aircraft, or cope with the arrival and departure of hundreds of passengers at a time. Others argued that the loss of such an aircraft would be catastrophic for the future of air travel, much like the sinking of the *Titanic*. Nonetheless, Boeing went ahead with the project. Its confidence was to be amply rewarded.

The C-5A in perspective

The first Lockheed C-5A flew on 30 June 1968 and entered operational service two years later in June 1970. However, although it represented a major step up in strategic airlift capability, the aircraft was to have a long and problematic period of development. Cost overruns at one stage amounted to more than $1 billion – a record at that time. As a result the contract was reduced by twenty-nine aircraft. But cost was not the only problem. During the test programme wing cracks appeared, which resulted in a restriction to 80% of the maximum design loads, and by 1980 normal operational cargo loads had been reduced to just 50,000lb (22,700kg) and airframe life reduced to just 8,000 hours. This triggered two major Congressional investigations into technical problems and cost overruns, jeopardising the continued existence of the Lockheed Aircraft Corporation.

Something had to be done about the C-5A, and in 1978 a programme began to replace the C-5A's wing primary structures. Over the next nine years the seventy-seven surviving C-5As had these replaced, and their fuselages strengthened at a total cost of $1.5 billion, restoring the aircraft to full operational capability. Congress additionally authorised a new USAF contract under the Reagan Defense build-up to reopen the production line, placing an order for fifty C-5B aircraft. As well as the structural changes, the C-5B incorporated many other improvements in the aircraft's systems, including slightly more powerful TF39-GE-1C engines.

Two further upgrade programmes followed. The Avionics Modernization Program (AMP) was the first in 1998, which greatly enhanced the aircraft's systems; the Reliability Enhancement & Re-Engining Program (RERP) was the second, which replaced the TF39 engines with the General Electric CF-6-80C2 engines having 52,500lb (233kN) thrust. The first aircraft to have completed the latter programme – now designated the C-5M Super Galaxy – first flew on 19 June 2006. Compared with the earlier aircraft, the C-5M has a 30% shorter take-off roll, a 27% improvement in unrefuelled range, and a 14% increase in maximum payload, taking it up to 284,000lb (128,940kg).

So, despite all its problems the C-5 eventually became the aircraft that the Army and Air Force had always wanted, and it is currently planned to be in service until at least 2040 – *more than 70 years* after its first flight. Nonetheless, it is interesting to contrast Lockheed's experience to that of Boeing, whom it narrowly beat to win the CX-HLS competition. While the Boeing 747 airliner may not have been extensively based on the company's losing airlifter proposal, it would certainly have drawn heavily on the design experience. Moreover, had it won the C-5A contract, Boeing would not have had the resources to work on a similar-scale commercial project. As it was, the investment required by the Boeing 747 stretched the company's finances to the limit.

The Boeing 747 ushered in the era of mass long-haul air travel. It also became the mainstay of long-haul airfreight. Having first flown in 1969, it is still in production today (in its freighter version), with more than 1,500 examples delivered. By contrast Lockheed built 131 C-5s. In retrospect it could be argued that CX-HLS was a good competition to lose.

BELOW Lockheed's second-built C-5A on a test flight. *US Air Force photo*

Chapter Three
Pursuit of VTOL

The late 1950s to late 1960s: Ambition outstrips practicality

ABOVE A depiction of the Boeing Model 900 VTOL airlifter. *Boeing*

In many ways the 1950s represented the golden age of aviation progress. As turbine technology matured and the understanding of high-speed aerodynamics spread, new designs – for all types of military and commercial aircraft – proliferated. Every aspect of performance progressed. By the end of the decade passengers were routinely flying the Atlantic at speeds that were close to the world record at the decade's start.

While progress was taking place to provide US military forces with strategic airlift capability, designers were pursuing another long-sought aeronautical design goal – the development of transport aircraft with Vertical Take-Off and Landing (VTOL) capability. VTOL was already well established with helicopters, but rotary-winged aircraft had inherent limitations that restricted speed and forward flight efficiency.

The attractions of runway-independent flight were obvious. For the military it held out the prospect of operating aircraft close to a moving battlefront, while also eliminating the vulnerability of fixed runways. For the commercial world it offered the prospect of city-centre to city-centre operations. By the late 1950s advances in engine power-to-weight ratios gave every expectation that non-rotary-wing VTOL operations were just around the corner. The concept figured prominently in a multitude of books and articles from that period that claimed to forecast the future of aviation.

There seemed no shortage of ways to achieve this capability. Engine thrust could be deflected, small additional lift-engines could be attached, or the engines themselves could be tilted – indeed, whole wings could be tilted. Rotor blades could also be tilted, or used for vertical flight, then stopped and even stowed away once horizontal flight was achieved. Moreover, any of these ideas could be used in combination. The possibilities (and studies) seemed endless, and resulted in no end of imaginative designs. In practice, however, efficient and cost-effective VTOL was to prove to be an elusive goal.

The earlier years of VTOL technology

Rather surprisingly, it was the Army and not the Air Force that spearheaded most of the research and development effort in the 1950s. Helicopters certainly had a part to play for the Army, but the military needed heavier and faster air transportation. VTOL offered the potential to deliver troops and equipment quickly to almost anywhere on the battlefield, to keep them supplied, and to extract them when necessary.

The advent of nuclear weapons in 1945 pushed the Army towards VTOL technology in several ways. The Army had to fight the perception that nuclear weapons would dominate warfare (in the form of the Massive Retaliation doctrine), making ground forces obsolete. This doctrine led to massive funding for the Air Force's nuclear weapons and their delivery systems, while the Army struggled for relevance. This issue was diminished somewhat by the Korean War (or 'police action'), with its conventional battles fought across inhospitable terrain. It was in Korea that planners finally began to appreciate the helicopter's wartime advantages.

With the advent of the 'Flexible [Nuclear] Response' concept in the mid-1950s, the Army planned in earnest to fight and win on a nuclear battlefield. A major thrust was the adoption of the Pentomic system. Its name reflected two of the major concepts of the reorganisation – 'penta' (an organisation based on five major subordinate units) and 'atomic capability' (to include low-yield tactical nuclear weapons on the battlefield).

Mobility was central to the so-called Pentomic Army – slow-moving infantry on foot or in trucks would otherwise be easily destroyed by an enemy's tactical nuclear weapons. Aerial mobility would be the key. By 1955 Army planners laid out requirements in three tranches:

Role	Application
Single-person mobility	Helicopter (rotocycle) or lift-fan platform
Two-person scouting	Aircar/airjeep (lift-fans)
Transport	Various VTOL methods

But the Army faced another challenge in that it had neither the charter nor the capability to develop and procure these new weapons; these were reserved for the Air Force when that service was separated from the Army in 1947. After all, neither the Air Force nor the Navy was to be in the tank-building business. The exact division of responsibilities between the Air Force and Army was contentious through the 1950s. One Air Force view held that it alone should be responsible for *all* air vehicles. The Army ceded many air missions, but felt that it needed scout and transport capability under the direct control of local battlefield commanders.

Key dates of an uneasy peace: the shifting aviation boundary between the Air Force and the Army

1942: The Army Ground Forces are authorised the use of light aircraft, distinct from the Army Air Force.

26 July 1947: As part of the National Security Act of 1947, the Army Air Force is separated from the Army, becoming the Air Force, equal in stature to the Army and the Navy.

21 April 1948: The seminal 'Key West Agreement' is signed by Secretary of Defense Forrestal and delineates roles and mission of the armed services. Section VI, Paragraph A 5 states that the Air Force is 'To furnish close combat and logistical air support to the Army, to include air lift, support, and resupply of airborne operations, aerial photography, tactical reconnaissance, and interdiction of enemy land power and communications.'

20 May 1949: The Bradley-Vandenberg Agreement (codified as Joint Army and Air Force Regulation 5-10-1) sets roles for Army aircraft and enacts weight limitations: 2,500lb/1,134kg empty weight for fixed-wing and 3,500 to 4,000lb (1,588 to 1,814kg) for helicopters (rotary wing).

23 March 1950: The Air Force is assigned primary responsibility for Army aircraft administration (Army Regulation 700-50/Air Force Regulation 65-70). The Army can only procure Air Force-developed aircraft, commercial aircraft certified by the Civil Aeronautics Administration (CAA), or modified commercial aircraft certified by the CAA and approved by the Air Force. The Air Force is responsible for preparing specifications, conducting research and development at the Army's request, and making type classifications in coordination with the Army. It is to handle the purchase, acceptance and inspection, and other activities related to testing, supply and maintenance of aircraft and associated equipment. The Army retains the authority to determine the aircraft requirements, and funds Air Force activities performed on its behalf.

The long saga of changing responsibilities, for battlefield aviation, provided a window for extensive Army involvement in the evolution of VTOL. By the mid-1950s, years of disputes and negotiations had resulted in loosened restrictions on the Army and pointed to the eventual ability to have greater control over its aviation affairs. An important step occurred in 1955, when the Army obtained permission to use Navy expertise and personnel to contract for aviation research and development. This was done in reply to complaints that the Air Force set Army requests at low priority. The Navy had the Army work through the Office of Naval Research (ONR) rather than the Bureau of Aeronautics (BuAer), which handled aviation development for the Navy and Marine Corps. Nonetheless, this was to prove to be a productive partnership.

Funded by the Army, the ONR began by issuing major study contracts in 1955 to five companies: Bell, Fairchild, Hiller, Ryan and Vertol (recently renamed from Piasecki). Fairchild and Vertol undertook parametric studies that examined six different concepts each, with Fairchild concentrating on STOL designs in its Model M-221 family, and Vertol evaluating VTOL designs. In-depth examinations were done by Bell Aircraft (tilt-duct) and Hiller (tilt-wing) as specific point designs. The scope of Ryan's study is uncertain, but probably led to the subsequent contract to build the Ryan Model 92/VZ-3 deflected-thrust test bed.

Under its study contract, Bell Aircraft designed a tilt-duct point design, the Model D-181. Progressing from an initial design powered by Wright T49 turboshafts, Bell settled on a four-duct layout, powered by six Allison 550 B-2 turboshaft engines. This aircraft, perhaps the largest tilt-duct aircraft designed by Bell, featured a spacious pressurised fuselage carrying fifty-nine troops or fifty-two litters – far above the Army requirement.

The Hiller Helicopter Company of Palo Alto, California, was a small firm that had been established by Stanley Hiller at the end of the Second World

1955 Army heavy VTOL study requirements

a) Payload	8,000lb (3,629kg) outbound; 4,000lb (1,814kg) return
b) Take-off distance	0ft over a 50ft (15.24m) obstacle
c) Cabin size	8ft x 9ft (2.44m x 2.74m) cross section
d Cargo	35 combat troops or equivalent weight of vehicles or equipment
e) Hover ceiling	6,000ft (1,829m) altitude at 95°F (35°C)
f) Cruise speed	300mph (261kn, 483km/h) (minimum)
g) Radius of action	425mi (369nmi, 684km)

Bell Aircraft Model D181 Ducted Propeller Assault Transport (Configuration D181-960-11)

Powerplant	6 x Allison 550-B2 turboshafts* @ 4,219shp (3,416kW); 1 x GE J85 turbojet @ 2,450 lb (10.90kN) thrust
Wingspan	97ft 8in (29.77m)
Length	81ft 1in (24.71m)
Height	33ft 11in (10.34m)
Gross TOW	67,380lb (30,563kg)
Payload	8,000lb (3,629kg)
Cruise speed	300kt (556km/h)
Max speed	410kt (759km/h)
Mission range	369nmi (683km)
Ferry range	2,802nmi (5,189km) (overload)

* outboard engines are paired in duct centre body

2 October 1951: A special Memorandum of Understanding (MOU), known as the Pace-Finletter Agreement, is signed by the Army and the Air Force, which eliminates the aircraft weight limitations and replaces them with a definition of permitted Army aircraft in terms of the functions to be performed.

4 November 1952: A second Pace-Finletter MOU replaces the agreement of 1951 and favours the Army point of view. It establishes a 5,000lb (2,268kg) empty weight limit on Army fixed-wing aircraft, but leaves helicopters unrestricted. The document stipulates that the weight limit can be reviewed by the Secretary of Defense on the request of either service secretary (which leaves the door open for specific waivers). The MOU also clearly defines the functions to be performed by Army aircraft and those operated by the Air Force

1955: In response to continuing difficulties, the incremental transfer of all Army Aviation supply and maintenance responsibilities from the Air Force to the Army is approved.

1955: The Navy is authorised to conduct research and development at the Army's request (and funded by the Army).

26 November 1956: Continued disputes and doctrinal changes lead Secretary of Defense Charles E. Wilson to modify the 1952 MOU. The size of the combat zone within which Army aircraft can operate is expanded to 100 miles on either side of the front lines and no restrictions are placed on their performance within that zone. Weight limits on Army fixed-wing aircraft remain and helicopters continue to be unrestricted (thus helping push the Army further into rotary-wing and other VTOL development). In addition, the fixed-wing weight limit is waived for the Army purchase of evaluation quantities of the de Havilland Canada DHC-4 Caribou, designated the AC-1 and later the C-7.

6 April 1966: The McConnell-Johnson Agreement has the Army relinquishing its claims to operating the de Havilland CV-2/C-7 Caribou, the CV-7/C-8 Buffalo and all future *fixed-wing* aircraft designed to fulfil the tactical airlift role. The Army will transfer these aircraft to the Air Force. In return, the Air Force will relinquish all claims for *rotary-wing* aircraft designed and operated for intra-theatre movement, fire support, and supply and resupply of Army forces. This does not preclude the Air Force from operating helicopters for search and rescue and special air warfare.

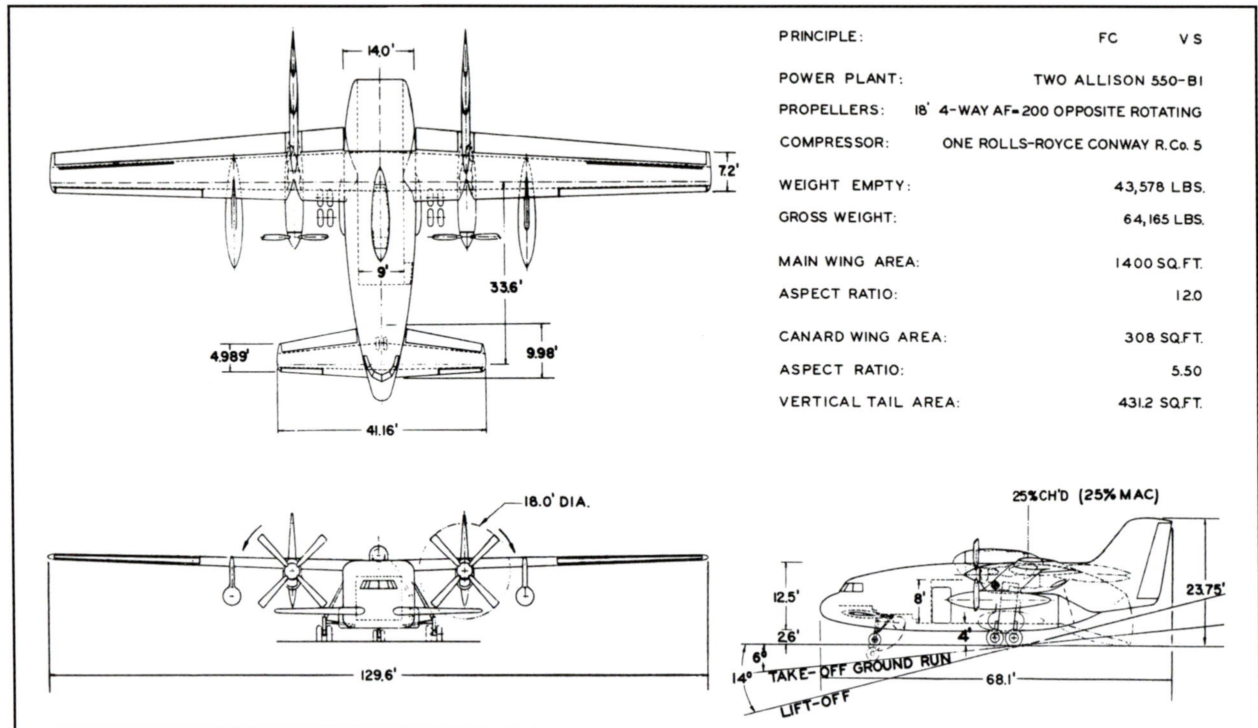

ABOVE **One of the six different Fairchild M-221 'High Speed Ratio STOL Aircraft' point designs was the canard-configured M-221C. The top-of-fuselage Rolls Royce R. Co. 5 Conway provided Boundary Layer Control (BLC) air for the wing, canard and tail. Two Allison 550 B-1 turboprops provided the prime power. Fairchild's focus and investments in STOL technologies left it poorly positioned to pursue Army VTOL development efforts.** *Fairchild*

BELOW **The Bell Aircraft D-181 six-engined ducted-propeller large VTOL transport studied in 1955 for the Army. Flaps on the intake of each duct opened to increase capture area and smooth the airflow to the propellers.** *Bell*

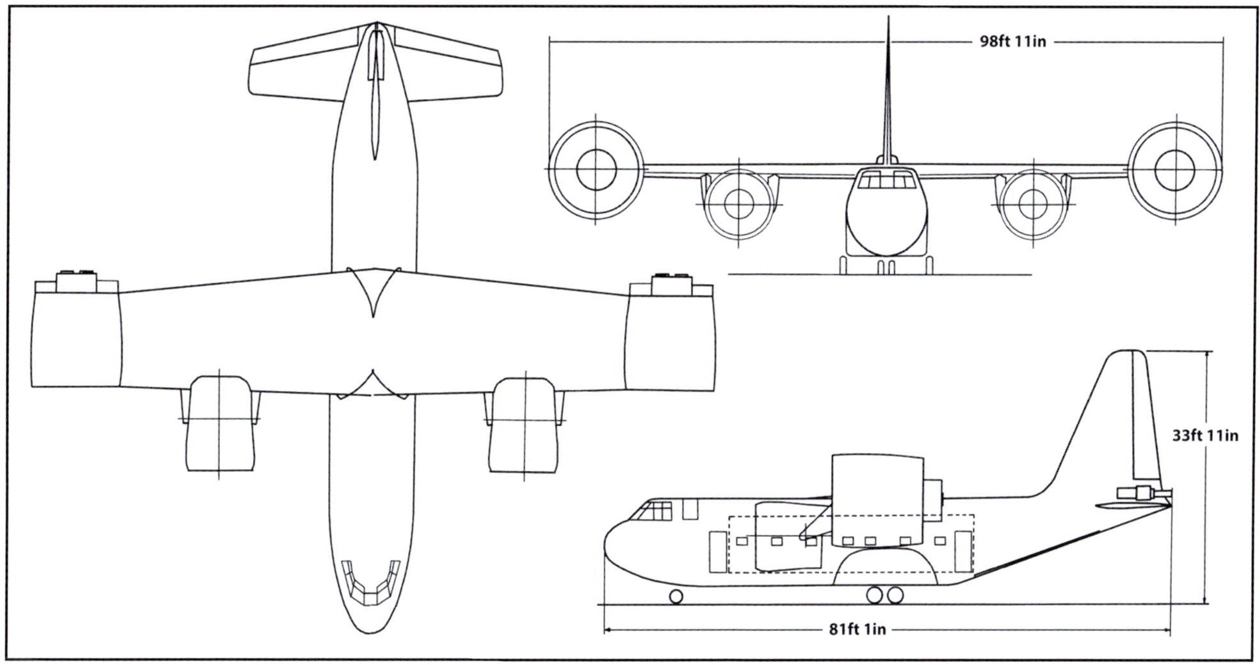

ABOVE Bell D181 general arrangement. The aircraft was to be powered by six Allison 550 B-2 turboshaft engines, one each in the inboard ducts and two each in the larger-diameter outboard ducts. *Bell*

War. By 1956 it featured a successful line of small helicopters sold to both commercial and military customers. But Hiller was concurrently pursuing a quiet but ambitious research programme focussed on other types of V/STOL aircraft. The Model 1048A was perhaps the largest of the company's tilt-wing concepts, developed under a March 1955 contract N(onr) 1657-00 administered through the ONR for the Army.

BELOW The Hiller Model 1048A Propelloplane, designed for an 8,000lb (3,629kg) payload with VTOL operations. *Special Collections & Archives, Wright State University*

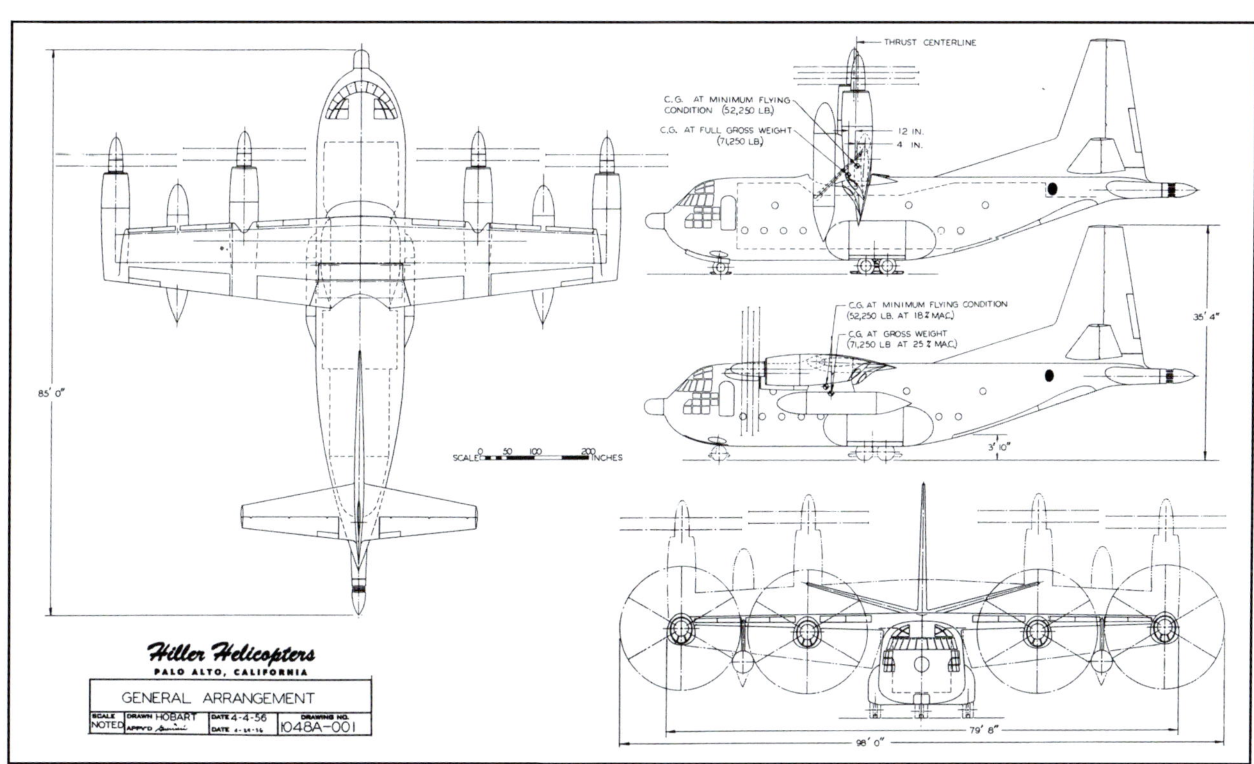

ABOVE The Hiller Model 1048A Propelloplane. *Dave Stern collection*

Hiller Model 1048A Propelloplane	
Powerplant	8 x '1965' turboshafts (paired)* @ 4,219shp (3,416kW); 1 x '1965' turbojet** @ 2,200lb (9.79kN) thrust (for pitch/yaw control)
Wingspan	98ft 0in (29.87m)
Length	85ft 0in (25.90m)
Height	35ft 0in (10.67m)
Gross TOW	71,250lb (32,318kg)
Payload	8,000lb (3,629kg)
Cruise speed	300kt (556km/h)
Max speed	410kt (759km/h)
Mission range	369nmi (683.3km)
Ferry range	2,802nmi (5,189.3km) (overload)

* Undefined, but generally resembles the design features of the Allison T40 with improved performance and efficiency.
** Undefined, but generally resembles the design features of the Fairchild J83 or GE J85.

Vertol performed a parametric study and comparison of six general design types for the ONR/Army in 1955-56: the tilt-wing propeller, tilting ducted propeller, vectored lift, special hovering turbojet (direct lift), Vertodyne (lift-fan), and Vectodyne (based on the Lippisch Aerodyne concept).

Of the six concepts examined, the Vectodyne had the heaviest weight, requiring nine Allison 550 B-1 engines to perform the specified mission. In comparison, the tilt-wing design was the lightest and only required four engines, with the tilt-duct design coming in second.

Vertol 'Special Hovering Turbojet'	
Powerplant	68 x GE J85 turbojets @ 2,450lb (10.90kN) thrust
Wingspan	90ft 0in (27.43m)
Length	92ft 0in (28.04m)
Height	35ft 0in (10.67m)
Gross TOW	107,266lb (48,655kg)
Payload	8,000lb (3,629kg) (vertical take-off)
Cruise speed	261kt (483km/h)
Mission radius	369nmi (683.3km)
Ferry range	1,364nmi (2,526km)

BELOW The Hiller Model 1095 was a 1958 Propelloplane concept that was repackaged to fit into the Navy/Marine Corps VTOL assault environment (including shipboard storage). When the ultimate TS-152 requirement was issued, Hiller decided to team with LTV and Ryan on what became the winning XC-142A proposal. *Special Collections & Archives, Wright State University*

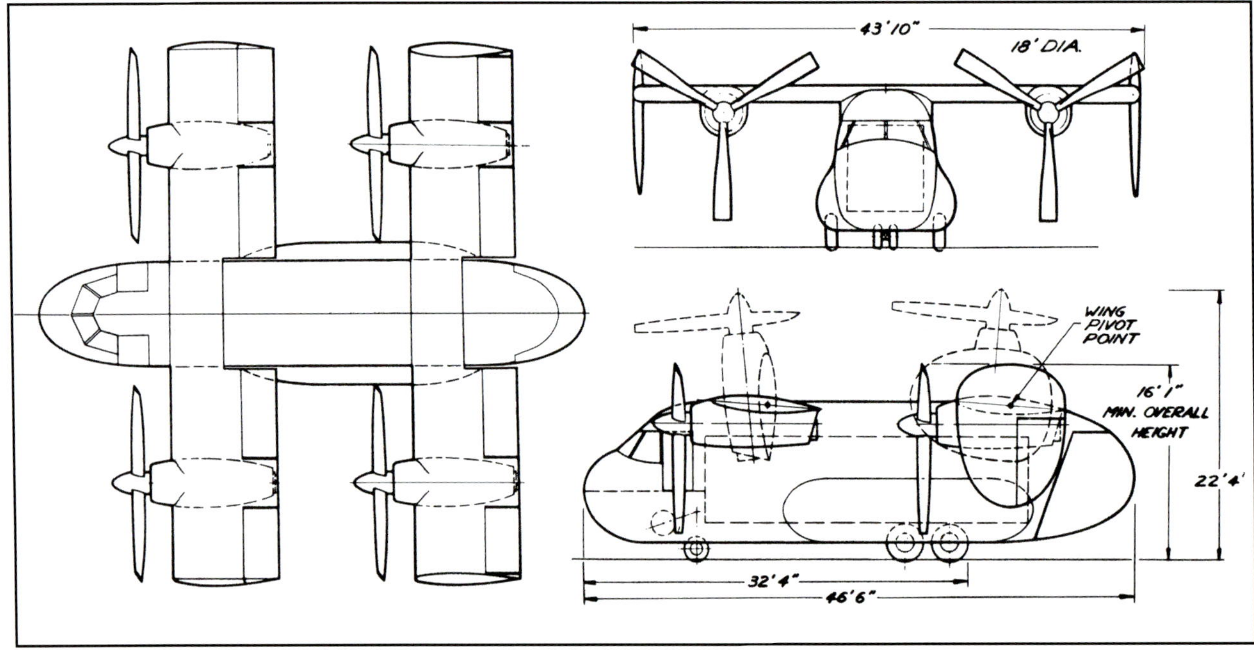

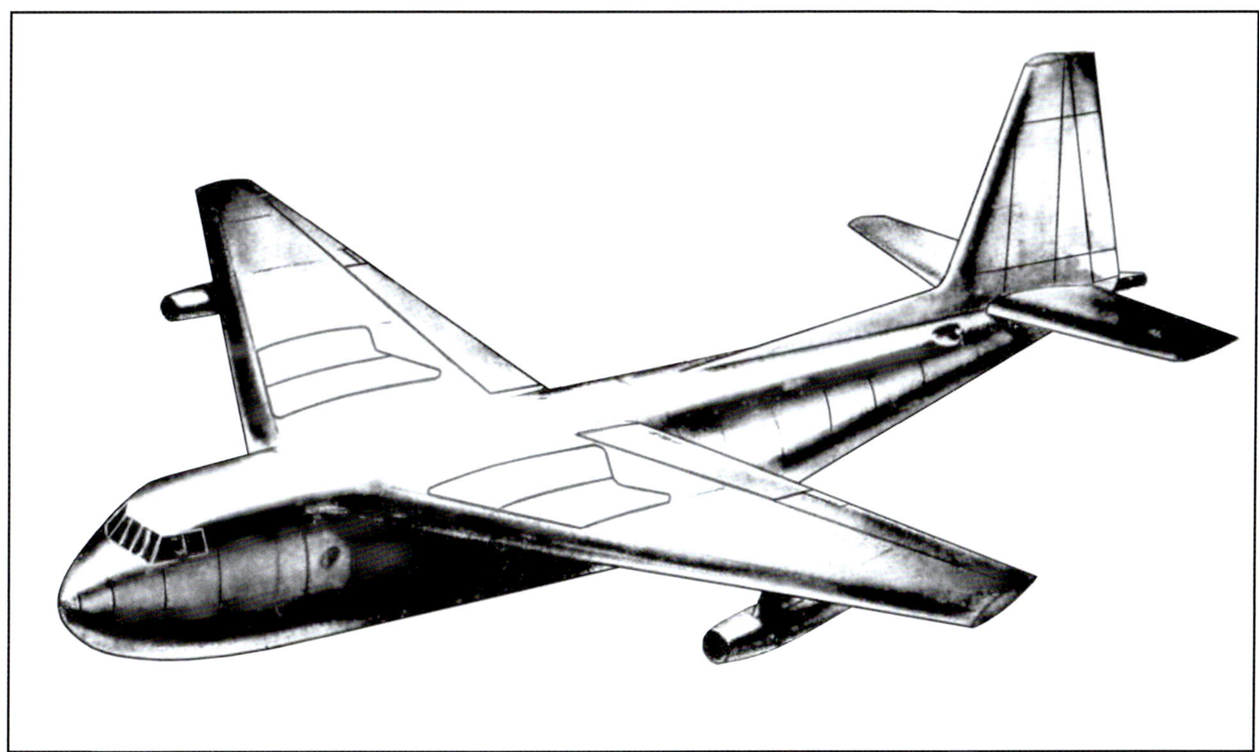

ABOVE At first glance, this Vertol direct lift concept looks quite conventional, although the doors in the wings could have covered lift fans. In reality, each wing contained thirty vertically mounted General Electric J85 turbojet engines in five groups of six. *Vertol*

BELOW In addition to the sixty J85 engines mounted vertically in the wing, three were housed in each external nacelle for horizontal flight, and two in the aft fuselage for pitch control (when hovering) or forward flight, for a grand total of sixty-eight engines. *Vertol*

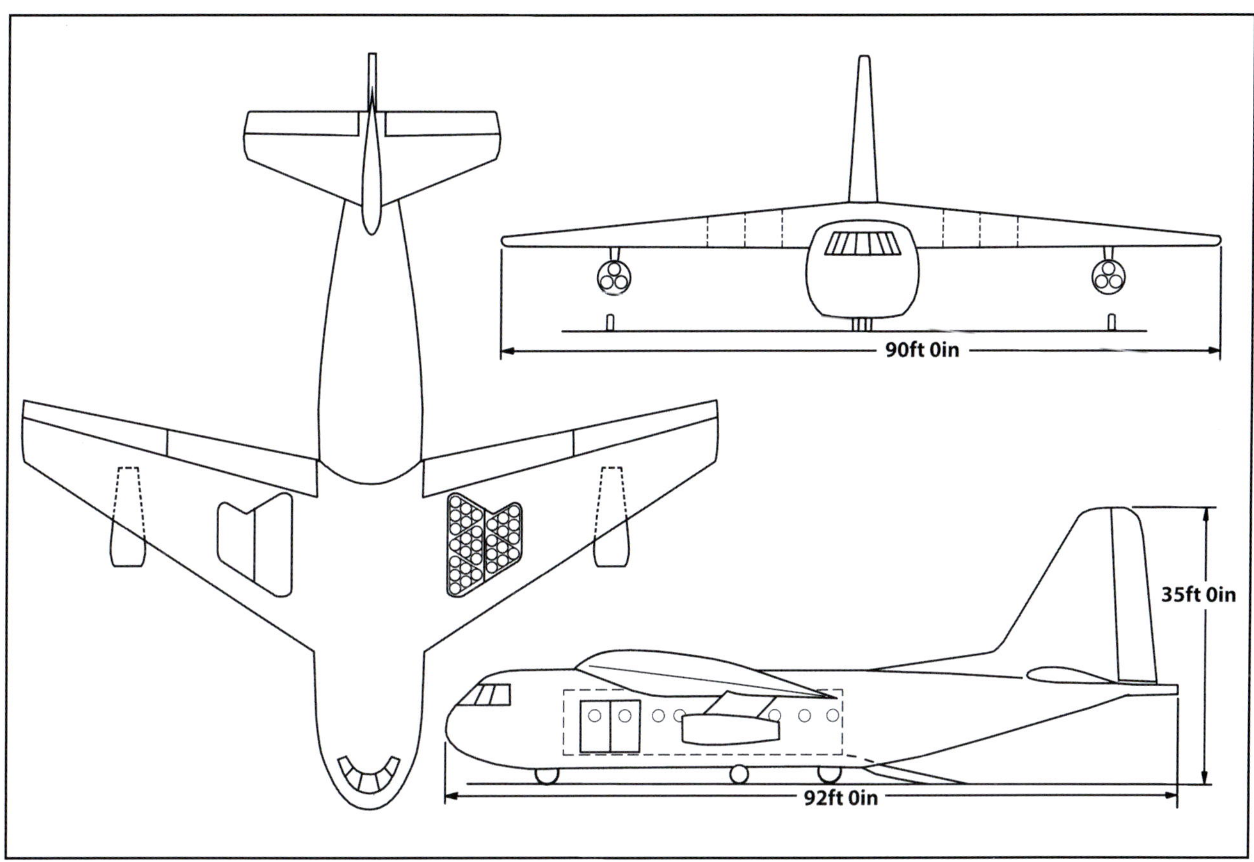

Into hardware: Technology test beds and demonstrators

The US Army sponsored a second wave of test beds managed through the Office of Naval Research (ONR) rather than the Air Force. VTOL test aircraft development proceeded in several categories that were of interest to the Army. Following are descriptions of the one Air Force and three Army aircraft whose configurations most directly supported the later Tri-Service VTOL programme.

Bell Helicopter Model 200/XH-33/XV-3

Bell Helicopter Company (under the same corporate umbrella as Bell Aircraft) had an early start with its Model 200. Bell submitted the design in response to a competition in August 1950 run by the Air Force for the Army. It won a development contract in May 1951 and the vehicle was designated the XH-33 in the 'Helicopter' series of designations. The first aircraft formally rolled out on 10 February 1955 with the XV-3 designation in the new 'V' design series, removing it from the 'H' – Helicopter – classification.

The first hover flight occurred on 11 August 1955, but repeated bouts of wing/pylon/rotor instability, and groundings for modifications, slowed flight test progress. The first aircraft crashed on 25 October 1956 due to severe rotor vibration. Fortunately, the pilot survived.

Development proceeded with the second aircraft, which featured a major change in the dynamic (rotor) system, with three-bladed prop-rotors replacing the two-bladed units. Flight testing resumed, interspersed with two extended sessions of piloted test runs in the NASA Ames facility 40ft by 80ft (12.2m by 24.4m) wind tunnel to diagnose and correct additional problems as they were encountered. The XV-3 finally achieved a full conversion in flight on 18 December 1958 – the world's first by a tilt-rotor fixed-wing aircraft. However, the achievement came at the cost of a long and difficult development effort – almost three times as long as its later competitors.

Doak Model 16/VZ-4

The tilt-duct principle was demonstrated by the small Doak Model 16 test bed, built by the equally small Doak Aircraft Company under a contract awarded 10 April 1956. Doak designed and built the aircraft quickly; it first hovered on 25 February 1958, followed by the first transition from vertical to horizontal flight on 5 May. Edwards AFB hosted the next round of testing, then the Army transferred the Model 16 to NASA at Langley on 5 May 1960 for further evaluation. NASA returned the aircraft to the Army on 21 August 1972, which later placed it on display at Ft Eustis.

Bell Aerosystems (the former Bell Aircraft) also competed for this effort, with the barebones Model D182A tilt-duct. The follow-on Model D182C proposal would have used major components of the Cessna T-37. Powerplants were to have been dual GE T58 turboshaft engines, with a gross weight of 6,270lb (2,844kg).

BELOW The surviving XV-3 in forward flight with the rotors partially tilted, near NASA's Ames Research Center. *NASA*

Army Aircraft Designations

The Army established a two-letter aircraft designation system in 1955, which was used up to 1962 when the current tri-service designation system was adopted:

First Letter (Type)	A = Fixed-wing aircraft, H = Rotorcraft, V = VTOL
Second Letter (Mission)	C = Transport, O = Observation, U = Utility, Z = Research

The one- or two-letter manufacturer's code was sometimes appended in contemporary usage – thus the use of VZ-4DO for the Doak.

RIGHT Doak's Model 16 (Army VZ-4) in its first hover flight at the Torrance, California, Municipal Airport. *Doak*

BELOW The Doak Model 16 (VZ-4) with tilt ducts is on the left, and on the right the Vertol Model 76 (VZ-3) with tilt wing and articulated propellers that drooped at rest due to the use of helicopter 'flap' hinges. A single, early Lycoming YT53 turboshaft engine located in the fuselage powered each technology demonstrator. *NASA*

Vertol Model 76/VZ-3

Vertol (formerly Piasecki Helicopter Corporation) received Contract N(onr) 2136(00) on 15 April 1956 to design, construct and flight test its Model 76, the Army's tilt-wing test bed. With Army designation VZ-3, the aircraft first flew on 13 April 1957, and its first transition was on 15 July 1958. In 1961 it was modified with the addition of a full-span trailing edge flap, added to prevent the wing from stalling during partial power descents. Flap deflection was programmed with wing tilt. The aft segment of the double-slotted Fowler flap also served as an aileron in conventional aircraft flight and as a yaw control device during hover and conversion. These modifications allowed the deletion of the small pitch and yaw fans in the tail in later designs. Flap hinges for the blades relieved the large moments of the rigid propeller operating at high angles of attack in the presence of a wing. Vertol omitted the conventional helicopter-type lag hinge, lessening the possibility of mechanical instability.

The aircraft completed its test programmes in 1966 and was donated to the National Air and Space Museum.

ABOVE The Vertol Model 76 (VZ-2) late in its life. Flaps were added and the ailerons were modified to 'droop' to prevent wing stall during low-speed/high angle-of-attack transitions, an endemic problem with the tilt-wing. *NASA*

Hiller Model 1051/X-18

Following its Propelloplane line of development, Hiller proposed the Model 1051 as the Tilt-Wing Flying Testbed. The Air Force placed Hiller under contract on 30 October 1957 to construct and test the X-18 (although Hiller had started design work in June 1956). Budget for the X-18 effort was very tight and existing components were used wherever possible. The largest of these was the fuselage, salvaged from an ex-boneyard Chase YC-122C, and Allison T40-A-6 engines from the Navy's Convair XFY 'Pogo' programme. The hybrid aircraft rolled out in December 1958 and began extended ground testing and validation at both Hiller's factory and nearby Moffett Field. It was then trucked to Edwards AFB, reassembled, tested and first flown on 20 November 1959 in conventional aeroplane mode.

Near disaster struck during the twentieth test flight on 4 November 1960, when the aircraft yawed, then flipped into an inverted spin due to a failed propeller control motor. Skilled piloting saved the aircraft but it was permanently grounded due to safety concerns before it could ever attempt a full transition in flight. However, the ground and flight data showed positive results for the tilt-wing concept and indicated that a practical service aircraft with such capability was well within reach.

BELOW X-18 general arrangement. *Hiller*

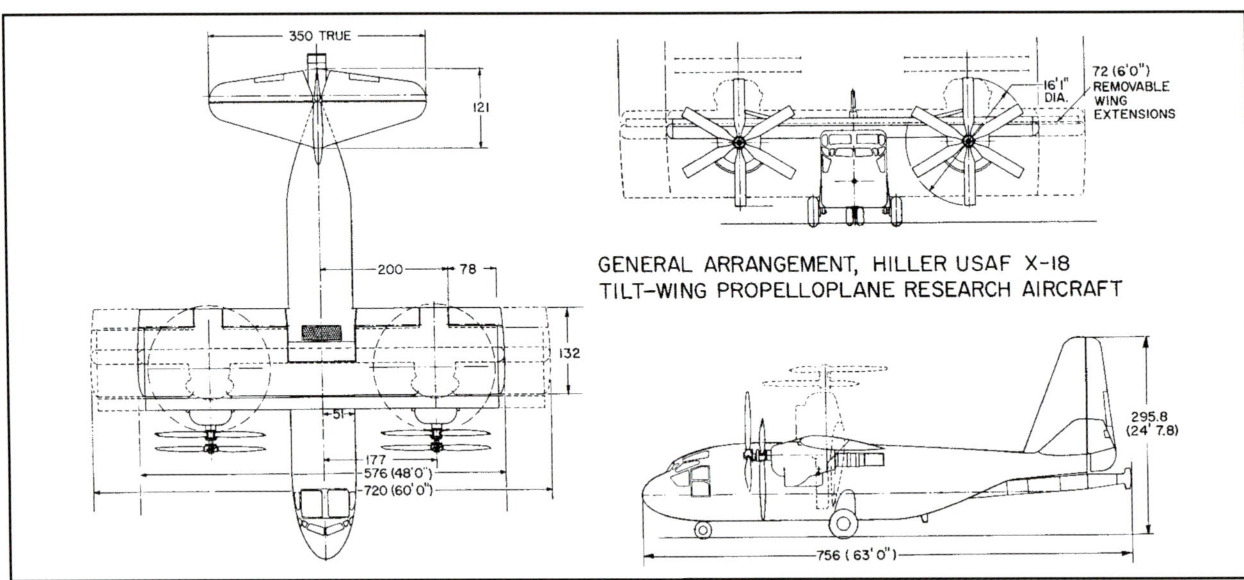

Selected VTOL test beds

	Bell Model 200, XV-3	Doak Model 16, VZ-4	Hiller Model 1051, X-18	Vertol Model 76, VZ-2
Technology	Tilt-rotor	Tilt-ducted prop	Tilt-wing	Tilt-wing
Sponsor	Army/Air Force	Army/ONR	Air Force	Army/ONR
Powerplant	1 x P&W R-985 piston radial @ 450hp (335.6kW)	1 x Lycoming YT53-L-1 turboshaft @ 860shp (641.3kW)	2 x Allison T40-A-14 turboprops @ 5,850eshp (4,362.3kW); 1x Westinghouse J34-WE-36 @ 3,400lb (15.12kN) thrust	1 x Lycoming YT53-L-1 turboshaft @ 860shp (641.3kW)*
Wingspan	31ft 4in (9.55m)	25ft 6in (7.77m)	48ft 0in (14.63m)**	24ft 11in (7.60m)
Length	30ft 4in (9.24m)	32ft 0in (9.75m)	63ft 0in (19.20m)	26ft 5in (8.05m)
Height	13ft 3in (4.04m)	10ft 0in (3.05m)	24ft 7.8in (7.51m)	15ft 0in (4.57m)
Gross weight	4,890lb (2,218kg)	3,200lb (1451.4kg)	33,000lb (14,968.5kg)	3,723lb (1,688.7kg)***
Max speed	160kt (296km/h)	230kt (426km/h)	220kt (407km/h)	184kt (341km/h)
First transition	18 December 1958	5 May 1958	n/a	15 July 1958

* Limited by transmission to 680shp (507kW)
** X-18 had provision for outer wing panel/wingtips to increase span to 60ft 0in (18.29m)
*** With ejection seat

The X-18 differed from the VZ-2 in both size and control systems. The X-18 used the Curtiss propellers developed for the XFY/XFY programmes, which were only controllable in blade pitch. The VZ-2 propellers had pitch control as well as a helicopter-like flapping hinge. (The Bell XV-3's tilt-rotor was the most helicopter-like, with the previously mentioned two-axis articulation as well as a lead-lag hinge for each blade. The prop-rotor had higher efficiency and required less power, but was the most difficult to develop.)

ABOVE The X-18 Tilt-wing V/STOL and the XROE Rotocycle (on the right) represented the largest and smallest Hiller products. *Hiller*

The culmination of Army V/STOL development

The possibility of practical applications of these (and more) Army transportation research efforts came in 1959 when the Army outlined three Army Study Requirements, or ASRs, to industry. Responses were to fulfil these major Army Aviation mission requirements during the 1960-to-1970 time period:

- ASR 1-60 Observation Mission
- ASR 2-60 Surveillance Mission
- ASR 3-60 Transportation Mission

Of these, ASR 3-60 called for an aircraft capable of transporting a 5,000lb (2,268 kg) payload over a mission radius of 217nmi (402 km), with a total hovering time of nine minutes.

At the close of the submission period on 1 February 1960, forty-five companies had responded with studies for 119 possible designs. Most were not detailed design proposals, but instead simply summaries that would allow the Army to analyse the alternatives. Additional opinions came from the DoD and NASA. On 19 March 1960 General Lymon Lemnitzer (the Army Chief of Staff) approved the Rogers Board recommendations with implementation for planning purposes.

For ASR 1-60, the result was the Light Observation Helicopter (LOH) competition (leading to the OH-6A and OH-58A helicopters). No specific aircraft platforms were recommended for ASR 2-60; instead, improved reconnaissance systems were to be developed (and these were later fitted to variants of the Grumman OV-1 Mohawk). No specific airlift aircraft was selected for ASR 3-60 either. Other recommendations included a further study to determine if the concept of air fighting units was practical, and if an experimental unit should be activated to test its feasibility.

The Army would meet its near-term airlift needs via two paths. Heavy helicopter transport duties would fall to the Vertol HC-1B helicopter (later the Boeing Vertol CH-47 Chinook), already under development under a contract issued by the Air Force in June 1959 on the Army's behalf. This ultimately proved fortuitous: the CH-47 was ready by 1965 for wartime use in Vietnam, while the XC-142A continued in flight trials. The Army's other need, for fixed-wing airlift, would fall to the de Havilland Caribou (which had received exemption from fixed-wing restrictions by the then Secretary of Defense, Charles E. Wilson).

Clearly, non-helicopter VTOL transport was close at hand, but not yet practical for production. The Army would continue to sponsor VTOL research into the mid-1960s with Lockheed's VZ-10/XV-4A (ejector flow), the GE/Ryan VZ-11/XV-5A (fan-in-wing), and evaluation of the Hawker Siddeley P-1127 Kestrel VZ-12/XV-6A (vectored thrust).

Ultimately, the Pentomic Army concept proved difficult to implement, and faded away as the Army pivoted towards air mobility (with helicopters) in Vietnam.

1961: The Tri-Service VTOL competition

Although the Army was not prepared to fund a full-scale VTOL airlifter development programme in 1960, the promising technologies drew attention from higher circles in the DoD. At the same time that the Rogers board was reaching its conclusions, a study panel commissioned by the DoD Director of Defense Research & Engineering (DDR&E), Herbert F. York, was in session. Chaired by Professor Courtland Perkins of Princeton, the panel was reviewing the full range of DoD VTOL development efforts.

The panel's April 1960 report suggested that a tilt-wing assault transport *could* be developed that met joint requirements of all three armed services. The DoD embraced the finding; a consolidated effort would eliminate duplication of research and development efforts. Despite the DoD's enthusiasm, however, the harsh reality was that each service had markedly mission requirements:

- Air Force: Combat Search and Rescue with a 1,500mi (2,413km) range (derived from the unfunded SOR-187 requirement that Bell had hoped to fill with its tilt-duct Model D190B)
- Army: Airlift with 400nmi (741km) range and an 8,000lb (3,629kg) payload or thirty-three combat troops
- Navy (serving as the procurement agent for Marine Corps): Assault/troop carrier (similar to Army) with 300kt speed, 200nmi (370km) range and shipboard, launch, recovery and storage (which resulted in stringent size and weight restrictions)

The service misgivings turned out to be immaterial; each initially fell in line under DoD direction and agreed to work towards a common design that met mission goals.

The competition and evaluation for a combined services VTOL airlift test aircraft was held under Navy technical supervision. The Navy completed Type Specification 152 (TS-152) in October 1960 and, after review and approval by the DoD, it was released to industry on 13 January 1961, quickly followed by a Request for Proposals on 1 February.

Given the state of the art at the time, this was quite a challenging set of requirements. Unlike most other competitions, however, there was no requirement for the contractor to submit details for a fully operational system, nor was there any commitment by the military to fund a follow-on production programme. The initial contract, worth

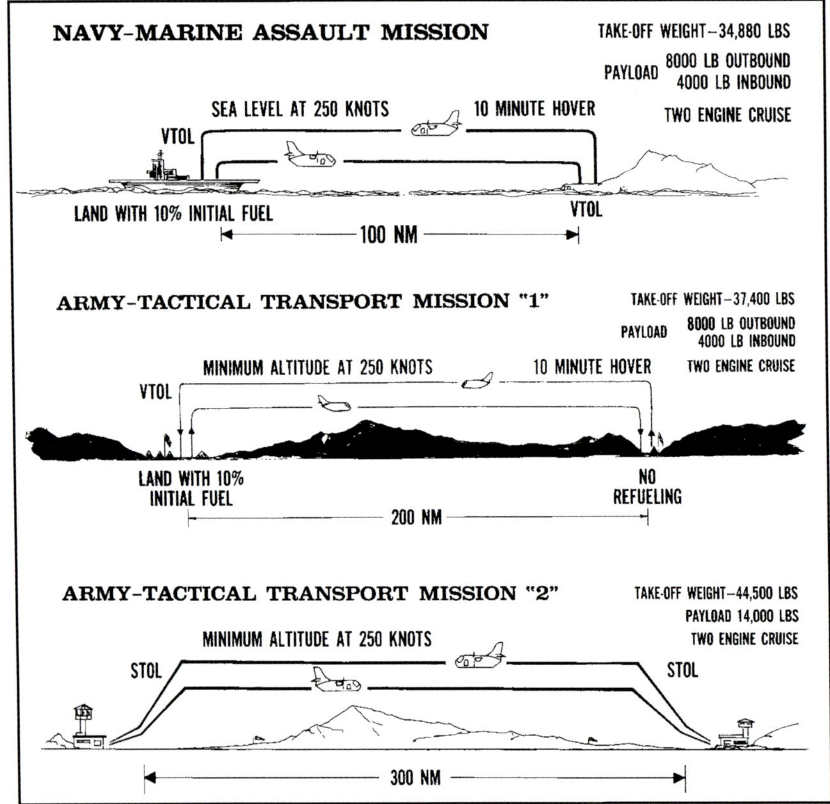

TS-152 (Tri-Service VTOL) requirements

Maximum airframe size for storage*	50ft (15.24m) long, 30ft (9.14m) wide, 17ft (5.18m) high
Cargo 'box' size	30ft (9.14m) long, 7.5ft (2.29m) wide, 7ft (2.13m) high
Maximum weight*	35,000lb (15,890kg)
Cruising speed at sea level	250-300kt (463-555km/h)
Maximum speed at sea level	300-400kt (555-740km/h)
Hover capability	6,000ft (1,829m), out of ground effect
Combat radius	200nmi (370km) with 32 combat-equipped troops
Useful load	Left to the bidder, but suggested as 8,000lb (3,629kg)
Minimum thrust-to-weight ratio	1.05:1

*Navy requirements for carrier operation

LEFT Mission profiles planned under TS-152. *LTV*

$1.9 million to the winning bidder, covered only the detailed design of the aircraft. The subsequent construction of five prototypes for testing under operational conditions as well as the static test article, fatigue test specimens and test rigs, was originally projected to cost $50.6 million.

There was intense interest in the opportunity. Indeed, of the major aircraft manufacturers, only three declined to respond: the Convair Division of General Dynamics, Northrop and Republic Aviation. Nine companies or consortia responded with full proposals, submitting eleven different designs between them. Not surprisingly, most sought to build on their previous research work, pursuing their individual approaches to VTOL.

Several other companies also submitted responses (some unsolicited), which, while not able to meet the stipulated requirements, sought research and development funds for projects they claimed to hold the necessary potential. For any company that had shown a previous interest in VTOL, this was too big an opportunity to miss.

Bell-Lockheed-Piasecki Model D2064

Bell Aerosystems (with team members Lockheed and Piasecki) proposed the Model D2064. Its configuration resembled Bell's previous experimental aircraft, the D2022, and employed four tilt-duct propellers, driven by four nacelle-mounted T64 engines. The ducts acted partly as aerofoils, reducing the required wing area.

The bulbous 'cab-over' design allowed the shortest possible fuselage. Fuel cells were to be installed above the cabin, which had primary access through two large 'petal' aft doors. Due to the compact design, only the 85sq ft (7.9m^2) outer-wing panels on the rear ducts and the upper vertical fin needed to be folded to meet the shipboard space requirements. It was the fastest of all the submissions to the competition with an estimated maximum speed of 385kt (712km/h) at 15,000ft (5,572m), while carrying the specified 8,000lb (3,629kg) payload.

In September 1961 Bell submitted a redesigned version of the D2064, designated the D2064A. Circulated just weeks after the Navy was allowed to withdraw from the Tri-Service VTOL programme, the design brochure showed a design without wing-folding or the 'cab-over' cockpit that was needed to meet the Navy's size requirements. In addition, the rear tilt-ducts were moved outboard to avoid exhaust gas ingestion from the forward engines.

Responsive Tri-Service VTOL proposals

Manufacturer	Model	Technology
Bell Aerospace, with Lockheed and Piasecki	D2064	Tilt-ducted prop
Bell Helicopter	D252	Tilt-rotor
Boeing Vertol	BV-137	Tilt-wing with rotor
Boeing Wichita	Model 900	Fixed lift-jet
Douglas	Model 828	Tilt-ducted prop
Grumman and Kaman	Model 242	Tilt-wing
McDonnell and Canadair	Model 175	Tilt-wing
North American (Columbus Division)	Not known	Tilt-wing
Sikorsky	Not specified	Tilt-wing with rotor
Vought-Hiller-Ryan	VHR-477	Tilt-wing

Additional Tri-Service VTOL proposals

Company	Model	Technology
Burnelli	n/a	Deflected lift-jet
Fairchild	M-351	Tilt-wing
Fowler	Model 20	Deflected propeller thrust
House of Kraft	PJ-VTOL HK-711	Lift-fan
Prewitt/Atlantic Research	Roto-Jet	Stopped-tandem rotor
Vanguard	Model 30	In-wing/fuselage lift fans
Verticraft	Verticar	Lift-fan
Wilford	n/a	Hot gas rotor

ABOVE Company artwork for the Bell Model D2064. *Scott Lowther/APR*

Bell Aerosystems Model D2064	
Powerplant	4 x GE T64-GE-6 turboshafts @ 2,850hp (2,130kW)
Wingspan	42ft 4.8in (12.93m)
Length	50ft 0in (15.25m)
Height	21ft 4.8 (6.53m)
Payload	8,000lb (3,629kg)
Max speed	385kt (712km/h)

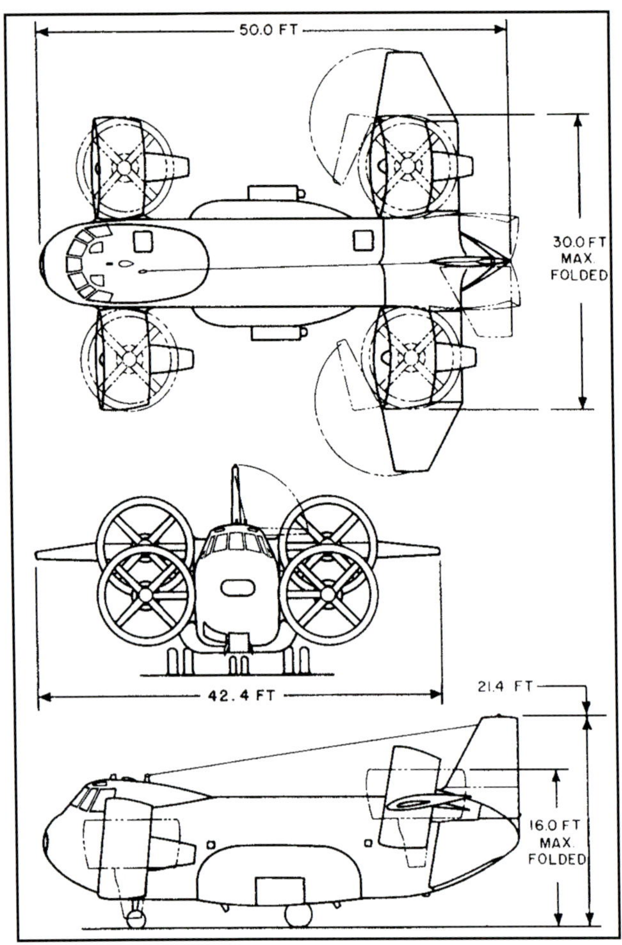

ABOVE Bell D2064 display model. *Tony Chong collection*

LEFT Bell D2064 general arrangement. *Scott Lowther/APR*

BELOW Bell D2064 internal details. The raised cockpit provided room for the cross-shafting and gearboxes for the forward engines and the nose landing gear. *Scott Lowther/APR*

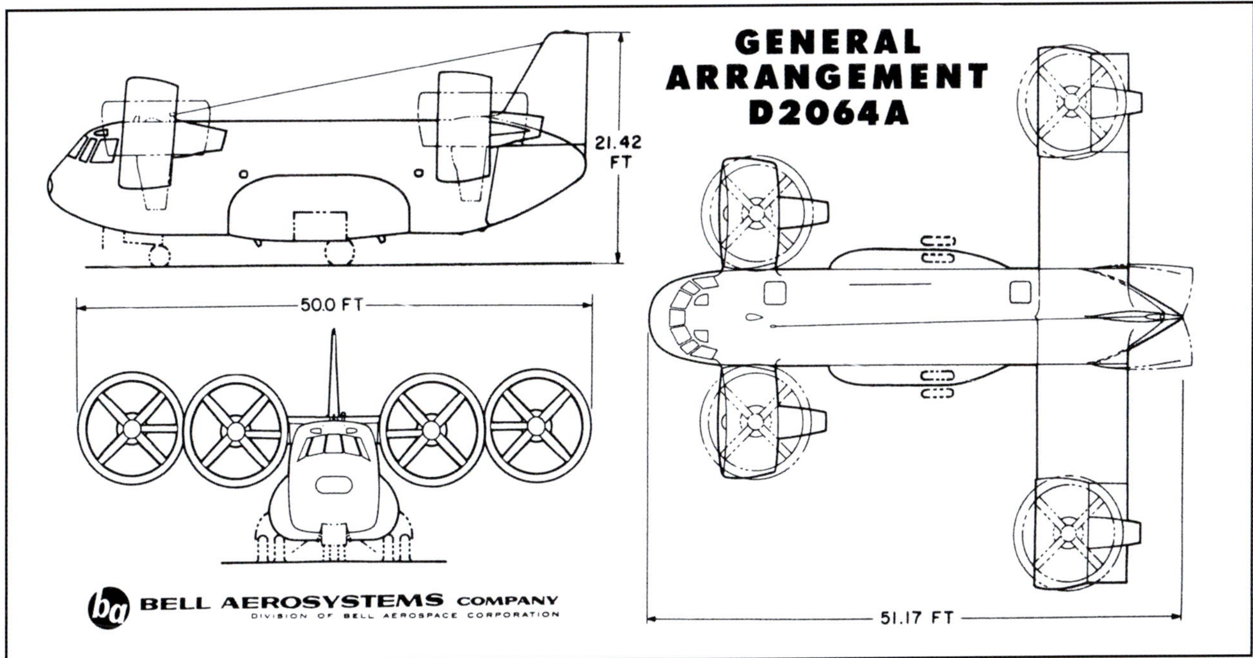

ABOVE Bell revised its tilt-duct design as the Model D2064A in September, 1961. *Scott Lowther/APR*

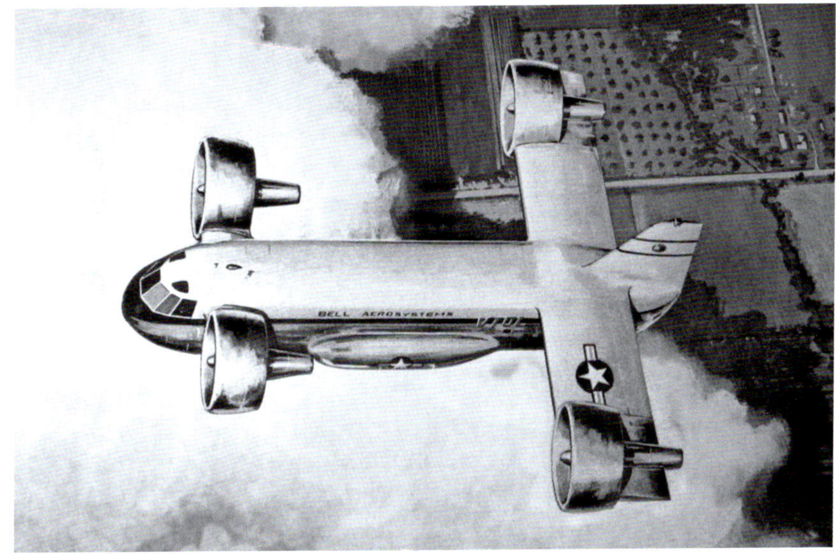

RIGHT Freed from the Navy/Marine Corps carrier fit and folding requirements, the later D2064A was a sleeker aircraft. *Scott Lowther/APR*

Bell Helicopter Model D252

Bell Helicopter's tilt-rotor submission was based on tilt-rotor technology pioneered on its XV-3 research aircraft. Designated D252, the design was dominated by two large tilt-rotors on swivelling engine nacelles mounted at the tips of the low-set fixed wing. The large swept area of the tilt rotors allowed low disk loading (and low downwash) and high power loading. This efficient conversion of engine torque through utilisation of the large-diameter tilt-rotors allowed the use of only two of the cross-shafted T64 engines rather than the four required by the other competitors. Despite the lower installed power, the D252 met the cruise speed requirement of 250kt (463km/h), and was only 2 knots slower than the required maximum speed of 300kt (555km/h). The weight saved could be traded for extra fuel or payload capacity.

BELOW Bell Helicopter Model D252 general arrangement. *Tommy Thomason*

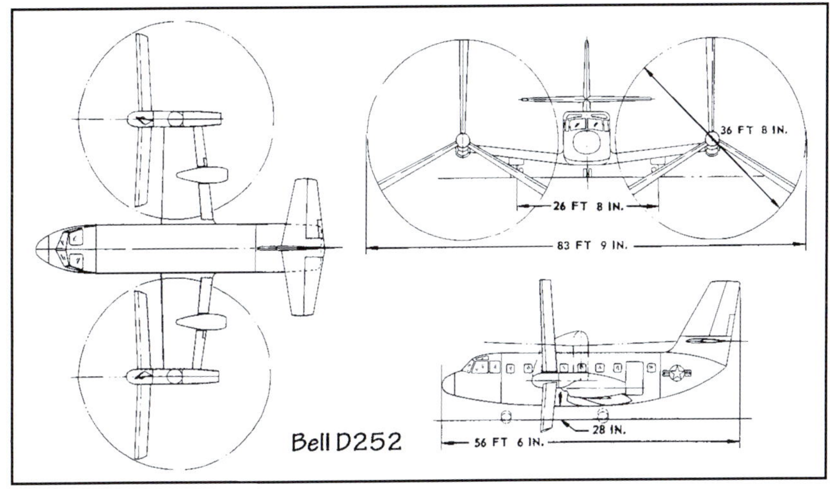

Bell Helicopter D252	
Powerplant	2 x GE T64-GE-6 turboshafts @ 2,850hp (2,130kW)
Span (including rotors)	83ft 9in (27.06m)
Length	56ft 6in (17.23m)
Height	n/a
Rotor Diameter	36ft 8in (11.18m)
Payload	8,000lb (3,629kg)
Cruise speed	250kt (463km/h)
Max speed	298kt (551km/h)

To enable the smallest possible shipboard footprint, the fuselage was designed to fold into three, approximately equal, elements. The tilt-rotor blades folded to reduce span and the vertical tail folded to reduce the overall height. All folding operations were to be hydraulically powered. Cargo could be loaded into the centre fuselage with the nose and/or tail folded, as well as through the aft fuselage ramp; the cargo floor was 50in (1.27m) above ground/deck level. The main landing gear retracted into fairings that extended aft from the rear spar of the low-set wing, affording the widest tread of any of the competitors.

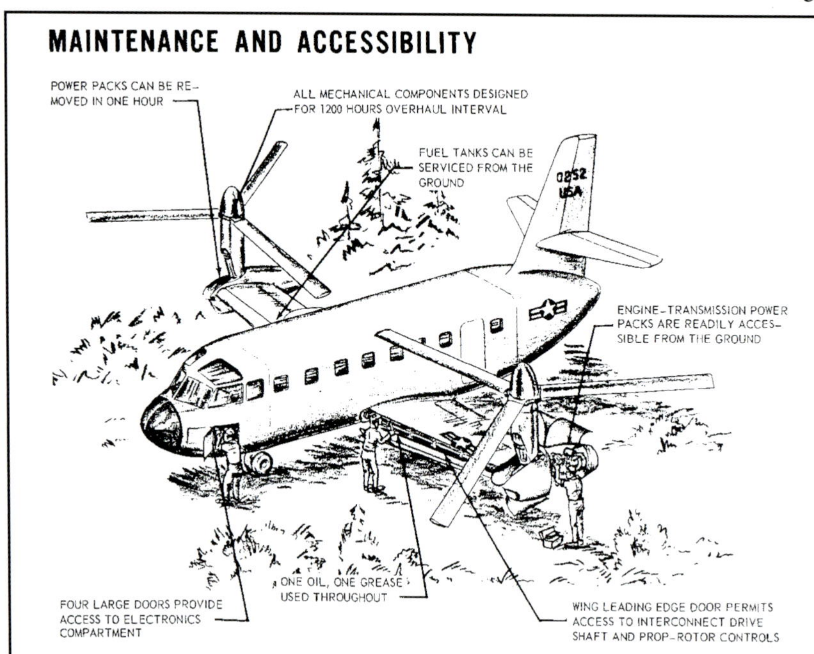

ABOVE The design features shown in this Bell D252 promotional artwork include ground-level access to the engines. *Tommy Thomason*

BELOW The design of the Bell Helicopter D252 carrier stowage arrangement had the unique combination of a fixed wing and folding fuselage to meet requirements. *Tommy Thomason*

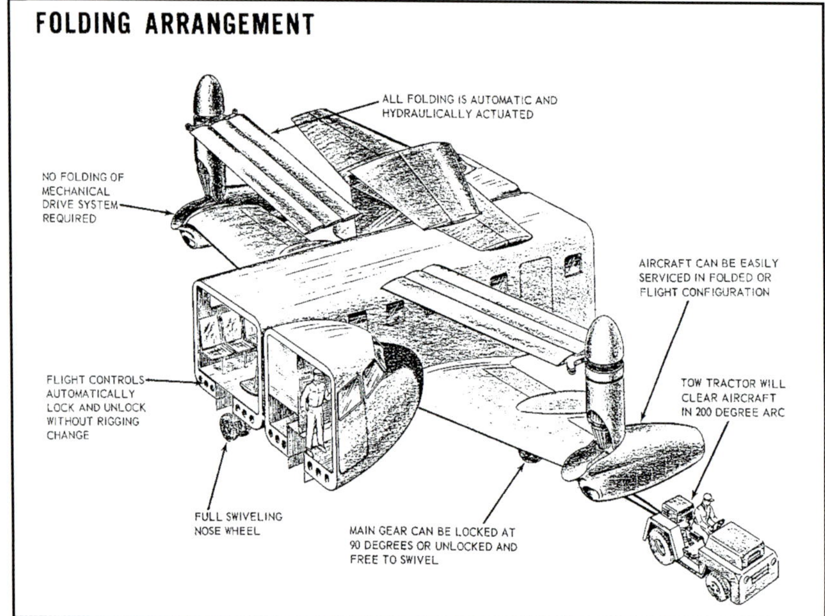

Boeing Vertol Model 137

The Boeing Vertol entry built on the experience gained from the Boeing Vertol Model 76, or VZ-2. The BV-137 was powered by four T64 engines, podded in pairs beneath the wings and coupled together to power two large, three-bladed flapping prop-rotors. These were linked by a cross shaft as a safeguard against failure of any individual engine. The wings incorporated leading edge slats and double-slotted flaps. The 24ft (7.32m) diameter of the rotors offered low disk loading, but there was insufficient ground clearance to permit conventional take-offs and landings (as in today's V-22 Osprey).

Boeing Vertol 137	
Powerplant	4 x GE T64-GE-6 turboshafts @ 2,850hp (2,130kW)
Rotor diameter	24ft 0in (7.32m)
Wingspan	55ft 0in (16.78m)
Length	50ft 0in (15.25m)
Height	23ft 0in (7.02m)
Cargo bay	7ft 0in (2.14m) high x 7ft 6in (2.29m) wide x 30ft 0in (9.15m) long

BELOW Promotional artwork for the Boeing Vertol Model 137. *Boeing*

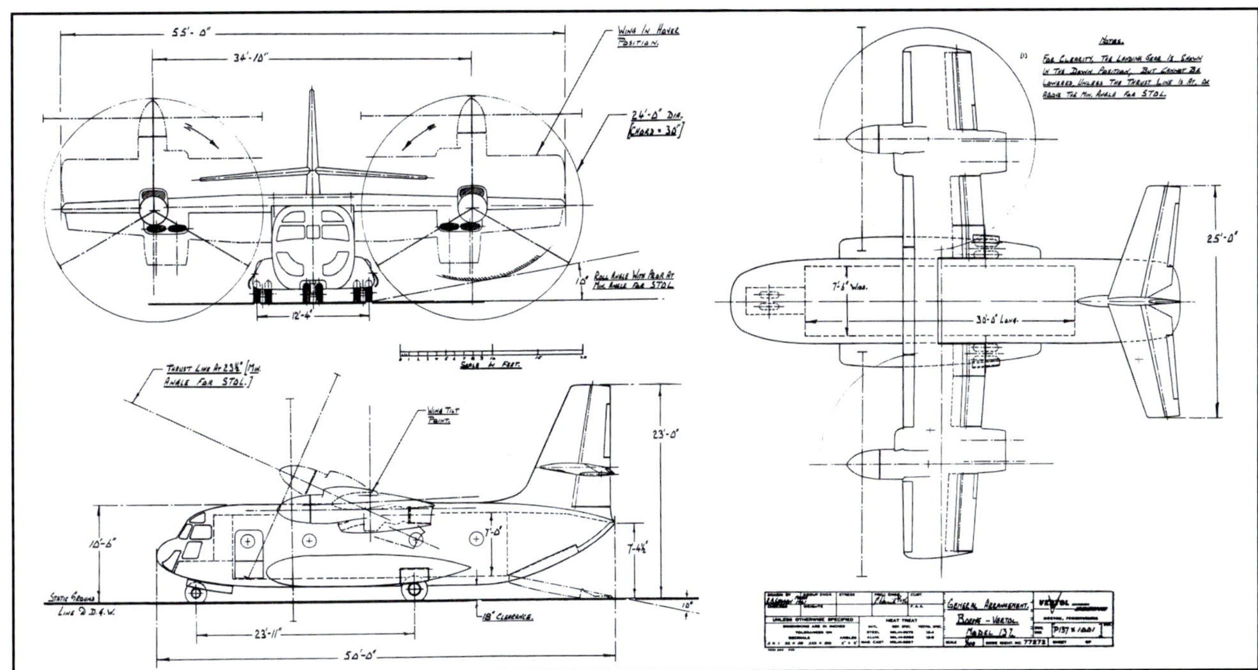

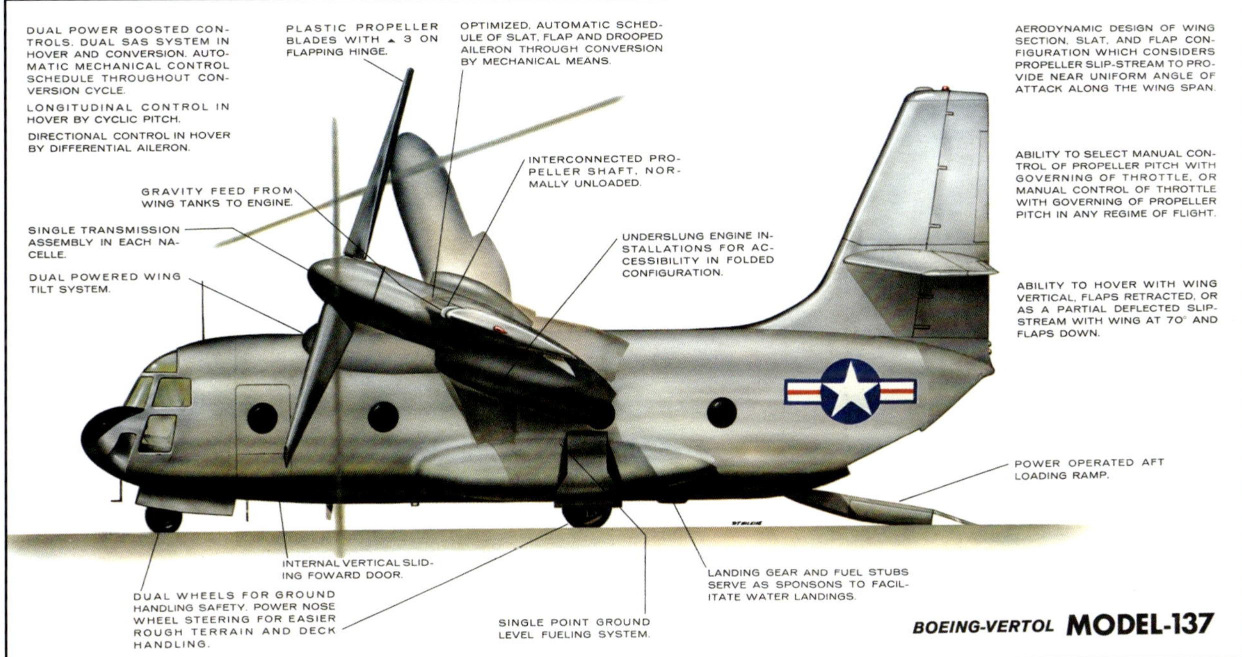

TOP BV-137 general arrangement. *Boeing*

ABOVE BV-137 general features. *Boeing*

BELOW The BV-137A for the Navy and Marine Corps with wide-track landing gear and sponsons, and the wing/tail folding arrangement. *Boeing*

Boeing Vertol hedged a bit on the design, offering the baseline BV-137 for shore-based applications and the navalised BV-137A for the carrier-based Marine Corps assault transport mission. This version had folding wings and a vertical tail for shipboard storage. It also housed the main landing gear in larger sponsons to increase track width.

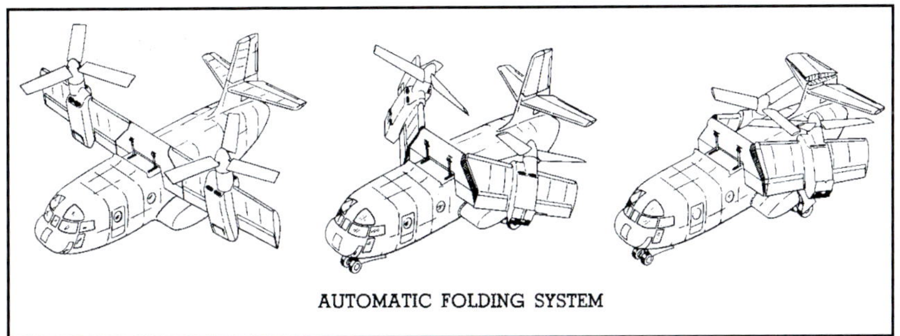

ABOVE This display model of the Boeing (Wichita Division) Model 900 shows the exhaust louvres of six of the twelve lift-jets. *John Aldaz photo*

LEFT The Boeing (Wichita Division) Model 900 had a relatively large canard and a small wing. *John Aldaz photo*

Boeing Wichita Model 900	
Powerplant	12 x LE-4000* turbofans @ 4,000lb thrust (17.8kN) for vertical lift; 2 x CF700 (Advanced) turbofans @ 4,800lb thrust (21.3kN) for forward thrust
Wingspan	49ft (14.95m) or 28ft 8in (8.74m) folded
Length	52ft 7in (16.04m) or 50ft 0in (15.24m) folded
Height	25ft 6in (7.78m) or 17ft 0in (5.18m) folded
Max TOW	38,550lb (17,486kg) with 6,000lb (2,722kg) payload
Max TOW (overload)	43,600lb (19,790kg) with 8,000lb (3,629kg) payload
Max speed	360kt (666km/h)
Ferry range	2,200mi (4,070km)

* 'LE-4000 engine' represents an engine in the class of the General Electric SF 145 or the Bristol BS 59/9

Boeing Wichita Model 900

The Model 900 was the second of two Boeing entries; each was developed independently, a point stressed in the submissions. Indeed, Boeing Wichita's Model 900 took a completely different approach from all the other entries, employing separate engines for lift and cruise purposes.

Twelve dedicated LE-4000 engines, mounted in sixes in nacelles along either side of the upper fuselage, provided vertical lift. Thrust could be deflected by 15° to assist low-speed manoeuvrability and transitional flight. Reaction control jets, mounted at the extremities of the wings and fuselage, provided low-speed control, while two GE CF700 (Advanced) turbofans provided cruise flight.

The failure of any one lift engine was compensated for with increased thrust from the remaining eleven. With one engine out, the aircraft was still able to hover at 3,200ft (976m), half of its normal ceiling. The redundancy eliminated the complexity and weight of the engine cross-shafting featured in other submissions.

Boeing proposed constructing two 'Initial Prototypes', powered by twelve General Electric SJ 132 turbojets and two CF700-2B turbofans (based on the J85 turbojet). These would be followed by 'Advanced Prototypes' powered by twelve 'LE-4000' (either General Electric SF 145 or Bristol 59/9) turbofans and two GE CF700 (Advanced) turbofans.

Jet exhaust velocity at sea level was estimated at 300ft/sec (91.5m/sec) with a temperature of 300°F (149°C), making it suitable for steel-decked carrier operation with both the wings and the fin folded. The wings folded outboard of the propulsion engines, making it possible to taxi in this configuration.

The Model 900 promised impressive performance, including a claimed speed of 360kt (666km/h) at sea level, a ferry range of 2,200nmi (4,070km) and the ability to hover at an overload gross weight of 43,600lb (19,790kg). In a competition populated exclusively by unconventional designs, however, it was one of the more high-risk submissions. Notably, although the era saw many proposals and several prototypes employing combinations of separate lift/propulsion engines, no successful production aircraft has ever used this combination.

The Model 900's unusual approach may have resulted from the leader of its design team, Richard Vogt. Vogt had been chief designer for Kawasaki in the 1930s. He subsequently joined Blohm und Voss in a similar capacity, and during the Second World War oversaw the design of the highly unconventional, asymmetrical BV 141 together with several concepts for early jet fighters. After the war Vogt migrated to the USA under Operation Paperclip. He later joined Boeing, where he is credited by some with inventing the winglet.

Douglas Models D-828 and D-829

Douglas developed two designs, Models D-828 and D-829, each powered by four T64 engines. The primary difference was that the Model D-828 utilised a six-bladed, 8-foot-diameter variable-camber propeller in a tilting duct (Douglas preferred the term 'turbo-duct'). In contrast, the Model D-829 utilised larger, slower-turning un-ducted 14.5ft (4.42m)-diameter variable-camber propellers and had a larger vertical tail.

Douglas Tri-Service V/STOL

	Model D-828 'turbo-duct'	Model D-829 tilt-prop
Powerplant	4 x GE T64 turboshafts @ 2,850hp (2,130kW)	4 x GE T64 turboshafts @ 2,850hp (2,130kW)
Span	48ft 5in (14.77m) or 30ft (9.15m) folded	48ft 5in (14.77m) or 30ft (9.15m) folded
Length	50ft 0in (15.25m)	50ft 0in (15.25m)
Height	25ft 5in (7.75m) or 16ft 3in (4.96m) fin folded	28ft 4in (8.64m) or 16ft 3in (4.96m) fin folded
Wing area	355sq ft (33.01m²) including aft ducts	364sq ft (33.85m²)

BELOW Boeing Model 900 general arrangement. *Boeing*

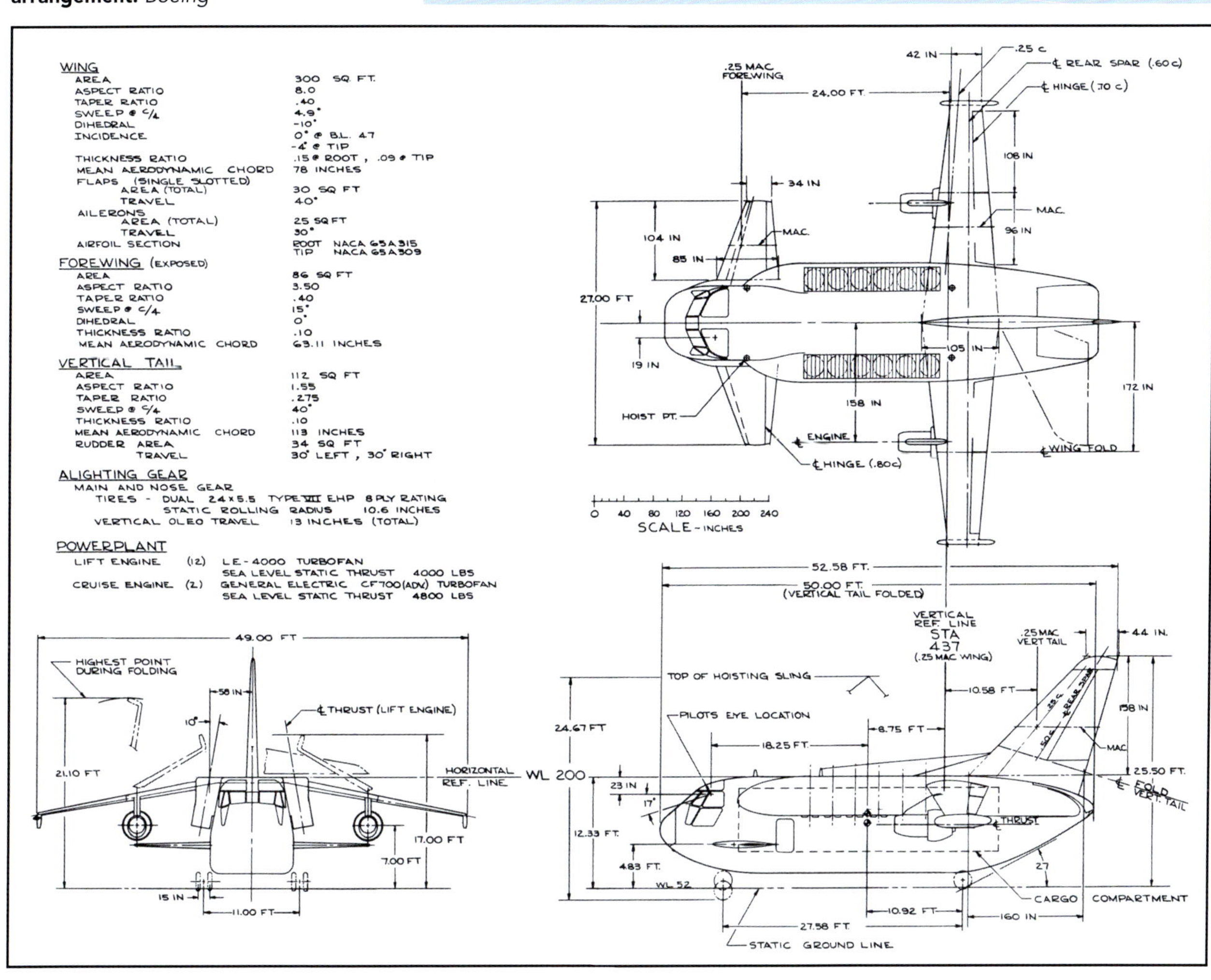

Douglas's aircraft differed from the Bell D2064 in having the engines mounted in the fuselage, and staggering the turbo-ducts (or propellers) horizontally. This arrangement eliminated hot gas ingestion and the propeller-induced turbulence that doomed the Bell proposal. Douglas submitted only one of its designs – the Model D-828 – in response to the Tri-Service VTOL competition, presumably feeling that it was better suited to carrier operations. The company later proposed its Model D-829N to NATO, in July 1961.

Previously, Douglas's Santa Monica Division developed two- and four-engined tilt-wing designs under the Model 1886 project designation, but discontinued this line of development after reports were issued in October 1955.

The 1960 turbo-duct designs drew heavily on the work of Doak Aircraft of Torrance, California. Doak had been established in 1939 by Edmund Doak, a former Douglas engineer and El Segundo Division plant manager. The company had successfully flown its Model 16 tilting-ducted-fan demonstrator since February 1958. Impressed by the initial results, the Army and NASA continued to test the aircraft, now designated VZ-4, until 1960.

At this point the 'roles and missions' issue emerged again; the Army was reminded that it could only develop helicopters. Unfortunately for Doak, the DoD classified the VZ-4 as an aeroplane and, unlike the Army, the USAF showed no interest in its development. Having lost its only major customer, Doak closed down. Douglas bought out the patents and engineering data, hiring several Doak engineers into the advanced design team to assist with the Tri-Service VTOL proposal, responding to Navy interest in the ducted fan.

ABOVE LEFT Company artwork for the Douglas Model D-828. *Boeing*

LEFT The Douglas Model D-829N (for NATO) painted by R. G. Smith. *Boeing*

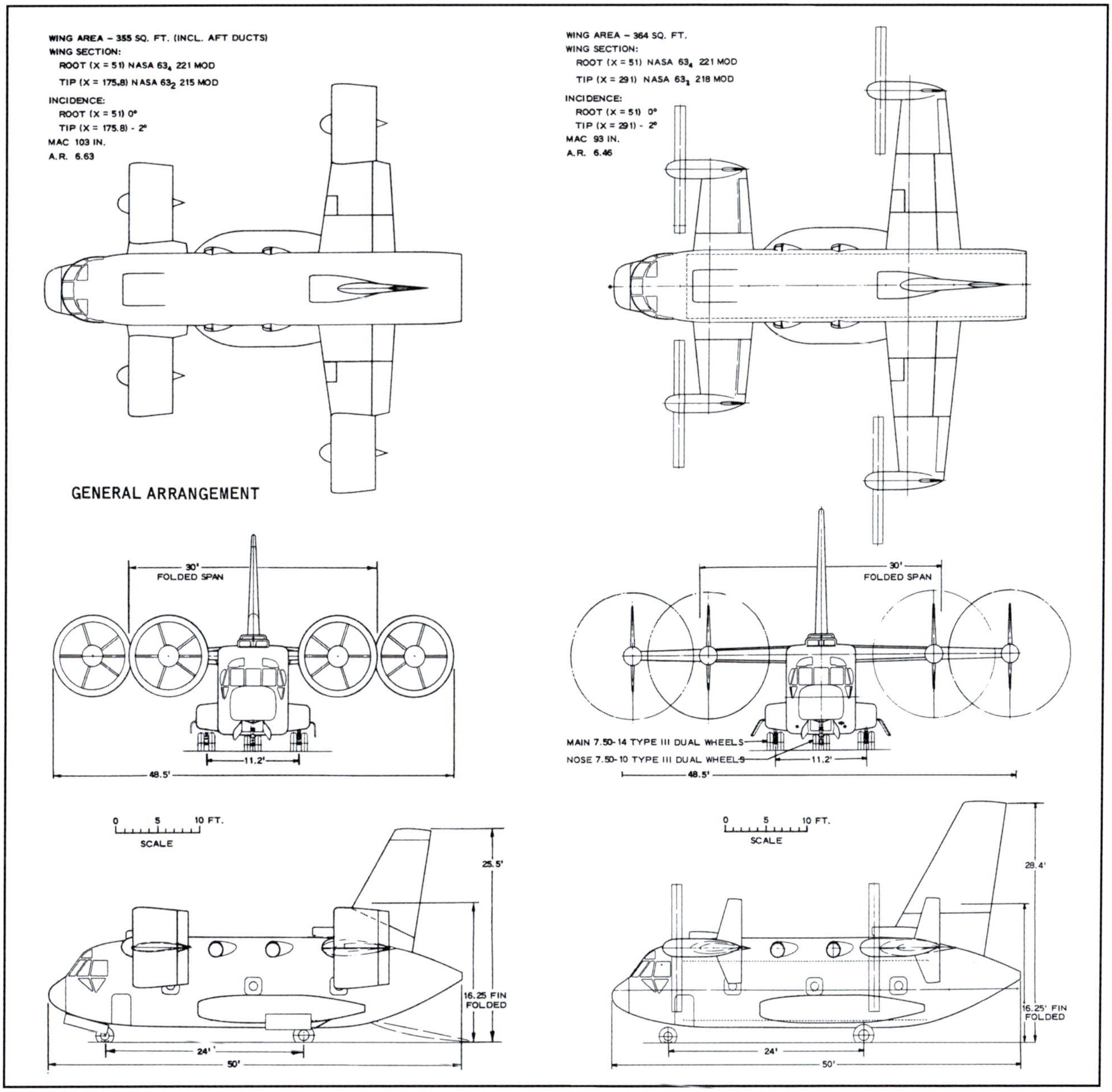

ABOVE Douglas Models D-828 (left) and D-829 (right). The higher efficiencies of the of the turboducts used in on the D-828 allowed smaller prop diameters and a smaller vertical tail that the D-829. The D-829 open prop design offered a lower velocity downwash reducing dust and soil/rock erosion during land-based operation. *Boeing*

RIGHT A powered model of the D-828 undergoes flow visualisation testing. The multitude of tuft directions indicates the confused airflow as the model simulated hovering close to the ground. *Boeing*

ABOVE A display model of the Doak Model 22. *Author collection*

BELOW Grumman-Kaman G-242 general arrangement. *Special Collections & Archives, Wright State University*

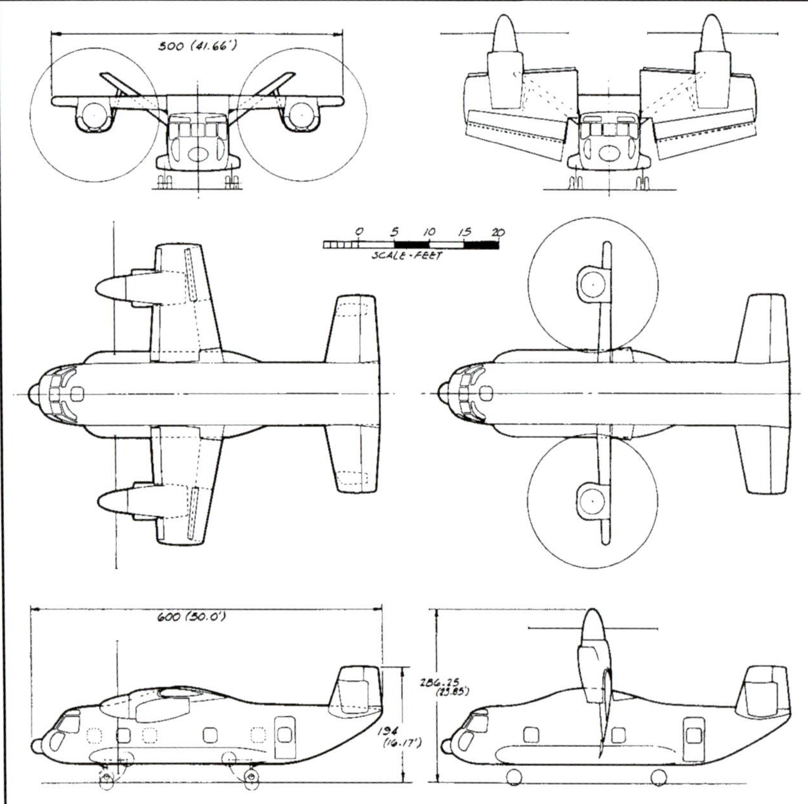

Grumman-Kaman Model G-242

Grumman teamed up with Kaman Aircraft Corp to produce a tilt-wing proposal designated as the G-242. Grumman led the design team, but relied on Kaman's 'propulsive variable-camber rotor' technology previously prototyped on the K-16B tilt-wing experimental aircraft. The K-16B had married a Grumman JRF-5 Goose fuselage to a tilt-wing/deflected-slipstream arrangement, powered by two General Electric YT58-GE-2A engines. Extensively tested in a wind tunnel, it suffered lengthy delays during ground evaluations. By 1962 it still had not flown, leading the Navy to cancel the project.

The G-242 design had a relatively conventional fuselage with a four-strut, dual-wheel landing gear. The wing had a 'cut-away' centre section that – with leading edge slats and Fowler flaps – promised stall-free performance at the high angles of attack that the wing would experience during transition from vertical to horizontal flight. The V-tail provided sufficient area for transitional stability and the canted vertical surfaces added to the area needed for high-speed flight. Apart from minimising drag, the small tail area also had the benefit of being a simple non-folding lightweight structure. Grumman opted for a 'roll-up' aft cargo door with a construction similar to that used on the bomb-bay doors of the B-24 bomber. The fuselage incorporated separate, manually installed ramps, which brought a further estimated weight saving of 207lb (94kg).

Grumman-Kaman G-242	
Powerplant	4 x GE T64-GE-6 turboshafts @ 2,850hp (2,130kW)
Span	41ft 8in (12.71m) (including propellers)
Length	50ft 0in (15.25m)
Height	16ft 2in (4.91m) to top of fin, or 23ft 10.5in (7.27m) with engines vertical
Max speed	351kt (650km/h)

ABOVE Company artwork for the Grumman-Kaman G-242. *Special Collections & Archives, Wright State University*
BELOW The G-242 in Marine Corps markings. *Special Collections & Archives, Wright State University*

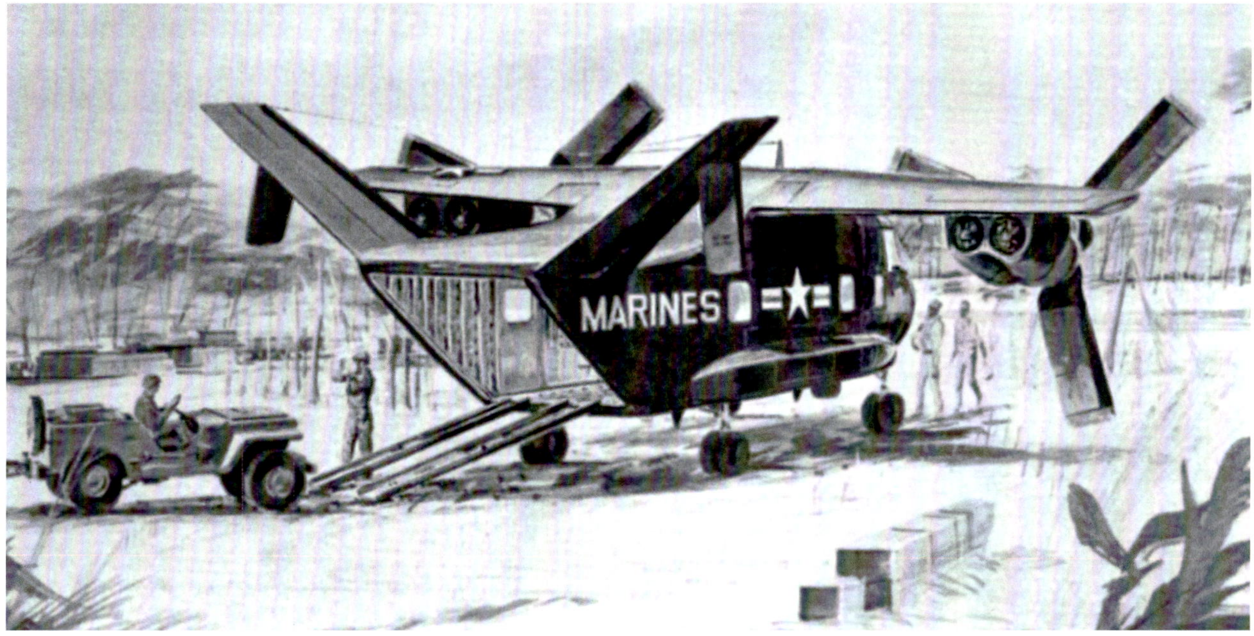

The G-242's propellers were 18.75ft (5.72m) in diameter. Each of the three blades used a flap at the 50% chord line, extending from the tip to the half span, to increase the propulsive force.

Grumman expended considerable effort in support of the proposal. The company built mock-ups of the forward fuselage/cockpit and wing centre section control system, then constructed a test rig to evaluate downwash/ground erosion. It also proposed an alternative cockpit design featuring advanced video displays similar to those pioneered on the A-6A and later used on the F-14A.

ABOVE Company artwork for the McDonnell-Canadair Model 175. *Terry Panopalis collection*

McDonnell-Canadair Model 175

McDonnell initiated design studies under three model numbers on 12 December 1960, undoubtedly after seeing a pre-release copy of the TS-152 specification. The Model 169 was described as a quadrafoil (four wings) design with tandem tilt wings and four engines driving Hamilton Standard variable-camber six-blade propellers. Model variations ran from 169A to F. The subsequent Model 170 investigated tilt-duct technology, with iterations from Model 170A to G and an airline version called the T-70A. The Model 171 investigated four-engine tilt-wing options.

A further variation was added to the effort on 29 December in the form of the Model 172, which was to use tilting ducted tip-driven fans. The Model 174, a tilt-wing deflected-flap quadrafoil, followed on 20 January 1961. The final option, the Model 177, was introduced

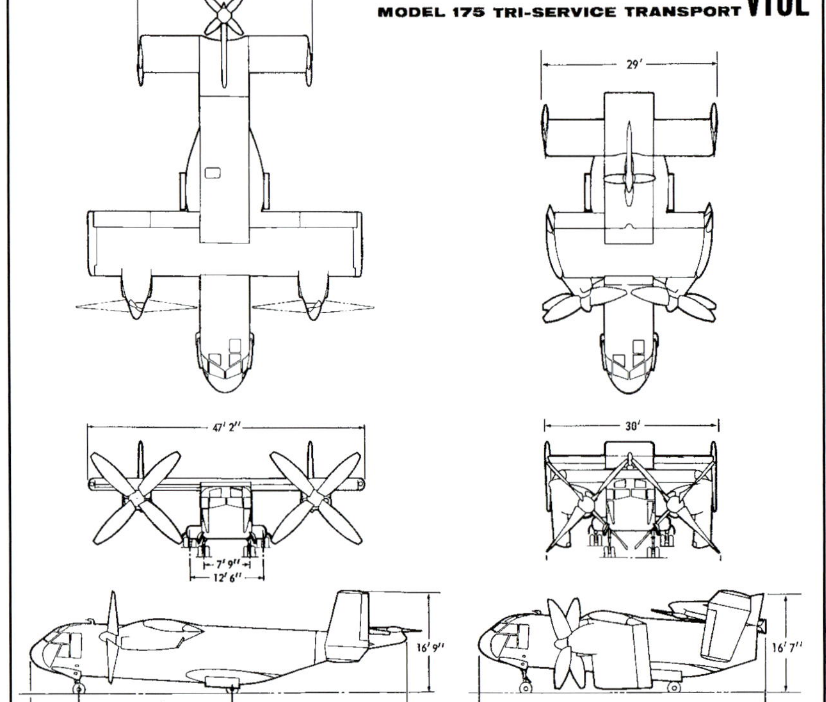

LEFT McDonnell-Canadair Model 175 general arrangement. *Terry Panopalis collection*

McDonnell-Canadair Model 175	
Powerplant	4 x GE T64-GE-6 turboshafts @ 2,850hp (2,130kW)
Span	47ft 2in (14.39m) or 30ft 0in (9.15m) folded
Length	66ft 6in (20.28m) or 50ft 0in (15.25m) folded
Height	16ft 9in (5.11m) or 16ft 7in (5.08m) folded
Max speed	340kt (629km/h)
Cruise speed	259kt (480km/h)

on 14 February and represented the culmination of a decade of 'hot rotor' studies and proposals. It evolved from the earlier McDonnell Model 113P compound helicopter. That design had used a pressure jet-driven (hot gas) rotor for take-off, hover and landing, but operated as an autogyro in forward flight.

McDonnell ultimately rejected these designs and selected the Model 175 (first announced on 8 February 1961), which it developed in cooperation with Canadair, taking advantage of the latter's expertise in tilt-wing turboshaft aircraft design. Canadair had been working in this field since 1956 and had studied a variety of VTOL techniques under the CL-62 model number. These had culminated in the CL-62B, which was submitted in response to the Army ASR 3-60 request.

In planform, the aircraft looked like an enlarged version of Canadair's later CL-84 with two very large, wide-chord, fibreglass propellers, and twin vertical fins. Like the NAA entry, the aircraft had a horizontal tail rotor for slow-speed pitch control. Cruise speed was estimated to be 259kt (480km/h), with a maximum speed of 340kt (629km/h).

Four T64 turboshaft engines provided power, paired in each of two nacelles and cross-shafted. Each set of engines connected to a combining gearbox that drove a propeller 14ft (4.27m) in diameter.

Landing gear was a 'quadracycle' type with four struts. All four sets of wheels were fully retractable, but also extendable to raise the aircraft for ground clearance during wing-folding. In addition to wing-folding, the aft fuselage (including the pitch propeller and the empennage) was hinged to fold upwards by about 180° to shorten the aircraft by 16.5ft (5.03m). An Auxiliary Power Unit (APU) located in the left aft sponson provided self-starting, power, and air capabilities, with cabin heating and ventilation systems housed in the right aft sponson.

North American Aviation Tri-Service tilt-wing VTOL

The Columbus Division of North American Aviation submitted a tilt-wing design with four separate engines and a small, horizontal shrouded tail rotor used for pitch control at low speeds. The twin vertical tails were placed clear of the disturbed airflow caused by the wing centre section during transition. They were mounted on a variable-incidence (up to 10°) horizontal stabiliser. The tilt wing was positioned by rotary actuators similar to those used to fold the wingtips on

BELOW **NAA Tri-Service tilt-wing VTOL general arrangement.**
Special Collections & Archives, Wright State University

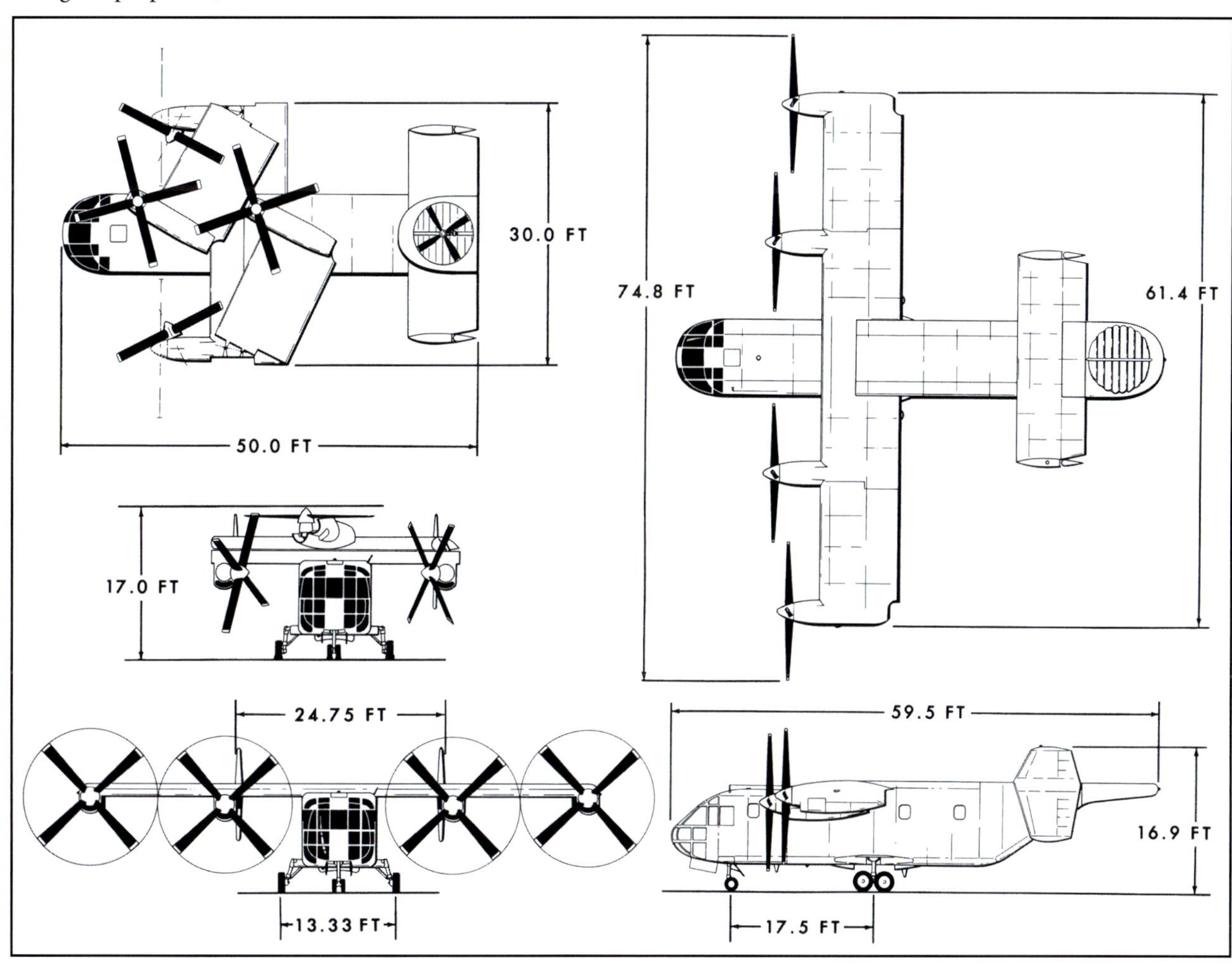

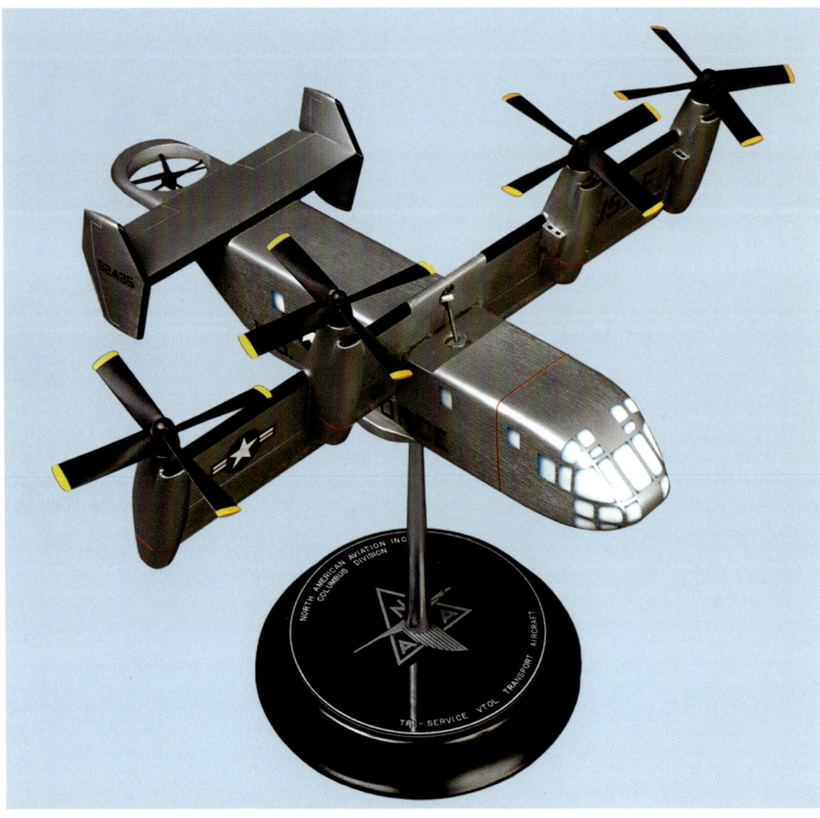

ABOVE The complex NAA folding design allowed the inboard engines to be run for deck spotting.
Special Collections & Archives, Wright State University

LEFT A display model of the NAA Tri-Service tilt-wing proposal.
John Aldaz collection

North American Aviation Tri-Service tilt-wing VTOL

Powerplant	4 x GE T64-GE-6 turboshafts @ 2,850hp (2,130kW)
Wingspan	61ft 4.8in (18.73m) to wingtips
Span including rotors	74ft 9.6in (22.81m) or 30ft 0in (9.15m) folded
Length	59ft 6in (18.15m) or 50ft 0in (15.25m) folded
Height	16ft 10.8in (5.15m) or 17ft 0in (5.19m) folded

BELOW NAA Tri-Service tilt-wing VTOL internal structure.
Special Collections & Archives, Wright State University

TRI-SERVICE VTOL TRANSPORT

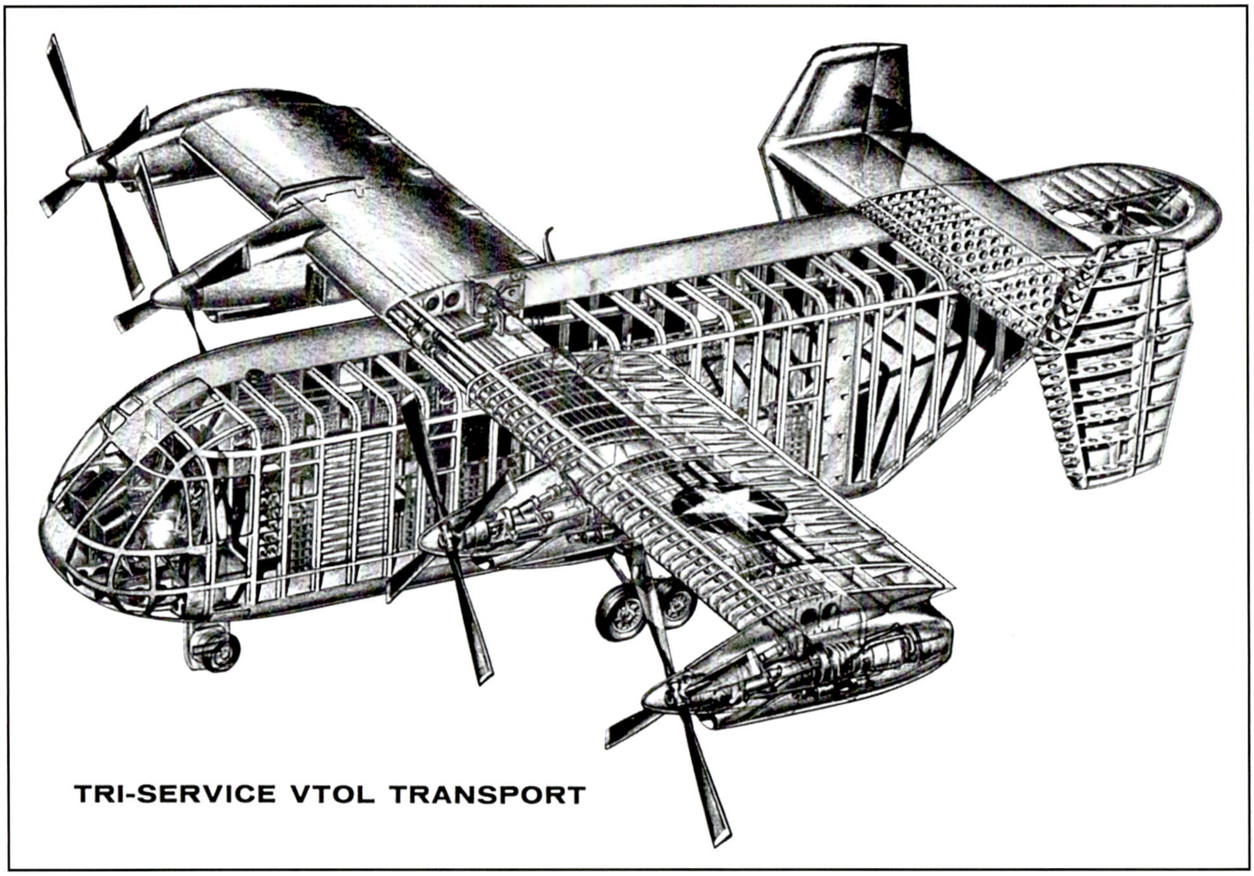

the company's XB-70A. This was unlike the other tilt-wings in the competition, which used conventional linear actuators. The two-spar wing featured full-span Fowler flaps, with the outboard sections used as ailerons in conventional flight. A dual cross-shafting system between the four engines was included.

Despite other advantages, the twin-tail configuration created challenges for aircraft carrier stowage. The dual vertical stabilisers forced North American to adopt a rather complicated wing and propeller folding system. All four propeller assemblies, 16ft (4.88m) in diameter, folded for storage, with the outboard assemblies folding downward (or upward on the folded, inverted wing panel), and the inboard propellers rotating inwards by approximately 70°. The extreme aft fuselage, sprouting the pitch control shrouded propeller, rotated up and forward to reduce the fuselage length to the mandated 50ft (15.25m).

ABOVE Promotional artwork for the Sikorsky DS-109 tilt-wing.
Special Collections & Archives, Wright State University

Sikorsky DS-109 tilt-wing

The Sikorsky entry envisaged a conventional aircraft configuration but with tilting wings. The two propeller/rotors, 24ft (7.32m) in diameter, were driven by two pairs of T64-GE-6 engines. Power output from each set would drive a single propeller through a gearbox, and each gearbox would be cross-shafted to the other.

Sikorsky DS-109 tilt-wing

Powerplant	4 x GE T64-GE-6 turboshafts @ 2,850hp (2,130kW)
Span	59ft 8in (18.19m) or 30ft 0in (9.14m) folded
Length	53ft 2in (16.22m) or 50ft 0in (15.24m) folded
Height	23ft 0in (7.01m) or 17ft 0in (5.18m) folded
Mission gross weight	35,000lb (15,890kg)
Max speed	352kt (651km/h)
Cruise speed	233kt (431km/h) with 2 engines or 324kt (600km/h) with 4 engines

The DS-109 was designed to cruise at 233kt (431km/h) using power from just two of the four engines, at its mission gross weight of 35,000lb (15,890kg) at sea level. Cruise speed with all four engines operating rose to 324kt (599km/h), albeit at a higher rate of fuel consumption, with maximum speed rising to 352kt (651km/h).

BELOW Sikorsky DS-109 tilt-wing airlifter internal details.
Special Collections & Archives, Wright State University

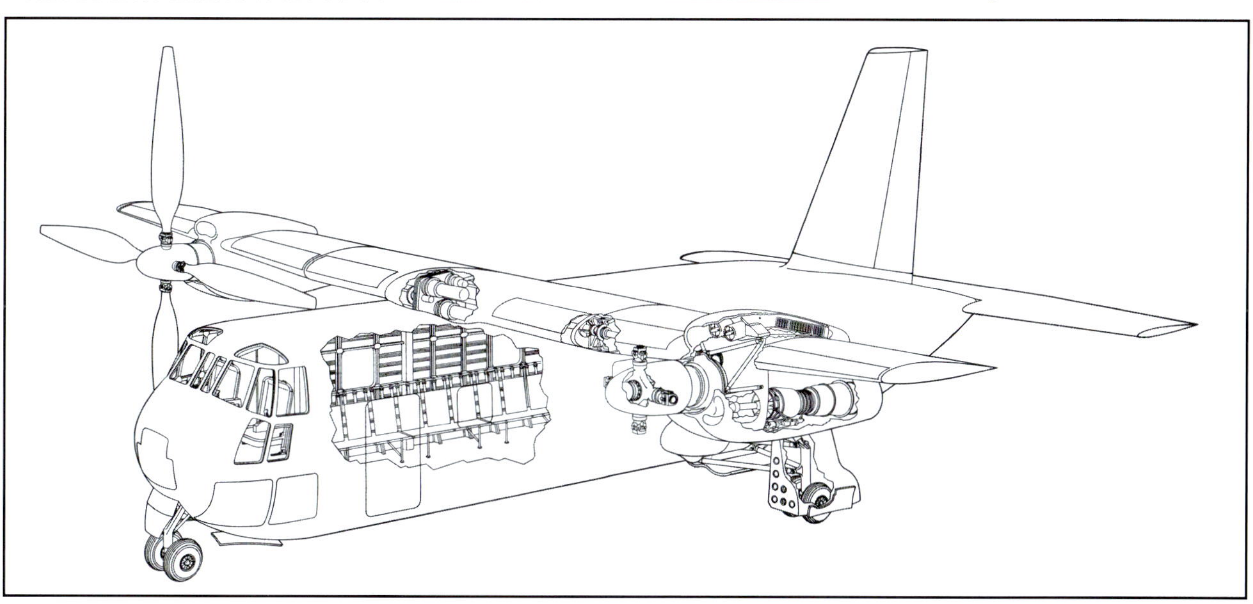

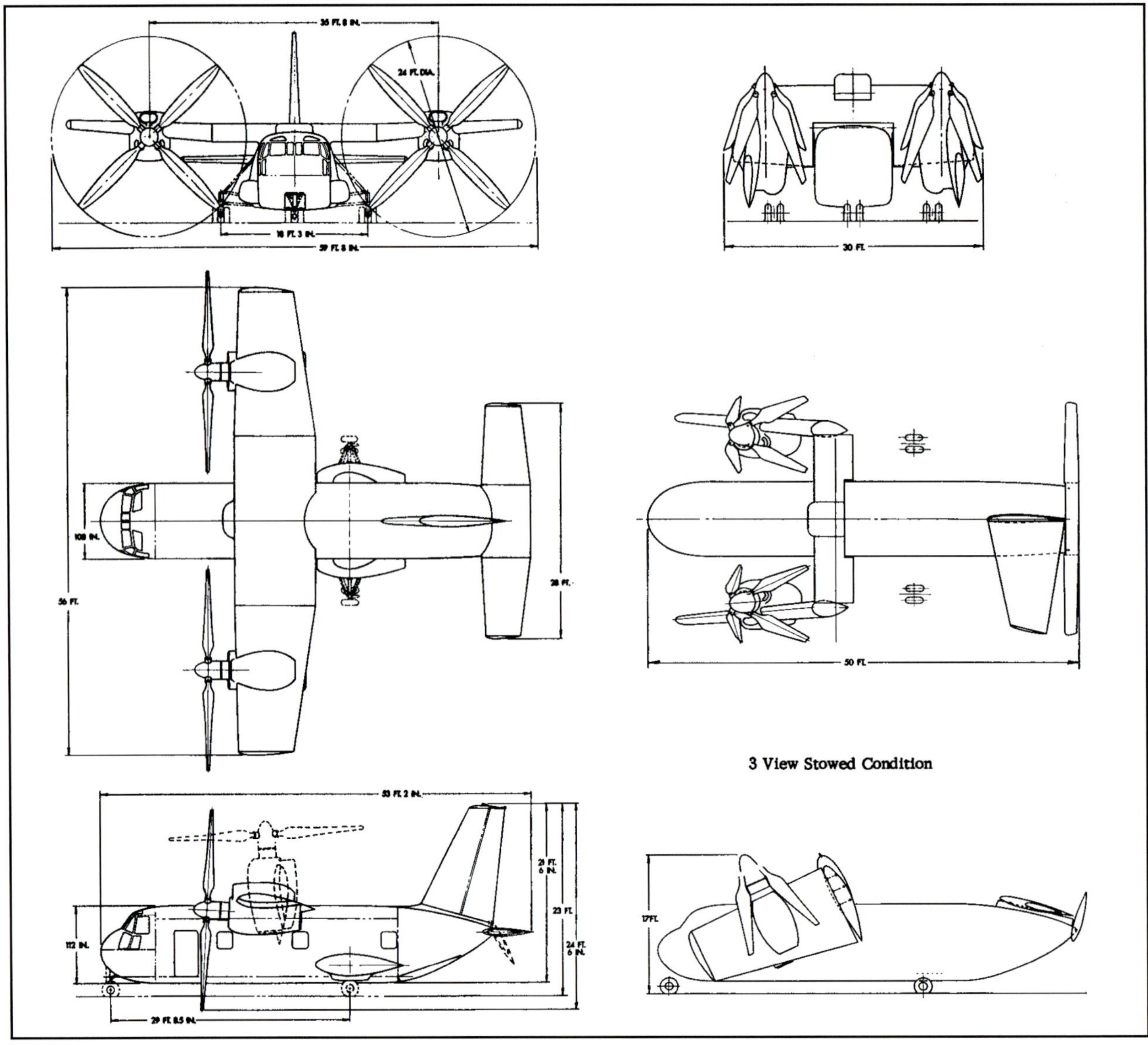

ABOVE Sikorsky DS-109 tilt-wing general arrangement and folding outline. Rather unusually, the wings folded forward.
Special Collections & Archives, Wright State University

In common with the BV-137 and the D252, the diameter of the propellers would have made it impossible to land or take off in conventional flight mode. Also, in common with the designs from the other helicopter manufacturers, cyclic control of the propellers was used for pitch control, eliminating the aft-mounted pitch-control propeller seen in many other tilt-wing designs.

For shipboard storage, the propeller blades would be folded, the wing raised to the 65° position, and the outer wing panels folded forward. The vertical tail folded to the port side and the all-moving horizontal stabiliser folded to the vertical, nose-down position.

Vought-Hiller-Ryan VHR-447 (XC-142A)

The VHR-447 entry was a joint bid by Vought (subsequently consolidated as Ling-Temco-Vought and known as LTV) with Hiller Helicopters and Ryan. It was a tilt-wing aircraft, building on Hiller's X-18, the largest and most powerful tilt-wing aircraft to fly up until that time. Ryan contributed deflected thrust expertise gained from its VZ-3 test bed.

Vought-Hiller-Ryan VHR-447 (XC-142A)	
Powerplant	4 x GE T64-GE-6 turboshaft @ 2,850hp (2,130kW)
Span	67ft 6in (20.59m) or 30ft (9.15m) folded*
Length	58ft 4in (17.79m) or 58ft 1in (17.72m) folded*
Height	26ft 1in (7.95m) or 16ft 6in (5.03m) folded*
Wing area	534.5sq ft (49.67m²)
Max TOW VTOL	41,000lb (18,610kg)
Max TOW STOL	44,500lb (20,200kg)
Payload VTOL	8,000lb (3,629kg)
Payload STOL	12,000lb (5,450kg)
Max speed	375kt (694km/h)
Cruise speed	250kt (463km/h)
Operational radius (VTOL)	200nmi (370km), original estimate, or 48nm (89km), actual

* Proposed; requirement deleted

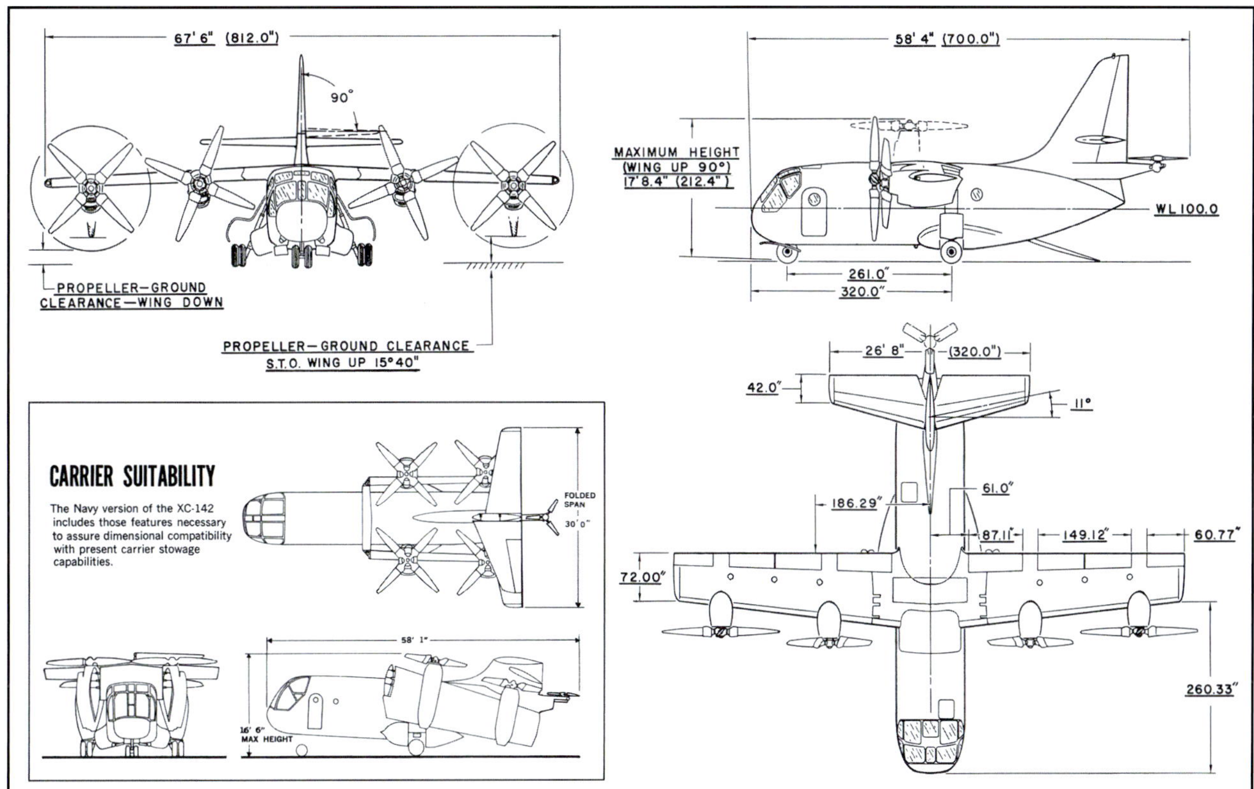

ABOVE Vought-Hiller-Ryan VHR-447 general arrangement. *LTV via Bill Spidle*

RIGHT Illustrations attached to the Burnelli lifting-fuselage proposal letter. *NARA II*

The VHR-447 was a much larger aircraft than the X-18 and could accommodate an 8,000lb (3,629kg) payload or thirty-two fully equipped troops. It was powered by four T64 engines and incorporated cross shafting, together with direct control of propeller pitch to improve handling during the hover. The tilt wing incorporated leading edge slats and double-slotted flaps to increase lift during low-speed and transitional flight.

Burnelli Lifting-Fuselage Adaption

A two-page letter undersigned by Chalmers Goodwin, President of the Burnelli Avionic Corporation, announced that the company was unable to respond to the stipulated requirements, but stated that '…we do believe we have a property that can be modified to meet most of the stated and required characteristics.'

Attached to the letter was a sketch showing the company's current prototype aircraft, modified to use the 'Bristol Rotatable Thrust Ground Effect' engine. It was claimed that two such engines would enable the company's aircraft, with its distinct 'body-lift' shape, to meet most of the Tri-Service competition requirements. Although unidentified, the engine appeared to be the Bristol Siddeley BS.53 as used on the Hawker P.1127, accommodated in a semi-submerged belly installation. However, Goodwin added that, 'Naturally any hovering would be restricted to the area employing the ground effect principle and this would rule out the higher hover ceiling stated in your specifications.'

Given that the two-page letter did not begin to approach the level of documentation required by the RFP, it is not surprising that the proposal evaluation team found the Burnelli concept to be 'non-responsive' and did not consider it further.

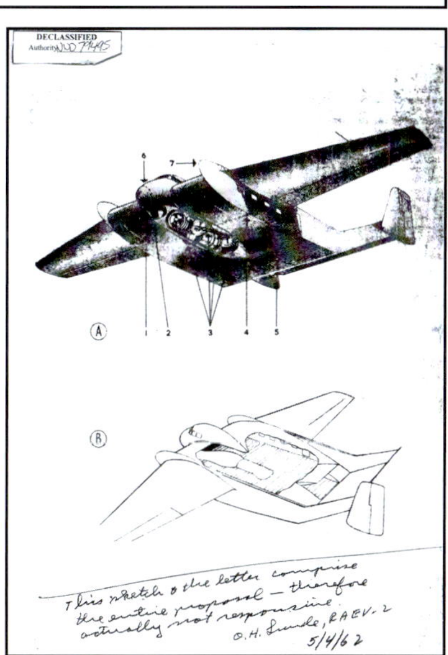

Fairchild Model 351

Fairchild declined to submit a fully responsive proposal. Instead it suggested an approach that was 'in partial fulfilment of the requirement'. It argued that as a result of the company's activities in the field of VTOL aircraft, extending back to 1954, '…the principal problem inherent in this type of aircraft is the attainment of adequate control and stability in the low-speed range.'

Fairchild Model 351	
Powerplant	4 x GE YT64-GE-8 turboprops @ 2,850shp (2,130kW)
Span	51ft 10in (15.50m) (centreline of No 1 nacelle to centreline of No 4 nacelle)
Length	42ft 6in (12.96m)
Height	21ft 0in (6.40m)

The company further argued that the solution was to concentrate the entire low-speed control system in the propellers and wing, eliminating '...all extra gadgetry ... and the penalties in weight, performance and reliability.' Fairchild proposed to reduce pitch inertia by

> '...freeing the wing relative to the fuselage around the pitch axis while in the VTOL configuration. The wing alone is controlled and flown while the fuselage, including the payload, is suspended essentially level at all times with only a variable damping connection between the two which alleviates pendulum type oscillations.
>
> 'Longitudinal control is accomplished by wing tilt as a function of differential propeller thrust, made possible by placing the propellers forward and aft of the pivot point when the wing is at maximum tilt angle. Directional control is accomplished by a combination of differential propeller torque, deflection of ailerons in the slipstream and deflection of the engine exhaust stream. Inertia about the yaw axis is held to a minimum by installing all engines in inboard nacelles. Roll control is obtained in the conventional manner, by differential propeller thrust with respect to the axis symmetry.'

The staggered propeller arrangement (above and below the wing) provided differential pitch control in VTOL mode. This allowed Fairchild to dispense with the tail rotor seen in most other tilt-wing designs. This not only reduced weight, but also eliminated the 'negative lift' that was needed during transition to push the tail down (and the nose up) in other designs.

Fairchild proposed that a test programme for the M-351 (which embodied the new control technique and likely met the stipulated programme requirements) be carried out in parallel

BELOW **Fairchild M-351 general arrangement.** *NARA II*

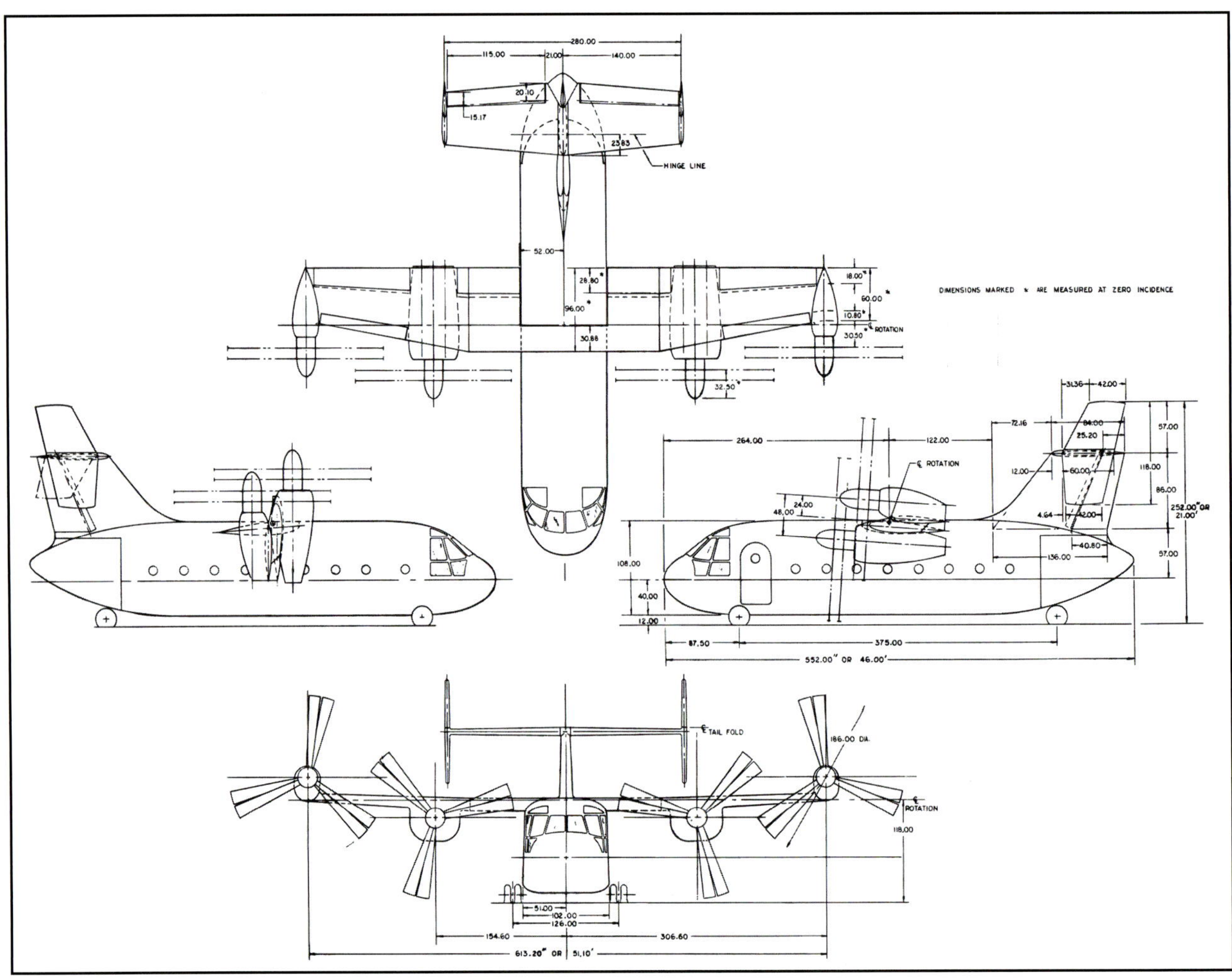

with the Tri-Service evaluation programme. The M-351 met all of the sizing requirements in the specification by folding the wings outboard of the fuselage and by folding down the upper portion of the vertical stabilisers. A 'quadracycle' landing gear allowed the fuselage to sit low to the ground. The four engines (GE YT64-GE-8s being mentioned as a possibility) were mounted in the two inboard nacelles, while shafting and gearboxes tied together all four sets of counter-rotating propellers. Fairchild selected Hamilton Standard six-blade, variable-camber propellers that were under development at the time.

There is no evidence of interest in Fairchild's proposed test programme by the evaluation team, since it would have required additional funding to run in parallel with the Tri-Service VTOL programme.

Fowler Model 20 (deflected-slipstream Breguet 941 VTOL development)

A 'dark horse' response to the competition came from inventor Harlan Fowler in California. He proposed a version of the French Breguet 941 STOL transport modified for vertical take-off with his patented Fowler 'Draguration Flap System'. He additionally proposed increasing the engine power efficiency by adding large ducts around the propellers. Far from being some crackpot inventor, Harlan Fowler was a highly respected aeronautical engineer who had earlier created the Fowler flap. While much of his career was spent as an independent consulting engineer, he had worked for the US Army Signal Corps, Pitcairn Aircraft, the Army Air Corps, Martin and the Air Force in various engineering positions.

Fowler was apparently surprised when he learned that he had been placed on the bidder's list. With a scant three weeks to prepare a response, he based his design on his previous studies of 'Conversion of Breguet's STOLs to VTOLs'. In his cover letter to the Navy, he stated that 'it is hoped the Tri-Service Committee will nevertheless carefully review the contents of this study, not as a competitor to those who are qualified to execute any development contract, but as a matter of being informed of the possibility of converting the Breguet 941 STOL.'

BELOW Fowler proposed an adaptation of the Breguet 941 with shrouded propellers and an enlarged flap system to deflect the thrust for vertical lift. *NARA II*

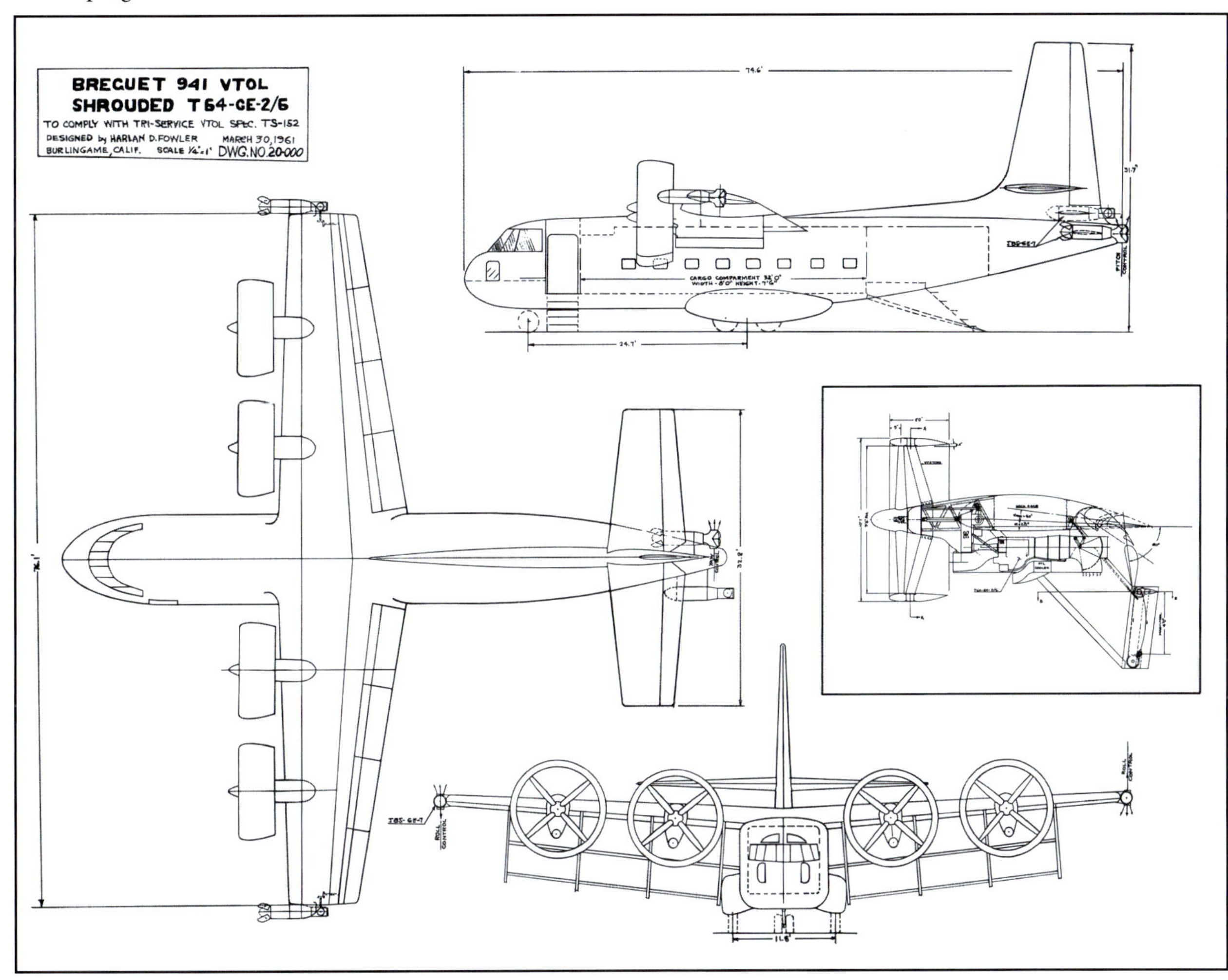

Fowler Breguet 941	
Powerplant	4 x shrouded GE T64-GE-2s @ 2,810hp (2,100kW) or 4 x T64-GE-6s @ 2,850hp (2,130kW); 4 x J85-GE-7s @ 2,450lbst (10.9kN) thrust for Reaction Control System
Span	76ft 1in (23.23m)
Length	74ft 6in (22.72m)
Height	31ft 7in (9.63m)

He further noted, 'It should be emphasised that the Breguet Company has not been contacted for information or data of any kind by applicant [Fowler], and are therefore unaware of this proposal.' He submitted his design just before the Breguet's first flight on 1 June 1961. A conventional aircraft with four turboprop engines mounted on a high wing, it achieved its short-field performance by slipstream deflection over extended flaps.

House of Kraft HK-711

Possibly the most unusual design came from the 'House of Kraft Nuclear and Consulting Engineers' of Lynchburg, Virginia, which submitted an unsolicited proposal detailing its HK-711 PJ (Peripheral Jet) VTOL. It would divert the thrust from two Pratt & Whitney TF30-P-2 turbofan engines to drive four lift-fans for vertical flight. The compressed airflow was to be applied to a fluted core rotor attached to the fans (in essence 'core-driven' rather than 'tip-driven' as in General Electric lift-fans). In an initial submittal, tip clearance of the rotors was electromagnetically controlled. In case of engine failure, batteries would take over to power the electromagnetic field, which could also be used to maintain rotor rotation. Kraft later elected to replace the electromagnetic system, noting that it had '...designed a compressed air system incorporated in the ducting similar to JATO, to minimise the "Dead Man's Curve".'

The design had a high wing over a 50-foot fuselage equipped with loading doors 8ft (2.44m) tall. The very broad chord wing had a fixed centre section of 30ft (9.15m) span with outer-wing panels of

House of Kraft HK-711	
Powerplant	2 x P&W TF30-P-2 turbofans @ 14,560lb (64.77kN) thrust
Span	40ft 0in (12.20m) with outboard sections horizontal or 30ft 0in (9.15m) with outboard sections vertical
Height	17ft 0in (5.18m)
Length	44ft 5in (13.55m)

BELOW House of Kraft HK-711 general arrangement. *NARA II*

9ft (2.75m) span. Both panels folded down and inboard. Each float also folded inboard. The aircraft sported twin underhung vertical stabilisers. At least one contained a tail rotor/fan to ensure directional control during hovering flight.

In the proposal cover letter, Kraft noted that the HK-711 was also amphibious, although this was not required in the Type Specification. Kraft stated, '...however, we feel this craft is of a more useful nature since it is to be used as an assault aircraft based on carriers and its use can be extended to more efficient sea rescue work.'

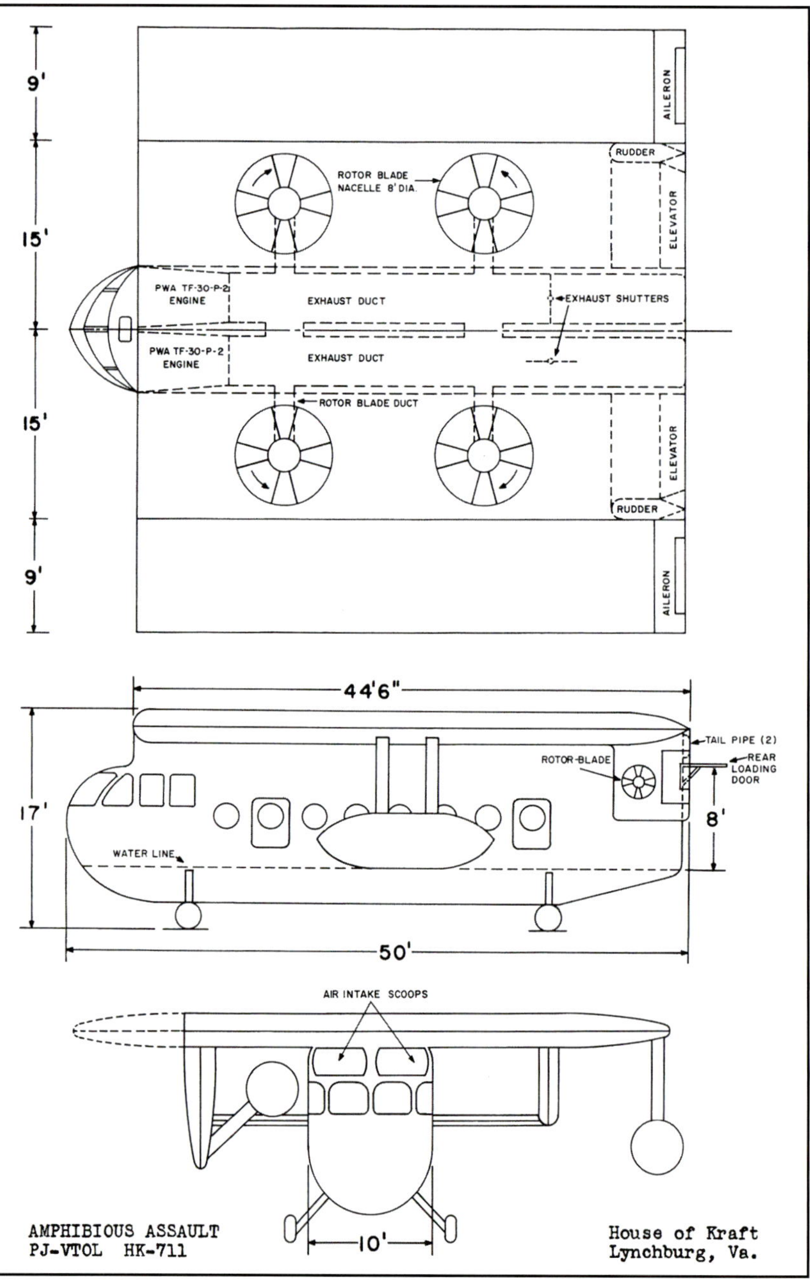

Prewitt Roto-Jet

Richard Prewitt was another rotary-wing pioneer, whose Prewitt Aircraft Company built rotor blades for Piasecki. Prewitt Aircraft evolved into Prewitt Plastics Company before its acquisition by Atlantic Research Company. It was there on 3 April 1961 that Prewitt submitted an unsolicited proposal 'to be reviewed in conjunction with the evaluation of the Tri-Service VTOL Aircraft.'

Prewitt proposed an '...experimental jet airplane, with substantially symmetrical airflow during conversion between tractor propeller and fixed-wing configurations, having VTOL characteristics.'

The Roto-Jet was specified to hover at 6,000ft (1,830m) on a hot day with a rotor having a disk loading of 5lb/sq ft (24.2kg/m²). The rotor blades could be converted rapidly to fixed wings. As an aircraft in flight it was to have a wing loading of 70lb/sq ft (339kg/m²). As a VTOL aircraft it was similar in size and operation to the Fairey

Prewitt Roto-Jet	
Powerplant	2 x unspecified turbofans, possibly GE CF-700s @ 4,200lb (18.68kN) thrust
Span	47ft 0in (14.34m) in aeroplane mode
Length	64ft 0in (19.52m)
Height	23ft 0in (7.02m)
Payload	8,000lb (3,629kg)
Max speed	400kt (740km/h)

RIGHT **Promotional art for the Prewitt Roto-Jet.** *NARA II*

BELOW **Prewitt Roto-Jet general arrangement in different modes.** *NARA II*

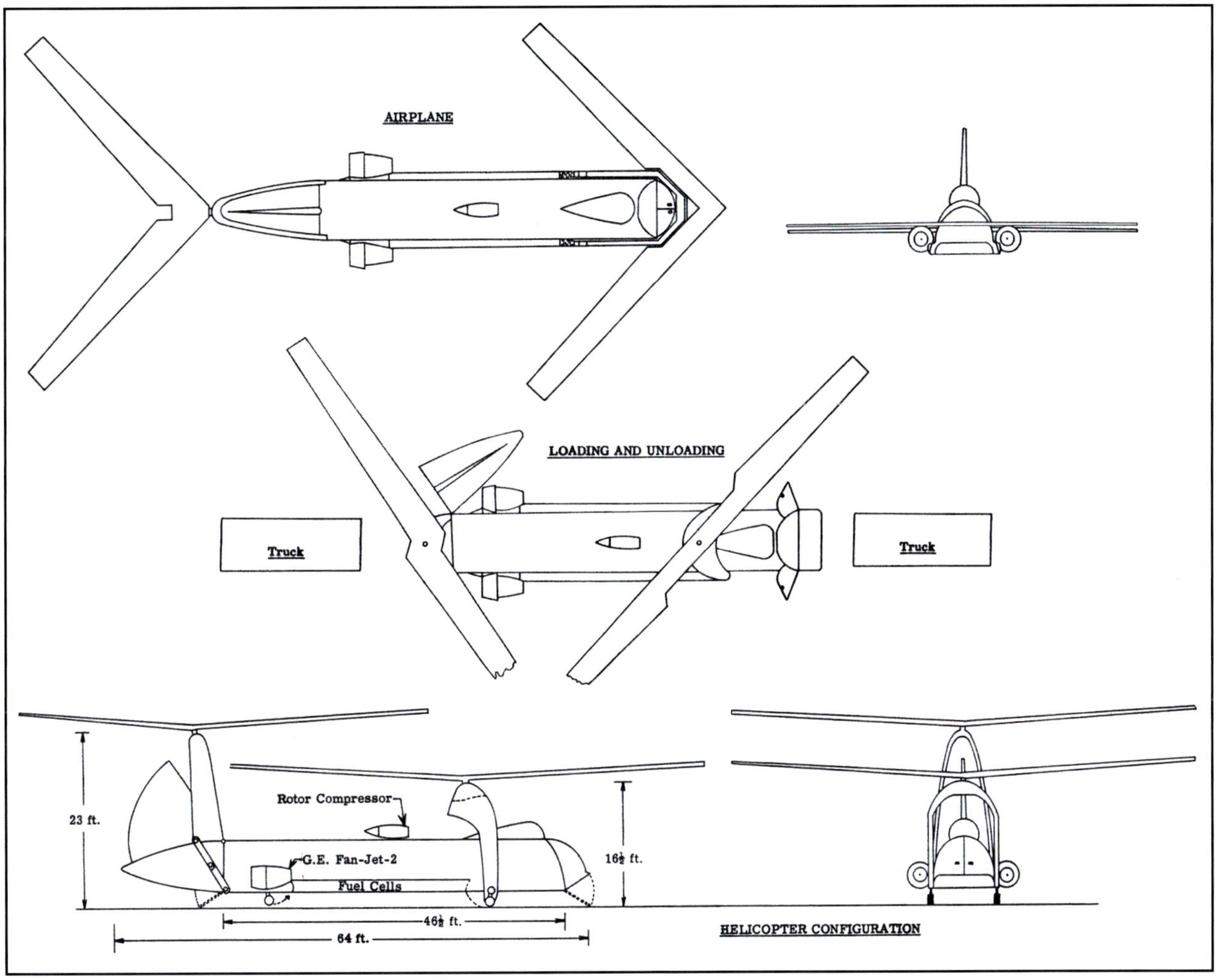

AIRPLANE

LOADING AND UNLOADING

Truck

Truck

23 ft.

Rotor Compressor

G.E. Fan-Jet-2

Fuel Cells

16½ ft.

46½ ft.

64 ft.

HELICOPTER CONFIGURATION

Rotodyne, while its low-speed flight operation was similar to the McDonnell XV-1 and the McDonnell 120 jet-rotor-propelled aircraft.

Of the several designs submitted by Prewitt, the one that best fitted the Tri-Service VTOL RFP requirements looked at first glance to be similar to the Piasecki XH-16 helicopter. After vertical lift-off, however, the design converted to a fixed-wing aircraft. The first conversion step involved stopping the jet-driven rotors and rotating one of the two blades 180° so that the leading edge would face forward. Then both blades would be swept aft at an angle of about 40°. Both rotors were mounted on movable yoke-like structures that rotated 90° forward (for the forward rotor) and 90° aft (for the aft rotor) for wing-borne flight. Thrust for forward flight would be provided by two 'G.E. Fan Jets', most likely the CF-700.

The proposal evaluation board determined that Prewitt's submission was incomplete and therefore nonresponsive to the RFP. No further development was pursued.

Vanguard Model 30

The Vanguard Model 30 was the second of the two designs in the competition to incorporate lift-fans in the wings, a configuration then under development with the GE/Ryan VZ-11 (later XV-5A) concept demonstrator for the Army.

The contractor, Vanguard Air and Marine Corporation based in Radnor, Pennsylvania, was formed in February 1959 by Edward J. Vanderlip and John L. Schneider, former Piasecki engineers, to design and build an executive VTOL aircraft. They had been developing a fan-in-wing aircraft for the three years prior to the competition, and in the course of this work they carried out extensive wind tunnel testing of the Model 2C Omniplane at the Ames Research Laboratory, jointly sponsored by the USAF and NASA.

Vanguard Model 30	
Powerplant	4 x Allison 501-H2 turboshafts @ 4,350shp (3,244kW)
Wingspan	58ft 5in (17.82m)
Length	72ft 0in (21.96m)
Height	21ft 7in (6.58m)
Max TOW	30,600lb (13,880kg)

BELOW Vanguard Model 30 general arrangement. *NARA II*

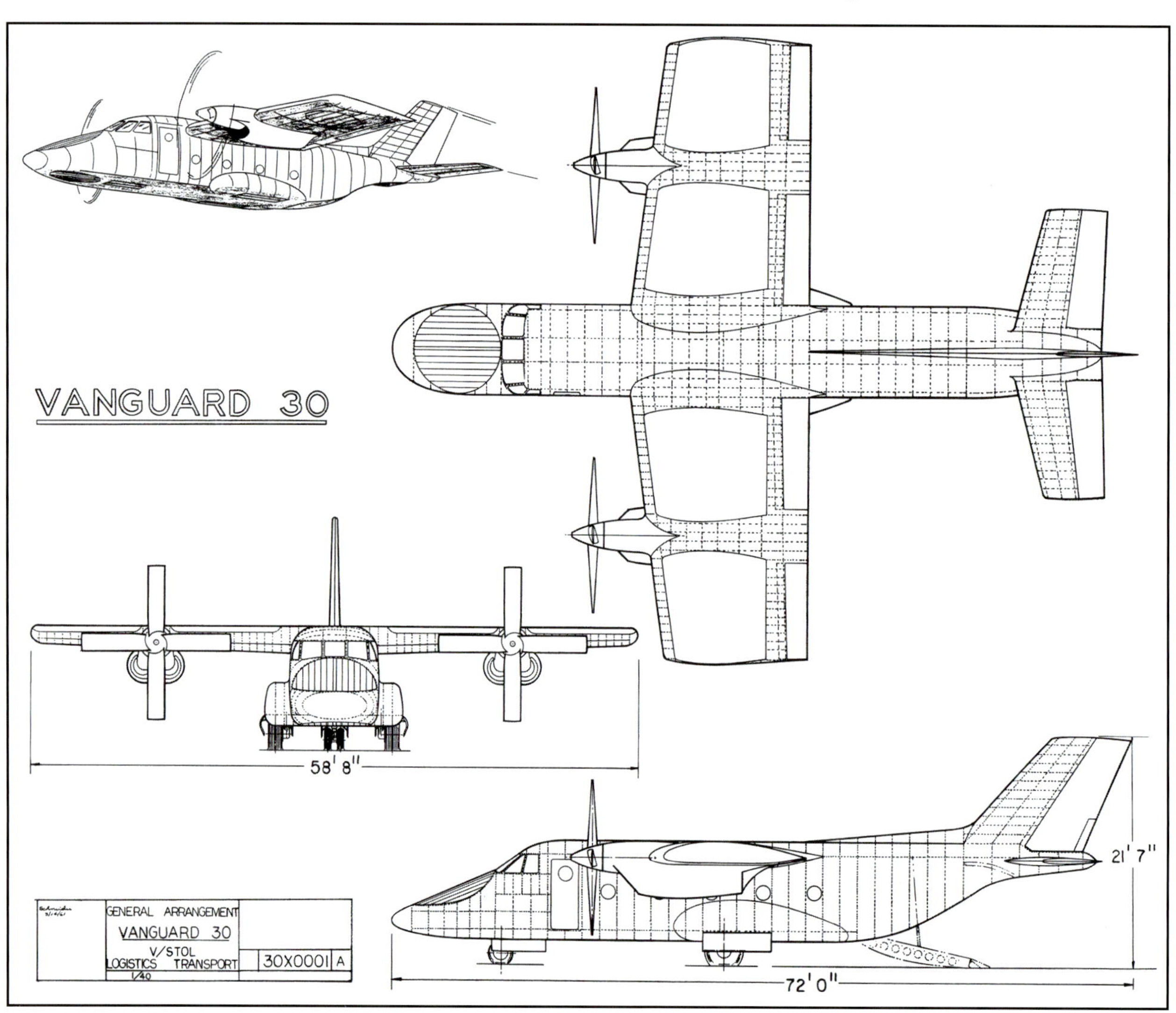

While the company claimed that these tests proved highly promising, it felt that it was not yet ready to submit a full proposal meeting the requirements of the competition. Instead, it submitted a design study for an aircraft that, given development time, could meet the specification. It stated, 'It is this Contractor's firm conviction that continued testing and evaluation of the fan-in-wing principle will prove its desirability over all other concepts.' The submission further stated that although unable to respond fully to the immediate competition, Vanguard intended to submit a subsequent unsolicited proposal for an operational aircraft fully meeting the TS-152 specification.

The Model 30 used four Allison 501-H2 turboshaft engines (paired two to a nacelle) to drive Vanguard-designed gearboxes, which provided power to the four 8ft (2.44m)-diameter fans in the wings and the single fan in the nose for vertical lift, as well as to two 14ft 6in (4.42m) propellers for normal flight. The wing fans incorporated single-piece upper closures that rose to allow air to enter the fans. Airflow was then directed by vanes below the fans for attitude and directional control.

ABOVE Promotional artwork for the Vanguard Model 30 in civil markings. *NARA II*

BELOW An illustration of the Verticraft Verticar proposal. *NARA II*

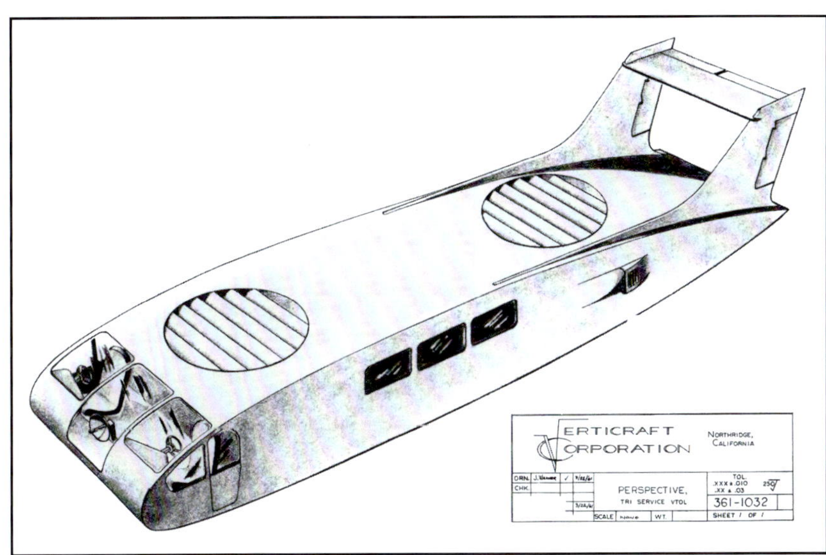

Verticraft Verticar

Alexander Krivka, President of the Verticraft Corporation (inventers of the Verticar, Vertibus and Vertidyne air vehicles), submitted a letter regretting the company's inability to submit a full proposal due to late receipt of the RFP. He further wrote, 'Verticraft, however, feels it has a very unique vehicle in that it offers high forward speeds in a true VTOL aircraft and would like to know if a proposal could be submitted at some future date.'

The fuselage of the two-duct Verticar was shaped like an airfoil, generating lift for horizontal flight. Two air ducts, located in the fuselage's front and aft, housed the counter-rotating propellers that provided vertical lift. The propellers were to be shaft-driven from two Pratt & Whitney JFTD12A-3 turboshaft engines with bypass modifications directing the exhaust gases straight aft during forward propulsion.

Krivka went on to explain:

'The vehicle is controlled in vertical flight through control vanes in each air duct and in the engine exhaust ducts. In horizontal flight, control is achieved through a conventional rudder/elevator system plus the control vanes in the exhaust ducts. Four wheels are provided for road travel with the front wheels being steerable and the rear wheels

Verticraft Verticar	
Powerplant	2 x P&W JFTD12A-3 turboshaft engines @ 4,500shp (3,356 kW); 1 x [unspecified] four-cylinder air-cooled motor for road travel
Span	10ft 0in (3.05m)
Length	48ft 0in (14.64m)
Height	13ft 0in (3.96m)
Max TOW	29,700lb (13,470kg)
Max speed	420kt (695km/h)

being driven by a four-cylinder air-cooled engine. In order to increase cargo area, load carrying capacity, and/or improved performance, two or more vehicles can be locked together … and controlled manually by a single operator.'

There is no evidence that the evaluation board wished to pursue this proposal. Although a smaller, single-fan Verticar prototype had been built, no further development is known to have taken place.

Wilford Convertiplane	
Powerplant	2 x Allison T56 turboprops (assumed) @ 4,350hp (3,245kW), plus unspecified cold air compressors
Span	60ft 0in (18.30m)
Length	75ft 0in (22.88m)
Height	10ft 0in (3.05m)
Rotor diameter	100ft 0in (30.5m)
Payload VTOL	8,000lb (3,629kg)
Payload STOL	12,000lb (5,450kg)
Max speed	350kt (648km/h)
Cruise speed	275kt (509km/h)
Range	1,000nmi (1,851km)

Note: tabular data and data in images do not match.

Wilford Convertiplane

E. Burke Wilford was another early pioneer of the aviation industry. He had been involved in applied research and development in the field of aeroplanes, helicopters and convertiplanes since 1926 as a private designer, investor, and aeronautical engineer. Wilford had twelve related patents granted in the 1920s and 1930s, primarily in the areas of gyroplanes, other aircraft designs and control systems.

His Wilford Aircraft Corporation submitted several convertiplane designs to the Tri-Service competition.

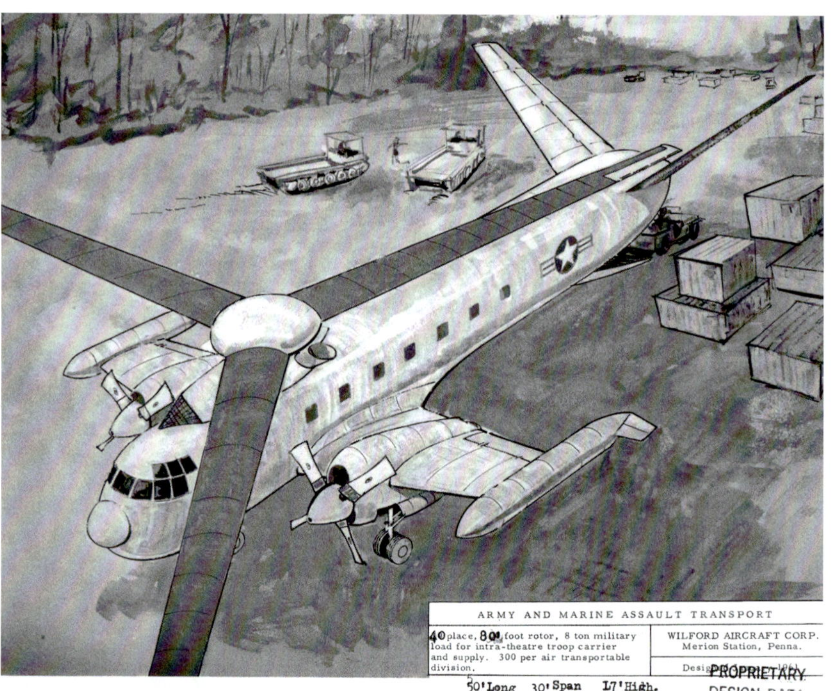

BELOW **The Wilford Convertiplane.** *NARA II*

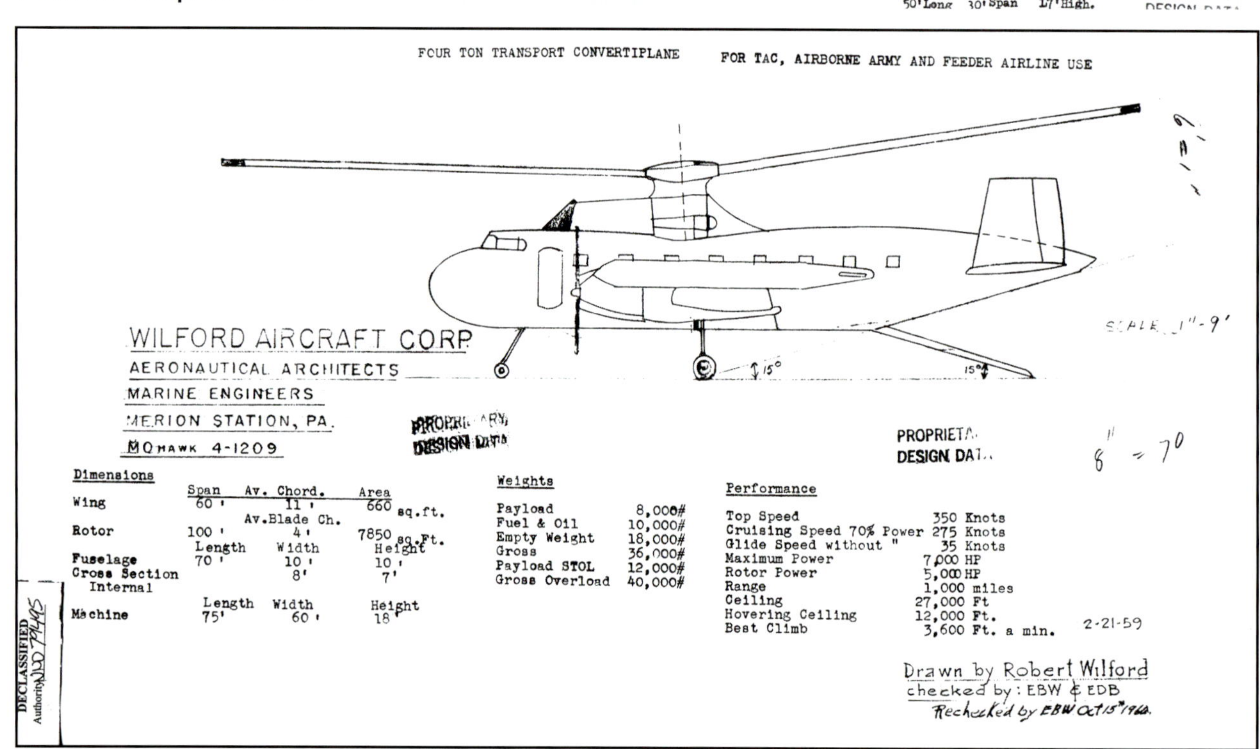

BELOW **Promotional artwork for the Wilford Convertiplane.** *NARA II*

Accompanying drawings illustrated a variety of one-, three- and four-bladed cold-jet convertiplanes using a fuselage similar to the Convair Model 240. Propulsion for wing-borne flight appeared to be Allison T56s while the cold-jet compressors were not specified.

While the claimed performance broadly met the RFP specifications, the 70ft (21.35m) length, 60ft (18.3m) span and 100ft (30.5m) rotor diameter, without provision for folding, clearly exceeded the maximum size requirements (though a somewhat smaller version is shown in Wilford artwork).

The Tri-Service competition winning bid

Senior DoD management had high hopes for the programme, but the view from the working levels was not so sanguine. George Spangenberg (the Navy's head of evaluation) ruefully recalled:

> 'The Tri-Service Transport then was just as impossible as TFX was. We were a little ahead of TFX time-wise I think. But it was the same kind of a mess. The Marines had their requirement which was basically the CH-53D requirement as far as number of troops and so on for the fifty mile radius but they wanted it done at 300 knots, about where we are today with the V-22, over thirty years later. The Army requirement ... was a medium range distance requirement coupled with a heavy lift requirement, probably well beyond the Marine lift requirement. The Air Force came up with an air-sea rescue mission that they would go 750 miles to pick up a pilot that had ditched... You knew it couldn't be met by any single airplane.'

The Army favoured a tilt-wing turboprop arrangement; the Navy felt that this was unsuited to carrier operation and wanted a rotatable ducted-fan system. Initially, the USAF sided with the Navy viewpoint, but later came round to the Army's way of seeing things, opposing tilt-rotor designs. Industry failed to come to a consensus, with the individual contractors selecting options that posed them the least risk. The conventional airframe manufacturers chose tilt-wing designs with pitch-control propellers, while the helicopter manufacturers adopted the familiar cyclic-control techniques used in helicopters.

Returning to Spangenberg's recollection:

> 'The designs came in and we had all kinds of airplanes... Lots of configurations. All of them were better for one service than another. Those twin tandem ducted fans were the best for the Marines. The ones with big wings, the tilt wing device was best for the Air Force and you really couldn't meet the Army requirement with anything that would meet the other two.
>
> 'At the end of the preliminaries we agreed that the Army would go do their evaluation, the Air Force would do their evaluation, we would do ours and we'd get together at the end. It was the only competition of this nature we ever had where the winning design by one service was ruled unacceptable by the other two.
>
> 'We ended up by going to the Assistant Secretaries of the Air Force, Navy and Army and saying we can't get there from here with this proposal. We told you before we couldn't do it, now we've got proof that we couldn't do it. The Navy position was we will withdraw. Let's let the three services get their VTOL money and do research that serves a useful purpose. The Air Force and Army secretaries said no, we've been told to do it, we'll go ahead. Eventually we got DDR&E Brown's permission for the Navy to withdraw.'

While the Navy played no further active part in proceedings, it was stated that the programme would still consider meeting the Navy's needs '...when the state of the art permits'. This, one suspects, was little more than a fig leaf. The Navy was tacitly allowed to proceed on its own path, and within eighteen months would be holding its own competition for a tilt-duct VTOL test aircraft. This was competed for between the Douglas Model D-850 and the Bell Model D-2127, won by Bell and eventually flown as the X-22A. Meanwhile, for the Tri-Service programme the Navy withdrawal simplified matters by removing the need for folding wings and tails.

This development path notwithstanding, the Navy had already hedged its VTOL bets. On 27 March 1961 the Chief of Naval Operations (CNO) issued a revised developmental characteristic (AO-17501-3) for a medium assault transport helicopter for the Marine Corps with essentially the same requirements as the Tri-Service VTOL (AO–17501–2). Cruise speed was reduced to 150kt (278km/h), within comfortable reach for a helicopter. RFPs were issued to Kaman, Sikorsky and Boeing Vertol on 7 March 1962, with the latter two companies submitting proposals. Sikorsky was announced as the winner on 24 August 1962 with its S-65 design, later designated as the CH-53A Sea Stallion.

After the Air Force takeover of responsibility for the programme, the choice narrowed to either the North American or the Vought tilt-wing design. The North American bid was $88 million (including a separate subscale test bed aircraft), whereas LTV's cost amounted to $52.5 million. The LTV consortium won the competition, and its VHR-447 tilt-wing proceeded into detailed design as the XC-142A, to be followed by a contract for five prototypes.

Perhaps there was an element of playing safe in this decision, since a large tilt-wing technology demonstrator (the X-18) had already

ABOVE The XC-142A in a vertical hover. *LTV via Bill Spidle*

BELOW The XC-142A in 'up and away' horizontal flight. *LTV via Bill Spidle*

successfully flown. Moreover, unlike the tilt-rotor bids, the VHR-447 was capable of conventional take-offs and landings. The XC-142A's first flight was actually made in this fashion on 29 September 1964. Hovering flight was achieved three months later and the first horizontal-to-vertical transition carried out on 11 January 1965.

Evaluation results were mixed. Vertical take-off and landing and 'up and away' performance were acceptable, with the aircraft being overpowered for level flight. On the other hand, the airframe was about 2,500lb (1,135kg) heavier than specified (even after the deletion of the heavy wing and tail folding mechanism required during the early design phase), and fuel consumption was higher than promised. This resulted in the calculated (VTOL) combat radius with full load being 48nmi (88.9km) rather than the original goal of 200nmi (370km).

Flight testing also revealed numerous lesser problems, one of which was excessive vibration. With the pressure to reduce weight to a minimum, all V/STOL aircraft of the time were designed with a lightweight structure more like that of a helicopter, with a resulting lack of rigidity. Reportedly strobe lights were used during testing to detect the shaking of hydraulic pipes. The cross shafting in particular proved to be a cause of excessive noise and vibration, and in one instance the failure of a component in the pitch linkage controlling the tail rotor led to a fatal crash. Indeed, four out of the five prototype aircraft suffered accidents.

Nonetheless, the XC-142 demonstrated the concept's viability and potential. Consequently, in early 1966 the USAF requested a proposal for a C-142A production version. LTV modified the design with a lengthened 'chin' fairing on the forward fuselage to house a weather radar, and with no requirement for ejection seats the cockpit glazing was changed to a more conventional layout without the large overhead windows. Designers slightly widened the fuselage to accommodate the standard 463L pallet, and raised the horizontal tail to improve control effectiveness during hover in ground effect.

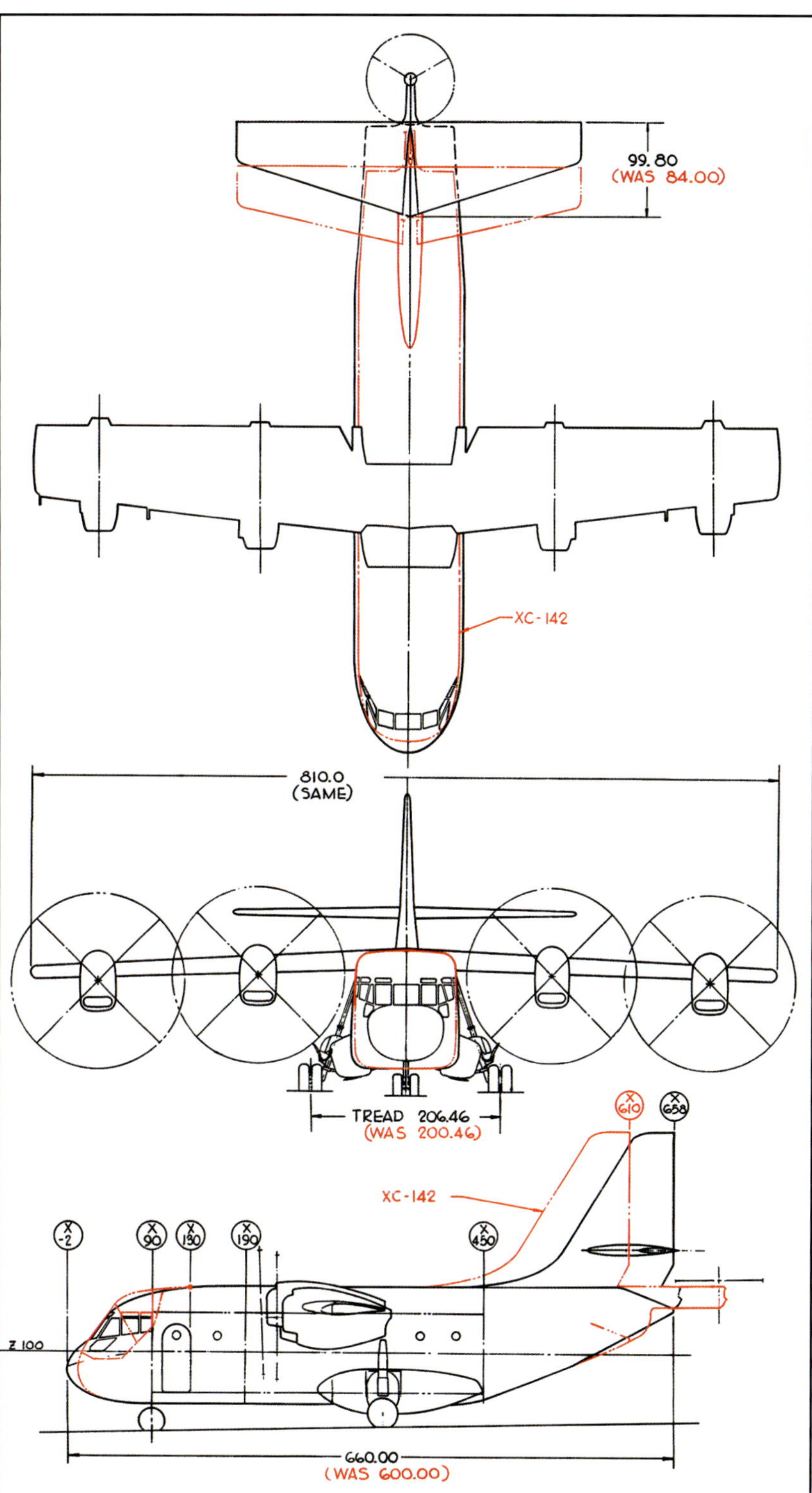

ABOVE A comparison of the XC-142A (in red) and an early C-142A design prior to relocation of the horizontal tail. *Greater St Louis Air and Space Museum via Mark Nankivil*

Submitted on 8 November 1966, the proposal was rejected by the evaluation team. Although the C-142A was potentially acceptable with much development, a new programme, known as CX-6, held greater promise for the Air Force.

ABOVE An artist's depiction of the production C-142A. The fuselage was lengthened to add troop doors. The high-mounted horizontal stabilator would not need to tilt for landing or take-off. *LTV via Bill Spidle*

BELOW A model of the proposed C-142A showing the revised cockpit and high-mounted stabiliser. *Greater St Louis Air and Space Museum via Mark Nankivil*

The XC-142 was one of those aircraft that 'almost made it'. Had the design been developed with the same tenacity as was later shown with the V-22 Osprey, it might well have led the way for a whole new category of similar military transports.

In 1978 the Defense Science Board set up a Task Force on V/STOL aircraft, reviewing the status and future of the technology. It was chaired by Dr Courtland Perkins who, interestingly, had led the similar exercise in 1959 that had provided the impetus for the Tri-Service VTOL competition. The final report was issued in November 1979. With benefit of hindsight and some irony, he wrote in the preface:

> 'V/STOL has been a technical capability of interest for many years, but except for a very few cases, this interest has been developed primarily by technologists rather than military operators. There have been many studies such as this one. The first for the Department of Defense was undertaken in 1959 for Dr Herbert York, then Director of Defense Research and Engineering (DDR&E). This study group upon reviewing V/STOL technology and service requirements recommended the development of a V/STOL logistic aircraft… [It] was a tilt-wing turboprop, considered by a majority of the technical community of that day as perhaps the most feasible solution… [These] aircraft flew and proved
>
> '(a) that the technology wasn't quite as ready as the enthusiasts believed,
>
> '(b) that an airplane with a vertical take-off and landing capability would about double its payload if allowed a short (500ft) ground roll and, most importantly,
>
> '(c) none of the three Services were really interested in the airplane – they didn't want to pay the additional cost … in dollars, handling qualities or complexities.
>
> 'A number of operational capabilities peculiar to V/STOL were demonstrated in the XC-142 program. However, these capabilities were not judged to be sufficiently attractive at that time to offset the cost penalties associated with V/STOL capability.'

The XC-142A, with its tilt-wing configuration, proved to be a cul-de-sac along the path of American airlifter design. However, the TS-152 Tri-Service competition was not to be the last chapter in the 1960s quest for a V/STOL transport.

Chapter Four
The Air Force Turns to V/STOL

1963 to 1972: The goals change, the challenges remain

ABOVE This concept art depicts Boeing Model 743-147B airlifters in action. *Boeing*

Even as the Tri-Service VTOL programme with an 8,000lb (3,629kg) payload was getting under way in 1961, the armed services were already working on a requirement for a larger, more useful V/STOL transport aircraft. In October 1961 the Army prepared a Qualitative Materiel Requirement (QMR) for a vehicle able to operate from a 1,000ft (305m) airstrip, carrying a payload of 20,000lb (9,072kg), with an operational radius of 500nmi (925km). This document outlined the Army needs to the Air Force.

Specific Operating Requirement 198

This was closely followed by the drafting of a Specific Operating Requirement (SOR) by the Air Force, with a slightly lower 16,000lb (7,257kg) payload, but capable of a vertical first landing. At the same time there were apparently discussions taking place with Britain's Royal Air Force about a joint project that could also meet the latter's requirements for an aircraft carrying a 35,000lb (15,876kg) payload, able to operate off a 1,500ft (457.2m) airstrip initially as a STOL aircraft, but with the potential to develop into a V/STOL transport in due course.

These goals and requirements eventually merged into SOR 198 and called for the following:

- Payload/radius: 16,000lb (7,264kg) both ways at 500nmi (925km)
- Minimum cruise speed: Mach .70 at 25,000ft (7,620m)
- Sea level dash: 300kt (555km/h)
- Ferry range: 3,500nmi (6,475km)

- Minimum thrust-to-weight at first landing: 1.2:1
- Minimum body cross section: 31ft x 9ft x 9ft (9.46m x 2.75m x 2.75m)

The intended usage was as follows:

Army: Tactical support of ground forces

- Transport of men and equipment
- Air-drop or ground delivery at minimum preparation site
- Ability to operate between general theatre depot and combat zone

Air Force: Support for missile installations

- Support for VTOL fighter sites

CX-6: The 10-ton V/STOL assault transport

Allocations for an aircraft to fulfil the requirements of SOR 198 were scheduled for inclusion in the Fiscal 1965 budget with the hope of some prior funding being added to the project. The eventual effort became known as the CX-6 programme (not to be confused with the C-6/VC-6 Beechcraft King Air used for transport into President Johnson's ranch in Texas).

Air Force Research & Development 'Cargo-X' designations of the 1960s

Designations	Mission	Eventual aircraft
CX	Jet airlifter	C-141A
CX-2	Aeromedical evacuation	C-9A
CX-3	Unknown	n/a
CX-4	Heavy logistic support	C-5A
CX-5	Unknown	n/a
CX-6	V/STOL assault transport	none
CX-HLS	Heavy logistic support	C-5A
CX-X	Heavy logistic support	none

An initial competition was held in 1964 to select contractors to begin Phase-Zero Conceptual studies. In June 1965 it was reported that both Boeing and North American Aviation had been awarded research contracts valued at $350,000.

There was no shortage of enthusiasm or ideas from the two aircraft companies concerned. These ideas, however, tapped into or expanded upon years of ongoing work that unsurprisingly produced iterations instead of clean-sheet designs. Moreover, much of this work was done with an eye on the civil market, pursuing the concept of an inter-city STOL airliner.

Boeing Model 732-22-2 V/STOL airlifter (1959)

Powerplant	8 x Allison Model 550 E4 turboshafts @ 8,500shp (6,338kW)
Wingspan	147ft 0in (44.81m)
Length	108ft 2in (32.97m)
Height	38ft 6in (11.73m)
VTOL gross TOW	210,000lb (95,524kg)
VTOL payload	50,000lb (22,680kg)
STOL gross TOW	260,000lb (117,934kg)
STOL payload	54,000lb (24,949kg)
Cruise speed	290kt (537km/h)
VTOL range	900-3,000nmi (1,667-5,556km)
STOL range	2,300-4,500nmi (4,260-8,334km)

As CX-6 studies got under way, there were signs of impatience (perhaps disillusionment) within the military at the slow development of an operational V/STOL capability. Later, at the first National V/STOL Aircraft Conference Symposium, former Army General Hamilton H. Howse recalled in his keynote address that at a meeting back in 1962 an Air Force officer predicted that by 1969 *all* USAF aircraft in Northern Europe would have V/STOL capability. In reality there was no likelihood of *any* such aircraft having this capability.

Prior Boeing studies for Study Requirement SR-175

Starting in the mid-1950s, Boeing developed a diverse range of designs under its Model 732 series of designations. Divided into small, medium and large groups, the Boeing Wichita Division studied the small and medium sizes (leading to the Model 900 submission in the Tri-Service VTOL competition). The Boeing Transport Division in Renton studied designs for an aircraft with a gross weight of more than 50,000lb (15,250kg). The most promising of these were summarised in a report submitted in response to what became defined as Air Force SR-175 (Study Requirement-175) in February 1960. The Model 732-22-2 represented the heavier end of the VTOL range, using an unusual parasol-wing arrangement to allow the fuselage to be closer to the ground while maintaining clearance for the propellers. The eight propellers, 24ft (7.32m) in diameter, were to be powered by Allison T61 turboshaft engines (a growth version of the Model 550 B-1 engine).

BELOW The Boeing Model 732-22-2 had tractor propellers that tilted upward and pusher propellers that tilted downwards for VTOL flight. The high parasol wing allowed propeller clearance and a low fuselage deck level for loading and unloading. *Boeing*

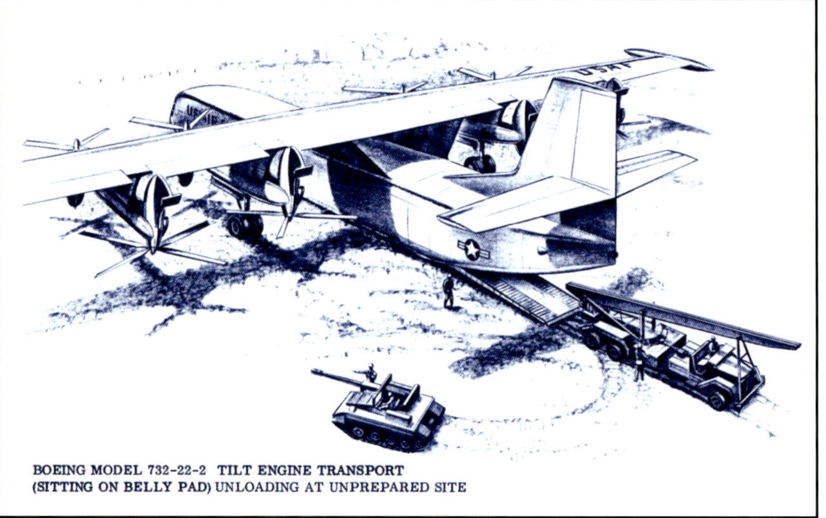

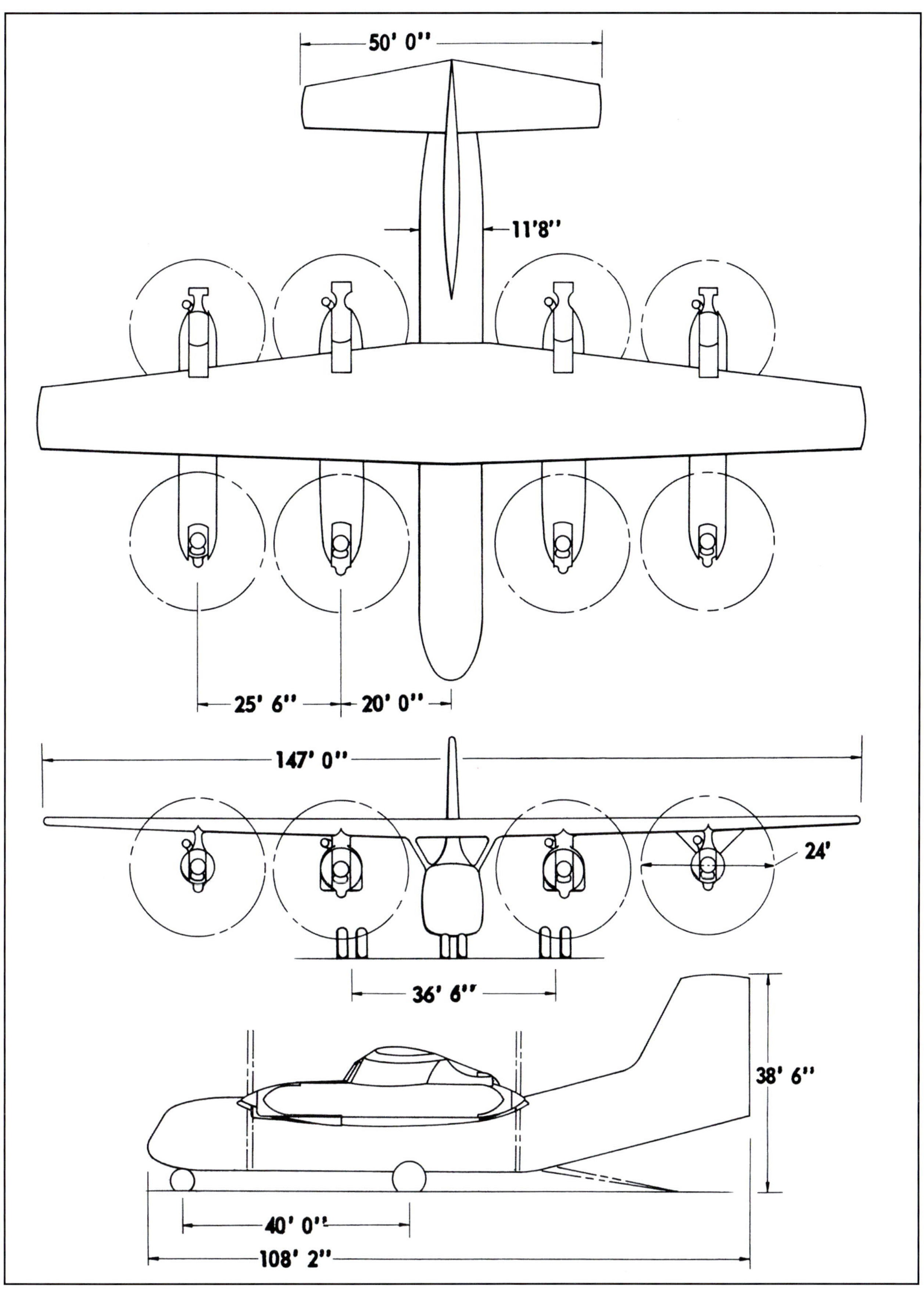

ABOVE Boeing Model 732-22-2 general arrangement from September 1959. *Boeing*

Boeing CX-6 studies

Although not submitted in the SR-175 report, Boeing also investigated a wide range of lift-fan designs. The establishment of the CX-6 programme in 1962 seemed an ideal opportunity to capitalise on and further extend this work, which was being conducted under the Model 743 number. It represented a major step-up in scale – and ambition – compared with the ongoing XC-142A programme.

Having created the basic set of designs with differing lift methods, a trade-off study was then undertaken to look at the potential effect of redesigning the aircraft to make use of a short ground roll on take-off or landing. This was based on the observation that (from the limited amount of experience available at the time) VTOL aircraft appeared regularly to make use of a short ground roll anyway. The aircraft did this to minimise ground erosion, avoid hot gas re-ingestion and to overcome visibility problems when using unprepared surfaces.

This study looked at two of the existing Boeing designs with payload sizes of 24,000lb (10,896kg) and 35,000lb (15,890kg), and examined the effect on each if they were redesigned for roll distances of 0, 250, 500 and 750ft (0, 76.25, 152.5 and 228.6m). Obviously, the longer the ground run, the less vertical thrust was needed, hence fewer lift engines were required. It was found that the weight saving was offset to some extent by the need for high-lift devices on the wing and a slight increase in the vertical fin size.

The results also showed a rather dramatic and perhaps somewhat surprisingly negative outcome, namely that designing the aircraft for a short ground roll instead of VTOL resulted in only '...a rather modest weight saving and rapid loss of VTOL payload capability.'

For example, the 35,000lb (15,890kg) payload aircraft, with its design optimised for a 750ft (228.6m) ground roll, showed a saving of 18% in gross weight, but could only carry a payload of less than 4,000lb (1,814 kg) if it was also required to operate in the VTOL mode. The 24,000lb (10,896kg) payload aircraft could not lift any payload if it was redesigned to use a similar ground roll or even fly the basic VTOL mission. In other words, relaxing the CX-6 requirement by allowing the option of a short ground roll simply eliminated the ability to use the same aircraft in VTOL mode.

In contrast, the concurrent experience with the British Hawker Harrier showed that the introduction of a short ground run transformed the operational capability of what was originally a VTOL aircraft. In this case it allowed a far heavier load of weaponry and/or fuel to be carried. The difference between the two was due to the technologies used. The Harrier/AV-8 was essentially a conventional airframe where all or part of the propulsive engine thrust could

CONFIGURATION STUDY

PROPULSION SYSTEM — CRUISE	FAN	TURBOJET	TURBOJET	TURBOJET	TURBOFAN	FAN
LIFT	FAN	FAN	LIFT JET	LIFT JET	TURBOFAN	FAN
CONCEPT						
GROSS WEIGHT	124,000	131,500	132,000	132,000	140,000	125000 (aprox)
O.W.E.	72,000	74,000	70,600	72,900	75,000	-
FUEL WEIGHT (BASIC MISSION)	36,000	41,500	45,400	43,100	49,000	-
NUMBER OF:						
GAS GENERATORS	4	7	12	12	4	8
CRUISE/LIFT	2 at 13,000#	4 at 9,500#	4 at 10,500#	4 at 10,500#	4 at 37,000#	4 at 7,600#
FAN DRIVE	2 at 13,000#	3 at 12,400#	0	0	0	4 at 7,600#
LIFT	0	0	8 at 11,750#	8 at 11,750#	0	0
FANS	5	6 (3 CONTROL)	0	0	0	4
VTOL T/W	1.20	1.20	1.30	1.30	1.20	1.33
f (FT²)	26.25	27.45	27.9	24.5	31.3	31.0

NOTE: MISSION REQ. NOT MET.
1. NO ENGINE OUT CAPABILITY
2. NO C.G. TRIM CAPABILITY
3. 3.4 MIN. VTOL TIME (8.0 MIN. USED ON OTHER CONFIGURATIONS)

ABOVE Model 743 V/STOL configurations studied in December 1962. *Boeing*

BELOW The Boeing Model 743-100-42 concept used two tilting ducted cruise-fans and three lift-fans. *Boeing*

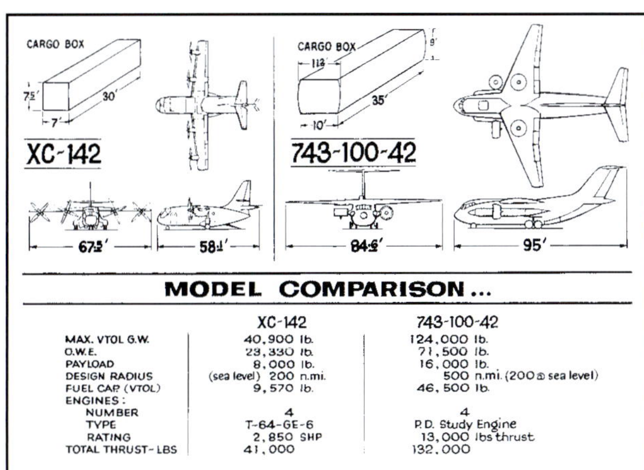

MODEL COMPARISON ...

	XC-142	743-100-42
MAX. VTOL G.W.	40,900 lb.	124,000 lb.
O.W.E.	23,330 lb.	71,500 lb.
PAYLOAD	8,000 lb.	16,000 lb.
DESIGN RADIUS	(sea level) 200 n.mi.	500 n.mi. (200 @ sea level)
FUEL CAP (VTOL)	9,570 lb.	46,500 lb.
ENGINES:		
NUMBER	4	4
TYPE	T-64-GE-6	P.D. Study Engine
RATING	2,850 SHP	13,000 lbs thrust
TOTAL THRUST-LBS	41,000	132,000

ABOVE **The Boeing Model 743-100-42 compared with the XC-142A. Doubling the payload caused the gross weight to triple.** *Boeing*

ABOVE RIGHT **Another December 1962 Boeing Model 743 design explored the combination of twelve lift engines in the wing root fairings and four deflected-thrust cruise turbofans.** *Boeing*

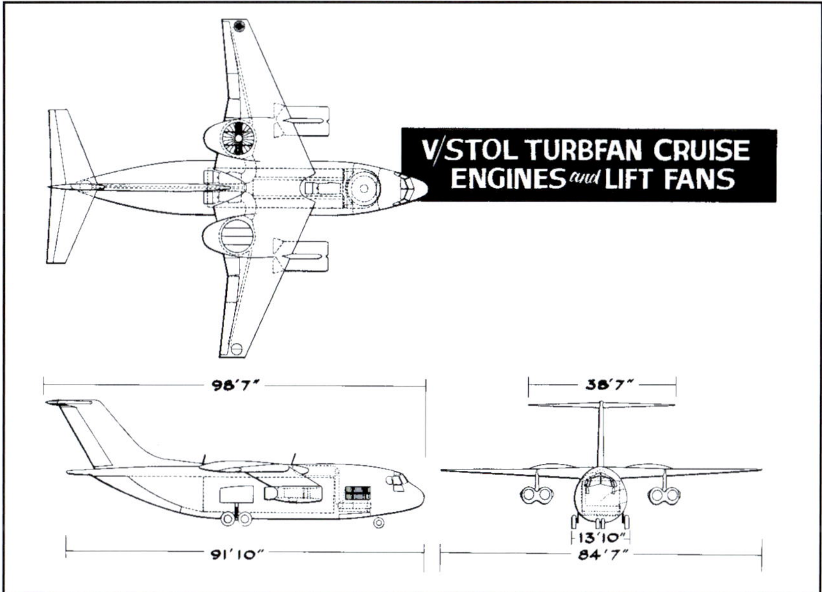

RIGHT **This Boeing Model 743 concept offered four deflected-thrust turbofans in wing pods and three primary jet-driven lift fans, one in the nose aft of the cockpit and two in the trailing edge of the wing root. Two much smaller fans were located in the wingtips for roll control.** *Boeing*

be deflected to give lift. As such, it was perfectly capable of being operated as a conventional aeroplane. A short ground roll simply boosted the total lift available.

On the other hand, the CX-6 projects were unconventional configurations, with separate lift engines and wings not sized for horizontal take-offs and landings. In those instances, the penalties for redesigning the projects to take advantage of a short ground roll were shown to outweigh the benefits. When it came to proposals for CX-6, it was a case of VTOL or nothing – adaptation to V/STOL use was not an option.

RIGHT **The forward lift-fan was located in the forward fuselage between the cockpit and cargo compartment and was fed by lateral intakes in the sides of the fuselage.** *Boeing*

ABOVE An alternative Boeing Model 743 version employed four lift-fans in extended wing root fairings and four podded turbofans. *Boeing*

Boeing continued to work extensively on a series of designs under the family of model numbers 743-100-81 to -83 dating to August 1965. The 743-100-81A featured four 'flip-out' gas-driven lift-fans and four deflected-thrust cruise jet engines. The gas generators for the lift fans were placed above the cargo bay, fore and aft of the centre wing section.

By June 1966 Boeing's studies converged into a small family of designs in the 743-147 to 743-154B range, mostly differing in wing planform and engine layout and location. The gas-driven lift-fans were placed in fixed positions, buried in the wing root. Hover control considerations were addressed by using a hot-gas reaction control system. Called 'bleed and burn', air was bled off from the engines and ducted to the control ports where fuel was injected and burned to increase thrust.

Despite the simplification of the fan system and other optimisations compared to the Model 743-100-81A, the estimated Operating Weight Empty (OWE) increased from 88,600 to 91,350lb (40,224 to 41,473kg). At the same time, take-off gross weights decreased. With the payload goal steady at 24,000lb (10,896kg), this meant that the fuel load (and therefore range) also decreased, a worrying trend.

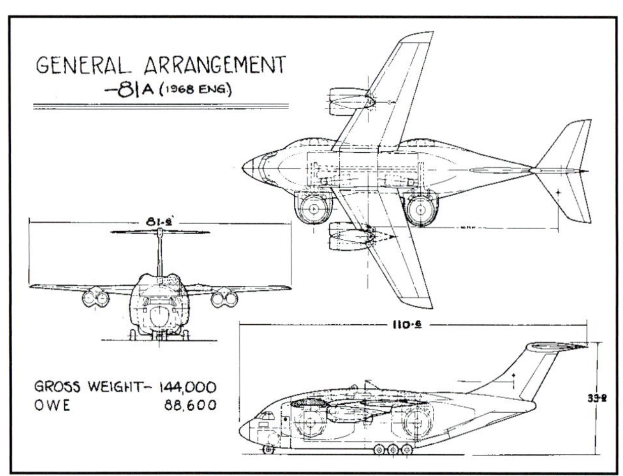

BELOW Boeing Model 743-100-81A general arrangement from August 1965. *Boeing*

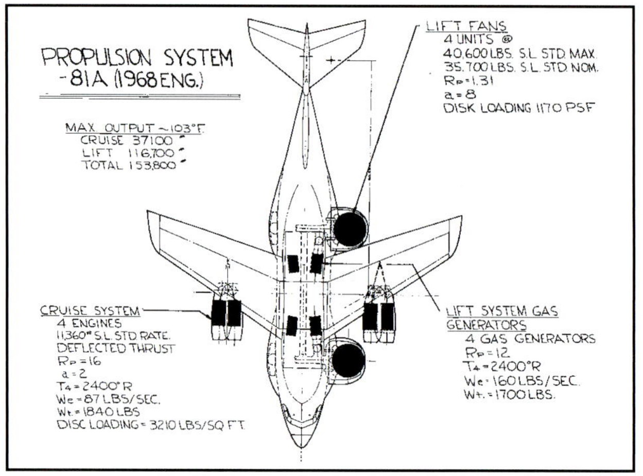

BELOW The Boeing Model 743-100-81A with details based on engine technology projected for 1968. *Boeing*

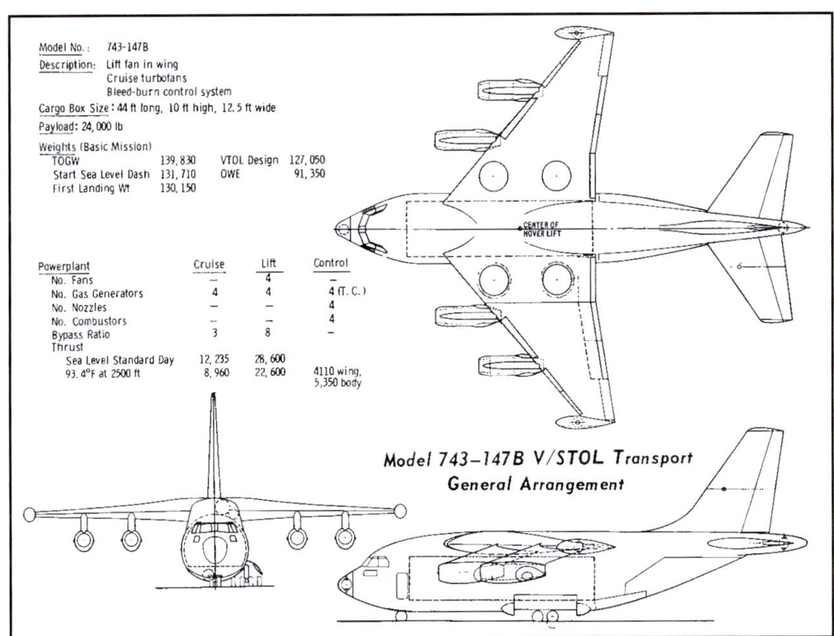

ABOVE **Boeing Model 743-147B general arrangement from June 1966.** *Boeing*

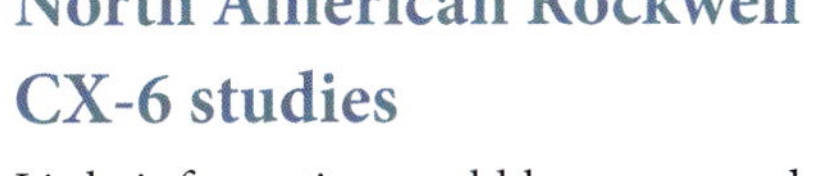

North American Rockwell CX-6 studies

Little information could be uncovered regarding North American's CX-6 studies. A model exhibited by the company at the 1965 Paris Air Show, however, portrayed a small VTOL transport, with small high-mounted, sharply swept wings, two deflected-thrust engines and two sets of lift engines, mounted below the wing roots.

Company artwork also showed the fan-in-wing concept, which reached hardware in the form of a large wind tunnel test model with operating GE engines driving lift-fans at NASA's Ames Research Center.

RIGHT **The North American CX-6 concept with four large lift-fans in the mid-wing nacelles.** *Dave Stern collection*

BELOW RIGHT **The NAA CX-6 concept with lift-jets in wingtip nacelles and two turbofan engines for horizontal flight.** *Special Collections & Archives, Wright State University*

BELOW **A NASA wind tunnel model configured with wing fans for early North American Aviation tests. Six GE X-376 lift-fans, driven by the exhaust from two YJ85-5 turbojet engines, were completely enclosed in the wing.** *NASA*

The CX-6 programme fizzles out

Despite early momentum, the CX-6 programme was dead by January 1967 (as was the TS-152-inspired XC-142A). This was partly in response to the rising costs of the Vietnam War, but it also reflected increasing loss of confidence in the promise that VTOL could be accomplished. In a telling statement, a contractor official related in 1965 that 'we've been saying for the past four years that it [the CX-6A] is technically feasible. In retrospect, it might not have been true four years ago, but I think we can prove it now.'

This brave enthusiasm made little impact on Defense Secretary McNamara, who was burdened by the conflicting demands of the Vietnam War and the repeatedly demonstrated inability of the defence contractors to execute their technically advanced programmes within their promised costs. According to *Flight* magazine (22 February 1967), McNamara 'felt that VTOL had not yet demonstrated its superiority in any field sufficiently well to justify support of any particular operational requirements.'

In addition, some of the Air Force mission requirements demanded that VTOL transports faded away; there would be no field-deployed VTOL nuclear-strike fighters needing logistical support, as had been forecast in 1961.

This disillusionment bore consequences. The LTV XC-142A and Bell X-22A programmes were only allowed to continue until their already committed funds were exhausted. Moreover, the CX-6 transport studies were ended, citing the lack of availability of a suitable powerplant. In retrospect, this was the key technical point that hobbled the CX-6. It demanded four to eight engines (gas generators) with the necessary thrust, weight and efficiency to drive the large lift-fans. These did not exist and would have taken five to six years to develop. The only existing hardware in 1965 were the lift-fans (a technology pioneered and heavily marketed by General Electric) powered by the J85 with 3,000lb (13.4kN) thrust – a far cry from the 13,000lb (57.9kN)-class thrust gas generators required by CX-6.

The conclusions in the Boeing final report of June 1966 included the following observations, which would be reflected in the trends of later studies:

- 'Sophisticated aerodynamic high-lift devices are not necessary or desirable for very short field performance. Very little lift is developed by the wing during the shorter ground roll since take-off velocities are low. The high-lift devices are not efficient at very low forward speeds and tend to unnecessarily add weight to the airplane. It is easier to get the required lift by increasing lift thrust
- 'Larger airplanes have better payload-to-gross-weight ratios than smaller airplanes'

A November 1970 NASA report on behalf of the FAA entitled 'Conceptual Design Study of a V/STOL Lift Fan Commercial Short Haul Transport' reflects much of the CX-6 debate on the merits of the different configurations. One of the earlier Boeing Model 743 designs even appeared in colourful artwork in the guise of a civilian 'Intercity Transport'.

'Light Intra-Theatre Transport' (LIT) V/STOL cargo aircraft

Although the 1968 Defense Budget and DoD opposition curtailed VTOL transport development, it did not halt USAF interest in the more practical options of V/STOL. This was embedded in a requirement for what it termed a 'Light Intra-Theatre Transport V/STOL Cargo Aircraft' (LIT) as a replacement for existing de Havilland C-7s (recently transferred from the Army) and Fairchild Hiller C-123s.

This aircraft concept grew directly from the requirement to deal with conflicts such as that in Southeast Asia. It was assumed, as a result of the Vietnam War, that at least 80 per cent of these conflicts would involve small-to-medium-sized forces in Asia, Latin America or Africa in an environment where airfield denial was a possibility. The Air Force considered five potential LIT concepts: lift-fans, pure jets, rotors, tilt-wings, and the LTV ADAM (Air Deflection And Modulation) concept.

An initial round of LIT programme studies ran from February to August 1967. The first study, by Lockheed-California, proposed a single stoppable/stowed rotor along the lines of its previous work. The second study was done by a team of United Aircraft's Sikorsky Aircraft Division and North American Rockwell's Los Angeles Division, which suggested a twin lateral/tilting/stowed-rotor configuration. Published concepts from the late 1967/early 1968 period showed tilt-rotors and folding-blade helicopter designs shared with the CARA (Combat Aircrew Recovery Aircraft).

As the LIT concept definition progressed, however, disagreement reportedly surfaced between the USAF and the Army on one hand, and the Department of Defense on the other, over exactly what kind of aircraft would be sought. The former envisaged a tilt-wing V/STOL, based on XC-142 technology, which could carry 8-10 tons (8,128-10,160kg) as a VTOL, or twice that payload in STOL mode. As such it would serve alongside the C-130s and new C-5s, until further funds were available to replace the C-130s in a separate effort. The DoD on the other hand wanted a larger aircraft that would also replace the C-130s. (It is interesting to note, looking back from today's vantage point, that the C-130 is still in production almost fifty years later and that the Air Force does not field an aircraft in the class of the C-7/C-123.)

By mid-1968 the Air Force put three companies under contract to study more conservative concepts for LIT: Boeing-Vertol, LTV and McDonnell Douglas. Contractor efforts soon converged on relatively conservative tilt-wing designs to achieve STOL performance.

ABOVE The Sikorsky tilt-rotor LIT concept from 1967. Forward speed was to be boosted by the turbofans the wings. *Author collection*

Boeing Vertol's tilt-wing aircraft was described as having propeller/rotors 26ft (7.93m) in diameter and a horizontal stabiliser with a very large incidence range. The VTOL cargo capability was given as 10,000lb (4,540kg), and an STOL payload of 34,000lb (15,436kg). Its speed range was listed as 0 to 400kt (740km/h), with a STOL approach speed using a partly tilted wing of 30-45kt (56-84km/h).

LTV also studied a tilt-wing concept that proceeded to wind tunnel testing under the V-506 designation. Conceptually similar to the XC-142 (whose test programme was drawing to a close), the V-506 provided many refinements, including the deletion of the pitch control tail rotor, replacing it with two small turbojet engines.

Hedging its bets, LTV also studied STOL transports with small turbofan engines, a fixed wing and externally

BELOW The Boeing Vertol LIT in action. *Dave Stern collection*

ABOVE The LTV V-506 wind tunnel model. *LTV via Bill Spidle*

LTV V-506	
Powerplant	4 x unspecified turboshafts; 2 x unspecified turbojets
Wingspan	95ft 10in (29.21m)
Length	82ft 0in (24.99m)
Height	35ft 9in (10.9m)

ABOVE LTV's Model V-506 illustrated in a hover. *Greater St Louis Air and Space Museum via Mark Nankivil*

BELOW LTV V-506 tilt-wing compared with an ADAM (Air Deflection And Modulation) point design concept with additional flip-out lift-fans. ADAM concepts were extensively studied by LTV, but were considered by the Air Force to be too exotic and untested to remain in the running for the CX-6. *LTV via Bill Spidle*

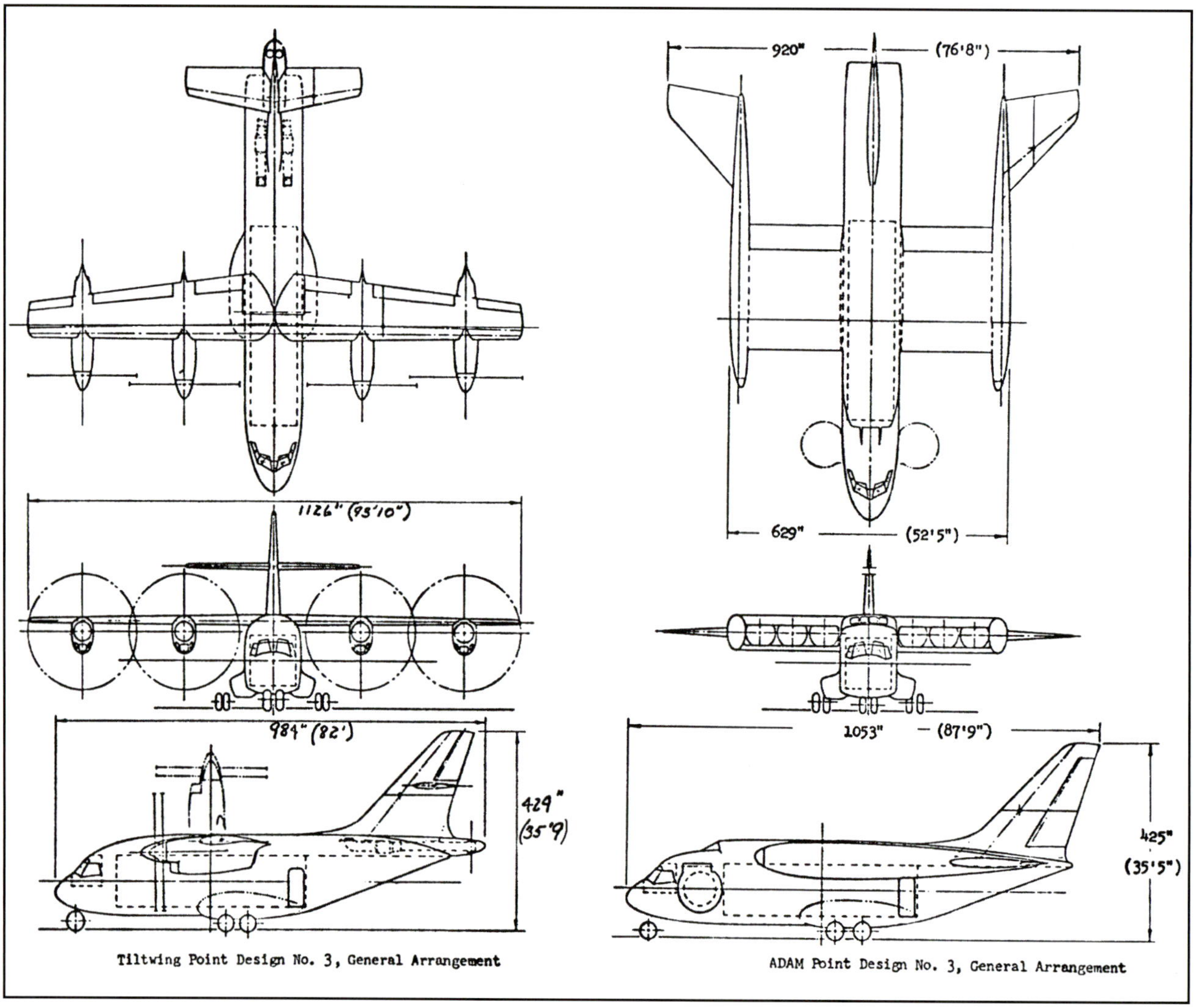

1126" (95'10")
984" (82')
429" (35'9)
Tiltwing Point Design No. 3, General Arrangement

920" (76'8")
629" (52'5")
1053" (87'9")
425" (35'5")
ADAM Point Design No. 3, General Arrangement

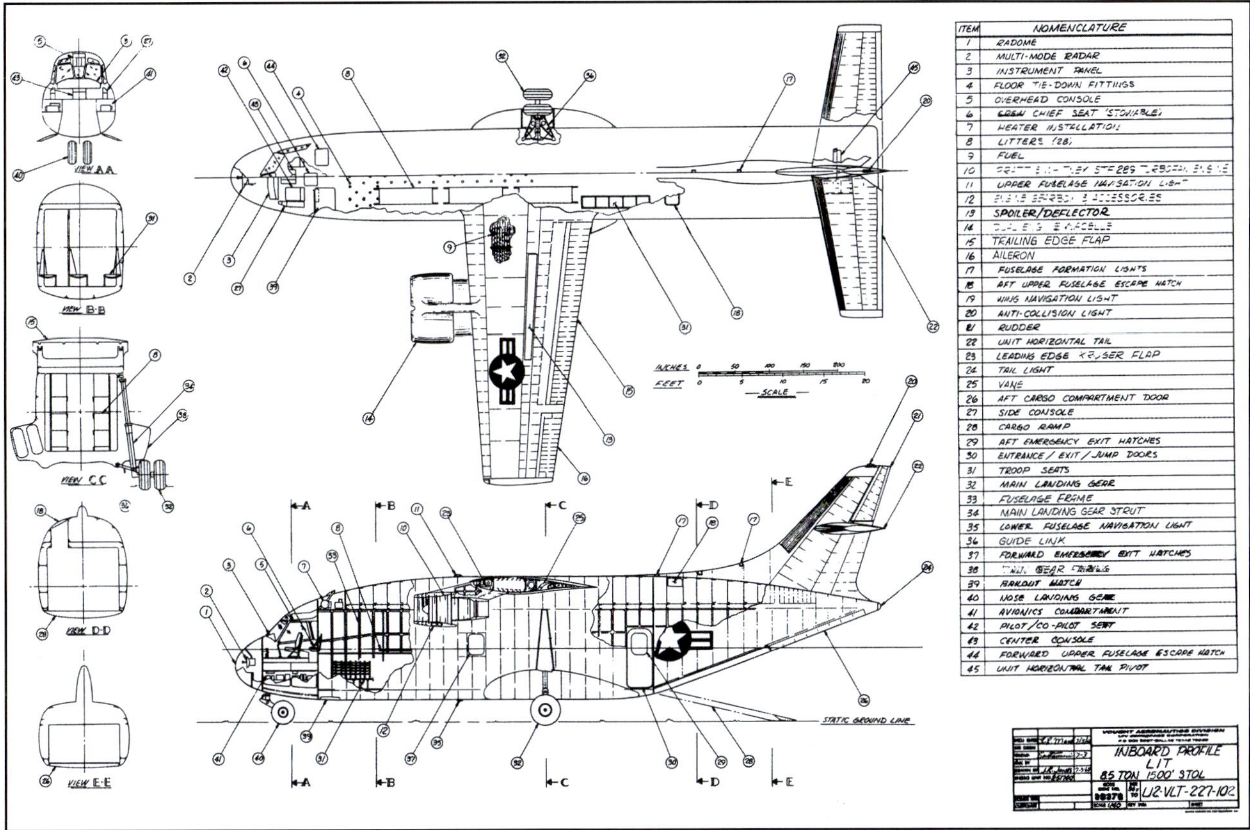

ABOVE The LTV 8.5-ton payload, four-turbofan STOL LIT concept. *Greater St Louis Air and Space Museum via Mark Nankivil*

blown double-slotted flaps. With a 17,000lb (7,780kg) payload and a 1,500ft (478m) take-off run, it offered little advantage over the C-123 in these areas.

McDonnell Douglas continued its association with the basic Breguet 941, advancing the design to its Model 188E. It was reported that the company wanted to have an STOL product that it could offer to the commercial market by the early 1970s, '...regardless of the action taken by the Air Force on its LIT programme'. Planned to be introduced as an STOL freighter (the Model 188E) to gain experience with STOL operations, a re-engined passenger version would follow, followed again by a larger passenger aircraft, the McDonnell Douglas Model 210E.

North American Rockwell continued its research and development efforts from the CX-6 programme with apparently two STOL concepts in development for the LIT programme, but would offer commercial versions '... only if the military buys one of them'. One of these proposals worked via thrust deflection by means of extensive wing-flaps. Interestingly, it incorporated the

RIGHT A prototype Breguet 941 undergoes refit in February 1969 at McDonnell's St Louis facility, with F-4J Phantoms under construction in the background. McDonnell marketed the aircraft as the Model 188. *Author collection*

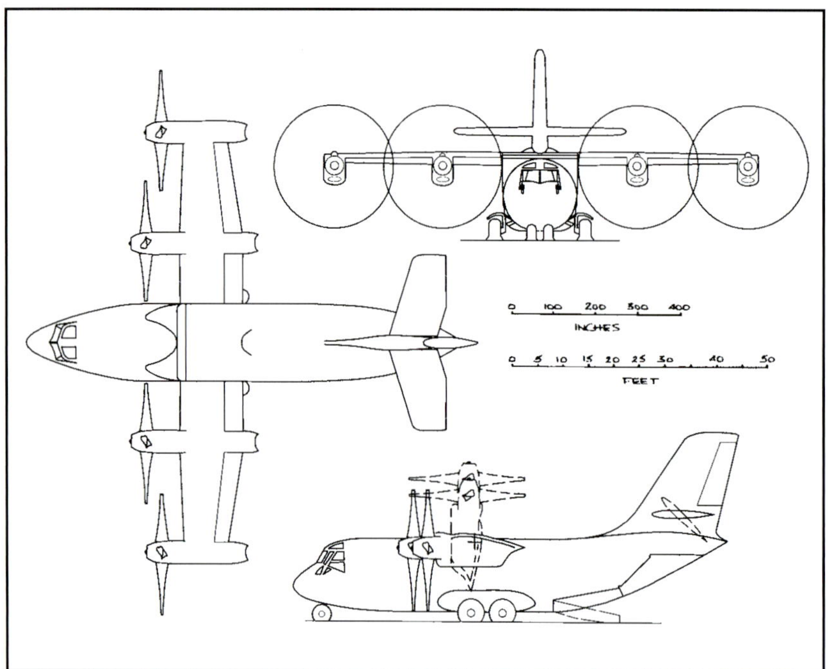

ABOVE The Canadair/General Dynamics CL-284-1A11 tapered-wing LIT design from November 1968. *Scott Lowther/APR*

expertise in tip-driven fans developed in CX-6, but rather than using them for lift it utilised them for prime propulsion. Turned so that the thrust line was horizontal, the engines had an effective bypass ratio that was unequalled in that thrust class at the time.

Canadair and General Dynamics/ Convair Division also performed conceptual studies. Two designs were defined under the Canadair CL-284 project number, the 1A10 version with a parallel-chord wing and the -1A11 with a tapered-chord wing.

There was clearly no shortage of designs for the USAF's LIT requirement, most of which were less exotic and ambitious than those studied under the CX-6 programme. Moreover, many employed the tilt-wing, which had been extensively explored over the previous decade. To the outside observer, it appeared in 1969 and 1970 that the USAF might at last be on the path to getting an operational V/STOL aircraft with a cargo compartment 9ft high by 9ft-wide by 36ft long (2.74m by 2.74m by 11.0m), a 30,000lb (13,608kg) STOL payload and a 250nmi (463km) mission radius.

In reality, LIT was dogged by two interrelated issues – size and VTOL capability. The DoD desire to consolidate aircraft types had the effect of forcing consideration of the larger, more capable C-130-sized (or larger) solution, which could not be reasonably satisfied by VTOL technology. That basic disagreement over the size and capacity of the LIT was overshadowed by the question of whether VTOL was still worth pursuing, or if STOL gave most of the benefit for a much lower complexity and cost.

This discord was well apparent to the industry. Various news snippets and trade magazine reports on the LIT programme revealed that the aircraft companies were hedging their bets with regards to V/STOL as opposed to STOL. To quote an unidentified Boeing-Vertol official, 'Everybody's going crazy trying to assess the additional price you pay for vertical lift, but we all know you don't get "V" for free.'

Further adding to the headwinds facing the LIT programme was General William W. Momyer, commanding general of the Tactical Air Command. In his previous role as the deputy commander for air operations and Seventh Air Force commander in Vietnam, he formed the 834th Air Division to ensure the management and control of airlift within Vietnam. In fact, the transfer of the de Havilland C-7 Caribous from the Army to the Air Force took place under his command.

His strong opposition to LIT was based on the observation that the Army continued to supply the front lines using heavy helicopters under it's 'Airmobile' concept, and that the LIT duplicated that Army functionality. He saw no need in spending the decreasing Air Force budget to duplicate this Army function. Instead, he saw that an airlifter larger than LIT was needed to bring cargo to airfields further from the battlefield, where the CH-47s would then take over, bringing the cargo to the front lines.

Because of eroding military support for the LIT, declining top-line Defense budget and competing demands from other programmes, the US House of Representatives deleted further LIT studies from the draft 1971 budget in November 1969. The Secretary of the Air Force and the Chief of Staff announced in March 1970 that funding for the LIT was to be deferred. In practice, this meant concluded.

The Air Force regroups: LST and MST STOL cargo airlifter programmes

With the abandonment of aspirations for vertical flight, attention turned to the more practical goal of achieving much-improved STOL capability. Two separate efforts were laid out: the Light STOL Transport (LST) and the Medium STOL Transport (MST), which would eventually replace the C-130.

LST: Light STOL Transport

By early 1970 the Air Force Systems Command (AFSC) was proposing light STOL transports to replace the C-7 and C-123 and to be used until the MST could be procured in numbers. The LST was initially envisaged as a readily available, if not off-the-shelf STOL aircraft requiring a minimum of development. Five possibilities were short-listed:

- Canadair 'CX-84' (growth development of the tilt-wing CL-84-1)
- de Havilland C-8 Buffalo
- Fairchild Hiller M-541, a modified C-123 with T64 engines
- Lockheed C-130 (STOL version)
- McDonnell Model 188 (licensed and developed Breguet 941)

At about the same time, airlines had become interested in STOL airliners to serve the heavily travelled Northeast Corridor via easy-to-access 'STOLPorts'. By the summer of 1970 American Airlines, in conjunction with the FAA, issued requests to thirteen airframe manufacturers for a forty-eight-passenger, turboprop STOL transport design. With the agreement of the Air Force, the RFP also specified compatibility for use by the military.

The Air Force thinking was that it was feasible to develop a common propulsion system, wings, empennage and landing gear, differing only in fuselage design. Following this approach, Canadair proposed the CL-246 STOL airliner with four engines and fuselage sizes from a basic forty-eight passengers in four-abreast seating to enlarged versions accommodating six-abreast seating for eighty.

Airlines wanted to have the aircraft in the 1972-75 time period and the Air Force hoped to have its LST in service by 1974. Combined requirements of the airlines in the Northeast Corridor probably would have amounted to about fifty aircraft, with the USAF needing eighty.

These requirements were for an aircraft with capabilities similar to the Light Intra-Theatre Transport of the late 1960s, which TAC had strongly opposed. The Light STOL Transport failed to come to fruition due to this opposition and poor justification for spending money on a 'temporary' solution.

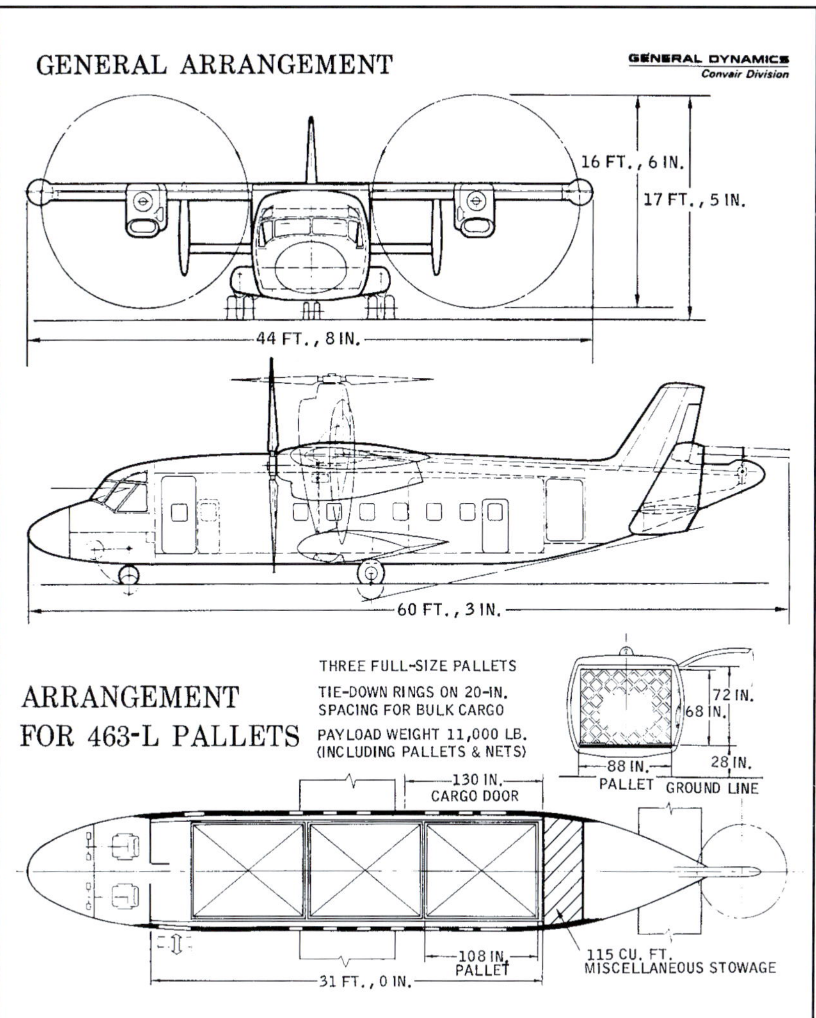

ABOVE Canadair developed an enlarged airlifter derivative of the CL-84 for the Air Force's abortive LST program with twin GE T64-GE-7 engines. *San Diego Air and Space Museum*

BELOW The Canadair Light STOL Transport design as marketed by parent company General Dynamics' Convair Division. *San Diego Air and Space Museum*

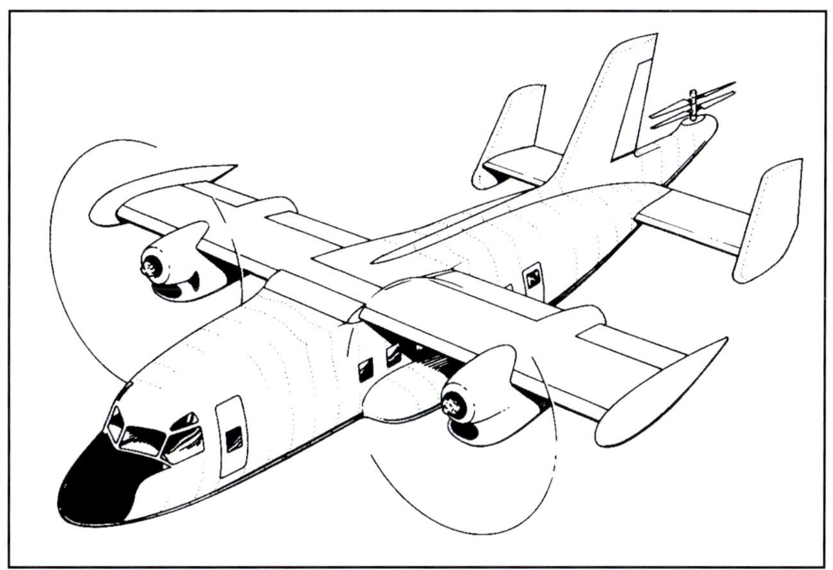

MST: Medium STOL Transport

In 1968 the Tactical Air Command (TAC) identified the need for a transport aircraft capable of supporting rapid battlefield air mobility – the capability to deliver outsized combat vehicles to forward deployed troops (something that neither the C-130 LIT nor LST aircraft could do). TAC's need was formalised as a Required Operational Capability (ROC) issued on 6 May 1970. The ROC 52-69 requirements were:

- Able to carry 28,000lb (12,700kg) cargo over a 3,600nmi (6,667km) unrefuelled mission, while cruising at Mach 0.75, above 20,000ft (6,100m)
- A cargo compartment 45ft long, 12ft wide and 12ft high (13.7 by 3.7 by 3.7m)
- Truck-bed-height loading, and able to accommodate standard 463L pallets

This new MST requirement stated a need to augment strategic airlift by providing a 3,600nmi ferry range and a 2,600nmi range with a useful payload, a requirement that has since been revised and made more specific in the current Military Airlift Command (MAC) ROC 9-75.

Boeing had been working on concepts through the late 1960s as the MST programme requirements crystallised. These studies – under the Model 953-200 series family of designation – went through numerous iterations and variations. These included over-wing, slipper and under-wing engine positions. Engine selections included the TF34, CF6, JT3D, JT8D-15 and F101. STOL technologies investigated included internally and externally blown flaps and vectored/deflected thrust, and numerous different designs were developed to investigate cargo compartment size and loading options.

Boeing was not alone, as General Dynamic/Convair was also pursuing studies. And Douglas had re-entered the fray. A year after losing the competition for the C-5, Douglas restarted advanced design studies in the tactical STOL area.

LEFT An unidentified early Boeing Model 953-200 series design is depicted in this concept art. *Boeing*

BELOW This chart enumerates configurations explored in the Boeing Model 953-200 family, including the 953-280, which became the YC-14. Each bubble is a different aircraft configuration that was generated and evaluated. *Boeing*

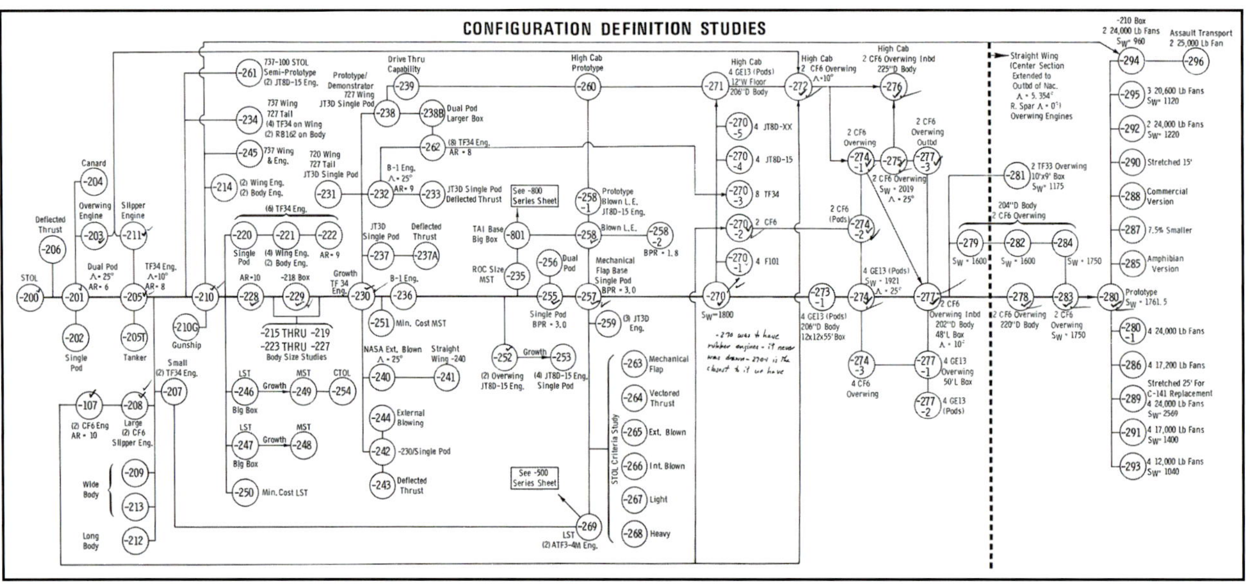

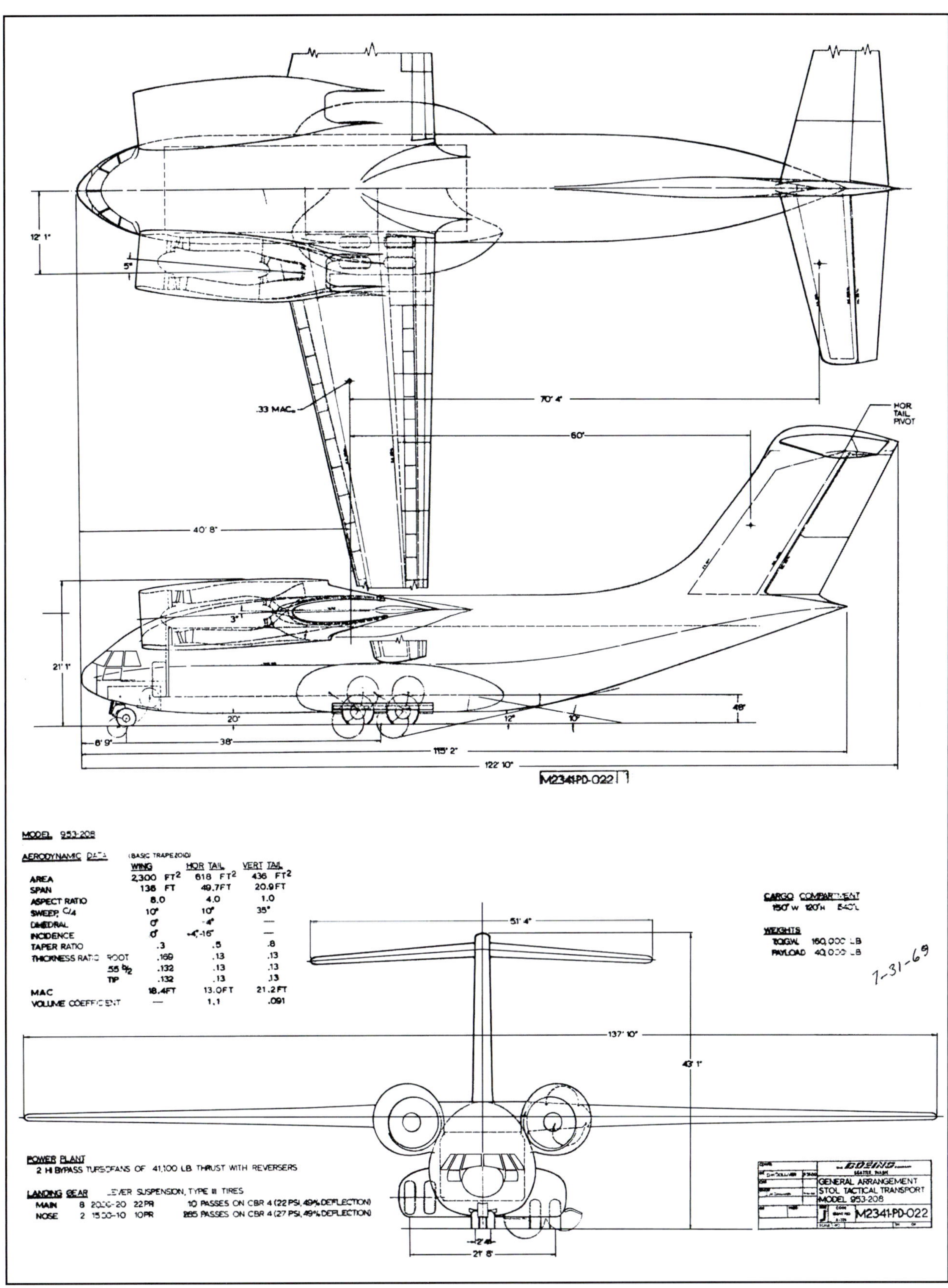

ABOVE **This Boeing Model 953-208 design dates from July 1969 and looks similar to the eventual YC-14, but the engine exhaust flows both above and below the wing. The engine nacelles are anchored to the fuselage and the cockpit is low-mounted to provided side visibility under the engines.** *Boeing*

ABOVE The Boeing Model 953-233 featured four JT3D engines with deflected thrust. *John Aldaz photo*

ABOVE Boeing studied a MST adaptation of the Japanese Kawasaki XC-1 with four TF34 engines replacing the dual JT8Ds. *John Aldaz photo*

Its first step was to reserve internal specification numbers D-915 to D-919 for design studies on 15 December 1966 (and in doing so perhaps unwittingly reused some of the C-5 project numbers).

Douglas was able to draw upon a great deal of effort that it had invested earlier in developing a series of STOL projects. These started with the Model 1906 in 1957, which by 1957 had progressed through a series of iterations to include the Models 1906A/B/C and other derivatives. These, in turn, were succeeded by a series of proposals running from 1962 to 1964 that were designed to replace the C-123. Unfortunately for Douglas, its technically conservative approaches of using high-lift wings with full-span, double-slotted flaps and slats to achieve STOL found little favour in a time period when VTOL concepts were in the ascendency. Douglas ended these efforts in 1964 and chose not to compete for the CX-6 effort in order to concentrate the company's resources and money on the C-5 competition.

BELOW The McDonnell Douglas Model 915B MST from June 1970. *Boeing*

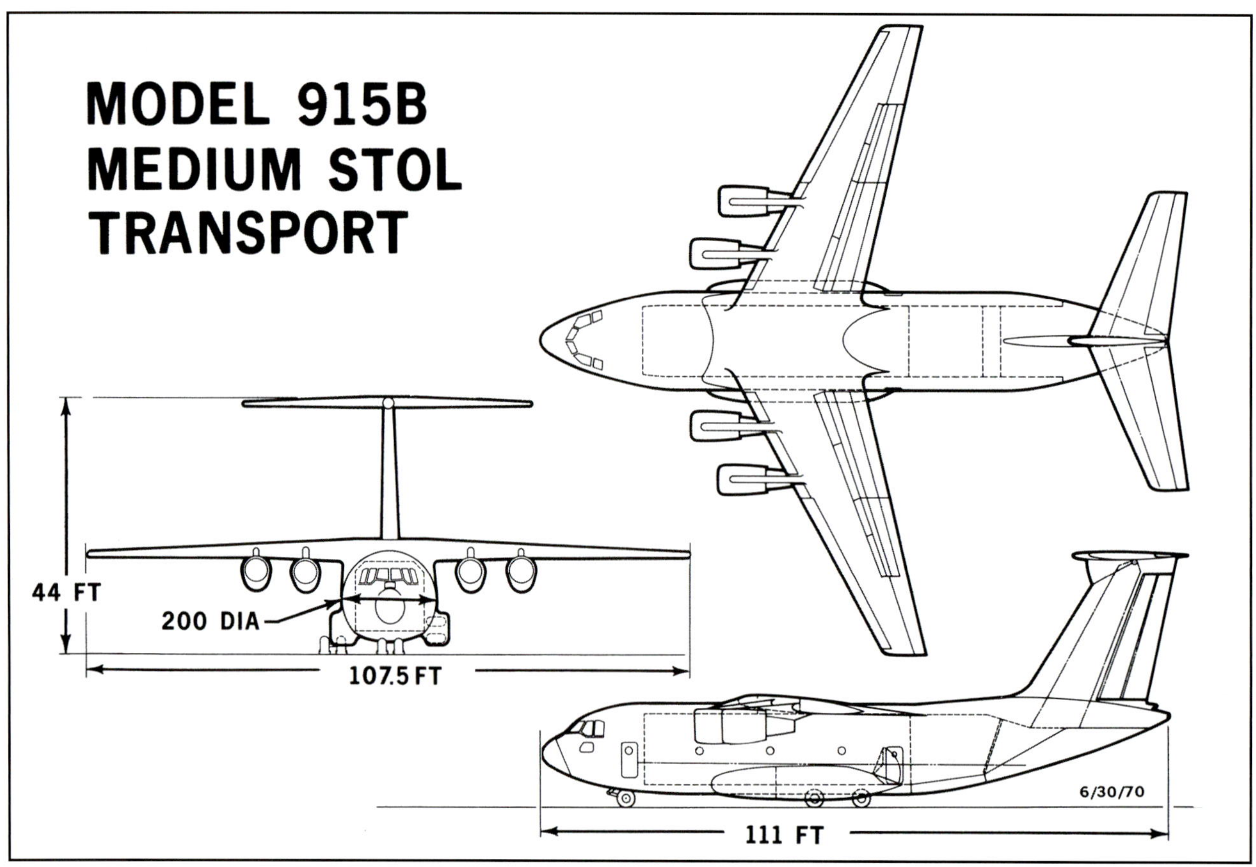

ABOVE A McDonnell Douglas wind tunnel model exploring the exhaust effects of the high-bypass turbofans on wide-span externally blown flaps, from June 1968. *Boeing*

VTOL: A promise unfulfilled

The 1960s started out with an expectation that VTOL aircraft were an inevitable operational reality. The need for this capability, in both attack aircraft and fighters, was obvious to the Air Force and the Army, while the rapidly advancing 'state of the art' promised near-term delivery. The only question seemed to be which of the many emerging technologies would prove the most effective.

In practice, it didn't happen. Despite successive efforts and extensive research, the decade ended without a single non-helicopter VTOL aircraft in operational service and, with the sole exception of the AV-8A Harrier for the Marine Corps (created in the UK as the pioneering Hawker P.1127), none was in prospect. Indeed, it would be nearly forty years before a winged VTOL transport (the V-22 Osprey) would enter service.

The reasons were threefold:

- Firstly, the rotary-winged helicopter successfully occupied many of the roles to which other VTOL airlifter concepts aspired, albeit without the speed or the range. Indeed, by 1970 both the Army and Marine Corps had been flying VTOL transports with an 8,000lb (3,632kg) payload for years (the CH-47 and CH-53 helicopters, respectively)
- Secondly, the technological challenge – mainly in terms of hovering performance and transitional flight – proved more difficult in practice than had been imagined in 1960. To quote from a 1984 NASA review, looking back at VTOL developments (NASA Technical Memorandum 85938 'VSTOL Concepts in the United States – Past, Present and Future'):

'Most of the aircraft suffered in several ways from ground effects. Re-ingestion of engine exhausts lowered take-off thrust, and resulted in aerodynamic suck-down for most jet-powered concepts. Ground erosion was a major problem for all turbojet operations. Noise from the turbojet engines was a major deficiency for commercial operation. Recirculation of the propeller slipstream resulted in performance degradation and stability and control problems for tilt-wing types. *The significance of these ground-effect problems was not appreciated at the aircraft design stage.*'

Moreover, much of the needed technology (primarily engines in the appropriate power class) did not exist and, if progressed, would require VTOL projects to bear the full cost of their parallel development. [Authors' emphasis]

- Thirdly, with the helicopter assuming the 'easier' missions, a heavy VTOL airlift capability appeared to not be worth the cost, complexity and penalty in terms of conventional flight performance

Making things more difficult in the late 1960s was the competing demands for funding. The DoD was already grappling with cost overruns on the C-5, Minuteman ICBM and F-111. It was also facing impending demands to finance the high-priority A-X, AWACS, B-1 and F-15 development (and their eventual procurement) – all in an era of austerity being imposed by the new Nixon administration, not to mention the funds being consumed by major civilian projects such as the SST and Apollo programmes.

The pursuit of VTOL had taxed engineers to the full and produced some of the most imaginative designs in airlifter history. Would any of them have succeeded in becoming effective operational aircraft had the will been there and the funds made available? As with the scores of other proposals described in this book, one can only speculate. However, it seems doubtful. Even the much later V-22, designed and built after the state of the art had moved on considerably, saw a long and problematic development period, taking sixteen years (1989-2005) from first flight to eventual operational acceptance.

The 1960s ended with dismal prospects for practical VTOL airlift, beyond the capabilities already offered by helicopters. The 'V' component of V/STOL was simply too complex and demanded too much of a compromise in conventional flight performance. STOL, however, was another matter.

The advantages of being able to deliver supplies and combat vehicles to forward-deployed troops using short, unpaved strips became ever clearer through experience in Southeast Asia.

Moreover, this consideration did not apply to just that theatre. Europe was still in the grip of the Cold War, with the ever-present threat of conflict between NATO forces and the Warsaw Pact countries. Should war break out, it was inevitable that major airfields would be targeted and bombed within the first few days of hostilities. This meant that the US Army would be heavily dependent on aircraft that could use parts of damaged runways, smaller airfields or unpaved airstrips for its rapid deployment and resupply.

Other factors were also leading to a demand for a new type of aircraft. The large-capacity C-5 was about to introduce a new class of strategic airlift capability to the US Armed Forces. The first C-5A was handed over to the Air Force in December 1969 and deliveries were to be complete by 1973. This meant that huge quantities of weapons and supplies could be delivered over transcontinental distances. However, the usefulness of this capability was greatly impeded if that cargo could not be rapidly distributed. One major problem was that the size of US Army combat vehicles had grown over the previous decade, and many vehicles that were easily transported by the C-5A were too large to fit into the C-130 or C-141 (which had the same fuselage cross section). Moreover, even loads like those carried by these medium airlifters needed to be broken down and repackaged to fit smaller tactical supply aircraft like the C-7 Caribou.

In summary, strategic airlift capacity was about to outstrip tactical capability, and a medium-to-heavy STOL capability was high on the tactical requirements list.

BELOW A General Dynamics/Convair MST concept with external-blown flaps and high-flotation landing gear. *Convair*

Chapter Five
Routes to the C-17 and KC-10

1971-1992: Two decades of impressive designs and stuttering progress

ABOVE Bell Aerosystems' proposed ACLS (Air Cushion Landing System), as adapted to the Boeing YC-14, would have combined STOL and off-runway capability. *Dave Stern collection*

By the start of the 1970s the Air Force had its long-sought new strategic airlifter, the C-5, in production, complementing the capabilities of its C-141s and C-130s. However, two requirements were becoming pressing. One was for a large assault transport able to operate from short semi-prepared airstrips, and the other for a tanker to replace, or at least supplement, the KC-135s. The industry ultimately met both of these requirements, but the path proved both long and difficult.

MST to AMST: The Advanced Medium STOL Transport

The course of the Medium STOL Transport (MST) changed under a new DoD policy of 'fly before buy' – which was also seen as a return to prototyping. Deputy Secretary of Defense David Packard (one of the founders of Hewlett-Packard) advocated this approach, partly in response to major cost overruns on earlier projects in the 1960s, including the C-5. The goal was to iron out engineering difficulties and uncertainties before making any commitment to a production contract.

In response, the Air Force then initiated the 'USAF Advanced Prototype Program' to evaluate worthwhile candidates. Some 220 proposed projects were screened, resulting in six finalists:

- Advanced Medium STOL Transport (AMST)
- Advanced Remotely Piloted Vehicle (ARPV)
- Large tanker aircraft (Boeing 747 evaluation)
- Lightweight Fighter Aircraft (LWF)
- [Acoustically] Quiet Aircraft
- Very Low Radar Cross Section (RCS) vehicle

From these, the Air Force selected AMST and the LWF for prototyping; the Boeing 747 tanker evaluation proceeded under different funding. The AMST programme was formally launched in December 1971, and the subsequent RFP specifications were similar to the MST ROC but extended the length of the cargo area to 55ft (16.8m).

Boeing and Lockheed had previously submitted proposals under the Advanced Prototype Program for STOL transports. Boeing's approach was to prototype an entirely new aircraft employing a newly designed wing with high-lift devices, augmenting the latter with thrust vectoring. Boeing also offered several options that adapted existing commercial 727 and 737 wings to avoid the requirement for a wholly new aircraft. Lockheed suggested modifications to the C-130E to a STOL configuration using either improved turboprop or turbofan propulsion. As an alternative, Lockheed proposed modification of the C-141 to a STOL configuration using higher-performance engines. These efforts ended when the AMST programme began.

In parallel with the AMST initiative, NASA was running a competition for a Quiet Short Haul Aircraft, or QUESTOL. Several firms responded to this. Because NASA was looking for a technology demonstrator rather than an aircraft intended for a subsequent production contract, the proposals adapted elements from existing aircraft as much as possible. McDonnell Douglas, for example, offered a modified DC-9 with a high wing, four underslung engines, and blown flaps; Lockheed took a similar approach based on its S-3A Viking; and Boeing eventually won the competition with a design based on the C-8A Buffalo using an upper-surface blown (USB) system. There were suggestions that that QUESTOL and AMST should be combined, but NASA declined and ran a successful pure research programme on its own.

In response to the AMST RFP, six firms submitted seven proposals between them: Bell, Boeing, Fairchild, Lockheed, Lockheed and North American Rockwell (jointly), and McDonnell Douglas.

ABOVE For 'powered lift' wind tunnel tests, NASA Langley repurposed an existing C-5 model using new wings and empennage. This configuration explored underslung engines and blown, triple-slotted flaps. *NASA*

BELOW The same model was reconfigured for upper surface blowing. The full-span flaps induced a strong nose-down force, necessitating inverted leading edge flaps on the horizontal stabiliser to balance it. *NASA*

Bell Aerospace Company AMST proposal

Bell's AMST submission proposed a two-step approach: a low-cost demonstrator using a C-130 fuselage, with a new wing and pylon-mounted TF33 engines and a T-tail assembly, which would be followed by an operational aircraft able meet all the requirements of the RFP. Both were to be twin-engine aircraft employing Cold Thrust Augmentation (CTA) for short-field performance.

RIGHT Bell pursued a pure test bed approach for its AMST prototype, using a C-130 fuselage. *Tony Chong collection*

BELOW Bell AMST prototype general arrangement. *via Scott Lowther/APR*

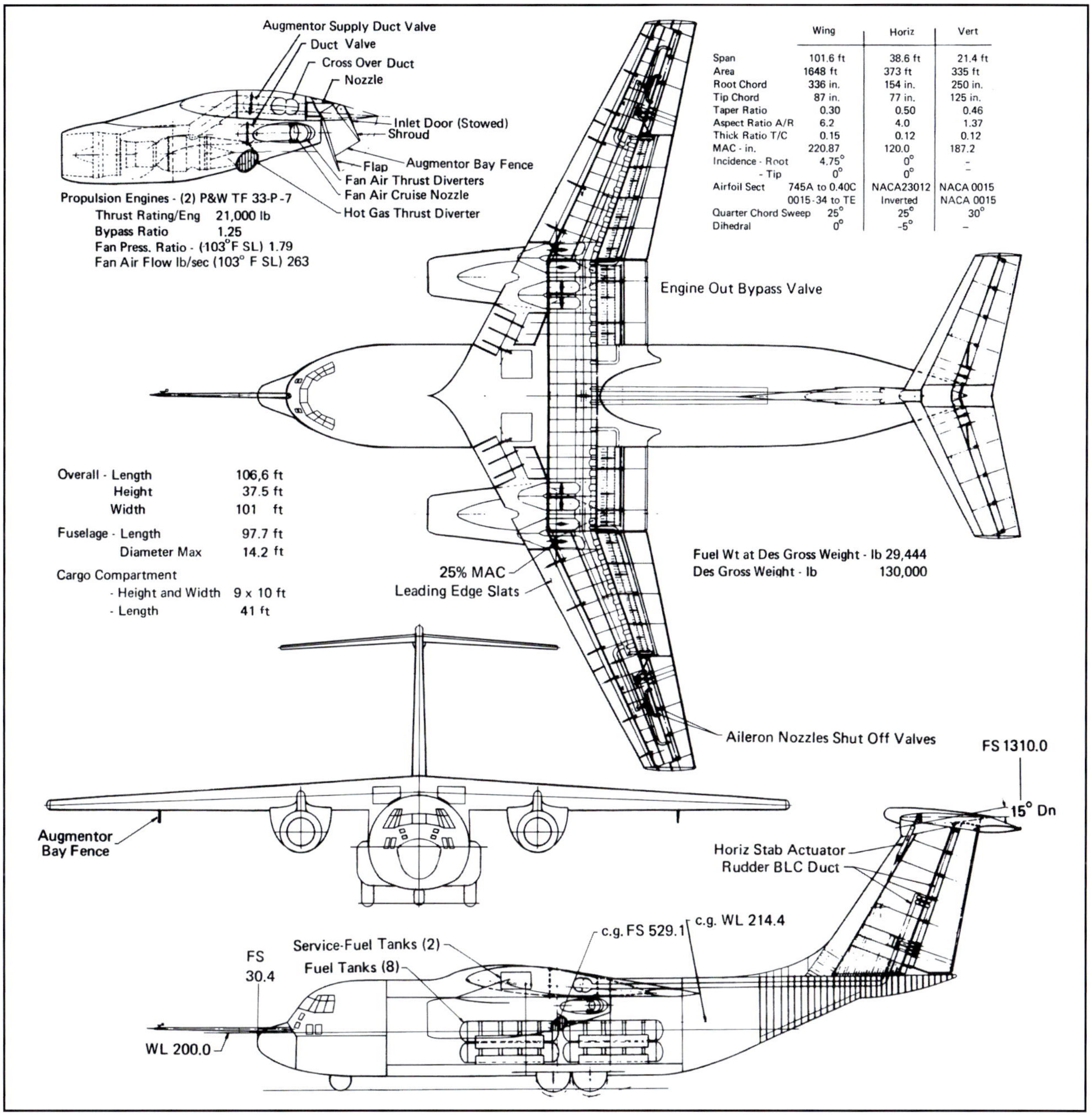

Augmentor Supply Duct Valve
Duct Valve
Cross Over Duct
Nozzle
Inlet Door (Stowed)
Shroud
Flap
Augmentor Bay Fence
Fan Air Thrust Diverters
Fan Air Cruise Nozzle
Hot Gas Thrust Diverter

Propulsion Engines - (2) P&W TF 33-P-7
Thrust Rating/Eng 21,000 lb
Bypass Ratio 1.25
Fan Press. Ratio - (103°F SL) 1.79
Fan Air Flow lb/sec (103° F SL) 263

	Wing	Horiz	Vert
Span	101.6 ft	38.6 ft	21.4 ft
Area	1648 ft	373 ft	335 ft
Root Chord	336 in.	154 in.	250 in.
Tip Chord	87 in.	77 in.	125 in.
Taper Ratio	0.30	0.50	0.46
Aspect Ratio A/R	6.2	4.0	1.37
Thick Ratio T/C	0.15	0.12	0.12
MAC - in.	220.87	120.0	187.2
Incidence - Root	4.75°	0°	–
- Tip	0°	0°	–
Airfoil Sect	745A to 0.40C 0015-34 to TE	NACA23012 Inverted	NACA 0015 NACA 0015
Quarter Chord Sweep	25°	25°	30°
Dihedral	0°	-5°	–

Engine Out Bypass Valve

Overall - Length 106,6 ft
Height 37.5 ft
Width 101 ft
Fuselage - Length 97.7 ft
Diameter Max 14.2 ft
Cargo Compartment
- Height and Width 9 x 10 ft
- Length 41 ft

25% MAC
Leading Edge Slats

Fuel Wt at Des Gross Weight - lb 29,444
Des Gross Weight - lb 130,000

Aileron Nozzles Shut Off Valves

FS 1310.0
15° Dn

Augmentor Bay Fence

Horiz Stab Actuator
Rudder BLC Duct

c.g. FS 529.1
c.g. WL 214.4
Service-Fuel Tanks (2)
Fuel Tanks (8)
FS 30.4
WL 200.0

The CTA system had been under development by the Air Force Aerospace Research Laboratories over the previous five years. The system utilised the turbofan's bypass airflow, diverting it into wing-ejector flaps. Fairchild had proposed this arrangement for the company's M-270 (described in *American Secret Projects 2*) a decade earlier. As with the M-270, the air would flow via pylon ducts past the inner-wing structure before being ejected through the jet flaps. One drawback was that this arrangement left little or no room in the wing for fuel. As a consequence, Bell's prototype carried its fuel in eight large tanks permanently installed on the cargo deck with two feeder tanks in the fuselage-to-wing fairing. This limited the prototype to being an aerodynamic test bed, without any possibility of being used for cargo loading or carriage tests.

Bell Aerospace Company (Division of Textron) AMST prototype	
Powerplant	2 x P&W TF33-P-7 turbofans @ 21,000lb (93.45kN) thrust
Wingspan	101.6ft (30.98m)
Length	106.6ft (32.49m)
Height	37.5ft (11.43m)
Wing area	1,648sq ft (158.10m²)
Design gross weight	130,000lb (58,967kg)

Boeing AMST proposal	
Powerplant	2 x GE CF6-50D turbofans @ 50,300lb (223.75kN) thrust
Span	130ft 2in (39.67m)
Length	134ft 6in (41.0m)
Wing area	1761.5sq ft (163.65m²)
Max TOW	215,000 lb (97,520kg)

At the time of its submission in 1972, Bell felt that there was only one suitable engine available: the P&W TF33-P-7 with 21,000lb (93.45kN) thrust and a bypass ratio of 1.29. However, it was stated that either the P&W/Rolls-Royce Pegasus 102 or P&W TF33 'Configuration 9' might be available in time for the prototype.

Boeing Model 953-280

Boeing proposed an aircraft with high-mounted straight wings and a T-tail. It was powered by two General Electric CF6-500 engines, each rated at 50,300lb (228.3kN) static thrust. These were mounted above and forward of the leading edge of the wing, with upper-surface blown flaps. Exploiting the Coandă effect, the airflow stayed attached to the surface as it passed over the deeply

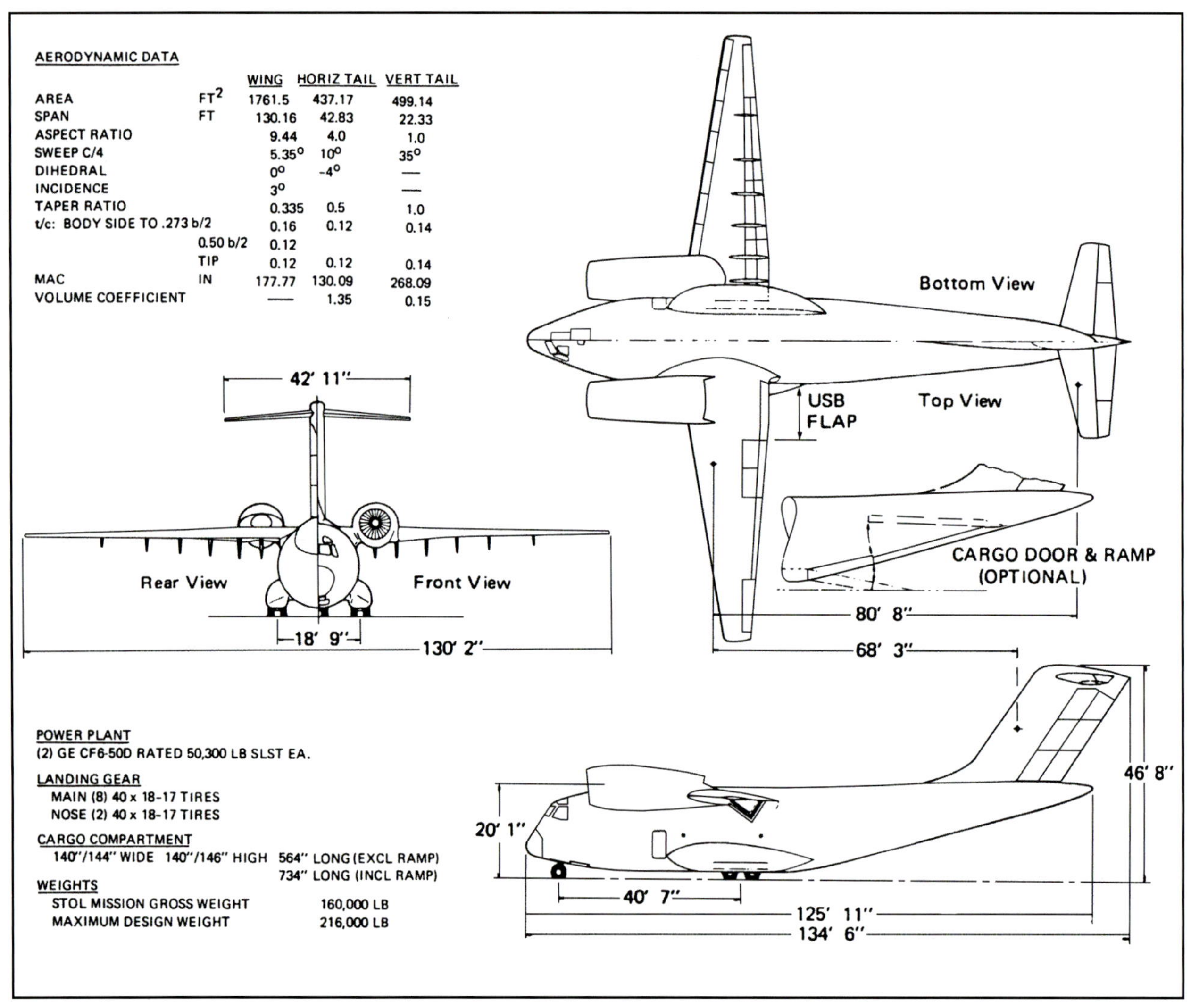

BELOW **The Boeing YC-14 prototype would evolve in detail from this initially proposed baseline design.** *Boeing*

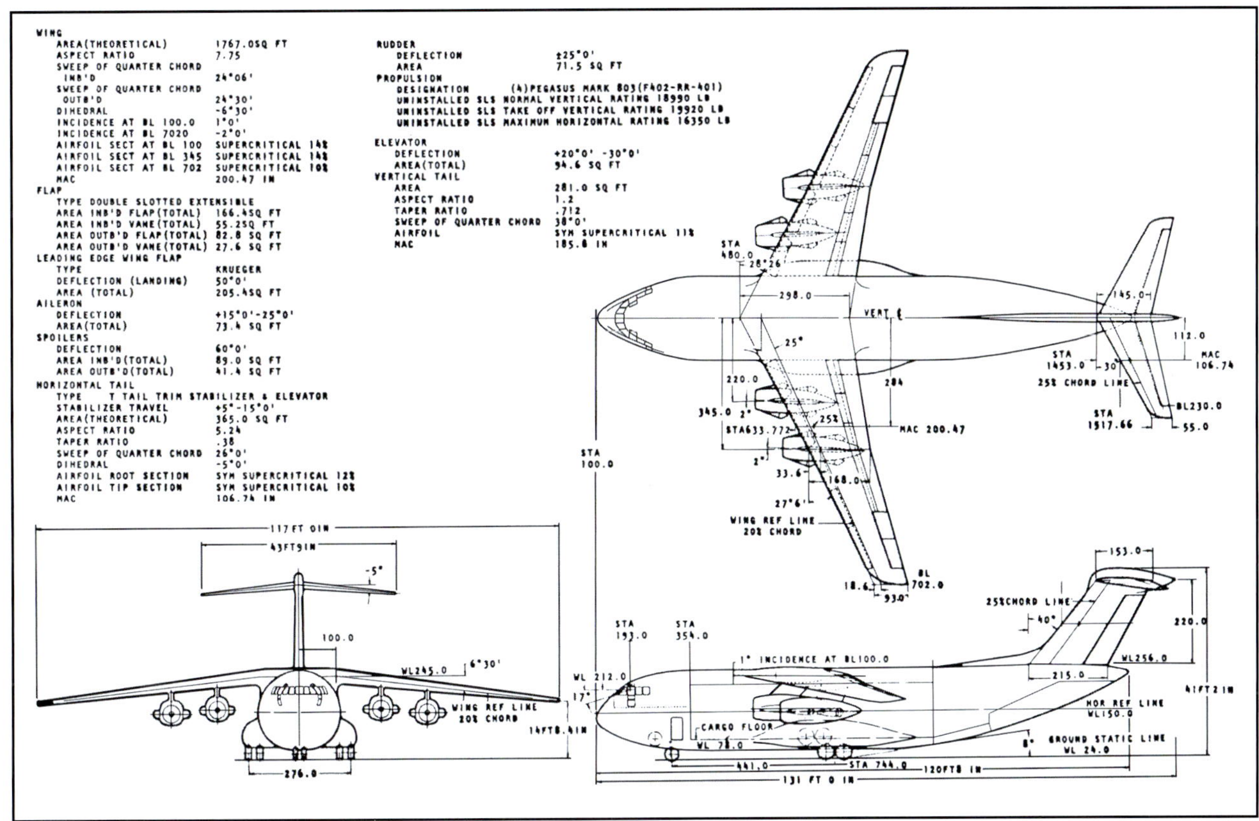

ABOVE Fairchild AMST proposed general arrangement. *Fairchild*

curving trailing edge flaps, being deflected downwards and enhancing lift.

Fairchild AMST proposal

Fairchild proposed using vectored thrust to provide its STOL capability, employing four Rolls-Royce Pegasus engines, a powerplant already in use with the Hawker Harrier and on order for the AV-8A. Despite the proven reliability of the engine, a failure in any one of the four engines must surely have been cause for concern. Of note, only one transport aircraft using this engine got as far as a flying prototype, the German Dornier Do-31, which had first flown some six years earlier but never went into production.

Fairchild AMST proposal	
Powerplant	4 x RR Pegasus Mk 803 (F402-RR-401) turbofans @ 19,900lb (88.52kN) (vertical thrust)
Span	117ft (35.66m)
Length	131ft (39.93m)
Height	41ft 2 in (12.55m)
Wing area	1,767sq ft (164.16m²)

Lockheed Model AMST proposals

Lockheed submitted two proposals. The first was Lockheed-Georgia Corporation's LG-203, with the proposed AMST prototype being the LG-203X. A surviving display model shows vectored thrust nozzles on the engines, though these are not evident

BELOW Lockheed LG-203 general arrangement. *Lockheed*

	WING	H. TAIL	V. TAIL
AREA SQ.FT.	2180	427	485
ASPECT RATIO	7.0	5.25	1.24
TAPER RATIO	0.4	0.4	0.6
SPAN FT.	123.5	47.3	24.5
MAC FT.	18.7	9.6	20.2
SWEEP (c/4)	10°22'	13°46'	35°

123.5 FT
43.6 FT
124.0 FT
136.4 FT

ABOVE **A Lockheed LG-203X desk model.** *Author collection*

BELOW **An artist's concept of the Lockheed/North American Rockwell AMST.** *Author collection*

Lockheed-Georgia LG-203X AMST proposal	
Span	123.5ft (37.64m)
Length	136.4ft (41.57m)
Height	43.6ft (13.29m)
Wing area	2,180sq ft (202.53m²)

in the three-view drawings. The model also shows a degree of sweepback to the wings and tailplane that is absent from the drawing; it is not clear which represents the later version of the design.

Lockheed's second AMST entry, presumably from Lockheed California (CALAC), was a joint bid with North American Rockwell. It featured a high-wing, T-tailed configuration with the large vertical fin typical of aircraft designed for a slow-speed approach and take-off. It was powered by four engines with the jet efflux directed onto slotted flaps. This design may have shared the Rockwell advanced design designation of D516 with previous versions studied under the MST effort.

McDonnell Douglas Model D-915 AMST proposal

McDonnell Douglas AMST proposed a four-engine aircraft with a conventional airlifter layout, featuring high-mounted swept wings and a T-tail. It employed an externally blown slotted-flap system to

provide the STOL capability. With externally blown flaps, the jet exhaust from the engines impinges on the underside of the flaps, spreads spanwise and flows through the flap slots, thereby augmenting flap effectiveness.

As did the other bidders, McDonnell Douglas proposed both a prototype and a production version of the aircraft. The former would be intended as a flight test vehicle only, stripped of nonessentials such as autopilot, all-weather avionics, cargo handling, air-drop systems or in-flight refuelling. The engine selected for the prototype was the Pratt & Whitney TF33-P-7. However, the possibility was raised of subsequently switching to the General Electric GE13/F10 (based on the GE-SNECMA CFM-56, itself derived from the F101 engine planned for the B-1). Repositioning the engines would accommodate any change to a large high-bypass powerplant.

Although the prototype would be heavier than the production aircraft (as a result of the latter taking advantage of composite materials in its construction), both had the same maximum STOL take-off weight of 160,300lb (72,710kg) and a maximum STOL payload of 28,000lb (12,700kg). Douglas also offered a slightly smaller 'minimum cost' aeroplane in addition to the 'recommended' AMST version.

RIGHT The McDonnell Douglas Model 915 for AMST submission. *Boeing*

BELOW The McDonnell Douglas AMST proposed prototype design. *Boeing*

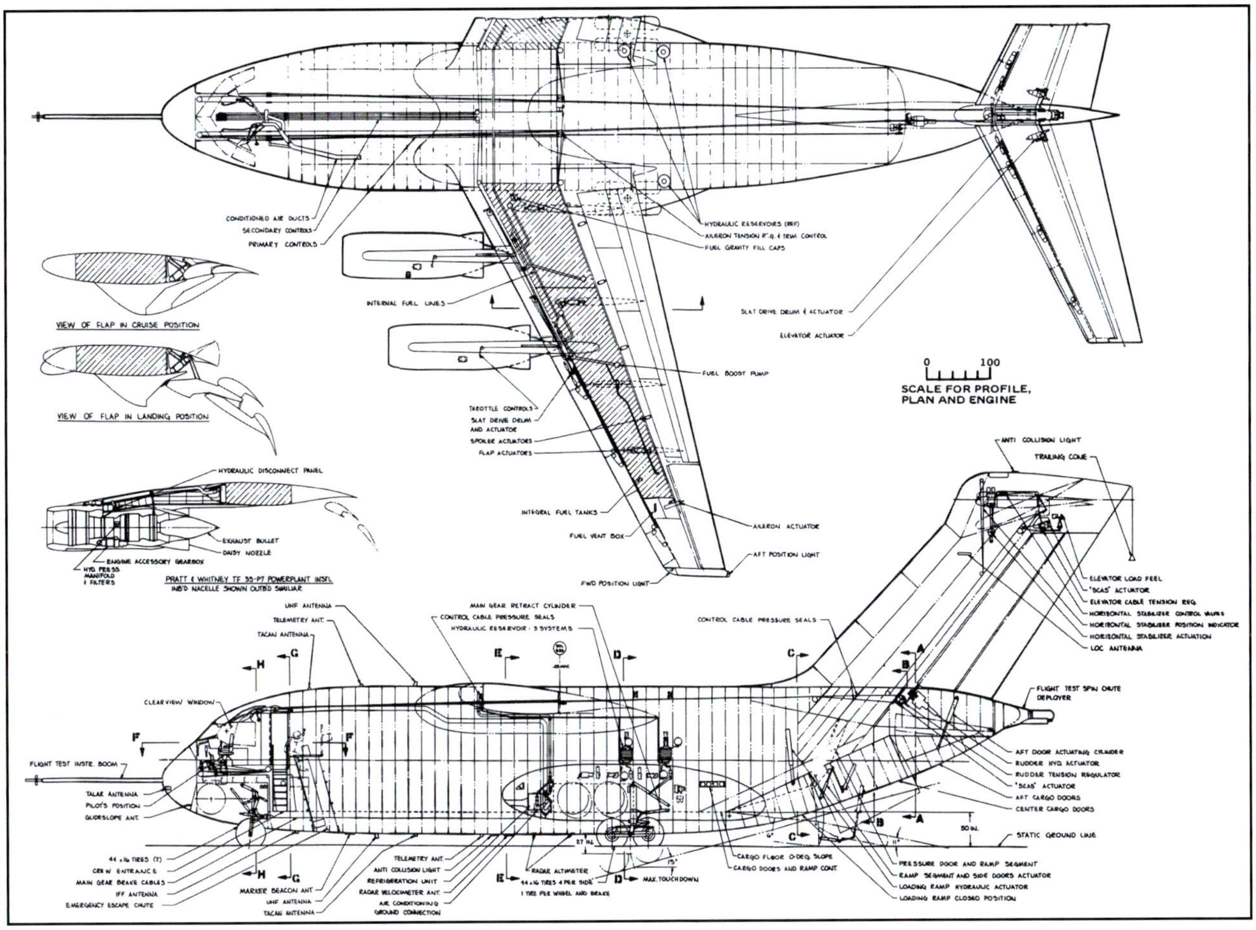

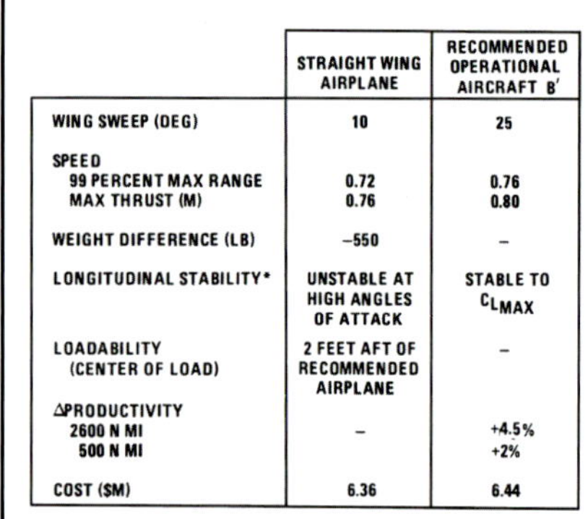

	STRAIGHT WING AIRPLANE	RECOMMENDED OPERATIONAL AIRCRAFT B'
WING SWEEP (DEG)	10	25
SPEED		
99 PERCENT MAX RANGE	0.72	0.76
MAX THRUST (M)	0.76	0.80
WEIGHT DIFFERENCE (LB)	−550	–
LONGITUDINAL STABILITY*	UNSTABLE AT HIGH ANGLES OF ATTACK	STABLE TO $C_{L_{MAX}}$
LOADABILITY (CENTER OF LOAD)	2 FEET AFT OF RECOMMENDED AIRPLANE	–
ΔPRODUCTIVITY		
2600 N MI	–	+4.5%
500 N MI		+2%
COST ($M)	6.36	6.44

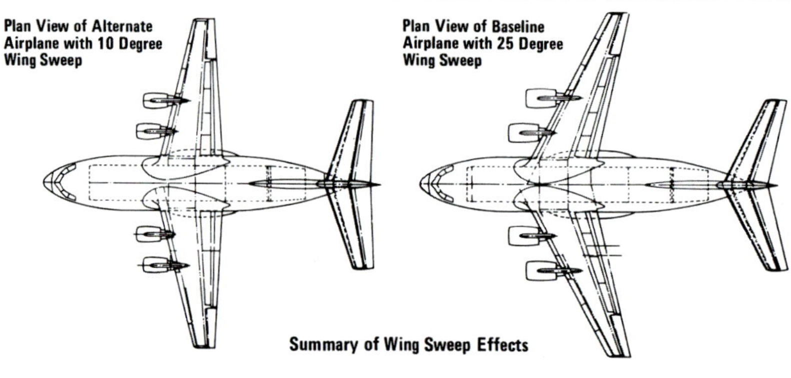

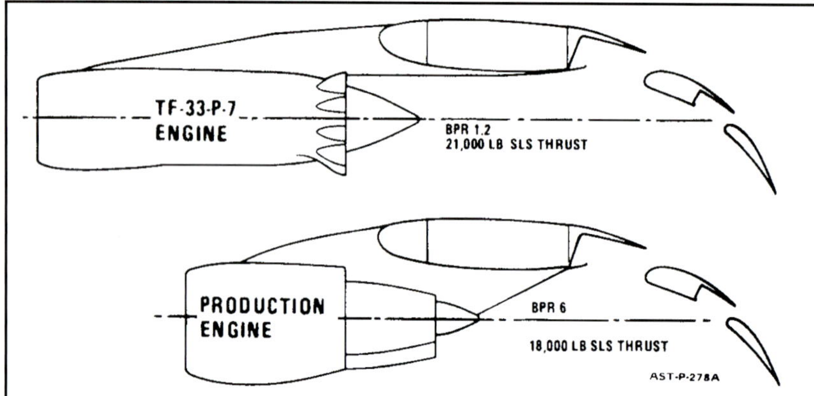

ABOVE Although a swept-wing was preferred by McDonnell Douglas, the straight wing was less expensive to build. *Boeing*

LEFT McDonnell Douglas D-915 alternate engine positioning and blown flap system. *Boeing*

McDonnell Douglas Model D-915P (proposed AMST production version)	
Powerplant	4 x GE13 derivative turbofans @ 18,000lb (80.07kN) thrust
Span	112ft 3in (34.21m)
Length	124ft 9in (38.02m)
Wing area	1,800 sq ft (167.2m²)
STOL TOW	151,450lb (68,697kg)
Payload	28,000lb (12,701kg)

The AMST competition winners: YC-14 and YC-15

While the basic configuration of the AMST proposals gave them a superficially similar appearance, the approaches to achieving STOL capability were quite different. They included:

- Deflected thrust
- Internally blown flaps
- Externally blown flaps
- Mechanical flaps plus vectored thrust
- Upper-surface blown flaps

On 10 November 1972 Secretary of the Air Force Robert Seamans authorised contract awards to Boeing and McDonnell Douglas, whose proposals used upper-surface blown flaps and externally blown flaps respectively. The contracts required each contractor to build two AMST prototypes for comparative testing, to be designated YC-14 and YC-15 respectively.

Boeing YC-14

The Boeing YC-14 as built had evolved considerably in detail from the proposed Model 953-280. The aft fuselage was redesigned with the lower profile being 'kinked' to provide additional clearance for cargo loading and unloading. Engineers made numerous changes to reduce cost, such as revising the vertical tail to a non-tapered design, which meant that all the ribs could be identical. In addition to the upper-surface lift provided by the engine exhaust, boundary layer control was provided across almost the entire span of the wing, from ports aft of the Krueger leading edge flaps. The wing also incorporated a supercritical airfoil for drag reduction.

Boeing YC-14 prototype	
Powerplant	2 x GE CF6-50D (F103/F2) turbofans @ 48,6800lb (217kN) thrust
Span	129ft (39.32m)
Length	131ft 9in (40.13m)
Height	48ft 2in (14.68m)
Wing area	1,762.4sq ft (163.84m²)
Max STOL TOW	169,500lb (76,880kg)
Max TOW	225,000lb (102,060kg)
Cruise speed	Mach 0.64
Range	2,630nmi (4,870km)

The first YC-14 was rolled out on 11 June 1976, with the first flight taking place on 9 August from Boeing Field, Seattle. The second aircraft followed on 21 October, and both were ferried to Edwards AFB for testing by mid-November.

The intended production C-14A had a number of small differences from the prototypes, including bracing struts between the engines and the fuselage as a weight/cost reduction measure. The YC-14 nacelle main structure had to deal with a cantilevered, pendulous mass that was in essence a gyroscope. The addition of the bracing strut enabled a lighter forward engine mount. The company also revised the nose contours, possibly to accommodate the production radar system. Boeing dropped the use of BLC on the C-14A and chose more conventional slats to replace the variable-camber Krueger flaps. Aft fuselage changes were made to address the drag

TOP RIGHT The first YC-14 in flight near Edwards Air Force Base. *Air Force Test Center History Office*

MIDDLE RIGHT Three desk models of YC-14 and C-14 aircraft. *John Aldaz photo*

BOTTOM RIGHT Boeing proposed the KC-14 KCX tanker to replace ageing Marine Corps KC-130Fs. Ultimately, neither the KC-14 nor the F-14A entered Marine Corps service. *Boeing*

problems encountered in fight testing. An APU was to be added in the forward right landing-gear sponson.

Boeing also proposed a variety of further applications for the aircraft, such as the KCX air-refuelling tanker for the Marine Corps requirement to replace its aging KC-130F Hercules.

McDonnell Douglas YC-15

The YC-15 differed in many details from the earlier McDonnell Douglas AMST proposal. Most importantly, reflecting Air Force pressure to minimise aircraft unit cost, it featured a straight rather than a swept wing. Other cost-saving features included the use of the DC-10 cockpit design, C-141 main landing gear and a non-tapered vertical tail. The first YC-15 flew on 26 August 1975 from Long Beach, California, with the second following on 5 December. They were initially tested at Douglas facilities in Yuma, Arizona, until the Air Force was ready to conduct the side-by-side comparison following the YC-14's first flight on 9 August 1976.

After completion of the Air Force's initial evaluation, McDonnell Douglas proposed a 'Phase II' flight effort to include the installation of a new wing with an increased root chord and span increased to 132.6ft (40.4m). Both prototypes flew initially with a wing of 110.3ft (33.6m) span. The company used the opportunity to evaluate alternate powerplants. On the first YC-15, the No 1 JT8D-17 engine was replaced with a GE/SNECMA CFM-56, returning to flight testing on 16 February 1977. A similar change was made to the second YC-15 to test a prototype Pratt & Whitney JT8D-209; that aircraft returned to the air on 4 March 1977.

LEFT The McDonnell Douglas YC-15 is seen in flight near Yuma, showing the retrofitted large wing and the large CFM-56 engine in the number one position. *Boeing*

BOTTOM Wing growth in the C-15 programme: as initially flown (left, 110.33ft/33.6m); the new wing as retrofitted and flown on YC-15 No 1 (centre, 132.6ft/40.4m); and as planned for C-15A production with CFM-56 engines (right, 146.6ft/44.6m). *Boeing*

BELOW A comparison of the Transall C-160, McDonnell Douglas C-15 and Lockheed C-130. *Boeing*

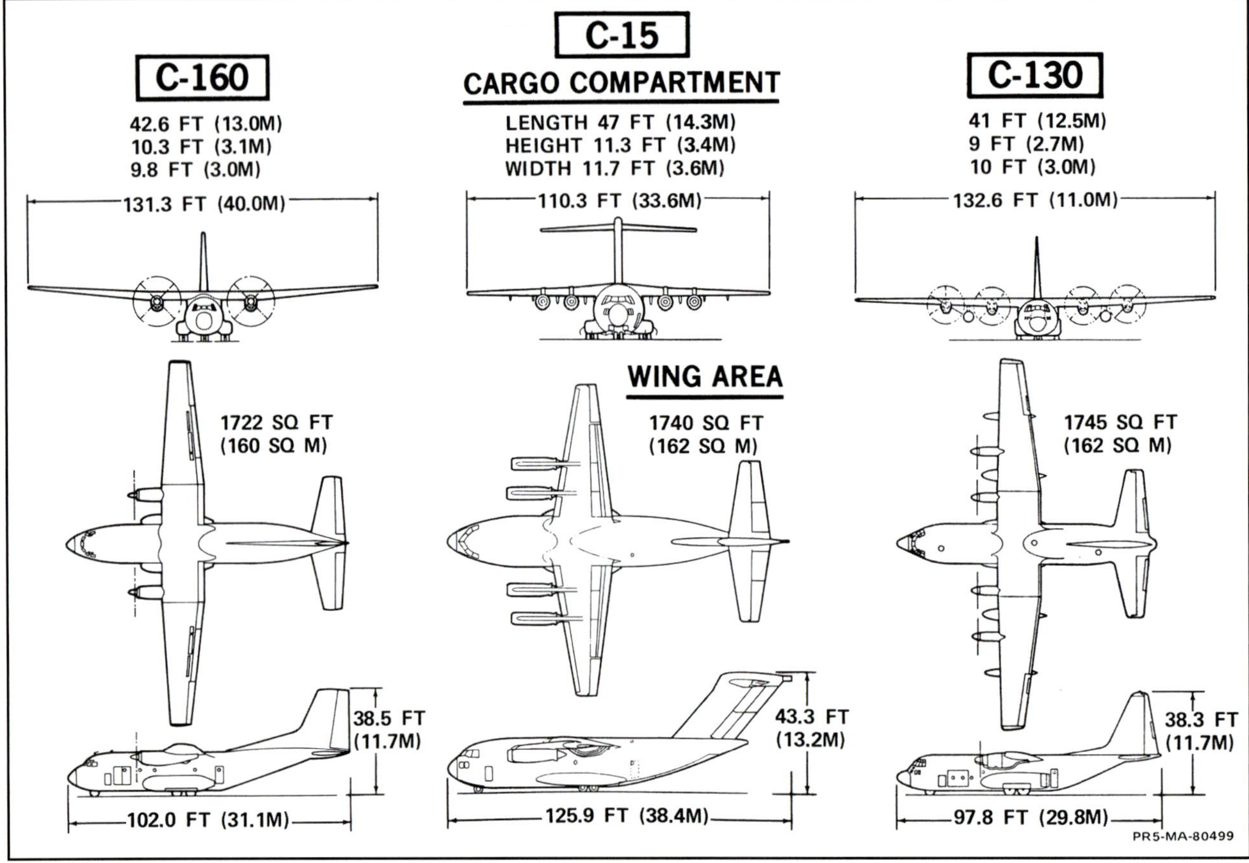

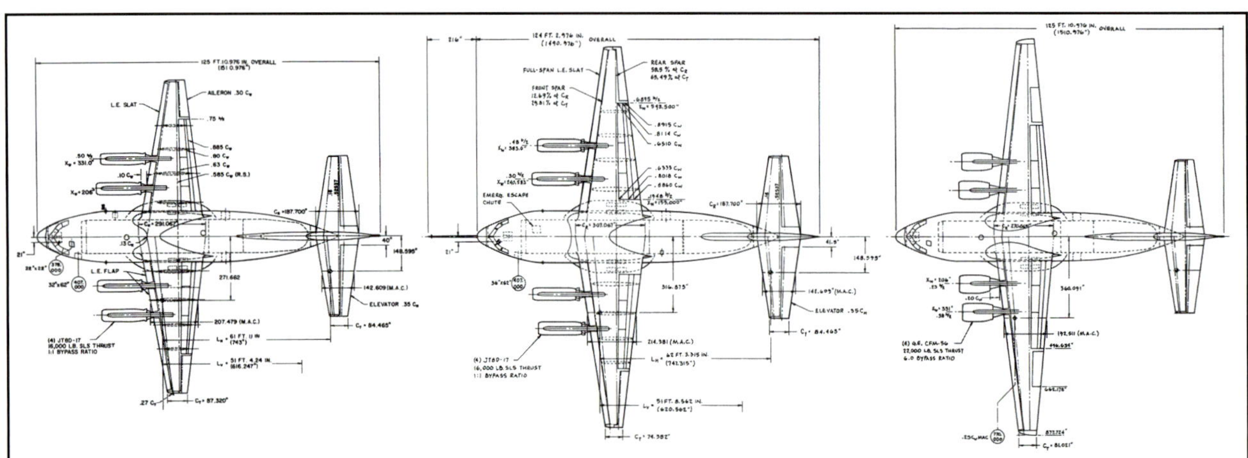

McDonnell Douglas YC-15 prototype	
Powerplant	4 x P&W JT8D-17 turbofans @ 15,500lb (68.95kN) thrust
Alternative engines	1 x CFM-56 (retrofitted to first prototype); 1 x JT8D-209 (retrofitted to second prototype)
Wingspan	110.3ft (33.6m)/132.6ft (40.4m) (retrofitted to first prototype)
Length	124.2ft (37.8m)
Wing area	1,740sq ft (161.7m²)/2,107sq ft (195.8m²) (retrofitted to first prototype)
Cargo compartment	47.0ft (14.33m) long x 11.7ft (3.57m) wide x 11.3ft (3.44m) high
Max TOW	216,680lb (98,370kg)
Payload	78,000lb (35,400kg)
Cruise speed	543mph (874km/h)
Range	1,760nmi (3,260km) or 2,426nmi (4,492km) (with enlarged wing and fuel capacity)

Although designed against specific STOL transport requirements, McDonnell Douglas proposed a number of further potential applications for the aircraft. These included the KC-15 Air Refueller, a STOL Airborne Surgical Hospital (SASH), Cruise Missile Launcher, and Remotely Piloted Vehicle (RPV) Launcher/Controller.

Additionally, McDonnell Douglas investigated commercial derivatives of the C-15 (Model D-915-2) under the Model D-3210 family. Initial work under the 'Stolmaster' name was done in 1975. This was followed up by work

Selected McDonnell Douglas YC-15 commercial derivatives (Model D-3210)	
'Stolmaster'	
D-3210-31	No stretch, 4 x GE/SNECMA CFM-56
D-3210-39	12ft (3.66m) stretch, 4 x GE/SNECMA CFM-56
D-3210-32	22ft (6.71m) stretch, 4 x GE/SNECMA CFM-56
D-3210-49	30ft (9.14m) stretch, 2 x GE CF6-50C engines
D-3210-52	38ft (11.58m) stretch, 2 x Pratt & Whitney JT9D-59 engines
'Jet Trader II'	
D-3210-62	38ft (11.58) stretch, passenger/cargo convertible

ABOVE The DC-15 Remotely Piloted Vehicle (RPV) carrier as proposed to the Government of Iran. The RPVs were from the Teledyne Ryan Model 124/147 family. *Boeing*

BELOW McDonnell Douglas KC-15 proposed tanker version. *Boeing*

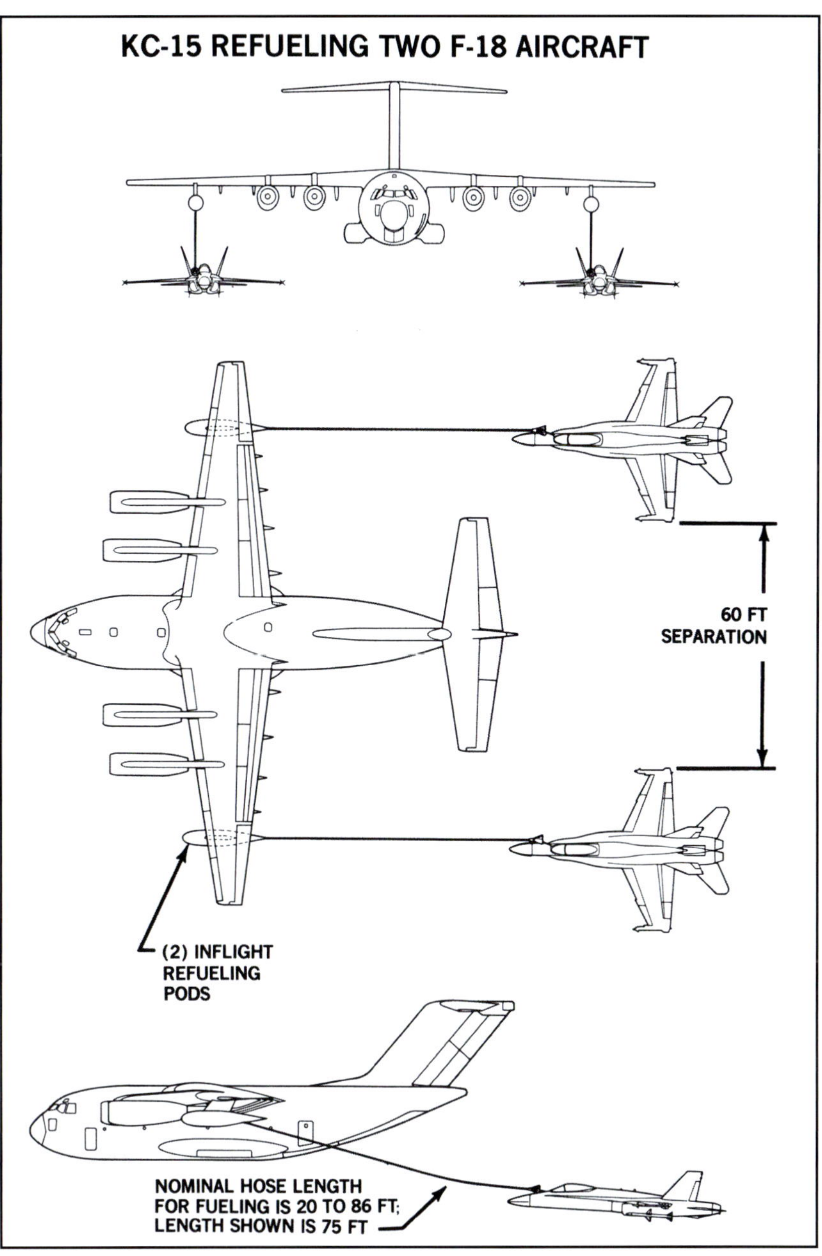

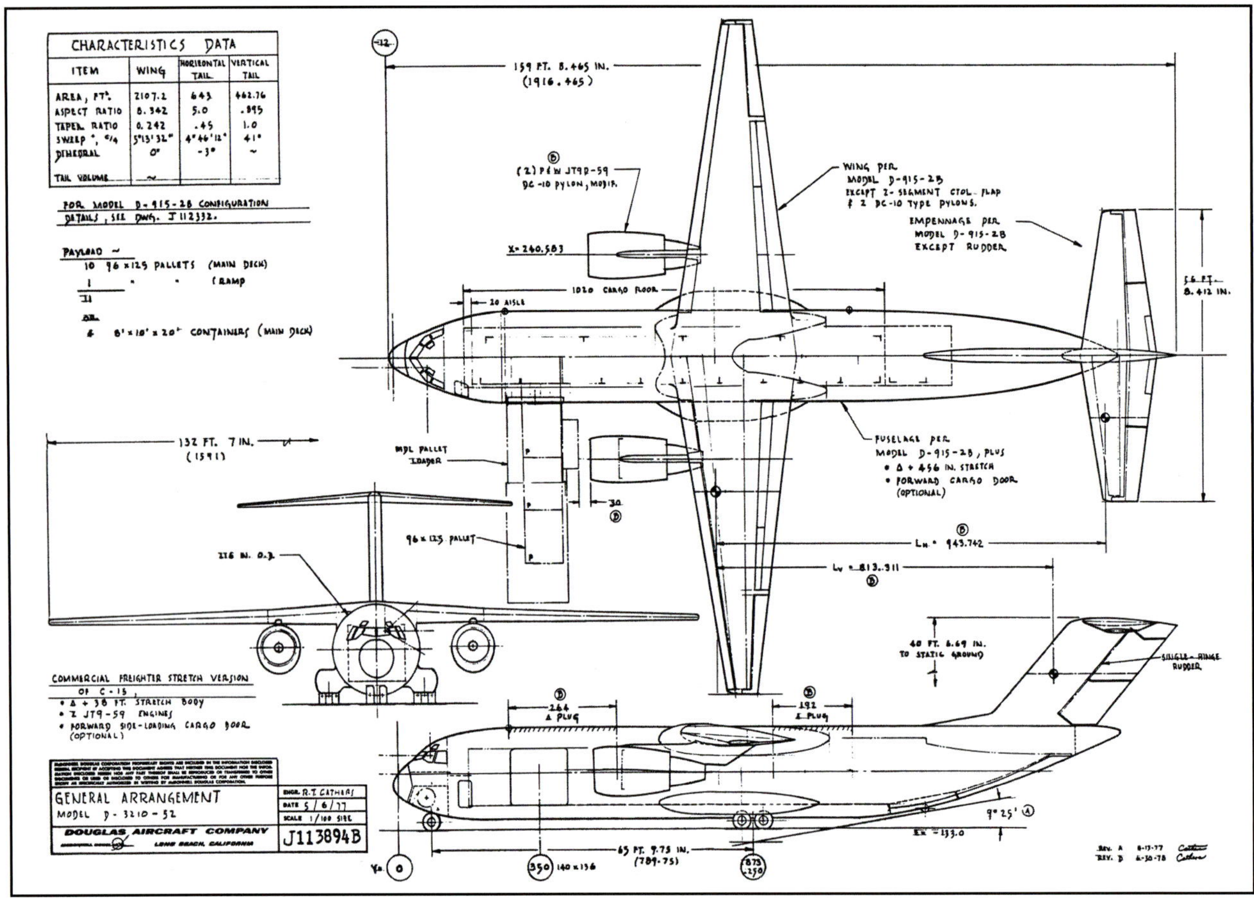

ABOVE The largest C-15 Stolmaster civil stretch was the Model D-3210-52, with two Pratt & Whitney JT9D-59 engines. The pylons and nacelles were to be modified versions of those used on the DC-10. *Boeing*

under the 'Jet Trader II' name in 1978, culminating in a public unveiling at an industry forum where airline comment and feedback was solicited. Although discussions with Flying Tiger Line followed, the project did not proceed further due to the eventual cancellation of the AMST programme.

AMST: An impressive program overtaken by events

During flight testing, both the YC-14 and YC-15 exceeded their specified performance goals and, when the test programme concluded, the Air Force's Test & Evaluation Command found both aircraft to be satisfactory. The Air Force Systems Command (AFSC) initiated the source selection process with the technical proposals due on 15 November 1977. The selection process was to take ninety days with the award of a Full Scale Development (FSD) contract set for April 1978. But that didn't happen.

Circumstances had changed, causing a rethink of the AMST concept. The Arab-Israeli War of 1973 exposed the need for the United States to have a better global response capability. While MAC had been able to fly urgent supplies to Israel using its fleet of C-5 and C-141 aircraft, it had been hampered by the vast distances that needed to be covered – on average 6,450 miles (10,380km) either way – without en route facilities or sufficient air-refuelling capability. This highlighted the need for greater strategic airlift capability.

At the same time, the Office of the Secretary of Defense (OSD) and Congress were beginning to ask whether the C-130 might do most of the intended job of the AMST for less money. Faced with these pressures, MAC issued a revised Required Operational Requirement in December 1975, ROC 9-75, broadening the mission of the AMST and giving it more of a strategic role. However, the political battles continued, with the Air Force pushing for its revised AMST, Lockheed lobbying directly for the continued production of the C-130, and the Army wavering in its support for the AMST as it was in competition for funds with its heavy-lift helicopter requirement.

The AMST programme was also competing for funds against other, pressing demands. The recent Middle East conflict had highlighted the need to add air-refuelling capability to the C-141 and to provide much greater tanker capability in the form of ATCA (discussed below). Adding to the pressure, the C-5 fleet needed an extensive wing modification effort to restore its capability.

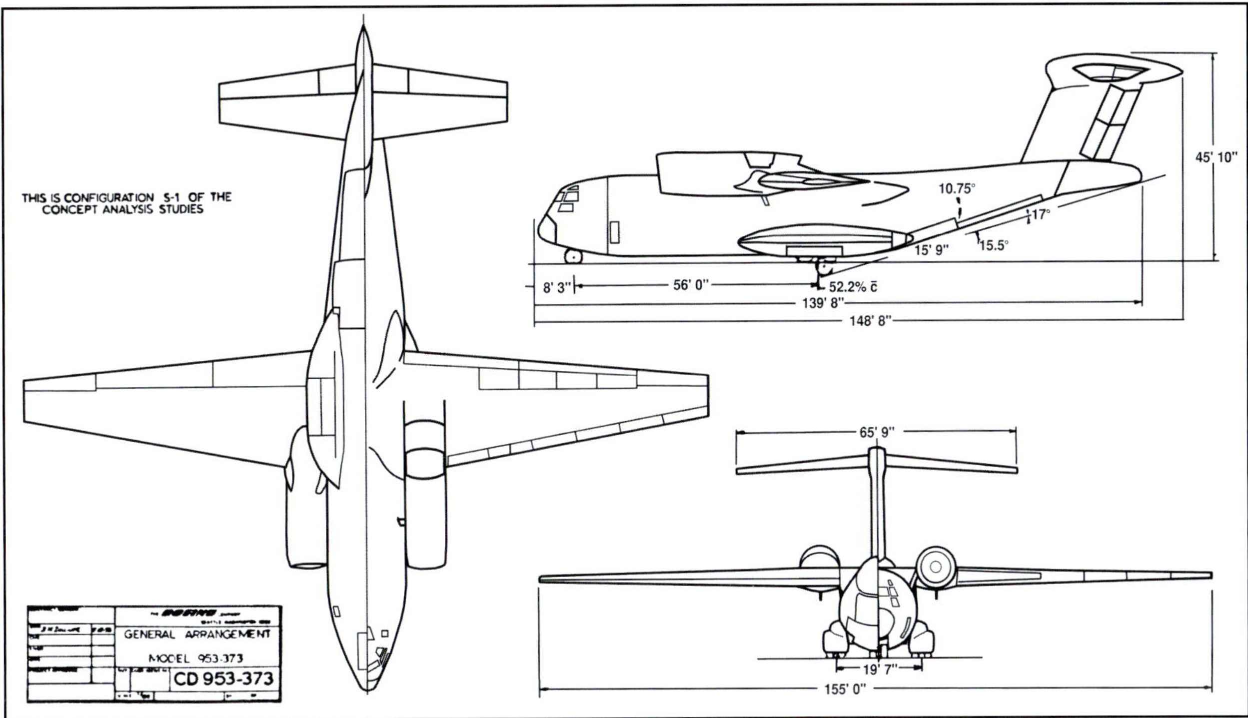

ABOVE **The Boeing Model 953-373 was one of many studies of stretched airlifters based on the YC-14. The overall length was increased by 16ft 11in (5.16m) and the wing was simplified and span increased by 26ft 1in (7.95m). Conversely, the vertical tail was reduced in height by 2ft 4in (71m).** *Boeing*

BELOW **General arrangement of the stretched C-15B with four high-bypass turbofans (either the GE/SNECMA CFM-56 or the Pratt &Whitney JT10D). The proposal added six feet to the fuselage ahead of the wings and eight feet aft, together with an enlarged wing.** *Boeing*

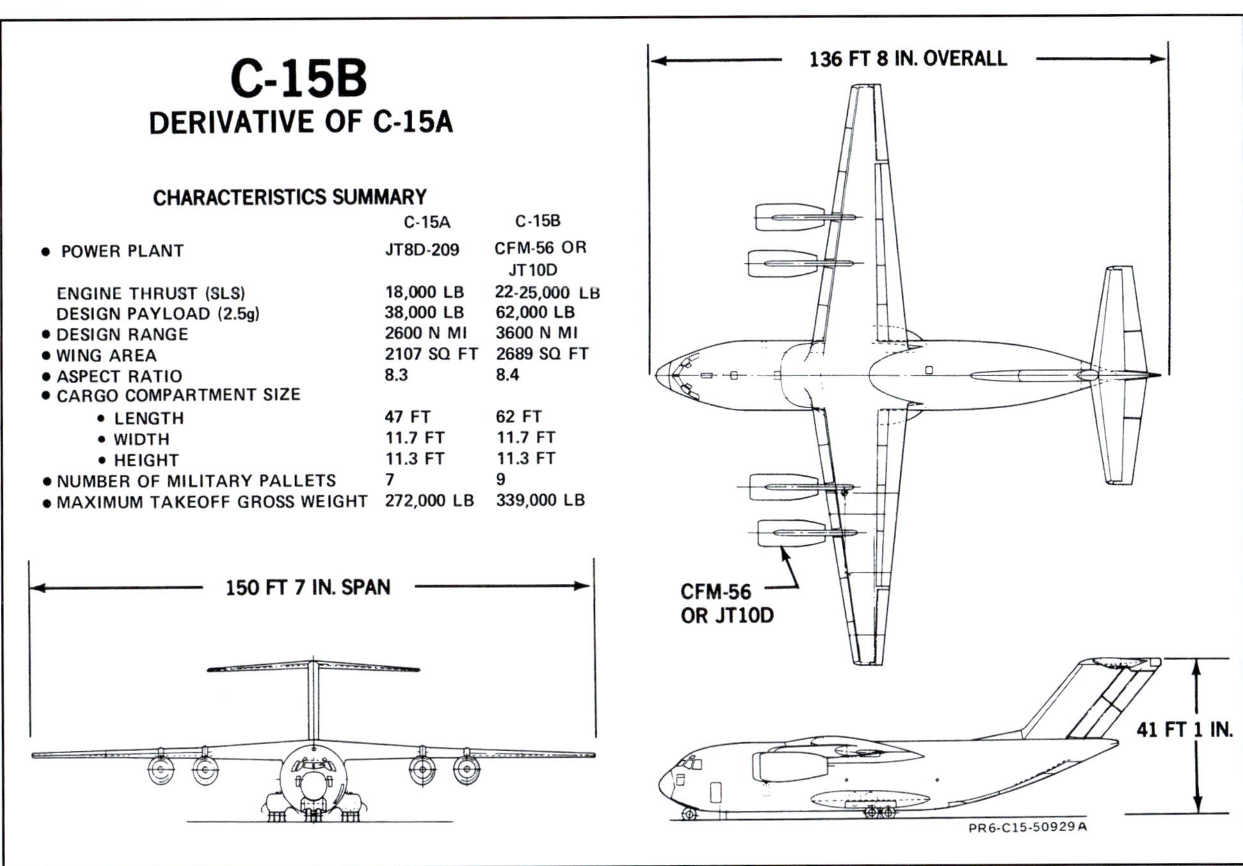

	C-15A	C-15B
• POWER PLANT	JT8D-209	CFM-56 OR JT10D
ENGINE THRUST (SLS)	18,000 LB	22-25,000 LB
DESIGN PAYLOAD (2.5g)	38,000 LB	62,000 LB
• DESIGN RANGE	2600 N MI	3600 N MI
• WING AREA	2107 SQ FT	2689 SQ FT
• ASPECT RATIO	8.3	8.4
• CARGO COMPARTMENT SIZE		
• LENGTH	47 FT	62 FT
• WIDTH	11.7 FT	11.7 FT
• HEIGHT	11.3 FT	11.3 FT
• NUMBER OF MILITARY PALLETS	7	9
• MAXIMUM TAKEOFF GROSS WEIGHT	272,000 LB	339,000 LB

LEFT A display model of the proposed C-15B showing the stretched fuselage. Less obvious are the repositioned CFM-56 engines and the enlarged wing. *Boeing*

Moreover, given the newly redefined need for an AMST derivative to fulfil a strategic role, there was no way that either the YC-14 or YC-15 could be ordered into production. The new aircraft would need both a longer range and a larger cargo floor, which in turn would mean new wings and more powerful engines – resulting in a substantially different aircraft.

The final nail in the AMST coffin came with the political change in Washington, bringing in President Carter who, in an effort to reduce defence expenditure, withdrew funding for the AMST in the 1978 budget. The AMST programme as originally conceived was effectively dead.

However, the effort would be far from wasted. The Air Force began to consider the need for a wide-body airlifter to supplement or ultimately replace the C-141 that might have at least double the range of the AMST-class aircraft. At the same time McDonnell Douglas began to study how to expand its aircraft to fit the new requirements. The Air Force titled this new program 'C-X', for Cargo Experimental. As described later, it eventually led to the C-17, arguably the most capable airlifter yet flown.

Postscript: EC-15 Airborne Command Post prototype

By 1980 the Air Force was studying possible paths to replacing its various models of converted KC-135 Airborne Command Posts. McDonnell Douglas Corporation (MDC) saw its nascent C-X as a prime contender, and stressed that to provide the operational flexibility for survivability the replacement aircraft would need:

- Short-field take-off and landing capability
- Unprepared field operations capability
- Specified payload weight and volume capacity (allowing for growth)
- Fuel efficiency
- Long-term dispersal and live-aboard capability

To reduce programme risk, MDC suggested retrieving one of the YC-15s from desert storage at Davis Monthan AFB and converting it into a test bed for the production configuration for the yet-to-be developed C-X airframe. Given an immediate C-X go-ahead, MDC projected that the production EC-X could be in service by 1986. This offer was not accepted, but led to extended studies of the EC-17 version of the C-17, which. as described below, would become the eventual winner of the C-X competition.

1980: The C-X programme

The original AMST specification may have been overtaken by events, but the underlying need for a greatly enhanced airlifting capability remained. Notwithstanding the AMST programme's imminent cancellation in December 1979, both the armed forces and the aircraft companies were already working on the kind of aircraft that should succeed it. The only aircraft that could carry the Army's outsize equipment was the C-5, but it was limited to operating only from substantial, fully prepared airfields; the only aircraft that

BELOW The inboard profile of the projected EC-15 test bed, showing the Advanced Refuelling Boom that was being developed by McDonnell Douglas under separate contract. *Boeing*

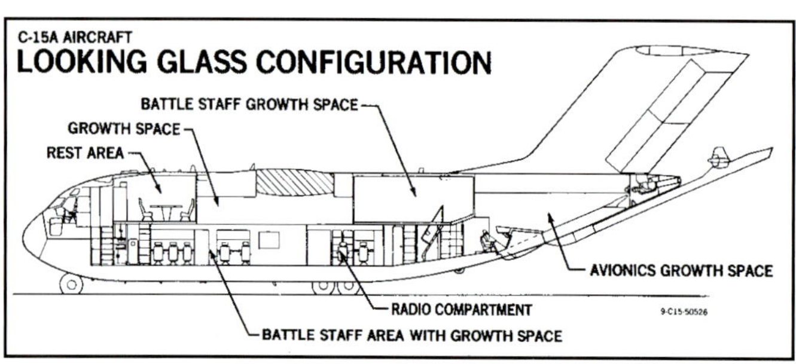

BELOW Internal arrangements of the McDonnell Douglas EC-15 test bed. *Boeing*

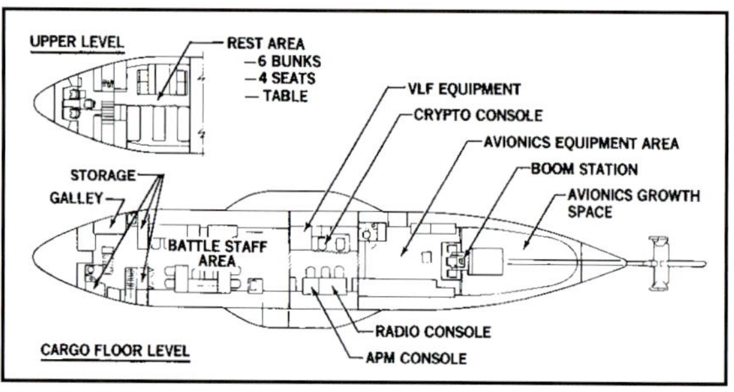

could operate from forward airfields was the C-130, but it could not carry the XM-1 tank or various other outsize items of infantry equipment.

The decision by President Carter and his Defense Secretary Harold Brown to cancel AMST was not supported by those who fully understood the situation. The Army Chief of Staff, General Bernard Rogers, and General Alexander Haig (who commanded the United States Army in Europe) both voiced their opposition to the decision, expressing their views to the Senate Armed Services Committee.

Appearing before the House Budget Committee, Air Force Secretary John Stetson and Chief of Staff General Lew Allen expressed the view that it was 'essential to identify and produce a new wide-body tactical airlift aircraft to replace the C-130 and to keep pace with Army requirements.' Despite the strength of these views, the Carter government nevertheless cancelled AMST. However, momentum was already building for the kind of aircraft that would be needed.

In the last quarter of 1979 the Air Force's requirements crystallised into a new project designated the C-X. The USAF documented its needs for additional airlift capability in a Mission Element Statement (MENS), which was formally approved by the Department of Defense on 28 November 1980. This stressed that the capability to operate out of a small austere airfield was a desirable feature, but only if it did not impose a penalty on the primary mission of 'intertheatre airlift'. The overall aim was to combine the Air Force's strategic and tactical requirements in a single aircraft, capable of replacing the C-141 while also being able to operate out of short, semi-prepared airstrips.

Meanwhile, the Air Force had issued a Request for Proposals (RFP) for C-X during October. The requirements called for a strategic range of 2,400nmi (4,440km) with a 120,000lb (54,480kg) payload, coupled with the ability to operate from a 3,000ft (915m) austere airfield. The RFP allowed for either a newly designed aircraft or a derivative of an existing aircraft, provided the latter could meet all the requirements. In response, Boeing, Lockheed and McDonnell Douglas all chose to propose new aircraft.

Lockheed also proposed an adaptation of the C-5. Although this was unsuccessful, the C-5 was put back into production in 1985, in an unrelated decision.

Boeing Model 1050 C-X proposal

Capitalising on its experience with the YC-14, Boeing's starting point in its response to the C-X competition was its Model 953-921. This was essentially a bridge between the earlier aircraft and the eventual submission, which Boeing promoted as the C-16. (It should be noted that this was not an official designation assigned by the Air Force – the 'C-16' title had been reserved for four different projects at one time or another before being permanently skipped.) However, the path to the Boeing C-X encompassed several different design families, all under the generic designation of Model 1050. As part of this process, Boeing evaluated two-engine (Model 1050-2xx), three-engine (Model 1050-3xx) and four-engine (Model 1050-4xx) variants in parallel, before opting for a three-engine configuration.

The eventual aircraft, the Model 1050-307, showed more external resemblance to the YC-14 than some of the intermediate designs, which had a more conventional appearance. However, it was a much larger aeroplane than the YC-14, with a third engine mounted at the base of the T-tail. Boeing emphasised the survivability advantages of such a configuration, with the engines being set well apart and fed by separate fuel systems, and with the aft engine shielded from ground fire.

Boeing Model 1050 C-X proposal	
Powerplant	3 x GE CF6-80A1 turbofans @ 48,000lb (213.51kN) thrust
Wingspan	159ft (48.5m)/165ft (50.3m) with winglets
Length	183.8ft (56.06m)
Height	52.0 ft (15.85m)
Wing area	3,299sq ft (353m²)
Max TOW	497,700lb (266,000kg)
Payload	48,870lb (22,190kg)

BELOW General arrangement of the Boeing Model 953-921; the company's initial C-X design. While retaining elements of the C-14 fuselage and stretching it, the new wing and engines abandoned the previous STOL design. *Boeing*

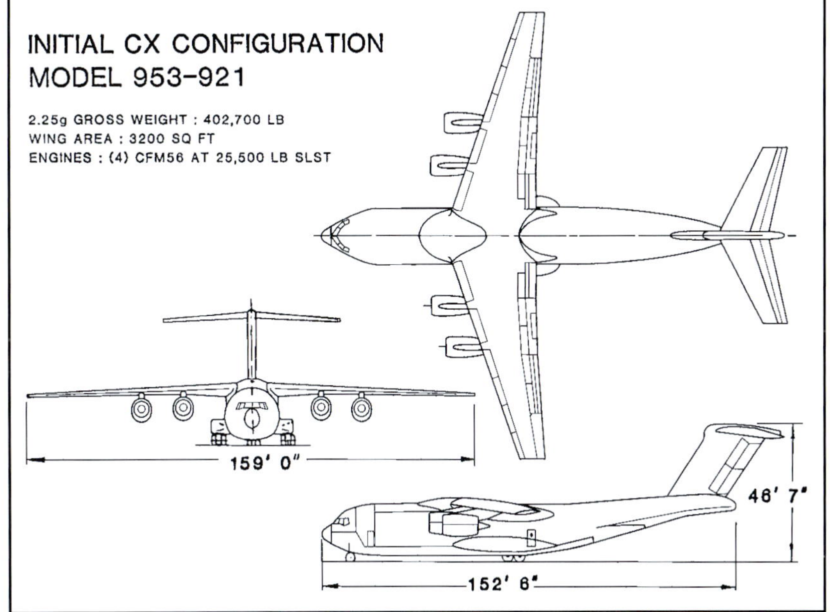

AIRPLANE/ENGINE OPTIONS
SMALL
400-450K
MEDIUM
450-500K
LARGE
500-600K
-011,-921
-016,-018
-009
CF6-80A
JT9D-7R4D
-004
CFM56
JT10D-232
-006A
CF6-32
JT10D-236
RB211-535
-005
CF6-32C
JT10D-236
RB211-535
-007A, -017
CF6-80A
JT9D-7R4D
-008
CF6-80C
JT9D-7R4H

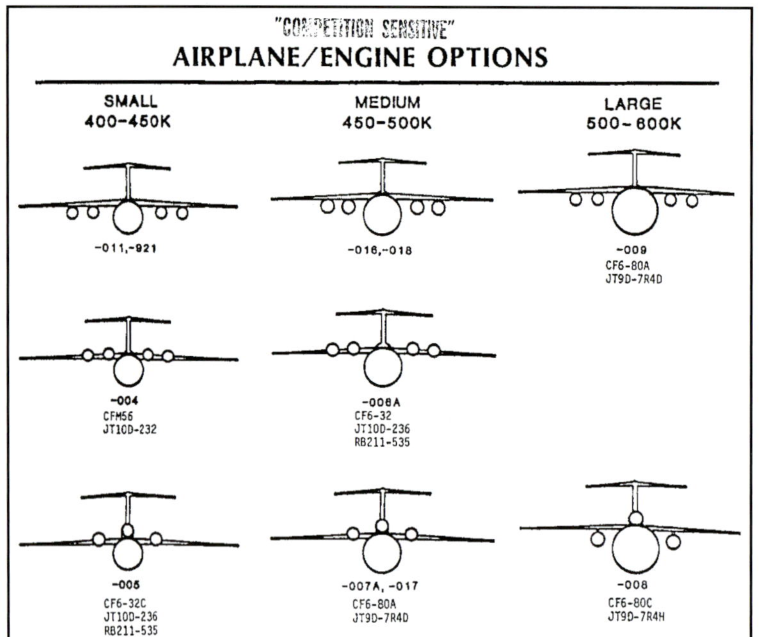

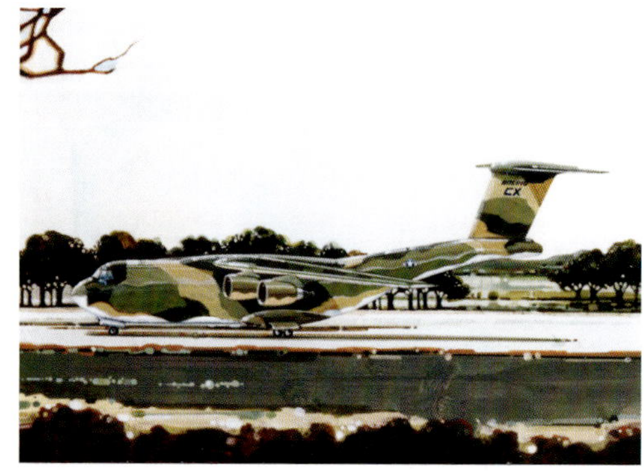

ABOVE Artwork depicting the Boeing Model 953-921. *Boeing*

LEFT This chart shows some of the C-X design and engine options considered by Boeing in April 1980, before the Air Force finalized its requirements. Neither the fuselage diameter nor the gross weight had been decided. Boeing designations for these preliminary designs were in the Model 1050-0xx series. *Boeing*

BELOW General arrangement of the Boeing Model 1050-201, a twin-engine C-X design. Twin-engine aircraft were in the -2xx series, three-engine in the -3xx range and four-engined designs were in the -4xx range. *Boeing*

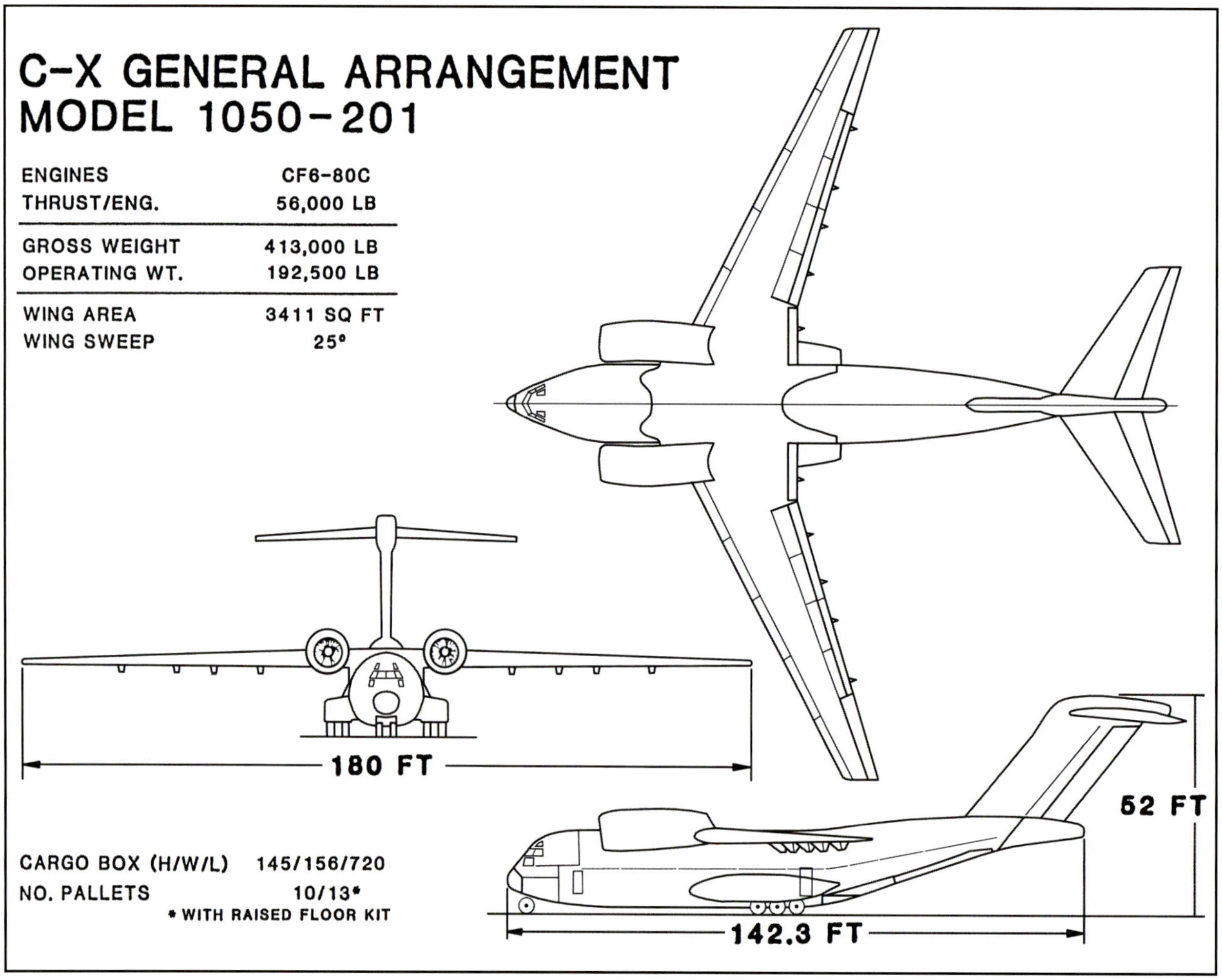

C-X GENERAL ARRANGEMENT
MODEL 1050-201
ENGINES CF6-80C
THRUST/ENG. 56,000 LB
GROSS WEIGHT 413,000 LB
OPERATING WT. 192,500 LB
WING AREA 3411 SQ FT
WING SWEEP 25°
180 FT
52 FT
142.3 FT
CARGO BOX (H/W/L) 145/156/720
NO. PALLETS 10/13*
* WITH RAISED FLOOR KIT

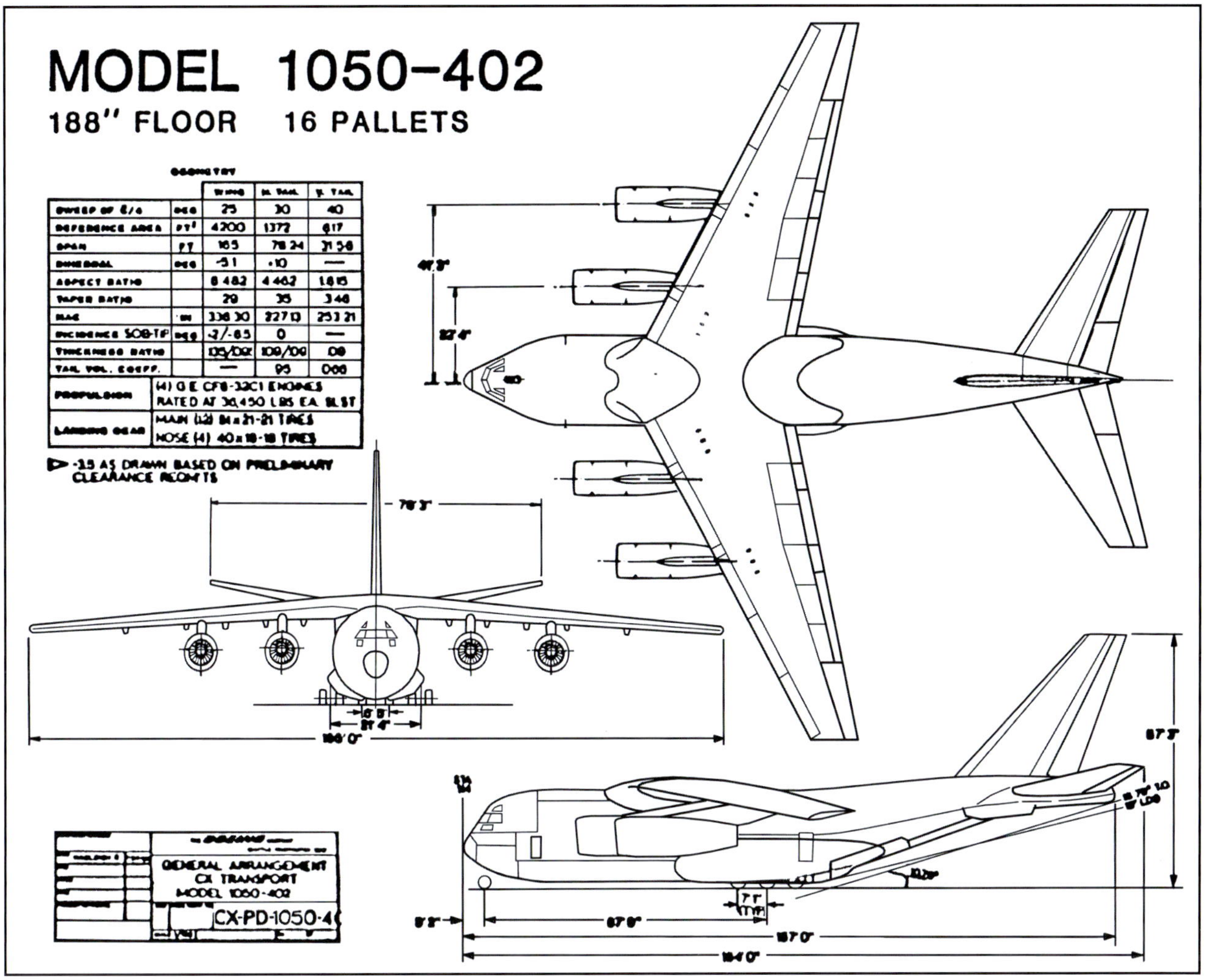

MODEL 1050-402

188" FLOOR 16 PALLETS

GEOMETRY

		WING	H. TAIL	V. TAIL
SWEEP OF C/4	DEG	25	30	40
REFERENCE AREA	FT²	4200	1372	617
SPAN	FT	165	78 24	31 58
DIHEDRAL	DEG	-3 1	+10	—
ASPECT RATIO		6 482	4 462	1 615
TAPER RATIO		29	35	346
MAC	IN	336 30	227 13	253 21
INCIDENCE SOB-TIP	DEG	-2/-6 5	0	—
THICKNESS RATIO		135/092	109/109	09
TAIL VOL. COEFF.		—	95	066
PROPULSION		(4) G E CF6-32C1 ENGINES RATED AT 36,450 LBS EA SLST		
LANDING GEAR		MAIN (12) 54 x 21-21 TIRES NOSE (4) 40 x 18-18 TIRES		

-3.5 AS DRAWN BASED ON PRELIMINARY CLEARANCE REQM'TS

GENERAL ARRANGEMENT CX TRANSPORT MODEL 1050-402

CX-PD-1050-4

ABOVE General arrangement of Boeing Model 1050-402, a four-engined C-X design. By September 1980, Boeing had focussed on the tri-jet option for further development and suspended work on the two- and four-engine alternatives. *Boeing*

BELOW General arrangement of Boeing's Model 1050-307; this was the basis for Boeing's proposed Model 1050 as the 'C-16'. The 'C-16' designation was used by Boeing but was never formally issued by the Air Force. *Boeing*

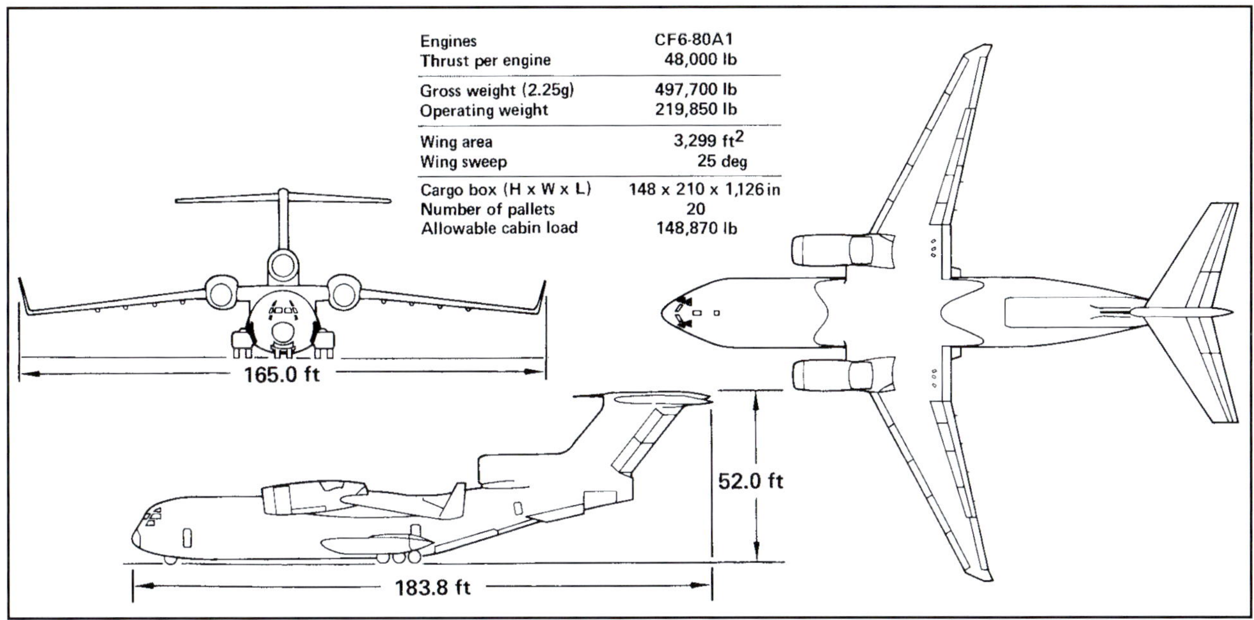

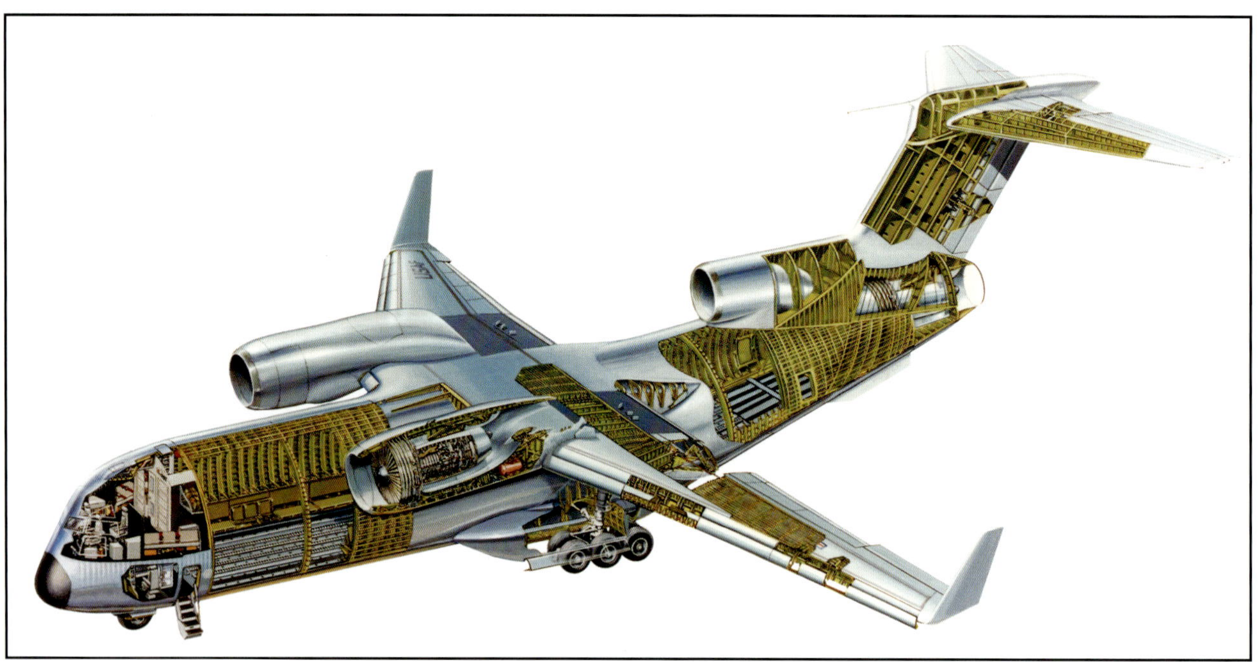

ABOVE A cutaway view of the proposed 'C-16'. *Boeing*

BELOW A side view of a Boeing 'C-16' model painted in the 1980s 'European One' camouflage scheme. *John Aldaz collection*

BELOW The Boeing 'C-16' posed with YC-14 and 727-200 models. *Boeing*

BELOW This head-on view emphasizes the 'Tri-Jet' layout of the Boeing Model 1050. *Boeing*

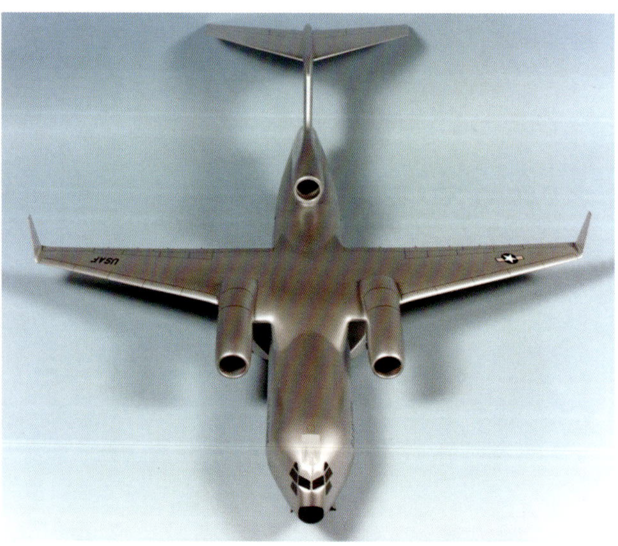

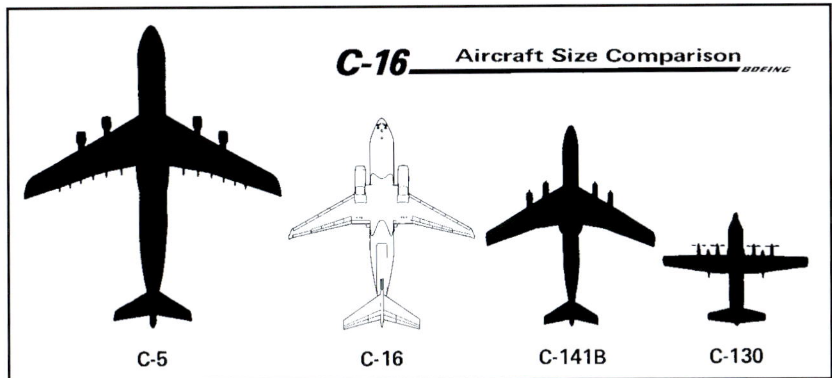

ABOVE A size comparison between the Boeing 'C-16' and other contemporary airlifters. *Boeing*

McDonnell Douglas Model D-9000 C-X proposal (C-17A)

Douglas responded vigorously to the opportunity offered by the C-X programme. After receiving the RFP, the company halted nearly all work on its proposed commercial Advanced Technology Medium Range transport (ATMR) to concentrate on the C-X response. The significance of this move lies in the fact that just a few months earlier the company had scaled down its work on potential stretched versions of the DC-10, switching resources to the ATMR programme; it was intending the ATMR to compete with the Boeing 757 in the Boeing 727 replacement market.

Douglas studied five basic design options, starting with what was essentially its earlier YC-15 aircraft and progressively scaling it up by broadening the fuselage, then increasing the wing sweep to 25°. All of these designs had the same basic configuration, with high-mounted wings carrying four podded engines, and a T-tail. In each case engineers evaluated the design with both the GE/SNECMA CFM-56 engine rated at 25,500lb (11.3kN) thrust and the more powerful P&W JT10D rated at 32,000lb (14.25kN). (During the course of the programme in November 1980, Pratt & Whitney rebranded its engine product line, with the JT10D becoming the PW2037. Thrust was increased to 37,000lb (164.58kN) with the PW2037, and 40,400lb (179.71kN) with the PW2040, which received the military designation of F117-PW-100 for use on the C-17.)

McDonnell Douglas Model D-9000 C-X proposal (C-17)	
Powerplant	4 x P&W PW2037 turbofans @ 37,000lb (164.58kN) thrust
Wingspan	165ft (50.29m)/169.8ft (51.76m) with winglets
Length	159.1ft (48.49m)
Height	55.1ft (16.79m)
Wing area	3,800sq ft (353m²)
Max TOW	585,000lb (265,300kg)
Max payload	169,000lb (76,640kg)

BELOW The McDonnell Douglas C-X Configurations 0 to 3 were based on the C-15 and were incrementally enlarged in size and capability. *Boeing*

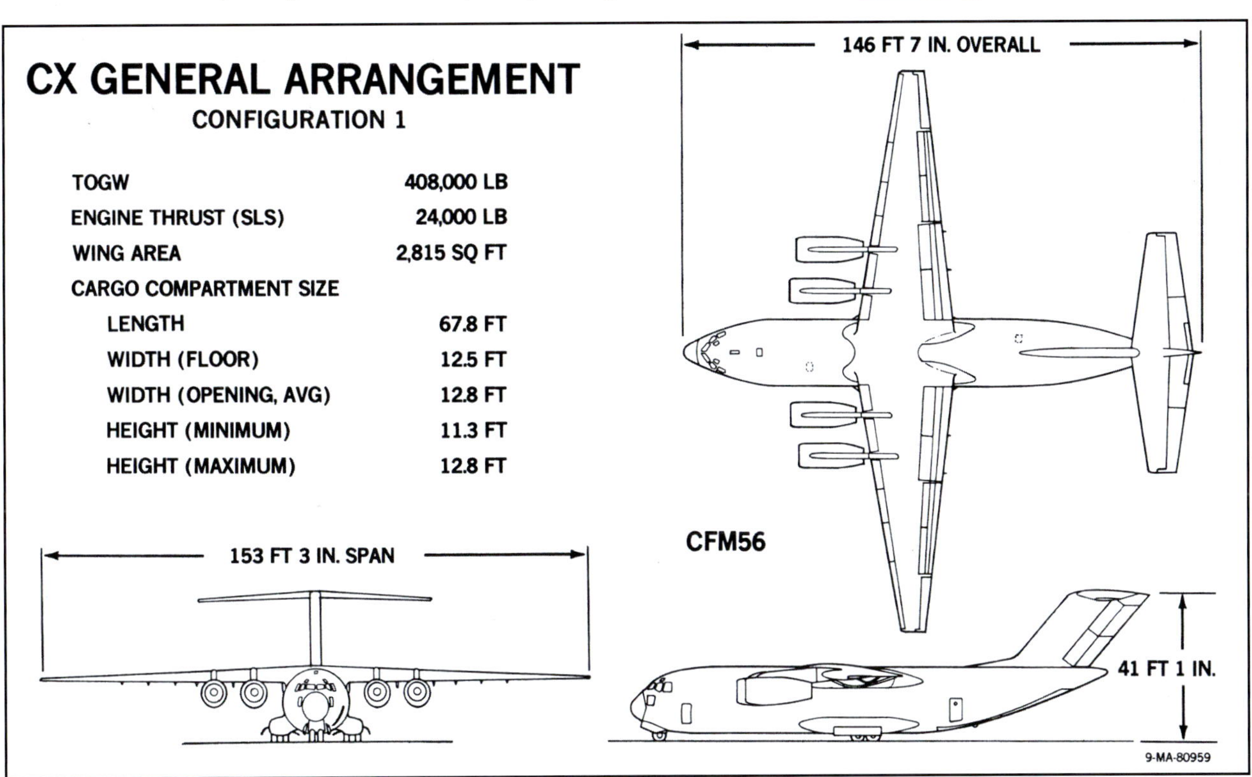

CX GENERAL ARRANGEMENT

CONFIGURATION 4

TOGW	530,000 LB
ENGINE THRUST (SLS)	32,000 LB
WING AREA	3,460 SQ FT
CARGO COMPARTMENT SIZE	
LENGTH	67.8 FT
WIDTH (FLOOR)	15.7 FT
WIDTH (OPENING, AVG)	14.5 FT
HEIGHT (MINIMUM)	11.3 FT
HEIGHT (MAXIMUM)	12.8 FT

164 FT 8 IN. OVERALL

169 FT 10 IN. SPAN

JT10D

43 FT 9 IN.

9-MA-80958

ABOVE **The McDonnell Douglas C-X Configuration 4, put forward at the end of 1979, was the largest option and the only one with a swept wing.** *Boeing*

BELOW **A McDonnell Douglas 'narrow-body' C-X wind tunnel model with extended forward fuselage and 'long duct' engine nacelles.** *Boeing*

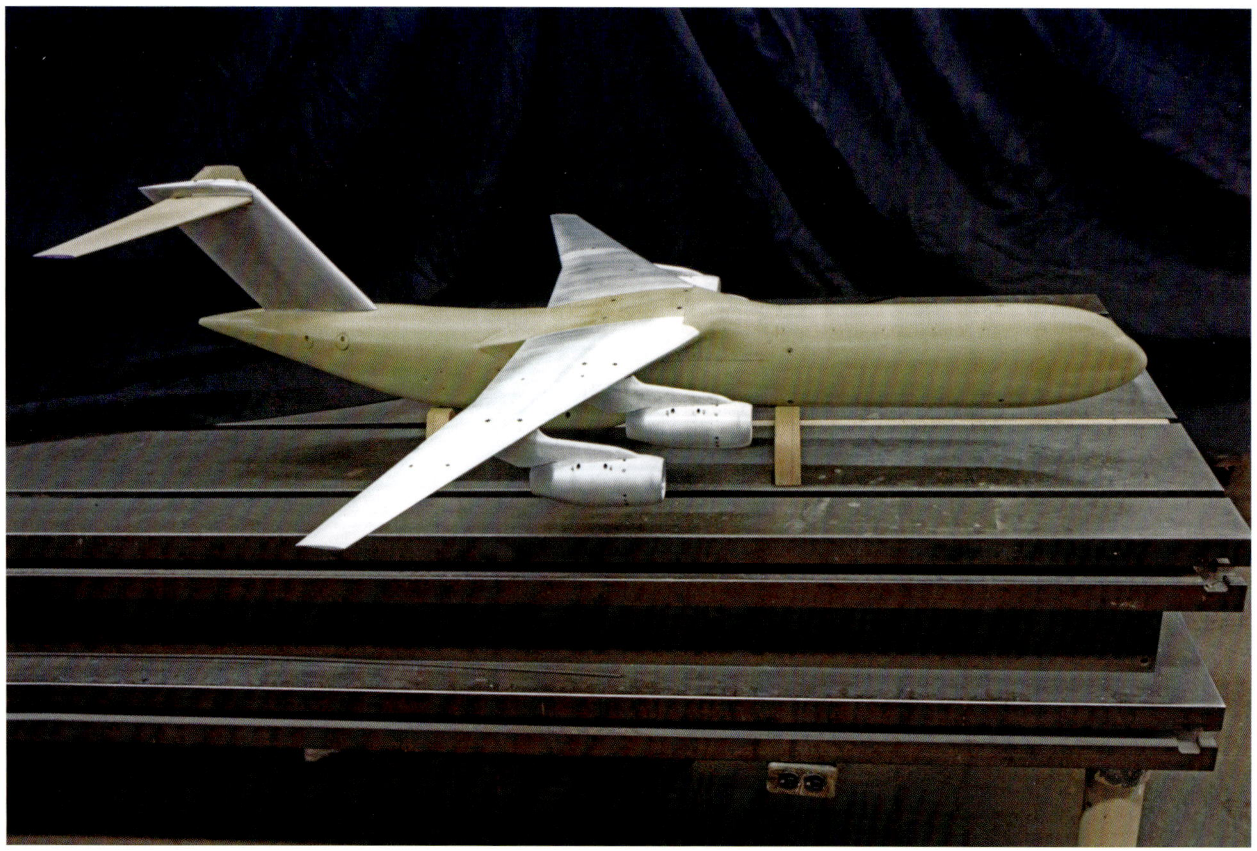

ABOVE This cutaway artwork shows the McDonnell Douglas Model D-9000 C-X submission. The APU in the tailcone would later be moved to the landing gear sponson for accessibility. *Boeing*

Lockheed ATA variants

	Small	Medium	Large
Powerplant	2 x GE/SNECMA CFM-56 22,000lb (97.86kN) thrust	2 x GE/SNECMA CFM-56 22,000lb (97.86kN) thrust	4 x GE/SNECMA CFM-56 22,000lb (97.86kN) thrust
Wingspan	93.2ft (28.41m)	121.0ft (36.88m)	150.0ft (45.72m)
Length	117.6ft (35.84m)	132.3ft (40.33m)	162.4ft (49.50m)
Height	32.6ft (9.94m)	39.0ft (11.89m)	39.0ft (11.89m)
Floor length	43.3ft (13.20m)	53ft (16.15m)	83ft (25.30m)
Wing area	1,450sq ft (134.7m^2)	2,069sq ft (192.2m^2)	2,746sq ft (255.1m^2)
Max TOW	128,979lb (58,504kg)	237,600lb (107,774kg)	304,000lb (137,892kg)
Range	1,000nmi (1,850km)	n/a	3,340mni (6,190km)
Payload	32,000lb (14,520kg)	55,000lb (24,950kg)	72,5000lb (32,660kg)

Lockheed Model LG-610 C-X proposal

Lockheed-Georgia proposed the LG-610 design for the C-X competition. It was a conventionally configured airlifter that shared the high wing and T-tail, both derived from research carried out for the LG-603 Advanced Transport Aircraft (ATA).

Revealed in 1974, Lockheed positioned its ATA concept as a family of cargo transports; they shared a near-common wing but featured different fuselages to optimise a particular operational need. The designs all incorporated what is now regarded as a first-generation supercritical wing.

Lockheed never brought the ATA programme to fruition, although it continued design work for the rest of the decade. And later, when the C-X

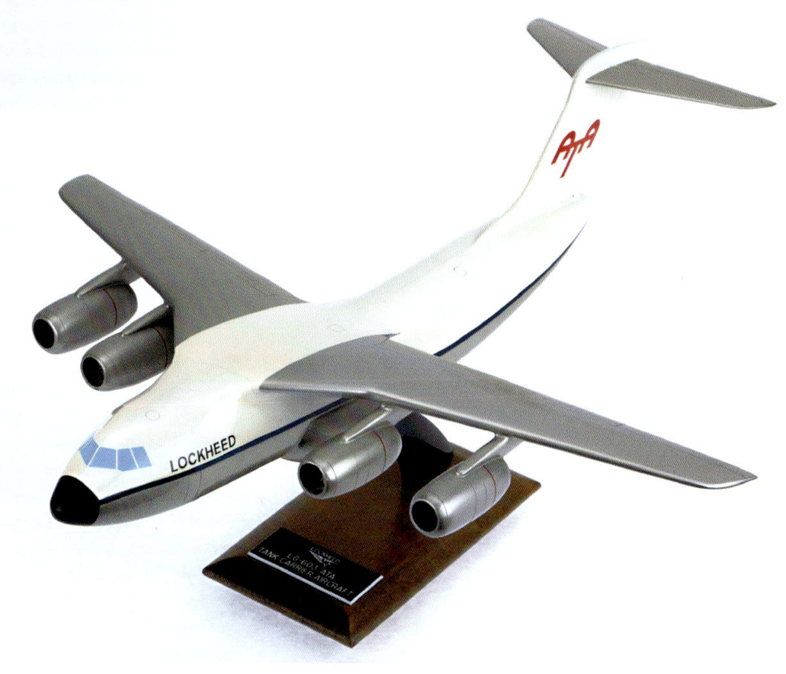

RIGHT A display model of the Lockheed LG-603 Advanced Transport Aircraft (ATA). *John Aldaz collection*

programme began, engineers were able to use ATA as the basis for C-X design work, designating the project as the LG-610. During the refinement process, the LG-610 configuration team decided to increase the cargo hold width by nearly one-third, extended the fuselage tailcone to reduce drag, and increased the size of the wing-to-fuselage fairings.

Lockheed LG-610 C-X proposal	
Powerplant	4 x P&W PW2037 turbofans @ 37,000lb (164.58kN) thrust
Wingspan	169.47ft (51.65m)
Length	177.4ft (54.1m)
Height	49.78ft (15.17m)
Max TOW	480,000lb (217,720kg)
Payload	130,000lb (58,970kg) at 2,500nmi (4,630km) range

Despite the Air Force's technical interest in drag-reducing winglets, Lockheed chose not to include them, citing wind tunnel results where '...the anticipated induced drag improvement was easily obtained but this was largely offset by increases in profile drag.' Lockheed cited additional drawbacks, including difficult construction and displacement of an aileron mass-balance weight. It appears that the company's entry was eliminated at an early stage of the C-X competition.

The outcome of the C-X competition

In April 1981 the Secretary of the Air Force announced that Lockheed's C-5 proposal did not meet the minimum C-X requirements and would not be considered further in the competition, but would still be considered as a separate, alternative airlifter. As a result, Lockheed submitted several unsolicited C-5 proposals to both the USAF and the Secretary of the Air Force, culminating in September 1981 with a design known as the C-5N. At the same time, Boeing proposed the 747 as an alternative.

In August 1981 the Air Force completed its evaluation of the C-X proposals and announced McDonnell Douglas as the winner, giving the aircraft the designation of C-17. However, despite having carried out a formal procurement competition with a clear winner meeting all the originally specified requirements, no immediate full-scale development order was forthcoming.

Budgetary constraints only allowed limited development funding for the new aircraft, forcing the Air Force to look for alternative means of meeting its short-term airlift requirements. These included ordering more C-5s or KC-10s, ordering the 747, or expanding the Civil Reserve Air Fleet. Congress allocated $50 million for this option, but that prompted an 18 December 1981 letter from the US General Accounting Office expressing concern that, because no formal competition existed to satisfy this new requirement, there was a danger of making single-source awards for multi-billion-dollar contracts.

ABOVE The Lockheed LG-610 C-X proposal. *US Air Force*

BELOW Lockheed LG-610 general arrangement. *Lockheed*

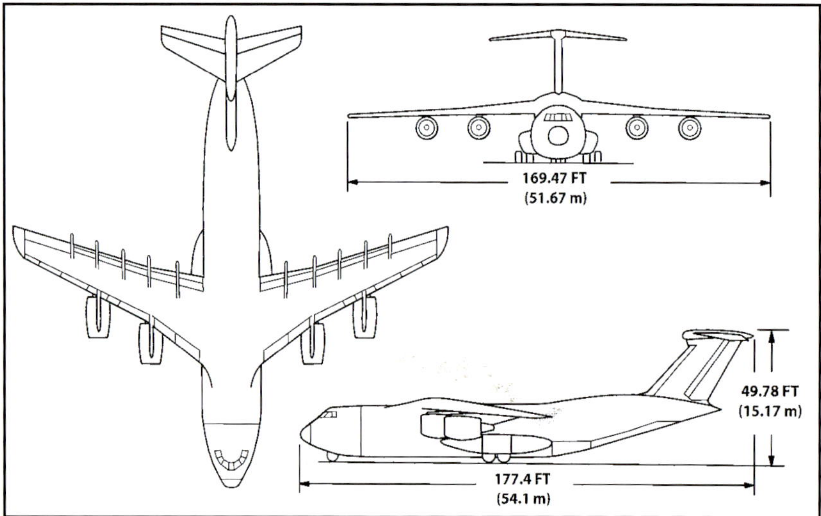

McDonnell Douglas EC-17 Advanced Airborne Command Post

The McDonnell Douglas C-17 would have a protracted gestation period. Due to restricted government funding, MDC was initially awarded a limited development contract and had to work at a reduced pace until December 1985, when a full-scale development contract was finally authorised. In the meantime, the company looked to further exploit the aircraft's capabilities, which coincided with the Air Force's need to replace the EC-135 in the role of World-Wide Airborne Command Post (WWABNCP).

ABOVE This McDonnell Douglas EC-17 model displays the all-white anti-flash paint scheme in common with the Boeing E-4 Airborne Command Post, and a SATCOM antenna radome on top of the fuselage. *Boeing*

ABOVE An early concept for the McDonnell Douglas EC-17 as an Airborne Command Post with a large SATCOM antenna radome and no refuelling boom. *Boeing*

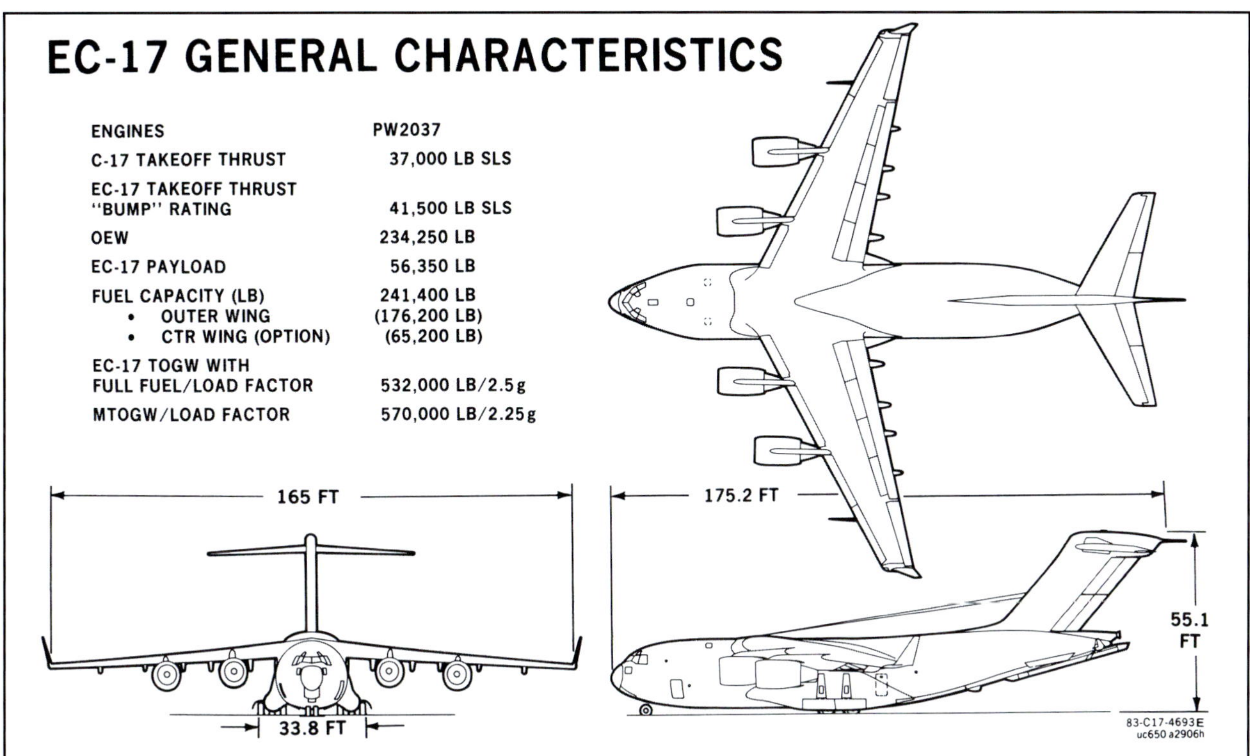

ABOVE McDonnell Douglas EC-17 general arrangement. *Boeing*

SAC had identified the need to replace the well-worn EC-135s in 1980, and the following year this had been ratified by the Chiefs of Staff in a Joint Mission Element Need Statement (JMENS). The Statement identified the C-17, still under development, as the aircraft best suited to meet this requirement, and in February 1985 the Air Force contracted with McDonnell Douglas for a detailed design study of the EC-17.

The modifications from the standard C-17 included the use of a centre-wing tank that could carry fuel, diesel oil or water. Another significant modification was the addition of an air refuelling system for both taking on and offloading fuel. It borrowed the KC-10 boom but, unlike the KC-10, where the operator sat at the back of the fuselage, able to directly view the receiving aircraft through large mirrors and a huge window, the EC-17 operator sat in the crew rest area and steered the boom remotely using a large stereo TV screen. McDonnell Douglas had patented and test-flown the system on a KC-135; decades later Boeing would incorporate it in the KC-46A.

The additional centre-wing fuel tank allowed the EC-17 to fly fourteen-hour missions while carrying a thirty-strong crew of two pilots, a boom

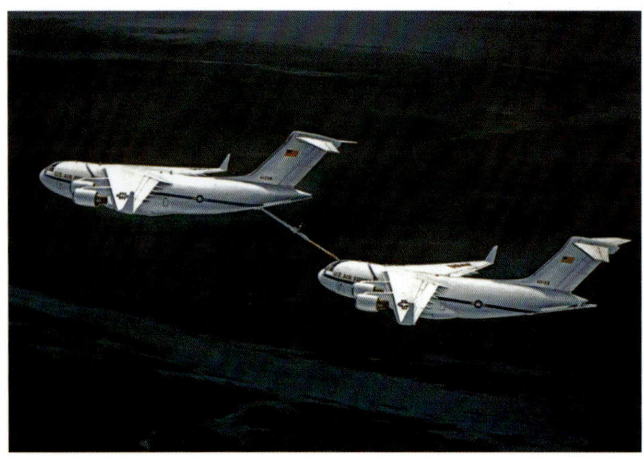

ABOVE **An EC-17 transfers fuel to another EC-17 in a depiction during part of a mission.** *Boeing*

EC-17 AIR REFUELING SYSTEM
FUEL LINES TO CENTER WING FUEL TANK
150.51
107.30
RAMP HORIZONTAL
CARGO DOOR HINGE POINT
BOOM HINGE POINT
CAVITY FOR VLF/LF LTWA
UTILIZES EXISTING KC-10 BOOM AND CONTROL SYSTEM
PROVIDES RAMP CLEARANCE FOR ON/OFF LOADING CONTAINERS
REMOTE STEREO TV BOOM OPERATOR STATION

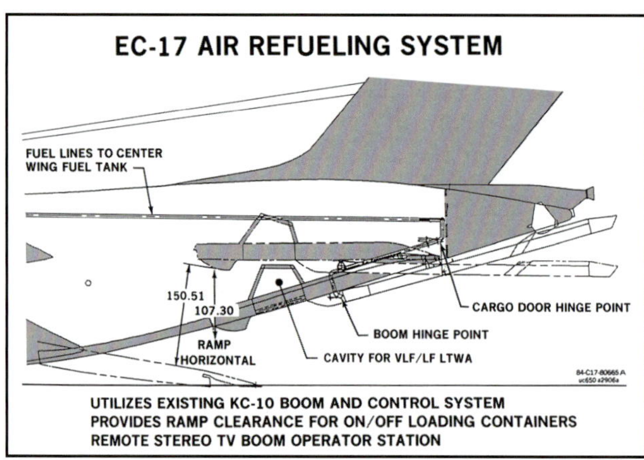

ABOVE **The EC-17 refuelling boom would have attached to the upper cargo door. The tailcone housed dual Wankel rotary motor-driven APUs for extended ground operation, underneath the fairing for a retractable VLF/LF trailing wire antenna.** *Boeing*

BELOW **One of several internal arrangements proposed for the McDonnell Douglas EC-17.** *Boeing*

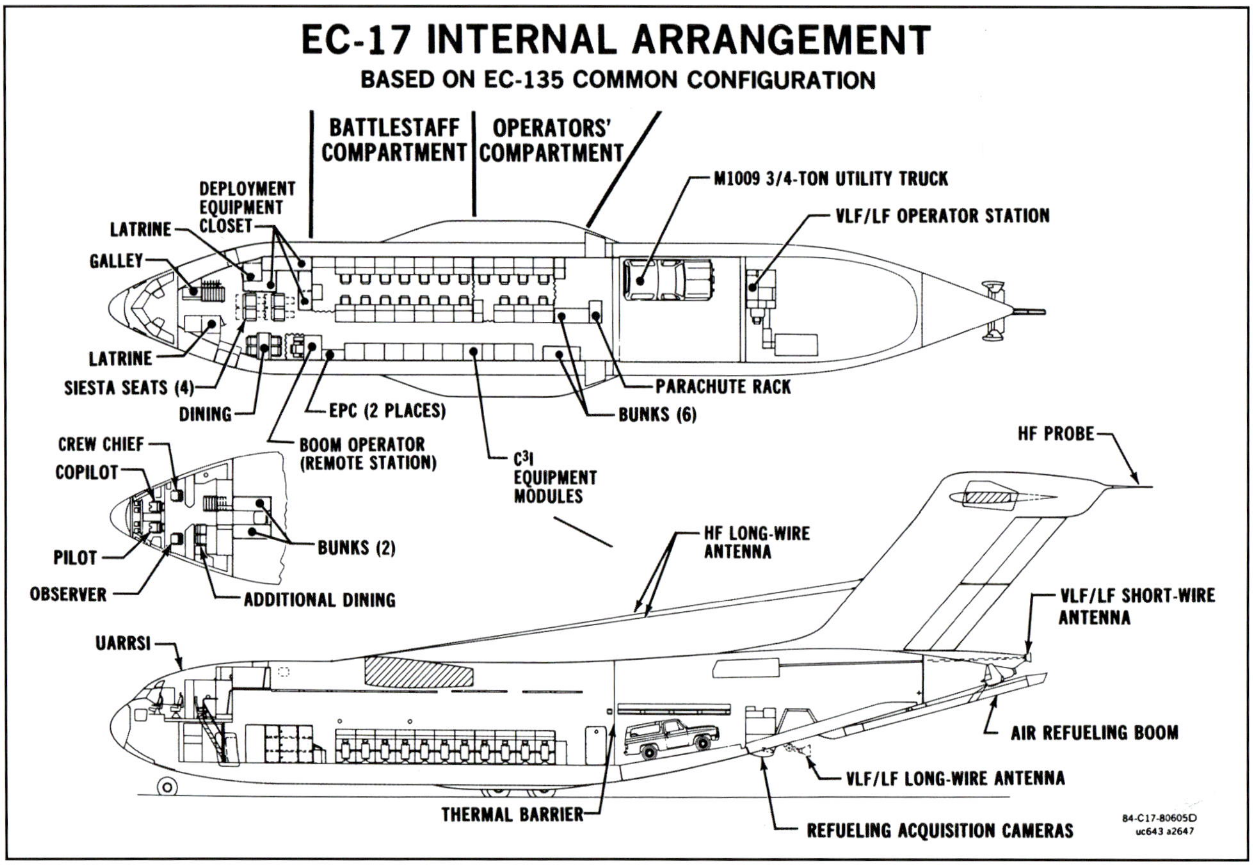

EC-17 INTERNAL ARRANGEMENT
BASED ON EC-135 COMMON CONFIGURATION
BATTLESTAFF COMPARTMENT
OPERATORS' COMPARTMENT
DEPLOYMENT EQUIPMENT CLOSET
LATRINE
GALLEY
M1009 3/4-TON UTILITY TRUCK
VLF/LF OPERATOR STATION
LATRINE
SIESTA SEATS (4)
DINING
EPC (2 PLACES)
PARACHUTE RACK
BUNKS (6)
CREW CHIEF
COPILOT
BOOM OPERATOR (REMOTE STATION)
C³I EQUIPMENT MODULES
HF PROBE
PILOT
OBSERVER
BUNKS (2)
ADDITIONAL DINING
HF LONG-WIRE ANTENNA
VLF/LF SHORT-WIRE ANTENNA
UARRSI
AIR REFUELING BOOM
VLF/LF LONG-WIRE ANTENNA
THERMAL BARRIER
REFUELING ACQUISITION CAMERAS
84-C17-80605D
uc643 a2647

operator and twenty-seven mission team members, together with a three-person maintenance crew. Designers optimised the aircraft's survivability and deployment capabilities, building in self-sufficiency for two weeks.

The end of the Cold War undermined the case for a 'Looking Glass' replacement. The EC-17 was not developed further, and the EC-135s were retired without a direct replacement. Air Force and Navy missions were eventually combined in refitted E-6B 'Mercury' aircraft that won the follow-on TACAMO mission, beating the Lockheed ECX-130.

After a delay of four years, in December 1985 McDonnell Douglas received a full-scale development contract for 210 aircraft. But development problems, combined with funding constraints, led to delays, and in April 1990 the Secretary of Defense reduced the order to 120 of the new airlifters.

The C-17 prototype flew on 14 September 1991 but the following year static test airframe tests revealed

ABOVE Flash forward: the first-built C-17A climbs out on its retirement flight from Edwards AFB to the National Museum of the Air Force on 23 April 2012. *Author photo*

structural issues. The resulting redesign and requalification programme cost an additional $100 million. Flight testing revealed additional problems, and in mid-1994 the Department of Defense seriously considered terminating the entire programme after delivery of the initial order of forty aircraft. However, McDonnell Douglas managed to persuade the DoD that the problems were soluble. And so it proved.

The C-17, now named Globemaster III, entered service on 17 January 1995 – nearly twenty years after the first flight of the YC-15, the aircraft on which it was originally based. The USAF finally had the flexible, long-range strategic and tactical airlifter that it had long sought.

With the success of the programme, the original order for 120 aircraft was reinstated and was followed by another multi-year procurement of eighty aircraft. Later another twenty-three were procured, exceeding the original programme plan. The aircraft was also ordered by the Royal Air Force and the air forces of Australia, Canada, Qatar, India and Kuwait.

The Advanced Tanker/Cargo Aircraft (ATCA)

Throughout the long developmental cycle that led to the C-17, the Air Force was also pursuing options for an aircraft to supplement its ageing KC-135 tanker fleet.

This formal effort began back in December 1973 when it issued a Required Operational Capability (ROC) for an Advanced Tanker/Cargo Aircraft, or ATCA. This capped a lengthy process that began in June 1967, when the Strategic Air Command (SAC) had first documented the need for an 'Advanced Capability Tanker' to replace or supplement the existing KC-135 fleet, the oldest having reached ten years of service. This aircraft would also respond to an additional – and growing – air-refuelling requirement from the Tactical Air Command (TAC). While SAC needed to fly long-range penetration missions, TAC's US-based fighters had to deploy across oceans. The desired aircraft became known as the 'KC-X'.

In May 1967 Boeing submitted 'Aerial Refuelling Tankers for the 1970 Requirements' to SAC. The report extensively documented the need to support operational bomber missions with tankers, and suggested different ways and costs of doing so. It put forward and compared five different aircraft: three substantially modified versions of the KC-135A, a tanker version of the Boeing 747, and an entirely new aircraft, the Model 954-100. Some of the KC-135 derivatives had the following modifications:

KC-135 Mod 'D'
New, larger wing with two GE TF39 engines

KC-135 Mod 'H'
Re-engined with scaled-down P&W JT9D-1s plus four lift engines

KC-135 Mod 'I'
Re-engined with scaled-down P&W JT9D-1s with a wing incorporating the Boeing Model 707-320B leading edge and the 720B leading edge glove

All three KC-135A derivatives had the same maximum take-off weight as the original aircraft, 301,600lb (136,800kg).

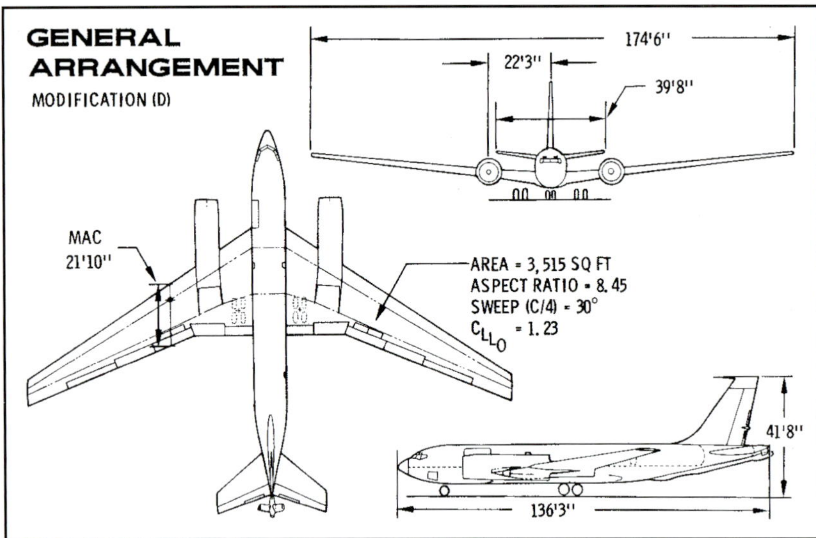

ABOVE The Boeing KC-135A 'Modification (D)' had a new wing and two TF39 engines *Boeing*

BELOW The Boeing Model 954-100 advanced tanker. *Boeing*

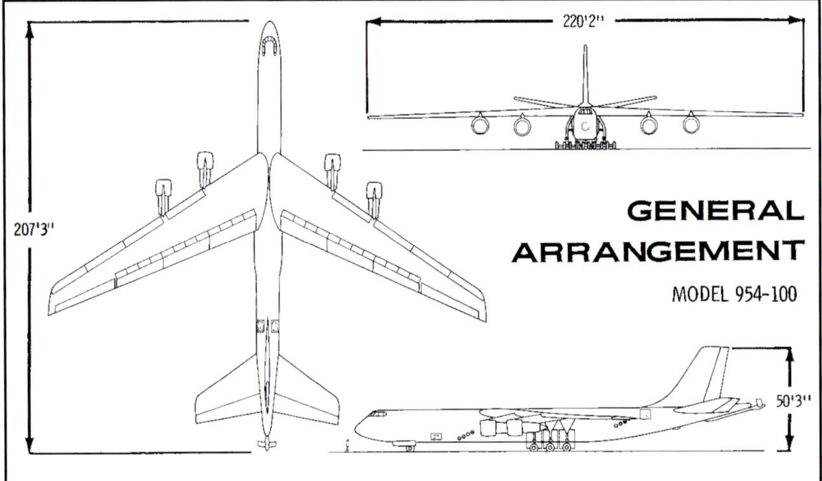

The Model 954-100 was perhaps the ultimate option. It was a large aircraft that grafted KC-135 features onto Boeing's B-52 planform. Four JT9D-1 turbofans provided primary power while eight lift-jets (of 10,000lbst, 44.49kN each) were installed in the fuselage to reduce take-off runs to less than 6,000ft (1,830m), a requirement for operation from dispersal airfields. The Model 954-100 was to have an 800,000lb (362,870kg) MTOW – significantly heavier than the notional KC-747, which was given as 680,000lb (308,440kg). Although the manufacturers had proposed a wide variety of imaginative designs, the USAF declined to pursue any of them.

While the need for more air-refuelling capacity was abundantly clear – and growing – the decision-making and funding process was only slowly rumbling forward. The Air Staff wondered if the requirement could not be more efficiently met with existing production aircraft such as the Boeing 707-320, Boeing 747B or Lockheed C-5A. However, resultant analyses became bogged down in a tangle of conflicting requirements, budgetary constraints and competing, higher-priority demands. TAC, for example, sought multi-point hook-ups capable of simultaneously refuelling, while SAC needed a tanker with just one 'flying' boom able to transfer masses of fuel to a single bomber at a time.

In addition, defence planners noted one more reason to build a new tanker. In the event of hostilities in Europe, NATO's fuel supply system, comprising ocean-going tankers, pipelines and ground storage facilities, would be highly vulnerable to attack by the Warsaw Pact forces. A fleet of high-capacity tankers could largely counter this threat. Given these many uncertainties about exactly what was needed, and with the austere budgets for FY71 and FY72, the lack of progress was not surprising.

Despite the grumpy fiscal environment, Boeing vigorously pushed an unsolicited proposal to sell fifty KC-747 tankers to the Air Force in 1971. However, it does not appear to have met an enthusiastic response, partly because it only satisfied one aspect of the USAF's requirement and partly because of the unavailability of funds. The proposal's sole result was a research project that fitted a refuelling boom (a 'dry installation' not actually able to transfer fuel) onto a 747 to demonstrate the feasibility of transforming very large existing aircraft into aerial refuellers.

The new tanker effort languished until 1973, when it received new impetus and an expanded mission. Given the cost of developing both a new tanker and a new large cargo aircraft, planners started to examine the feasibility of a flexible, dual-mission aircraft. Studies quickly followed that centred on three existing wide-bodied aircraft: Boeing's 747, the McDonnell Douglas DC-10, and Lockheed's L-1011.

The idea was given a further boost later that year by the Arab-Israeli conflict. That war highlighted the urgent requirement for a rapid worldwide response capability, together with the need to decrease US dependency on overseas bases. Seizing the opportunity, the Air Force issued a new ROC for an 'Advanced Multipurpose Tanker' on 15 December. Within the month this had been renamed the 'Advanced Tanker/Cargo Aircraft', or ATCA. However, funding was not forthcoming to launch a design competition.

ABOVE The first Boeing 747 built was modified to physically demonstrate tanker compatibility with existing receiver aircraft (an SR-71A is seen here), although fuel could not be transferred. Two ex-TWA 747-131s were later converted as tankers for the (then) Imperial Iranian Air Force. *Author collection*

RIGHT The rear-looking 'boomer' control position is seen as it remains today on Boeing's prototype 747 on display in Seattle. *Author photo*

In 1975 the Air Force Chief of Staff, General David C. Jones, proposed leasing aircraft to test their capabilities. Only two aircraft types were available for such a leasing arrangement: the Boeing 747 and McDonnell Douglas DC-10. For a time this 'try out the possibilities on the cheap' idea was in play, but was dropped in favour of 'a competitive paper-source selection leading to the direct procurement of 41 wide-body freighter aircraft'.

On 27 August 1976 the USAF issued an RFP to industry. Four candidates were short-listed: the Boeing 747, McDonnell Douglas DC-10, Lockheed C-5, and Lockheed L-1011. By mid-1977 the field had narrowed to two, with the C-5 eliminated because it was not in production, and the L-1011 because there was no pre-existing variant with a large cargo door in the fuselage.

Boeing 747 ATCA and ATOCA

In many ways the Boeing 747 was well suited, if not over-qualified, for the requirement. By the middle of 1977 the company had already delivered close to 350 747s, including a number of freighter versions, together with three E-4 Advanced Airborne Command Posts (based on the 747) to the USAF.

The 747 ATCA was to have a maximum overload take-off weight of 870,000lb (394,630kg). The 747-200F, the model upon which the ATCA was based, was already available to commercial customers at a maximum take-off weight of 820,000lb (371,950kg). Boeing stated that by installing new engines and improving the undercarriage, and with minor strengthening of the fuselage, this could be increased to 930,000lb (421,840kg). Furthermore, by introducing a larger, more efficient wing (which Boeing was studying) there was the potential to raise the maximum take-off weight to 960,000lb (435,450kg).

Boeing further proposed an alternative, outsize-cargo version, which it termed the 'ATOCA' ('O' for 'Outsize').

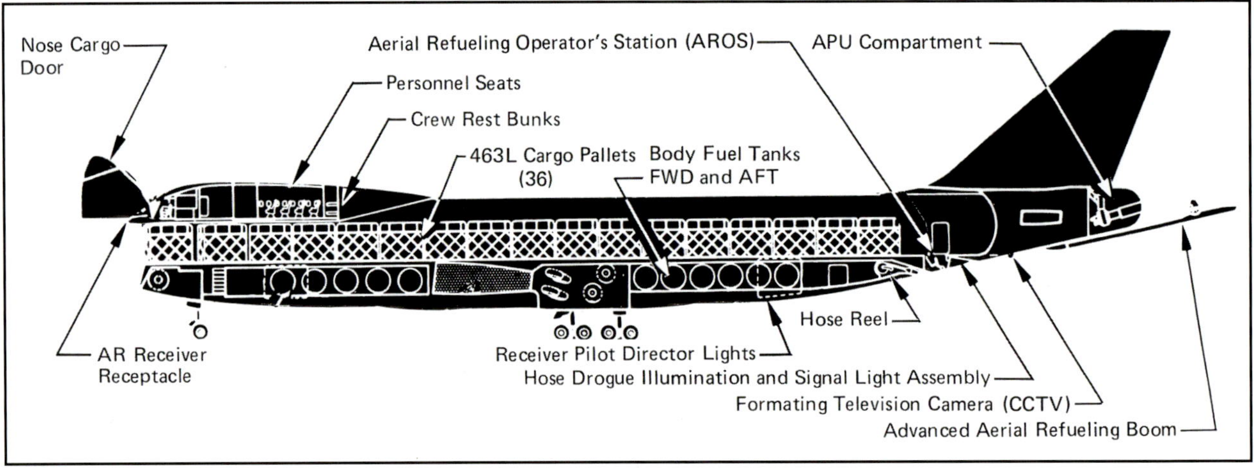

ABOVE Boeing 747 ATCA internal configuration. *Boeing*

The aircraft was externally similar to the ATCA with the exception of the forward fuselage, which was widened and heightened to provide a cargo bay of constant cross section, enabling it to carry outsize loads such as M-60 or XM-1 tanks.

Boeing also outlined a variety of other potential future uses for its 747, promising a high degree of fleet standardisation covering a variety of missions, ranging from airlift to surveillance and even airborne missile launches.

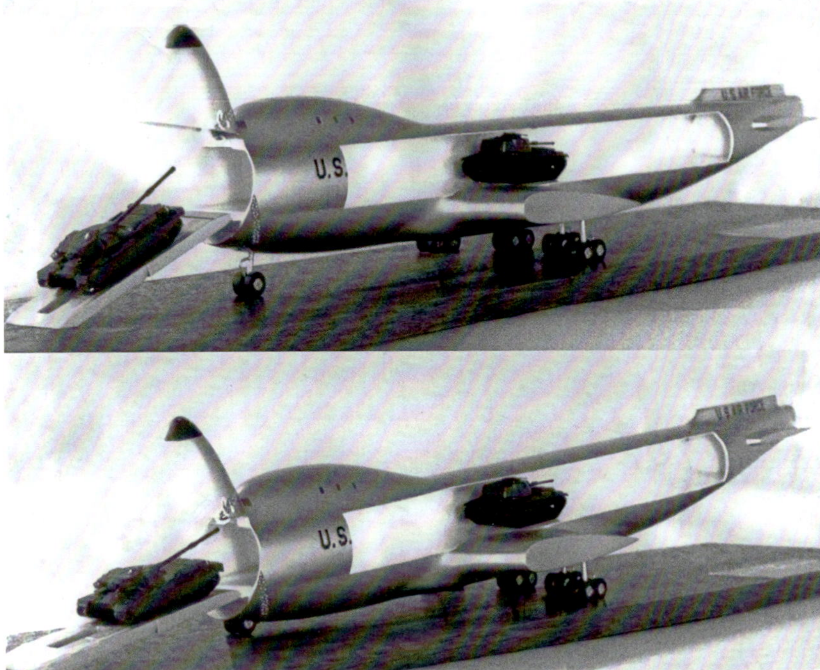

ABOVE Unveiled in February 1974 and later named the 'ATOCA', this Boeing 747 military derivative featured a wider and taller forward fuselage and a kneeling nose gear. *Boeing*

BELOW Reconfiguring the forward fuselage of the Boeing 747 ATOCA created a constant width and height inside the main 747 cargo compartment, to accommodate main battle tanks. *Boeing*

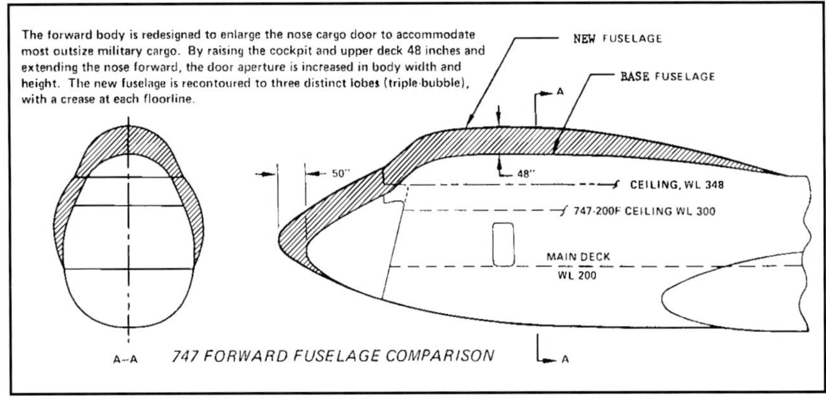

McDonnell Douglas DC-10 ATCA

McDonnell Douglas based its ATCA submission on the commercial freighter version of its DC-10-30CF, powered by three General Electric CF6-50C2 turbofans, each rated at 52,000lbst (231kN). Its maximum take-off weight was the same as that of the commercial aircraft, 590,000lb (267,860kg). As with the Boeing submission, McDonnell Douglas emphasised both the proven operational record and the potential for future variants able to undertake a wide variety of missions.

Modifications for the ATCA role included:

- An air-refuelling station with both a boom and a hose-and-drogue air-refuelling system in the lower rear fuselage

Boeing 747-based ATCA and ATOCA

	ATCA	ATOCA
Powerplant	4 x P&W JT9D-7J turbofans @ 50,000lb (22,680kN) thrust	4 x P&W JT9D-70D turbofans @ 56,000lb (25,401kN) thrust
Wingspan	195ft 8in (59.60m)	195ft 8in (59.60m)
Length with boom	245ft 3in (74.75m)	249ft 5in (76.02m)
Height	63ft 5in (19.30m)	63ft 5in (19.30m)
Wing area	5,500 sq ft (511 m²)	5,500 sq ft (511 m²)
Max TOW	800,000lb (362,870kg)	855,000lb (387,820kg)
Payload	243,200lb (110,310kg)	232,800lb (105,230kg)

McDonnell Douglas DC-10-30CF-based ATCA

Powerplant	3 x GE CF6-50C2 turbofans @ 52,500lb (236kN) thrust
Wingspan	65ft 4.5in (50.41m)
Length	181ft 7in (55.35m)
Height	58ft 1in (17.40m)
Wing area	3,958sq ft (367.71m²)
Max TOW	590,000lb (267,620kg)

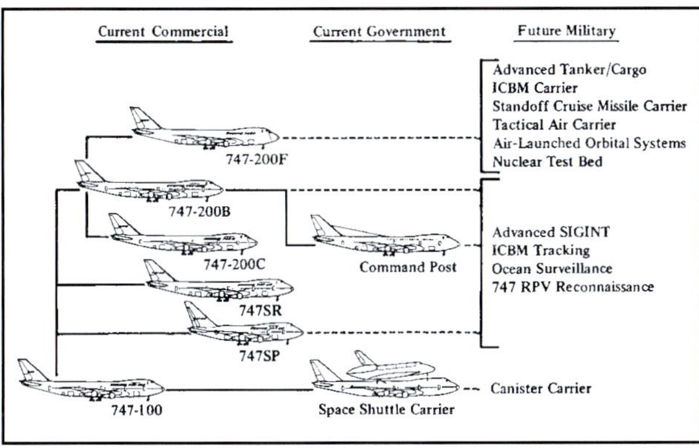

ABOVE **The Boeing 747 family tree with potential military derivatives.** *Boeing*

ABOVE **A Boeing concept model of the 747 ATCA showing the centreline and remotely operated wing refuelling booms.** *John Aldaz collection*

ABOVE **The McDonnell Douglas DC-10 ACTA concept in the originally planned bare metal colour scheme.** *Boeing*

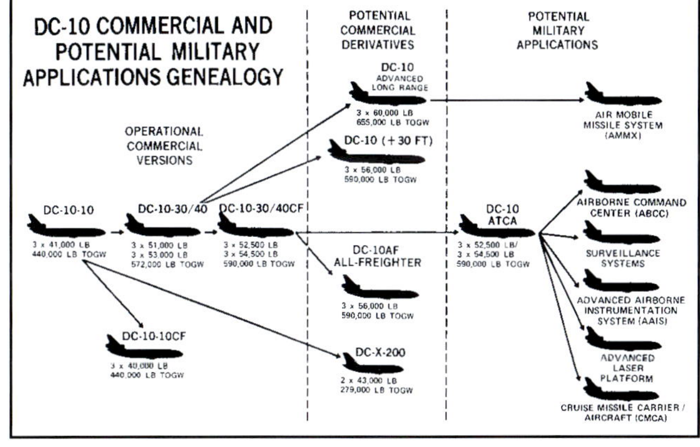

ABOVE **The McDonnell Douglas DC-10 family tree with potential military derivatives.** *Boeing*

- Seven fuel cells between special frameworks in the strengthened lower cargo deck
- An air-refuelling receptacle over the cockpit
- A standard DC-10-30C 8ft 7in high by 11ft 7in wide (2.61m by 3.56m) upper deck cargo door in the left forward fuselage
- A cargo handling system on the main deck, with ball-mats, power rollers and a winch
- Military avionics

The ATCA decision

For a programme designed to minimise cost, complexity and timescale, the ATCA competition proved a remarkably lengthy process that eventually concluded with Source Selection on 19 December 1977. The two aircraft were evaluated in six different scenarios that compared capabilities and costs, and the DC-10 was named winner. McDonnell Douglas also won a contract for the aircraft's logistics support, leaving the Air Force responsible only for flight-line maintenance. All the other support would come from the McDonnell Douglas commercial network – a highly innovative arrangement for the time.

The intention from the outset had been to buy an aircraft that was, as far as possible, an 'off the shelf' product. Nonetheless, substantial modification was necessary, dropping DC-10

ABOVE Its advanced refuelling boom extended, the first-built KC-10A banks away from the camera plane. In flight test configuration, the tanker has a test boom on the left wingtip and a trailing cone at the top of the tail, and wears the 'N10KC' civil registration. *Boeing*

BELOW Prior to the ATCA decision, McDonnell Douglas proposed the DC-10 for many military roles. Here, a DC-10 derivative (note the passenger windows in the aft fuselage) is depicted as a replacement 'Rivet Joint' electronic surveillance aircraft. This could have resulted in an 'RC-10' replacing the RC-135V 'Rivet Joint' aircraft. Instead, some forty years after this painting was completed, the existing 'Rivet Joint' RC-135 airframes continue in service. *Boeing*

commonality to 88%. Perhaps inevitably, McDonnell Douglas soon proposed the 'KC-10B', with a cargo door enlarged to 10ft high by 14ft 1 in wide (3.05m by 4.32m) to allow loading of outsized cargo. However, the USAF declined to pursue this concept, evaluating it as too great a departure from the original concept of buying an 'off the shelf' aircraft, and not worth the programmatic risks.

The first KC-10A 'Extender' rolled out on 16 April 1980, with a first flight on 12 July. Test flights proved that the aircraft retained the excellent flying characteristics of its DC-10 cousin, and fears that the middle engine might interfere with air-refuelling the T-tailed C-5 proved groundless. The first of sixty production KC-10As was delivered on 17 March 1981 – some fourteen years after the need for a bigger and more capable tanker than the KC-135 had been first formally identified. It is expected to remain in service till 2030 and its currently planned replacement by the Boeing KC-46A Pegasus.

ABOVE Another proposed DC-10 conversion appears to have been a replacement for the Lisa Ann/Rivet Amber RC-135E ballistic missile warhead tracking aircraft that crashed on 5 June 1967 with the loss of all those aboard. The side-mounted phased-array radar was rated in the several megawatt range of emitted power. *Boeing*

Extending the existing fleet

Two efforts began in the 1970s to extend the existing fleet of cargo and tanker aircraft in lieu of creating new aircraft. The first effort centred on lengthening the fuselages of the existing MAC C-141A fleet, and the second, in the late 1970s, examined re-engining SAC's KC-135 fleet.

Stretching the Starlifter

Although Lockheed had previously proposed a stretched production version of the Starlifter, the Air Force declined the opportunity. As seen in *American Secret Projects 2*, the 444in (1,127.7cm) stretch would have resulted in a gross weight increase that required a new, six-wheel main landing gear housed in redesigned sponsons, together with a strengthened centre fuselage.

What became the C-141B configuration originated in 1964 as a civil stretch of the C-141A, named the L-300B. This version was neither as long nor as heavy as the 1961 stretch, and retained the existing main landing gear and centre fuselage structure. However, there was insufficient interest in the civil models for production to begin, so the concept languished; meanwhile, Lockheed's commercial Hercules variant went into production in 1965, with its successive stretches.

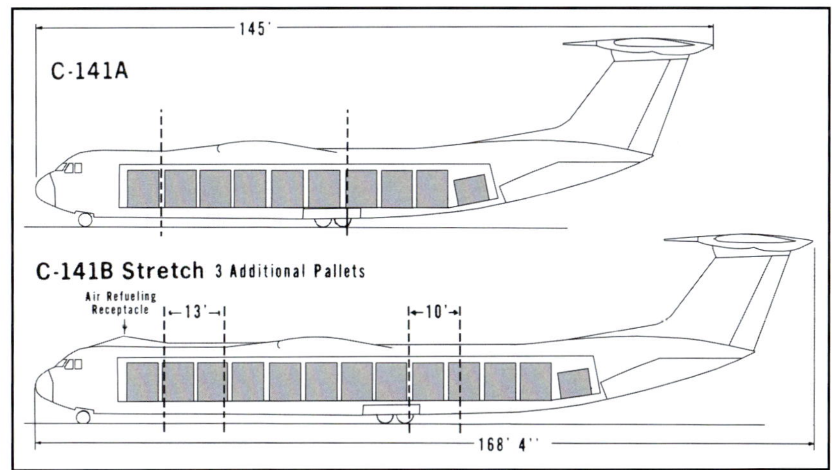

ABOVE The 23ft (7.0m) stretch of the C-141 increased the cargo deck area by 233sq ft (21.65m²) and the number of standard 463L pallets that could be carried by 25%. *Author collection*

The stretched C-141 was reconsidered (as a conversion of existing airframes) in the wake of the 1973 Arab-Israeli War, when US airlift capability to support Israel was severely strained, both in capacity and by the loss of intermediate ground refuelling airports that were closed to the US. The design was constrained by cost, ruling out the new main landing gear and centre fuselage; as a result, the maximum gross weight could not

ABOVE A stretched C-141B (left) and a C-141A share the ramp at Norton AFB in the morning haze prior to their missions. *Paul Minert photo*

exceed that of the C-141. Consequently the conversion was limited to stretching the fuselage by 160in (460.4cm) forward and 120in (304.8cm) aft of the wing, together with retrofitting an externally mounted Universal Aerial Refuelling Receptacle Installation (UARRSI) atop the forward fuselage.

The Air Force issued a contract to Lockheed in June 1975. The prototype YC-141B rolled out in January 1977 and flew on 24 March. The first production conversion was delivered to the 60th Military Airlift Wing on 11 April 1980 and the conversion effort was ramped up to a rate of ten aircraft per month, concluding in 1983 with a cost underrun. MAC converted its entire fleet of 271 aircraft, effectively adding a cargo space that was the equivalent of ninety C-141As.

Refurbishing the KC-135

As the ATCA programme wound its way through the Defense Department and Congressional thickets, studies continued to address the deficiencies of the KC-135A. Originally positioned as an interim tanker, to be replaced by a later, more advanced Lockheed design in the 1950s, the KC-135 had become the only tanker, rapidly replacing the piston-engined KC-97 in first-line SAC service, despite not fully meeting the requirements of the 1955 KC-X competition.

For while the Boeing Model 367-80 and KC-135 aircraft were the best designs possible with 1952 technology, the airframes were sized to the best engine of the time, the J57. The equivalent civil Model 707-100 series aircraft were equally hobbled by the relatively low thrust and small wing, both combining to limit weight and fuel, and therefore range. The 707 did not become a true success until the debut of the 707-300 series, whose larger wing and higher thrust/more fuel-efficient first-generation turbofan engines made true intercontinental range finally possible.

Boeing and the USAF undertook three programmes to improve the KC-135A. The first centred on the lower wing skins, replacing the lighter (but less durable) 7178-T8 aluminium alloy with the much tougher 2024 series metal – an improvement that nearly tripled the aircraft's life. A second initiative focused on the J57 turbojet powerplants; originally promoted as a 'wonder engine' when introduced twenty years earlier, it was now viewed as an obsolete, dirty and noisy fuel-guzzler that had to be replaced. Third, Boeing partnered with NASA to investigate possible wing drag reductions (and fuel savings) promised by newly invented winglet technology.

The KC-135R

Together with re-engining, engineers examined the replacement of the entire wing to allow much higher gross weights – thus increasing fuel loads, which translated to either a longer range or more fuel to be transferred at shorter ranges. Seven possible configurations emerged:

Re-engined KC-135 proposals

	KC-135P-7*	KC-135RF**	KC-135ME***
Powerplant	4 x P&W TF-33-P-7 turbofans @ 21,000 lb (93.41kN) thrust	4 x P&W JT8D-207 turbofans @ 19,000lb (84.51kn) thrust	2 x GE/SNECMA CFM-56 turbofans (inboard) @ 21,000lb (93.41kN) thrust, 2 x P&W J57 turbojets (outboard) @ 13,000lb (57.83kN) thrust
Wing	'KC-135'	'KC-135'	'KC-135'
Wingspan	130ft 10in (39.88m)	130ft 10in (39.88m)	130ft 10in (39.88m)
Wing area	2,433sq ft (226m²)	2,433sq ft (226m²)	2,433sq ft (226m²)
Max TOW	315,400lb (143,063kg)	317,800lb (144,154kg)	n/a

* KC-135P-7 uses 'TF-33-P-7' engine
** KC-135RF uses JT8D-209 'Re-Fanned' engine
*** KC-135ME uses 'Mixed Engine' configuration

Re-engined and re-winged KC-135 proposals

	KC-135H	KC-135X	KC-135Y
Powerplant	4 x P&W TF-33-P-7 turbofans @ 21,000lb (93.41kN) thrust	4x GE/SNECMA CFM-56 turbofans or 4 x P&W JT10D turbofans @ 20,000 lb (88.96kN) thrust class	4 x GE/SNECMA CFM-56 turbofans or 4 x P&W JT10D turbofans @ 20,000lb (88.96kN) thrust class
Wing	'707-300'	'707-300'	'New supercritical'
Wingspan	142ft 5in (43.44m)	142ft 5in (43.44m)	approx 175ft (53.3m)
Wing area	3,101sq ft (288.8m²)	3,101sq ft (288.8m²)	n/a
Max TOW	374,400lb (169,827kg)	376,400lb (107,735kg)	424,000lb (192,326kg)

KC-135P-7:

Installation of Pratt & Whitney TF33-P-7 engines on existing KC-135s, a new horizontal stabiliser (enlarged from 500 to 545sq ft [46.4 to 50.6m²] at the outboard tips as on the 707), and new landing gear struts.

KC-135RE:

Installation of the Pratt & Whitney JT8D-209 'Re-Fanned' engine. The -209/-217 family of engines had been developed from the basic JT8Ds (used by the airlines) primarily for use on the stretched McDonnell Douglas DC-9-80, and was now becoming available.

KC-135ME:

The KC-135ME – 'Mixed Engine' – was to use two different engine types on the same aircraft. The inboard engines would be the 'Ten-Ton class' General Electric/SNECMA CFM-56 turbofans, while the outboard Pratt & Whitney J57 turbojets would remain in place. Other changes included new landing gear struts for higher gross weights and a horizontal stabiliser of increased span for greater pitch authority. This option offered the lowest conversion costs of all the studies.

KC-135H:

The engines would be replaced by Pratt & Whitney TF33-P-7s and the 2,433sq ft (226m²) wing would be replaced by the 3,101sq ft (288.8m²) wing used on the 707-300 series of airliners.

KC-135X:

This variant was a KC-135A with four GE/SNECMA CFM-56 or Pratt & Whitney JT10D engines installed, with the 707-300 wing.

KC-135R (KC-135TT*, later KC-135RE)**

Powerplant	4 x GE/SNECMA CFM-56-1B1 (F108-CF-100) turbofans @ 21,634lb (96.27kN) thrust
Wing	'KC-135'
Wingspan	130ft 10in (39.88m)
Wing area	2,433sq ft (226m²)
Max TOW	322,500lb (146,000kg)
Max fuel capacity	200,000lb (90,718kg)

* KC-135TT – 'Ten-Ton' class engine
** KC-135RE – 'Re-Engine'

BELOW The ultimate path taken towards fleet renewal was the 'KC-135TT', which became the KC-135R engine-replacement programme using the CFM-56. *Author photo*

As with the KC-135H, the landing gear would be improved and a horizontal stabiliser of increased-span installed.

KC-135Y:
This would use CFM-56 or JT10D engines and a new reduced-sweep, supercritical wing. It would have the same miscellaneous airframe improvements as the KC-135X.

The final re-engining option was the 'KC-135TT', which replaced all four engines with the GE/SNECMA CFM-56 turbofan in the 'Ten-Ton' thrust class and kept the KC-135 wing. And that is ultimately what the Air Force chose to do. The 're-winged plus re-engined' options had the highest costs, and analyses showed that the performance increases (for the price) did not match those offered by the simpler engine substitution. The first modified aircraft rolled out on 22 June 1982. In addition, the KC-135Q (previously modified for refuelling the SR-71A) received the same conversion, becoming the KC-135T.

The KC-135E

Even as the CFM-56 re-engining engineering effort was under way, the Air Force encountered an unexpected windfall – airport noise regulation. The phase-in of US Federal Aviation Regulation (FAR) 36 Part 2 noise regulations helped drive the fleet retirements of Boeing 707 and 720 aircraft by airlines, since these aircraft would be banned from operating in the US by 1985. This drove down the aircraft prices, and the Air Force took advantage of the situation by purchasing 187 of these JT3D turbofan-powered aircraft at bargain prices. The airliners were ferried to the Aerospace Maintenance and Regeneration Center (AMARC) at Davis Monthan Air Force Base, and were then stripped of the JT3Ds, nacelles, pylons and other parts.

Boeing Wichita received the conversion contract in August 1981 and the first aircraft in the programme flew with its new engines in January 1982, beating the KC-135R into the air. The civil JT3D-5A/8A engines were converted to the TF33-PW-102 configuration and used to re-engine 187 KC-135As, which were redesignated as KC-135Es. Although the turbofans could not meet the noise regulations in the civil market, the military was exempt from the noise rules and the TF33s were quieter than the J57s that they replaced. In addition, the KC-135Es were found to be 14% more fuel efficient than the KC-135As and could offload 20% more fuel.

As the KC-135 fleet was drawn down in the 2000s, most of the Air National Guard and Air Force Reserve KC-135Es were retired, being replaced by KC-135Rs drawn from active duty squadrons. However, some eighteen KC-135E aircraft were re-engined yet again with CFM-56s to return to duty as KC-135Rs, thus having flown with three completely different engine types during their careers. Other non-tanker versions such as the various RC-135 reconnaissance models were converted to use the new engine.

BELOW The first large aircraft application of aerodynamicist Richard Whitcomb's winglet concept was tested on the KC-135A in a joint Air Force/Boeing/NASA programme. *NASA*

The KC-135A winglet test programme

The third effort to improve the KC-135 saw winglets installed on a test aircraft. Developed by NASA's Richard T. Whitcomb (inventor of the 'area rule' and the supercritical wing), the winglet harnessed the powerful wingtip vortex to reduce drag. First tested on a Learjet Model 28, flight testing of the winglet on the KC-135 was supported by the Air Force, Boeing and NASA, with the tanker flying in August 1979.

Flight testing showed that the winglet improved cruise efficiency by 6% at optimum conditions. Although effective, it was not adopted for the KC-135 fleet because, while improving fuel efficiency by lowering drag, it did not address the engine deficiencies of the KC-135/J57 combination. In addition, the winglets' aerodynamic loads required costly strengthening of the outer wing panels. The Air Force decided that the re-engining programmes provided the most benefits for the cost.

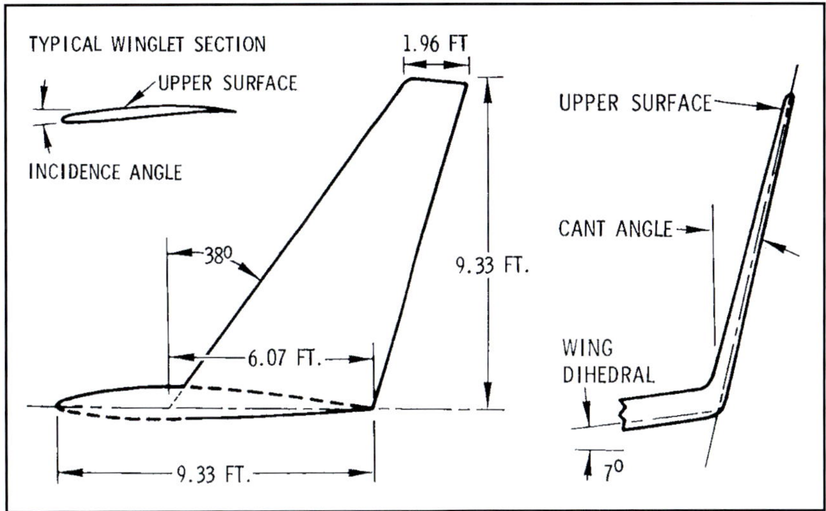

ABOVE The KC-135 winglets were tested at several cant and incidence angles. The best results were obtained at 15° cant and -4° incidence. *NASA*

Two decades in perspective

Contrary to plans at the beginning of the 1970s, the US military heavy airlift fleet ended the decade with a quite different mix of aircraft either in service or under development.

The light-to-medium airlift role was largely filled by the same aircraft – the C-7, C-123 and C-130 – that had been in service in 1970. None had been replaced, though the C-7 and C-123 force had been transferred from front-line to reserve operation. The Air Force had completely withdrawn from the battlefield air cargo/air assault mission, with the Army taking over this role using CH-47 helicopters.

The most dramatic airlift evolution occurred in the Medium STOL Transport segment. Over the decade's course, the original concept had steadily morphed into a near-strategic airlifter. Its size, range and payload were much greater, while its STOL capability had been scaled back to the point where it still required a 3,000ft (823m) landing strip – though, of course, still much less than the 9,000ft (2,743m) needed by the C-5.

It is instructive to compare the requirements expressed in the original MST ROC, issued in 1970, with the C-17 airlifter that eventually emerged from the C-X competition some twenty years later, as set out in the accompanying table.

During the same decade, the requirement for additional tanker capability – which triggered the Advanced Tanker Cargo Aircraft (ATCA) programme – yielded a formidable range of proposals based on extending or adapting existing aircraft. Despite some very creative proposals, the ultimate solution arrived in a more mundane – though highly effective – form.

Limited numbers of KC-10s were ordered to supplement (though not replace) the KC-135 tanker fleet. Implemented in the 1980s, this move very successfully improved air-refuelling capability. It was a critical accomplishment, considering that the tanker-supply mission had evolved from supporting a range of conflicts around the world to creating a massive air bridge to Europe in the event of a Soviet invasion. In addition, the re-engining of the KC-135 fleet proved very successful.

At the upper end of the airlift scale, the Air Force finally had a truly strategic transport, the C-5, although structural deficiencies initially imposed performance limitations. The Air Force, obligated to meet ever-increasing commitments, looked at either (1) replacing the C-5's primary wing structure, or (2) stretching the C-141, as originally proposed in 1961, to increase its cargo volume.

In the end it had to do both. By the start of the 1990s the Air Force had the fleet of airlifters that it had long sought, either in service or on order, but it had been a long and difficult process, with many imaginative proposals falling by the wayside.

MST ROC requirements and C-17 capabilities compared

	MST (ROC) 52-69 requirements	C-17 capabilities
Max cargo load	28,000lb (12,700kg)	169,000lb (76,657kg)
Max range	3,600nmi (6,667km), unrefuelled	4,700nmi (8,704km), unrefuelled
Speed	Mach 0.75, above 20,000ft (6,100m)	Mach 0.74-0.77
Landing length	2,000ft (610m) with 18,000lb (8,165kg) cargo	3,000ft (823m) with 160,000lb (72,575kg) cargo
Cargo box	45ft long x 12ft wide x 12ft high (13.7m x 3.7m x 3.7m)	88ft long x 18ft wide x 13ft high (min) (26.8m x 5.5m x 4.0m)
Truck-bed height loading	Use standard 463L pallets	Use standard 463L pallets

Chapter Six
Carrier On-Board Delivery

Airlift on the high seas

ABOVE A tailhook-equipped Fairchild C-123 is depicted approaching an aircraft carrier as it performs the COD mission. *Fairchild*

Transporting key personnel and materials to and from aircraft carriers at sea poses special challenges to military air transportation. Apart from the normal requirements of any transport aircraft, it also demands the ability to land and take off from a small, moving deck, and the ability to stow compactly once on board.

The quest for this capability – known as Carrier On-Board Delivery (COD) – has resulted in a wide variety of unique designs. Because of the limited prospective production runs, most of the proposals have either been adaptations of existing aircraft originally designed for other purposes, or specialised variants of multi-purpose aircraft.

The start of COD activities

COD activities started during the Second World War, albeit in a modest way, using the Grumman J2F Duck amphibious biplane. In the early post-war years the role was fulfilled using modified versions of the Grumman Avenger – a carrier-based torpedo bomber – to deliver personnel, mail and small high-priority cargo. General Motors was a second-source manufacturer of the Avenger under the TBM designation. Some of these aircraft were converted to the TBM-3R; modifications included removing the gun turret and glazing over the area to provide either passenger seats or a cargo space. Two additional passengers could also be seated, low down in the rear fuselage, giving a maximum of six, though hardly travelling in great comfort. The bomb bay could also be used for cargo.

In 1950 Douglas proposed its AD-5 Skyraider for the role. The AD-5 had started life as a 1949 proposal to combine the two previously separate Anti-Submarine Warfare (ASW) missions – hunter and killer – within a single aircraft. However, this highly versatile aircraft was subsequently utilised by the Navy for many other missions. While the general utility version would have given a marginal increase in capability over the TBM-3R for COD duties, it was not assigned to transport squadrons dedicated to the COD role.

What the Navy needed was an aircraft with significantly greater load-carrying capability, particularly for large items like spare engines for the jet aircraft then coming into widespread carrier service. In a late-1951 response Grumman started to look at a design based on its much larger S2F-2 Tracker anti-submarine aircraft. The design retained the S2F-2's wings, engines and empennage but married these to a deeper fuselage.

The new aircraft could carry nine passengers or 3,500lb (1,589kg) of cargo. However, concerned with more pressing needs, the Navy did not show an immediate interest in the project and it was not until 1953 that it started to seriously consider the potential introduction of a twin-engine COD transport. At this point the Navy specified that it required an aircraft capable of carrying a payload of 8,000lb (3,632kg) with items up to 10ft 8in (3.25m) long and 5ft 1in (1.55m) wide; these dimensions were determined by the need to accommodate nuclear weapons.

Both the desired payload and compartment size were beyond the capability of a straightforward variant of the S2F, so Grumman responded by proposing an enlarged fuselage with a double-folding door in the port-side aft section. It also built a mock-up of the arrangement to demonstrate its effectiveness. The company's efforts paid off and a contract was awarded for forty-five aircraft under the designation TF-1. The Trader, as it was to become known, first flew on 19 January 1955 and entered service in October the same year. Later redesignated as the C-1A, the aircraft had an incredibly long service life, with the last examples not being retired until 1986. This earned the C-1A the distinction of being the last piston-engine aircraft to serve at sea with the US Navy.

ABOVE The General Motors TBM-3R had the gun turret removed and the area glazed over as part of the conversion to the COD role. *National Museum of Naval Aviation*

BELOW Seating arrangements on the TBM-3R. *Tommy Thomason collection*

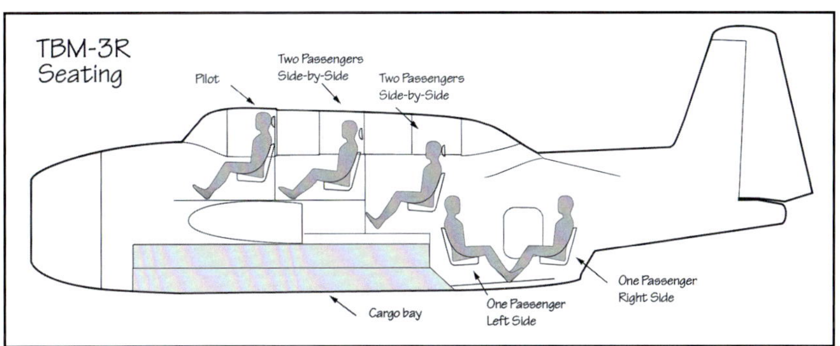

BELOW A Grumman TF-1 in flight, showing the cabin windows and side cargo doors. *Courtesy of Northrop Grumman Corporation*

The need for greater capability

The TF-1/C-1A represented a major step forward, but the Navy felt it needed an even bigger aircraft; the wide-scale introduction of a new angled, or 'through-deck', layout on aircraft carriers would be able accommodate it. The requirements were informally communicated to aircraft manufacturers, although as far as is known no official Invitation to Bid was issued. Both Douglas and Fairchild submitted proposals for consideration, Douglas with its Model 1906A and Fairchild with successively modified versions of the C-123.

Douglas Model 1906A

The Douglas Model 1906A was a conventional, high-wing transport aircraft design, powered by four Lycoming T55 turboshaft engines. It was proposed both as a COD aircraft for the Navy and as an assault aircraft for the Marines.

ABOVE This Douglas concept art shows the Model 1906A being unloaded at sea. *Boeing*

BELOW A Douglas Model 1906A 'traps' aboard an aircraft carrier. *Boeing*

Rather than coming from the Douglas El Segundo Division (with its track record of supplying the US Navy with combat aircraft), the proposal originated from the company's Santa Monica Division. Initial concepts included a bow-loading design with a slab-sided fuselage, but this evolved into a sleeker configuration with a low-level cargo floor and a rear loading arrangement. Designated the Model 1906A, Douglas proposed the aircraft to the Navy on 1 August 1957, competing with the Fairchild M-255.

The Model 1906A was designed to carry a payload of 15,000lb (6,810kg) or fifty-eight fully equipped troops over a range of 1,500nmi (2,777km). Of particular note was its take-off and landing capability. Although fitted with an arrester hook mounted under the upper cargo door, the 1906A could land on a carrier without using the hook at a wind-over-deck (the combination of wind-speed and carrier speed into wind) of 10kt (18.5km/h). Indeed, it was claimed that with a 25kt (46.3km/h) wind-over-deck, it could stop within 190ft (58m) using wheel-braking and reverse thrust alone. In similar conditions it could also take off to return to shore with no payload in just 85ft (25.9m) without using catapult assistance.

This performance resulted from a high thrust-to-weight ratio coupled with a high-lift wing incorporating leading edge flaps and virtually full-span trailing edge flaps. To permit the latter installation, spoilers rather than ailerons were used to provide lateral control.

Douglas D-1906A	
Powerplant	4 x Lycoming XT55-L-1 @ 1,651shp (1,231.6kW)
Span	102ft 5in (31.24m)
Length	88ft 2in (26.89m)
Height	36ft 8in (11.18m)
Wing area	1,300sq ft (119.4m²)
Max TOW	67,000lb (30,420kg)
Payload	15,000lb (6,810kg) or 28 passengers
Max speed	270kt (500km/h)
Cruise speed	243kt (450km/h) at 20,000ft (6,100m)
Range	1,500nmi (2,776km)

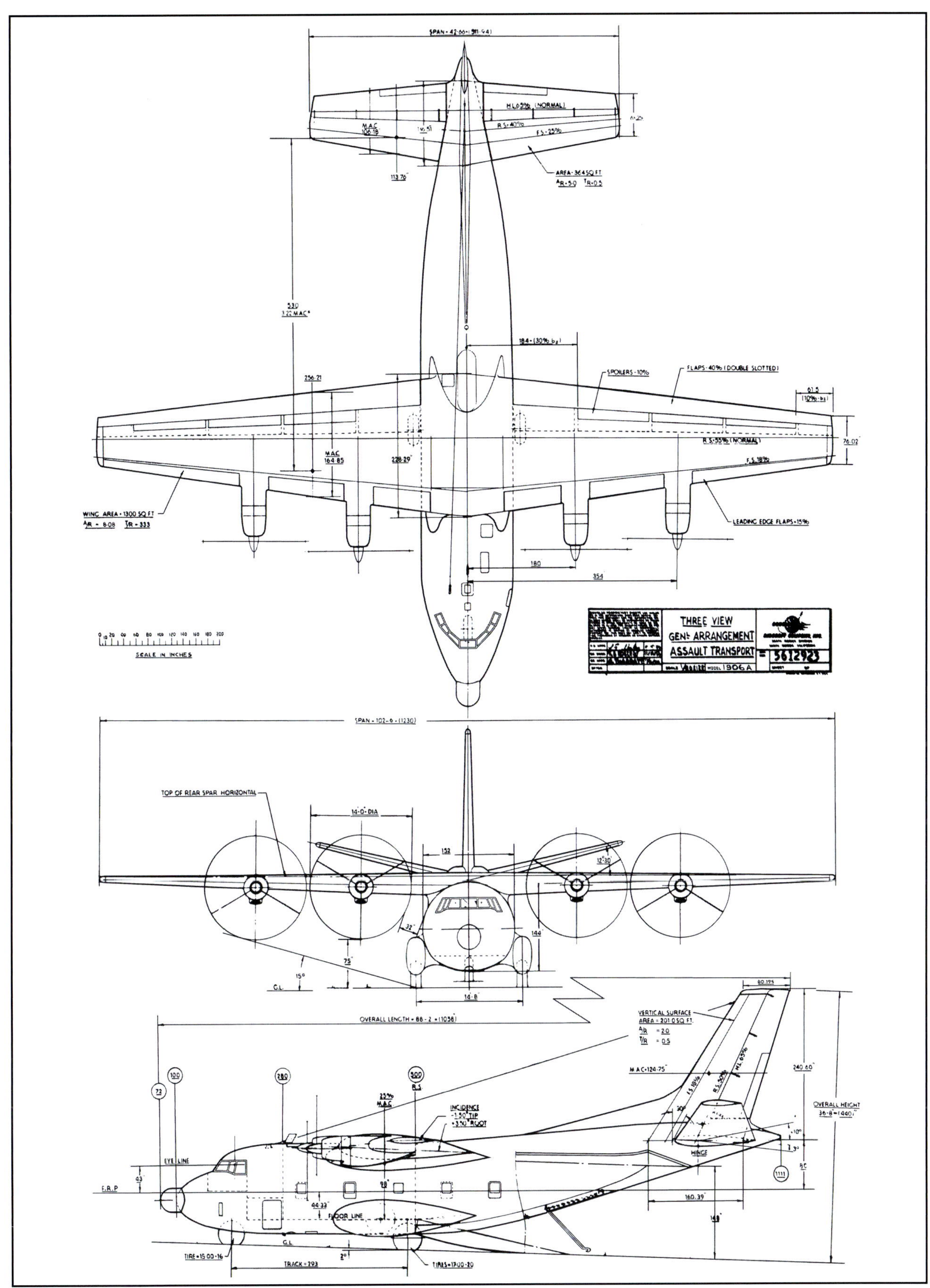

ABOVE Douglas Model 1906A general arrangement. *NASM*

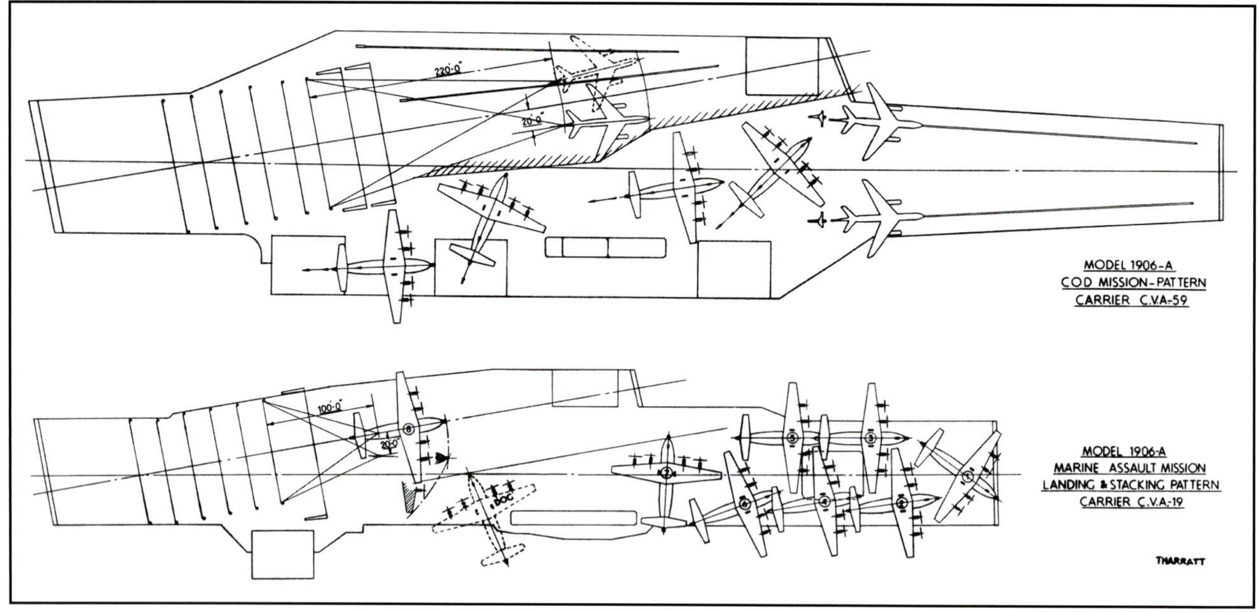

ABOVE Deck spotting diagrams for the Model 1906A COD on the large-deck *Forrestal* (above) and the Marine Assault version on a modified 'Essex' class carrier (below), showing recovery positions after an assault mission. Lack of wing-folding would likely have proven to be an operational challenge. *Boeing*

As initially presented to the Navy in November 1956, the Model 1906A did not have folding wings or tail, so it could not be taken to the hangar deck for parking, storage or repair. Douglas presented revised studies in July 1957, modifying the Model 1906A-1 for Assault/COD and the Model 1906C-1 for AEW (Airborne Early Warning) with folding wings and tail. A surviving desk model shows that the fin was intended to fold to the port side and that both wings were designed to fold back horizontally from hinges just outboard of the inner engines. Aircraft payloads and gross weight did not change, and the effect of the added structure and actuating systems on the projected empty weight was not identified. The model number 1906B was allocated for a version to be marketed to the Air Force.

Douglas Model 2007

Following its submission of the Model 1906A/1906A-1, Douglas went on to propose a smaller aircraft tailored specifically for the COD mission, designated the Model 2007. To quote the preliminary study report of 20 September 1957: 'This size aircraft has been studied in response to interest by some elements within the Navy favouring a smaller aircraft.'

The Model 2007 resembled a scaled-down version of the Model 1906A, but unlike the larger aircraft it incorporated a swing-tail loading arrangement. This allowed the elimination of the upswept aft fuselage with its taller tail. Only the flight crew compartment was pressurised.

BELOW A display model of the revised Douglas 1906A-1, showing the wing and tail folding arrangement. *John Aldaz collection*

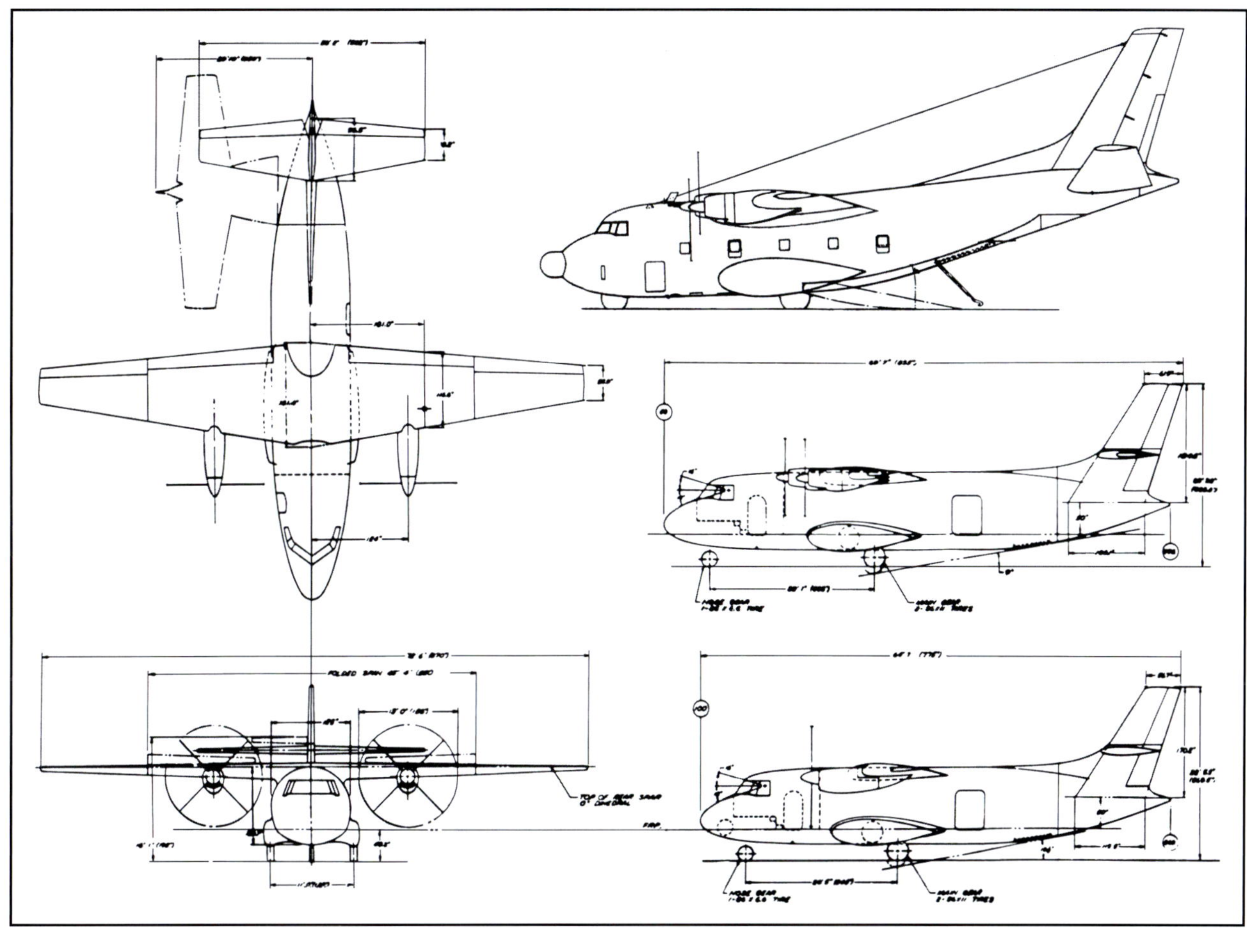

ABOVE The Douglas Model 2007-2 twin-T64-engine version, with the Model 1906A top right and the four-T53-engine Model 2007-1 middle right. *Boeing*

Douglas Model 2007

	'-1' Four-engine version	'-2' Twin-engine version
Powerplant	4 x Lycoming T53 turboprops @ 1,451shp (1,082kW)	2 x GE T64 turboprops @ 4,330hp (3,290kW)
Span	78.6ft (23.97m)	72.5ft (22.11m)
Length	68ft (20.60m)	63.33ft (25.60m)
Height	23ft 7.5in (7.21m)	23ft 5.5in (7.13m)
Wing area	765sq ft (71.14m²)	650sq ft (60.45m²)
Max TOW	46,300lb (21,020kg)	40,4000lb (18,342kg)
Payload	8,000lb (3,640kg)	8,000lb (3,640kg)
Cargo area	76in high x 104in wide x 443in long (1.93m x 2.64m x 11.25m)	76in high x 104in wide x 387in long (1.93m x 2.64m x 9.83m)
Max speed	257kt (476km/h)	310kt (574km/h)
Cruise speed	236kt (437km/h)	236kt (437km/h)
Range	1,500nmi (2,777km)	1,500nmi (2,777km)
Ferry range	2,875nmi (5,322km)	2,820nmi (5,220km)

The design was offered in two versions; the larger and heavier Model 2007-1 featured four Lycoming T53 powerplants, and the smaller and lighter Model 2007-2 used two General Electric T64s. The 860shp (645kW) T53 had the benefit of already being in operational service, while the higher-powered 3,080hp (2,300kW) T64 was still under development. Either model could carry a payload of 8,000lb (3,632kg) over a distance of 1,500nmi (2,777km).

Fairchild Models M-216 and M-255

After Fairchild had been awarded the Air Force contract for C-123B production in October 1953, the company began an intensive effort to widen the sales opportunities for the aircraft by adapting it for new missions. This resulted in a naval version designated the M-216. The company named this the 'Flying Lighter', a 'lighter' in naval terms being a flat-bottomed barge used to ferry goods to and from ships in harbour.

The M-216 was initially proposed with a tail-hook and other naval adaptations, but to avoid the associated weight penalties these did not include folding wings or tail. This precluded storing it in the hangar deck. The main changes to the standard C-123B were the installation of a new trailing-beam main landing gear and an arrester hook, together with structural reinforcement. New mooring (tie-down) and hoisting points were positioned mid-wing and on the nose.

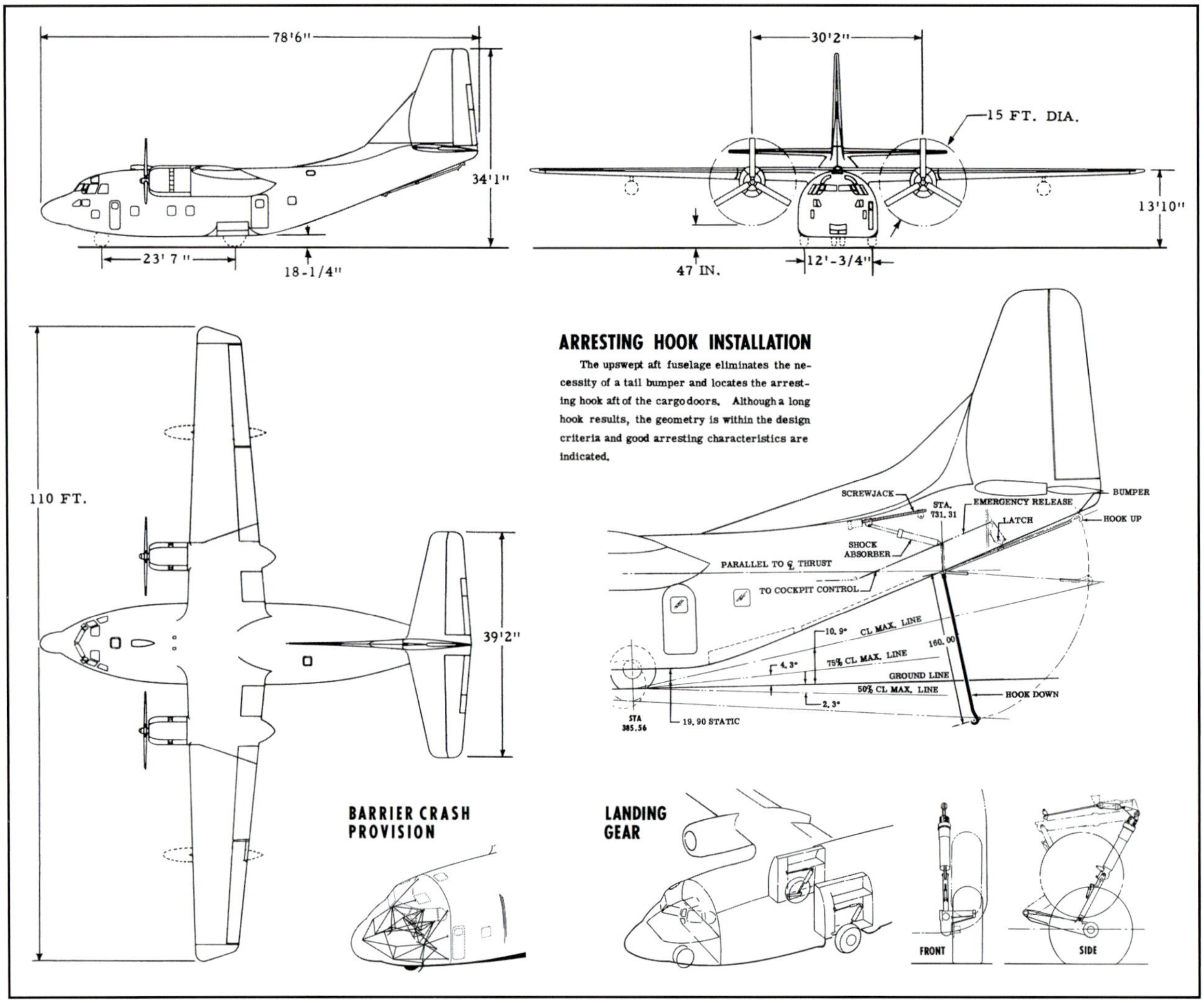
78'6"
34'1"
23' 7"
18-1/4"
30'2"
15 FT. DIA.
13'10"
47 IN.
12'-3/4"
110 FT.
39'2"
ARRESTING HOOK INSTALLATION
The upswept aft fuselage eliminates the necessity of a tail bumper and locates the arresting hook aft of the cargo doors. Although a long hook results, the geometry is within the design criteria and good arresting characteristics are indicated.
SCREWJACK
EMERGENCY RELEASE
BUMPER
LATCH
HOOK UP
SHOCK ABSORBER
PARALLEL TO ℄ THRUST
TO COCKPIT CONTROL
CL MAX. LINE
75% CL MAX. LINE
GROUND LINE
50% CL MAX. LINE
HOOK DOWN
19. 90 STATIC
BARRIER CRASH PROVISION
LANDING GEAR
FRONT
SIDE

ABOVE **Fairchild M-216 general arrangement.** *NARA II*

THE FAIRCHILD M-216 FLYING LIGHTER
FOR ADEQUATE CARRIER-ON-BOARD DELIVERY

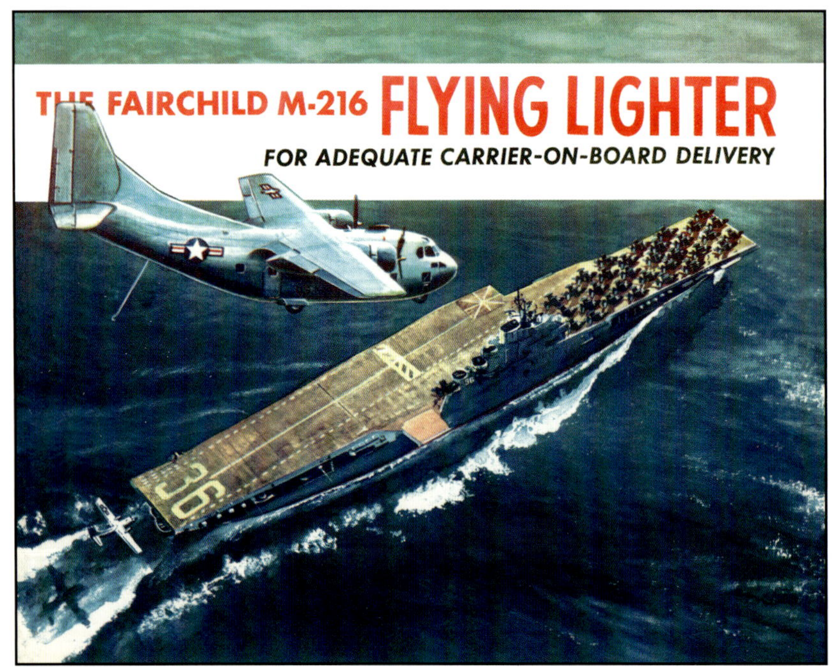

LEFT **Brochure cover artwork for the Fairchild M-216, a minimal modification of the C-123B.** *NASM*

This changed in Fairchild report OER-8 of July 1955, which outlined three C-123-based concepts for the Navy and Marine Corps. These were a stock C-123 for both shore transport use and the Marine Corps assault mission; the carrier-capable M-216 (which now incorporated wing and tail folding); and, building on the M-216, the M-220, which was designed to serve as a flying picket/CIC (Combat Information Center) equipped with height-finding and azimuth (ranging) radars.

Fairchild described the M-216 as 'A version of the proven C-123B especially designed for high seas delivery'. The aircraft was claimed to be capable of delivering 16,000lb (7,260kg) of payload to a carrier 1,200

miles (1,930km) out to sea, or even as far as 2,000 miles (3,220km) with 10,000lb (4,540kg) of fuel carried in external tanks. Mounting small Fairchild J44 jet engines on the wingtips was suggested as a further performance-enhancing option.

Based on comments from the Navy, Fairchild then refined the concept in 1957 with a further modified version of the C-123 under the M-255 designation. Refinements included the relocation of fuel from external drop tanks to internal wing tanks, and the repositioning of the J44 jet engines to the rear of the R-2800 engine nacelles (due to Navy concerns about their location on the folding outer wing panels). Additional stabilising surfaces were added to the ends of the horizontal tail.

Fairchild further recommended that instead of a single aircraft delivering only essential supplies, the Navy should utilise a fleet of aircraft, largely replacing carrier-supply ships. An 'Essex' class carrier would be able to accommodate twelve M-255s on the deck, while 'Midway' and 'Forrestal' class carriers would be able to handle even more. Out of each normal battle group of four carriers, one would be designated to handle the logistics task. Aircraft could land, unload and refuel in about ten minutes. Aircraft carriers would no longer have to retreat from the combat zone to transfer supplies from vulnerable transport ships in a safer rear area.

The concept envisaged the entire fleet quickly flying in, folding their wings as each one was unloaded and refuelled, then rapidly departing in quick succession. Although the folding-wing arrangement would permit the use of the carrier's elevator, it was envisaged that such a step would only be employed in the event of aircraft unserviceability, thus avoiding deck obstruction. A later refinement of the plan added a fifth carrier that acted as a floating warehouse for the whole fleet, distributing supplies to the other carriers, destroyers, cruisers and submarines by helicopter. The M-255s would be based at sixteen already established US land bases around the world.

Clearly, Fairchild was not just proposing a new COD aircraft; it was suggesting a whole new system for carrier support. The company envisaged that this could take over supply of everything currently provided by ships, excepting only the vast amounts of bulk fuels and lubricants required by the aircraft carrier and its Air Wing. The system would, of course, require establishing air superiority during time of war, but to be fair the existing system of ship-to-ship supply was itself a vulnerable process. It was a bold and imaginative concept, but perhaps just too big a step for the Navy to take.

Fairchild Model M-216 'Flying Lighter'	
Powerplant	2 x P&W R-2800-99W radials @ 1,900hp (1,417kW) normal, or 2,500hp (1,864kW) on take-off with water injection
Span	110ft (33.55m)
Height	34ft 1in (10.39m)
Length	78ft 6in (23.94m)
Wing area	1,223sq ft (110m²)
Payload	16,000lb (7,260kg) or 26 passengers
Range	1,200mi (1,930km), or 2,000mi (3,220km) with 10,000lb (4,540kg) fuel In external tanks

Fairchild Model M-255	
Powerplant	2 x P&W R-2800 radials @ 2,300hp (1,716kW), 2 x Fairchild J44 turbojets @ 1,000lb (4.45kN) thrust
Span	110ft (33.55m)
Span (folded)	42ft (12.81m)
Height	34ft 1in (10.39m)
Length	78ft 6in (23.94m)
Operating radius	1,500mi (2,413km)

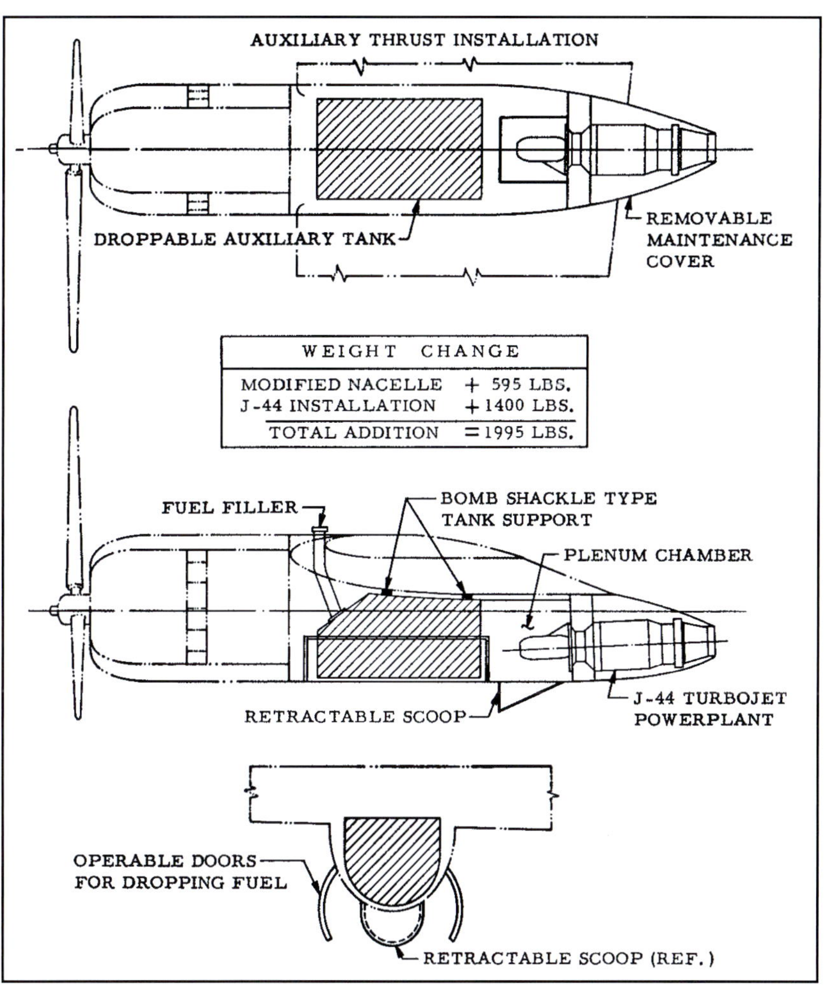

RIGHT Installation of the additional J44 engine and auxiliary fuel tank in the Fairchild M-255 nacelles. *NARA II*

The view at the end of the 1950s

None of the COD designs described above were pursued further, which is not surprising when viewed against a backdrop of larger issues. Three factors argued against their development.

Firstly, and of greatest significance, Grumman was already producing an adequate COD aircraft and delivering it to the fleet. It had the advantages of low cost and a high degree of commonality with the similar Grumman S2F ASW and WF-1 AEW aircraft.

Secondly, the thought of putting the C-123 and Model 1906A-sized aircraft on the decks of aircraft carriers as small as the modified Second World War-vintage 'Essex' class was not an easy 'sell'.

Thirdly, the contractors were attempting to sell common designs to two customers with different plans, yet needing the support of both if the programme was to go ahead. Indeed, Fairchild sensed in its discussions with Marine Corps officers that the Marines were in a delicate position. While the modified C-123 was adequate as an interim assault aircraft, the service did not want to jeopardise its long-term plans to buy the Lockheed C-130 for that mission.

The case for a large COD was not sufficiently convincing. Moreover, Navy opinion was fragmented; some officers (including the CNO) accepted the argument for a fully carrier-capable aircraft, while others were prepared to settle for non-folding wings and tail as a cost-saving expedient.

All of these considerations appear to have been overtaken by the 1958 budget cutbacks that forced the Navy to make hard decisions, such as choosing between the F4H Phantom II and the highly capable F8U-3 Crusader III. Budget pressure caused by the simultaneous development of the Polaris A-1 ICBM and the 'George Washington' class SSBN submarines to carry them, resulted in the cancellation of two other high-profile naval aviation programmes, the P6M-2 SeaMaster and the SSM-N-9 Regulus II supersonic cruise missile (together with the bespoke submarines required to launch it). Under these circumstances, the Grumman TF-1 (later C-1A Trader) remained a 'good-enough' solution for the time being.

Large COD: A postscript to the 1950s deliberations

Although the Navy had baulked at the idea of a large COD aircraft in the 1950s, a dramatic demonstration that this was not an unrealistic concept was soon to take place, albeit having nothing to do with a COD proposition.

In November 1963 the Naval Air Test Center proved the feasibility of operating a large transport aircraft at sea by demonstrating C-130F deck landings and take-offs from the USS *Forrestal* – without the benefit of an arrester hook or catapult gear. This particular aircraft was borrowed from the Marines, the only modifications being a different metering pin in the nose-wheel strut oleo, the addition of higher-capacity brakes, and the removal of the external fuel tanks.

Two carrier-qualified fighter pilots performed the tests, following C-130 check rides with a Lockheed test pilot; a Marine Corps C-130 flight engineer accompanied them. The crew made several landings and take-offs, up to the maximum take-off weight of 121,000lb (54,930kg); none presented any problems.

However, it was a limited trial, simply designed to establish the ability of a C-130 carrying a substantial payload to land and take-off from a carrier, in the event that this ever became necessary for a long-range supply mission. It was perceived as being too high-risk a procedure for routine operations, with the danger that the aircraft would become unserviceable after landing, greatly restricting the carrier's capability to continue launching and recovering aircraft. In fact, the *Forrestal*'s commanding officer reportedly warned the test team that if the aircraft went unserviceable during the trials and he had to resume normal operations, he would order the C-130 pushed overboard.

LEFT A Lockheed C-130 undergoing carrier landing trials in November 1963. *Mark Aldrich collection*

McDonnell Model 188E (Breguet 941)

After McDonnell's loss to LTV in the Tri-Service VTOL competition, it signed a technical agreement with the French manufacturer Breguet in the autumn of 1961. This was followed on 6 June 1962 by a licence agreement to develop the Model 941 for American use. The Breguet Model 941 was a

STOL transport aircraft developed from Breguet's prototype Model 940, and first flew in June 1961. Preliminary design of McDonnell's Model 188 was completed in the spring of 1963, and the Breguet 941.01 toured the East Coast of the United States in June-July 1964, being demonstrated to the Air Force and Army, before returning to France on 16 April 1965.

The Model 188E was also seen as being suitable for carrier flight-deck operation, being proposed to the Navy in September 1964. Offering a large cargo hold, it had very slow approach and take-off speeds, did not require catapult rig or arresting hook, and was operable on a pitching carrier deck without strength modifications to the landing gear. However, the Demonstrator did not offer wing or tail folding, so would be restricted to the flight deck. From the Navy point of view, the Model 188E offered few advantages over the Douglas and Fairchild designs evaluated five years previously. So far as is known, no actual carrier demonstrations were performed.

McDonnell Model 188E (Breguet 941)	
Powerplant	4 x Continental 261-5 turboprops (licensed Turbomeca Turmo III D3) @ 1,465shp (1,092kW), or 4 x General Electric T-58-SIB turboprops @ 1,500shp (1,119kW)
Span	77ft 11in (24.75m)
Length	76ft 8in (23.37m)
Height	30ft 11in (9.42m)
Wing area	897sq ft (83.34m²)
Max TOW	58,422lb (26,500kg)
Payload	17,500lb (7,938kg)
Cruise speed	200kt (370 km/h)
Radius	400nmi (740.8km) @ max payload
Ferry range	3,040nmi (5,630km) with ferry fuel tanks

ABOVE The prototype Breguet 941 (as the McDonnell Model 188E Demonstrator) flies over the NASA Langley Research Center. *Greater St Louis Air and Space Museum via Mark Nankivil*

BELOW Breguet 941 general arrangement. This aircraft was the basis for the McDonnell Model 188. *Breguet*

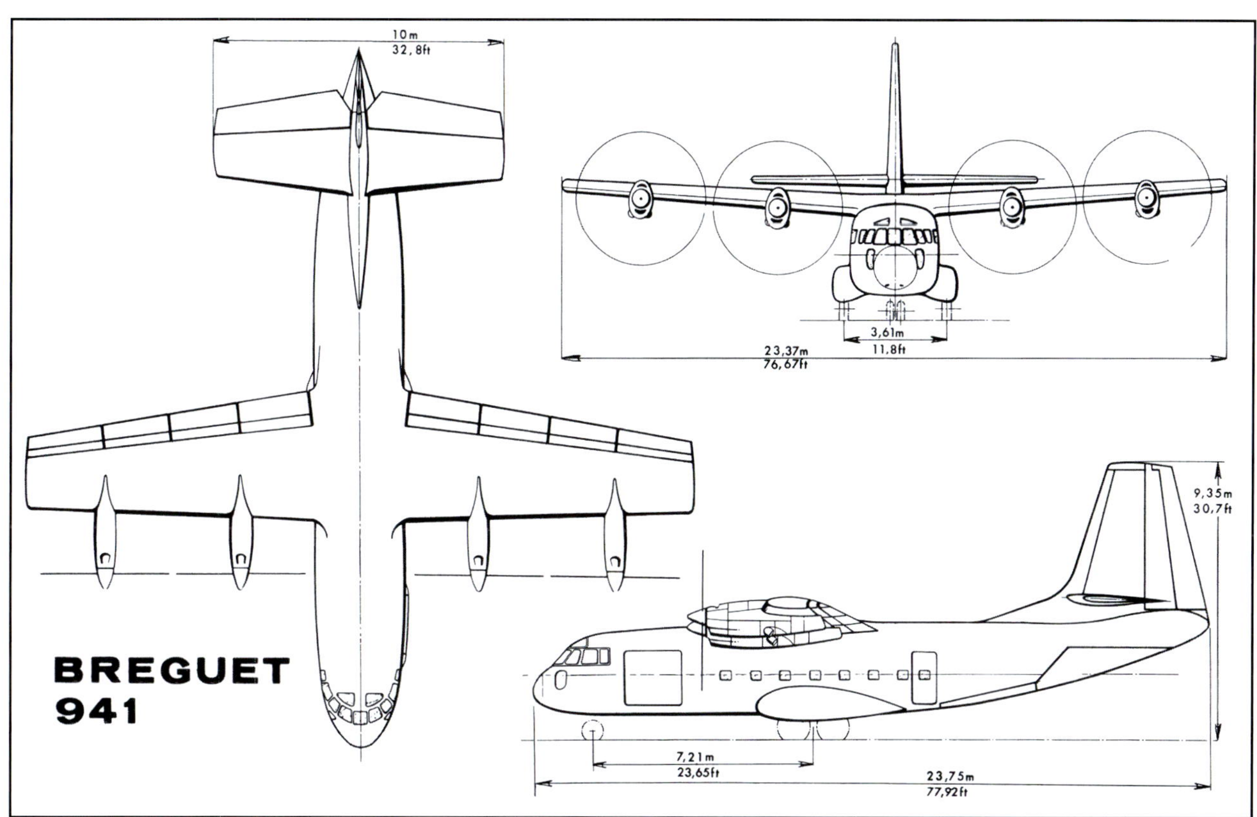

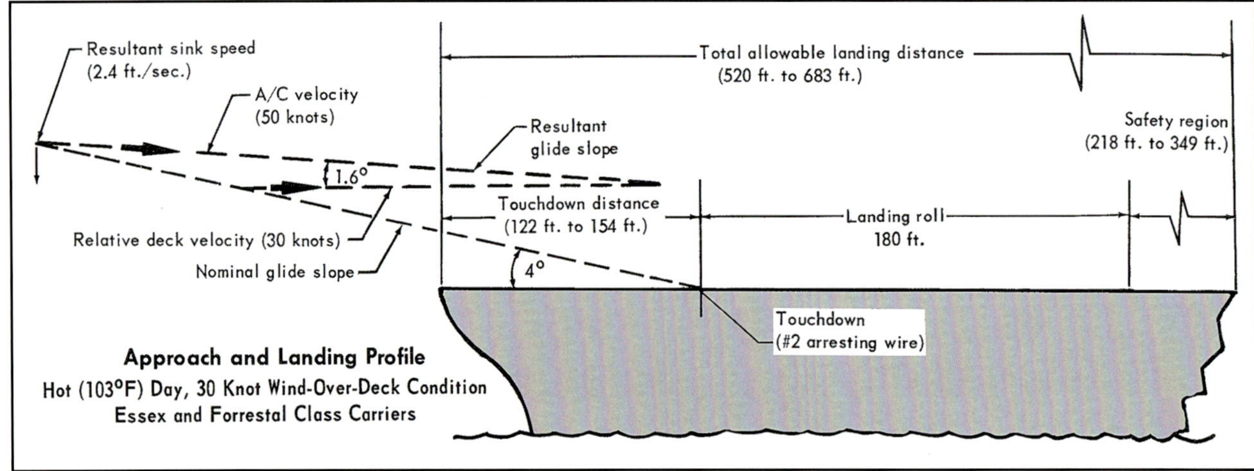

ABOVE The McDonnell Model 188's low approach speed, coupled with the wind-over-deck, was to result in a carrier landing roll of only 180ft (54.86m) using reverse thrust only (no wheel brakes or arresting gear). *Boeing*

McDonnell persisted with development despite the lack of interest from the US military, touring the second Breguet 941S as the Model 188 STOL airline demonstrator in 1968 with the goal of marketing the ultimate Model 210 STOL airliner. However, the STOL airliner market did not expand as expected, and the small niche that existed was filled by the de Havilland Canada DHC-7.

The 1960s: The Navy opts for the Grumman C-2A Greyhound

While the piston-powered C-1 Traders were providing yeoman COD service, by the early 1960s their limitations had become obvious. Significantly, they were unable to transport the bigger jet engines now powering Navy fighters. There was an additional need for an aircraft with greater range. This resulted in the Navy finally implementing a programme to supplement the C-1 in 1964.

Instead of opting for one of the large aircraft options described above, or initiating an industry-wide competition for a new aircraft, the Navy entered into a single-source, fixed-price contract with Grumman to adapt its in-production, carrier-based E-2A AEW

BELOW The early C-2 concept with an enlarged slab-sided fuselage, cabin portholes and the standard E-2A tail assembly. *Grumman History Center*

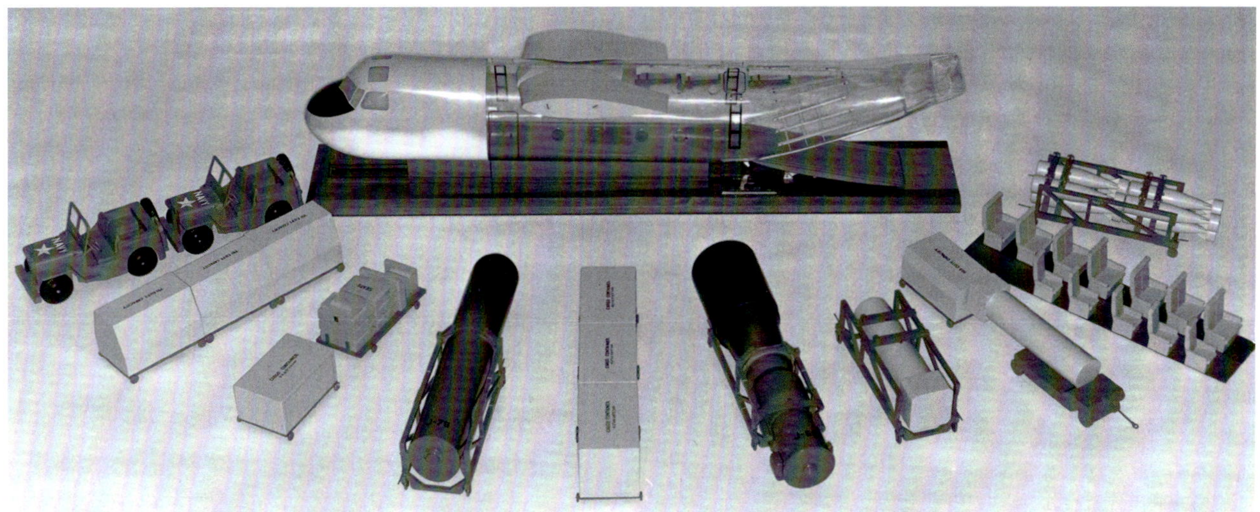

ABOVE A C-2 fuselage model with projected payloads. *Courtesy of Northrop Grumman Corporation*

BELOW The first C-2 was converted from a prototype E-2A; the all-new reshaped fuselage and modified tail is noticeable. *Courtesy of Northrop Grumman Corporation*

Hawkeye as its new COD aircraft. Originally developed as an ECP (Engineering Change Proposal) to the E-2A, it became known as the C-2A Greyhound.

The early design of the C-2 introduced a new slab-sided fuselage with multiple cabin windows, retaining the E-2A's wings, engine and tail assembly. However, designers later removed the latter's horizontal dihedral to retain hangar height clearance after the rear fuselage had been redesigned to raise the tail for better ramp access. It may have also matched the geometry of the wing lock to the outboard fin when folded, since the C-2's wing was mounted at a slightly greater angle of incidence.

The C-2 entered service at the end of 1966. However, to reduce cost it lacked several of the originally planned features. These deletions included in-flight refuelling capability, external drop tanks mounted on the fuselage inboard of the engines, weather/navigation radar, a fully integrated auxiliary power unit, mechanised 463L pallet handling, and litter provisions for the sick or wounded. The first batch of C-2s totalled only nineteen aircraft, including the prototypes converted from the first two E-2As.

Grumman C-2A Greyhound	
Powerplant	2 x Allison T56-A-8B turboprops @ 4,050shp (3,020kW)
Span	80ft 7in (24.60m) or 29ft 4in (8.94m) folded
Length	56ft 10in (17.30m)
Wing area	700sq ft (65m²)
Max TOW	54,354lb (24,650kg)
Payload	20,608lb (9,350kg) or 26 passengers
Cruise speed	251kt (465 km/h)
Range	1,300nmi (2,400km)

The 1970s: The Navy takes a further look at COD aircraft

By 1972 the Navy recognised the need, and the potential, to supplement its C-2s. Moreover, although it had previously looked at – and rejected – the possibility of using large aircraft for the COD role, it was now ready to revisit the concept. The attraction of expanding the mission of aerial fleet supply at sea – acquiring an aircraft with greater range than the C-2, with more speed and capacity – outweighed concerns about interfering with normal deck operations.

The Navy described its ideal requirements for the aircraft as follows:

- Carrier compatible
- Jet-propelled

- Cargo/passenger convertible
- Capable of in-flight refuelling
- Able to internally carry either two aircraft engines (without afterburners attached) or helicopter rotor blades/transmission systems

It should also have (in order of decreasing acceptability for trade-off):

- Commonality with contemporary aircraft
- A cruise speed of at least 330kt (611km/h)
- An unrefuelled range of 2,200mni (4,072km)
- A payload of 10,000lb (4,540kg)

However, overriding all these considerations was a requirement that the flyaway cost (less engines and avionics) should be about $5 million. Proposals for either studies or prototypes were due at Naval Air Systems Command by 1 September 1972. Presumably to make the cost constraint less of a disincentive to contractors, the Navy further stipulated that 'An aircraft readily adaptable for use in other military and civil roles is highly desirable.'

As far as is known, this remarkably broad solicitation for proposals was the only formal communication of the Navy's COD requirements issued in the 1970s. Not surprisingly, it drew a very wide range of responses, from development of existing carrier aircraft and the adaptation of well-established airliners such as the Boeing 737, DC-9 and Hawker Siddeley HS 748, to wholly new aircraft designs. While it might seem surprising, operating modified airliners was generally practical and within the catapult and recovery capability of the largest carriers. Boeing also put forward several entirely new designs in the C-2 size class, these being in the Model 953-500 family – one of the few purpose-designed COD proposals ever conceived.

Notwithstanding the Navy's stipulation that it required a jet-propelled aircraft, Bell Helicopter submitted a tilt-rotor proposal. It is also reported that General Dynamics proposed a new light COD aircraft, its Model 300, but the authors could find no details of this project.

As a result of industry interest, the Navy had no shortage of options, and as the decade progressed more would arise from a series of studies to explore the potential for a range of VTOL aircraft. One of these studies focused on a multi-purpose vehicle whose role would encompass COD. As a result, there were multiple prospective COD programmes running concurrently, but they were so different in nature that it would be hard to call them direct competitors. Nonetheless, this must have made decision-making more difficult, particularly given the funding constraints that were to be introduced within the austerity and diminished military expenditure of the Jimmy Carter administration.

Bell Helicopter Model D305

Despite the Navy's expressed interest in a jet-propelled aircraft, Bell proposed a V/STOL tilt-rotor aircraft as a solution for the COD requirement. The Bell D305 drew on experience gained with the XV-3 experimental tilt-rotor aircraft and extensive follow-on research and analysis. It had a twin-boom configuration allowing an easily accessed and fully usable fuselage for cargo, passengers or special equipment, as well as compactness when folded.

With foldable rotor blades and forward-folding booms hinged immediately behind the wings, the aircraft was capable of using the standard 30ft by 60ft (9.15m by 18.30m) carrier elevator and being stowed within the standard hangar deck height of 20ft (6.10m).

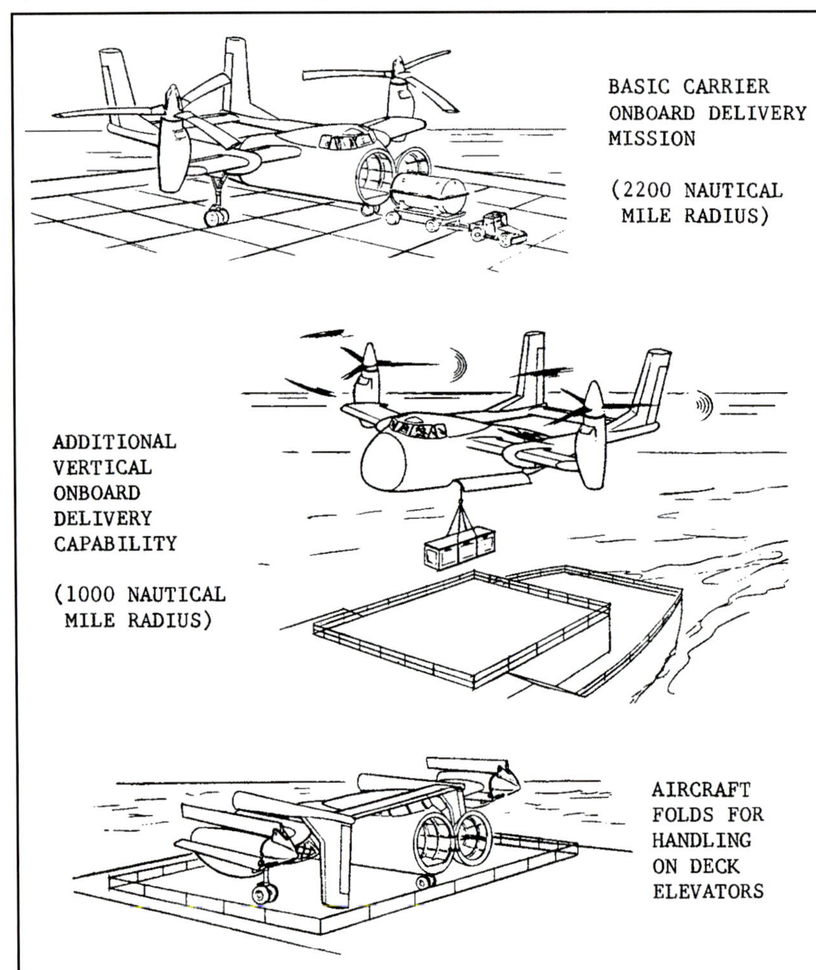

LEFT Illustrations of the Bell D305's capability. *Tommy Thomason collection*

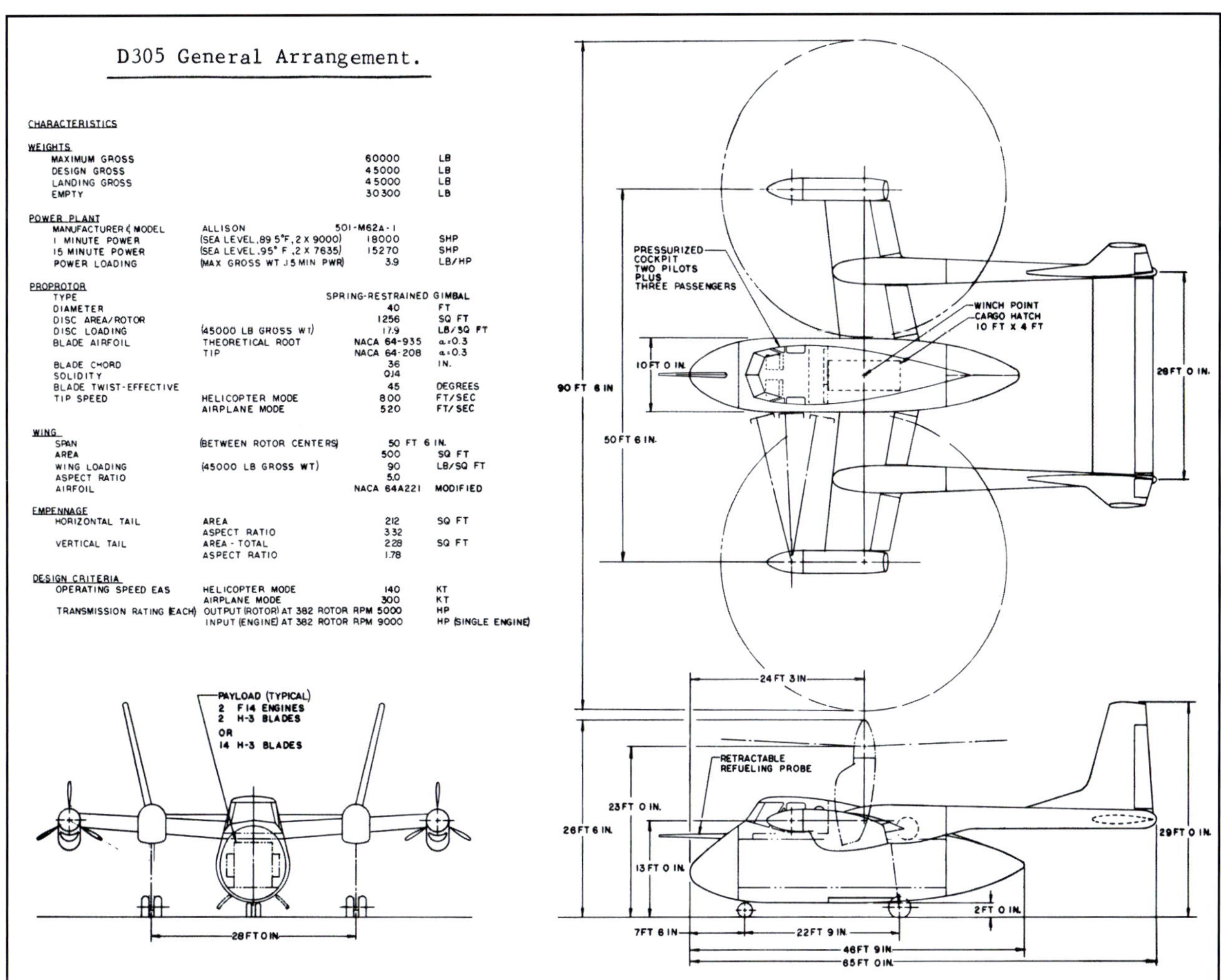

ABOVE General arrangement of the Bell D305. *Tommy Thomason collection*

Bell Helicopter Model D305	
Powerplant	2 x Allison 501-M62A-1 turboshafts @ 18,000shp (13,429kW) for 1 minute, or 15,270shp (11,387kW) for 15 minutes
Wingspan	50ft 6in (15.40m)
Rotor diameter	40ft (12.20m)
Width	90ft (27.45m), 59ft (18m) folded
Length	65ft (19.82m), 29ft 3in (8.92m) folded
Height	29ft 6in (9.00m), 19ft (5.80m) folded
Wing area	500sq ft (46.5m²)
Max TOW	60,000lb (27,240kg)
Payload	20,000lb (9,080kg)
Operating speed	300kt (555km/h) in aeroplane mode, 140kt (259km/h) in helicopter mode
Range	2,200nmi (4,070km)

Bell stressed that it could not only meet the stipulated COD requirements but also, uniquely, provide Vertical On-board Delivery (VOD) by loading and unloading through a fuselage floor hatch while hovering. Thus it could directly support any ship in the fleet, not just aircraft carriers. Despite these advantages, the tilt-rotor concept was relatively unproven at that point. The Navy was very unlikely to take a chance on it when there were more conventional and faster COD alternatives.

Boeing 737 and 727

Boeing's Model 737 short-range airliner had first flown on 9 April 1967 and had already secured a place in the commercial market – though few could have guessed how successful it would become, with its advanced descendants still attracting orders more than fifty years later. However, the production backlog was relatively small in the early 1970s, even with the benefit of an Air Force order for nineteen aircraft as navigation trainers (designated T-43A).

Boeing had already proposed the Model 737-CXL as a land-based transport for the Navy (losing to McDonnell Douglas's DC-9-30-based C-9A Nightingale), and this model possibly formed the basis of Boeing's submission. The opportunity of offering it to the Navy as a COD aircraft, therefore, came at an opportune moment as the production rate was down to one aircraft per month as a result of the 1972-73 economic recession.

Although much larger than the carrier-based C-1s and C-2s, the 737 was within the prevailing maximum weight limits for arrested landing and catapult-assisted take-off. Whether the 737 COD

ABOVE A Boeing 737 with the hook down is about to 'trap' on an aircraft carrier. *Boeing*

had folding wings is not known, though a promotional illustration shows a Boeing 737 on approach to a carrier with an arrester hook lowered. Boeing was sufficiently interested in the prospect to conduct a preliminary carrier-landing evaluation at nearby NAS Whidbey Island, using an aircraft carrier's visual-approach system located at the end of a runway that was marked out as an angled deck with 600ft (288m) between the target touchdown area and its far end. Boeing's test pilot, using a company 737, was reportedly able to touch down and stop within that distance, with 41ft (12.5m) to spare, without benefit of a tail-hook or arresting gear.

Remarkable though it may seem, Boeing also proposed its larger 727 for the COD role. The company made the proposal in 1965 as part of a wider campaign to promote the Model 727 as a military aeroplane. This initiative was based on adapting the 727C (Convertible cargo/passenger) model to become the proposed 727M (Military) equivalent. Boeing marketed the aircraft for several different missions:

- Navy COD
- USAF and USMC aerial tanker
- US Army/USMC assault transport
- military staff and command transport
- aeromedical transport

LEFT A depiction of a Boeing 727-100 COD being catapult-launched from the USS *Enterprise*. *Boeing*

ABOVE Boeing display model of the 727 COD proposal. *John Aldaz photo*

RIGHT A 'Fleet Support' adaptation of the Boeing 727 (with a tail-hook) is shown launching one of the six AQM-37A under-wing target drones. *Boeing*

Boeing Model 727M	
Powerplant	3 x P&W JT8D-1 turbofans @ 14,000lb (62.3kN) thrust
Span	108ft (54.9m)
Length	133ft 2in (40.62m)
Height	34ft (10.37m)
Wing area	1,650sq ft (154.41m²)
Max TOW	170,000lb (77,180kg)
Max speed	632mph (1,017km/h)
Cruise speed	570mph (917km/h)
Range	1,700mi (2,735km) with 38,000lb (17,250kg) cargo, 2,300mi (3,700km) with 55 passengers, 3,110mi (5,000km) max

Boeing Models 953-507 and 953-517

The Boeing Models 953-507 and 953-517 evolved from Boeing's work on the AMST programme in the early 1970s. Like the company's submission for that programme, which led to the YC-14, the designs produced extra lift using the jet efflux exiting over, and following the curvature of, the upper surface of the wing, thereby taking advantage of the Coandă effect. Boeing termed this its Upper Surface Blowing (USB) arrangement. At the time the company had high hopes for the system and described it as 'a break-through in aircraft design [that] will spawn … a family of aircraft for both military and commercial application.'

The Model 953-507 was similar in layout and wing planform to the YC-14, but featured a different tail configuration and could be either two- or three-engined. A range of engines was offered with consequent variations in operating weight. In its three-engine configuration, the third engine sat on top of the fuselage in line with the other two. This also necessitated the use of a 'butterfly' tail, rather than the usual vertical fin and horizontal stabilisers, which had the additional advantage of reducing the overall height, thus eliminating the need to have a folding fin.

The wings folded just outboard of the two wing-mounted engines. The variant powered by three General Electric GE TF34 turbofans, rated at 9,280lb (41.3kN) thrust, was estimated to be capable of carrying a payload of 10,000lb (4,540kg), with a cargo bay capable of accommodating three 463L pallets.

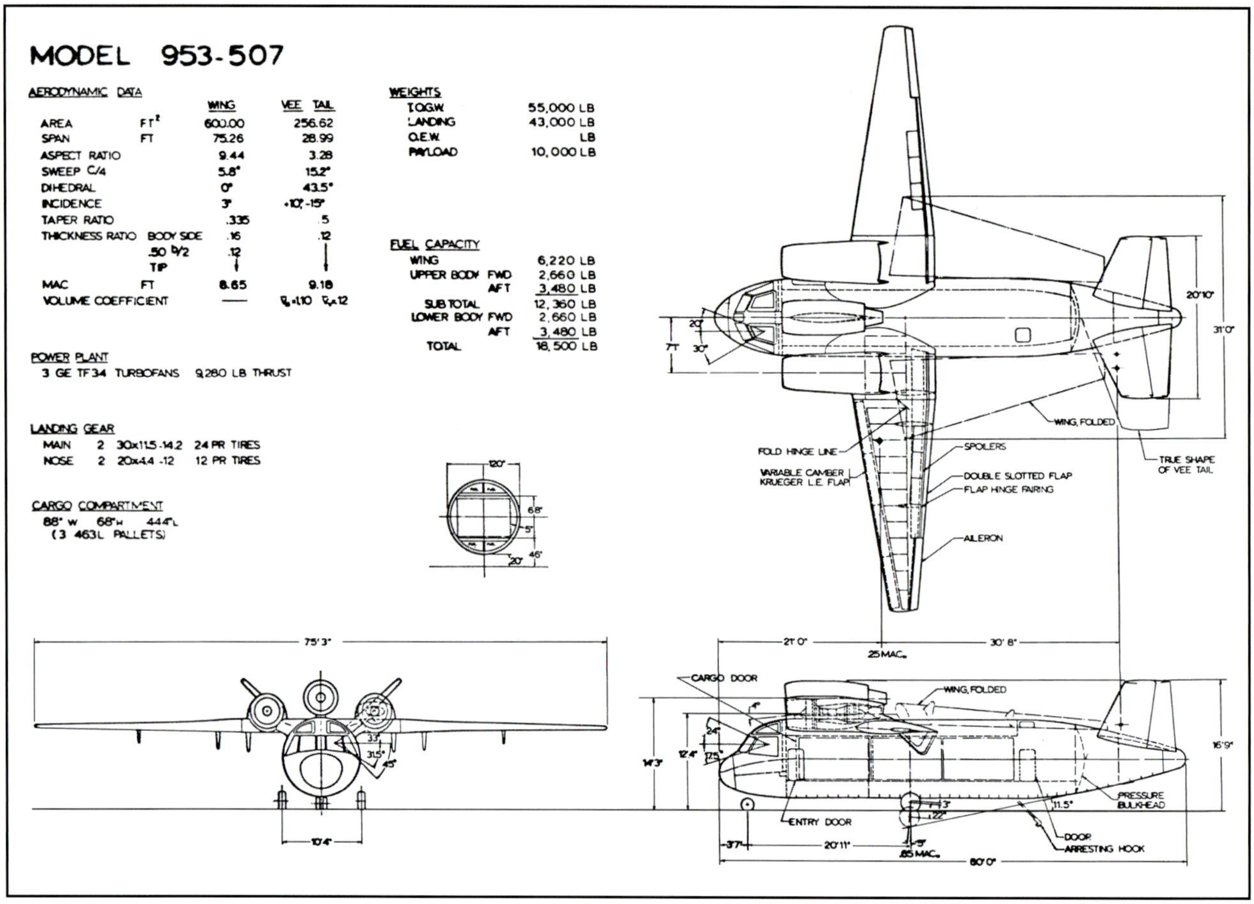

MODEL 953-507

AERODYNAMIC DATA

		WING	VEE TAIL
AREA	FT²	600.00	256.62
SPAN	FT	75.26	28.99
ASPECT RATIO		9.44	3.28
SWEEP C/4		5.8°	15.2°
DIHEDRAL		0°	43.5°
INCIDENCE		3°	+10°,-15°
TAPER RATIO		.335	.5
THICKNESS RATIO	BODY SIDE	.16	.12
	.50 b/2	.12	
	TIP		
MAC	FT	8.65	9.18
VOLUME COEFFICIENT		—	$\bar{V}_h$=.110 $\bar{V}_v$=.12

POWER PLANT
3 GE TF34 TURBOFANS 9,280 LB THRUST

LANDING GEAR
MAIN 2 30x11.5-14.2 24 PR TIRES
NOSE 2 20x4.4-12 12 PR TIRES

CARGO COMPARTMENT
88" W 68"H 444"L
(3 463L PALLETS)

WEIGHTS

T.O.G.W.	55,000 LB
LANDING	43,000 LB
O.E.W.	LB
PAYLOAD	10,000 LB

FUEL CAPACITY

WING		6,220 LB
UPPER BODY	FWD	2,660 LB
	AFT	3,480 LB
SUB TOTAL		12,360 LB
LOWER BODY	FWD	2,660 LB
	AFT	3,480 LB
TOTAL		18,500 LB

WING, FOLDED
FOLD HINGE LINE
VARIABLE CAMBER KRUEGER L.E. FLAP
SPOILERS
DOUBLE SLOTTED FLAP
FLAP HINGE FAIRING
AILERON
TRUE SHAPE OF VEE TAIL
CARGO DOOR
ENTRY DOOR
PRESSURE BULKHEAD
DOOR
ARRESTING HOOK
75' 3"
10' 4"
21' 0"
30' 8"
25 MAC
20' 10"
31' 0"
16' 9"
14' 3"
20' 11"
80' 0"

ABOVE Boeing Model 953-507 general arrangement, powered by three TF34 turbofans. *Boeing*

BELOW Boeing Model 953-517 general arrangement. With four TF-34 turbofans, this was Boeing's preferred design. *Boeing*

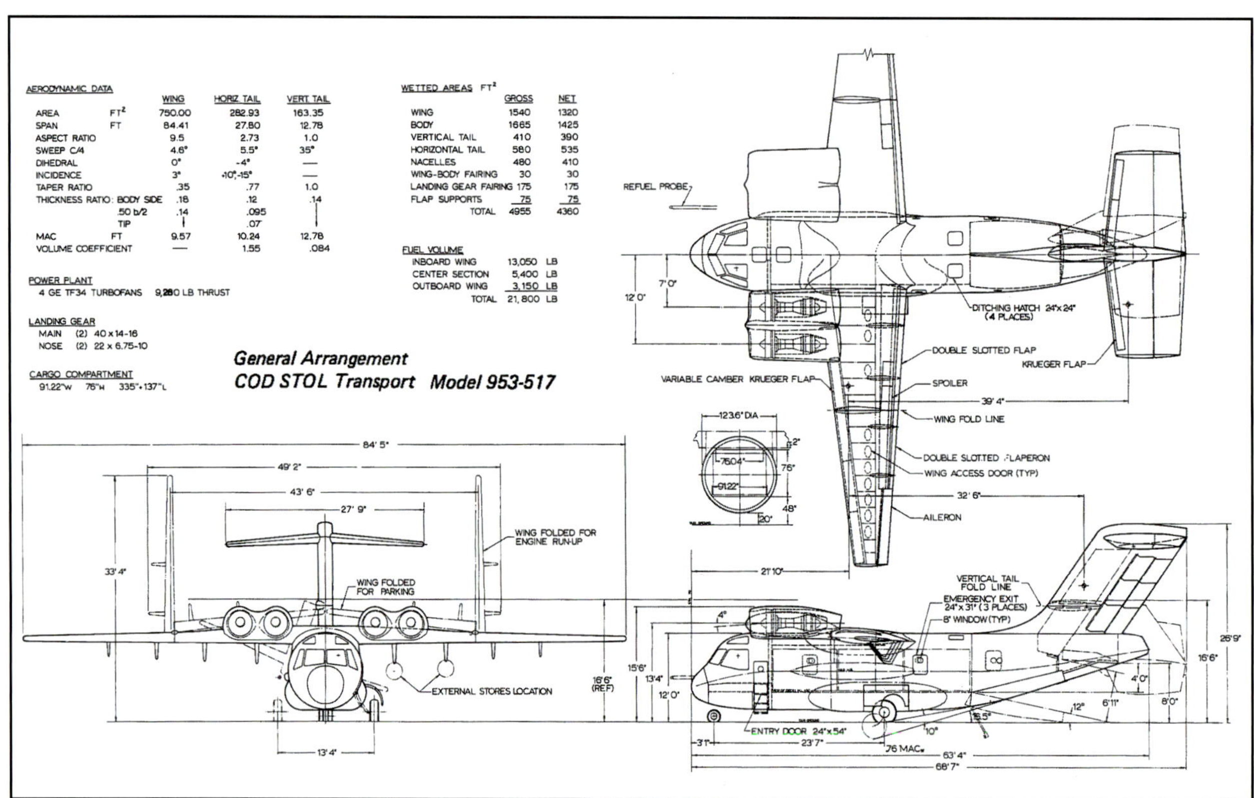

Boeing Model 953-507	
Powerplant	3 x GE TF34 turbofans @ 9,280lb (41.3kN) thrust
Span	75ft 3in (22.95m)
Length	60ft (18.3m)
Wing area	600sq ft (55.80m²)
Max TOW	55,000lb (24,970kg)
Payload	10,000lb (4,540kg)
Cargo hold	88in wide x 68in high x 444in long (2.57m x 1.73m x 11.28m)

Boeing Model 953-517	
Powerplant	4 x GE TF34 turbofans @ 9,280lb (41.3kN) thrust
Span	84ft 5in (25.77m), 49ft 2in (15.0m) folded
Length	68ft 7in (20.92m)
Height	26ft 9in (8.27m), 33ft 4in (10.61m) folded
Wing area	750sq ft (69.75m²)
Cargo hold	91.2in wide x 76in high x 512in long (2.31m x 1.92m x 13.01m)

ABOVE The Grumman Model 614 VRCX adaptation of the C-2A; to be fitted with four Garrett ATF3 turbofan engines. *Mark Aldrich collection*

The Model 953-507 was certainly one of the most innovative designs put forward for the COD role, but it was handicapped by the cost of developing a completely new airframe and the fact that most of the engines identified were either in the early stages of development or as yet only paper proposals.

However, Boeing eventually proposed to the Navy a larger version of the aircraft, the Model 953-517, powered by four engines, with a T-tail. At the same time it also offered a land-based equivalent, the Model 953-518.

Grumman Model 614 (turbofan-powered C-2A)

When production of the C-2A ended in 1967, only nineteen aircraft had been delivered, including the two prototypes converted from E-2 Hawkeyes. Responding to the Navy's interest in a turbofan-powered replacement, Grumman proposed a new-build, much-modified version of the C-2A. Designated the Grumman Model 614 VRCX (Experimental design for the VRC squadrons), it featured four Garrett AiResearch ATF3 turbofans rated at 4,000lb (17.8kN) thrust. While the ATF3 was under development and had not flown yet, it offered much better fuel economy than other turbofan engines. These engines were mounted in twin pods under each wing. The aircraft was also equipped with an in-flight refuelling probe.

The Navy expressed interest in the concept, but it proceeded no further. However, as will be seen later in this chapter, proposals for more turbofan-powered C-2 derivatives would follow.

Hawker Siddeley Type 849 (H.S. 748) COD

British manufacturer Hawker Siddeley put forward an adapted COD version of the H.S.748 twin-turboprop aircraft. This had started life as an airliner, flying for the first time in 1960, before being developed into a multi-purpose military transport to meet a Royal Air Force requirement, in which guise it first flew on 9 July 1965. The 748 had been designed from the outset to have good short-field performance and to be able to operate in difficult conditions from bases with limited maintenance facilities.

RIGHT A promotional illustration of the Type 849 in US Navy colours. *Avro Heritage Centre*

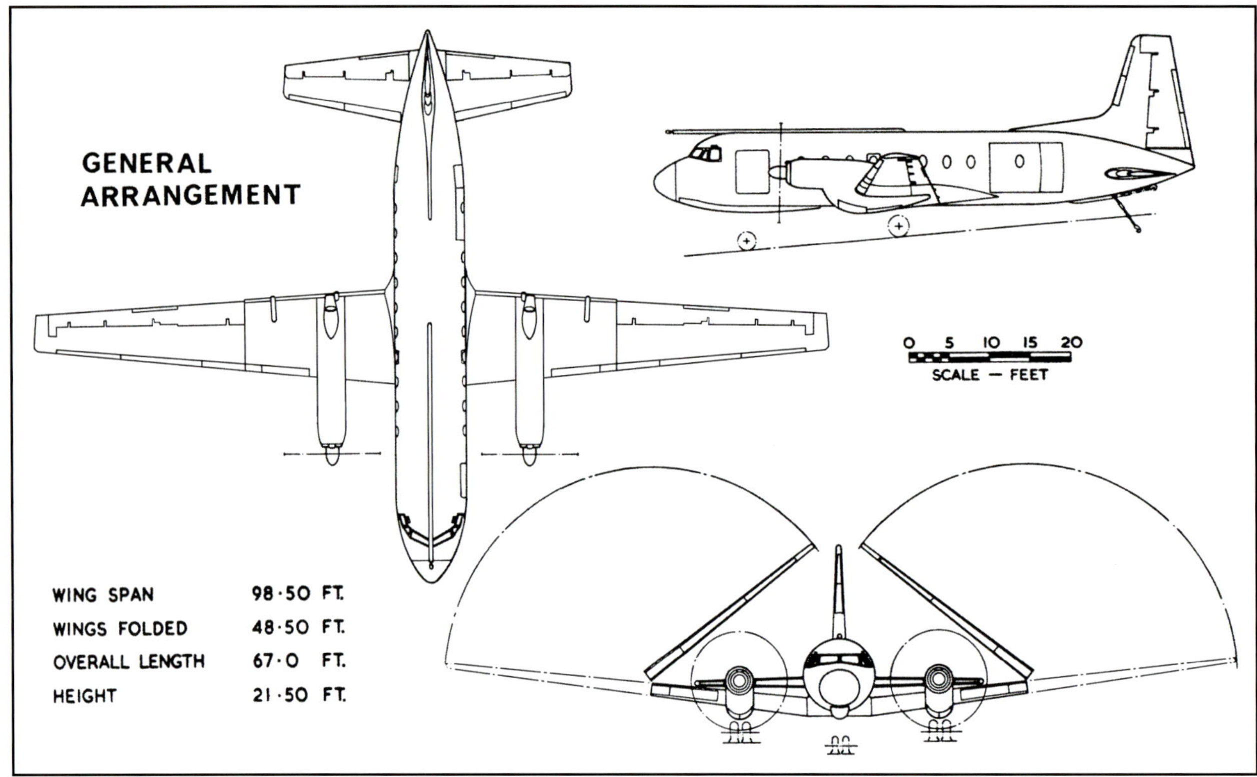

ABOVE Hawker Siddeley Type 849 COD.
Avro Heritage Centre

Hawker Siddeley Type 849 COD	
Powerplant	4 x Rolls-Royce Dart R.Da.7 Mk 532-2L turboprops @ 2,280shp (1,700kW)
Span	98.5ft (29.55m), 48.50ft (14.70m) folded
Length	67.0ft (20.30m)
Max TOW	50,000lb (22,700kg)
Max payload	9,850lb (44,720kg)
Range	1,380nmi (2,550km) with max payload, 2,200nmi (4,070km) with 4,400lb (2,000kg) payload

Assigned the Hawker Siddeley designation of Type 849, the COD proposal was a modification of the basic H.S.748 rather than the RAF Andover transport aircraft (which had an upswept aft fuselage and a rear loading ramp). The changes to the H.S.748 included folding wings, fuselage modifications to accommodate an arrester hook, strengthened landing gear with a longer stroke nose-wheel, and additional double doors in the port side, aft of the wings.

The overall dimensions were identical to the H.S.748 with the exception that the effective height on the ground was reduced by the 'tail-down' sit, resulting from the longer nose-wheel strut. Its engines were slightly more powerful versions of the Rolls-Royce Dart turboprops, and at 50,000lb (22,700kg) the all-up weight was a little higher.

Hawker Siddeley claimed that the Type 849 was capable of carrying a payload of 9,850lb (4,470kg) over a range of 1,380nmi (2,550km) or 4,400lb (2,000kg) over a range of 2,200nmi (4,070km). It was also fitted with an in-flight refuelling probe.

S-3 COD (Lockheed Model CL-1276)

Both Lockheed and the Navy had already envisaged that the company's S-3 Viking ASW aircraft, which was under development and would enter service in 1974, could be modified for the COD mission. Lockheed explored several variations on the theme and proposed two to the Navy. The first was dubbed the 'S-3 Utility COD' and was a lower-cost, minimum-change variant. More ambitious was the 'S-3 COD'.

The S-3 COD incorporated a mostly new, enlarged fuselage, while retaining the cockpit module, wings, engines and empennage of the basic S-3 aircraft. First explored under the Lockheed California designation of Model CL-1276, the project had both two- and three-engine options for the COD and VPX (Fixed-wing Patrol) missions.

Integral to both designs was the cargo compartment, which was to be 6ft (1.83m) wide, 6ft (1.83m) high and have a flat, unobstructed floor 26ft (7.92m) long. Total cargo compartment volume in the full COD design was 785cu ft (22.23m^3), including the aft cargo loading ramp, which was stressed to carry medium-weight loads when closed. Lockheed stated that the use of preloaded cargo containers could achieve a thirty-minute turnaround time on board a carrier. This 'quick-turn' capability would reduce interference with shipboard Air Wing aircraft launch and recovery, and permit increased utilisation of the COD aircraft.

In the mixed passenger/cargo configuration, the passengers boarded through a door on the forward right side of the S-3 COD fuselage and sat in the front of the compartment, ahead of the cargo containers, allowing simultaneous cargo loading and unloading through the aft ramp. Lockheed designed movable barriers that could be used fore and aft of the containers to prevent them from shifting during high-G catapult launch and carrier landings. The new main landing gear units were moved outboard and housed in sponsons to keep the wheel wells from intruding into the cargo compartment.

There was little difference in payload between the two, from 11,580lb (5,257kg) to 12,562lb (5,703kg), but a massive difference in weight, from 55,344lb (25,080kg) to 90,545lb (41,107kg). This was due to the substantial increase in internal fuel, from 17,222lb (7,819kg) to 44,572lb (20,236kg) in the patrol/ASW version, which would have yielded a much greater range.

Lockheed S-3 Utility COD

As the least expensive variant, the S-3 Utility COD would have been created by inserting a 70in (1.78m) plug into the existing forward fuselage, providing an area ahead of the wings able to accommodate small package cargo or twelve passengers. This internal space was augmented by externally accessible cargo compartments replacing the former weapons bays.

The Navy's basic COD requirement called for the ability to carry a 10,000lb (4,540kg) payload over a range of 2,200nmi (4,072km). The S-3 Utility COD could not meet this payload target; internal carriage was only 5,854lb (2,658kg), though this could be increased to 7,384lb (3,352kg) by two under-wing cargo pods. It was claimed that these pods could also be used to transport spare engines, either for the S-3A or the Grumman F-14. The range, however, at 2,389nmi (4,422km) exceeded the requirement, while being reduced to 2,000nmi (3,702km) if the external pods were used.

As well as being less costly than the S-3 COD, this simpler conversion also had the advantage of requiring a much shorter development time. Lockheed

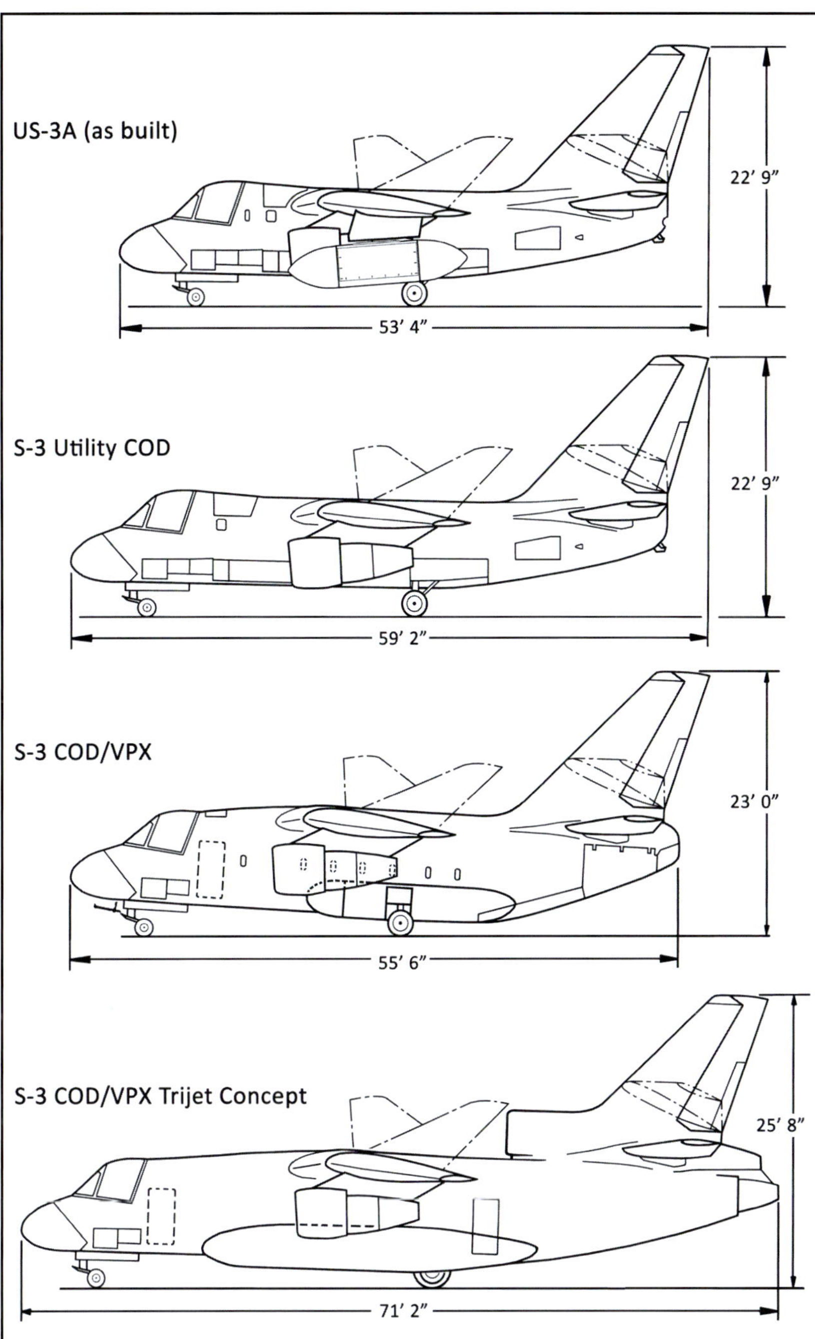

ABOVE The Lockheed US-3A (as converted), with the S-3 Utility COD (modified CL-1650 AEW), Twin-Jet CL-1276 'S-3 COD/VPX' and Tri-Jet CL-1276 COD/VPX versions. *Lockheed*

Lockheed CL-1276 Twin-Jet and Tri-Jet

	Lockheed CL-1276 Twin-Jet	Lockheed CL-1276 Tri-Jet
Powerplant	2 x GE TF-34 turbofans @ 9,280lb (41.3kN) thrust	3 x GE TF-34 turbofans @ 9,280lb (41.3kN) thrust
Span	68ft 8in (20.93m)	68ft 8in (20.93m)
Length	59ft 2in (18.03m)	71ft 2in (21.69m)
Height	23ft 0in (7.01m)	25ft 8in (7.82m)
Max TOW	55,344lb (25,080kg)	90,545lb (41,107kg)
Payload	11,580lb (5,257kg)	12,562lb (5,703kg)

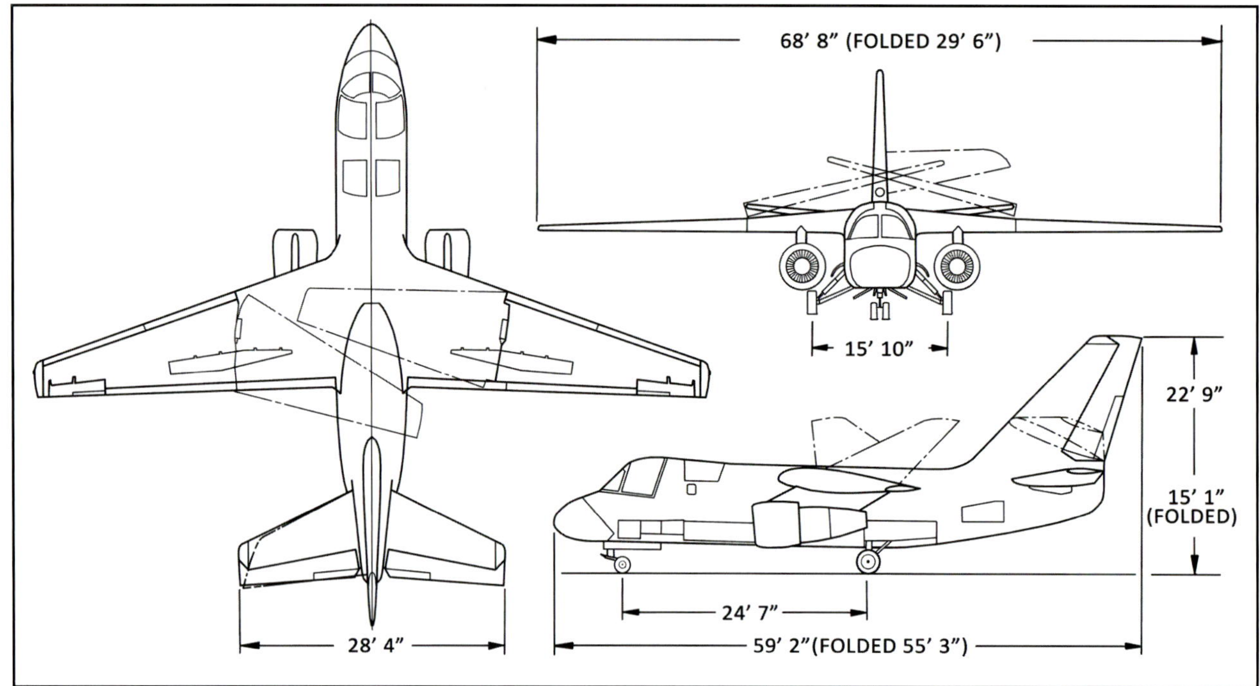

ABOVE **Lockheed S-3 Utility COD general arrangement.** *Lockheed*

BELOW **Lockheed S-3 Utility COD internal arrangement.** *Lockheed*

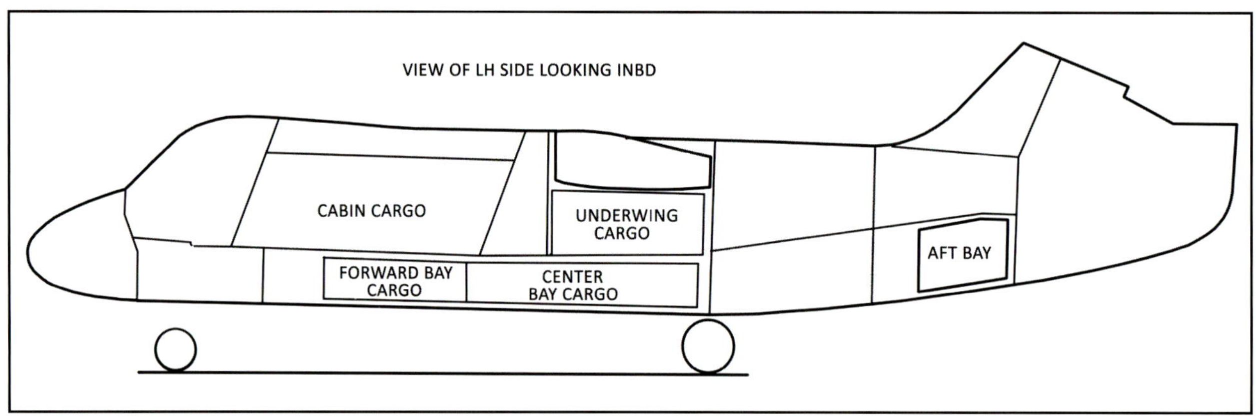

Lockheed S-3 Utility COD	
Powerplant	2 x GE TF-34-GE-2 turbofans @ 9,275lb (41.27kN) thrust
Span	68ft 8in (20.93m)
Length	59ft 2in (18.04m)
Max TOW	44,142lb (20,040kg)
Payload	5,854lb (2,653kg)
Range	2,389nmi (4,422km)
Max speed	442kt (818km/h)
Cruising speed	351kt (650km/h)

suggested that the two original S-3A prototypes, which were still fully instrumented for flight testing, could be converted to serve as the S-3 Utility prototypes.

McDonnell Douglas DC-9/C-9 (COD)

The US Navy had ordered the commercial 'off the shelf' DC-9-30 under the 'CXL' requirement (winning over the Boeing 737) as a shore-based transport aircraft in 1973. Designated the C-9B Skytrain II, the aircraft was to replace Navy and Marine Corps Convair C-131F/Gs and Douglas C-118s. It was, therefore, natural for the company to propose a carrier-compatible variant to meet the COD requirement.

Again fighting the stigma of being thought too large to operate aboard the aircraft carrier, the C-9 (COD) was in fact no larger than a C-130F. Being based on the smallest DC-9 variant, its maximum take-off weight of 98,400lb (44,630kg) and landing weight of 72,000lb (32,660kg) were under the 'max cat' and 'max trap' catapult and arrester gear capability given its take-off and approach speeds and a reasonable wind-over-deck. Further, the JT8D engines were highly reliable and it was claimed that even if one should fail, the C-9 (COD) could be launched with sufficient safety margin.

The aircraft was to be a hybrid of the DC-9-10 fuselage modified with the C-9B cargo door and the DC-9-20 wing with leading edge slats. The main

ABOVE The McDonnell Douglas C-9 (COD) with refuelling probe. *Author collection*

modifications were the introduction of a relocated, strengthened and extendable nose-wheel strut with a catapult tow/holdback, and the addition of an arrester hook and in-flight refuelling probe. Selected fuselage skins and longerons were re-gauged (thickened) to withstand the additional stress of launch and landing. The addition of a wing-folding mechanism was proposed as a study item. Cargo capacity was rated at 10,000lb (4,540kg) at a range of 2,200nmi (4,070km). The fuselage had space for seating twenty passengers in the rear cabin and space for bulk items such as two afterburner-fitted TF30 jet engines or four standard 463L cargo pallets in the forward cabin.

Douglas C-9 (COD)	
Powerplant	2 x P&W JT8D turbofans @ 14,000lb (62,30kN) thrust
Span	93.3ft (28.46m)
Length	104.4ft (31.84m)
Height	26.8ft (8.17m)
Wing area	1,300sq ft (117m²)
Max TOW (land)	110,000lb (49,900kg)
Max TOW (carrier)	104,000lb (47,170kg)
Payload	10,000lb (4,540kg) at TOW of 98,400lb (44,630kg)
Range	2,200nmi (4,070km) with 10,000lb (4,540kg) payload

ABOVE A C-9 (COD) is launched off the waist catapult of an aircraft carrier. *Author collection*

BELOW A display model of the C-9 (COD). *John Aldaz photo*

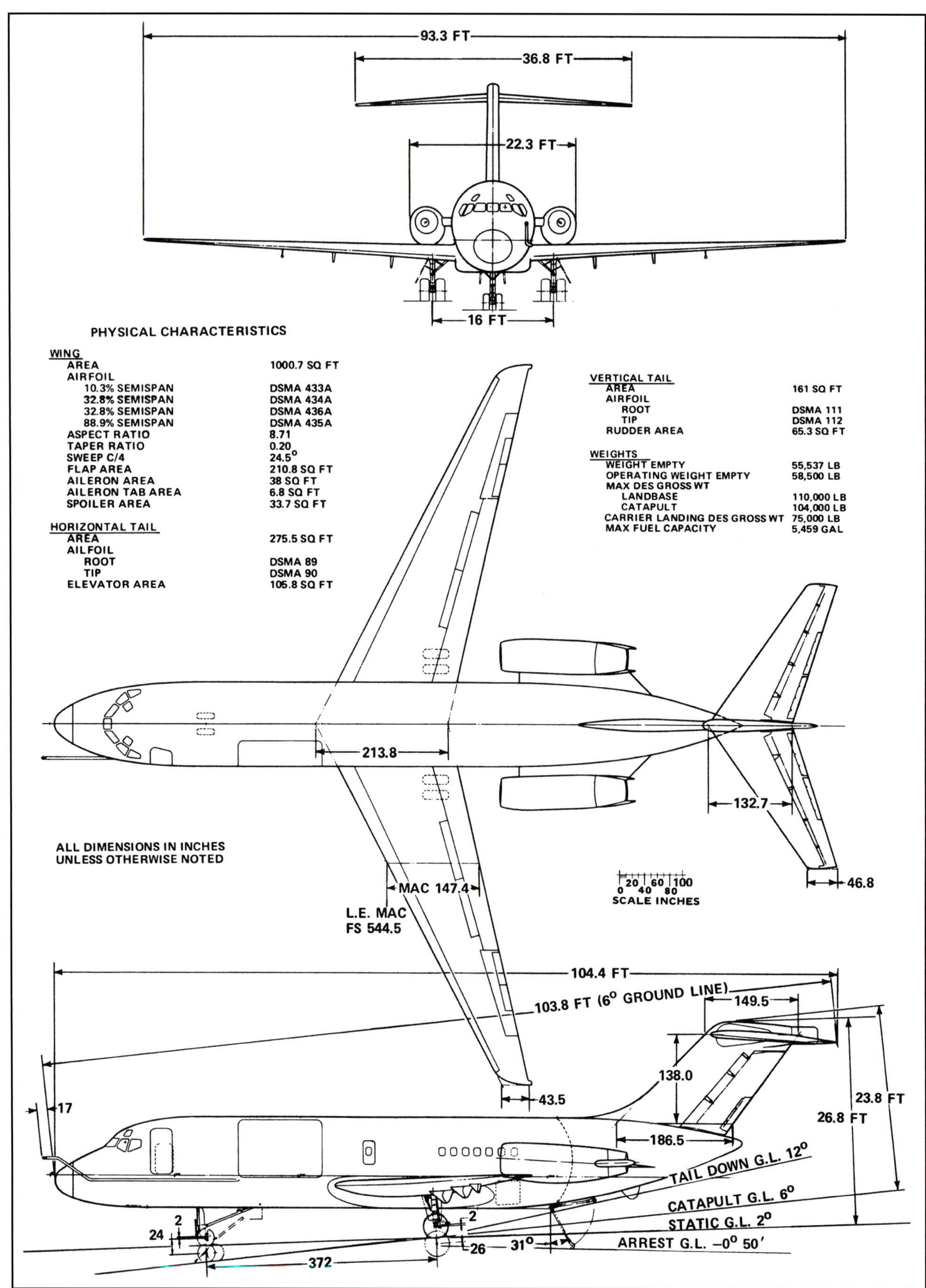

ABOVE **McDonnell Douglas C-9 (COD) general arrangement.** *Author collection*

The losing winner: Lockheed

After eighteen months of studies and evaluation, the Navy finally selected the S-3 Utility COD in September 1974, preferring this to the other finalists, the Grumman C-2 Derivative and S-3 COD. But although the decision had been made, funding still had to be found.

An initial production run of twenty-four aircraft was envisaged, with the possibility of this being extended later to thirty-six aircraft. According to AW&ST, the Navy promised a formal decision on procurement by October 1972; on this basis Lockheed believed that the S-3 Utility – reportedly the front-runner in the competition – could fly by the spring of 1976, with service deliveries starting in late 1978. However, the production contract would still be dependent on the 'fly before buy' policy then in vogue at the Defense Department.

A year later the Fiscal Year (FY) 1977 Defense Budget carried a $170 million line item for twelve S-3 Utility CODS, in spite of dissention within the Navy and the Defense Department. This funding was deleted in an amendment offered by House Representative M. Robert Carr, who pointed out that the 'stripped' utility version would cost $14 million per aircraft, $2 million more than the S-3A with the advanced avionics for Anti-Submarine Warfare. The fact that this cost also included a one-time charge for non-recurring engineering and testing for the COD version was ignored, and the budget amendment was passed without Navy or DOD opposition. Since the final S-3A funding had been provided the previous year, S-3 production was ending, so the chance to add the COD variant while the assembly line was 'hot' was lost.

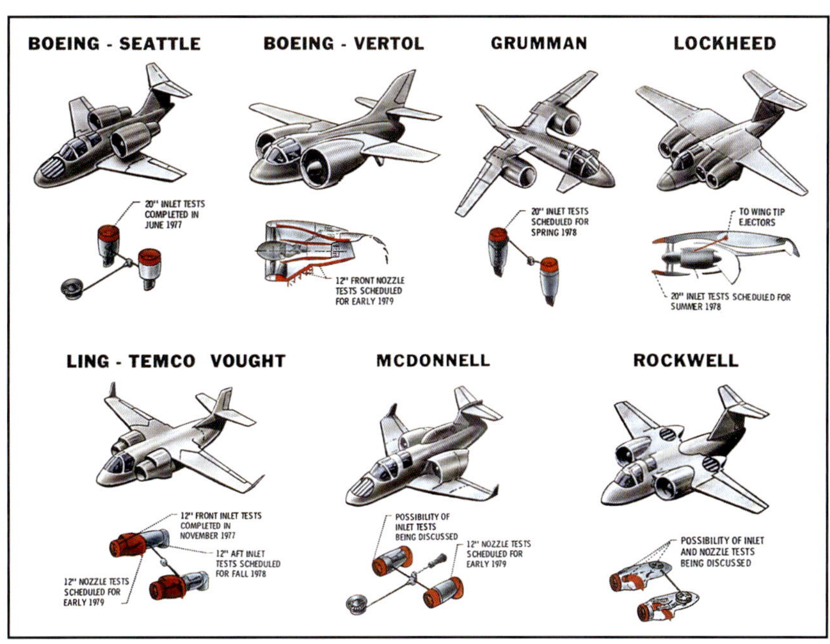

ABOVE Contractor propulsion concepts to meet Type A V/STOL requirements. *NASA*

Type A V/STOL: Vertical on-board delivery COD

Support for the conventional S-3 COD versions had perhaps been undermined by a simultaneous exploration of multi-mission V/STOL aircraft. The investigation of this concept was driven by the Navy's battle in the early 1970s to introduce a new type of ship: a 'light, inexpensive' (the terms being relative) aircraft carrier, termed the 'Sea Control Ship' (SCS). Initially conceived as a modern counterpart of the Second World War Escort Carrier (CVE), the SCS was sized at a displacement of 13,768 long tonnes (13,989,000kg). It was primarily intended to escort convoys to Europe and protect them from attacks by long-range Soviet Tu-95 'Bear' bombers. The SCS would also fill the gap caused by the impending retirement of the Second World War-vintage 'Essex' class aircraft carriers, most of the survivors having been converted to the Anti-Submarine Warfare role.

The theory – enthusiastically championed by the Chief of Naval Operations, Admiral Elmo Zumwalt – was that the smaller SCS, being less costly, could be deployed in greater numbers than the big nuclear and non-nuclear carriers. The SCS would possibly also be more survivable than its big sisters. In many ways it reflected the British concept of using smaller carriers as platforms for the Hawker Harrier and helicopters.

New V/STOL aircraft were central to the whole concept. The SCS would not be able to host the existing carrier-compatible fixed-wing aircraft; as a consequence new multi-mission V/STOL aircraft would have to be created. With this in mind, the Navy initiated an extensive series of studies in the mid-1970s. These explored what it defined as the 'Type A' and 'Type B' V/STOL aircraft. Type A investigated the concept of a support-aircraft family, capable of undertaking a wide variety of roles, while the Type B was a fighter.

There was also a 'Type C' requirement for a light anti-submarine helicopter, and 'Type D' for a light scout aircraft. However, neither of these requirements triggered the same volume of studies as the Types A and B.

Type A missions were to include ASW, AEW, marine assault, aerial tanker, long-range rescue, COD and vertical on-board delivery. The whole concept held out the prospect of a fleet of mission-specific aircraft, with a high degree of commonality providing savings in terms of design, development, procurement, training, spares and support equipment. Indeed, it was more of a family of aircraft than an individual design: each variant would be adapted for a specific role while making use of the same propulsion system and the 'high-value' common elements of the airframe such as the wings, nose and tail surfaces.

The Type A and B V/STOL programmes led to a number of Navy and NASA-commissioned efforts across an eight-year period of study and technology development. Boeing Seattle, Boeing Vertol, General Dynamics, Grumman, Lockheed, Ling-Temco-Vought, McDonnell Douglas and North American Rockwell were all awarded research contracts. Bell Helicopter was not included since tilt-rotor research had been separately funded, but responded nevertheless by pointing out the benefits of the latest in its family of tilt-rotor designs.

Most contractors studied several different types of lift methodology and airframe configurations, and their studies produced a wide variety of approaches to achieving V/STOL performance. This resulted in numerous proposed aircraft designs, of which only the COD/VOD variants fall within the scope of this book.

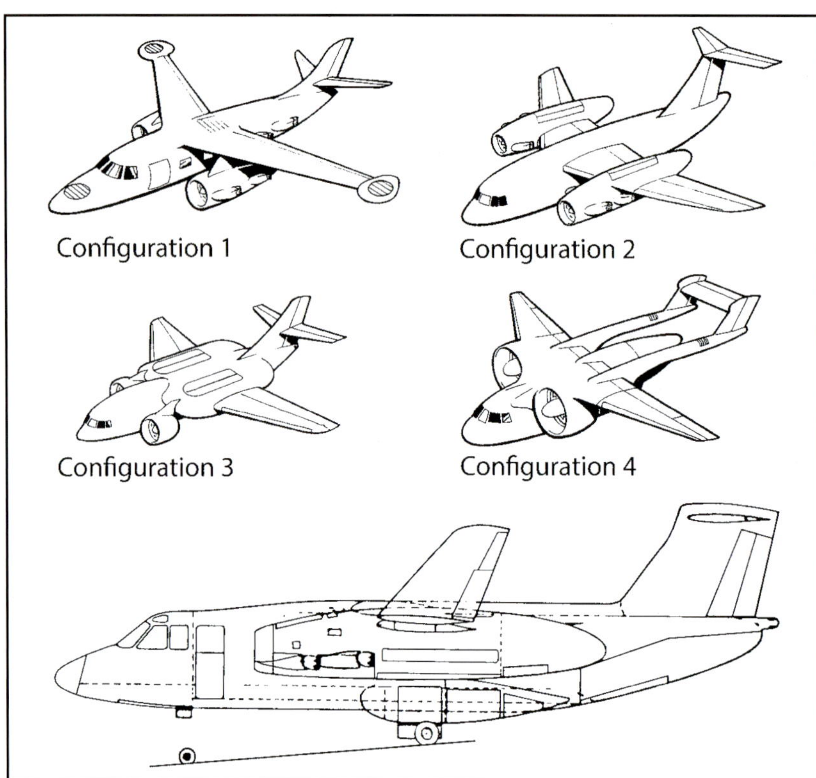

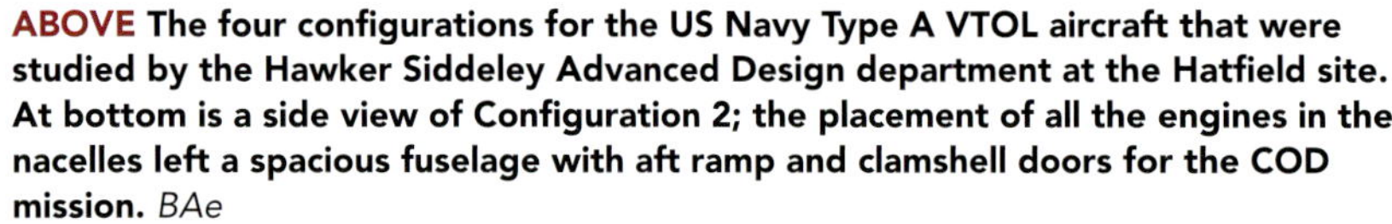

ABOVE The four configurations for the US Navy Type A VTOL aircraft that were studied by the Hawker Siddeley Advanced Design department at the Hatfield site. At bottom is a side view of Configuration 2; the placement of all the engines in the nacelles left a spacious fuselage with aft ramp and clamshell doors for the COD mission. *BAe*

BELOW Hatfield's Configuration 4 was held to have the most promise, but required new geared turbojet engines to drive the newly designed deflected thrust fans. *BAe*

BAe (Hatfield) Type A Design Studies

In a rather unusual move, the former de Havilland (later Hawker Siddeley, and finally BAe) Hatfield Future Projects Department responded to the American RFP. Four concepts were outlined by the British company:

- **Configuration 1**: was powered by three Rolls-Royce Pegasus vectored thrust engines, two being mounted under the wings. The third was located in the rear fuselage, fed by a flush intake in the upper fuselage that was covered by doors when not in use for VTOL and transition. Bleed air from the engines was used to drive fans at the wingtips and in the nose of the aircraft to provide additional lift and control in vertical flight. The design was quite large, with a length of 65ft 5in (19.95m), span of 70ft 4in (21.44m) and a height of 17ft 0in (5.18m)
- **Configuration 2**: was powered by two Rolls-Royce RB.193 vectored thrust engines mounted in wing nacelles, with each nacelle also accommodating two vertically mounted Rolls-Royce/Allison XJ99 lift jets for a total of six engines. This conservative propulsion design (using hardware demonstrated in the 1960s) was judged to require the least amount of development work, but had the drawback of high exhaust velocities and hot gas impingement on the landing deck

- **Configuration 3**: was powered by six Rolls-Royce RB.202 lift fans, two for both lift and propulsion (on swivelling pylons) and four in fuselage side fairings for vertical lift only. The conceptual RB.202 fan was driven by a light-weight engine core based on the RB.162 lift jet
- **Configuration 4**: was to be a twin-boom aircraft, powered by geared lift/propulsion fans which deflected airflow for VTOL and 'up and away' flight. Each fan was driven by a pair of geared, single spool gas turbines, one of which was mounted in the hub of each fan. For VTOL flight, an additional engine (reverse mounted in each boom and fed by an air intake in the upper rear of the boom) provided supplemental power to drive the fan. This design was considered to have the most potential for operational use of the four that were outlined

It appears that without interest from the US Navy or the UK MOD, development beyond these initial concepts was not pursued and formal HS project number(s) were not assigned.

Bell Helicopter tilt-rotor Models D319 and D321/323

Bell Helicopter elected to propose a tilt-rotor for the Type A V/STOL. The initial response to the RFI, the D319, incorporated fold-rotor technology; after take-off the rotors tilted forward for conversion to aeroplane mode, then the blades folded aft. Propulsion for normal flight was then provided by turbofan jet engines in the rear fuselage, which gave the dash speed presumed to be required by the ASW mission. Other missions utilised a more conventional tilt-rotor that incorporated much of the same drive train as the other designs. Bell subsequently argued that a higher dash speed was not necessary and proposed a relatively common and less complicated configuration for all the V/STOL A missions as the D321 (AEW and ASW) and D323 (Marine Assault and COD).

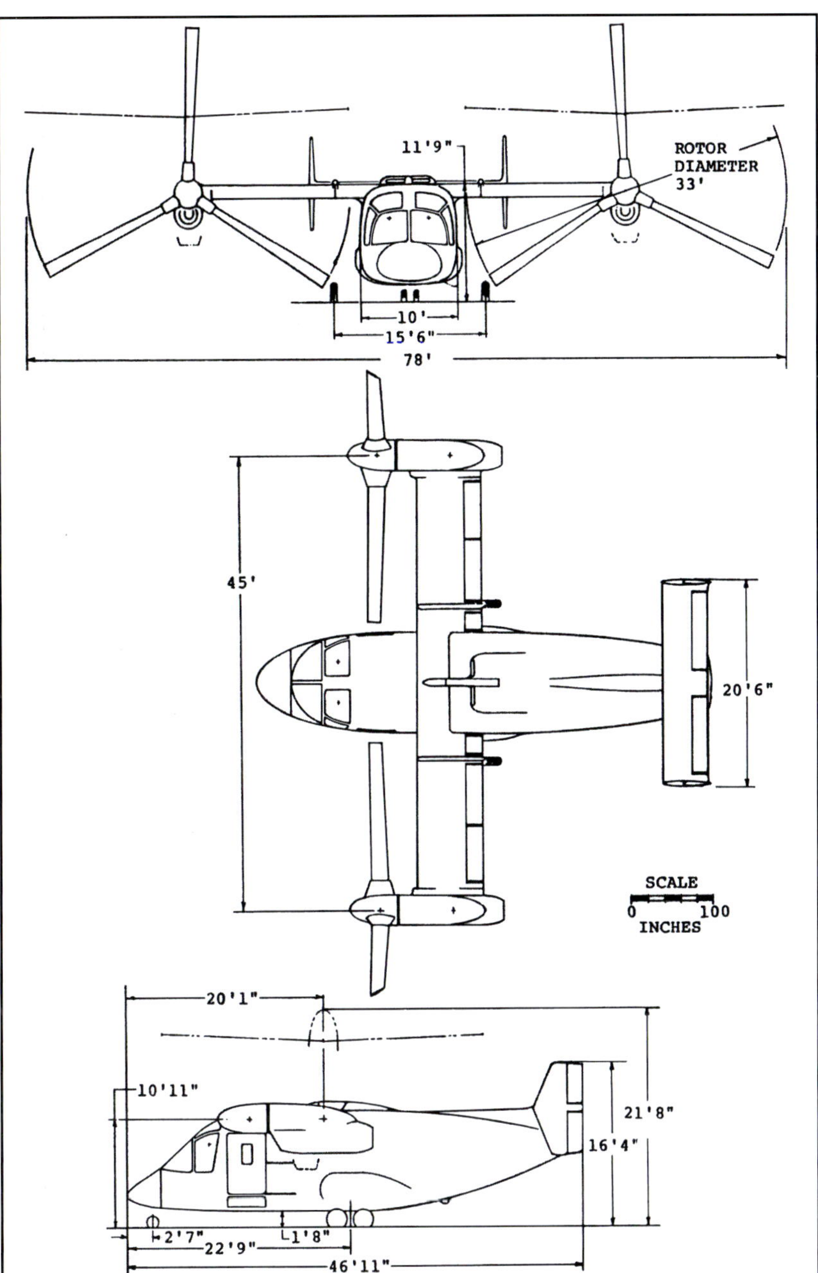

ABOVE Bell D319D general arrangement. *Tommy Thomason collection*

RIGHT A model of the Bell D321 in Navy markings. *Tommy Thomason collection*

ABOVE **The Bell 0323 was a growth version of the D321 going from a twin-engine design to four T64 turboshafts.** *Tommy Thomason collection*

Bell Helicopter Model D323	
Powerplant	4 x GE T64 turboshafts @ 4,330hp (3,290kW)
Span	45ft (13.72m)
Rotor diameter	32ft (9.76m)
Max TOW	42,000lb (19,068kg) VTOL, 46,000lb (20,884kg) STOL
Max speed	350kt (649km/h)
Max range speed	275kt (509km/h)
Range normal	1,000nmi (1,850km)
Range self-deploy	2,500nmi (4,630km)

Bell Helicopter Model D319D	
Powerplant	2 x undefined turboshafts @ 3,534shp (2,636kW)
Wingspan	45ft (13.90m) between rotor centres
Rotor diameter	33ft (10.20m)
Width (total)	81ft (24.70m)
Length	46ft 11in (15.38m)
Height	21ft 8 in (6.61m), engines vertical

General Dynamics/ Convair San Diego Model 84

Canadair Limited (then owned by General Dynamics) pursued V/STOL aircraft studies through much of the latter 1950s. Their efforts were rewarded when McDonnell Aircraft Corp selected their tilt-wing design for further development as the Model 175 for the Tri-Service VTOL airlifter in 1960, preferring this to the competing in-house McDonnell designs. Unfortunately, this combined effort lost to the Vought Hiller Ryan XC-142A.

BELOW **The GD/Convair Model 84 was an enlarged version of Canadair's CL-84 tilt-wing design.** *General Dynamics*

Canadair was not deterred and continued development of smaller scout-sized aircraft in the form of its Models CL-73 and CL-74 which had been studied earlier for the US Army requirements specified in ASR 1-60. Ultimately these led to a larger aircraft, the CL-84 which first flew on 7 May 1965. Unfortunately, this crashed on its 305th flight due to a gearbox failure on 12 September 1967. Three further developed CL-84-1 aircraft were built for Canadian service test as CX-84s and one was used by the US Navy for additional testing aboard the USS Guam (operating as a surrogate Sea Control Ship – SCS) in 1972.

The CL-84-8 was developed by Canadair as an enlarged variant to meet ASW and AEW requirements for the new SCS. This was to be about 30% larger geometrically and 50% heavier than the CL-84-1. Convair San Diego (also part of the General Dynamics Corporation) then took over leadership of the proposal effort having had significant experience in ASW equipment integration for the US Navy in their previous VS(X) work.

General Dynamics/Convair Model 84

	Canadair CL-84-1	Convair Model 84
Powerplant	2x Lycoming LTC1K-4C (T53) turboprops @1,500shp (1,118.6kW)	2x GE T64-GE-415 turboprops @4,380shp (3,266.2kW)
Span	33ft 4in (10.16m)	42ft 0in (12.19m)
Length	47ft 6in (14.48m)	53ft 7.5in (16.35m)
Height	17ft 6in (5.33m)	18ft 10.5in (5.75m)
Wing Area	233 sqft (57.5m²)	345.6sqft (105.3m²)
Max TOW VTOL	12,600lb (5,715.3kg)	29,000lb (13,154.2kg)
Max TOW STOL	14,500lb (6,577.1kg)	36,000lb (16,329.3kg)
Max Speed	260kts (481.5km/h)	382kts (707.5km/h)
Range	245nmi (453.7km)	n/a

Branded as the Convair Model 84 (out of sequence in their designation system) the proposed aircraft was to fulfil the Navy Type B requirements as one basic design, with several specialised variants: ASW, AEW, Marine assault troop carrier and COD/VOD.

Convair submitted a formal proposal on 5 June 1973, however this did not result in a contract as the Navy appeared to have a resistance to tilt-wing propeller aircraft (dating back to 1961 when they dropped out of the Tri-Service VTOL effort in opposition to the XC-142 design favoured by the Army and Air Force). However, Convair San Diego's advanced design activities diminished during 1975, and eventually ended when the Navy opted to pursue (and fund) the more sophisticated and speculative V/STOL technology efforts being proposed by other companies.

Boeing Model 1041

Initially, the Model 1041 VOD variant from Boeing Military Aircraft Company

BELOW Convair's Model 84 with a profile (bottom left) of the Canadair CL-84-1 as built and tested. *General Dynamics*

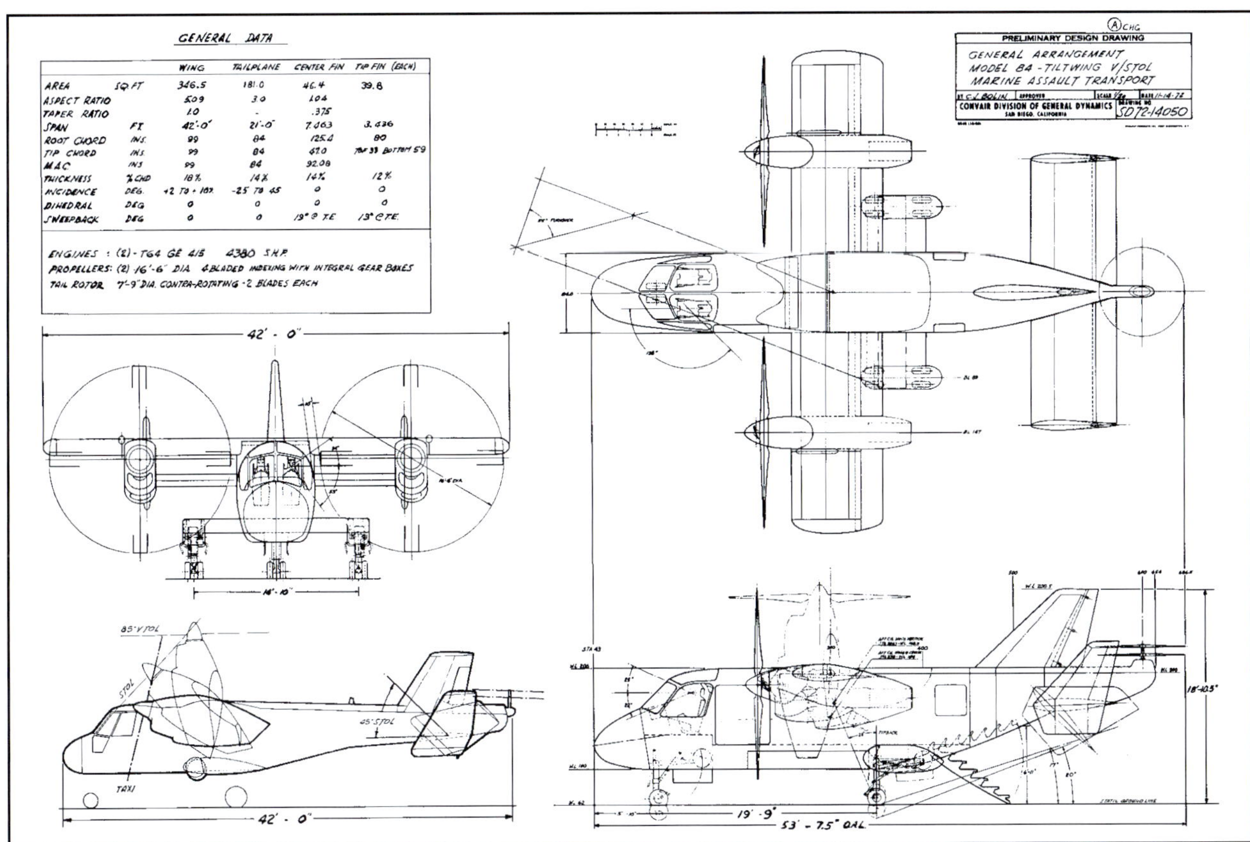

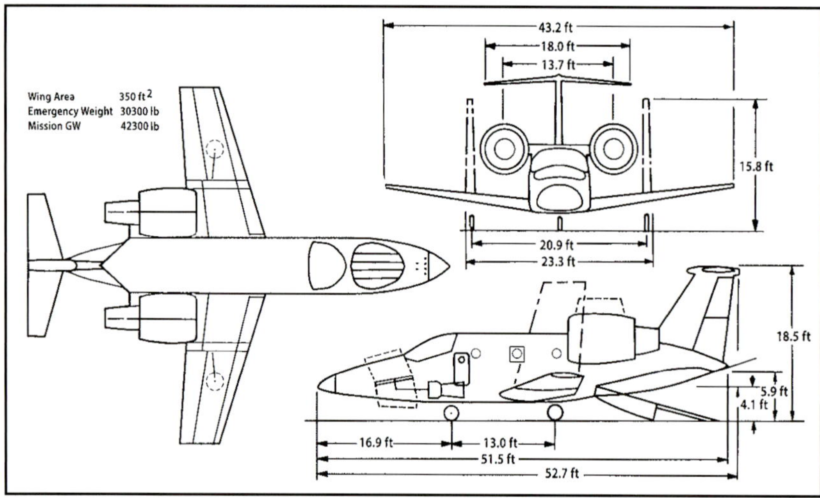

ABOVE Boeing Model 1041-130 general arrangement. *NASA*

BELOW The Boeing-Vertol Type A V/STOL proposal. *US Patent and Trademark Office*

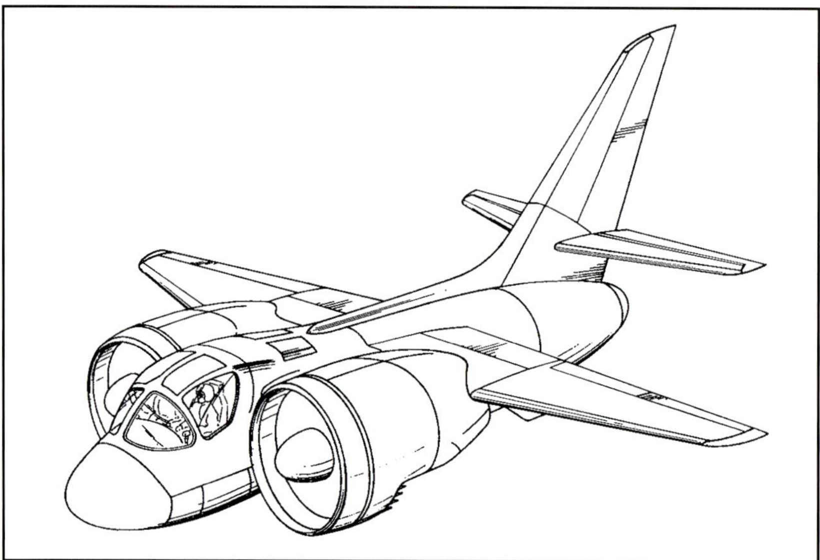

BELOW A three-view drawing of the General Dynamics 'Configuration A-311A' Type A aircraft. *NASA*

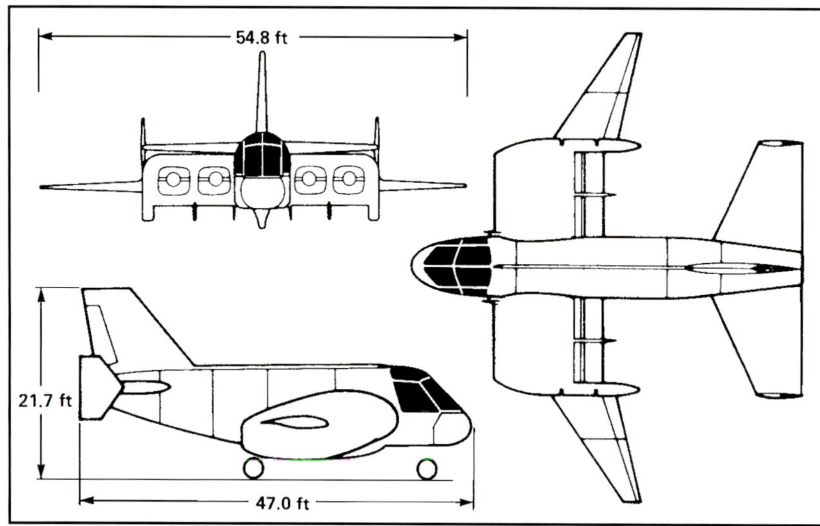

(Seattle) was planned as a two-engine aircraft powered by Allison T701 turboshaft engines with water injection, the engines being located in the fuselage aft of the wings. However, as the weight increased during the design process, a third engine was found necessary, and an additional T701 was added under the cockpit. These engines were mechanically cross-linked, with shafts driving a lift-fan in the nose and two fuselage-mounted lift/cruise-fans. The latter could be swivelled through 100° for vertical flight.

Boeing-Vertol Type A V/STOL proposal

The Boeing-Vertol study concept centred on large fans driving airflow through triple-slotted flaps in what it termed 'powered lift'. Part of the airflow from the fan would be exhausted from the bottom of the forward nacelle through louvres that would direct and control the airflow. Aft airflow (including the hot exhaust) would flow over the flaps. This concept would not have required articulating the engines and fans. The two exhaust streams from each engine would have yielded a 'four post' thrust pattern for greater stability in open ocean operations.

General Dynamics 'Configuration A-311'

General Dynamics conducted studies for its Type A concept at the Fort Worth Division. These explored a concept that the company dubbed 'ABLE' (Advanced Blown Lift Enhancement). This concept – very similar to the ADAM (Air Deflection and Modulation) concept pursued for a decade by LTV – used vanes in the engine nacelle to achieve thrust deflection. This was conceptually similar to the externally blown flap, except that the blown surfaces were an integral part of the propulsion system rather than part of the wing structure.

Company-funded studies began in early January 1977 in response to the Navy Request For Information (RFI). Initial configurations incorporated a three-engine arrangement, with two engines housed in round nacelles on the wings and one at the base of the tail. This initial design evolved into the A-302; an eight-engine design with four fan engines – two per nacelle under the wings – and four small turbine engines mounted above the aft fuselage. The original round engine nacelle was changed to a box-like 'lifting nacelle' that provided additional lift.

Continued optimisation and wind tunnel testing resulted in the A-311A with mid-wing nacelles. In this design, four 'notional' turbofan engines specified at 11,384lb (50.65kN) thrust were to be cross-shafted (for safety in the event of single-engine failure). A proposed test bed, designated the A-314, had a T-tail and utilised off-the-shelf Lycoming ALF-502L engines. For simplicity, this would not have had cross-shafting and, had it been built, it would have been limited to STOL operations.

ABOVE The COD/VOD was the same size as the A-311A ASW configuration. *NASA*

Grumman Model 698

The vertical flight capability of Grumman's proposal was based on a different technology from those used in most of the other Type A designs. Whereas the other proposals mostly opted for lift-fans, Grumman's approach used turbofan engines, augmented in some cases by an aft-fuselage-mounted turboshaft engine that helped to drive the turbofans.

The Model 698 initially featured a large canard for pitch control and two tilting turbofan engines mounted on the fuselage just ahead of the wings. The larger designs, such as the 698-311 for the Marine Corps assault mission, had a third turboshaft engine mounted in the aft fuselage supplying power to the fans via cross-shafting. Such was Grumman's faith in the design that it outlasted the Type A V/STOL study programme. The 698 concept demonstrator progressed through remote-controlled models to a full-scale TF34-powered wind tunnel model with a conventional T-tail empennage, and finally to a full-size mock-up displayed at the 1981 Paris Air Show.

BELOW The Grumman Model 698-311 COD variant with swing nose. *Courtesy of Northrop Grumman Corporation*

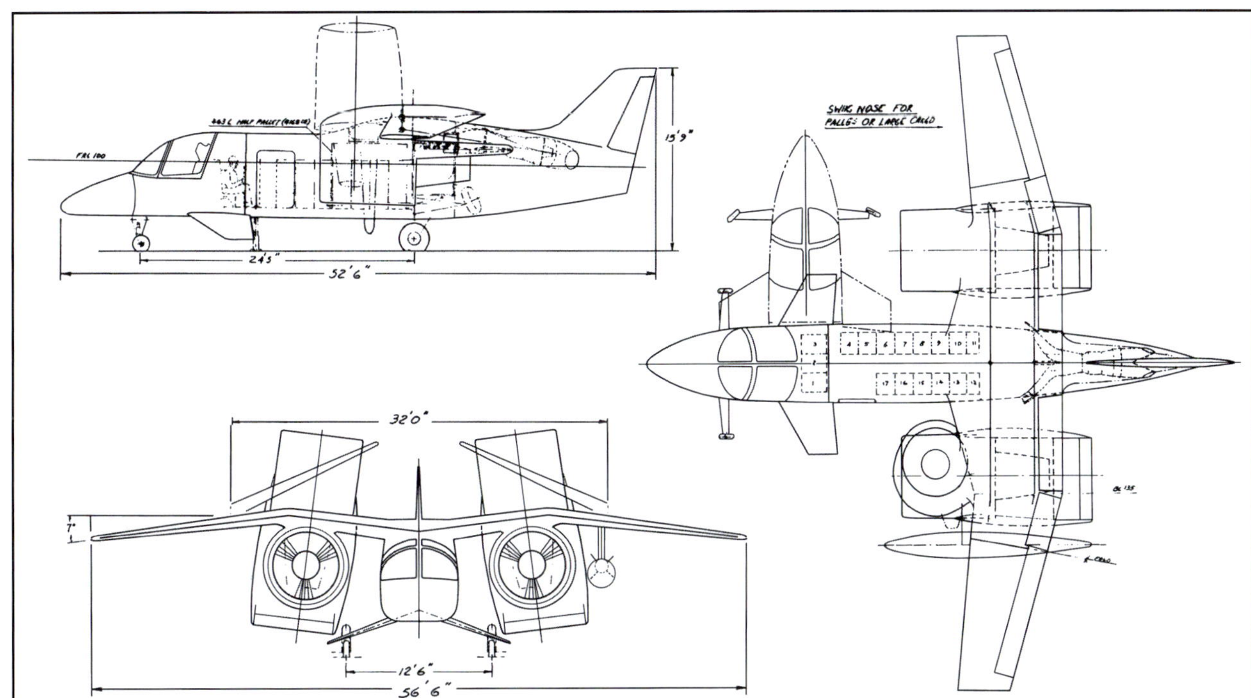

Grumman promoted the 698 as a multi-purpose, vertical-take-off aircraft suitable for a wide variety of civil and military applications. However, the Bell Helicopter tilt-rotor XV-15 (which became the predecessor of the V-22 Osprey) was also flying at the same time, and this was to prove of more appeal, particularly to the US Marines, its target customer. Part of the concern was that the downward hot jet blast of the 698 would make it less suitable for shipboard operations.

ABOVE The Grumman Model 698-300 series enlarged assault transport for the Marine Corps. *John Aldaz photo*

BELOW Grumman artist's concept of the Model 698 assault transport for the Marines in action; the COD version was to use the same fuselage. *Grumman*

Lockheed Type A V/STOL proposals

Lockheed explored a number of different options in response to the Type A V/STOL initiative, using a series of designations between CL-1677 and CL-1679.

The CL-1677 was a twin-engine, high-wing aircraft with a T-tail, using cruise-fan engines (with thrust deflection) in the front of two under-wing nacelles, and shaft-driven lift-only fans in the aft part of the same nacelles. Although there was cross-shafting between the engines, single-engine performance was poor in the critical transitional flight regimes, and the aircraft was judged as not being capable of making a vertical landing with one engine out.

Progressing on from the CL-1677, Lockheed eventually opted for a split-

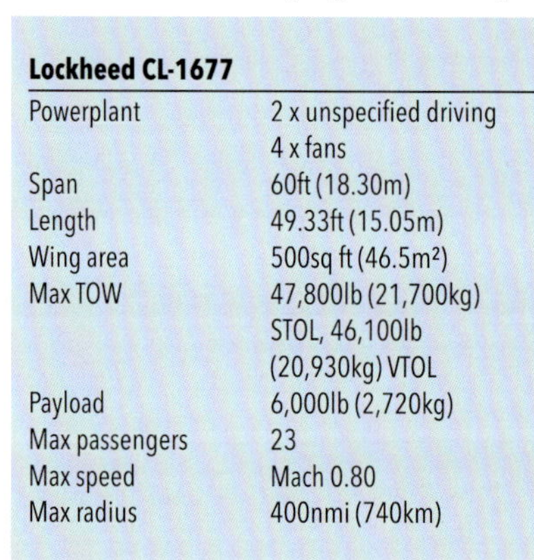
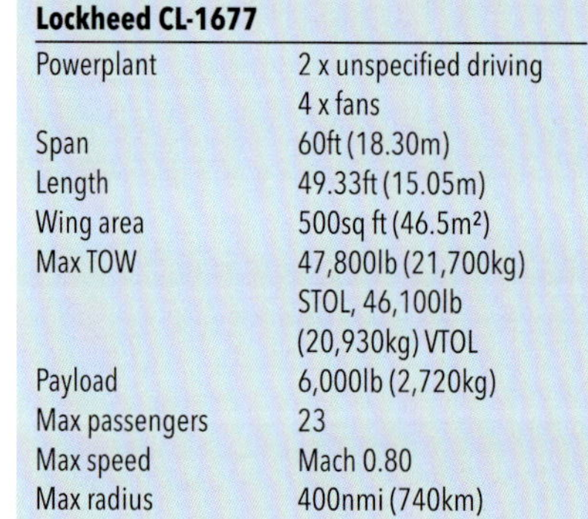

Lockheed CL-1677	
Powerplant	2 x unspecified driving 4 x fans
Span	60ft (18.30m)
Length	49.33ft (15.05m)
Wing area	500sq ft (46.5m²)
Max TOW	47,800lb (21,700kg) STOL, 46,100lb (20,930kg) VTOL
Payload	6,000lb (2,720kg)
Max passengers	23
Max speed	Mach 0.80
Max radius	400nmi (740km)

BELOW A display model of the Grumman Model 698 Demonstrator, in the 698-400 design series. *Author collection*

BELOW A Grumman 698 Demonstrator model with the twin TF34 turbofans positioned for VTOL flight. *Author collection*

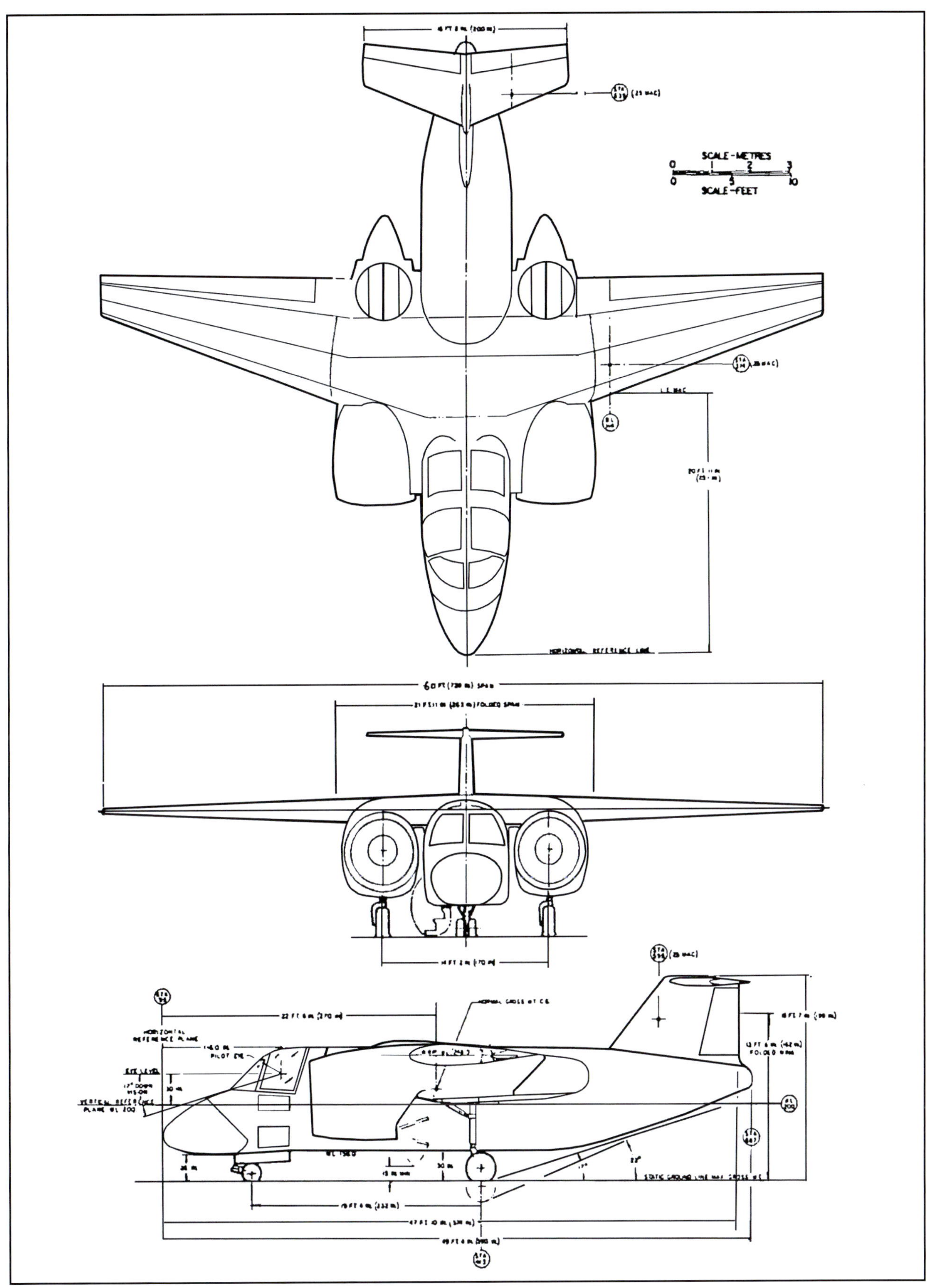

ABOVE **Lockheed CL-1677 design general arrangement.** *Lockheed*

LEFT **Promotional artwork for the twin-engine Lockheed CL-1677 Type A V/STOL study.** *Lockheed*

fan propulsion/lift system for its favoured Type A V/STOL approach. This was offered in both two- and four-engine versions.

Offering true One-Engine-Inoperative (OEI) performance, the Lockheed CL-1679 was a high-wing, T-tailed aircraft, powered by four high-bypass-ratio turbofans, mounted in twin nacelles on either side of the fuselage, flush with the top of the wing. The engine thrust was diverted from vertical flight to horizontal flight by a thrust deflector. An engine compressor bleed reaction system was used for pitch, roll and yaw control and for engine-out trim. Lockheed also explored the possibility of using wingtip ejectors for lateral control, and evaluated the advantages of cross-shafting between the engines.

McDonnell Douglas Model 260

McDonnell Douglas put forward a highly innovative proposal in the form of its Model 260. The largest variant fulfilled the VOD mission. Designed by the St Louis-based former McDonnell Aircraft Company (McAir), the Model 260 utilised a common propulsion system for a broad family of aircraft. It consisted of two J97 gas generators driving three identical 59in (1.5m) tip-driven fans, one in the nose and two in nacelles mounted alongside the fuselage towards the rear of the upper surface of the wings. The latter had swivelling exhaust ducts (termed D-Nozzles) to provide downward thrust for take-off

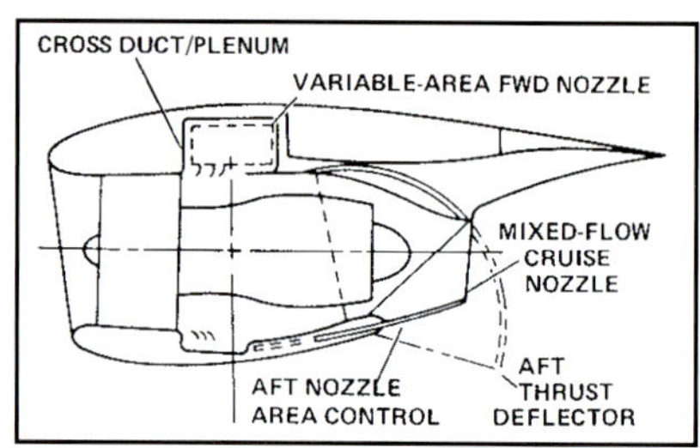

RIGHT **The thrust deflection arrangement for the Lockheed CL-1679 Type A V/STOL study.** *NASA*

BELOW **Lockheed CL-1679 Type A V/STOL study general arrangement.** *NASA*

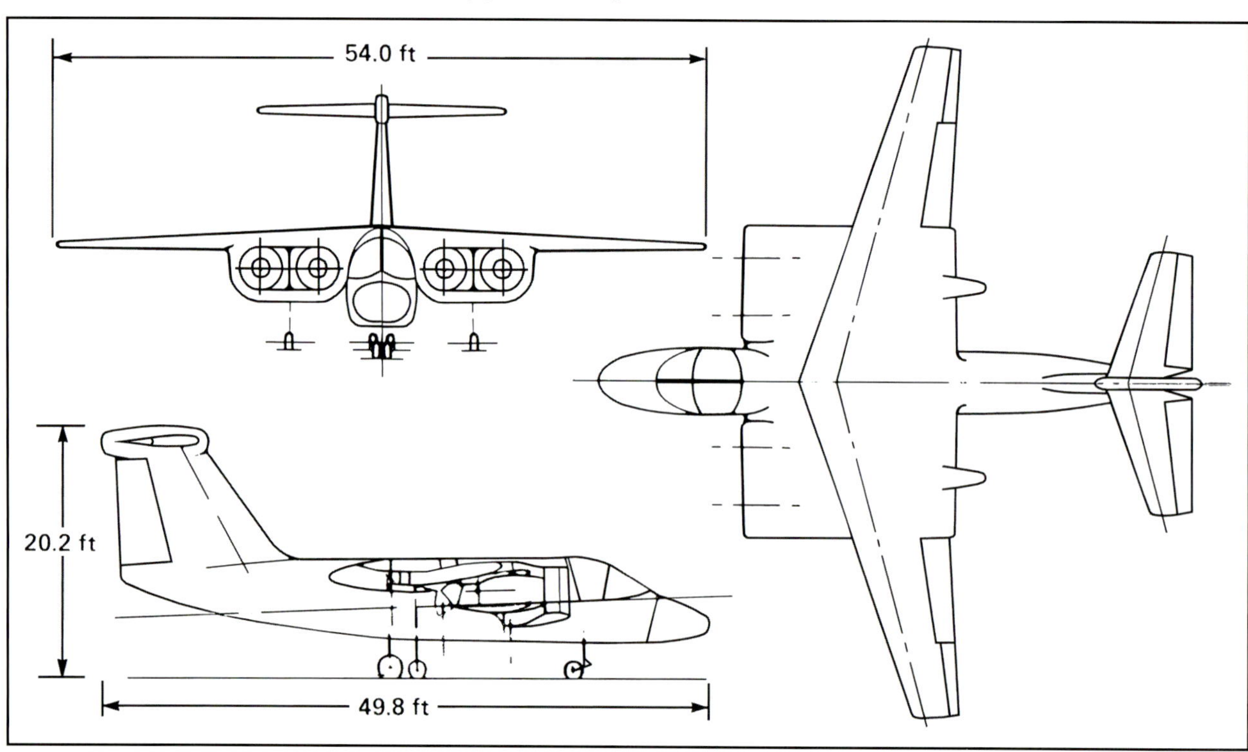

McDonnell Douglas Model 260 (baseline aircraft)	
Powerplant	2 x GE J97 turbojets driving tip fans
Span	41.1ft (12.54m), 17ft (5.19m) folded
Length	48.4ft (14.76m)
Height	17.0ft (5.19m)
Max TOW	33,000lb (14,980kg)
Max speed	Mach .85

and landing. The engines were linked and McDonnell claimed that in an 'engine-out' situation the system could still provide 57% of the normal two-engine lift.

Rockwell Type A V/STOL concepts, NA-420, NA-430 and NA-431

North American Rockwell explored a number of different Type A V/STOL proposals at both its Los Angeles and Columbus, Ohio, divisions.

The NA-420 reflected the Los Angeles Aircraft Division (LAAD) Advanced Design preference for a three-engine/two-fan arrangement. The advantages claimed were sufficient thrust available for safe engine-out operation and the ability to shut down an engine in flight for fuel-saving cruise and loitering. Designers chose a high-wing/twin-under-wing nacelle configuration to give maximum fuselage volume for passengers or cargo space.

In contrast to the LAAD effort, North American Rockwell's Columbus Division concentrated on its 'ejector in wing' propulsive lift concept, resulting in a proposed aircraft designated NA-431. Propulsion would be provided by two (alternatively four) cross-shafted gas generators driving fans in the nacelles. Exhaust flow would be discharged aft in forward flight or diverted into the wing-mounted ejector flaps for vertical lift. Ambient air would be drawn into the ejector airflow, increasing the total thrust generated.

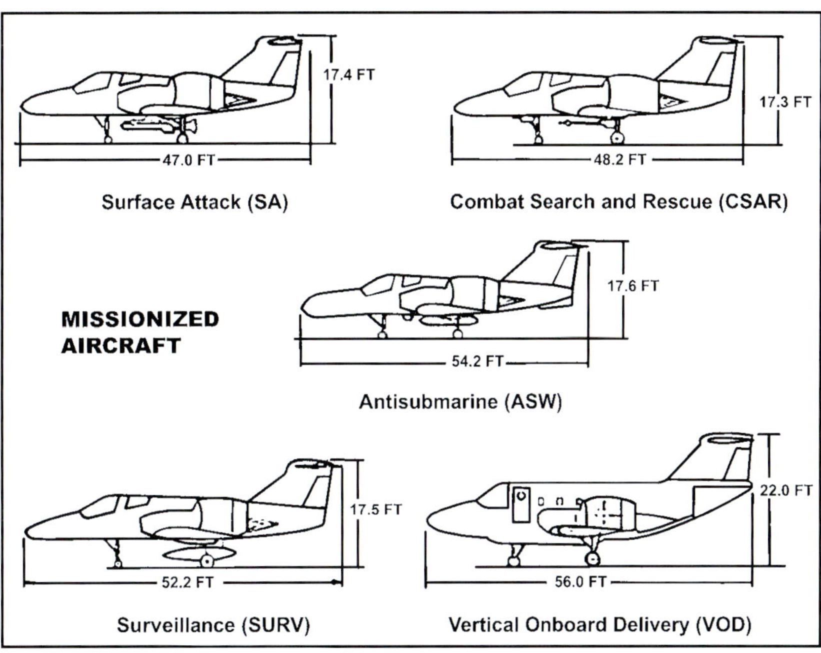

ABOVE The family of variants of the McDonnell Douglas Model 260. *Boeing*

BELOW The COD version of the McDonnell Douglas Model 260 is depicted over a Sea Control Ship. *Boeing*

RIGHT A display model of the McDonnell Douglas Model 260 in COD/Assault Transport configuration. *Author collection*

ABOVE **Artwork depicting the North American Rockwell NA-420.** *NASA*

BELOW **North American Rockwell Type A V/STOL COD/VOD general arrangement.** *Boeing*

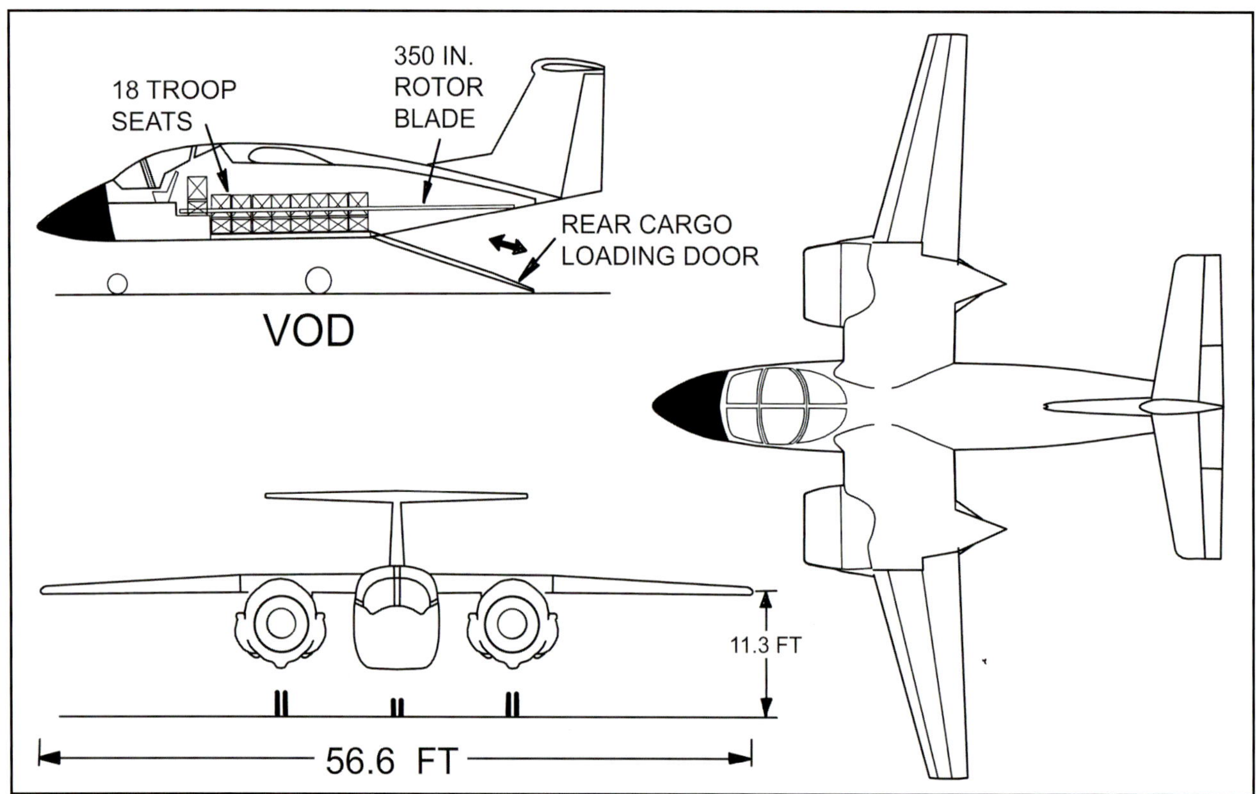

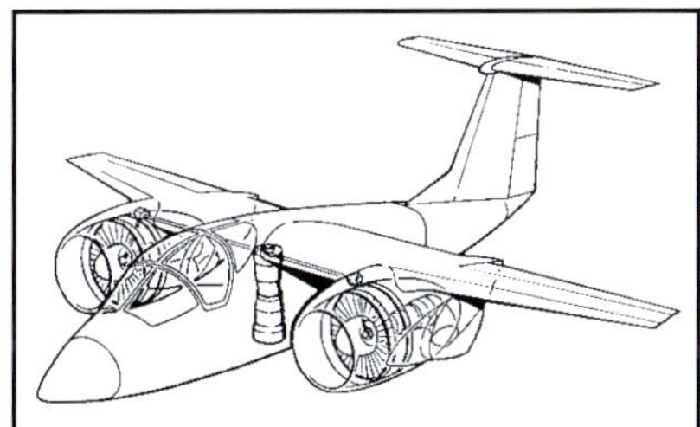

ABOVE The three-engine/two-fan arrangement of the NA-420. *Boeing*

However, by the time of the 1977 RFI it had become painfully evident that the ejector-lift arrangement was difficult to implement when applied to full-sized hardware, as was the case with the XFV-12A V/STOL fighter. The concept was quietly retired.

A further design to come out of North American Rockwell was the NA-430. This design progressed to the point where the company felt it was worth producing promotional artwork, but no further details of this design could be uncovered.

Vought V-530

Vought responded to the Type A V/STOL requirement with its Model V-530. Its basic configuration resembled the Lockheed S-3A, but with the propulsion system replaced by a tandem-fan arrangement, housed in large nacelles alongside the fuselage.

The tandem-fan arrangement minimised the required fan diameter. All four fans were the same size and each had its own air intake. Each pair of fans was to be driven by a common (unspecified) core engine. The airflow from the forward pair of fans was directed by a deflector door, that from the aft pair via a swivelling nozzle. The core engines also exhausted through the latter. The engines were cross-shafted, but this feature was only engaged in the event of engine failure or in circumstances where additional differential control was required for pitch, roll or yaw.

The V-530 wings folded forward and upside down, and the fin folded sideways. The proposal was also noteworthy for two features that anticipated future technologies: the

ABOVE The North American Rockwell NA-431. *John Aldaz collection*

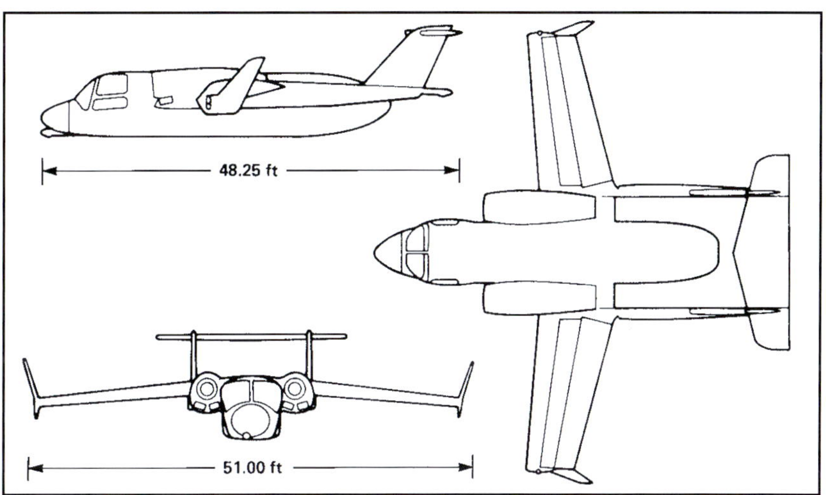

ABOVE North American Rockwell NA-431 general arrangement. *NASA*

BELOW Promotional artwork for the North American Rockwell NA-430. *John Aldaz collection*

ABOVE Promotional artwork for the Vought V-530. *LTV via Bill Spidle*

BELOW Vought V-530 general arrangement. *LTV via Bill Spidle*

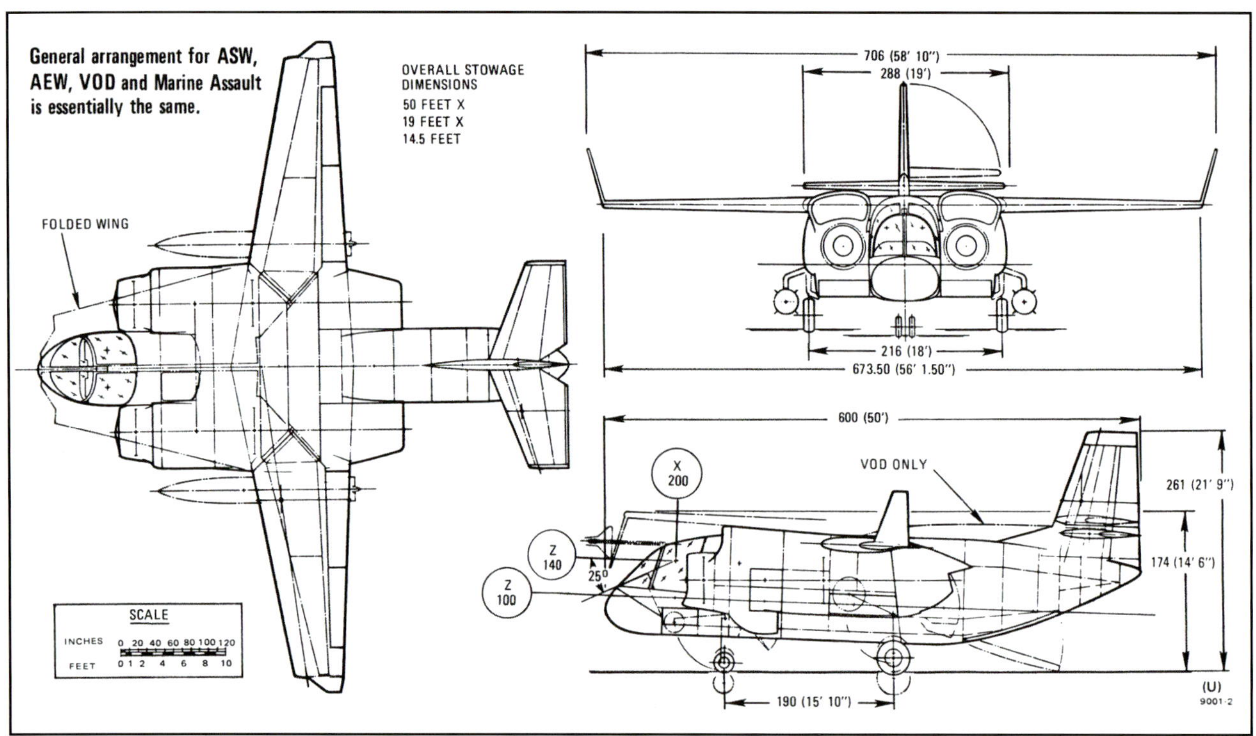

ABOVE A display model of the Vought V-530.
Mark Nankivil collection

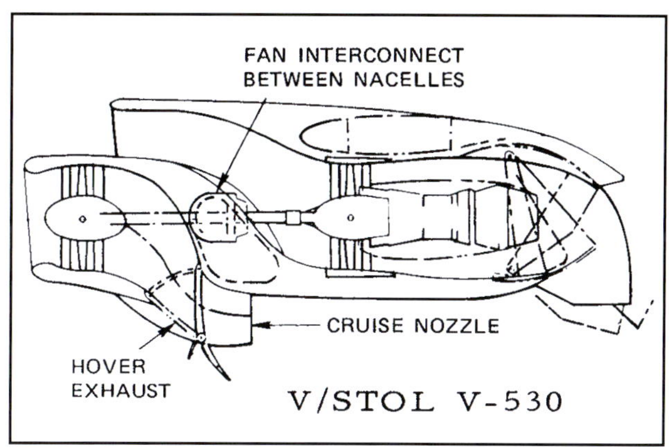

ABOVE Details of the Vought V-530 tandem-fan engine.
LTV via Bill Spidle

Vought V-530	
Powerplant	Unspecified core turboshaft driving 4 x fans of 51in (1.30m) diameter
Span	58ft 10in (17.94m), 19ft (5.80m) folded
Length	50ft (15.25m)
Height	21ft 9in (6.63m), 14ft 6in (4.42m) folded
Cargo bay length	21ft (6.41m)
Max TOW	35,000-45,000lb (15,890-20,430kg) depending on mission

introduction of vertical 'winglets' and the proposed extensive use of graphite/epoxy composite materials in the airframe's construction.

The Navy abandons Type A V/STOL

The SCS concept was dropped in 1975, to be replaced by a larger and faster type of craft, the V/STOL Support Ship or VSS, which would ultimately also be rejected. Meantime, the Navy already had VOD capability in the form of Boeing-Vertol CH-46 helicopters, which could carry cargo between ships, known as UNREP (Underway Replenishment) or VERTREP (Vertical Replenishment).

Despite the plethora of design studies carried out, the Navy terminated work on the Type A V/STOL programme in the second half of 1978 (although studies already contracted by the Navy and NASA would continue to their conclusion several years later). According to *Flight International* (15 September 1978), quoting unnamed US sources, the decision was actually taken by Zumwalt's successor as Chief of Naval Operations, Admiral James L. Holloway, just before he retired on 30 June.

The warning signs of diminishing support had come earlier. In February 1978 ADM Holloway had told the Congressional Appropriations Committee: 'We may find that we have set our sights too high in going for a Type A V/STOL that can do everything ... and we are re-evaluating our entire approach to V/STOL.' The Committee members were inclined to agree, observing that the programme's performance goals '...could probably never be met by today's technology'. It appears that the Navy had recognised the same problems that had been met by the USAF during its own abortive V/STOL CX-6 and LIT programmes during the previous decade (as discussed in Chapter Eight).

Flight International also reported that cost had been a major factor in the decision, with overall programme cost ranging from $5 billion to $8 billion out of the Aviation budget (shipbuilding cost not included). Another consideration would have been timing, with new conventional aircraft also being required to be available to replace types that would become obsolete by the early 1990s.

Despite all the studies carried out under the Type A initiative, the Navy would have to wait some years before it would acquire high-speed, long-range V/STOL capability. Ironically, it would be the concept that the Navy programme office had not expected to be proposed and about which it was not particularly enthusiastic – namely, the tilt-rotor.

The Navy stretches funding: The minimally modified US-3A

Even before cancellation, the Type A V/STOL programme was not going to meet the immediate need of supplementing the surviving Greyhound fleet of twelve aircraft. Having had the funding deleted for the new-build S-3 Utility COD, the Navy resorted to a minimally modified version that was tellingly designated the US-3A (for Utility) rather than CS-3A (for Cargo).

Although bespoke COD designs were sized around engines and nuclear weapons, the minimally modified S-3s addressed the more frequent requirement for out-of-stock avionics needed to get aeroplanes flightworthy and the crew's desire for mail, both of which could be accommodated in what amounted to the cubbyholes that constituted the S-3's cargo-carrying capability. The philosophy was one of making absolutely minimal modification to

ABOVE The Lockheed US-3A in company demonstrator markings with cargo/baggage pods. *Mick Roth photo*

the basic S-3. Its main virtue as a supplemental COD was that it was relatively long-legged and much faster than the propeller-driven C-2. However, it could not carry anything of significant size.

Work to modify the seventh YS-3A airframe as a prototype began in July 1975 and it first flew on 2 July 1976. Modifications included the removal of ASW and ESM equipment and deletion of the ECMO and TACCO electronics displays and ejection seats, to make room for six steerage-class passenger seats. Twin large external CNU-264/A baggage pods could also be carried on the external stores pylons to supplement what could be carried in the fuselage.

However, no major production or conversion order ever emerged. In all, just five more aircraft were modified into this configuration. Nonetheless, the US-3As performed a useful role right up until the last example was retired in 1998. They were used primarily in the Western Pacific and Indian Ocean areas where their speed and range were most beneficial. Notwithstanding Lockheed's expectation, a stopgap effort went to the other shortlisted option, with the Navy deciding to upgrade its remaining C-2A Greyhounds. This involved replacing the square-tipped propellers with new Hamilton Standard round-tipped examples and a structural service life extension, which involved strengthening the wing-box.

1980s: Meet the new COD, same as the old COD

By 1980 there were only twelve C-2s still flying (all of which would need to be retired by 1987 due to fatigue life limits) and although there were still forty-nine C-1s these had been in service for twenty-five years and carrier landings and salt air had taken their toll. Moreover, their piston powerplants were obsolete and they were the very last users of aviation gasoline on aircraft carriers.

According to *Wings of Gold* (Winter 1983 edition), in the late summer of 1980 the Chief of Naval Operations asked each of the fleet Commanders-in-Chief to define their COD requirements. The summarised result focused on two attributes. One was the ability to carry a replacement engine for the largest carrier-based aircraft planned for (at the time, the F-14's TF-30, weighing some 9,000lb or 4,000kg in its container). The other was for a range of 2,000 miles (3,220km). While useful, the US-3A could not conceivably meet the bulk cargo requirements, with conversions capped at six aircraft. In view of this, Lockheed revived plans for the S-3 COD and began marketing it, though once again to no avail.

Within two years a somewhat modest and more expedient solution had been funded and put into action, notwithstanding the last fifteen years of studies. The Grumman C-2 production line was reopened and thirty-nine Greyhounds were ordered, even though they were unable to meet the fleet's range requirement. Designated as the C-2A(R), for 'Re-procured', the aircraft were publicised as a minimally changed version of the 1960s-vintage C-2A. In actuality many small changes were made, such as using the strengthened wing of the E-2C then in production, installation of updated avionics, and a more capable APU installation. Other changes included uprated 4,910hp (3,661kW) T56-A-425 engines and incorporation of all of the improvements made to the existing fleet of aircraft during their Service Life Extension Program (SLEP) of the previous decade.

In the early 1980s the Navy also

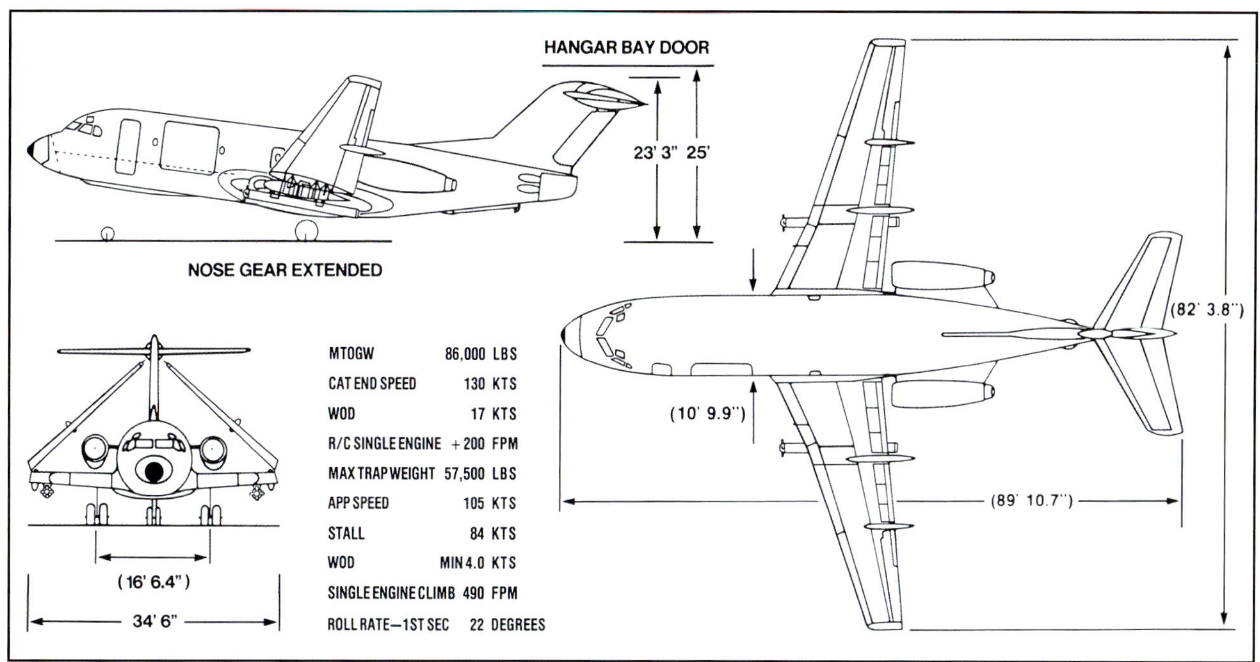

ABOVE Fokker F-28 COD general arrangement. *Tony Chong collection*

evaluated the addition of an in-flight refuelling capability to the C-2 in an effort to overcome its range limitation. An aircraft was modified for test purposes, but although more than 250 hook-ups were successfully completed, using a variety of tankers, the Navy concluded that the handling characteristics of the C-2 made it unsuitable for regular in-flight refuelling in a service environment.

Meantime, the Navy briefly revisited the idea of adapting an airliner for COD purposes, this time taking a serious look at the potential of the Fokker F-28.

Fokker F-28 COD

Following the success of the F-27 Friendship twin-turboprop airliner, Fokker had developed a twin-turbojet short-range airliner, the F-28 Fellowship, which first flew on 9 May 1967. In 1981 the company proposed a modified F-28 as an alternative to the restart of Grumman C-2A production.

The proposed modified aircraft was fully carrier-compatible with folding wings, a tail-hook and strengthened landing gear. It added a two-position nose-wheel strut to enable the nose to be raised for the catapult launch. This arrangement also lowered the tail to meet the height limit for below-deck stowage.

Fokker provided the Navy with several jet engine options for consideration: the Rolls-Royce Tay, Allison TF-41-A2 (a license-built Rolls-Royce Spey that powered the A-7), a non-afterburning GE F404 proposed for the A-6F, and the P&W TF30 that powered the F-14A, among others.

The proposal was considered seriously by the Navy. In 1983 the Naval Air Systems Command carried out a flight evaluation of the aircraft at both Fokker's facilities in the Netherlands and at NAS Sigonella, including 108 approaches using the visual landing system installed at the airfield. According to correspondence in the Naval Institute Proceedings

RIGHT The Fokker F-28 depicted during launch with two refuelling pods. *Tony Chong collection*

(December 1989), the Navy pilots and engineers concluded that '...the Fokker F-28 airplane has potential for the carrier-based carrier on board delivery, tanker or AEW mission.' The only major deficiency was inadequate lateral control on approach, which Fokker proposed to correct by increasing the span of the ailerons and the number of roll-control spoilers.

Grumman, however, had prevailed.

Fokker F-28 COD	
Powerplant	2 x Rolls-Royce Tay or non-afterburning GE F404 turbofans @ 13,850lb (62kN) or 11,000lb (48.9kN) thrust
Span	82ft 4in (25.11m), 34ft 6in (10.52m) folded
Length	89ft 11in (27.41m)
Height	23ft 3in (7.09m) (nose-strut extended)
Max TOW	86,000lb (39,040kg)
Max trap weight	57,500lb (26,110kg)
Cat end speed	130kt (241km/h)
Min wind-over-deck	4.0kt (7.4km/h)

BELOW General arrangement of the Boeing MPSNA with tractor prop-fans. *NASA*

1980s: New ideas explored – the prop-fan, and the Common Support Aircraft

While the above designs were being worked on, serious consideration was also being given to the potential for a new type of propulsion unit: the unducted fan or 'prop-fan' engine, sometimes known as the UHB (Ultra-High-Bypass) engine. The propulsive fan consisted of a series of relatively short, counter-rotating, curved blades mounted at the rear of the engine. Their high number, constrained diameter and curvature were adopted to avoid compressibility effects at the tips.

In theory – if the associated problems, largely relating to noise, could be solved – this promised greater efficiency than either the turboprop or the high-bypass turbofan.

Part of the pressure to investigate the potential of a much more efficient means of propulsion had resulted from the Middle East oil embargo in 1973. This affected fuel costs and also raised concerns about security of supply. As a consequence, in early 1975 the US Senate directed NASA to look at every conceivable way of economising on fuel consumption. NASA concluded that the prop-fan had the greatest potential. According to a subsequent NASA report, this 'was initially resisted almost entirely by US engine and airframe manufacturers, the airlines and the military'. One can, perhaps, understand the lack of enthusiasm for such an imposed disruption to the prevailing line of development.

Nonetheless, NASA began the MAPS (Multiple Application Prop-fan Studies) programme in the 1980s. Contracts were awarded to Beech (for a small business aircraft prop-fan) and to McDonnell Douglas, for a prop-fan design under its umbrella of ATT (Advanced Tactical Transport) studies. Additionally, under MAPS, and under NASA Lewis technical direction, the Navy funded three aircraft companies – Boeing-Wichita, Grumman and Lockheed-Georgia – to study a Multi-Purpose Subsonic Naval Aircraft (MPSNA) powered by prop-fans, with COD being part of the remit.

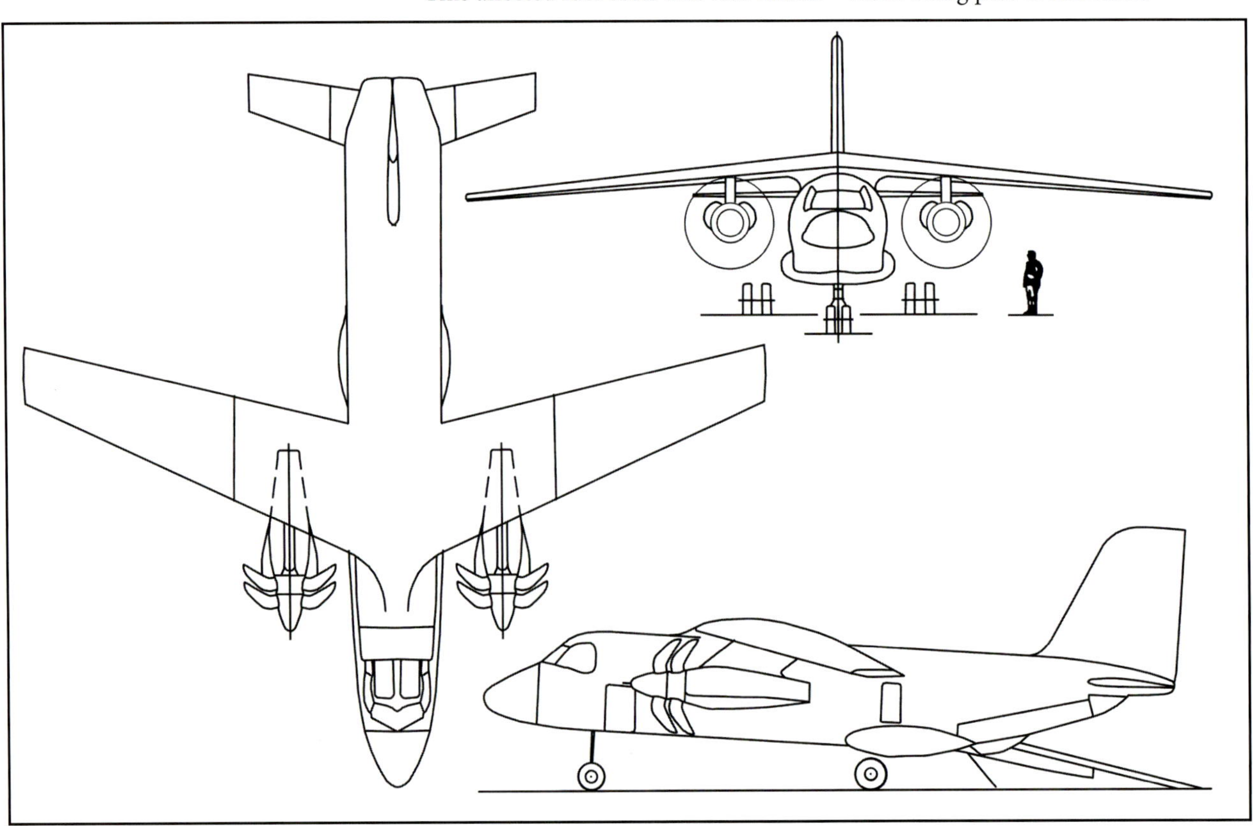

Each of the companies produced very different designs: tractor prop-fans, pusher prop-fans and conventional high-efficiency turbofans. MPSNA studies were completed by the end of 1986 and all concluded that the prop-fan offered an advantage in terms of loiter-time and range over conventionally powered aircraft.

On a parallel track, flight test of prop-fan hardware began with a McDonnell Douglas MD-80 and a Boeing 727 being used as test beds in 1988. These tests bore out the prop-fan efficiency claims, but to the present time the prop-fan remains a technology that has yet to have its day.

Also in the 1980s a new possibility arose for fulfilling the COD role when work started on what was known as the CSA (Common Support Aircraft). The new aircraft was intended to take on the roles of Carrier On-board Delivery, Tanker, Mine Warfare, Electronic Warfare (EW), Airborne Early Warning (AEW), C^3 (Command, Communication, Control), Anti-Submarine Warfare (ASW), Anti-Surface Warfare, Surveillance and Anti-Air-Warfare (AAW) – essentially the same commonality approach as the Type A programme, but without the V/STOL capability.

By the late 1980s this concept was being studied in the MPSNA programme, although many of the contractors had adopted their own names for their designs. A follow-on programme, MMVX ('Multi-Mission, Fixed Wing, Experimental' Aircraft) explored the concept further. These programmes produced a host of highly innovative designs, but none ever resulted in flying hardware.

Boeing MPNSA

Boeing chose to build its study around a large aircraft capable of meeting the full spectrum of missions, apart from ASW, which was met by a similar aircraft with a smaller fuselage.

The AEW/COD aircraft had a fuselage 9.5ft (2.90m) in diameter, which was sufficient to fit standard 463L pallets on a floor 88in (2.23m) wide in the COD version. The long cabin and tail ramp provided a cargo compartment 33ft (10.07m) long. Gross weight was estimated at 71,000lb (32,230kg) with a projected range of 2,100mi (3,379km) and a 15,000lb (6,810kg) cargo payload.

Engine placement drove significant differences in Boeing's aircraft configuration: the tractor prop-fan and turbofan engines were suspended from a high-placed wing, while the pusher Unducted Fans (UDF) were aft-mounted on the fuselage under a T-tail.

Grumman Model 719S MPNSA

Grumman studied two aircraft configurations: the wide-bodied Mission Requirements -1 (MR-1) and the smaller MR-2 design. The MR-1 fuselage was sized for the COD role and was capable of all other missions (with a size and weight penalty). The MR-2 was designed without regard to the COD or Tanker roles and as a result was smaller, lighter, and faster at low altitude.

The MR-1 was considered with the Pratt & Whitney STS-679 tractor and STS-743 pusher prop-fans rated at 11,047shp (8,250kW), and the P&W STF-686 high-bypass-ratio turbofan rated at 21,100lb (13,290kg). Grumman chose the aft-mount location for all engine options, explaining:

> 'Wing-mounted prop-fans cause considerable concern in the areas of carrier deck handling and safety, noise at crew station, conformal radar interference and weapons carriage and launch. Aft-mounted prop-fans (and turbofans) lead to lower aircraft spot size over wing mounting.'

BELOW A comparison between the Grumman MR-1 design and the E-2C, and the smaller MR-2 with the S-3A. *NASA*

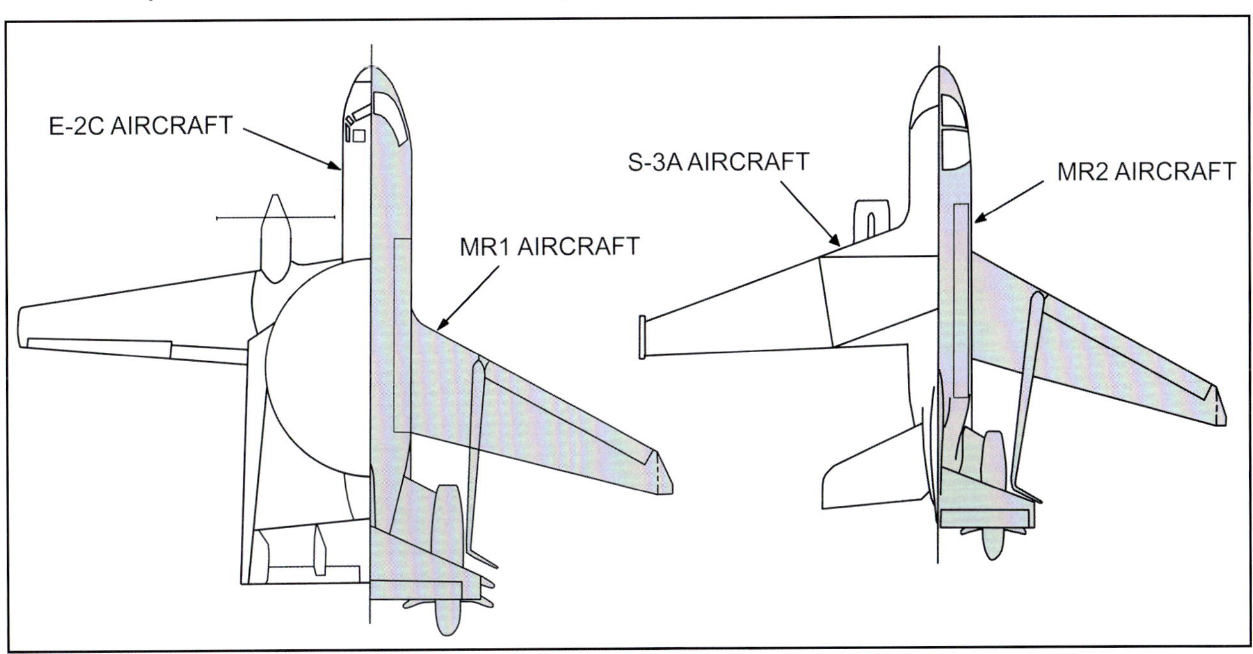

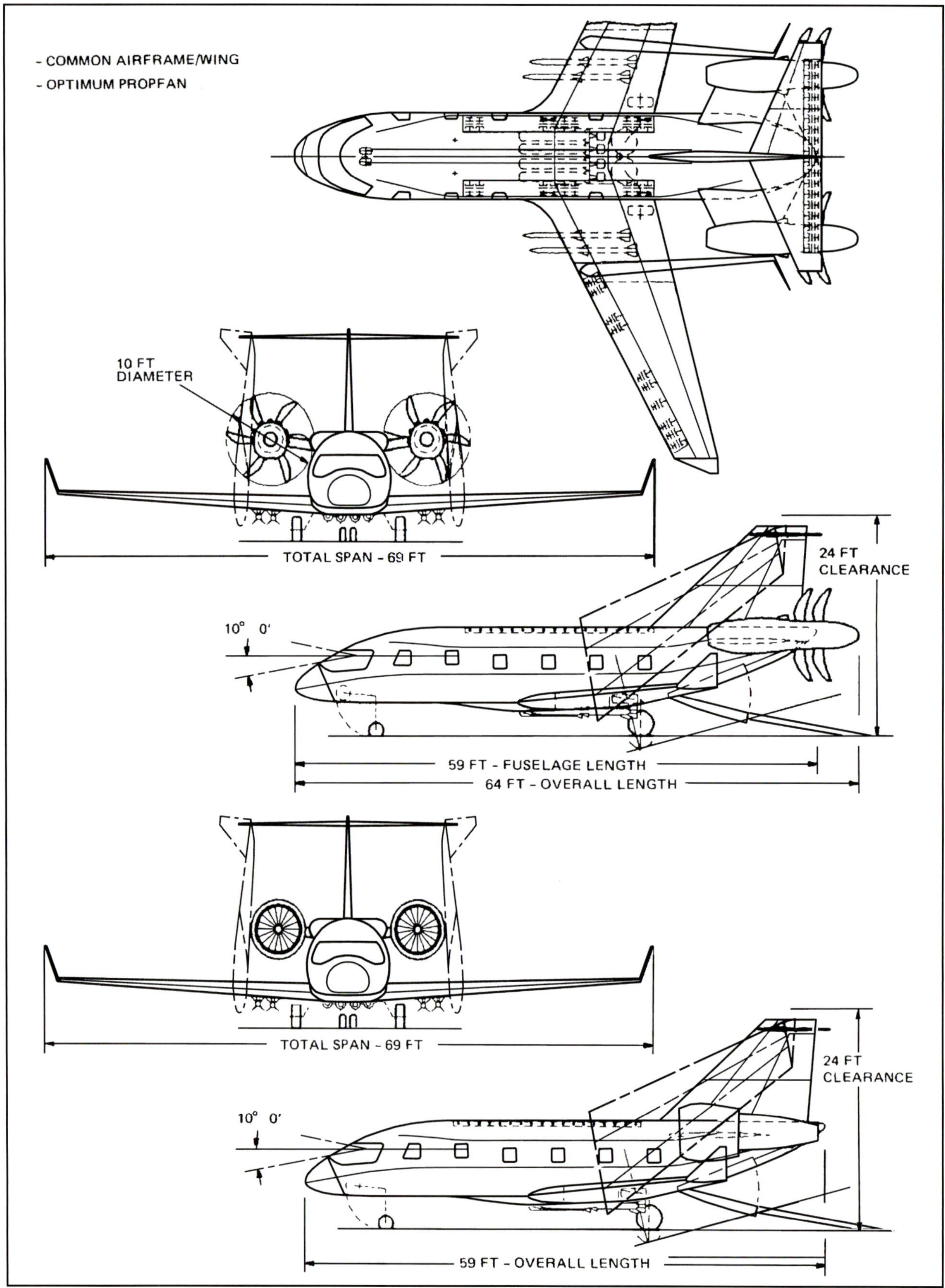

ABOVE The Grumman Model 719S MPSNA study aircraft for the MR-1 (Mission Requirements-1) configuration showing the pusher prop-fan and conventional turbofan variants. *NASA*

The MR-1 COD was sized for a 10,000lb (4,540kg) cargo payload and a 2,200mi (3,540km) range. While a specific MR-1 COD was designed, drawings show the baseline MR-1 design with all payloads including conformal radar array, external AMRAAM missiles and COD tail ramp.

Grumman Model 732 MMVX

Grumman explored a number of different configurations – many quite radical – for the MMVX design. These included a twin-turbofan with a wing that could best be described as delta with straight wings extending from the outboard extremities, and a canard aircraft powered by two prop-fans.

This MMVX version had the wide-body configuration in contrast to others in the ASW role. The very unusual tail and inboard wing layout was to accommodate internal conformal radar arrays. Each array was aimed 45° from the centreline of the aircraft, enabling a 360° total field of view.

Grumman Model 732 MMVX	
Powerplant	2 x unspecified turbofans
Span (estimated)	80ft (24.4m), 28ft (8.54m) folded
Length	61ft 6in (18.7m)

ABOVE A model of the wide-body Grumman MMVX design. *Courtesy of Northrop Grumman Corporation*

BELOW A Northrop N-381 AMSS desk model. *Author collection*

Northrop N-381 AMSS

Northrop, in line with its long tradition of designing tail-less aircraft, used a flying wing configuration – effectively a swept delta – for its AMSS (Advanced Multi-Sensor System) proposal. Given the project number N-381, it would have offered a direct replacement of the C-2 with somewhat less payload but significantly longer range and higher cruising speeds.

In terms of size, it had a very similar footprint to the S-3A (a point emphasised in the promotional material) and was similarly carrier-compatible. It was powered by two unspecified turbofan engines. An alternative version replaced the turbofans with twin pusher unducted fans. Loading, including pallets, was via large doors in the underside of the rear fuselage. There was no ramp – cargo would have to be hoisted in and out of the fuselage.

Northrop N-381 AMSS	
Powerplant	2 x unspecified turbofans or 2 x unspecified unducted fans
Span	70ft (21.35m)
Length	47.5ft (14.49m)
Height	17.96ft (5.48m)

Lockheed MPNSA adaptation for COD

Completed in March 1986, the Lockheed-Georgia study took a different approach from either Boeing or Grumman by focussing on the ASW role as the primary function for its multi-mission aircraft. That initial decision led to a smaller fuselage cross section as the starting point. This resulted in a smaller, lighter ASW aircraft than proposed by

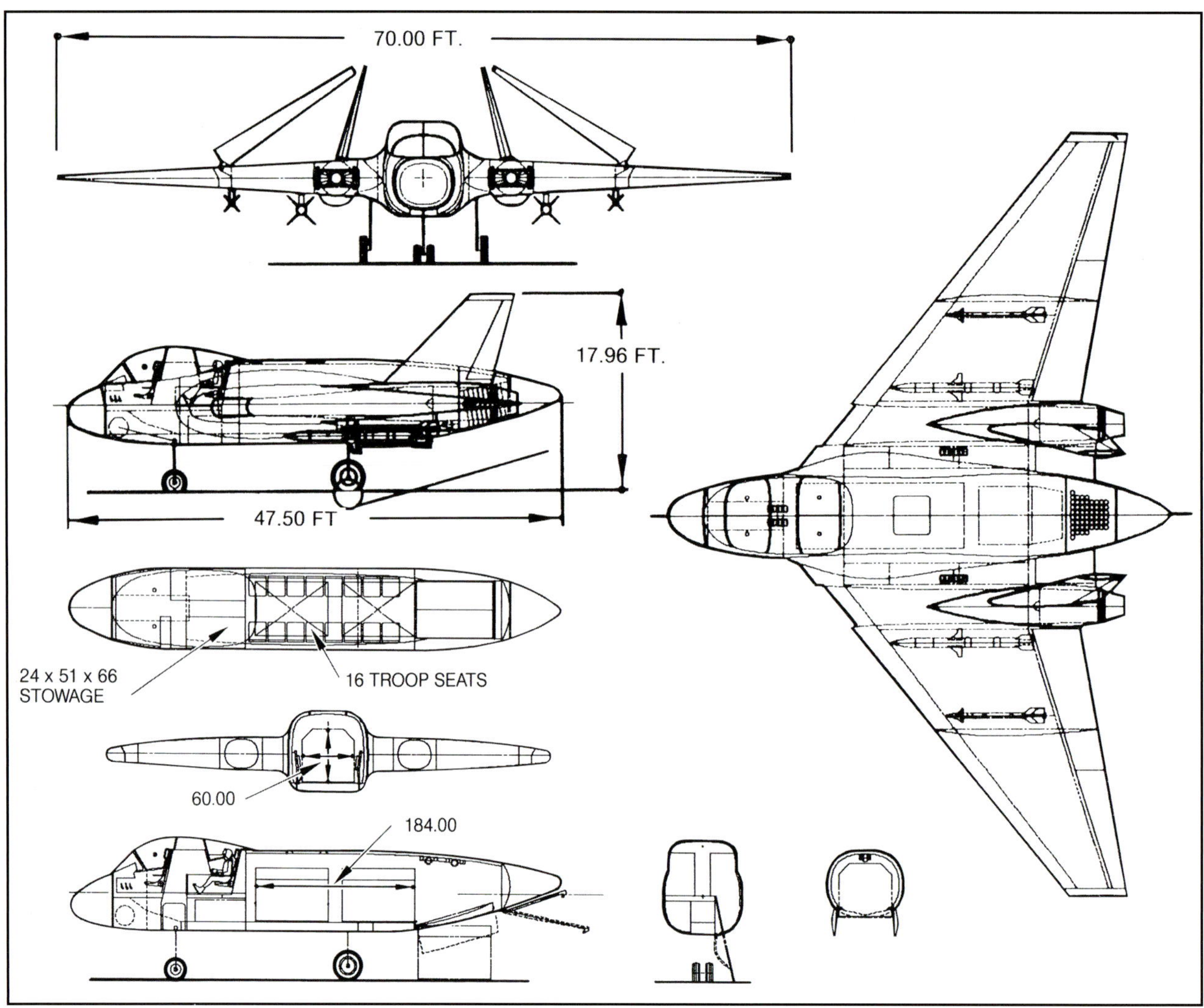

ABOVE Northrop N-381 AMSS general arrangement, configured for COD. *Courtesy of Northrop Grumman Corporation*

the other competitors, with one drawback – the design was only suitable for limited cargo carriage because no other internal space was available other than the weapons bays. These were re-faired to increase their internal area, with access through large, side-opening doors. Neither bulky items (such as aircraft engines) nor passengers could be carried in these areas. Lockheed admitted this up-front, stating that for true COD capability, a new fuselage would have to be designed.

The Lockheed ASW vehicle was a relatively compact design with the cockpit resembling that of a sleeker S-3 Viking. Gross weight was expected to be about 45,000lb (20,430kg) depending on mission. Lockheed chose a canard layout that moved the wing aft, in order to move the tractor prop-fans aft of the cockpit and cabin areas.

The prop-fans were driven by Pratt &Whitney STF678 engines, scaled to 8,700shp (6,488kW) and driving dual four-bladed counter-rotating props. The selected turbofan was the 'study' STF-686 with a thrust of 19,350lb (8,790kg). Engineers briefly studied the pusher-configured General Electric GE-36 but found that it was a poor match to the airframe. The nominal mission profile for the COD variant was to carry a 4,000lb (1,820kg) payload over a range of 2,200mi (3,540km).

While promising, the Common Support Aircraft programme faltered with little enthusiasm from either the Navy or Congress. The effort finally ended with the post-Cold War budget cutbacks, although the eventual need to plan for the replacement of the newer Greyhounds was still looming in the decade ahead.

COD development from the 1990s to date

Despite the many proposals presented in the 1980s, the Navy chose to pursue none of them, either as a dedicated COD transport or as one of the roles for a new multi-purpose aircraft. Further ideas emerged for more radical updating of the C-2 design and for essentially the resurrection (once again) of the S-3 COD. However, the Navy would not finally make a decision on its next COD procurement until 2015.

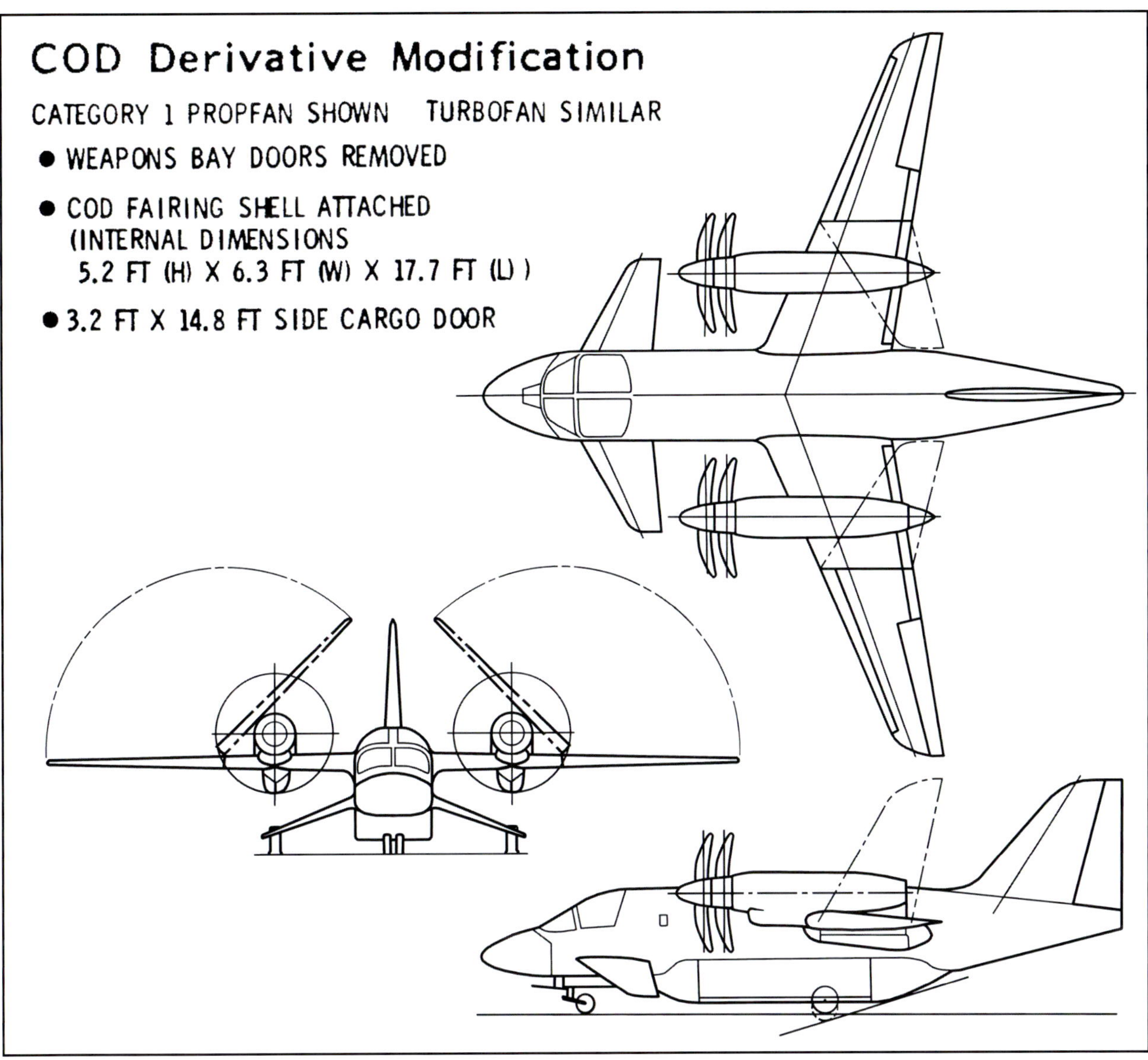

ABOVE **The Lockheed MPSNA concept with tractor prop-fans and expanded weapons bays for cargo carriage.** *NASA*

Northrop Grumman Greyhound 21

With the conclusion of the MMVX and MPSNA airframe efforts, the Navy and Grumman turned to examining how conformal radar array technology could be incorporated into the existing E-2 aircraft in 1987. Under the working designation of E-2X, configuration studies placed antennae on the sides or the fuselage and in the leading edges of the wings, and eliminated the distinctive E-2 rotodome. This change caused a decrease in pitch stability, which required the addition of a wing leading edge extension between the engine nacelles and the fuselage. This extra space did not go to waste, being used to carry additional fuel for the TF34 turbofan engines, which replaced the T56 turboprops.

However, detailed design work revealed that the challenges of fitting the new technology to an existing airframe were going to be hard to overcome. In particular it was going to be difficult to find space for, and to accommodate the weight of, the transmitter units, together with the additional cooling and power supply required. As a consequence, development of the E-2X derivative was halted.

Nevertheless, the E-2 features were once again carried forward and incorporated in another C-2 proposal. Dubbed 'Greyhound 21', the newly merged Northrop Grumman Corporation promoted the design as a multi-mission aircraft, capable of anti-submarine/anti-surface warfare, electronic surveillance and aerial refuelling, as well as COD duties. It was to be capable of carrying a 10,000lb (4,540kg) payload and had a range of 2,300mi (3,700km) ship-to-shore carrying outsized cargo items, without needing ferry tanks in the cabin.

With the exception of the replacement engines, the structure of

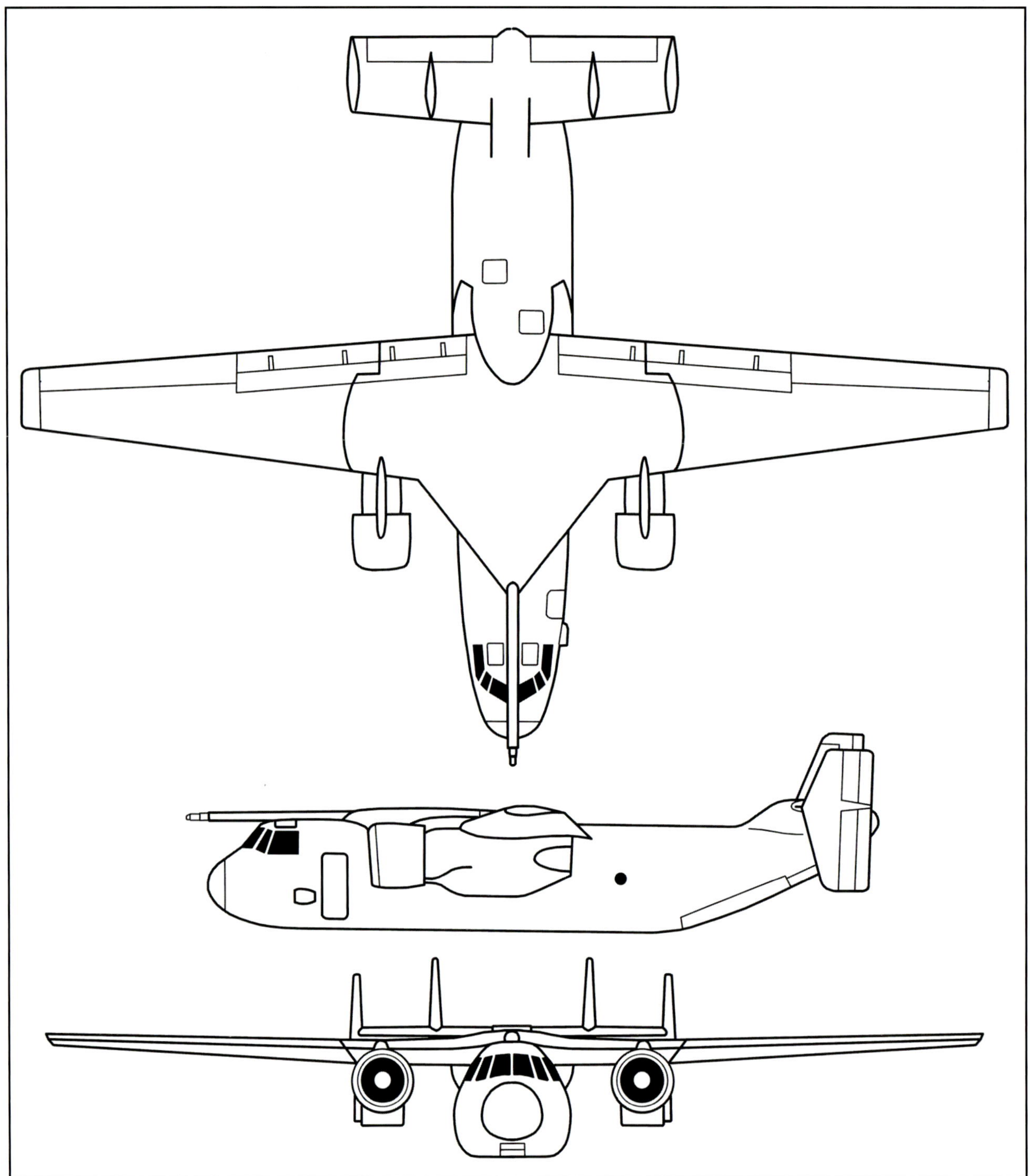

ABOVE Northrop Grumman Greyhound 21 general arrangement, with twin TF34 engines. *Courtesy of Northrop Grumman Corporation*

the aircraft appears to have involved minimum changes to the basic C-2A airframe, the main one being the forward extension of the wing leading edge inboard of the engines, a feature in common with the E-2X. Artwork shows an in-flight refuelling probe and the addition of fuselage-mounted drop tanks, a feature deleted from the original Greyhounds as a cost-saving measure in 1966. Despite continuing interest, the Navy did not proceed with this relatively costly variation on the basic C-2 design.

Lockheed Martin 'C-3'

Appreciating the lack of development funds for a wholly new COD aircraft, Lockheed Martin proposed to refurbish and restore a number of S-3 Vikings, as a 'partly new' replacement. By this time almost all of the retired aircraft were in storage at Davis-Monthan AFB in Arizona.

The 'C-3', as it was termed, would retain the earlier ASW aircraft's wings, engines and tail services, and marry these to a new fuselage similar to that proposed in the 1970s and 1980s. The fuselage around the cargo compartment would be 22in (0.56m) wider and 6ft (1.89m) longer than the original fuselage and could carry 10,000lb (4,540kg) cargo or twenty-eight passengers. Of great significance, it had a rear-fuselage ramp and the ability to load and carry a fully assembled P&W F135 engine for the F-35 strike fighter. Lockheed Martin also proposed a KC-3 air-refuelling tanker variant.

According to the US Naval Institute News (8 April 2014), at the same time that Lockheed Martin put forward its S-3 derivative (C-3) proposals, Northrop Grumman also offered a solution to the Navy's COD needs in the form of an upgraded C-2 using engines, wing components and cockpit from the company's E-2D Advanced Hawkeye aircraft – less ambitious than earlier proposals, but requiring little development and flight testing. Despite the advantages of these two proposals – and cost-effectiveness was surely one of them – neither found favour with the Navy.

ABOVE Brochure artwork for the Northrop Grumman Greyhound 21. *Courtesy of Northrop Grumman Corporation*

The Bell-Boeing V-22: Combining COD and VOD

Not until 2015 was action taken to replace the C-2 – nearly half a century after it first entered service. Its successor would be an entirely new type of aircraft, the tilt-rotor V-22 Osprey, designated CMV-22B. This brought together COD and VOD in one platform, combining the attributes of both a twin-rotor helicopter and a conventional turboprop transport aeroplane.

Moreover, with the aircraft already in service with the USAF and US Marines, the V-22 offered an advantage in terms of lower unit costs and the prospect of shared maintenance. The only notable external differences from the standard production V-22 are the enlarged external sponsons to provide for additional fuel, extending the aircraft's range, and antenna for long-range communications.

Taking off and landing as a helicopter, the tilt-rotor configuration avoids several major problems associated with the earlier deflected-thrust VTOL options, such as extremely high fuel consumption and high-velocity downwash while hovering.

The V-22's origins can be traced back to 1981 and the Joint-Service Vertical Take-off/Landing Experimental (JVX) programme. JVX resulted from the recognition that Bell Helicopter's proposed Type A V/STOL A with its tilt-rotor arrangement offered a unique capability for special operations and other missions that required a higher cruise speed and longer range than the helicopter could offer, while still retaining the ability to hover. This capability was demonstrated very effectively by the NASA/Army/Bell XV-15 tilt-rotor aircraft at the 1981 Paris Air Show.

Originally involving the US Army (electronic reconnaissance), USMC

BELOW Concept art of a 'KC-3' operating in a secondary aerial-refuelling tanker role. *Lockheed Martin*

(marine assault), USN (combat rescue), and USAF (special operations), the JVX programme was subsequently slimmed down to focus on the most urgent and justifiable requirement, the replacement of the obsolescent Marine Corps CH-46 helicopter.

The resulting V-22 was a joint Bell-Boeing venture, powered by two Rolls-Royce (at the time, still Allison) T406 turbo-shaft engines. Having first flown in helicopter mode on 19 March 1989 and successfully transitioned to fixed-wing flight on 14 September of the same year, the V-22 successfully completed sea trials in December 1990. Development of the V-22 was protracted by an incoming Secretary of Defense's attempts to cancel it, and not helped by two crashes, one fatal, which were caused by maintenance errors. Production was delayed as a result.

Two further fatal crashes during initial USMC evaluation of early production V-22s in 2000 also cast a cloud on its viability, even though both were attributed to pilot error. As a result, the first USMC V-22 and USAF squadrons did not become operational until 2007. Since then, however, the V-22 has become highly valued by both services for its combination of speed, range, payload, ability to hover and to make vertical take-offs and landings. Its safety record is now arguably better than most helicopters.

At the time of writing, thirty-eight CMV-22Bs are on order for the Navy, with initial operational capability (IOC) due to be reached in 2021 and full operational capability in 2024. The long-serving C-2A is planned to be completely replaced by 2026, and the Navy expects the full fleet of CMV-22Bs to have been delivered by 2028.

Critics of the decision to utilise the V-22 in the COD role point out that it has less range than the C-2 and a smaller cabin, which is barely able to accommodate the largest required single load, the engine for the F-35 fighter. The cabin is also unpressurised, meaning that oxygen has to be provided to passengers during flight above about 10,000 feet (3.05km). Against this, its proponents argue that its helicopter-mode capability provides greater mission flexibility, including the ability to operate from an aircraft carrier without needing to rely on its catapult or arresting gear.

BELOW The Bell Boeing CMV-22B COD/VOD prototype completed its first flight on 21 January 2020. *Bell*

Some have claimed that ordering the V-22 is a more costly solution than restarting C-2 production, though it seems unlikely given the Navy's record of reluctance to spend any more than is deemed absolutely necessary on COD. And, once again, the Navy's COD replacement decision – after being offered a wide range of options – has been to opt for minimal adaptation of an aircraft already in production.

COD in perspective

Looking back over the history of COD, the US Navy appears to have taken a remarkably conservative approach to meeting this particular mission requirement. Just two, highly conventional aircraft have fulfilled the COD role from the mid-1950s to the present day. This is despite the fact that the major aircraft companies have come forward with numerous proposals, both for adapting proven aircraft and for producing wholly new concepts for the role.

In many ways, this approach has been uncharacteristic of the Navy. In other areas the service was very much at the forefront of aircraft development and had no hesitation in adopting complex, high-performance aircraft for carrier service. The US Navy's more conservative approach to COD could probably be attributed to two things: firstly, competition for funds with higher-priority fighter, attack and ASW programmes, and secondly, the fact that the long-serving C-1 and C-2 simply did the job required. The last C-1 was not retired until September 1988 and the C-2 is currently expected to serve until 2024 – fifty years after the design's first flight.

Meantime, the Navy will be receiving its first combined COD and VOD aircraft, almost fifty years after first being presented with the concept. The V-22 brings an impressive new ability, yet still falls short of some existing C-2 capabilities such as maximum payload. So, while the immediate requirements may be satisfied, there is likely more to come in the history of COD.

Chapter Seven
Extending the Design Boundaries

Missile launchers, nuclear propulsion and aerodynamic concepts

ABOVE The Boeing Model 759-100 spanloader series began with Resource Carriers in the 1971-72 period. Pictured is the Model 759-153 in Boeing markings; later models would explore military adaptations. *Boeing*

Given the progressive development of very large, high-performance cargo-carrying aircraft, it is hardly surprising that a number of proposals have been made for either adapting them to other specialised roles, or for building on the latest experience to create even larger, more capable cargo airlifters. These studies have included:

- Airborne strategic missile launch
- Aircraft Nuclear Propulsion (ANP)
- Radical new aircraft configurations

This chapter reviews those proposals.

Airlifter airborne ballistic missile launchers

Defense strategy during the Cold War depended heavily on nuclear deterrence; at its heart was the ability to respond to a nuclear strike (or even a conventional armed invasion of Western Europe) with a massive retaliation. Initially this rested wholly on Strategic Air Command's bomber fleet. As Soviet air defence improved in the late 1950s, this role was increasingly spread to ICBMs (Intercontinental Ballistic Missiles) based across the USA, and SLBMs (Submarine Launched Ballistic Missiles), creating the modern triad concept. However, even housed in hardened silos, missiles remained vulnerable to a pre-emptive nuclear strike.

As a result, war planners looked to provide greater security by examining mobile basing concepts. One concept that was exhaustively evaluated was rail basing, where missiles could be launched by specially designed rail cars constantly travelling across the continental United States. Another mobility concept was to have them air-launched from large aircraft. A number of missiles could either be airborne at any one time, or be rapidly dispersed in times of heightened international tension. The concept was known as the ALBM (Air Launched Ballistic Missile). While the largest available bomber (the Boeing B-52) had the potential to carry such weapons, it was also a role to which large airlifters seemed well-suited; manufacturers responded with proposals that adapted several purpose-built designs.

Later in the 1970s, as cruise missile technology advanced – for conventional warfare as well as added nuclear deterrence – modified versions of airlifters were again proposed as potential launch platforms since they could carry large numbers of cruise missiles to within a stand-off range of targets. Indeed, virtually every large airlifter was considered at some time or other for one or both of these roles.

Skybolt ALBM launch platforms

The initial ALBM was a medium-range solid-fuelled missile that could be carried under the wing of the B-52 and released 1,000 miles away from the target, outside the range of Soviet air defences. The Douglas GAM-48 (later AGM-87) Skybolt, conceived in the late 1950s, was a two-stage solid-fuel rocket weighing 11,353lb (5,148kg), capable of carrying a single W-59 1 megaton warhead.

The Skybolt appeared to be the weapon of the future, countering advances in Soviet air defence and enhancing the role of the manned bomber – so much so that the British Government based the whole of its future deterrent strategy on its availability. Unfortunately, the prototype missiles suffered numerous failures in their early test firings and, with the advent of the first Submarine Launched Ballistic Missiles (SLBMs) the whole programme was unilaterally cancelled by Defense Secretary McNamara (and upheld by President Kennedy) in December 1962. After a firestorm of political protest in Britain, a compromise was worked out whereby Polaris missiles were to be made available to the Royal Navy, which then required a bespoke class of missile-carrying submarines to be created.

While intended for the B-52G and H, Skybolt's forthcoming availability led to a series of proposals for alternative, specially designed long-range carriers, based on either new designs or adapting existing aircraft. In September 1960, in response to the Air Force's System Study Directive (SSD) 17531 'Multipurpose, Long-Endurance Aircraft', Boeing submitted separate studies from several of its divisions. These included:

- Aero-Space Division: New aircraft development (Model 828 studies)
- Wichita Division: B-52 derivatives (Model 877 studies)
- Transport Division: Existing transport aircraft derivatives (Model 731 and 738 studies)

As an alternative to the Boeing proposal, Lockheed-Georgia offered the GL-207-45-26 with external

BELOW Boeing's Seattle Division proposed versions of airlifters currently under development (the 731-16M pictured), each capable of carrying four Skybolt missiles. *Boeing*

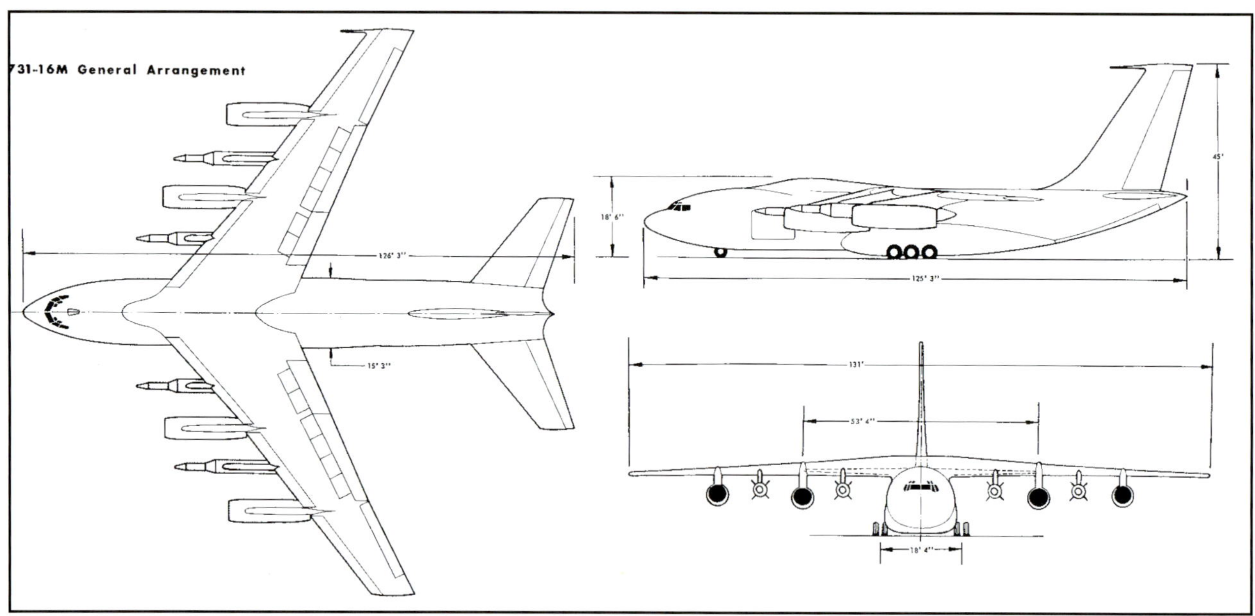

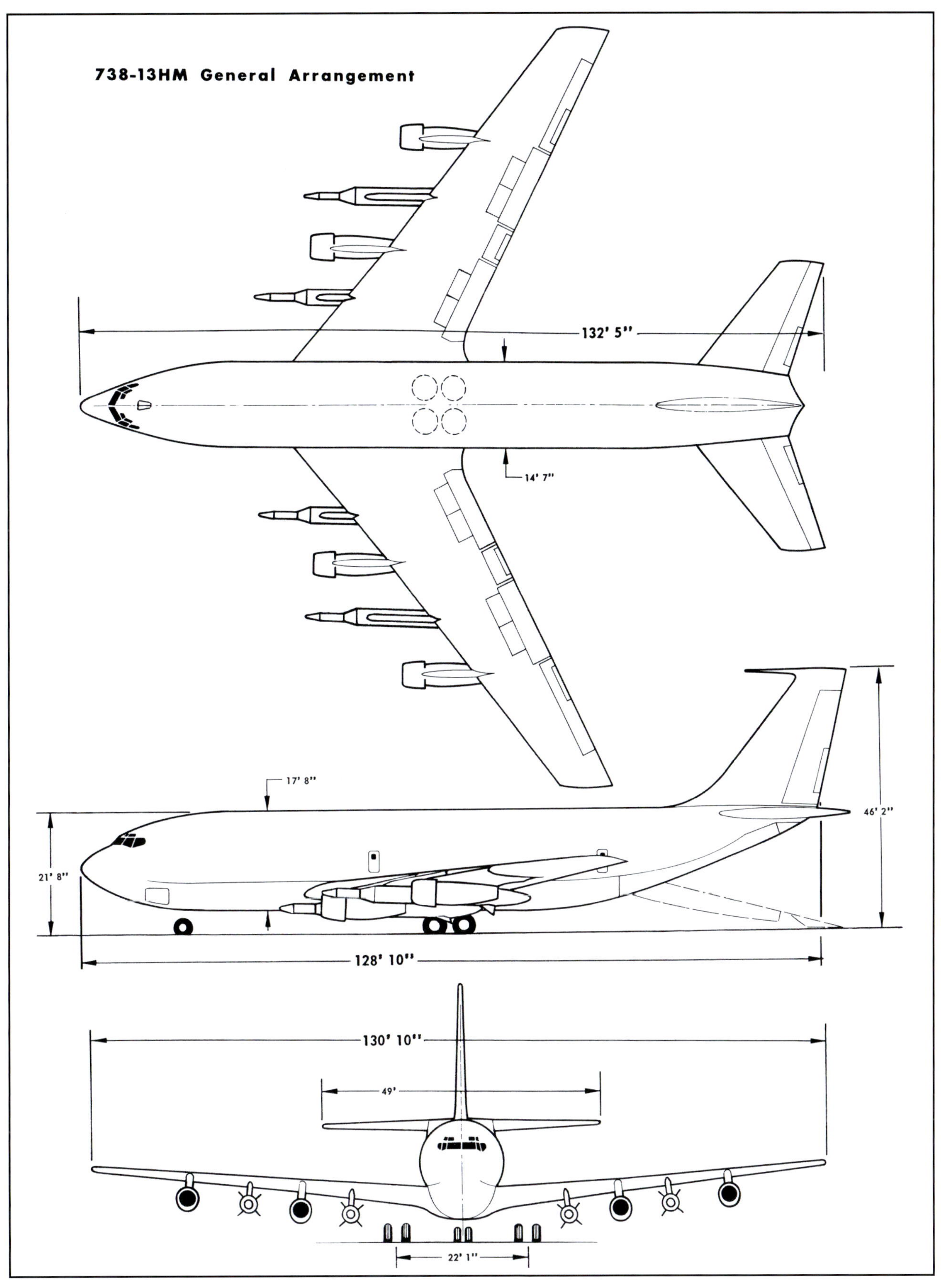

ABOVE Boeing's Seattle Division also proposed the 738-13HM (derived from the C-135 series tanker transports) capable of carrying four Skybolt missiles. *Boeing*

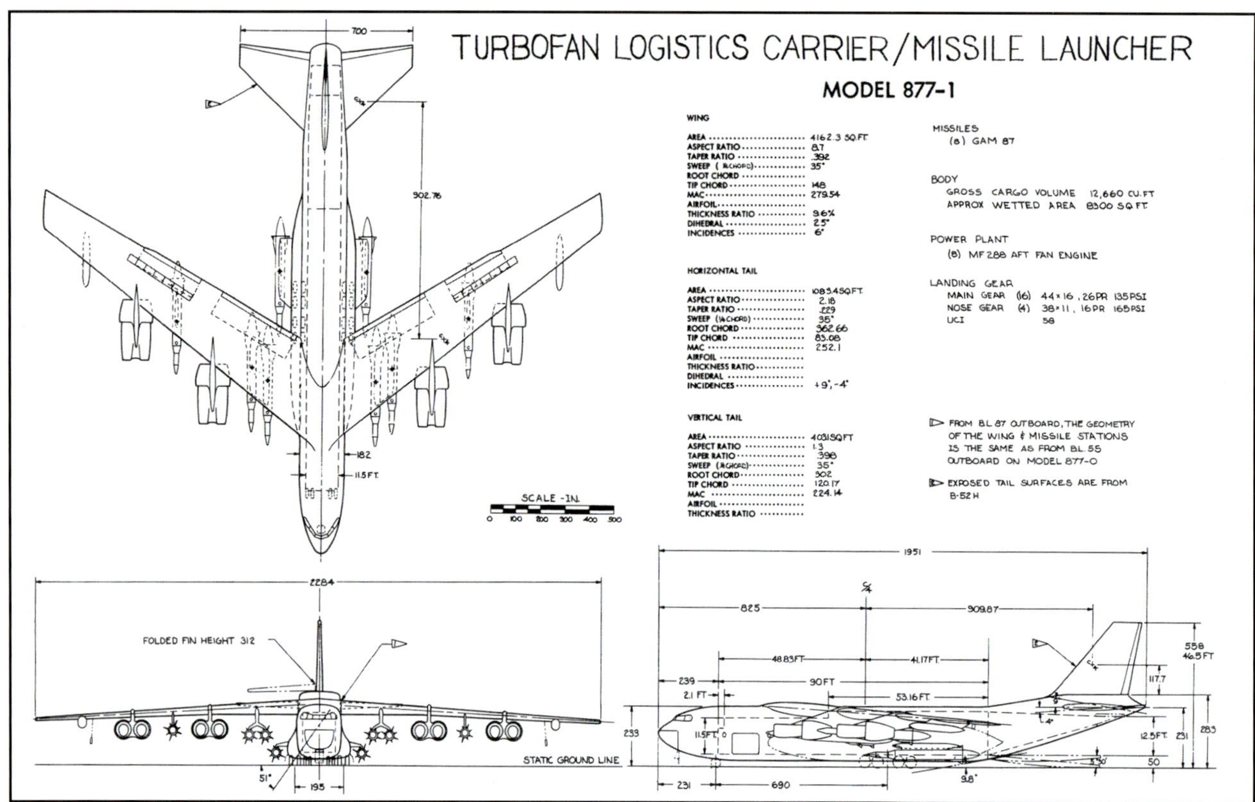

ABOVE **The Boeing Wichita Model 877-1 concept could carry eight Skybolt missiles externally, or cargo. Based on the B-52G, it was to be powered by eight GE MF-288 aft-fan engines** *Boeing*

BELOW **The Douglas Model 2205-D Long Endurance Aircraft (LEA) had a straight wing, two unspecified turboprop engines and internal carriage of two unidentified ballistic missiles, which would be released through belly doors. The cockpit structure shows DC-8 influence.** *Boeing*

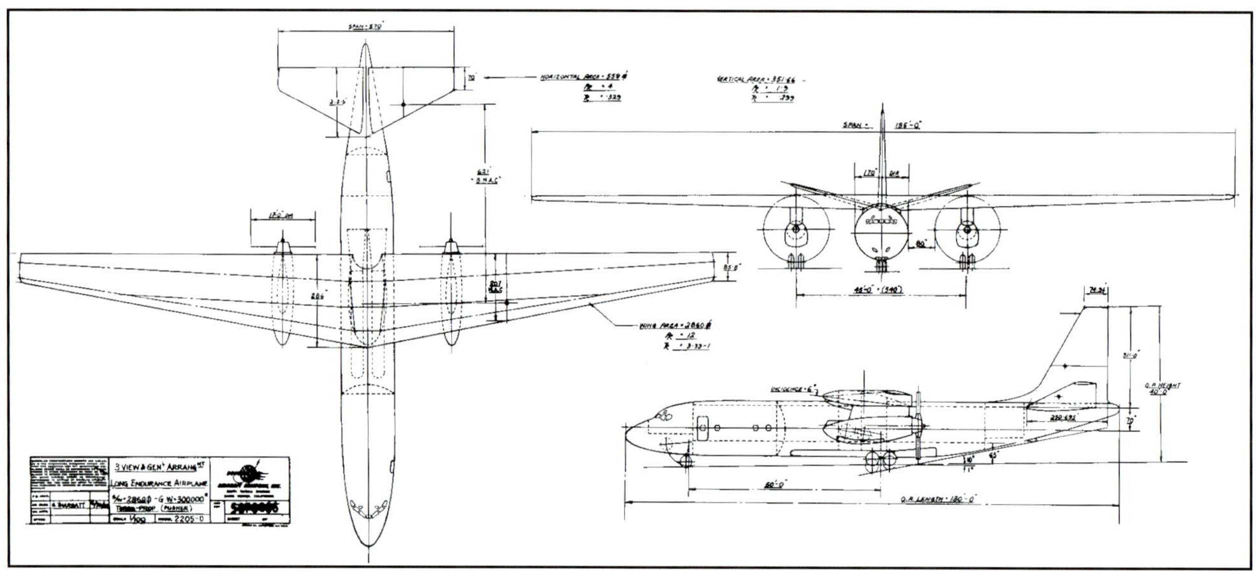

carriage of the Skybolt. While carrying the missiles externally would minimally affect the design's overall performance, it necessitated internal fuel tanks in the cargo area to achieve range goals. This addition both restricted the aircraft to a lower load factor of 2.0G and reduced the service life of the wing.

The cancellation of the Skybolt programme was not, however, the end of the road for the concept of ALBMs, nor for airlifter concepts that could launch them.

Proposals for purpose-built missile platforms returned again in 1963, under the Dromedary concept. This envisaged airborne platforms with highly efficient turboprop powerplants, enabling endurance missions of up to 120 hours. The powerplants were to be the

Boeing Model 877-1 MPLEA	
Powerplant	8 x GE MF-288 aft-fan turbofans @ 15,500lb (68.95kN) thrust
Span	190ft 4in (58.01m)
Length	162ft 7in (49.55m)
Height	46ft 6in (14.17m)
Wing area	4162.3sq ft (386.7m²)
Max TOW	390,000lb (176,900kg)
Payload (cargo)	100,000lb (45,360kg)

Douglas Model 2205-D	
Powerplant	2 x undefined turboprops
Span	185ft (56.39m)
Length	130ft (39.62m)
Height	40ft (12.19m)
Wing area	2,860qft (265.7m²)
Max TOW	300,000lb (136,080kg)

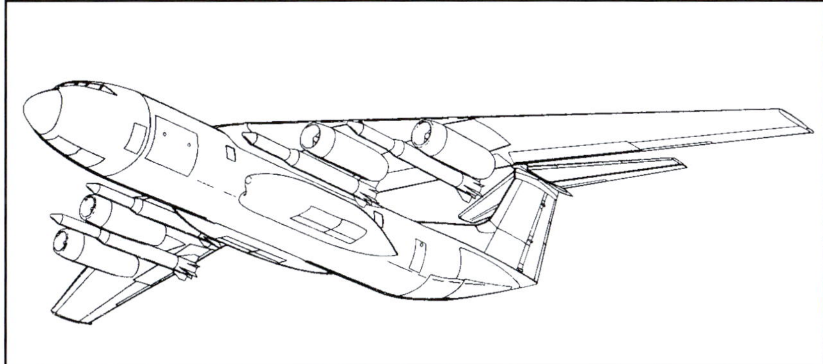

ABOVE The missile-carrying version of the Lockheed GL-207-45 was designed to carry four Skybolt ALBMs with little impact on aircraft performance. *Lockheed*

BELOW Northrop studied a missile-carrying multi-purpose aircraft with Laminar Flow Control. Propulsion was to be provided by four regenerative turboprops, and payload was to be four 10,000lb (4,536kg) air-to-surface missiles. *Courtesy of Northrop Grumman Corporation*

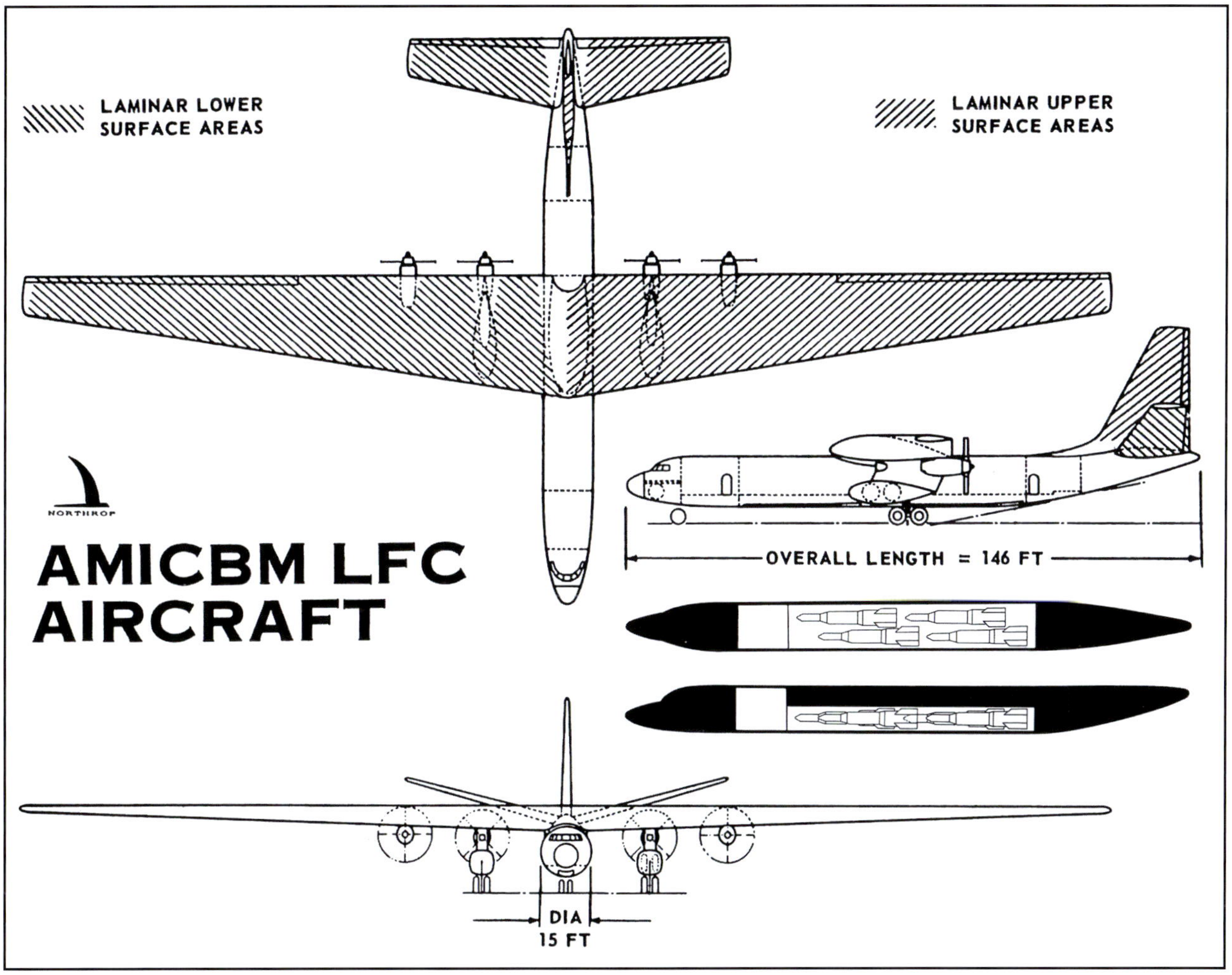

regenerative/recuperative turboprops that were later suggested for use in the CX-X programme (as discussed in Chapter Two).

Dromedary split into two initiatives. MAPLE/MPLE (Multi-purpose Long Endurance) remained in study status, while AMPSS (Advanced Manned Precision Strike System) moved forward, since it promised penetrating, precision strikes rather than just a stand-off capability with long endurance. The AMPSS studies eventually lead to the AMSA (Advanced Manned Strike Aircraft) – sometimes, somewhat unkindly, alleged to stand for 'America's Most Studied Airplane' – and to the B-1A at the beginning of the 1970s.

Strategic missile launchers of the 1970s and 1980s

By the early 1970s concerns were growing about the vulnerability of land-based forces to the increasing number and accuracy of Soviet ICBMs. Air-launched ballistic missile concepts returned again, viewed as survivable alternatives to ground-based launch from rail and fixed sites.

The feasibility of launching a ballistic missile from an airlifter was successfully tested in 1974, when a C-5A Galaxy launched an inert Minuteman I. The Minuteman system itself was not intended for future airborne deployment, but rather was being used to pave the way for a successor known as the 'Missile-X', or MX.

Boeing 747 ALBM platform

As before, studies of airborne launch platforms led in two directions: modifications of existing airlifter aircraft, and highly specialised single-mission-type platforms (the latter being beyond the scope of this book).

The C-5/Minuteman launch programme was primarily a

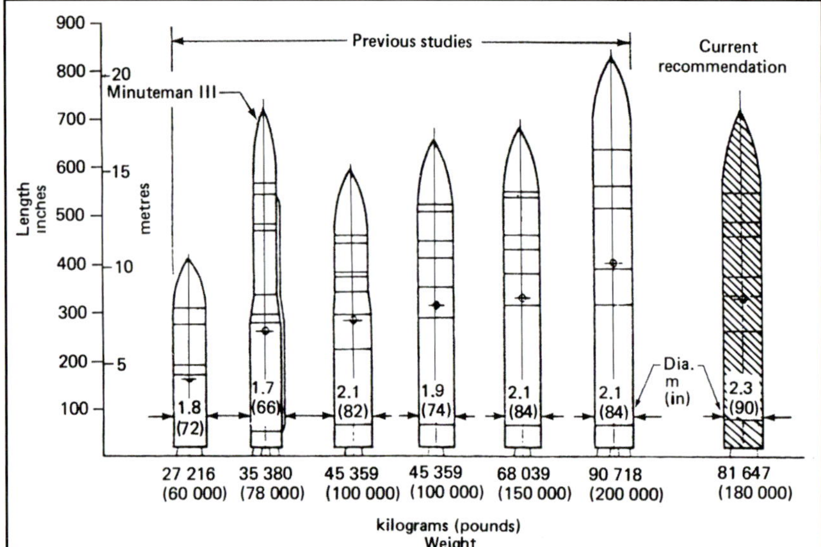

LEFT **MX missiles that could also be air-launched under study by Boeing in the mid-1970s.** *Boeing*

BOTTOM **A LGM-30B Minuteman ICBM is seen in its extraction cradle as it falls away from the C-5A on 24 October 1974. The cradle was then pyrotechnically separated and dropped away. After the missile reached a vertical launch attitude under a separate set of parachutes, the modified first stage fired for ten seconds to demonstrate powered, controlled flight. The other stages were inert and did not fire (and no warhead was carried).** *USAF*

BELOW **A series of eight flight tests resulted in an air extraction of an inert LGM-30A Minuteman I ICBM from a C-5A.** *USAF*

demonstration of ejection and parachute technologies, and not the kind of system envisaged for regular ALBM operational use, which would require substantial adaption of the carrier aircraft. Boeing described how a 747 could be modified for this role, carrying missiles in either the main or lower cargo deck, depending on the weapons involved. In the former configuration, the aircraft could carry two missiles up to 66ft (20m) long and weighing up to 200,000lb (90,720kg), which would move along rails to be launched by free fall from doors in the bottom of the rear fuselage. In the other configuration, the aircraft could carry four 100,000lb (45,360k g) missiles, 49.5ft (15.1m) long, mounted in two pairs at either end of the lower fuselage, each directly released via doors in the fuselage beneath them. In other words, it would be configured much like a large conventional bomber.

Without refuelling, the 747 could carry a 300,000lb (136,080kg) missile payload for more than five hours, loitering between 20,000 and 30,000ft (6,096 and 9,144m) at a speed of around Mach 0.62. A single air-to-air refuelling, taking the in-flight weight up to 1,200,000lb (544,310kg), could enable the aircraft to stay on station for an additional thirteen hours.

Lockheed ALBM launchers

A 1979 Lockheed missile launching proposal was a variant of its proposed LX-MRSA (Multirole Strategic Aircraft), itself a shortened version of the C-5. Making the maximum use of its investment in the prior C-5 programme and eschewing extended development, Lockheed projected that the aircraft could be in service by 1985.

Most notably, the proposed aircraft was 52.3 feet (15.94m) shorter, recognising that with dense and heavy payloads much of the C-5's internal volume went unused. For instance, when lifting two M-60 tanks (near the maximum weight capability of the

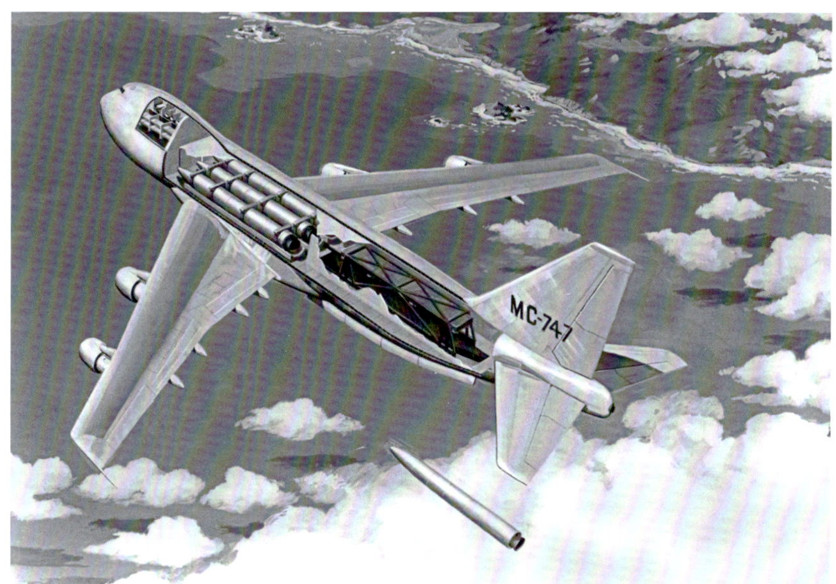

ABOVE **This Boeing cutaway art shows the notional internal arrangement of a 747 carrying four ALBMs.** *Boeing*

BELOW **Alternative arrangements for carrying and launching ballistic missiles from the Boeing 747. These were: translating (above), or in individual launch bays (below).** *Boeing*

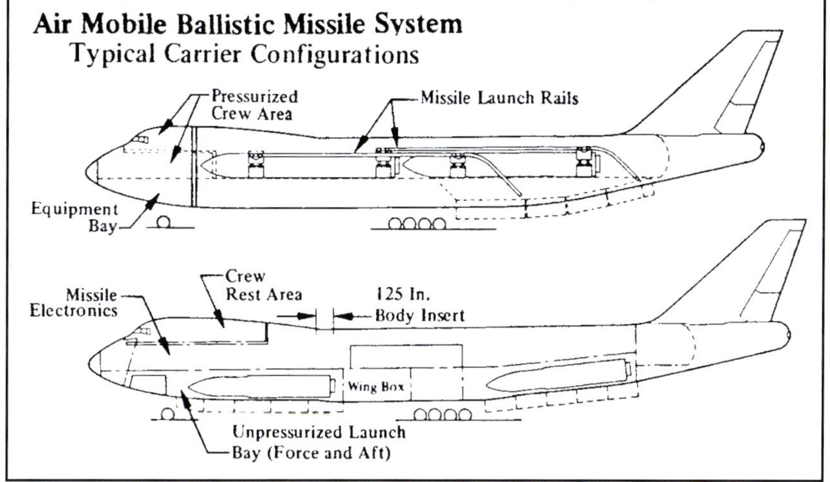

RIGHT **Boeing also proposed the C-14 as a missile launching platform.** *NARA II via Dennis R. Jenkins*

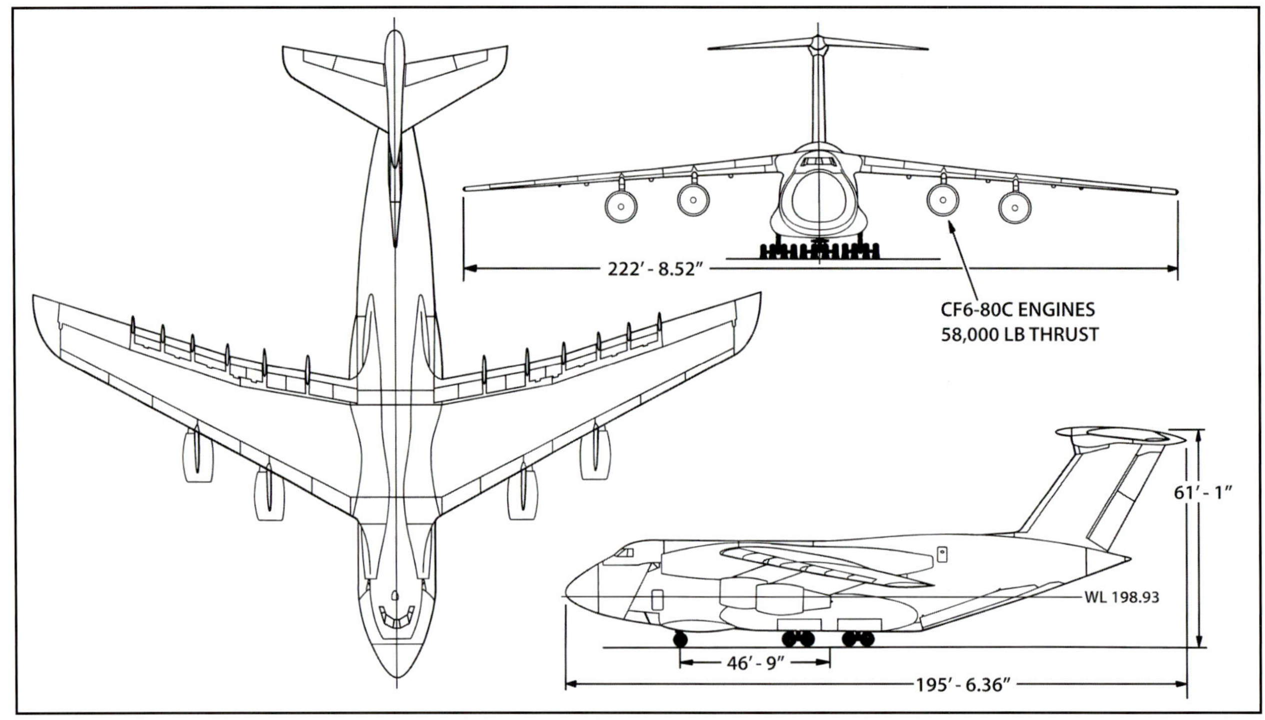

ABOVE The Lockheed MRSA (C-5 derivative) missile-launching variant. *Lockheed*

Lockheed LX-MRSA	
Powerplant	4 x CF6-80C turbofans @ 58,000lb (258.0kN) thrust
Span	222ft 8.52in (67.88m)
Length	195ft 6.36in (59.60m)
Max TOW	769,000lb (348,810kg) (at 2.5G load factor)
Payload	211,483lb (95,927kg)

aircraft), some 70ft (21.34m) of the cargo deck length was unoccupied. However, it would not be just a foreshortened version of the C-5, but an improved derivative incorporating new avionics, revised use of aluminium alloys and fasteners (for improved structural durability) and replacement of the TF39 turbofan engines with the more powerful and efficient CF6-80C.

BELOW Internal layout of the McDonnell Douglas DC-10 AMMX as it launches a ballistic missile. *Boeing*

McDonnell Douglas ALBM launchers

At different times McDonnell Douglas proposed ballistic missile-launching variants of all three of its airlifters: the DC-10, YC-15 and C-17. The ALBM adaptation of the DC-10 was proposed as the Air Mobile Missile System (AMMX) and was based on the Advanced Long Range version of the DC-10, itself a development of the DC-10-30/40. Only the forward fuselage would have been pressurised, since the missile compartment was to occupy two-thirds of the fuselage. The ICBMs were stored in inclined canisters over the wing carry-though structure and would have been deployed by a cold-gas ejection system through doors in the lower aft fuselage. This area was deepened, extending aft from the main landing gear to accommodate the missiles.

Boeing cruise missile launch platform

As well as studying how the 747 could be adapted as an ALBM launch vehicle, in the mid-1970s Boeing also studied adapting the 747 as a platform for Air

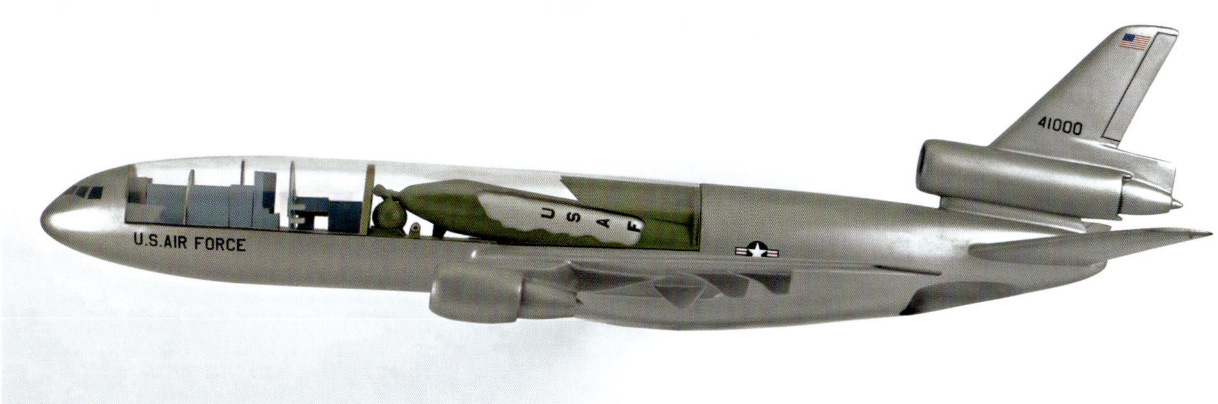

ABOVE **The McDonnell Douglas DC-10 AMMX was modified to carry two solid-fuelled ALBMs. The missiles would be ejected by pressurised cold inert gas through the openings under the horizontal stabiliser.** *John Aldaz collection*

BELOW **As did Boeing, McDonnell Douglas promoted an ALBM launcher variant of its AMST competitor aircraft, the C-15.** *Mike Machat*

BELOW **The McDonnell Douglas DC-10 AMMX launcher would have had a deepened and widened belly fairing to accommodate twin internal missiles. The model has the left ejection bay open and the right bay covered.** *John Aldaz collection*

Launched Cruise Missiles (ALCMs). ALCMs presented a different challenge, since their carrier would need to carry a large number of them internally, and eject them in quick succession. Engineers studied three 747 variants: militarised versions of the 747-200 and 747SP, and a 'quick change' version of the standard 747-200F commercial freighter. The latter would remain in normal service until required in response to a national threat, when it could be converted for military missions within forty-eight hours.

RIGHT **Promotional artwork for the McDonnell Douglas MC-17 ALBM launcher variant of the C-17.** *Boeing*

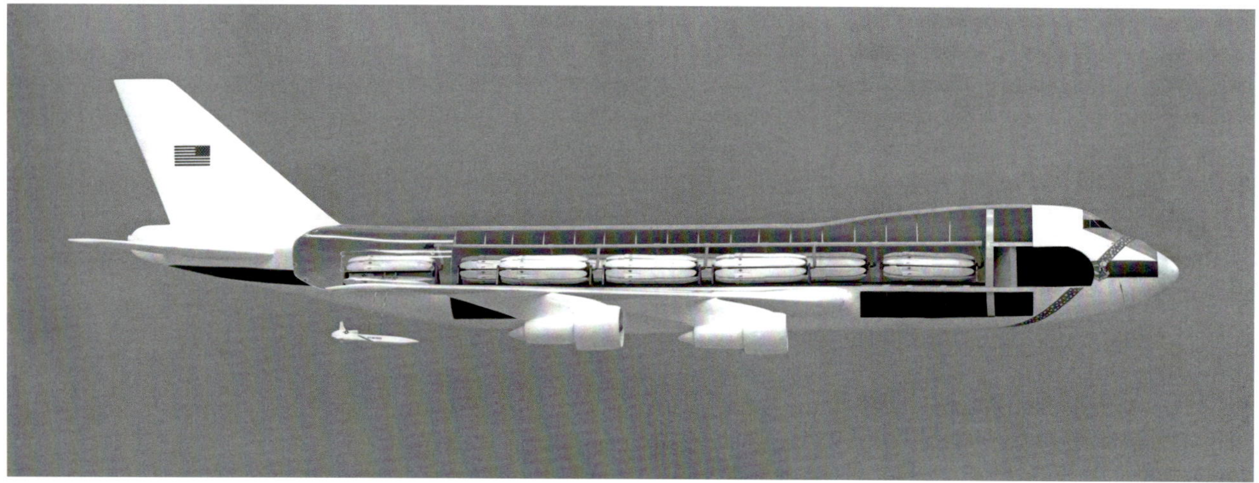

ABOVE **Cruise missile launch from a Boeing 747 aft main deck.** *Boeing*

BELOW **The cruise missile carriage proposed for the Boeing 747.** *Boeing*

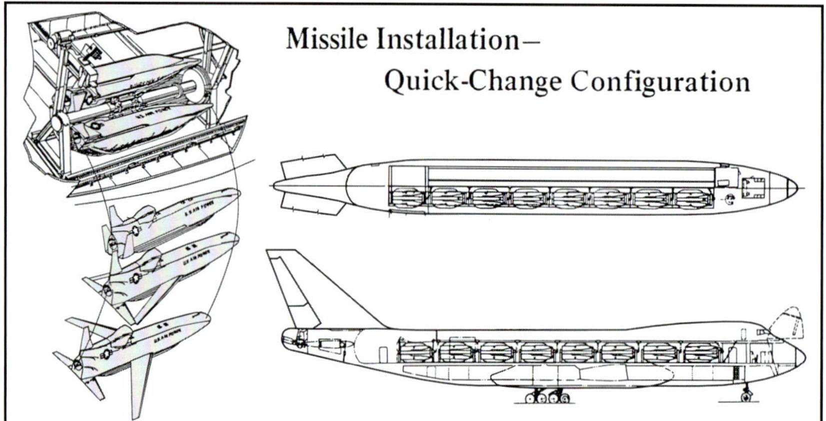

Boeing investigated three launch methods, using the University of Washington Aeronautical Laboratory wind tunnel:

- forward lower-lobe drop launch
- aft main deck eject launch from a simulated rotary launcher
- aft main deck drop launch from a side arm launcher

LEFT **The Boeing 747 arrangement for 'quick change' installation of AGM-86A cruise missiles, showing the side ejection and launch from the translated rotary launchers.** *Boeing*

The test programme examined launching the Boeing AGM-86A ALCM at simulated altitudes of 25,000ft (7,620m) and 30,000ft (9,144m) under long-range and endurance cruise conditions. All three launch methods proved feasible, with no adverse airflow interactions. The main deck ejection system required the least modification to the airframe, and was also suited to the 'quick change' arrangement for either of the commercial 747-200-based aircraft.

Investigators then examined three different launching options: translated rotary launchers, carousel rotary launchers, and a dedicated tube launcher. The first two options could handle either fifty-six Boeing AGM-86B or sixty-two General Dynamics AGM-109 Tomahawk weapons, the third just fifty-nine AGM-109s. However, as the last used up less fuselage space, it enabled the aircraft to carry an extra 52,000lb (23,590kg) of fuel. The proposed rotary launchers were based on those used in the B-52 and B-1A.

The translated multiple rotary launchers would be mounted on special track-based pallets. Two tracks ran alongside one another down the length of the hold, with the pallets moved around in flight to the launch position to eject-launch the missiles either via a bomb bay in the bottom of the forward fuselage or through launch doors in the sides of the rear fuselage.

The two carousel launchers were positioned in the fuselage, one fore and one aft of the wing box. Each contained a set of rotary launchers that were themselves rotated once they had discharged their load. This system gave the fastest launch rate – six seconds per missile, as opposed to the nine seconds for the other two systems – but it required greatly increased modification of the fuselage.

To minimise vulnerability, the aircraft would disperse to remote airfields and launch quickly in the event of heightened international tension. Planners estimated that missile-carrying 747s hangared in a dedicated hardened facility near the end of a runway could be airborne within ninety seconds.

ABOVE Promotional artwork for a Lockheed L-1011 cruise missile launcher. *Lockheed Martin*

ABOVE RIGHT A McDonnell Douglas DC-10-based CMCA is depicted launching Boeing AGM-86A cruise missiles through side-mounted bays. *Boeing*

Lockheed cruise missile launchers

Records show that Lockheed proposed its L-1011 for the ALCM role, ejecting cruise missiles from bays forward and aft of the wing box at the bottom of the fuselage.

McDonnell Douglas cruise missile launch aircraft

At different times McDonnell Douglas proposed missile-launching variants of all three of its airlifters: the DC-10, YC-15 and C-17. The first of these, the Cruise Missile Carrier Aircraft (CMCA), together with the later ATCA proposal, was derived from the DC-10-30/40CF.

Missile-launching airlifters in perspective

The proposals described above would almost certainly have developed into highly effective missile-launching systems. But not one was ever developed, quickly bypassed in favour of more

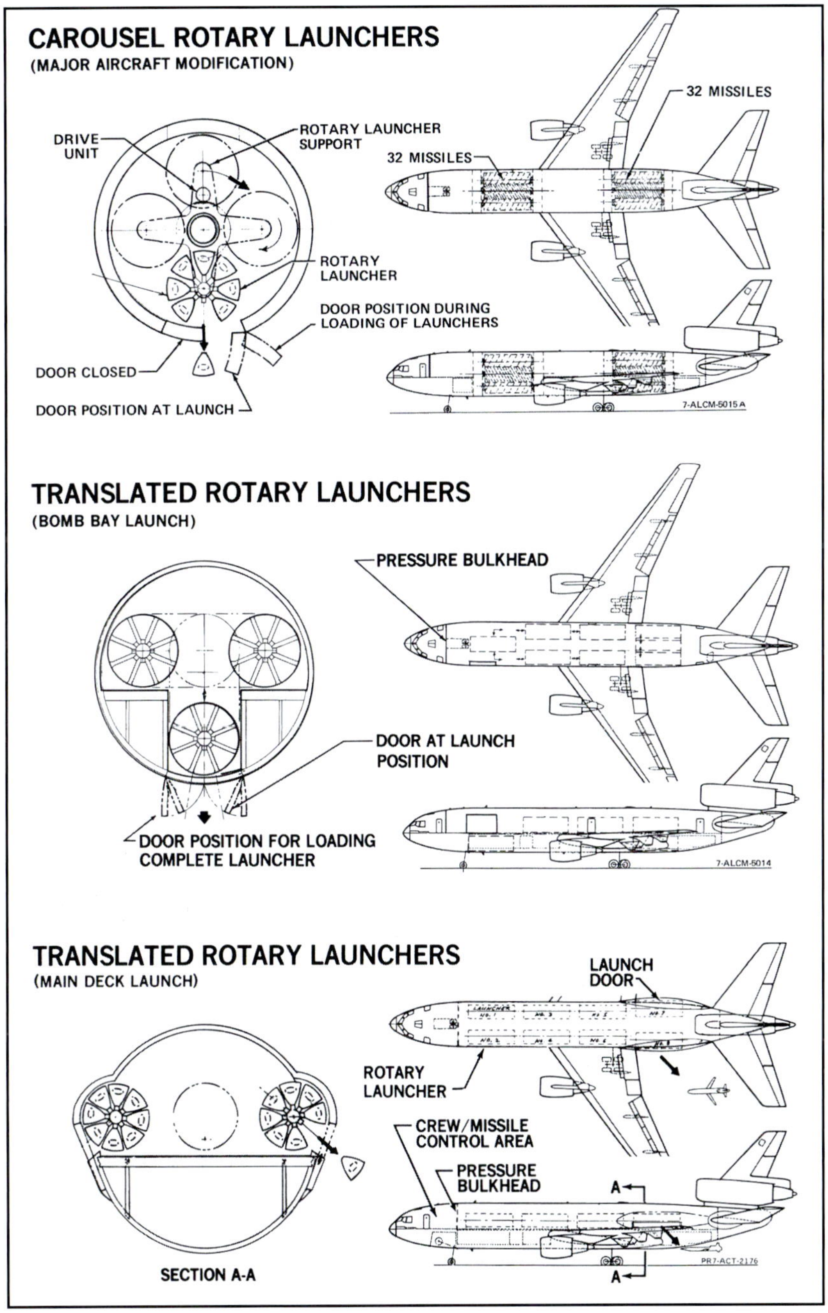

RIGHT Alternative rotary cruise missile launcher installations for the McDonnell Douglas DC-10. *Boeing*

ABOVE This retouched photo shows AGM-86B cruise missiles launching from a production McDonnell Douglas C-15A with CFM-56 engines. *Boeing*

BELOW BAe Systems' patent concept for a 747 equipped with vertical missile launchers. In the mission scenario seen here, an unusually configured high-altitude aircraft has targeted a threat missile system and relayed data via satellite to the ABVL 747, which then launches a missile, with boost-guidance updates. A precision munition is then deployed to attack the target. *US Patent and Trademark Office*

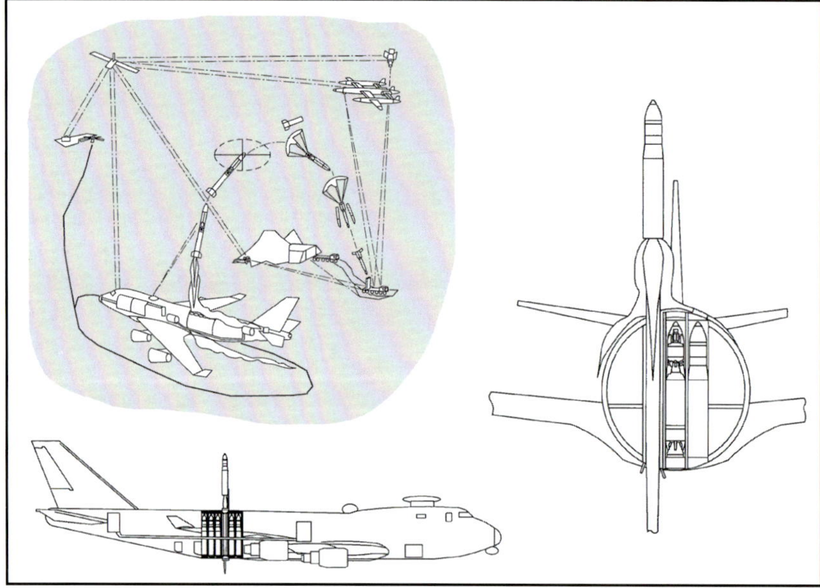

LEFT BAe Systems displayed this large model of an ABVL-modified 747-400 in April 2005. The model differed from the patent by having two launcher cell modules housing twelve missiles each. *Tony Chong photo*

advantageous military options. Air-launched ballistic missiles were ruled out in favour of survivable ground-launch options such as hardened silos and moveable platforms on either rail or wheels. And as submarine-launched missiles gained more range and accuracy, the Pentagon increasingly favoured them for rapid response to a nuclear first strike. There was simply no need to bear the expense or risk of a fleet of big aircraft constantly cruising overhead carrying fully armed nuclear ALBMs.

Additionally, the rapidly evolving cruise missile programme offered new options for conventional weapons delivery; they could be air-launched from SAC B-52s, surface ships and submarines. Their development closed the case against the need for large, purpose-built launch aircraft.

In 2005 BAe Systems proposed an ABVL (Air Based Vertical Launch) concept, with eighteen missiles carried in a cell matrix aft of the airlifter's wing. Initially intended to carry interceptor missiles for Ballistic Missile Defense, alternative payloads could be launched, including nano-satellites, deployable UAVs and re-targetable precision munitions.

Aircraft Nuclear Propulsion (ANP) programme

Viewed today, powering an aircraft with nuclear propulsion might seem somewhat bizarre. However, in the 1950s industry viewed the prospect as not only practical, but inevitable. The world's first nuclear submarine, the USS *Nautilus*, had begun construction in 1952 and was launched just two years later. The USS *Nautilus* revolutionised submarine capability, and went on to set numerous records in its twenty-six-year service life. For aircraft, nuclear power similarly promised virtually unlimited range and endurance.

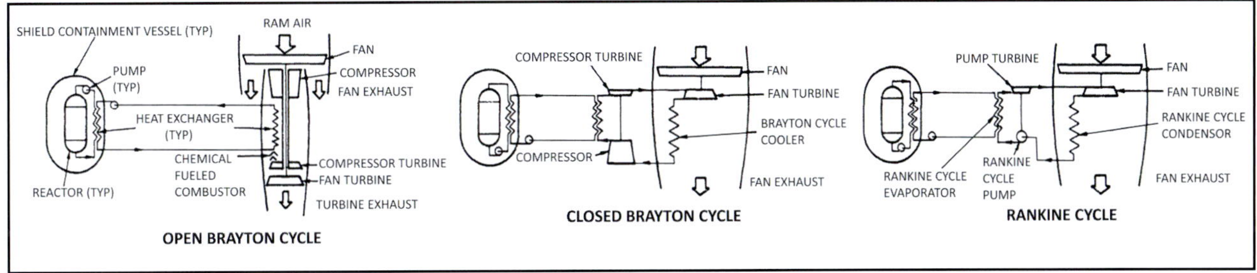

ABOVE Alternative ANP propulsion systems: the Open and Closed Brayton Cycles and the Rankine Cycle. *NASA*

The path to bring that capability to military aviation seemed clear: simply construct an aircraft large enough to carry a nuclear reactor, then shield the crew and payload from the reactor's radiation.

Engine options

In theory, a nuclear-powered aircraft engine works on the same principle as a turbojet or turbofan (or for that matter any other heat-cycle engine): air is compressed, heated and allowed to expand, driving a turbine and producing thrust in the process. The difference is that the airflow is heated by the reactor rather than by the burning of chemical fuel.

The engineering challenge centred on ways of how to transfer the energy (heat) from the reactor to the propulsion engine. There were two perceived options. The first Brayton Cycle option (Open Cycle) envisaged channelling the reactor coolant through a heat exchanger, transferring its energy to a further coolant, which in turn conveyed the heat to the airflow through the propulsion engine. The other options used the heated reactor coolant to drive a separate turbine system, which then drove the main engine compressor, thereby eliminating the need for a main engine turbine (Closed Brayton or Rankine Cycles).

Establishing the feasibility of Aircraft Nuclear Propulsion

The Air Force's interest in nuclear propulsion dates to the early post-war years, when it established the Nuclear Energy for Propulsion of Aircraft (NEPA) project. This initiative was subsequently joined by the Atomic Energy Commission, the Navy and NACA. The Open Brayton Cycle was selected for its reference aircraft. It also selected, for the initial effort, a liquid-metal (sodium/potassium – NaK)-cooled, fast reactor, since the technology was more proven and better understood than gas-cooled reactors. In comparison, almost all operational ground-based power-generation nuclear reactors use water as a heat transfer medium.

In 1951 NEPA was superseded by the enlarged Aircraft Nuclear Propulsion (ANP) programme. Studies quickly made clear the need for a flying test bed to demonstrate ANP's feasibility.

Initial studies by Fairchild and General Electric assumed the use of the Convair Advanced C-99 as a test bed since it would have both the unused volume and the weight-carrying capability necessary for the reactor and jet engines.

When the Advanced C-99 was not procured, engineers decided to convert a Convair B-36 bomber, the next largest available aircraft, into the test bed. Designated the X-6, it would carry a General Electric nuclear reactor powering four GE J53 turbojets, supplementing the B-36's six

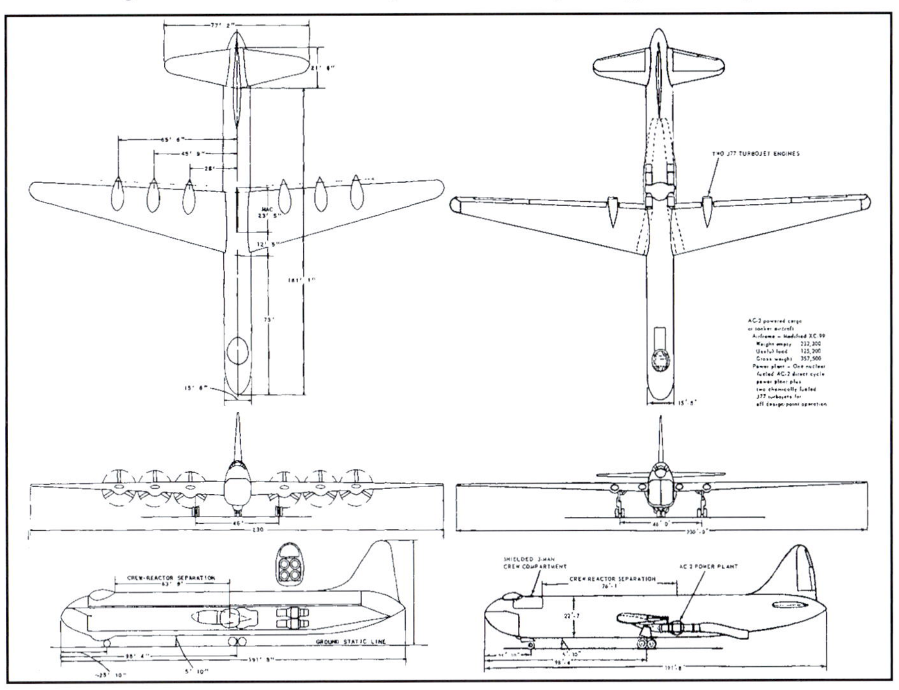

RIGHT Fairchild (left) and GE (right) notional designs using the Convair Advanced C-99 as a nuclear-powered test bed. Fairchild would have retained the six R-4360 piston engines; the later GE conversion would have supplemented the nuclear powerplant with two jet-fuel-powered J77 turbojets.
Fairchild, General Electric

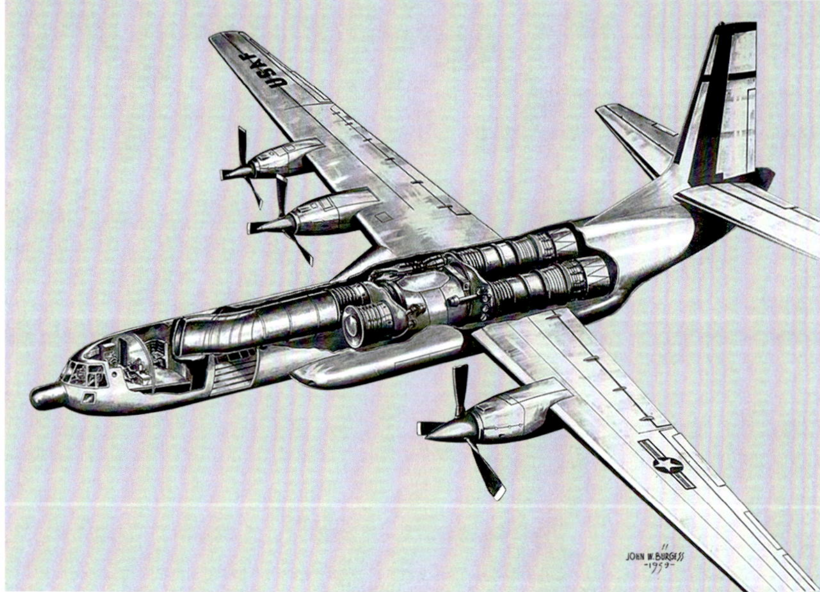

ABOVE The Convair NB-36H reactor shielding test bed in flight. *US Air Force*

LEFT This painting by GE artist John Burgess illustrates the installation of a General Electric X-211 turbojet powerplant in a test bed C-133. The inner port-wing section and No 2 turboprop engine have been deleted for clarity. *San Diego Air and Space Museum*

reciprocating engines. The additional weight was estimated to include the reactor at 10,000lb (4,540kg), reactor shielding at 60,000lb (27,220kg) and crew shielding at 37,000lb (16,780kg).

Although both the propulsion and the airframe components of the aircraft progressed satisfactorily, the programme ended in early 1953; the financially constrained US Administration foresaw insufficient military value in the project to justify the cost of the nuclear-powered (X-6) aircraft. By June 1953 all work had stopped on the X-6.

However, sufficient funds were left available to continue research and subsequently to support a less ambitious flying test bed/shield test aircraft at Convair. The company continued its efforts at solving shielding, radiation damage, airborne instrumentation, and ground handling problems. Most of the design, procurement and fabrication of a Ground Test Reactor, in connection with the X-6 programme, had been completed in 1952, and a full-scale nose mock-up of the shield test aircraft was built during that year. The problem of locating an aircraft for the project was resolved when a tornado struck Carswell AFB on 1 September 1952, damaging eighty-two B-36 aircraft. The most severely damaged bomber, with its forward fuselage badly mangled, was selected for the test bed role. Designated the NB-36H, this aircraft first flew in September 1955.

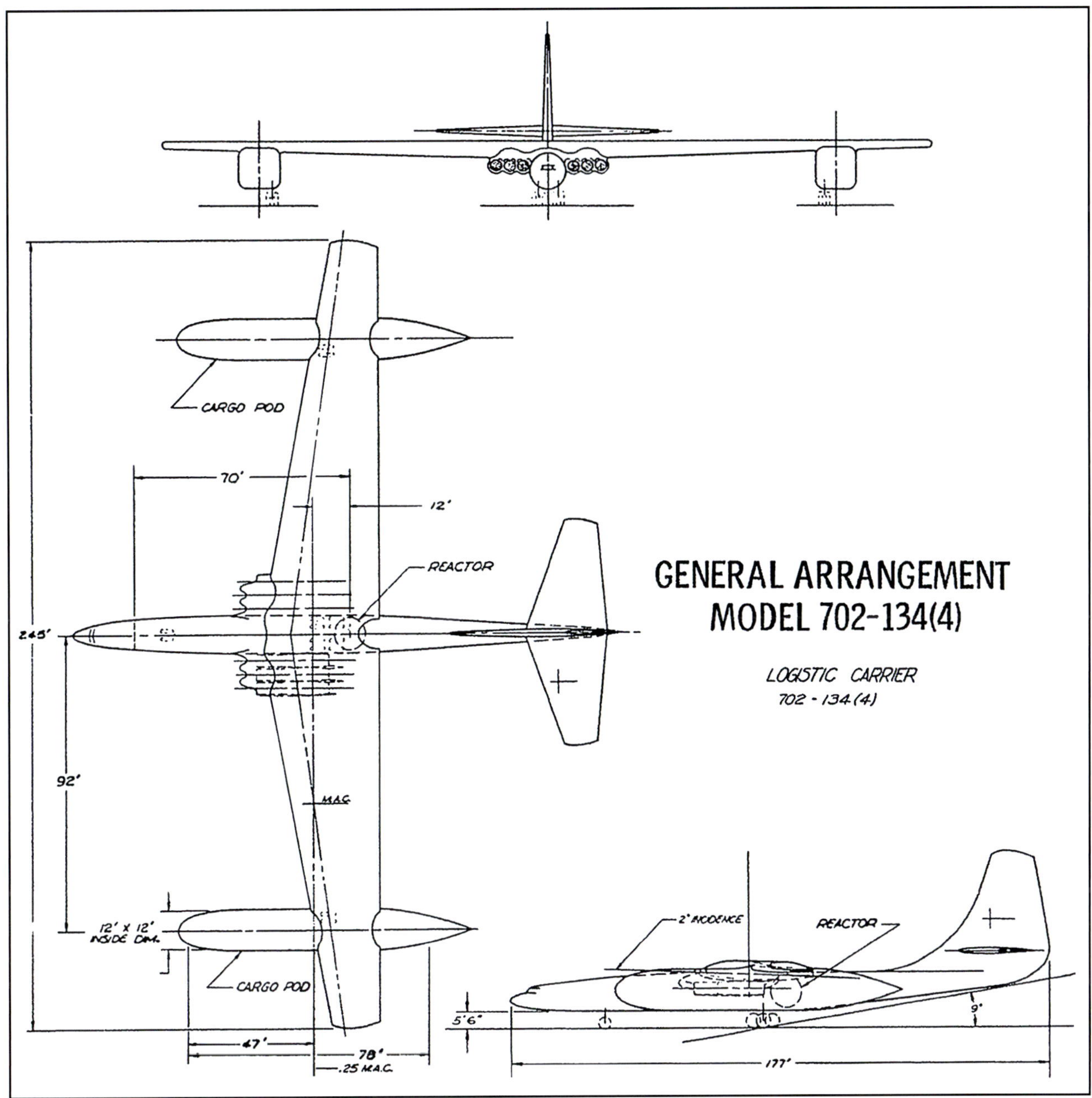

ABOVE **The nuclear-powered Boeing Model 702-134(4) general arrangement, from 1953.** *Boeing*

The three-megawatt air-cooled reactor that it carried played no active part in the aircraft's propulsion or any other aspect of its operational systems; its purpose was purely to test and demonstrate the facilities for shielding the crew of a nuclear-powered aircraft. This required replacing the entire B-36 forward fuselage, incorporating a new flight deck encased in thick lead and rubber shielding. The NB-36H carried out a successful flight test programme, which lasted until March 1957.

Boeing Model 702 and 716 ANP cargo aircraft

Boeing pursued initial ANP studies using the Model 702 number. While most were bomber studies, several were cargo aircraft studies. One was designated the Model 702-134(4), which used a single nuclear reactor to power six jet engines. Cargo was carried in twin outboard fixed pods with a 12ft (3.66m) square cross section.

Boeing records indicate that the model number 716 was allocated on 18 August 1955 for 'Study ... Nuclear Powered Transport' and the customer was the US Air Force. No data could be found on this project; however, it is likely that it was contemporary with the Douglas Model 1875 ANP effort of the same time.

Boeing Model 702-134(4) logistic carrier	
Powerplant	6 x turbojets driven by 1 x nuclear reactor
Span	245ft (74.7m)
Length	177ft (53.9m)

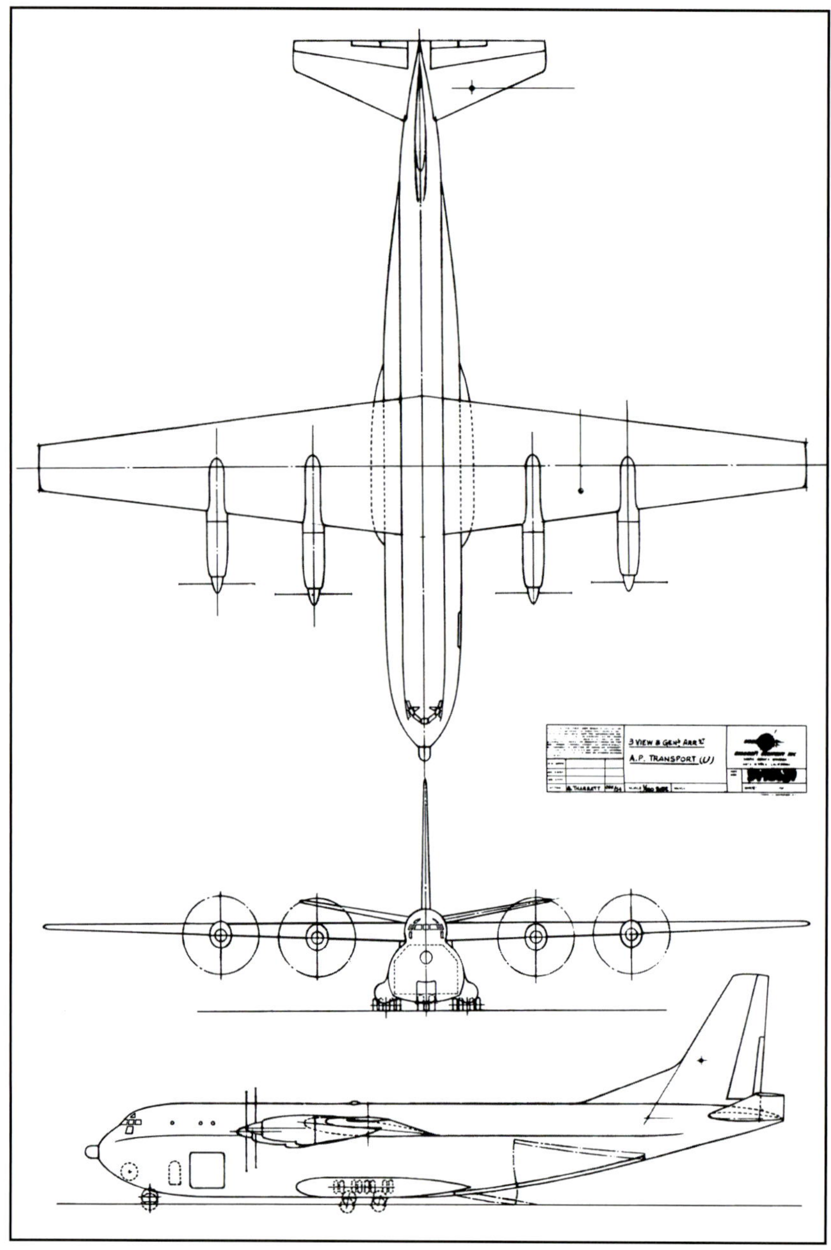

LEFT The initial Douglas 'A[tomic] P[owered] Transport' layout, dated December 1954, was derived from the XC-132. *Boeing*

Douglas Model 1875 ANP cargo aircraft

Between 1955 and 1957 Douglas (Santa Monica) under Air Force contract AF 33 (616)-2730 examined a number of design concepts for a large nuclear-powered military freighter under the overall designation of the Model 1875. Proposal efforts had started as early as December 1954 when a drawing of a modified XC-132 was generated with the innocuous title of 'A.P. Transport (U)'. The 'A.P.' signified 'Atomic Power' and the (U) meant that the drawing and title were sufficiently obscure as to be 'Unclassified'.

Douglas received a study contract and the initial effort began in early February 1955. The first task was to survey possible ANP logistic aircraft and engines to determine the most promising possibilities. Douglas reported that 'detailed studies should be concerned primarily with a turboprop carrier using a reactor size determined by cruise condition, which would operate at a design cruise speed between 300 and 400 knots at the minimum specified altitude of 20,000 feet.' After a down-selection of concepts, eight designs were drawn up in the sixty-day period starting in early March 1955. The first four were exploratory with dual pod, dual fuselage, dual boom and single fuselage layouts.

Parametric evaluations showed that the classic wing and tubular-body layout was superior in weight and drag to the other designs. Additionally, engineers determined that cruise flight required only 60% of the reactor power needed for take-off. If jet fuel could be used to provide supplemental thrust, the reactor could be scaled down to meet the cruise power requirement, reducing weight and increasing payload.

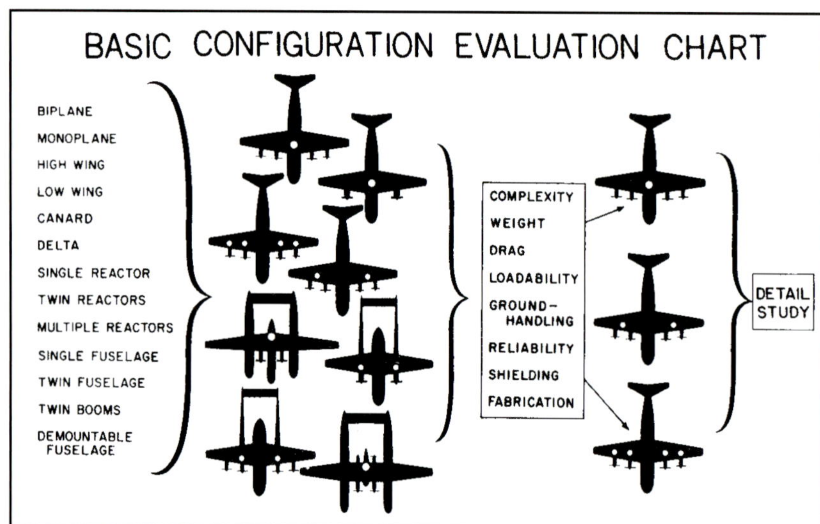

LEFT An overview of the initial ANP configurations studied by Douglas in 1955, which converged on a conventional 'wing-body-tail' layout with one, two or four reactors. The white dots indicate the number and location of the reactors. *Boeing*

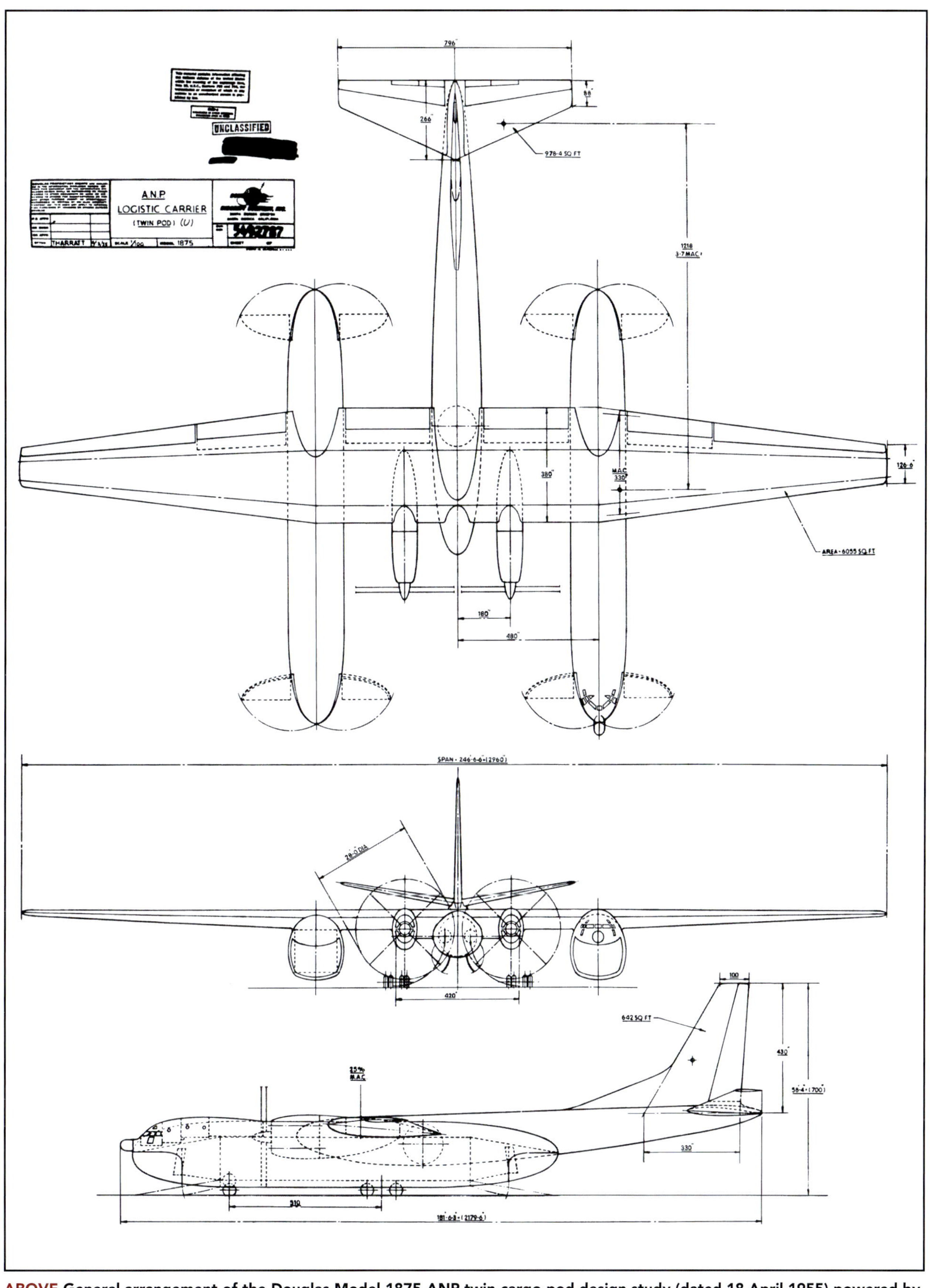

ABOVE General arrangement of the Douglas Model 1875 ANP twin-cargo pod design study (dated 18 April 1955) powered by a single nuclear reactor (the circle in the centre fuselage). *Boeing*

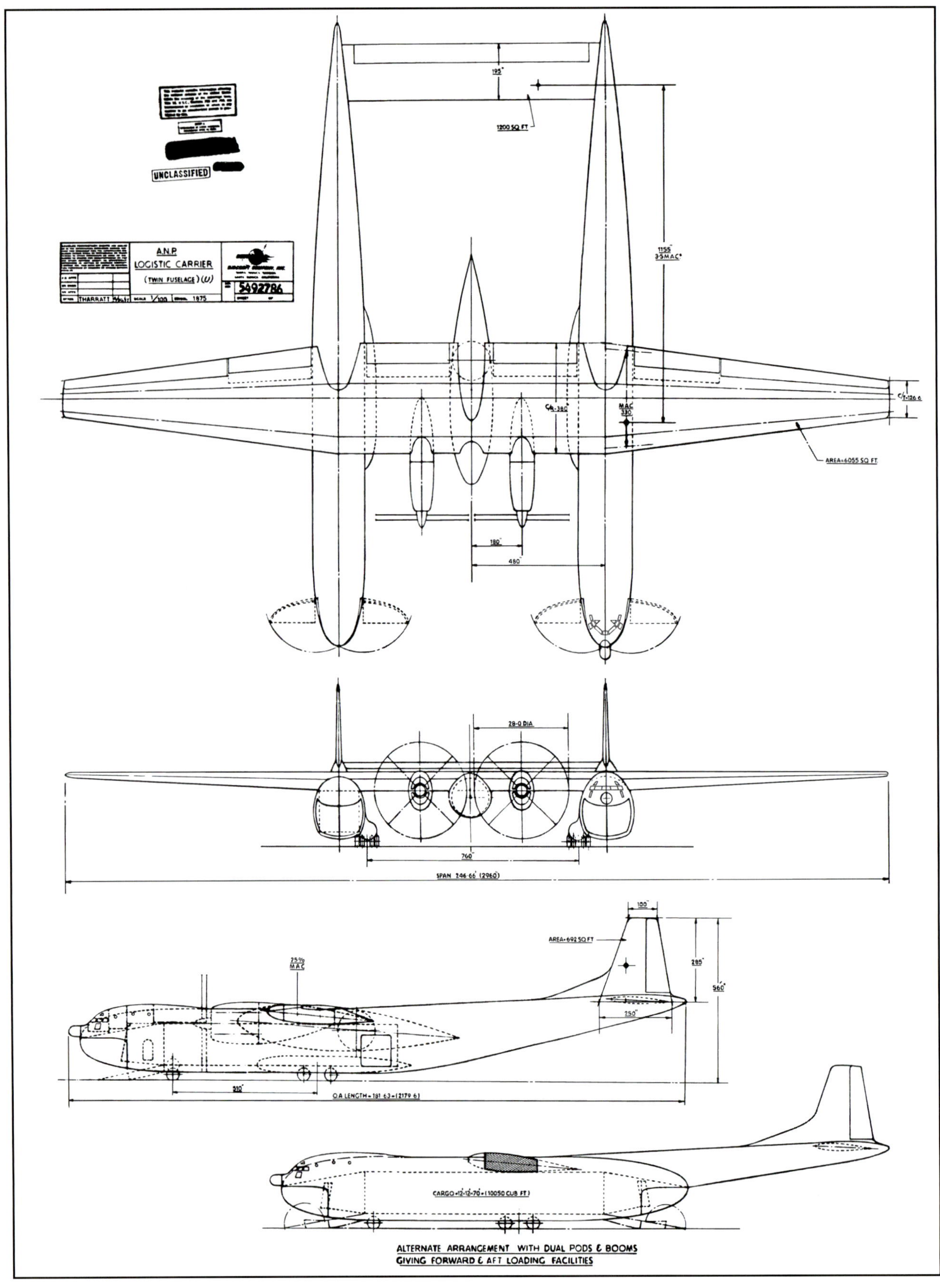

ABOVE General arrangement of the twin-fuselage Douglas Model 1875 ANP design study (dated 20 April 1955). The alternative side view (bottom) shows a variation with both forward and aft ramps. *Boeing*

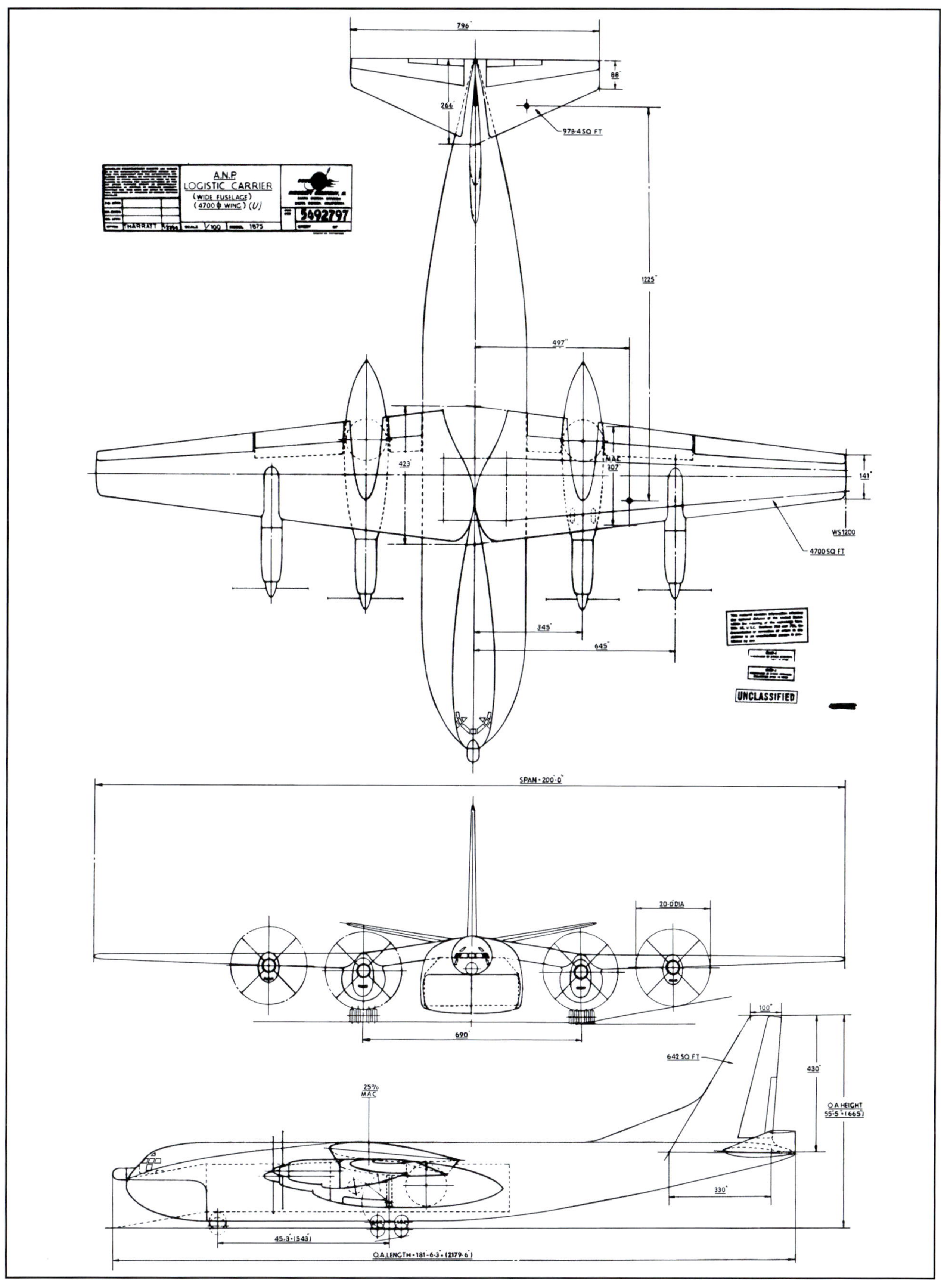

ABOVE **General arrangement of a wide-fuselage Douglas Model 1875 (dated 27 April 1955). The wingspan was 200ft (60.96m) and loading was from the nose only. A nuclear reactor was located in each of the inboard engine nacelles.** *Boeing*

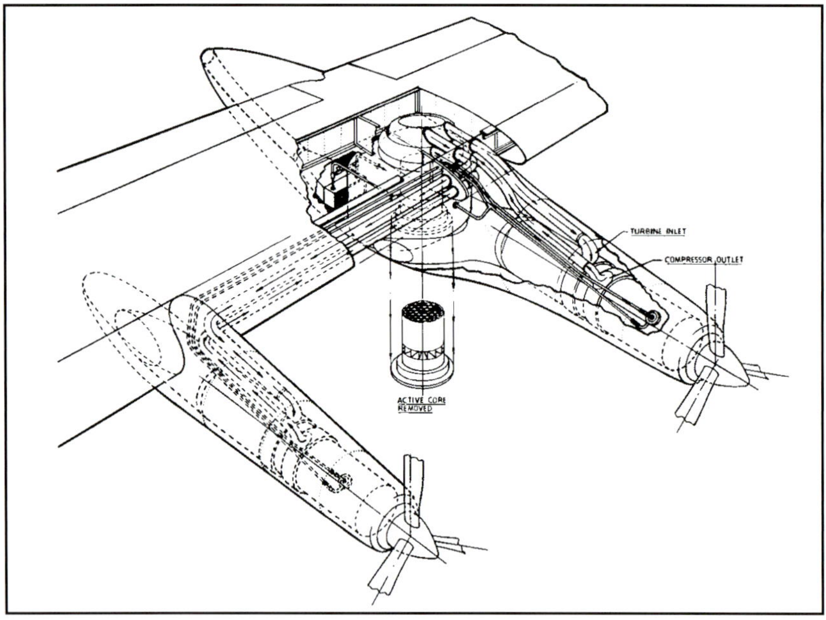

LEFT Direct Air Cycle reactors were evaluated in the Detail Study phase. As with the Indirect Cycle reactors, they were placed in the outboard nacelles for weight and for radiation attenuation. *Boeing*

Studies indicated the feasibility of an aircraft with a single reactor of 150 to 175MW or twin reactors of 60 to 75MW power, roughly equating to a power requirement of about 35MW per turboprop engine. This was significantly below the 125MW per jet engine required in the Boeing studies of 1953, which used bomber-sized powerplants. With the reduced reactor weights, payloads would be of the order of 100,000lb (45,360kg) to 200,000lb (90,720kg).

After analysis and trade-offs were completed, a Detail Study effort was launched in January 1956 and examined a common basic layout scaled to different fuselage cross sections, wing aspect ratios and overall sizes. Both Indirect Cycle (molten liquid sodium/potassium – NaK)

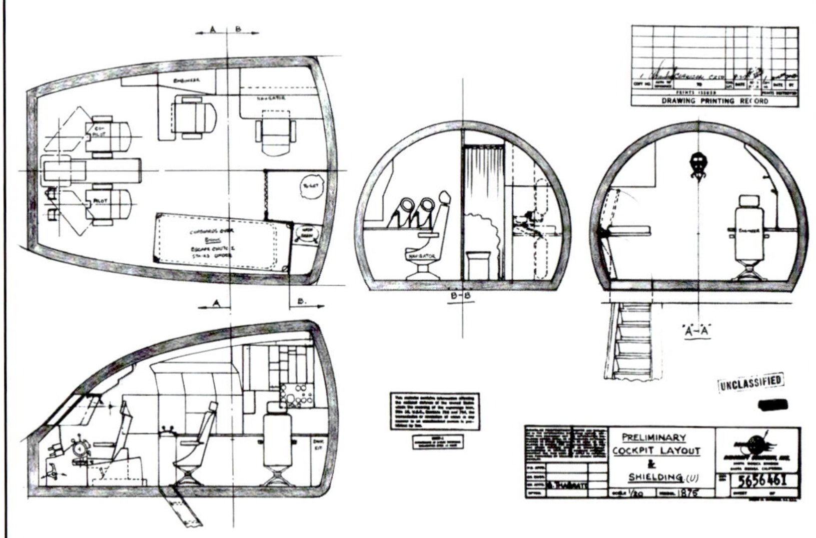

LEFT A Douglas sketch of the cockpit layout for its ANP transport. The thick outline indicates radiation shielding. *Boeing*

BELOW Passenger capacity for the large-fuselage Model 1875 variants would have been 572 troops seated on two decks. Power would be supplied by two AC-300-1 reactors. *Boeing*

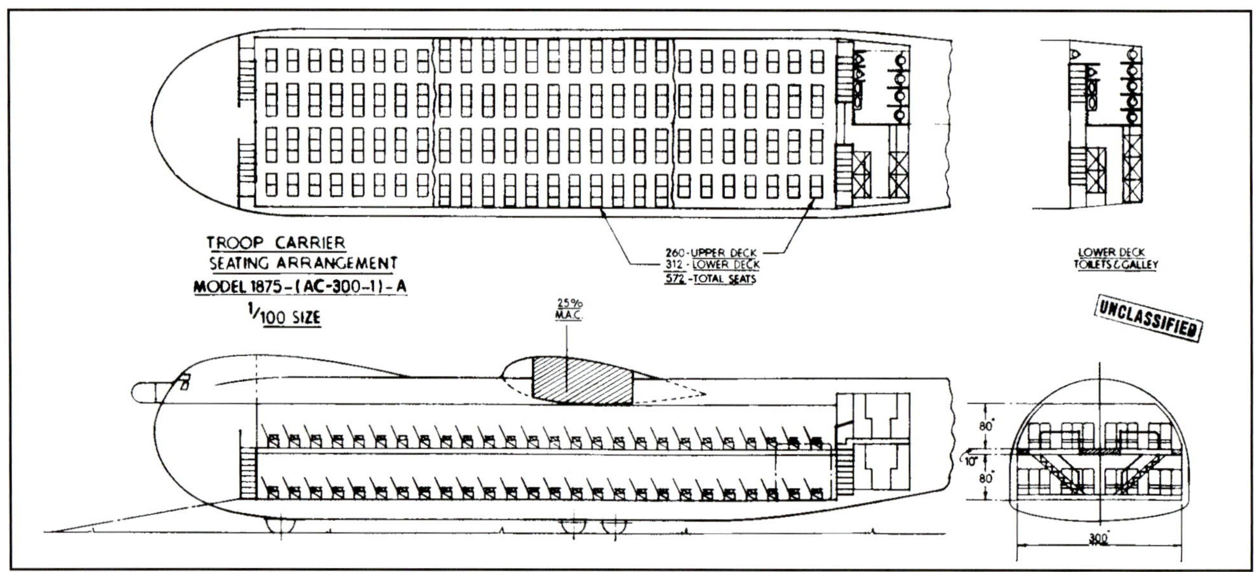

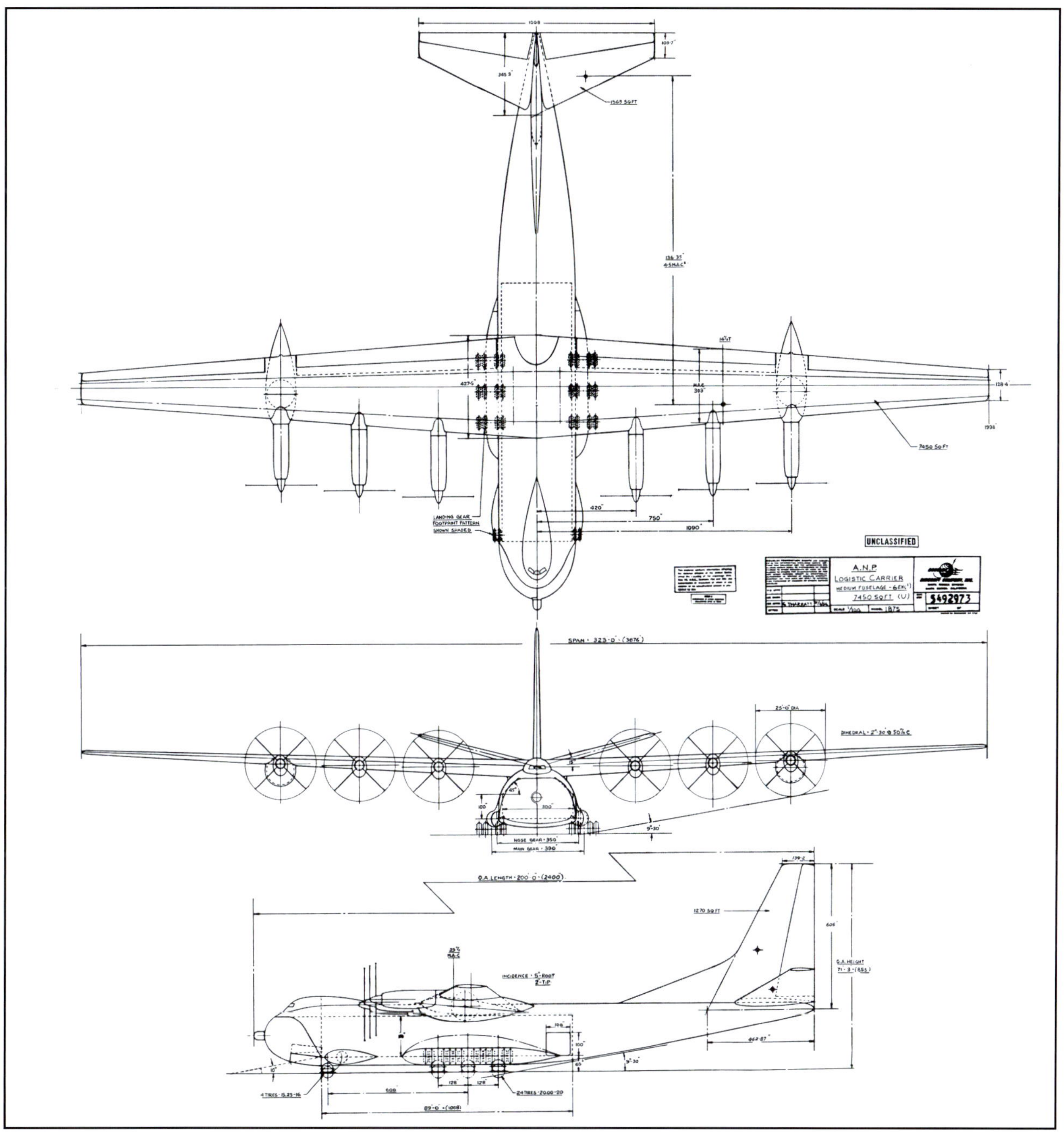

ABOVE General arrangement of the largest Douglas Model 1875 Study, Variation 4, with six engines. This was the largest of the studies, with the wing spanning slightly more than 323ft (98.55m). The twin nuclear reactors were located in the outboard engine nacelles, which gave a more favourable weight distribution across the wing. *Boeing*

Selected Douglas Model 1875 ANP airlifter designs

	Twin pod 18 April 1955	Twin fuselage 20 April 1955	Single fuselage 27 April 1955	Study No 4 8 February 1956
Powerplant	4 x turboprops 1 x reactor	4 x turboprops 1 x reactor	4 x turboprops 2 x reactors	6 x turboprops 2 x reactors
Span	264ft 8in (80.67m)	264ft 8in (80.67m)	200ft (60.96m)	323ft 4in (98.55m)
Length	181ft 6.3in (55.33m)	181ft 6.3in (55.33m)	181ft 6.3in (55.33m)	200 ft (60.96m)
Height	58ft 4in (17.78m)	46ft 8in (14.23m)	55ft 5in (16.89m)	71ft 3in (21.72m)
Wing area	6,055sq ft (562.5m²)	6,055sq ft (562.5m²)	4,700sq ft (436.6m²)	7,450sq ft (700.5m²)
Cargo hold (l x w x h)	70ft x 12ft x 12ft 21.34m x 3.66m x 3.66m	70ft x 12ft x 12ft 21.34m x 3.66m x 3.66m	80ft x 25ft x 12ft (est) 24.38m x 7.62m x 3.66m	89ft x 25ft x 14ft 2in 27.13 x 7.62m x 4.32m

ABOVE Artwork depicting a late Douglas Model 1875 ANP design study dated 8 February 1956, (possibly Study No 5A) with four turboprop engines. *Boeing*

reactors and Direct (Air) Cycle reactors were evaluated. At this time, Direct Air Cycle was better understood and was being tested in the GE XMA-1 turbojet powerplant, which was intended for use in the Convair NX-2 nuclear-powered bomber. The Direct Cycle was also appealing, since it did not rely on piping molten salt to as many as four engines and returning it to the reactor to be reheated.

A final design was drawn on 6 July 1956 and was labelled 'A.N.P. Logistic Carrier – Six P&W Nuclearized T57'. It was somewhat smaller than the No 4 design with a wingspan of 295ft (89.92m), but followed the same layout. Douglas completed a report titled 'Model 1444, Preliminary Study a Flight Demonstration Vehicle for a Nuclear Powered Turboprop' in February 1958, and the ANP study appears to have ended by 13 August 1958 when reports were submitted.

Termination of the ANP programme

Research, development and testing continued under the ANP programme throughout the 1950s, without any nuclear-powered aircraft actually flying. The overall programme received a major setback in 1958 when the Convair nuclear-powered bomber was cancelled and the ANP programme was reoriented to basic research. In 1961 the new US administration under John F. Kennedy reviewed then swiftly ended even the research components. Its view can be summed up in a message sent by President Kennedy to Congress on 28 March 1961, recommending the termination of the entire ANP programme: 'Nearly 15 years and about $1 billion have been devoted to the attempted development of a nuclear powered aircraft; but the possibility of achieving a militarily useful vehicle is still very remote.'

Subsequently, the Comptroller General of the United States reviewed the entire programme in a post-mortem report. Presented to Congress in February 1963, the report was highly critical of the programme's management, citing frequent changes in emphasis and direction.

The 1973 energy crisis and resurgent interest in nuclear propulsion

The 1973 oil embargo by the Organisation of Petroleum Exporting Countries (OPEC) and consequent economic shocks motivated the search for new ways to increase engine and airframe efficiency, together with alternative power sources. While early attempts to produce a nuclear-powered aircraft had consumed substantial funds without resulting in a flying demonstrator, nuclear propulsion still held out the enticing prospect of virtually unlimited range and of airborne systems that could stay aloft for weeks.

Both nuclear and aerospace engineering continued to advance and in 1975 Boeing submitted a proposal to adapt the Model 747 as a test bed. Boeing stated:

> 'A major obstacle in developing an airborne nuclear engine test bed has been the sheer weight and size of the reactor and its shielding. The 747 is the first airplane to put a feasible test bed aircraft within reach.'

Boeing offered a three-phased development plan. The first used separate engines for each phase of flight, with the normal four under-wing turbofans (using chemical power – JP fuel) employed for take-off and landing, and two fuselage-mounted nuclear-powered turbofan engines used for cruise. The second phase would have replaced the two inboard under-wing conventional jet engines with two dual-cycle engines, which could switch between jet fuel and nuclear power. The last phase would have removed the outboard conventional turbofans, with two nuclear turbofans mounted under the wing and two mounted on the sides on the mid-fuselage.

The proposal pointed out that the aircraft would need to carry a reactor weighing around 350,000lb. Adding to this, airframe modifications and new engines would require a further 80,000lb (36,290kg). Together these would add 430,000lb (195,050kg) to the weight of the basic aircraft. It was claimed that only the 747 had the ability to lift such a weight while still carrying full fuel and a useful payload. A growth version of the 747 was envisaged with a take-off weight of 1,070,000lb (485,340kg). This upgrade would have three times the useful payload of the current basic model (the 747-200) while enjoying virtually no range or endurance limitations.

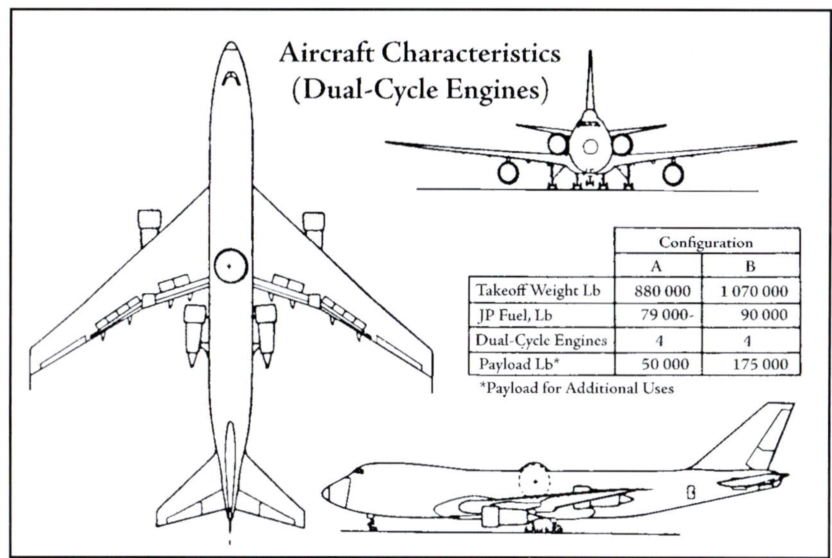

ABOVE **The 'Phase 3' Boeing 747 nuclear-powered test bed with four dual-cycle (kerosene and nuclear powered) engines.** *Boeing*

BELOW **The Westinghouse NuERA (Nuclear Extended Range Aircraft) nuclear reactor of the early 1970s was housed in a spherical containment vessel 18ft 4in (5.58m) in diameter, and provided the basis for the 747 test bed aircraft. The vessel contained not only the reactor but many of the support and control systems. Heat to drive turbofans was to be transferred to the engines by molten lithium (reactor coolant) and sodium/potassium as the working fluid being pumped to and from the engines. As can be imagined, plumbing and insulation were major aircraft design considerations.** *NASA*

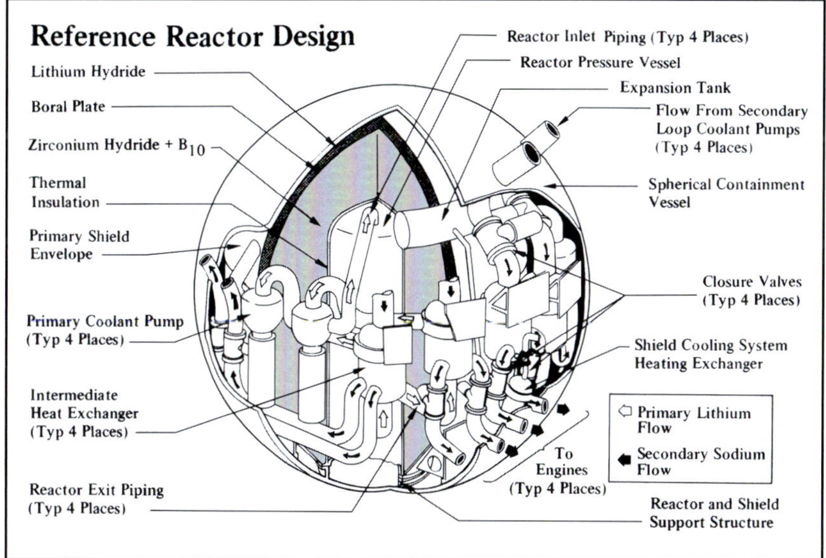

Boeing 747 nuclear test bed

Powerplant	4 x unspecified dual-cycle turbofans, 1 x NuERA nuclear reactor
Span	195ft 8in (59.60m)
Length	231ft 10in (70.66m)
Height	63ft 5in (19.30m)
Wing area	5,500sq ft (511m²)
Max TOW	1,070,000lb (485,300kg)
Payload	175,000lb (79,400kg)

Nuclear propulsion revisited: Innovative Aircraft Design Studies (IADS), 1976-77

The Boeing 747 test bed proposal was not taken up, but the company had correctly recognised the resurgence of interest in nuclear propulsion. Fifteen

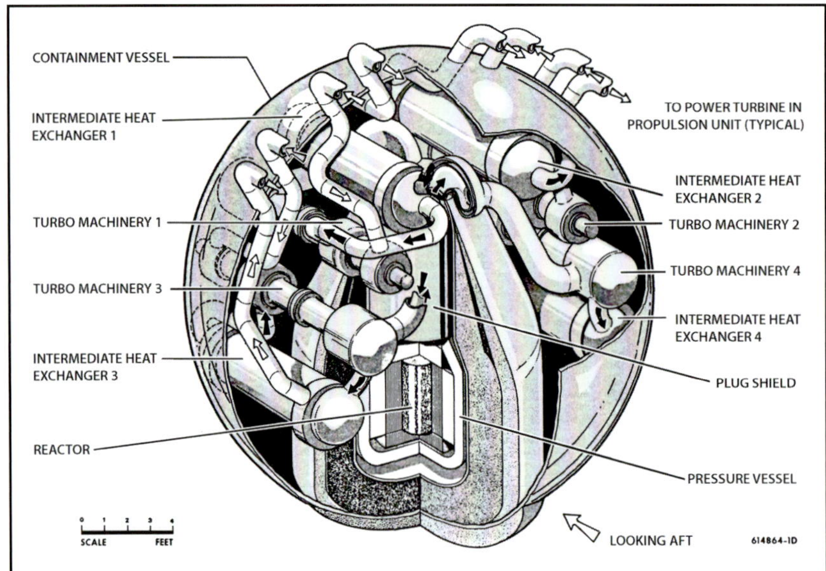

ABOVE The Westinghouse NuERA II gas-cooled reactor of 1975 was based on the NERVA nuclear rocket motor reactor core of the 1960s and used helium as the heat transfer medium instead of lithium and sodium/potassium. This design change, together with reactor and shielding optimisation, held the promise of reducing system weight by 75,000lb (34,019kg) even though diameter had increased to 20ft (6.10m). The power rating was 230 megawatts. *NASA*

BELOW Lockheed ANP baseline configurations at the start of the IADS study. *Lockheed*

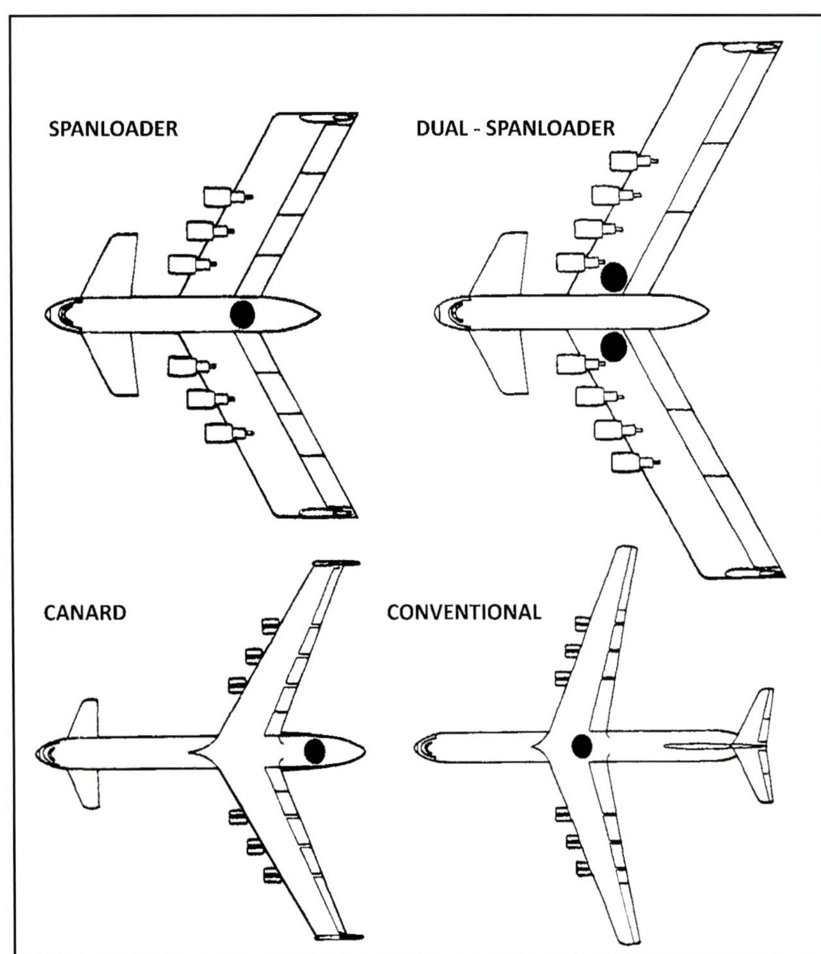

years after the termination of the ANP programme, the Air Force's attention again turned to the concept of nuclear-powered aircraft, this time looking specifically at the transportation potential.

In 1976 the USAF's Aeronautical Systems Division launched a series of 'Innovative Aircraft Design Studies' (IADS). These not only looked at nuclear propulsion possibilities but also at new approaches to designing a very large logistics aircraft. They were structured as follows:

- IADS Task I was performed by Lockheed and focussed on the study of a nuclear-powered airlifter
- IADS Task II was accomplished by Boeing and focussed on the conceptual design and evaluation of a conventionally powered military heavy logistics transport aircraft, as detailed later in this chapter

Lockheed started Task I on 24 June 1976 and its final report was presented on 15 April 1977. The objectives of the study were:

- To determine the best configuration for a minimum gross weight, multi-mission-capable nuclear aircraft, with consideration given to military/civil commonality
- To evaluate the selected configuration against the criteria for a defined reference mission, and to identify the most promising technologies that needed to be pursued and developed

From the onset, a purely nuclear-powered aircraft was never an option for this study. The engines would need to be dual-mode, able to burn conventional JP-4 fuel for take-off, climb and descent/landing, and also able to provide emergency capability in the event that the reactor needed to be shut down in flight. Interestingly, it was decided that the JP-4 fuel tanks could also be used as part of the reactor shielding.

The study set the same criteria as those for the parallel study of conventionally powered aircraft, basing it on two sizes of transport aircraft, with payloads of 400,000lb (181,440kg) and

RIGHT General arrangement of the refined Lockheed 600,000lb nuclear-powered spanloader aircraft at the end of the study. *Lockheed*

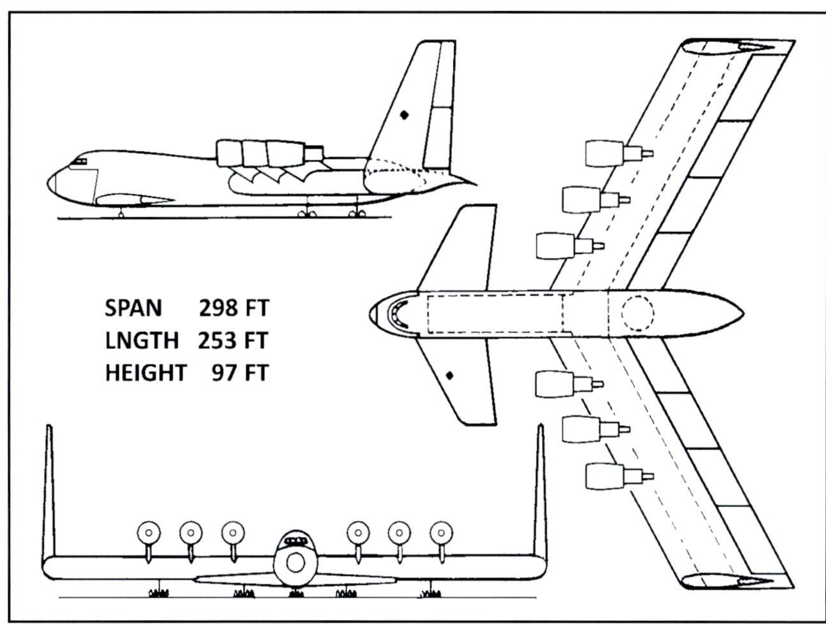

600,000lb (272,160kg), able to cruise at 0.75 Mach and operate from a 9,000ft (2,740m) field length. The mission range requirement for the nuclear aircraft was obviously inapplicable but the specification called for an emergency chemically refuelled range of 1,000nmi (1,850km).

The study examined four different aircraft configurations: conventional (similar to the C-5, albeit larger); canard; and both single- and twin-reactor spanloaders. The last two designs were intended to carry containerised cargo throughout the whole wingspan with a short fuselage for outsized cargo. The dual-reactor configuration was suggested as an alternative, distributing the reactor mass better and reducing the aircraft's overall structural weight. It also had the advantage of increasing wingspan with the aerodynamic advantages of increasing the aspect ratio and reducing induced drag.

For each nuclear-powered configuration, two options were developed, the first with a 400,000lb (181,4370kg) payload, the other sized for a 600,000lb (272,160kg) payload. This allowed analyses that compared their respective sizes and weights, and also permitted comparison with a conventionally powered aircraft.

The resulting differences in empty weight were not massive. A comparison of the designs showed that the canard aircraft had the lowest overall weight for carrying both payload sizes. For the lighter payload the canard was 4.8% and 9.8% lighter than the conventional and spanloader aircraft respectively. For the larger requirement, the canard was 1% lighter than the spanloader and 4.3% lighter than the conventional aircraft.

This resulted in the adoption of the canard configuration as the preferred option for a future nuclear airlifter. However, Lockheed noted that for smaller payloads, a conventional configuration might prove superior, and that for larger payloads the spanloader might have an advantage.

Conclusions of the Lockheed IADS Task I study

A nuclear-powered aircraft is not range-limited, but setting aside any strategic advantage that this might confer, the study looked at the crossover point – the mission range at which the take-off weight of a nuclear aircraft becomes less than that of a fully fuelled conventional aircraft. For the reference aircraft with the lower payload this point occurred at 9,200nmi (17,040km) and for the higher payload aircraft it came at 7,850nmi (14,500km). Beyond these distances, the nuclear aircraft was actually lighter than its JP-fuelled equivalent.

It also looked at the crossover point in terms of lifetime cost. This was more speculative because it rested on assumptions of the future cost of fuel. It concluded that if the latter remained unchanged the crossover points came at ranges of 11,950nmi (22,130km) and 11,000nmi (20,370km) respectively. However, if fuel prices were to rise by 300%, these would come down to 6,100nmi (11,300km) and 4,700nmi (8,700km). To quote: '…as the energy shortage becomes more severe in the future, the prospects for airborne nuclear propulsion improve.'

Nuclear-powered aircraft in perspective

Although the study produced a positive outcome, the development of a nuclear-powered aircraft went no further. The technological challenges may not have been insurmountable, but the attitude to nuclear power had changed over the years with greater understanding of the health hazard of exposure to radiation, particularly in the long term. By today's standards, the thought of military personnel being assembled to witness nuclear explosions, or aircrew being required to fly through mushroom clouds to collect samples – as happened in the early years of nuclear testing – seems hard to believe.

Moreover, events such as the Three Mile Island incident (1979) and the Chernobyl (1986) and Fukushima (2009) disasters have heightened public anxiety about the safety of nuclear energy. As a consequence the prospect of nuclear reactors being regularly flown around the globe has probably disappeared forever. Nonetheless, it is fascinating in terms of the history of airlifter design to see how yesterday's engineers explored the potential and mitigated the drawbacks of this technology.

Large airlifter studies of the 1970s

While the AMST programme (as discussed in Chapter Five) was progressing, another initiative was under way: development of a very large common commercial/military transport aircraft. The concept of a shared-purpose aircraft had existed for some time. Indeed, as related earlier, advocates had strongly argued in the late 1950s that military air transportation should be entirely contracted out to the airlines.

In 1974 the Military Airlift Command (MAC) outlined the concept of an aircraft suited both to augmenting the existing military airlift forces and to widespread application as a civilian freighter, thereby strengthening the Civil Reserve fleet. MAC gave it the 'placeholder' designation C-XX. The idea of a common cargo aircraft had much logic to commend it. Conceptually, it offered wider markets for the aircraft manufacturers, shared development costs, and a strengthened and more compatible Civil Reserve Air Fleet (CRAF). Because of the commonality of the freighter fleets, it also raised the prospect of substantial cost savings by contracting out all the maintenance activity to commercial sources with global support facilities.

CIVIL–MILITARY DESIGN COMMONALITY
KEY DIFFERENCES IN CURRENT DESIGNS

CIVIL
8'
- LOW WING, HIGH FLOOR (PASSENGER COMMONALITY)
- 8 × 8 AND LD CONTAINERS
- MODERATE FLOOR LOADING
- FIELD LENGTH = 3.7 km (12 000 ft)

MILITARY
4.1 m (13-1/2') HEIGHT CLEARANCE
- HIGH WING, LOW FLOOR (TRUCK BED LOADING)
- OUTSIZE CARGO
- HEAVY FLOOR SUPPORT
- SHORT FIELD CAPABILITY

ABOVE This NASA illustration shows the difficulty in meeting the disparate needs of the commercial and military user. A common design could create performance, weight and cost penalties to both users. *NASA*

BELOW Boeing's concept for a 747 with a 25ft (7.62m) extended body. *Boeing*

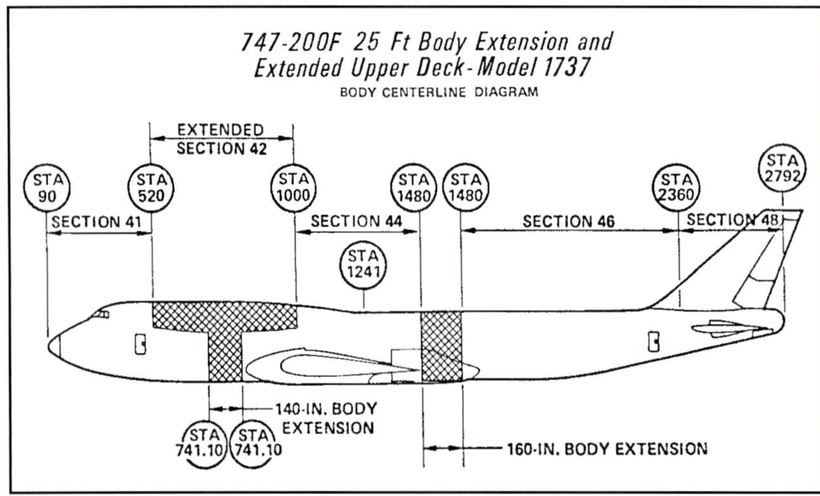

Boeing C-XX-747 proposal

Inevitably, Boeing's first – though by no means only – approach to the C-XX initiative was to base a response on its Model 747, since the freight version was already demonstrating its appeal in the commercial market. By September 1976 fifty-eight cargo or 'combi' (combined passenger/cargo) variants had been ordered, with thirty-five already delivered. Moreover, the airlines were already operating an extensive global support network, with spares and maintenance facilities sited around the world.

The first option was simply to increase the capacity of the standard 747 by inserting two 'plugs' in the fuselage, fore and aft of the wings, to extend the length of the aircraft from the standard length of 231ft 4in (70.56m) to 282ft 2in (86.06m). However, a more extensive adaptation, better suited to military freighter use, was to raise the wings to the top of the fuselage and to add a centre-wing section. This move extended the span from the standard 195ft 8in (59.68m) to 223ft (68.02m).

The change in configuration required a completely new, and somewhat strange, undercarriage system with two sets of main wheels, one set mounted at about 30% along the fuselage length, and the other at 64%, not so different from the tandem-undercarriage arrangement used on the company's B-52 bomber.

In addition to the nose door, which was increased in height compared with the standard 747 freighter, a rear fuselage ramp was fitted. Despite the significant changes in configuration, Boeing still felt that there was a high degree of commonality with the 747, which it emphasised by referring to the aircraft as the C-XX-747.

Boeing C-XX-747	
Powerplant	4 x unspecified turbofans
Span	223ft (67.97m)
Length	265.3ft (80.86m)
Height	66.3ft (20.21m)
Max TOW	980,000lb (444,520kg)
Payload	300,000lb (136,080kg)

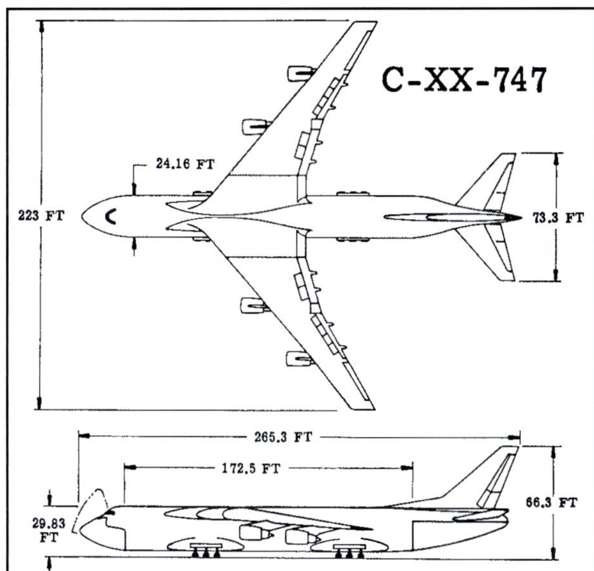

ABOVE The C-XX-747 was to use major components of the Boeing 747. *Boeing*

ABOVE A Boeing Trimotor concept model for the C-XX specification. *John Aldaz photo*

Boeing two- and three-engined C-XX studies

One of the most intriguing proposals to fulfil the C-XX requirement took the form of the Boeing design simply and obscurely titled 'Military/Commercial Three-Engined Freighter'. It is particularly interesting because of its unusual configuration. Design proposals normally tend to be part of a family, and one can see how they relate to other designs from the same source, either being developed from, or leading to, other aircraft – but not in this case.

BELOW Structural drawing of the Boeing Trimotor C-XX. *Boeing*

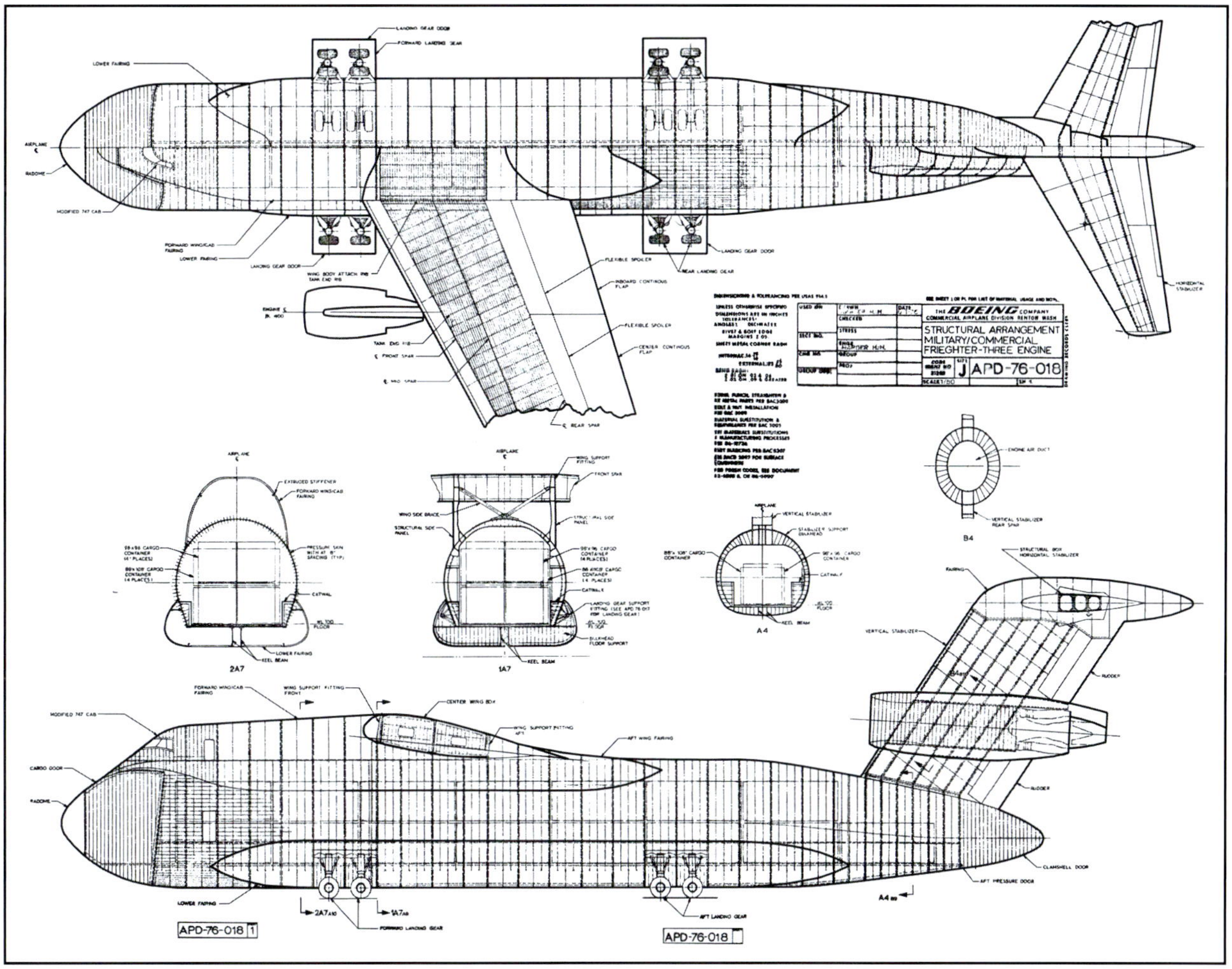

The aircraft had the upward-hinged nose, high-mounted wing and T-tail common to most airlifters, but there any similarity ended. The fuselage contours were unique and, unusually for a Boeing, it had three engines with the third mounted partway up the vertical fin. The cockpit cab was clearly adapted from the 747 and shared the same windshield arrangement. The aircraft was equipped with a quadracycle undercarriage, allowing the cargo deck to sit close to the ground.

Apart from the display model, only partial drawings have survived. The dimensions, therefore, can only be estimated. Based on known items like the size of the cargo containers shown in the drawings and the engine nacelle dimensions, it is believed that the span would have been around 262ft (79.6m). The three CF-6 turbofans engines of around 50,000lb (222.4kN) thrust each would indicate a maximum take-off weight in the order of 600,000lb (272,160kg).

Boeing Trimotor C-XX	
Powerplant	4 x CF-6 turbofans @ 50,000lb (222.41kN) thrust
Span	262ft (79.86m) (estimated)
Length	283ft (86.26m) (estimated)
Height	65ft (19.81m) (estimated)
Max TOW	600,000lb (272,160kg) (estimated)

Even less documented is an unidentified twin-engine heavy-lifter aircraft; a company model is the only available evidence. It may have been another C-XX proposition. Of note, the design appears to have major components of the commercial 767-200 design, which would date the project to 1978 or later. Common elements appear to be the wings, tail engines and cockpit cab, all grafted onto a new fuselage. The unusual vertical stabiliser profile is the result of reducing its effective sweep by the upward canting of the rear fuselage.

C-XX becomes ACMA

In the late 1970s leading figures in the Government, the Air Force and the aircraft industry expressed strong support for the dual-use concept. This resulted in a series of feasibility studies during which C-XX progressed to become ACMA (Advanced Civil/Military Aircraft). This was despite the fact that Air Force airlifters (other than the C-130) had failed to find a place in the civilian market. The C-141 had been certified under civil airworthiness standards as the L-300, but never found

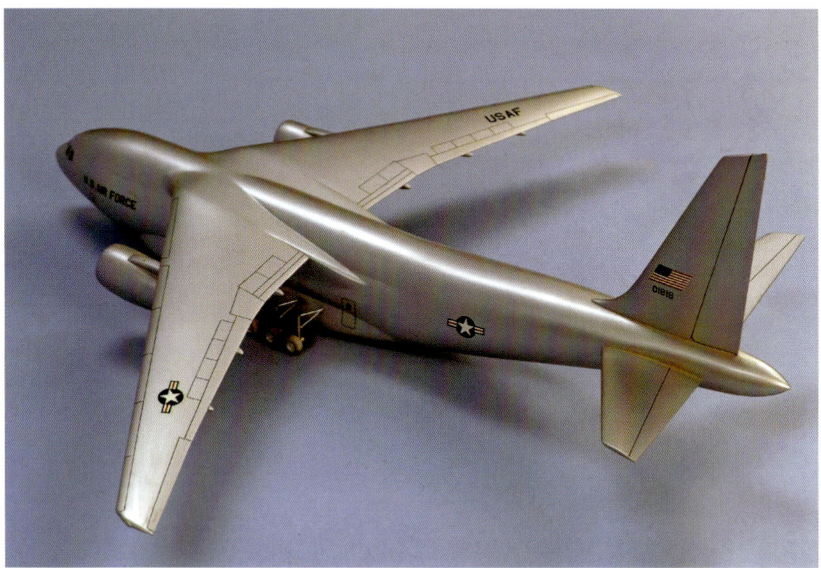

ABOVE The commonality with major Boeing 767 airliner wing and empennage structures is emphasised in this view. *John Aldaz photo*

BELOW The Boeing military/commercial twin-engined freighter. *John Aldaz photo*

a commercial user, and while the C-5 was capable of certification with minor modification, it too found no interest. It appeared that military requirements posed an unacceptable cost penalty to commercial users, and that the market of civil operators able to bear these costs without subsidy was either very small or non-existent. Further, the legal impact (on insurance, or leases, for instance) of using these aircraft in wartime was not covered by statue or case law.

Lockheed LGA-144

Under a series of designs within the generic designation of LGA-144, Lockheed studied a massive ACMA freighter that was conceptually a scaled-up version of the C-5A. The definitive version (the LG-144-400) had a maximum take-off weight of more than

Lockheed LGA-144 variations

Study Group	Designation	Study parameters and variations
Group I	LGA-144-1xx	Design Payload (which drove airframe sizing); variations from 315,000lb to 495,000lb (142,882kg to 224,528kg)
Group II	LGA-144-2xx	Loading/Unloading Aperture; Planform Shape of Cargo Compartment; Floor Height
Group III	LGA-144-3xx	Take-off Distance/Gear Flotation; Noise Characteristics/Engine-Out Climb Gradient
Group IV	LGA-144-4xx	Cargo Envelope (Maximum Height); Passenger Provisions; Maximum Structures Payload, Service-life Specification, Pressurisation

The C-5A and LGA-144-400 compared

	C-5A	LGA-144-400
Powerplant	4 x GE TF39-1 turbofans @ 41,000lb (182.38kN) thrust	4 x P&W STF477 turbofans @ 58,300lb (259.33kN) thrust
Span	223ft (68.0m)	288ft (87.8m)
Length	248ft (75.6m)	286ft (87.2m)
Design range	3,250nmi (6,020km)	4,000nmi (7,410km)
Gross weight	769,000lb (348,810kg)	1,038,600lb (471,100kg)
Design payload	220,000lb (97,790kg)	390,000lb (176,900kg)

BELOW The LGA-144-100 baseline and LGA-144-114 were the largest and smallest variations studied in the Design Options Study for ACMA. *Lockheed Georgia*

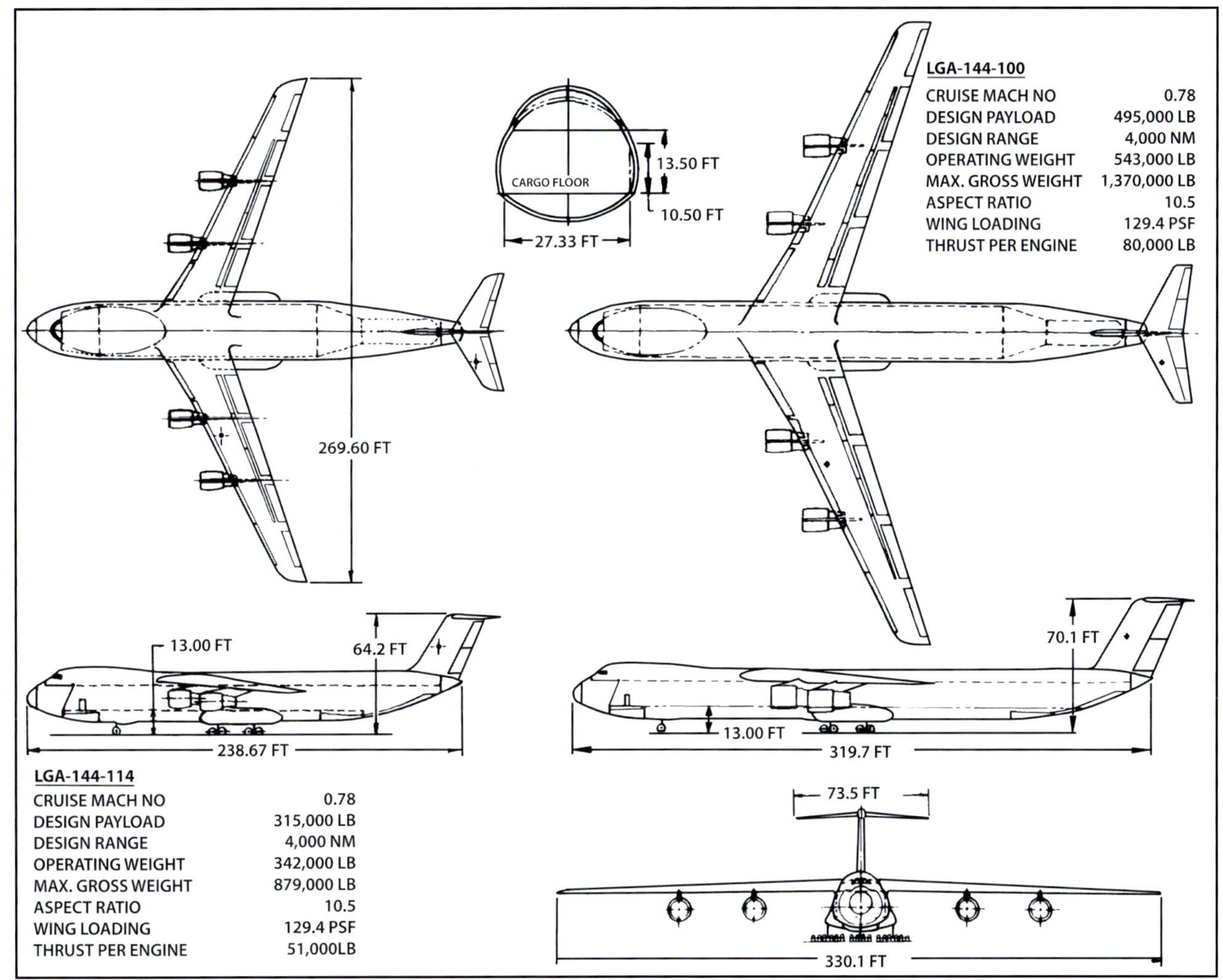

LEFT The Lockheed LGA-144-400 ACMA design cargo deck was sized to provide three 'lanes' of standard cargo widths. All loading was via the nose; the lack of a tail ramp enabled a symmetrical aft fuselage design, which lowered weight and drag. *Lockheed Georgia*

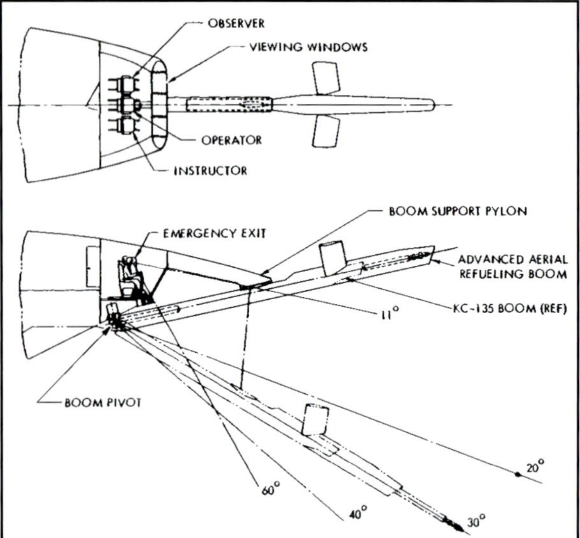

LEFT Originally designed for the proposed C-5B ATCA in 1977, this air refuelling 'tanker kit' could be added to the LGA-144-100 series aircraft, these being designated the -100T. A hose and drogue unit, to the left of the aircraft centreline, is not shown in this illustration. The weight penalty for the kit would have been 5,360lb (2,431kg). *Lockheed Georgia*

1,000,000lb (454,000kg) and was to have a 77% greater payload than the C-5A.

However, the studies began with an even larger baseline version, with a maximum take-off weight of 1,370,000lb (621,420kg) and a design payload of 495,000lb (224,530kg). Lockheed recognised that parallel development in other fields would be required, particularly new materials (60% of the structural weight was assumed to be composites) and propulsion technology along the lines of the proposed Pratt & Whitney STF-477 advanced-technology turbofans, rated at 80,000lb (355.86kN) thrust. With these requirements met, the company forecast an entry into service date of the mid-1990s.

BELOW The baseline design for the LGA-144-400 study variation. The dashed lines outline the cargo compartment, which had no tail ramp. *Lockheed Georgia*

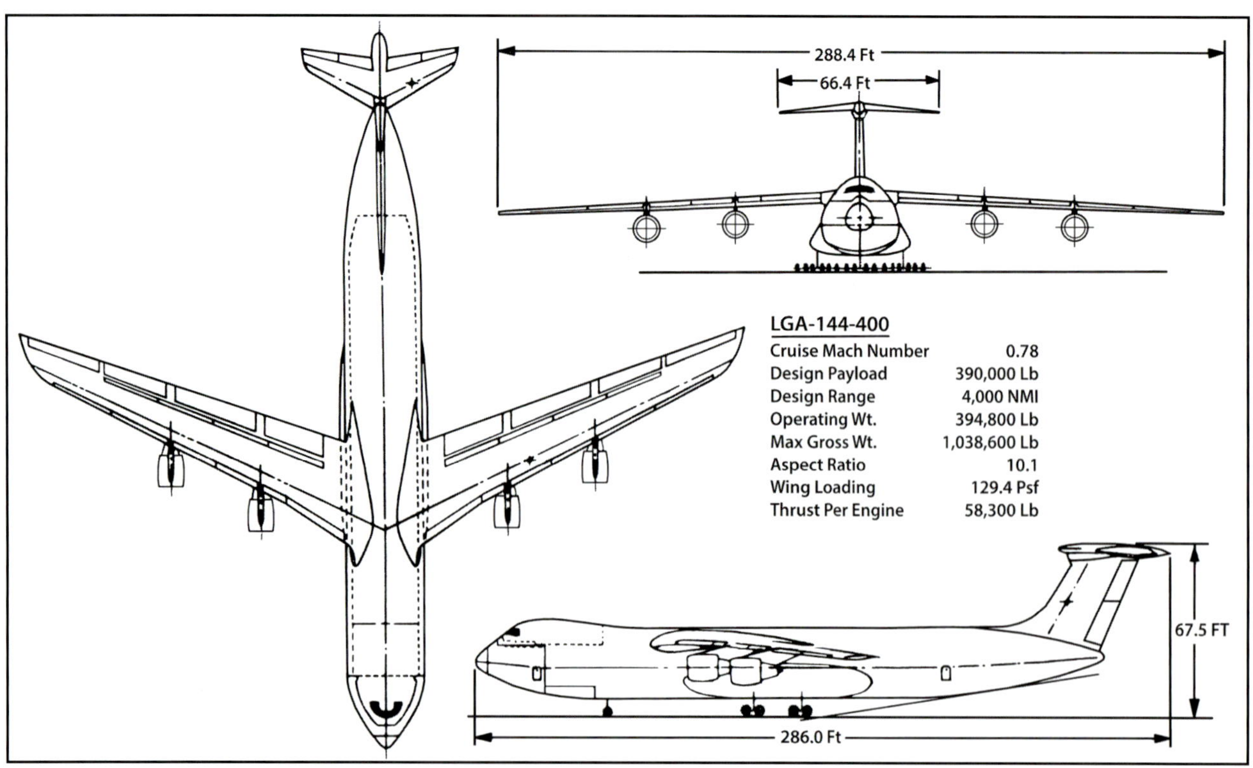

McDonnell Douglas CLASS Study and Model D-3133 'Nation Builder'

In 1978 McDonnell Douglas undertook a study for NASA termed the Cargo Logistics Airlift Systems Study (CLASS). It examined the feasibility of meeting a number of efficiency goals including a 45% reduction in total operating costs. Although the company was looking principally at future civilian requirements, it also had an eye on the capability of the Civil Reserve Air Fleet, and produced the final CLASS report in 1980.

Developed in concert with the CLASS study, McDonnell Douglas proposed the Model D-3133 'Nation Builder', a very large, advanced, all-freight aircraft. It anticipated future very heavy lift markets, since the austere economic climate in the 1970s pointed towards greater aircraft commonality between military and civilian transport aircraft. This would in turn strengthen the reserve capability available to the USAF through the Civil Reserve Air Fleet.

The D-3133 had a conventional 'airliner' layout, with four pylon-mounted turbofans slung underneath low, swept wings. The engines were unspecified but each required a thrust of 63,550lb (282.7kN). The whole of the nose, excluding the cockpit area, swung up to facilitate loading, and incorporated an integral powered-lift mechanism, shown in the display model. This ability compensated for the cargo deck being positioned very high above the ground.

McDonnell Douglas Model D-3133 'Nation Builder'	
Powerplant	4 x unspecified turbofans @ 63,550lb (282.7kN) thrust
Span	244.8 ft (74.62m)
Length	218.8ft (66.70m)
Height	76.9 ft (23.44m)
Payload	340,000lb (154,220kg)
Max TOW	976,260lb (442,820kg)
Range	3,700nmi (6,850km)

ABOVE **A large 'table model' of the McDonnell Douglas D-3133 showing its payload capability.** *Boeing*

BELOW **McDonnell Douglas Model D-3133 'Nation Builder' general arrangement.** *Boeing*

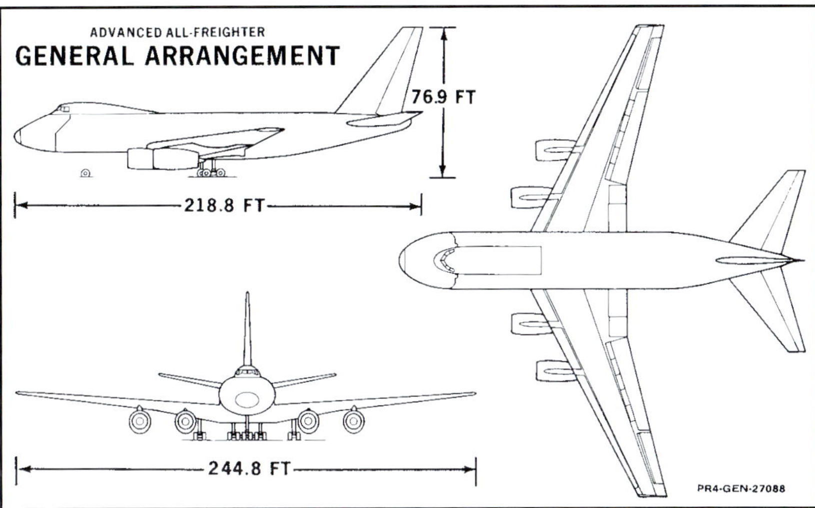

BELOW **A display model of the military version of the McDonnell Douglas 'Nation Builder'. The powered-lift loading platform eliminated the need for a long ramp and allowed the use of a low wing and underslung engines.** *Boeing*

The outcome of ACMA

Despite the impressive and potentially highly capable proposals arising from the C-XX/ACMA initiatives, none of them progressed beyond the drawing board. The concept was born in an era of tight funding and might be seen in hindsight as a largely political initiative: seeking a cheap way of augmenting military airlift capability. Although aircraft manufacturers put considerable design effort into ACMA studies, there seems to be little evidence of strong support from the commercial airlift industry, nor indeed from the Air Force. Moreover, operating a dual-owned transport of the type proposed would have meant moving into uncharted waters with respect to both US civil law and Federal Acquisition Regulations (FARs) – all this in the face of the impending airline deregulation of the 1980s.

It was not, however, the end of new airlifter studies.

Innovative Aircraft Design Studies (IADS) Task II Studies

As mentioned above, in 1977 the Air Force launched a series of 'Innovative Aircraft Design Studies' (IADS) sponsored by the USAF's Aeronautical Systems Division. At the same time as Lockheed was being awarded the IADS Task I contract to study the potential for a nuclear-powered airlifter, Boeing won the Task II effort. This investigated the conceptual design and evaluation of a military heavy logistics transport aircraft to be ready for service sometime between 1990 and 2000. The Air Force had earlier referred to this as the Inter-theatre Air Vehicle (IAV).

The specific objectives of the Task II study were to identify the most cost-effective logistics configurations for such an aircraft, looking at a variety of military missions and also at the commercial freight market. Since the aircraft would not enter service for twenty years, planners expected it to benefit from technology advances during that period. The parameters were very broad, with payloads between 200,000lb (90,720kg) and 600,000lb (272,160kg), and ranges between 3,600nmi (6,667km) and 7,200nmi (13,334km). Suitability for commercial applications was stressed as a major requirement.

The first round of IADS Task II (known as IADS-76) focused on an extremely large aircraft capable of carrying a payload of 400,000lb (181,440kg) over a 3,600nmi (6,667km) mission radius. As Boeing studies progressed, the point designs were grouped under the generic designation of Model 1044. Although examined in some depth, these designs were for comparative evaluation, rather than being full-blown proposals for actual aeroplanes.

Studies focussed on two different size groups – one with a payload of 200,000lb (90,718kg), and the other with 400,000lb (181,440kg) – and within these groups they examined two ranges – 3,000nmi (5,556km) and 6,000nmi (11,110km). The Boeing Model 1044-013 was the baseline for the larger aircraft. The designs were mostly of conventional configuration, but with variations in fuselage cross section and wing position. All aimed at a high degree of commonality between a military and a civil freighter, with some further exploration of using the same basic aircraft in a multi-role capacity.

BELOW **Boeing artwork depicting the Model 1044-013 from the IADS-76 Study.** *Boeing*

Boeing Model 1044-013	
Powerplant	4 x unspecified turbofans @ 81,800lb (363.9kN) thrust
Span	329ft 10in (100.53m)
Length	280ft 0in (85.34m)
Wing area	10,880sq ft (1,010.8m²)
Max TOW	1,480,000lb (671,320kg)
Payload	400,000lb (181,440kg)
Cruise speed	.81 Mach
Radius	3,600nmi (6,667km)

The following year a subsequent study, IADS-77, looked at smaller-sized transports, with payloads in the 115,000lb (52,160kg) to 200,000lb (90,720kg) weight range. This study ended in July 1978 and concluded that to break into either the freighter or the passenger-jet market of the 1990s, any new aircraft would have to offer a 20% improvement in direct operating costs over existing wide-body jets such as the Boeing 747 or DC-10.

A better-designed airframe simply was not sufficient; it would require extensive use of more advanced technologies, particularly new materials. It also concluded that it would be much

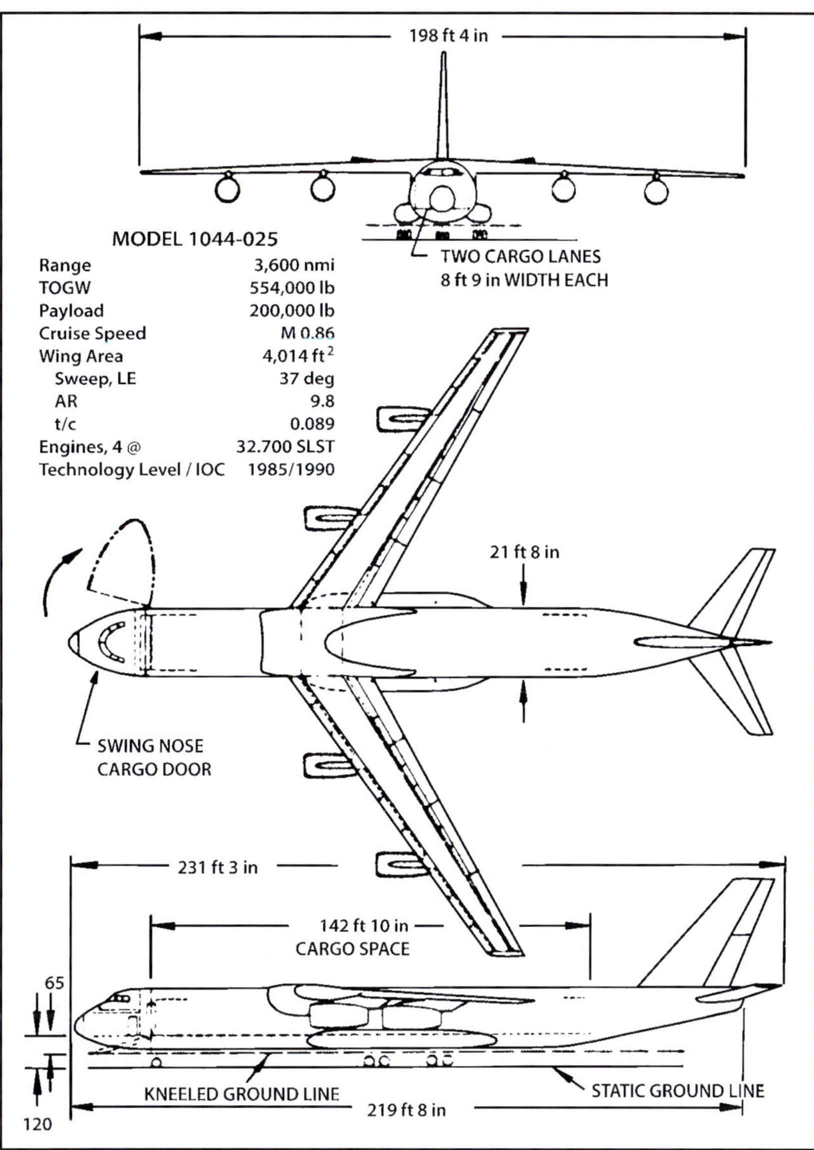

RIGHT General arrangement of the Boeing Model 1044-025 for the IADS-77 study. *Boeing*

more difficult to produce a competitive aircraft in the 100,000lb (45,360kg) payload category because the lower direct operating costs were not nearly as significant as they were for the larger-payload categories.

Boeing Model 1044-25	
Powerplant	4 x specified turbofans @ 32,700lb (145.46kN) thrust
Span	196ft 4in (59.84m)
Length	231ft 3in (65.00m)
Wing area	4,014 sq ft (372.90m²)
Max TOW	554,000lb (251,290kg)
Payload	200,000lb (90,720kg)
Cruise speed	0.88 Mach
Range	3,600nmi (6670km)

The IADS-77 study found that the military aircraft designed for a 3,500nmi (6,480km) radius with a payload of 115,000lb (52,160kg) was readily adaptable for alternative missions. The Model 1044-037, a conventionally configured aircraft in the lower weight category with a high-mounted, 45° swept wing, served as a baseline to investigate the potential for launching stand-off strategic missiles, for Anti-Submarine Warfare (ASW), for airborne warning and control, and for aerial refuelling.

Boeing Model 1044-037	
Powerplant	4 x unspecified turbofans @ 29,600b (131.7kN) thrust
Span	155ft 9in (47.47m)
Length	175ft 0in (53.34m)
Wing area	3,277sq ft (304.40m²)
Cruise speed	0.88 Mach
Max TOW	449,000lb (203,660kg)
Payload	115,000lb (52,160kg)
Radius	3,600nmi (6670km)

The Model 1044-034 stands out from the others, as a twin-boom cargo pod carrier, resurrecting an idea first

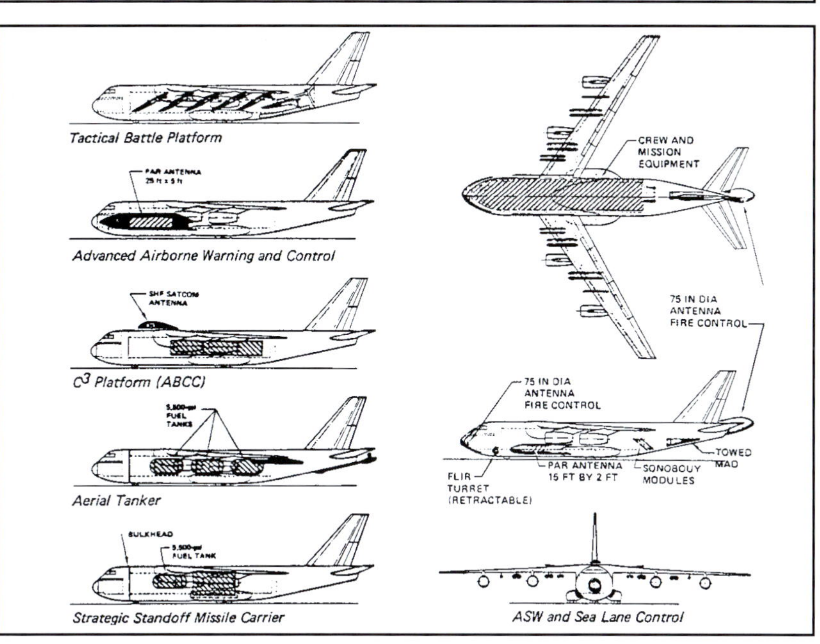

RIGHT Boeing Model 1044-037 variants: Tactical Battle Platform, Airborne Warning, Airborne Control Centre, Aerial Tanker, Stand-off Missile Carrier, and ASW. *Boeing*

Representative Boeing Model 1044 military airlifter designs

Model	Payload	Range	Configuration
Innovative Aircraft Design Study - Task II (IADS-76) - Air Force-funded			
1044-013	400,000lb (18,1440kg)	6,200nmi (11,482km)	Low wing, 27° sweep
Innovative Aircraft Design Study - Task II (IADS-77) - Air Force-funded			
1044-025	200,000lb (90,720kg)	3,600nmi (11,480km)	High wing, 37° sweep
1044-029	115,000lb (52,160kg)	3,600nmi (11,480km)	Low wing, 27°or 33° sweep
1044-030	115,000lb (52,160kg)	3,600nmi (11,480km)	Low wing, 27°or 33° sweep, engines above wings
1044-037	115,000lb (52,160kg)	3,600nmi (11,480km)	High wing, 45° sweep
1044-043	120,000lb (54,430kg)	4,600nmi (8,520km)	High wing, 30° sweep, twin booms, cargo pod
Advanced Strategic Airlifter Study (ASAS) - Boeing-funded			
1044-101A	250,000lb (113,400kg)	3,600nmi (11,480km)	High wing, 27° sweep, four engines
1044-102A	230,000lb (104,330kg)	3,600nmi (11,480km)	High wing, 27° sweep, three engines
1044-103A	345,000lb (156,490kg)	3,600nmi (11,480km)	High wing, 27° sweep, four engines

considered in the 1950s. Whatever the theoretical merits, it is difficult to see the civil market adopting an aircraft that would have required wholesale change in airport infrastructure and freight handling facilities.

Seeing potential in the Model 1044 series, Boeing followed the USAF-funded IADS studies with internally funded follow-on designs, terming the programme the 'Advanced Strategic Aircraft Study' (ASAS).

Design Options Study: Cargo pod and passenger module concept

On 29 February 1980 the Air Force published the final report of what was now called the Designs Options Study. The baseline design incorporated a composite graphite-epoxy primary structure, active flight controls, advanced engines, and new aircraft systems. Indeed, such developments were seen as essential for a viable new aircraft; separate NASA studies had emphasised that an advanced composite primary structure was a prerequisite for the Inter-theatre Air Vehicle (IAV) to succeed.

As well as looking at both conventional and span-loading aircraft configurations, the Design Options Study also examined an unorthodox concept: cargo pods and passenger modules, described in the final report on 29 February 1980. Based on an earlier NASA study, the cargo pod option evolved from the concept of a 'bolt-on' pod, easily attached to conventional commercial passenger aircraft in time of military emergencies.

The carrier aircraft would be the study's 'baseline' airliner/freighter, with a strengthened lower fuselage, built-in attachment fittings and systems connections, and the provision to attach tip fins to the tailplane. Estimates were that permanent provisions for conversions would add only 5,100lb (2,315kg) to the aircraft's weight, and that conversion could be carried out in fifty-eight hours. During this time the seats, lavatories, carpets, interior trim, entertainment and emergency systems would all be removed, together with aircraft's landing gear. The aircraft would then be lifted and placed on the cargo pod.

BELOW **The Boeing Model 1044-043 with a detachable cargo pod.** *Boeing*

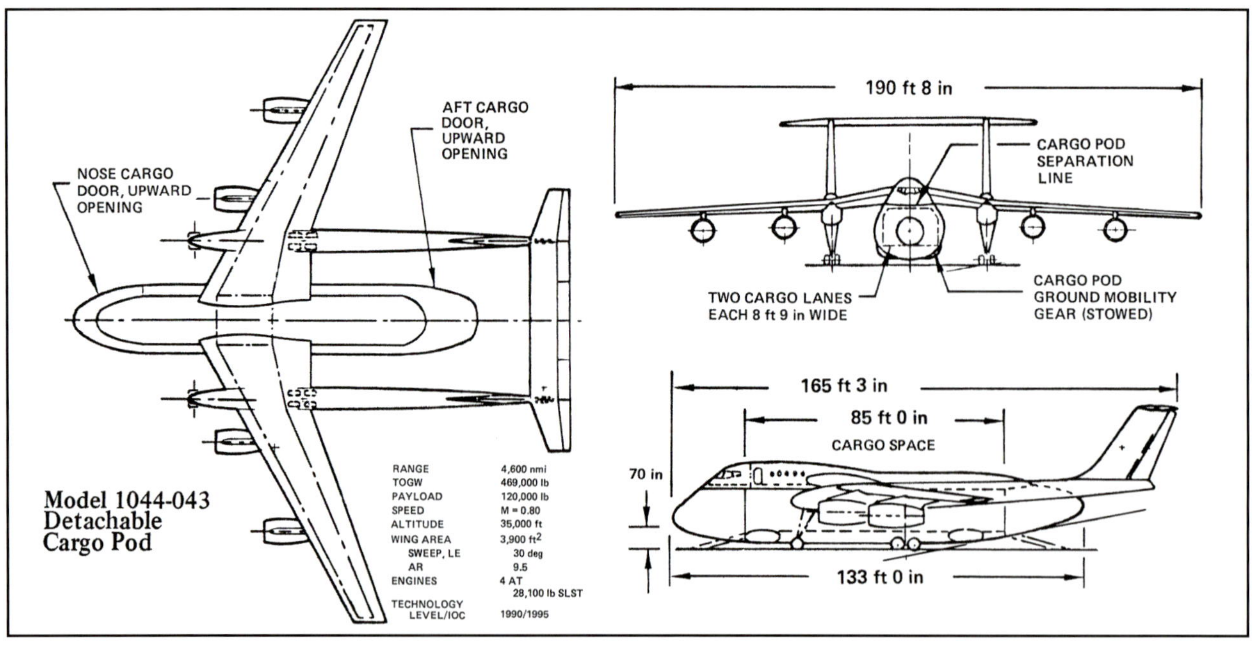

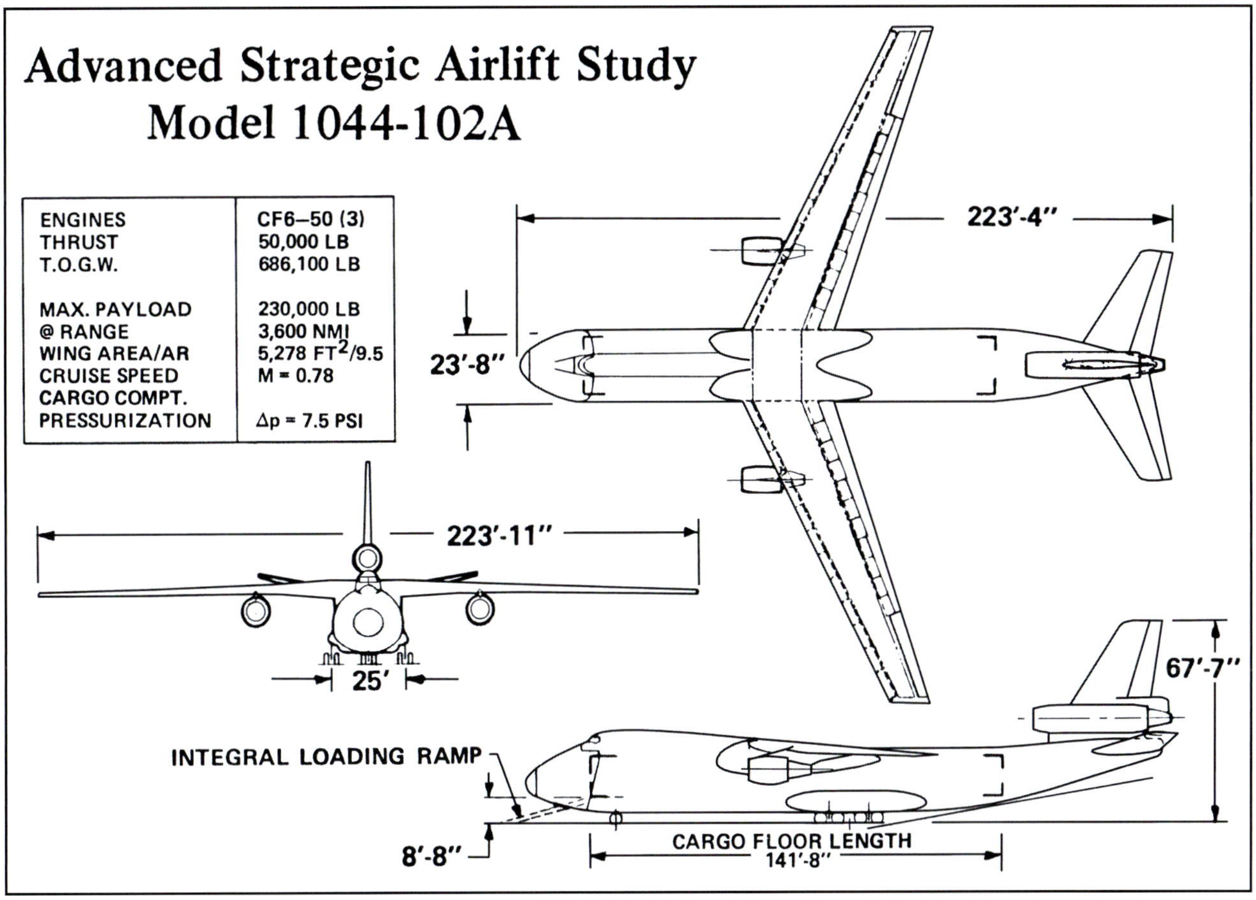

Advanced Strategic Airlift Study Model 1044-102A

ENGINES	CF6–50 (3)
THRUST	50,000 LB
T.O.G.W.	686,100 LB
MAX. PAYLOAD	230,000 LB
@ RANGE	3,600 NMI
WING AREA/AR	5,278 FT^2/9.5
CRUISE SPEED	M = 0.78
CARGO COMPT. PRESSURIZATION	Δp = 7.5 PSI

223'-4"
23'-8"
223'-11"
25'
67'-7"
INTEGRAL LOADING RAMP
8'-8"
CARGO FLOOR LENGTH 141'-8"

ABOVE **Boeing three-engined Model 1044-102A general arrangement.** *Boeing*

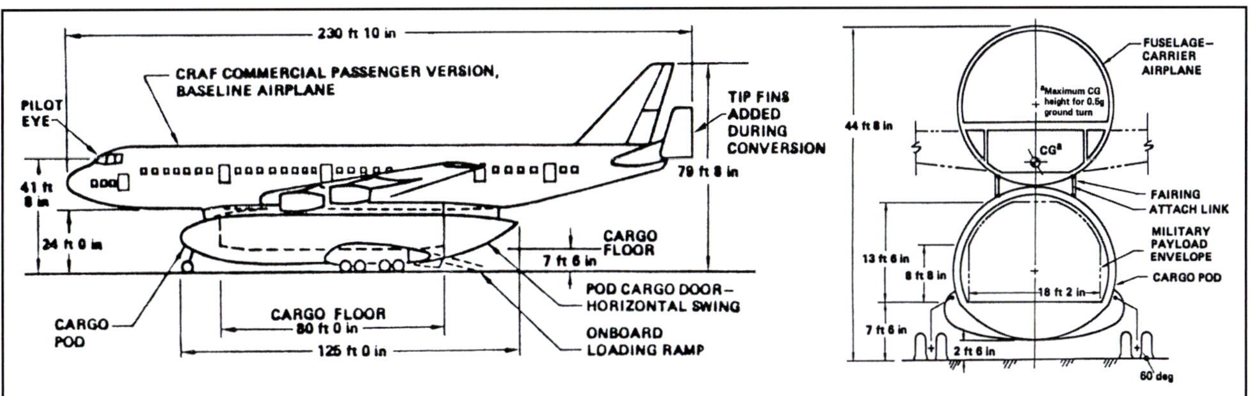

BELOW **The Boeing Model 1044-050-100 CRAF/commercial convertible aircraft with military cargo pod concept from the 1980 Design Options Study.** *Boeing*

While this might be possible for a single aircraft, one has to question the feasibility of converting a whole fleet of aircraft in the event of a national emergency, given the amount of hangar space and skilled labour required. The pod concept did, however, offer two significant advantages. First, it utilised commercial passenger aircraft rather than commercial freighters, offering a much larger available fleet for emergency use. Second, the pod offered adaptability for oversized loads.

The conclusion was that a commercial freighter could act as a productive military transport, but that the market for a new commercial aircraft – offering a capability way beyond that already available – was not immediately obvious. An aircraft with provisions to convert to an enhanced Civil Reserve Air Fleet freighter was certainly both achievable and attractive, but it incurred some penalty in both roles. This raised the unanswered question of how to incentivise commercial carrier participation in the aircraft's development and operation. Such incentives would require new enabling laws and regulations.

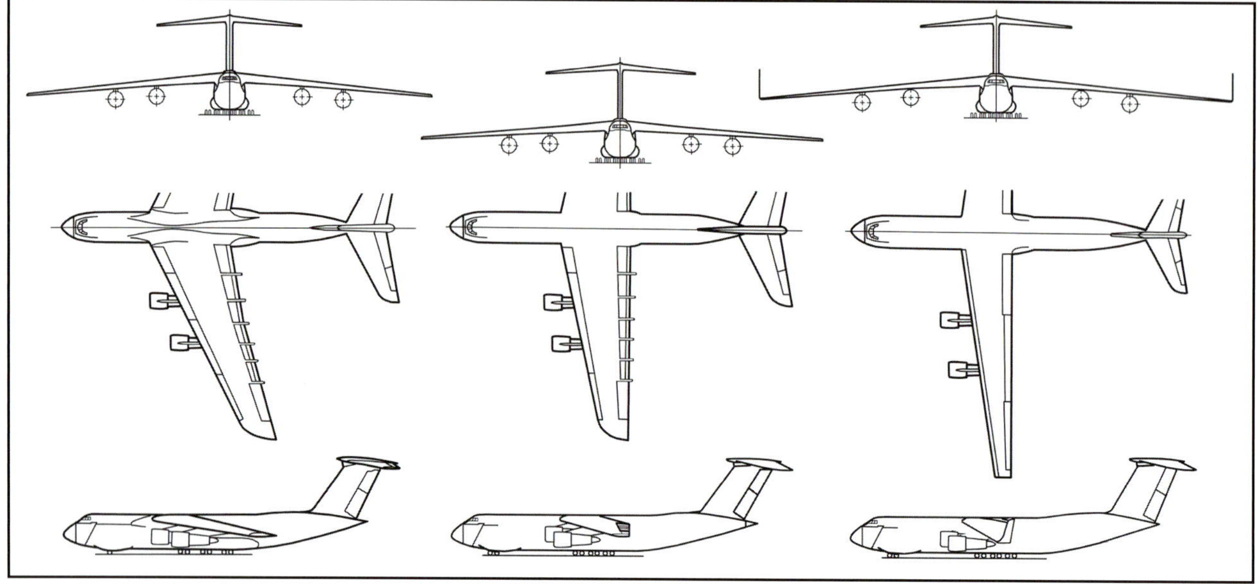

ABOVE **The Boeing Models 767-736, 767-738 and 767-700/767-740E.** *Boeing*

Boeing Advanced Aerodynamic studies: The Model 767-700 series

In late 1974 the Air Force Systems Command at Wright-Patterson AFB commissioned Boeing to assess potential gains in airlifter performance resulting from advances in aerodynamics. Titled 'Application of Advanced Aerodynamic Concepts to Large Subsonic Transport Airplanes', it was released on 17 November 1975.

The first phase of the study sought to identify the individual advanced aerodynamic concepts that might prove relevant, while the second examined aircraft configurations that could combine and exploit those that looked most promising. These included high-speed airfoils; Boundary Layer Control and extended laminar flow; compliant surfaces; aft movement of the centre of gravity; and refined wing-body contouring and winglets. All of these technologies were expected to be available by 1985.

As the basis for the second phase of the study, Boeing created a new aircraft sub-family under the 'engineering' Model 767-7xx designation (which is entirely unrelated to the 'commercial' Model 767 airliner). The study examined two versions of the basic aircraft, one optimised for range and the other for extreme endurance. The first had to be able to carry a payload of 250,000lb (113,400kg), unrefuelled, over a range of up to 10,000nmi (18,520km), while the other had to be able to take off with a payload of 400,000lb (181,400kg) and have loiter capability of up to twenty-four hours within 250nmi (463km) of base.

Engineers began by designing two reference versions of the aircraft, using technology employed on those such as the Boeing 747 and Lockheed C-5. These were then progressively refined, adding in the various advanced aerodynamic features. The reference versions were the long-range Model 767-736, incorporating High-Speed Airfoil, and the long-endurance Model 767-739 Conventional Aerodynamic Technology High-Endurance Airplane.

The final versions, which ended up with a common basic configuration, were known as the Models 767-700/767-740E Advanced Technology Long Range and High Endurance Airplanes. Their most distinctive feature was an unswept, very high-aspect-ratio wing, with large winglets.

The study concluded that there were huge advantages to be gained from the advances in aerodynamics. For the long-range aircraft these included a 63% fuel saving and a 42% weight reduction, and for the high-endurance model a fuel saving of 54% and a weight reduction of 28%.

In practice such gains have never become a reality – unlike the similarly projected advances in engine and materials technology. Extensive laminar flow control – the biggest contributor to the projected savings – remains elusive, and adaptive fuselage skins never became a practical proposition. However, one development that would find widespread use was the integration of winglets to reduce drag-inducing lateral airflow and vortex generation around the wingtips.

NASA airlifter studies

In parallel with the Air Force IADS studies – in part commissioned in response to political pressures – NASA also undertook studies in partnership with industry looking at the potential characteristics of the next generation of freighter aircraft. These were undertaken on the basis that 'NASA cooperates with USAF in searching for civil airplane concepts that could be used directly or with minimal modification for military airlift'. At the same time, the major manufacturers were individually assessing the future markets for both military and commercial freighters, particularly seeking opportunities (as always) to exploit their existing products.

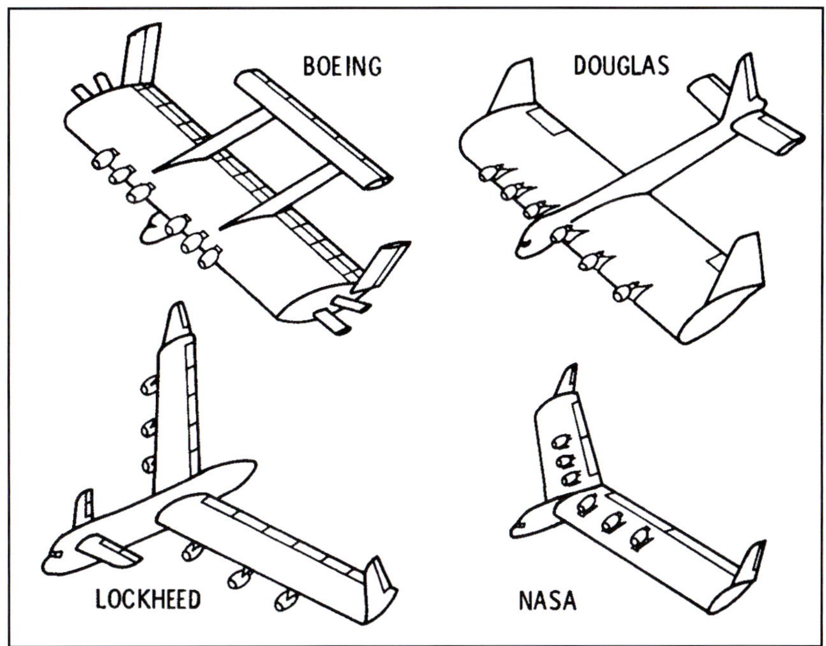

RIGHT Various airframe design approaches from the NASA spanloader study. *NASA*

All these factors combined to produce a plethora of conceptual designs. Given the long-term nature of the NASA-sponsored initiatives and the lack of the usual tightly specified operational requirements, these included many more radical ideas than would normally be the case. The late 1970s was thus a very fertile period for new, often highly imaginative airlifter designs. A selection of these projects follows.

Boeing Model 759 spanloader studies

Boeing explored a number of different configurations for a multi-mission transport aircraft under the designation of the Model 759, which had been summarised for staff members of the House Appropriations Committee in March 1974.

Designers grouped this large family of designs under two headings, 'conventional concepts' and 'advanced concepts'. In practice, as can be seen from the representative selection, the former were far from conventional, but simply less unconventional than the latter. They encompassed straight wings; high-aspect-ratio, pure flying wings; and low-aspect-ratio, multiple-payload spanloaders. The one characteristic they all shared was their large scale and the use of multiple engines – up to twelve in number.

The Model 759 designs were based on an aircraft with a fuel/cargo-carrying wing, multiple podded engines, and either a single- or a twin-boomed fuselage carrying a high-mounted tailplane on a single or twin fins respectively. The engines could be carried on pylons either above or below the leading edge of the wing. The concept used a highly modular approach, allowing a number of variations by simply adding engines and increasing the wingspan. The 'advanced designs' employed a similar philosophy.

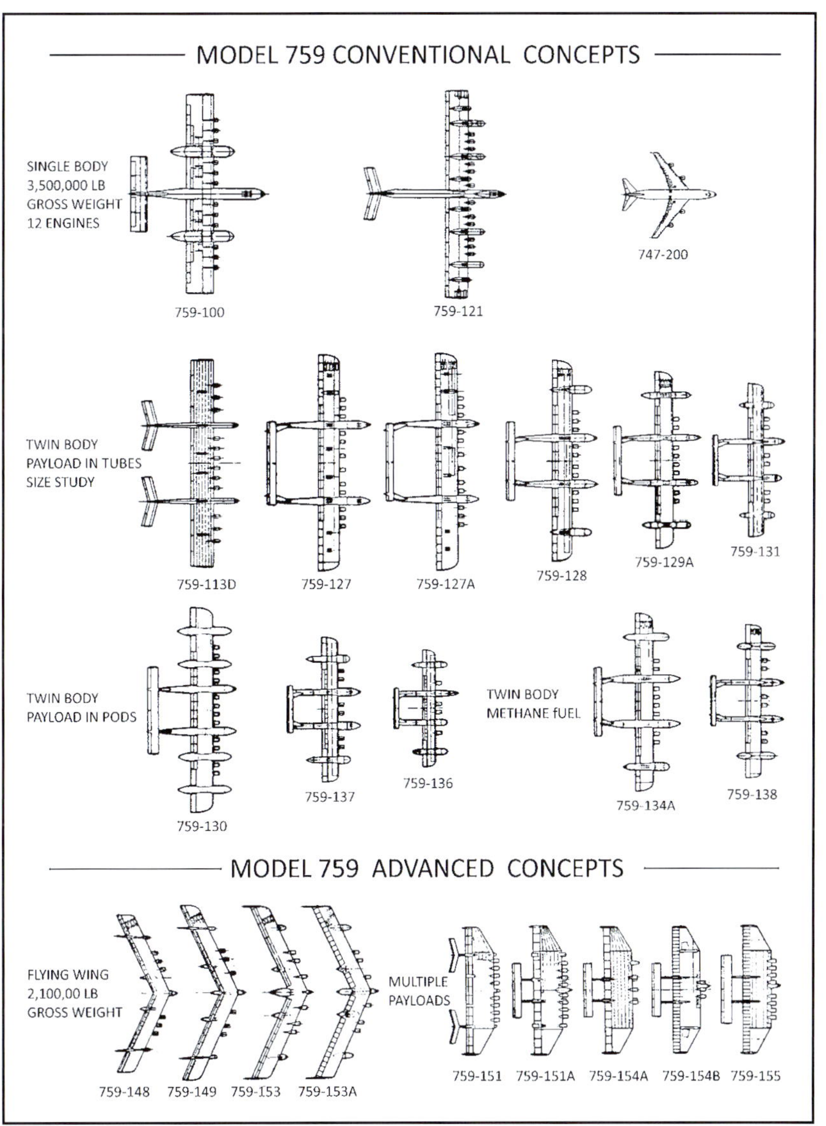

RIGHT Some of the Boeing Model 759 configurations explored for NASA. *Boeing*

Internal wing space could be used for cargo, in either military or commercial applications, while some military versions also incorporated an air-cushion landing arrangement.

Together with these studies, Boeing was also working with NASA to review the technical and economic feasibility of a large swept-wing, span-distributed-load freighter aircraft, to be ready for service by 1995. The Model 759-192M was the baseline military configuration with three span-wise cargo 'lanes'.

The final military spanloader iteration for this study was the Model 759-213M, which decreased the chord of the wing by removing one cargo 'lane' while increasing the span. Both measures increased the aspect ratio and thus aerodynamic efficiency. Outsized cargo could be carried in the centre afterbody.

Boeing Model 759-192M spanloader	
Powerplant	4 x unidentified turbofans @ 95,000lb (422.58kN) thrust
Span	301ft (91.75m) (with winglets)
Wing area	18,286sq ft (1,698.8m²)
Max TOW	2,655,000lb (1,204,290kg)
Payload	600,000lb (272,160kg)
Cruise speed	0.82 Mach
Range	5,500nmi (10.190km)

Boeing Model 759-213M military spanloader	
Powerplant	8 x unspecified turbofans @ 55,000lb (244.65kN) thrust
Span	417ft (127.1m) (with winglets)
Wing area	22,753sq ft (2,113.82m²)
Max TOW	1,957,000lb (887,680kg)
Payload	699,000lb (317,060kg)
Cruise speed	0.79 Mach
Range	5,500nmi (10,190km)

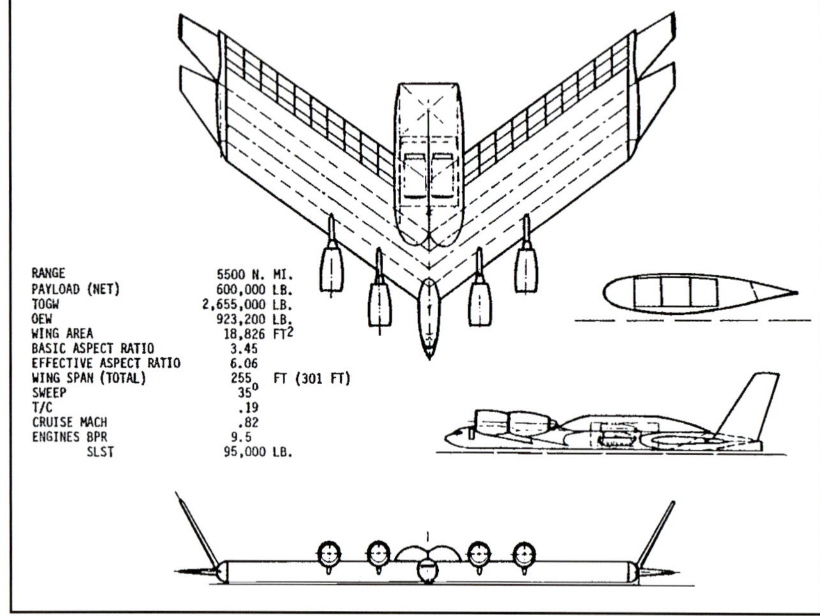

ABOVE The Boeing 759-192M (baseline military configuration). *Boeing*

Lockheed spanloader studies

As had Boeing, Lockheed also explored the possibility of freighters with a spanloading configuration. In 1976 the company carried out a study for NASA entitled 'Technical and Economic Assessment of Span-Distributed Loading Cargo Concepts'. The baseline was an aircraft intended to carry a payload of 600,000lb (272,160kg) over a distance of 3,000nmi (5,560km), cruising at Mach 0.75. Seven different spin-off configurations were examined and compared, varying from straight wings to wings with 60° sweep, and having either six or eight engines.

After extensive evaluation of the options, the study concluded that the optimum spanloaded aircraft would

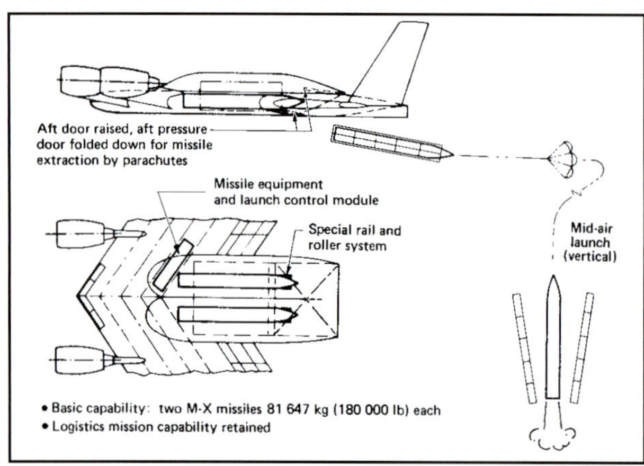

BELOW The Boeing 759-192M centre body fairing could be used for outsized cargo, or for air launch of the MX ALBM. *Boeing*

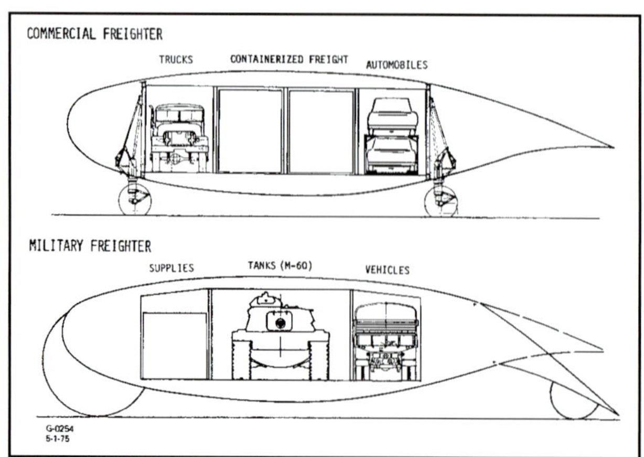

BELOW Boeing 759 internal configuration of span-wise wing cargo lanes. A variation of the military freighter featured an air cushion landing system (ACLS) with large airbags supporting the aircraft, rather than conventional landing gear. *Boeing*

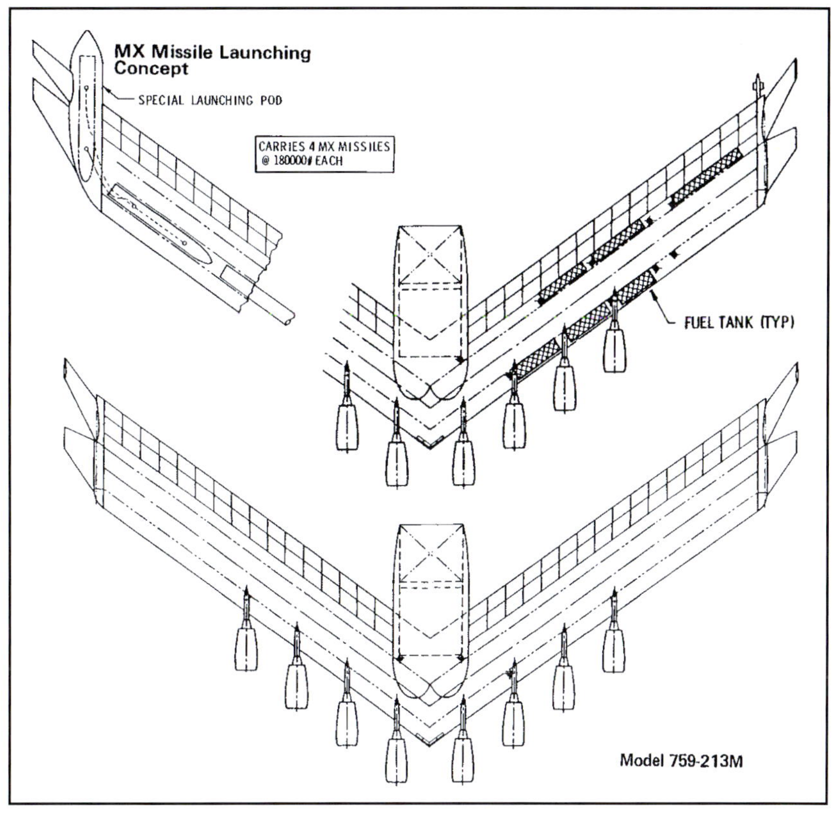

RIGHT The Boeing Model 759-213M was the endpoint of the military spanloader design study. An ALBM launching option (top left) and an aerial refuelling option (upper right) were also outlined. *Boeing*

have a gross weight of 1,540,000lb (698,530kg). The twin T-tails were deleted from the design due to adverse bending loads, and canards were substituted on an extended forward fuselage. Later in the study, Lockheed found that the highly swept vertical stabilisers were likely to have flutter issues, and replaced them with essentially unswept surfaces. Conventional landing gear replaced the air cushion landing system.

The entire 40° swept wing, of 331ft (100.89m) span with a constant chord and 22% thick, would carry two rows of containerised cargo, with additional containers or outsized cargo carried in a compartment in the fuselage section, 80ft (24.38m) long.

BELOW The initial Lockheed spanloader configuration at the beginning of the NASA study, with an air cushion landing system. *NASA*

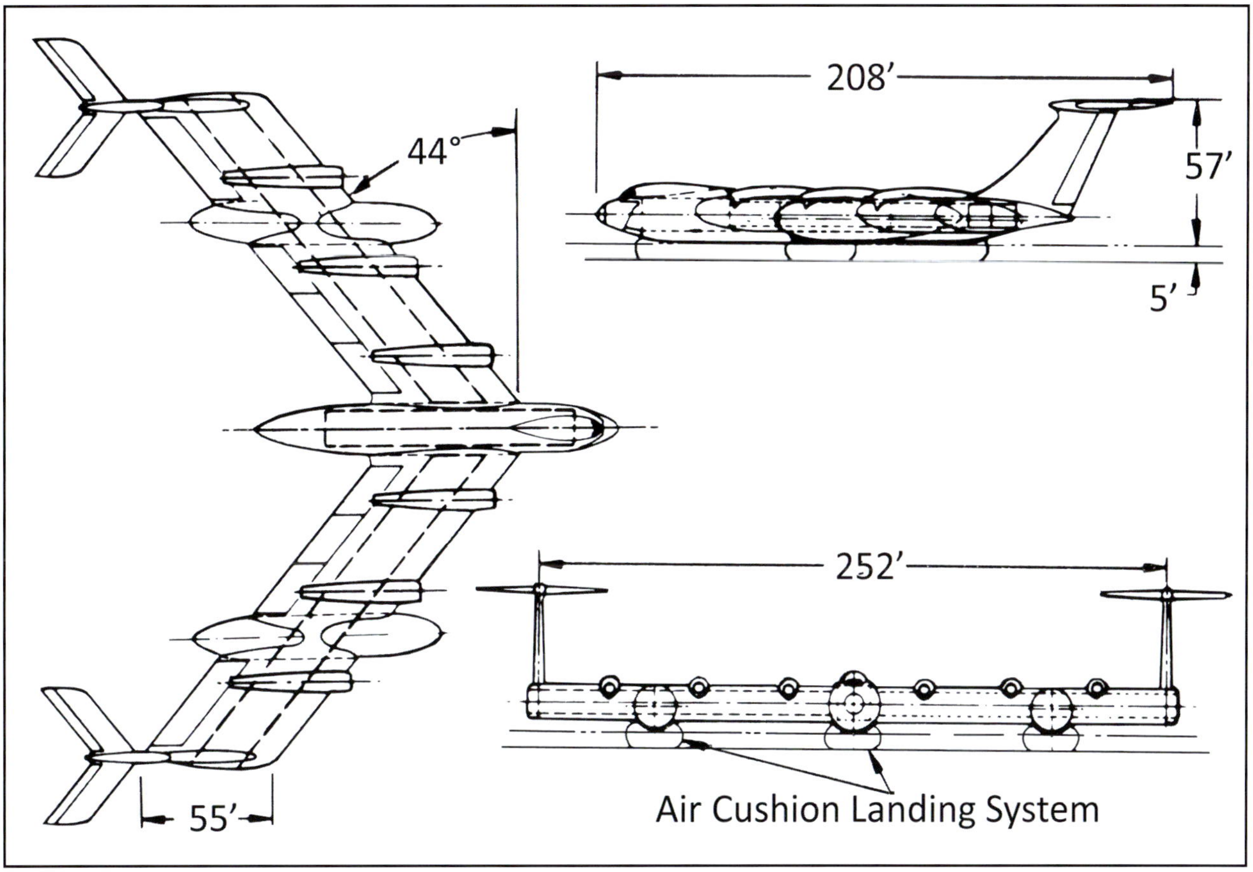

The Lockheed study, like others of the time, assumed the future availability of suitable engines, supercritical airfoils and composite materials. It estimated that compared to conventional aircraft the spanloader would have a 10.4% lower gross weight and 8.2% less fuel consumption. On the other hand, the 100ft (30.48) width of the main landing gear was incompatible with existing airport runways, taxiways and handling systems. In practice these would have been severe limitations from a military operations point of view. In an appendix, the study listed all airports in the US with runways 300ft (91.44m) wide; there were only eight, not counting the dry lakebed runways at Edwards AFB.

Lockheed spanloader	
Powerplant	6 x unspecified turbofans @ 64,000lb (284.69kN) thrust
Span	331ft (100.89m)
Length	297ft (90.53m)
Height	80ft (24.38m)
Max TOW	1,540,000lb (698,530kg)

McDonnell Douglas Model D-3135 spanloader	
Powerplant	6 x P&W JT9D turbofans @ 58,000lb (258kN) thrust
Span	285ft 5in (87.0m)
Length	202ft 6in (61.72m)
Height	73ft 8in (22.45m)
Wing area	18,314sq ft (1,701.4m²)
Max TOW	1,350,000lb (612,350kg)
Payload	637,000lb (288,940kg)

ABOVE The final Lockheed/NASA spanloader with a standard landing gear system. *NASA*

BELOW The McDonnell Douglas Model D-3135 spanloader illustrated in 'house colours'. A Model D-3133 'Nation Builder' is seen in the background. *Mike Machat*

McDonnell Douglas Model D-3135 spanloader studies

McDonnell Douglas also undertook spanloader studies for NASA. The Model D-3135 of October 1975 eschewed a flying wing configuration in favour of a conventional tailed layout, with a slim fuselage and an unswept 20% thickness wing. The six engines were podded, and mounted above and ahead of the leading edge. Cargo was loaded via the wingtips, with a capacity of forty-two intermodal containers.

Other unconventional military airlifter studies

Well before the C-XX programme, Boeing had been carrying out studies of the future commercial freight market. The company found a previous annual growth rate of 15% optimistic, and predicted a future growth of around 11%. Nevertheless, Boeing sensed the potential for a very large new airlifter.

Boeing had been working on a number of different configurations under the generic designation of the Model 754. In November 1976 designers selected the Model 754-172 from a short-list of four basic configurations as

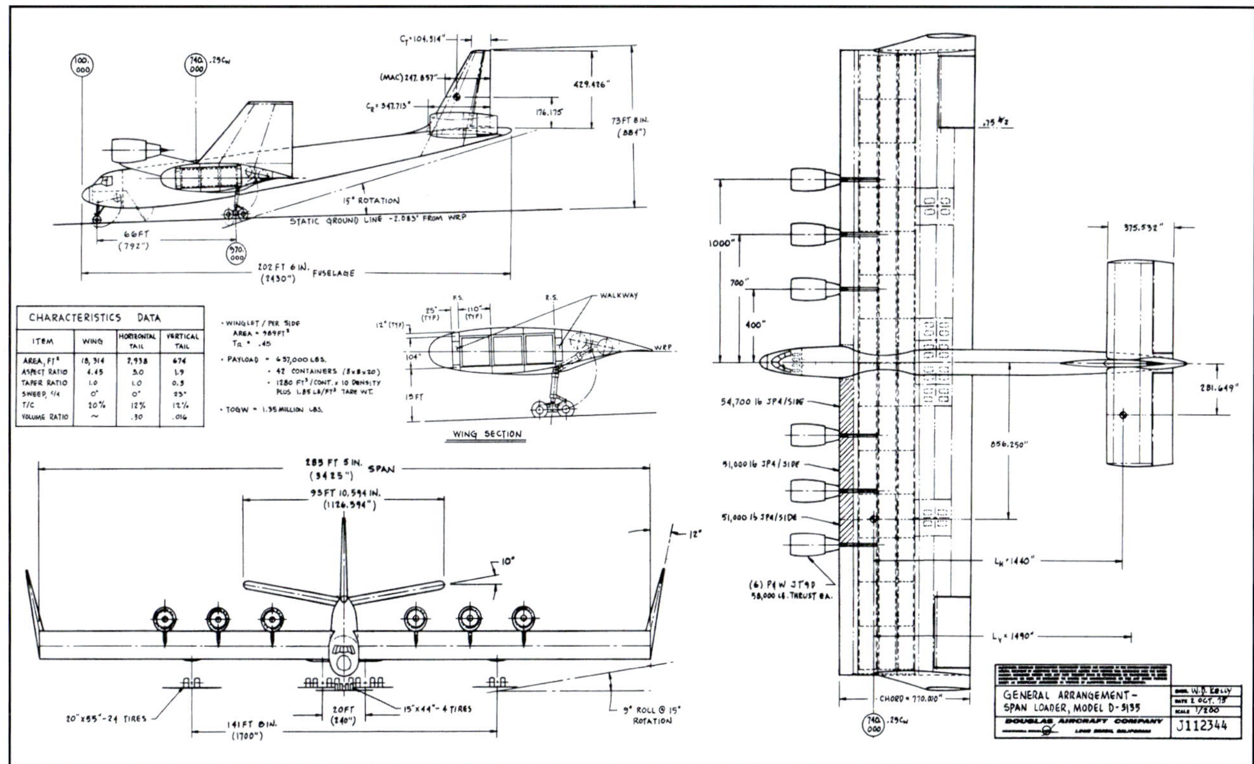

ABOVE **McDonnell Douglas Model D-3135 spanloader general arrangement.** *Boeing*

BELOW **The Boeing Model 754-172BP airlifter featured a double-lobe fuselage.** *Boeing*

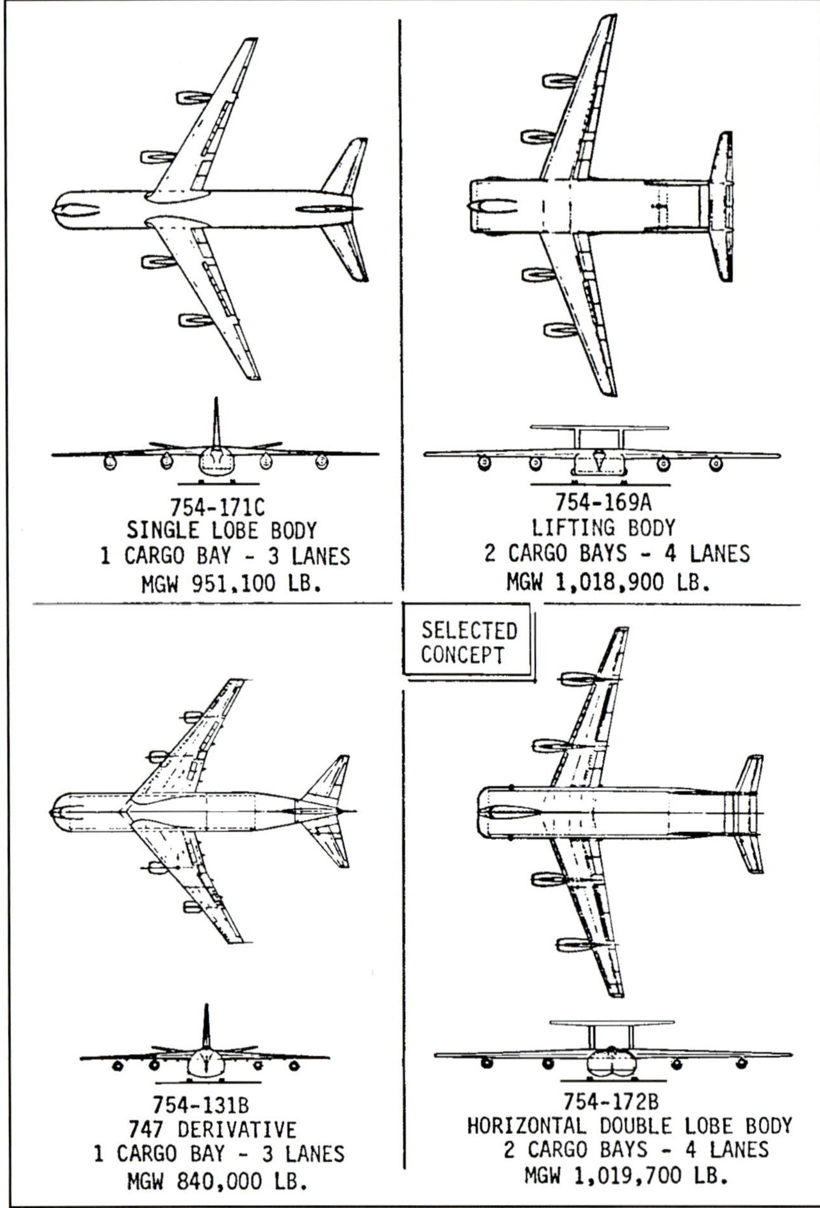

LEFT The four Boeing 754 configurations considered for the baseline model. *Boeing*

a baseline both for determining what was required, and for comparison with the existing 747 freighter.

The Model 754-172 had a high, moderately swept wing with four pylon-mounted turbofans, and a very wide, double-lobe fuselage containing two separate cargo bays and terminating with two fins, jointly supporting a T-tail. The proposed engines were General Electric CF6-50s, deemed sufficient to cope with a maximum take-off weight of more than 1,000,000lb (454,000kg).

Boeing Model 754-172BP

Powerplant	4 x CF6-50 turbofans @ 51,000lb (226.86kN) thrust
Span	298ft 9in (91.06m)
Length	236ft 11in (72.21m)
Height	50ft (15.24m)
Wing area	8,500sq ft (789.68m²)
Cruise speed	0.74 Mach
Max TOW	1,019,700lb (462,530kg)
Payload	357,400lb (162,110kg)

The capacious fuselage allowed easy stowage of the main undercarriage, eliminating the large external fairings common to high-wing transports. Indeed, the track of the main wheels was only 1ft (30.5cm) wider than that of the 747, making it possible to use existing airport runways and taxiways.

Boeing weighed a number of factors regarding the feasibility of producing a freighter suited to the commercial market, yet easily adaptable for military use. It would need to have a range at maximum payload of 2,775nmi (5,139km), a minimum cruise altitude of 28,000ft (8,540m) and a maximum approach speed of 140kt (259.3kph). It would also have to meet FAR civil aviation noise requirements.

To be suitable for military use at short notice, the aircraft would require the installation of conversion kits at dispersed depots. Operationally, the basic aircraft would need a loading

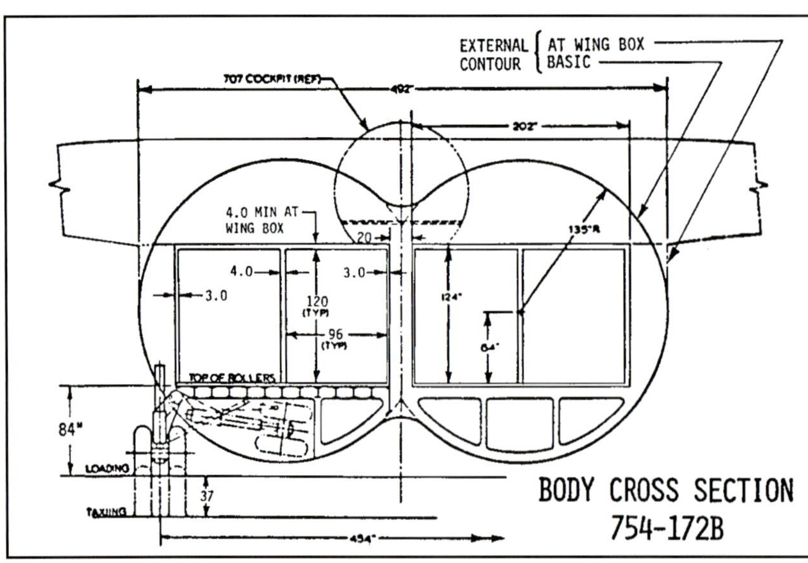

LEFT The double-lobe cross section of the Boeing 754-172B allowed four 'lanes' of cargo containers. *Boeing*

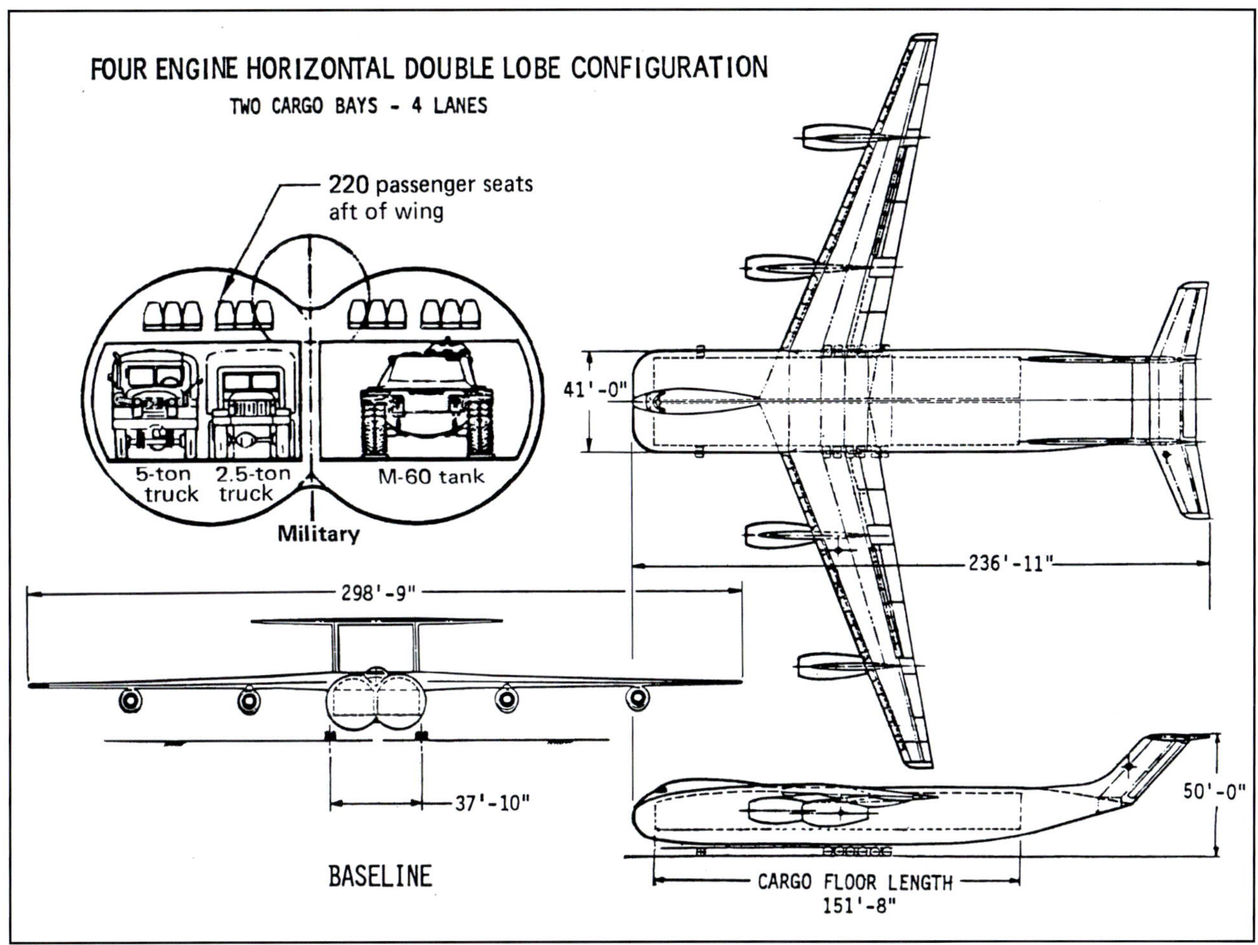

ABOVE Boeing Model 754-172BP general arrangement. The size of the aircraft allowed the carriage of passengers in side-by-side upper fuselage lobes aft of the wing. *Boeing*

facility that permitted drive-on of oversize items and the dual ability to handle military 463L pallets together with standard commercial Unit Load Device (ULD) airlift containers. It would also need a strengthened cargo deck to cope with the higher weight concentration of military loads. The question was – what sort of a penalty would this incur?

The overall outcome of the study was highly positive. It concluded that such an aircraft could meet all commercial requirements while also being capable of carrying all of an armoured division's oversize weight items and 96% of its outsize cargo elements, for a structural penalty of only 4,080lb (1,850kg), equating to just 1.2% of payload.

Lockheed Georgia Oblique Wing Military Airlifter

Although tracing its origins to pioneering aerodynamics work in Germany during the 1930s through the Second World War, the oblique wing (also known as the skewed or yawed wing) had R. T. Jones in the US as its primary proponent. He conducted early research efforts at the NACA Langley facility in the postwar period. These resulted in an elliptical wing design that when slewed, offered lower wave drag than comparable bilaterally swept wings at speeds of 0.6 to 1.4 Mach.

By the early 1970s, the research (and Jones) had been transferred to NASA's Ames Research facility and the concept was considered mature enough to have industry conduct specific configuration studies. The first was to Boeing for alternate SST (supersonic) configurations. This was followed by a study contracted to Lockheed Georgia of subsonic aircraft that was concluded in July 1976.

For this study, eight missions were initially defined and then narrowed to three: a commercial airliner, a Grumman Gulfstream-class executive transport and a military airlifter. The oblique wing configuration proved amenable to the airliner and executive transports, but the airlifter proved to be unusually difficult to adapt.

The 'Initial' configuration layout had a clean wing atop a nose-loading airlifter fuselage with four rear-mounted engines which had to have a thrust of 98,500lb (483.2kN) to meet the specified performance requirements. As there were no engines in this class were projected in the mid-1980s timeframe, six Pratt & Whitney STF-433 turbofans scaled to 67,610lb (300.7kN) were substituted.

This resulted in the 'Baseline' configuration which then had successive attempts to resolve engine location versus

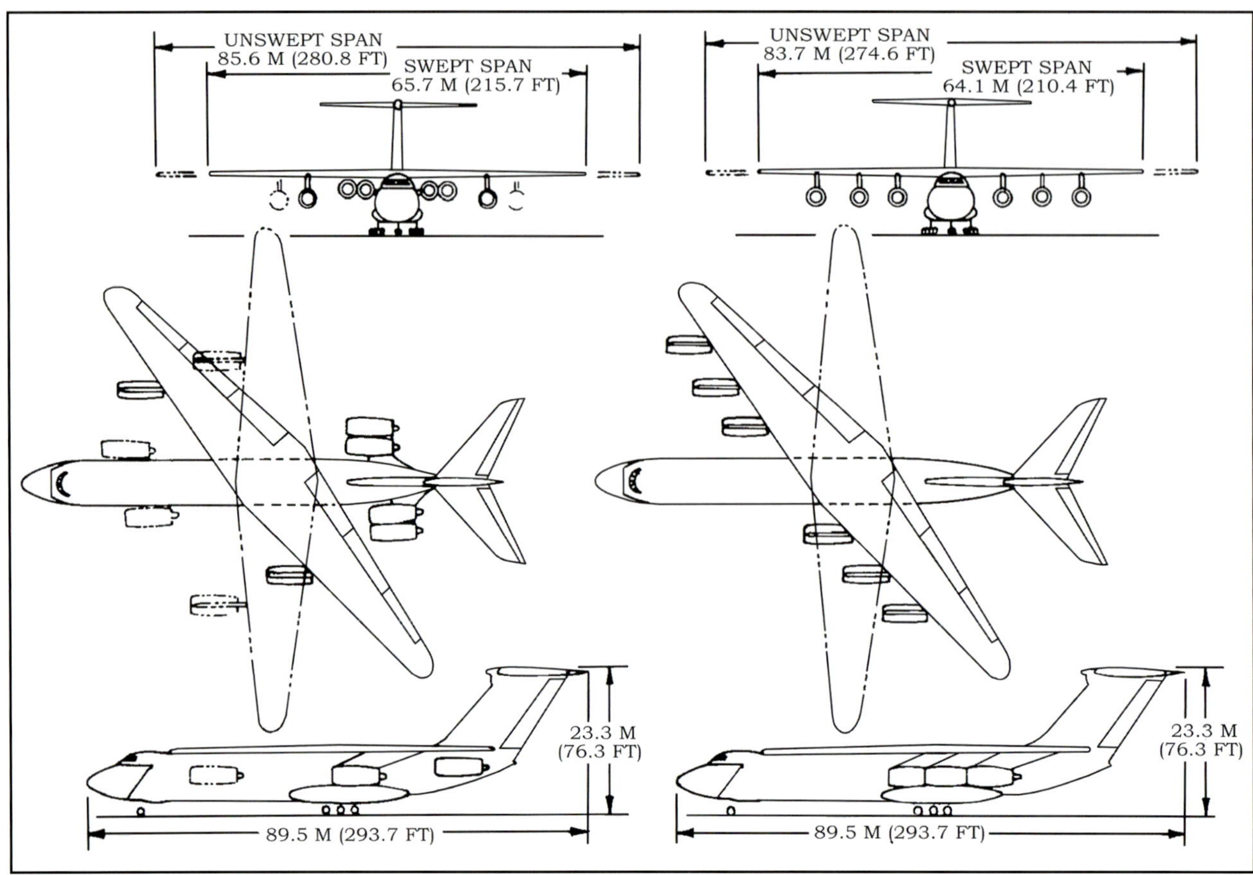

ABOVE The Lockheed Baseline (left) and Cycled Baseline (right) for the oblique wing military airlifter mission. Lockheed struggled with the forward fuselage and wing engine positions with the Baseline design. Moving the engines in the Cycled Baseline solved weight and balance problems but caused other intractable issues with the swivelling engines. *Lockheed*

weight and balance issues. Placement of all six engines on the aft fuselage (best for wing design) left the aircraft tail-heavy. Mounting the additional pair of engines on the fuselage near the nose resulted in their exhaust being ingested by the rear engines. Placing the pair on the wing still left the design tail-heavy.

The placement of all the engines on the wing resulted in the 'Cycled Baseline' design. This cured the fuselage weight, balance and loadability problems – at the cost of new mechanical, weight and reliability problems caused by the need to swivel the engines to keep them parallel to the fuselage as the wing was swept. The failure of one or more engines to swivel as the wing was swept and unswept would cause immediate stability and control issues probably leading to the loss of the aircraft. This was an unacceptable risk. Further, it was found that aerodynamic tailoring of the nacelles and pylons could only be optimized for one sweep angle, causing additional drag at any other wing position.

Lockheed-Georgia 'Cycled Baseline' Oblique Wing Airlifter

Powerplant	4x Pratt & Whitney STF-433 turbofans scaled to 62,411lb (227.62kN) thrust
Span (unswept)	274ft 7in (83.7m)
(swept)	210ft 5in (64.1m)
Length	293ft 8in (89.5m)
Height	76ft 4in (23.3m)
Wing Area	8,850sqft (822.2m²)
Cruise Speed	0.85 Mach
Range	3,500nmi (6,480km),
Max TOW	1,267,653lb (574,998kg)
Payload	350,000lb (158,757kg)
Cargo Bay Length	162ft 6in (49.53m)
Width	21ft (6.4m)
Height	14ft 6in (4.42 m)

Due these problems, Lockheed concluded that 'this mission/configuration combination is considered to be unsuitable for the Oblique Wing Concept'.

Lockheed Georgia Flatbed

Originating in 1978, the Lockheed-Georgia 'Flatbed' concept was a clever rework of the 'pack plane' concept first explored with the Fairchild XC-120 of the 1950s. As with the XC-120, it could carry alternative pods. However, its innovation was mounting payloads on top of the vestigial fuselage rather than slung below. This allowed a low-mounted wing and a short landing gear, saving weight. The aircraft could also 'kneel' to bring the deck closer to ground. (However, with the reduced ground clearance of the low-mounted wing, the four CFM-56 turbofans needed to be mounted on pylons above the wing.) The forward fuselage was hinged and swung to the right for unimpeded straight-in access to the cargo deck for loading and unloading.

The design envisaged a passenger pod housing 180 passengers, including twenty in first class. Lockheed admitted that the Direct Operating Costs (DOC) would be higher than a purpose-designed airliner, but noted that the penalty would be offset by the versatility of the multi-role airframe. The same airframe could carry payloads of multi-modal containers, either in a pressurised shell, an unpressurised shell, or exposed with aerodynamic transition fairings to reduce drag. The most eye-catching feature was the option to carry outsized equipment (such as Army tanks, bridging equipment or even earthmoving equipment) fully exposed.

In all, this was a highly imaginative way to encompass the dual civil-military role in one airframe. NASA sponsored a more in-depth study in 1980, but it went no further. Perhaps it was simply too bold.

ABOVE Early Lockheed Flatbed concept with a passenger module loaded (upper) and intermodal containers and fairings (lower). The design was later revised with a 'V' tail, which reduced structural weight by more than 1,000lb.
NASA via Tony Chong collection

BELOW The Lockheed military 'Flatbed' concept with an M-1 Abrams tank as a payload. Alternative configurations include: empty, an Army bridging unit, a passenger module, internal cargo modules, and exposed intermodal cargo containers.
NASA, assembled by authors

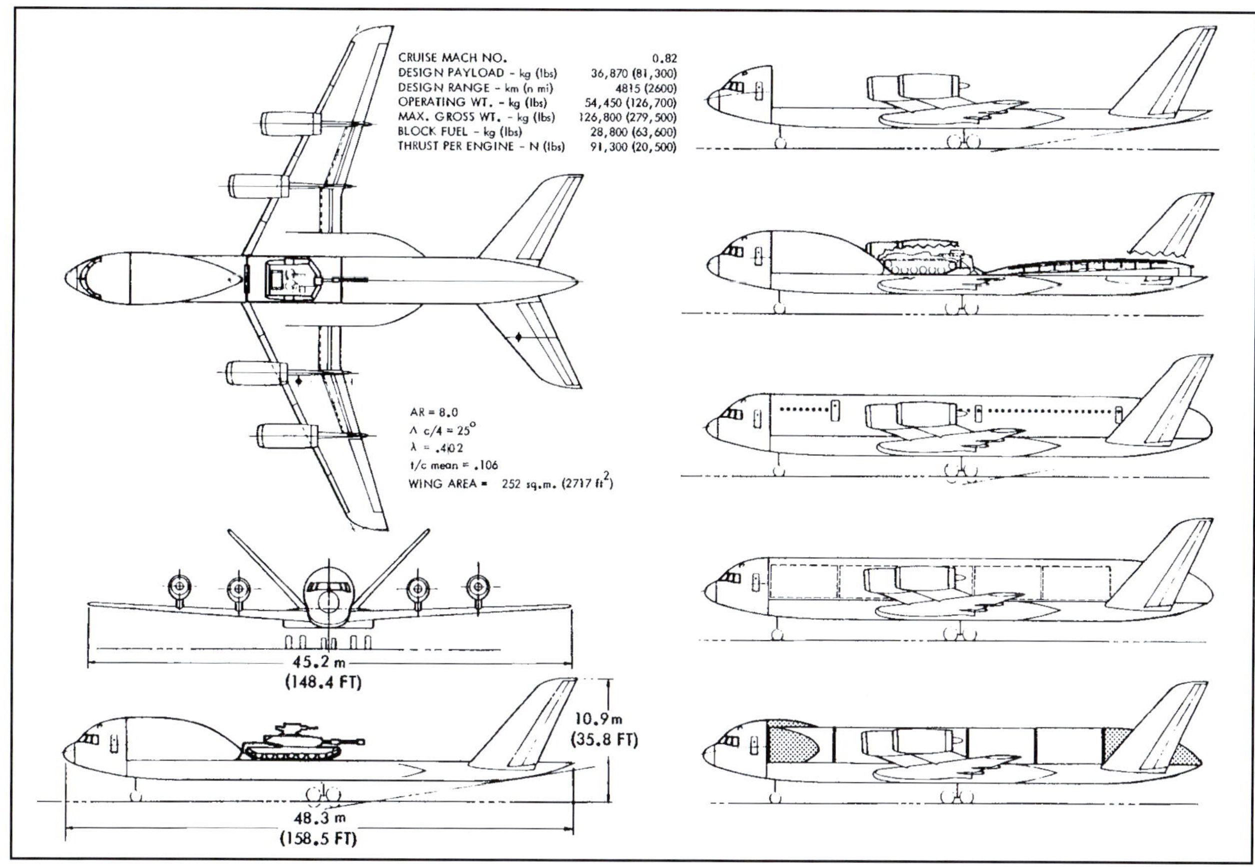

Lockheed-Georgia 'Flatbed'	
Powerplant	4 x GE/SNECMA CFM-56 turbofans @ 20,535lb (91.34kN) thrust (scaled)
Span	148.4ft 5in (45.2m)
Length	158.5ft 6in (48.3m)
Height	35.8ft 10in (10.9m)
Wing area	2,717sq ft (252m²)
Cruise speed	.82 Mach
Range	2,600nmi (4,815km) (commercial payload); 2,415nmi (4,473km) (military outsized cargo)
Max TOW	347,602lb (157,671kg) (M-1 Tank mission @ 2.0 load factor); 279,573lb (126,799kg) (passenger module mission @ 2.5 load factor)
Payload	115,000lb (52,163kg) (M-1 tank); 81,300lb (36,877kg) (passenger)

ABOVE Described as a Multi-role Global Length Aircraft (MGLA), this design was to have a range of more than 13,000nmi (24,776km), cruising at Mach .8. With a span of 227ft (67.2m), it was to have a take-off gross weight of 680,000lb (308,443kg) and a 150,000lb (68039kg) payload. It had pusher prop-fans and laminar flow control to achieve extended range. *Lockheed*

LEFT This NASA/ Lockheed Georgia 'braced' laminar flow wing concept was designed for extreme range. The struts allowed a lighter, more efficient structural wing design, while the winglets harnessed the tip vortices. The external fuel tank and engine placement spread weight across the wingspan to reduce bending loads. *NASA via Tony Chong collection*

BELOW Only a preliminary layout was done for this McDonnell Douglas canard and rear-wing very heavy airlifter. *Boeing*

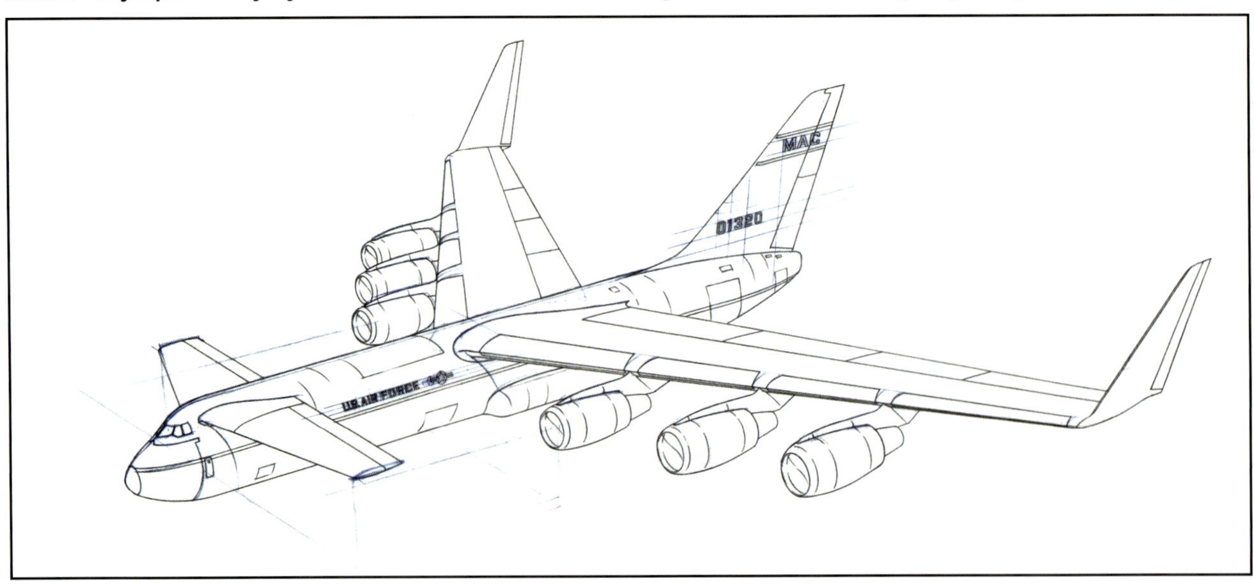

The airlifter studies of the late 1970s in perspective

In the latter part of the 1970s a number of factors converged to encourage the Air Force and NASA to seriously examine the potential for very large airlifters. One was recognition of the US Air Force's increasingly inadequate strategic lift capability; another was political pressure to develop a new aircraft that was suitable for both civil and military use, thereby strengthening the CRAF and also reducing development costs; and finally, there was the perceived potential increase in the global commercial freight market.

These forces led to an extensive number of studies, major programmes sponsored by the USAF, others by NASA, and yet others simply undertaken by the aircraft manufacturers looking after their own interests. They resulted in a host of highly imaginative designs, all aimed at producing massively capable new cargo aircraft that could be in service by the mid-1990s. Some of these were essentially scaled-up versions of conventionally configured airlifters, while others were more radical.

In particular, the NASA-backed studies convincingly argued that spanloading wings were far more efficient than the traditional aircraft configuration. For passenger-carrying, however, this layout presents inherent problems. Banking in a turn or even small deviations in roll due to turbulence causes extreme vertical displacement for anyone seated far from the centreline, although for cargo-carrying or tanker duties this becomes less of a problem. Nonetheless, no such proposal even progressed as far as detailed design, let alone to mock-up or prototype stage. The ground-handling problems and the necessary investment in airport facilities were just too great to justify. The debate continues to this day.

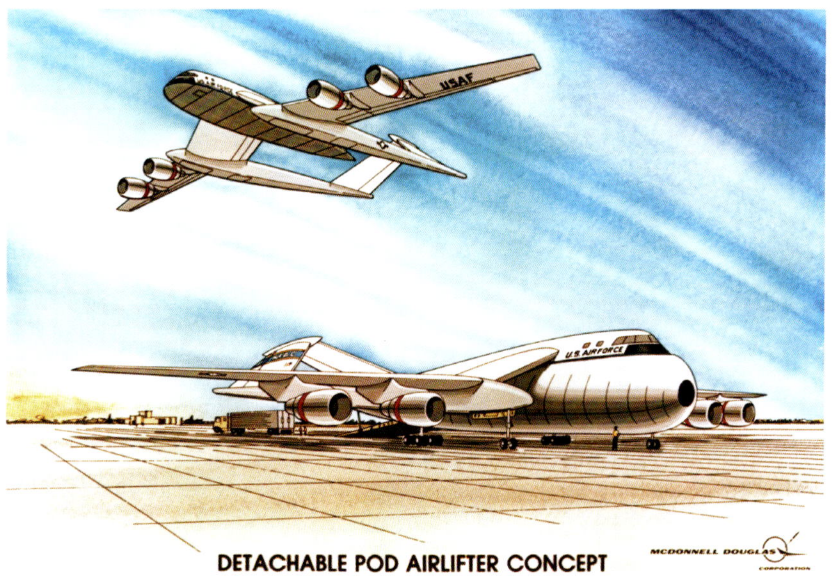

RIGHT AND OVERLEAF McDonnell Douglas released artwork depicting a series of concepts in the late 1970s, including a large prop-fan, solar-powered, pod-carrier and flying wing designs. *Boeing*

Less obvious is why none of the proposals for very large airlifters ever resulted in anything more than a design study. Interestingly, the foreseen prerequisites of advances in engine technology and composite materials were indeed realised. In subsequent decades the high-bypass-ratio engine of 100,000lb (45,360kg) thrust became a reality, as did the extensive use of composite materials in aircraft structures.

In retrospect it is not difficult to see why no large aircraft, capable of adaptation to cargo and passenger carriage, suited to both civil and military use, emerged. The various studies confirmed the feasibility of the concept but it would have required massive investment to turn it into a reality.

No aircraft company could risk going ahead on a speculative basis. It would have required substantial government funding – at least to cover development up to the prototype stage – for ACMA to have moved further forward. Although airlines were positive about the prospect, it would have been difficult to imagine them making a commitment to buy an entirely new category of aircraft a decade in advance of it becoming available. A similar government-funded approach had, of course, been taken with the United States SST programme ten years earlier, but in this case the requirements, while technologically challenging, were at least easy to define. With ACMA it was a case of speculating on both future military requirements and the emergence of a future global commercial market.

It is perhaps ironic that the large freighter that was to enjoy the greatest success in the commercial market (which is still in production today, some fifty years later) has been the Boeing 747 – an aeroplane repeatedly rejected by the USAF as either airlifter or tanker.

However, it would be wrong to assume that the studies described in this chapter led nowhere. They certainly added to the stock of aeronautical knowledge, but it often takes time for concepts to reach maturity. It is a matter of both waiting for other technologies to advance and also for the political, military or commercial environment to change. In the late 1940s it looked as though the flying wing bomber, exemplified by Northrop's B-35 and B-49, had been passed by, losing out to more conventional designs; fifty years later the Northrop B-2 Spirit was developed and entered service.

Perhaps an aircraft resembling some of the remarkable giant airlifters described above will one day replace the C-5.

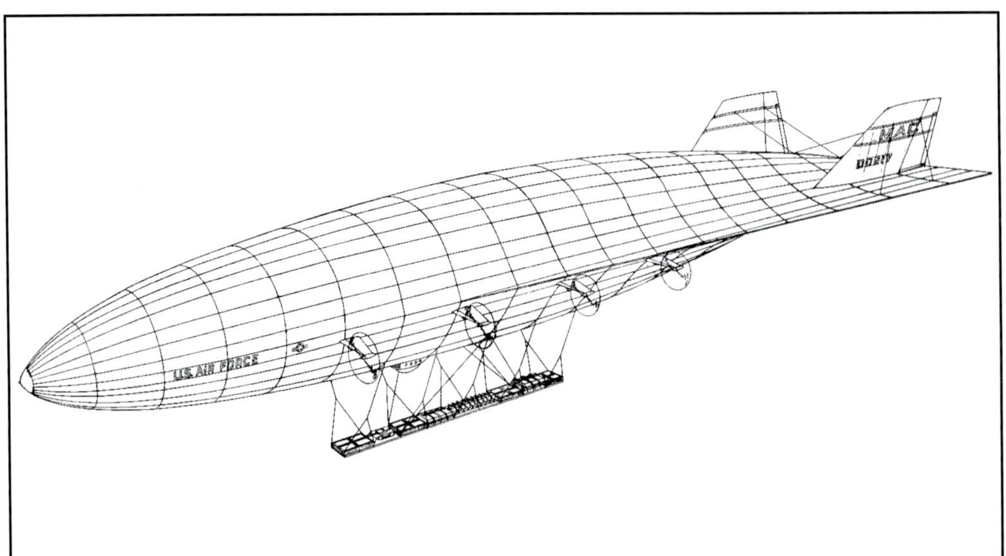

LEFT A McDonnell Douglas cargo dirigible design from the late 1970s, which would have traded speed for capacity. The cargo load pictured on the underslung gondola (one Main Battle Tank, four Infantry Fighting Vehicles, ten wheeled artillery pieces, three self-propelled guns and ten Conex containers of supplies) would have far exceeded the capability of any fixed-wing aircraft. *Boeing*

Chapter Eight

Extreme Outsized Airlifter Conversions

Exploiting heavy lift capabilities in new roles

ABOVE Artwork by Douglas Ettridge shows a notional Space Shuttle External Tank being loaded in a cargo pod carried by the Turbo-Three Corporation's Virtus. The Virtus used dual B-52 fuselages and their landing gear in this design variation.
Tony Chong collection

At the start of the 1960s the US aircraft industry – by then morphing into an aerospace industry – faced a significant new challenge. Successive Soviet 'firsts' in space, starting with the launch of Sputnik in October 1957, had created shock waves throughout the world, threatening America's established reputation for global technological leadership. The USA now found itself in what would become termed the 'Space Race'.

As part of the challenge of coordinating the design, construction and launch of the spacecraft themselves, the newly formed NASA faced an immediate logistics problem: transporting huge components over transcontinental distances between the different manufacturers, test sites and eventual launch facility. The ideal answer would be to airlift them, but nothing of this size had ever previously been transported by air. Although in the 1950s airlifters had been modified to accommodate ICBMs, these were only designed for the first generation of such missiles. It represented a huge challenge and it resulted in some highly imaginative proposals.

Defining NASA's challenge

It is easy to overlook the fact that when, in July 1962, President Kennedy made his bold declaration that America would land a man on the moon and return him safely to earth by the end of the decade, there was no clear view of exactly *how* this could be achieved. No decision had been made on the mission profile or the number or size of the launch vehicles involved.

There were three basic options for the mission profile:

- Earth orbit rendezvous, which assembled and possibly fuelled lunar spacecraft modules in Earth orbit. Various options required ten Saturn C-1 or up to fifteen Saturn C-2 rocket launches to place all the components into orbit for one mission
- Lunar orbit rendezvous, which envisaged that there would be a single launch of two spacecraft – an orbiter module and a specialised lunar lander – but rendezvous techniques had not yet been developed
- Direct ascent, which required the largest launcher of all – the 'Nova' class booster – to carry a spacecraft that combined the lunar lander and return functions.

Saturn stages to be transported	Designation	Diameter	Length
Saturn I (formerly Saturn C-1)			
First Stage	S-I Block 1	24ft (7.32m)	80ft 4in (24.49m)
Second Stage	S-IV	18ft (5.49m)	40ft 0in (12.19m)
Saturn IB (formerly Saturn C-1B)			
First Stage	S-IB	21ft 4in (6.53 m)	80ft 4in (24.49m)
Second Stage	S-IVB	21ft 8in (6.60 m)	58 ft 5in (17.81m)
Saturn V (formerly Saturn C-5)			
First Stage	S-1C	33ft 0in (10.06 m)	138ft 0in (42m)
Second Stage	S-II	33ft 0in (10.06 m)	81ft 7in (24.87m)
Third Stage	S-IVB	21ft 8in (6.60 m)	58ft 5in (17.81 m)

These options involved a truly bewildering number of rocket stages of differing capabilities, weights, diameters and lengths, which would come together to make up a single Saturn launcher. Moreover, the number of complete rockets that were needed was unknown. At one point it was possible to project that 150 Saturn C-2 launches would be needed to support ten moon missions (and each launch would require three rocket stages, each needing transport from the manufacturer to a test site, then to the launch site).

Initially, the Lunar Orbit Rendezvous concept was the least favoured of the three options, being viewed as the most

BELOW A Saturn S-I Block 1 stage with its eight H-1 engines looms over engineers at the Marshall Space Flight Center (MSFC) in 1960, illustrating the transportation challenge. The nominal diameter was *only* 24 feet. *NASA*

complex and highest risk – which is understandable in the light of the fact that in mid-1961 the rendezvous of two aircraft had yet to be achieved in Earth orbit, let alone around the moon. However, with tenacious promotion of the proposal by John Houbolt, an engineer working at NASA's Langley Spaceflight Center, it slowly became recognised that this was by far the most efficient way of carrying out the mission. Indeed, it could be accomplished by the launch of a single Saturn V rocket. In June 1962 it was adopted as the chosen mission profile

Transporting the Saturn V stages

Five contractors were involved in building the Saturn V, with Boeing being given responsibility for the S-1C stage. This was to be assembled just outside New Orleans, then transported to NASA's new launch facility at Cape Canaveral, Florida. Meantime, the S-II and S-IV/S-IVB stages were to be built in California and also shipped to Florida.

Early on, the chosen option was for waterborne conveyance by barge. However, the barge journey from California to Florida was painfully slow, taking about twenty-eight days through the Panama Canal. It was compounded by the fact that stages manufactured at the Marshall Space Flight Center in Alabama also needed to be transported to Louisiana for testing and back, before being sent on to Florida.

A mishap on 2 June 1961 pointed out the vulnerability of this system. The single lock at the Wheeler Dam (on the Tennessee River, downstream from Huntsville where the S-I stage was built) collapsed, trapping the barge *Palaemon* and its cargo. In response, NASA paid for roads to be built around the dam and moved the S-I to a hastily converted barge downstream for onward transportation to Cape Canaveral. This was completed in about eight weeks. This proved to be a prescient time-saving operation as the *Palaemon* remained trapped upstream for nine months until the rebuilt lock was opened.

ABOVE Concept artwork showing an early Douglas C-133 adaptation for carrying the Saturn S-IV stage. *Boeing*

BELOW A wind tunnel model of the C-133 with the initial tri-tail configuration carrying a Saturn S-I First Stage in March 1961. In this case the stage had only fairings fore and aft, with the rest of its structure left exposed. *Boeing*

The pressure was on to look at air transportation.

Douglas C-133 carrier studies

In 1960 NASA's Marshall Space Flight Center (MSFC) awarded a contract to Douglas to determine the feasibility of transporting the rocket stages by air, possibly as part of the contract won by Douglas to manufacture the S-IV stage used on various Saturn booster stacks.

The first study was submitted on 26 August 1960 and proposed 'piggyback' carriage on top of the C-133. Rather than replace the fuselage, a costly and time-consuming process to design, build and test, Douglas chose external cargo carriage. After evaluating whether to carry the stages with endcap fairings, Douglas opted for mounting the outsize items in a cargo pod or 'capsule', mounted on top of the aircraft. This required both a strengthening of the C-133 mid-fuselage and the addition of small vertical surfaces at the tips of the horizontal stabilisers to aid lateral stability.

On 15 May 1961 a follow-up report was submitted by Douglas adding the large S-I stage as a payload. After wind tunnel testing, the initial tail

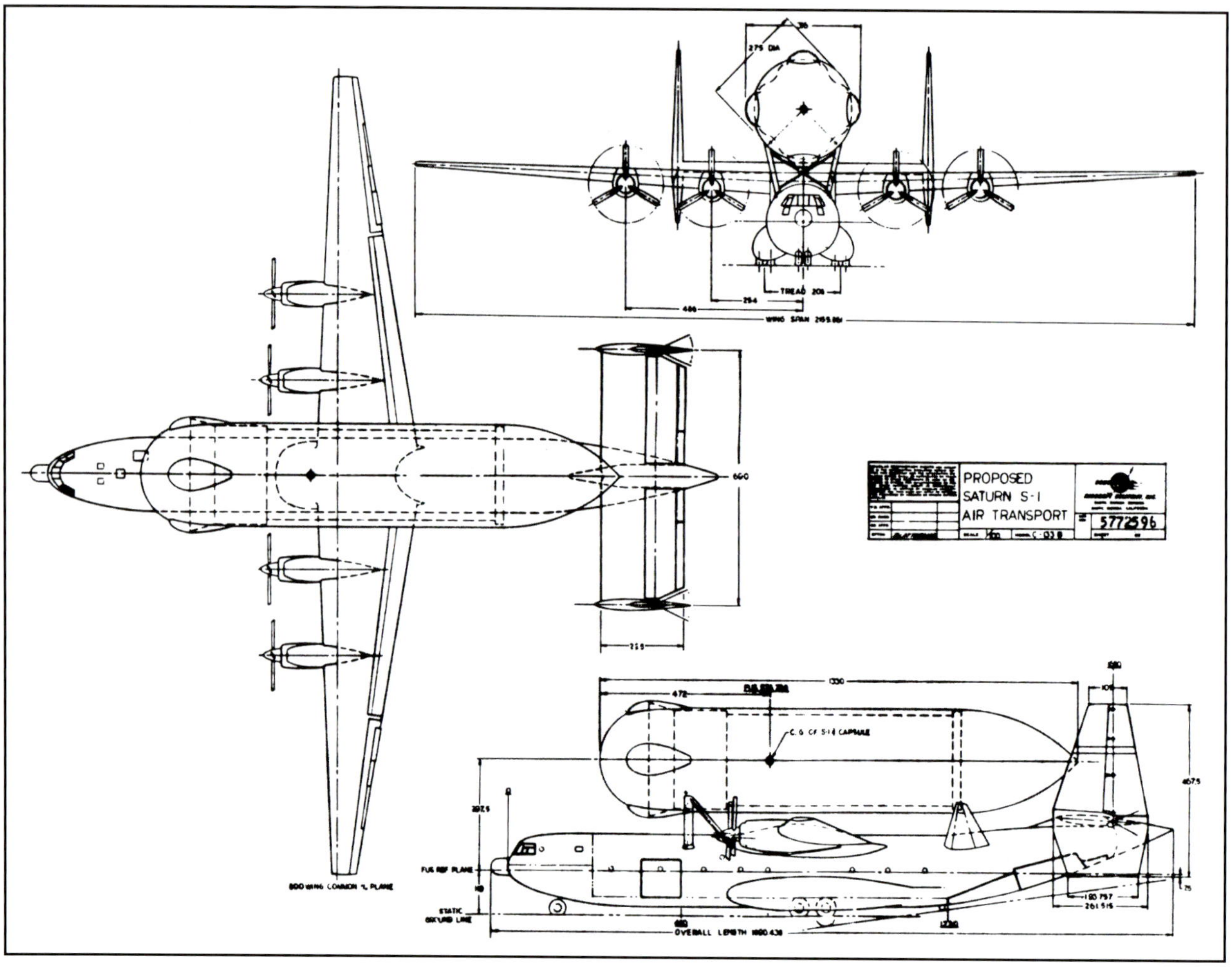

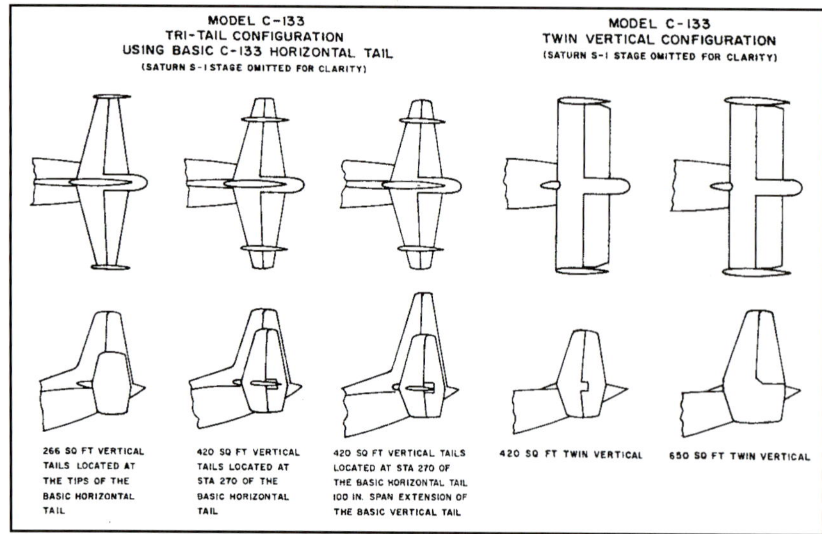

ABOVE General arrangement of the final C-133 configuration. The S-I stage was now carried aft-end forward in the cargo pod. The flared S-I Block 1 engine shrouds (blisters) were discarded in later booster configurations. *Boeing*

LEFT Evolution of C-133 tail configurations. *Boeing*

configuration with outrigger fins was replaced with large vertical fins mounted at the tips of a new horizontal stabiliser. The S-I stage (or other outsized cargo) was carried in a container pod, with the upper half of the centre section of the pod removable by crane to enable easy cargo loading. The flexibility of the new configuration allowed for a variety of different pods to be considered, depending on the cargo carried.

Douglas presented the study on 26 September 1961 at a meeting held in Tulsa, Oklahoma, attended by Wernher von Braun, Director of the Marshall Space Flight Center. Despite a comprehensive set of proposals, the Douglas idea of adapting the C-133 for this role was not pursued.

It is interesting to note that although the Douglas concept of an aerodynamic-shaped pod mounted on top of the fuselage was never adopted for use in the USA, the Soviet Union used this configuration for transporting its own outsized aerospace loads. The Myasishchev VM-T 'Atlant' was a conversion of the Myasishchev M-4 bomber (NATO codename 'Bison'), which carried

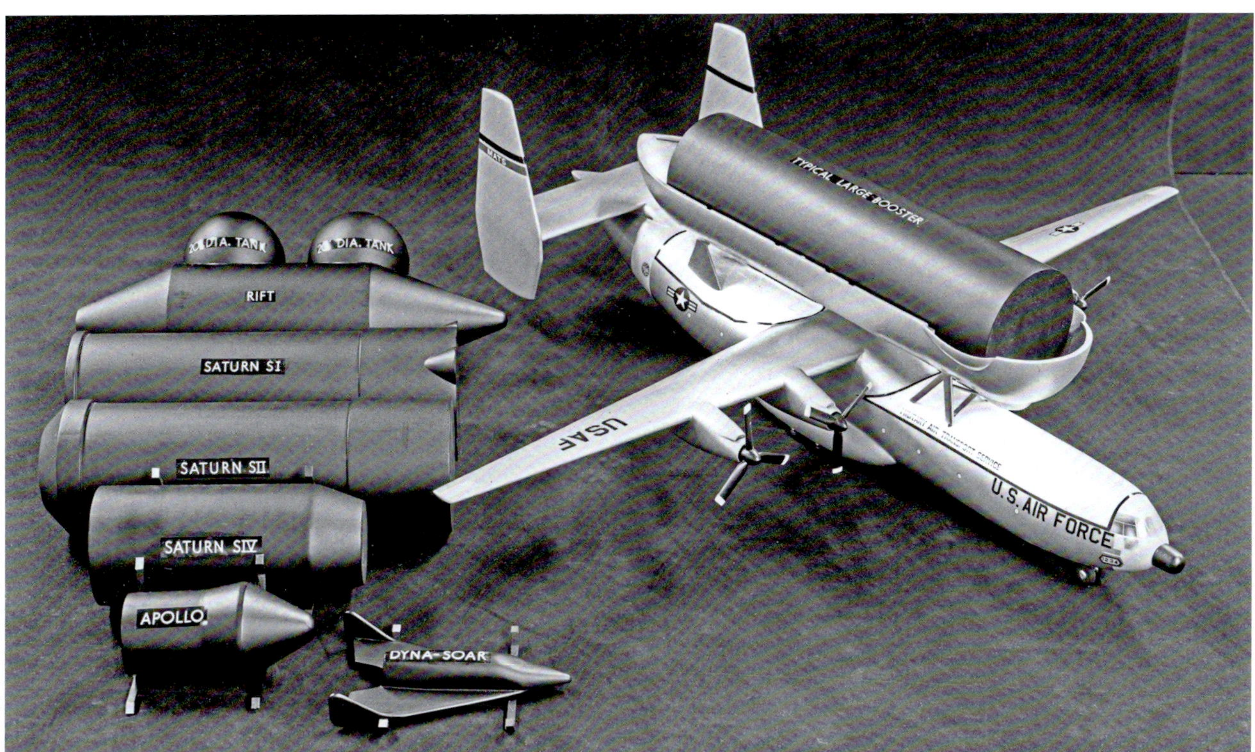

ABOVE A display model of the converted Douglas C-133 demonstrating the potential range of cargo loads, including a Dyna Soar spaceplane that could also be carried in the external capsule. *Boeing*

BELOW The Douglas C-133 Saturn carrier model. Use of the large cargo capsule required the replacement of the vertical tail with two large outboard surfaces, mounted on a constant-chord horizontal stabiliser. *John Aldaz collection*

either a cargo pod or – before being superseded in the role by the Antonov An-225 – the Soviet Space Shuttle.

'Large Booster' airlifters

In addition to the Douglas effort, NASA evaluated several other studies that addressed the air transportation problem. An unsolicited study (by Ling-Temco) was also received. This was performed in the 1959-60 timeframe and initially dealt with the proposed carriage of the C-1 and, later, S-II stages.

With the adoption of the Saturn C-5 (later Saturn V) configuration on 25 January 1962 and the Lunar Orbit Rendezvous plan on 11 July 1962, the numbers of stages to be transported became manageable. From the early requirement for fifteen Saturn C2s to build one moon mission, the total for the entire Apollo programme was reduced to eighteen Saturn Vs, of which three were non-flying test beds.

Plans for the even larger 'Nova' class booster never made it past a multitude of initial studies and faded away by 1965, probably to the relief of transportation engineers and planners.

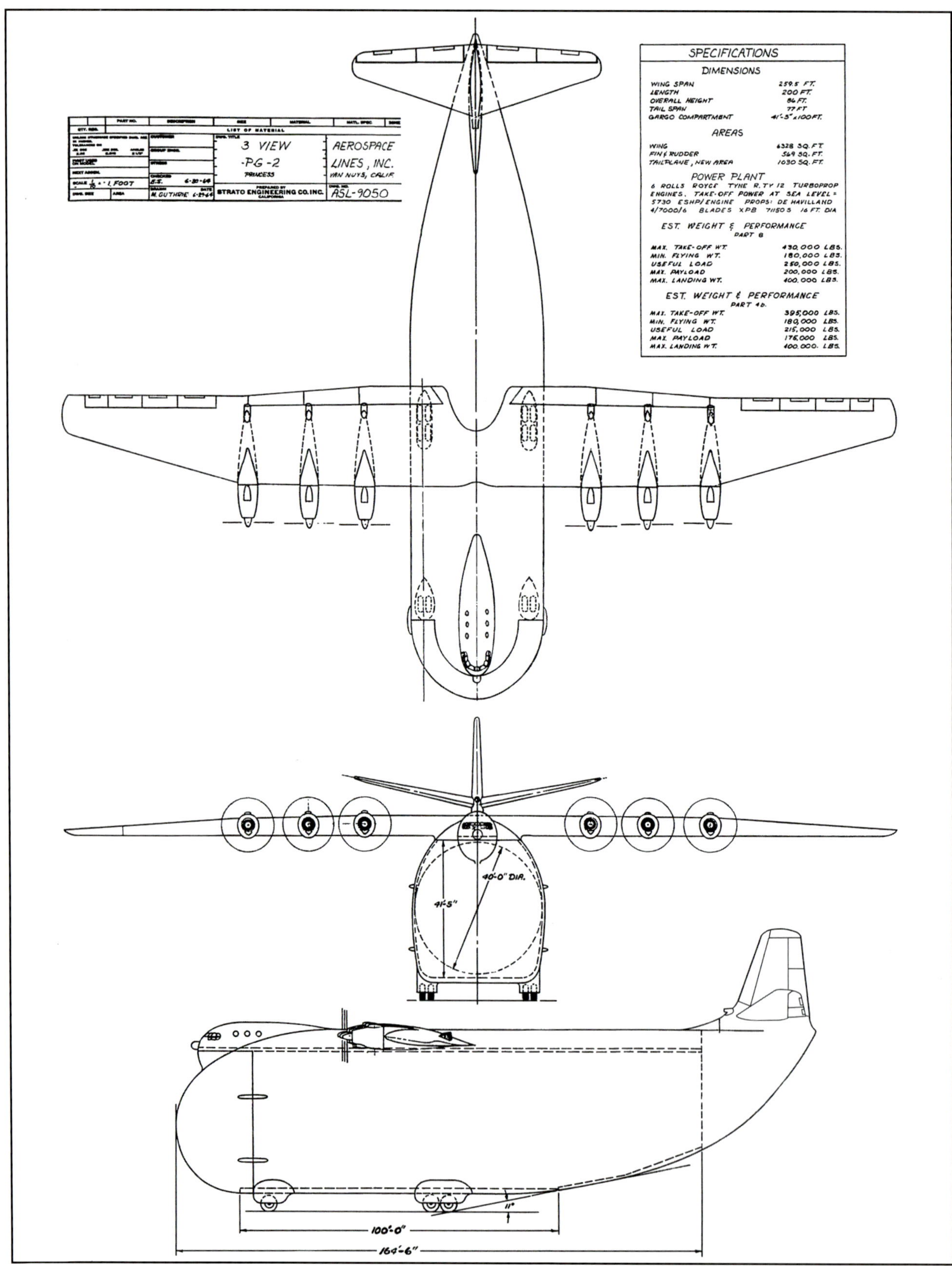

ABOVE **Labelled as the PG-2, the initial Conroy Princess Guppy was to use the wings and empennage of the Saro SR.45 Princess, replacing the ten Proteus turboprop engines (eight coupled in pairs and two as singles) with six Rolls-Royce Tyne turboprops. The fuselage featured a completely new structure, with the cockpit appearing to be from a Boeing Model 377 airliner.** *Via Scott Lowther/APR*

Saturn booster sizes were also settled upon, with the Saturn V S-1C First Stage and S-II Second Stage established at 33ft (10.06m) in diameter (this reportedly being set by the ceiling height at the NASA Michoud facility near New Orleans, Louisiana, where assembly of the S-IC was to take place). Moreover, as the shape of the moon programme solidified, it was decided that barge transport for the limited number of these stages would be acceptable. Only the S-II stages built by North American Aviation at Seal Beach, California, needed to make the long journey through the Panama Canal. The S-IC only had to travel from Louisiana and around Florida.

Further complicating the airlift plans, some in Congress were adamantly opposed to NASA building an aircraft specifically created for this purpose.

Aero Spacelines S-II carriers

The challenge of adapting an existing aircraft to accommodate the outsized loads that NASA had in mind was finding a large enough airframe with salvageable components. Aero Spacelines, under its president Jack Conroy, appeared to hit upon a promising solution when on 30 January 1964 it announced its intention to build a giant new cargo aircraft based on the Saunders Roe Princess flying boat.

Three Princesses were built, the first (and only one to fly) taking to the air initially on 22 April 1952. With ten Bristol Proteus turboprops, six of which were coupled in paired nacelles, a span of 220ft (67.1m) and a maximum take-off weight of 330,000lb (150,000kg), it was certainly a giant of its time. Flight testing proved successful but orders from airlines never materialised. There were two problems. First, the aircraft was seriously underpowered. While this could be rectified as more powerful engines became available, the other problem could not. In short, the anticipated future for long-haul passenger flying boats was not there. Flying ceased in June 1954 and all three aircraft were cocooned awaiting a buyer.

Conroy's press release made it clear that he was proceeding with an outsize-cargo adaptation of the Princess, stating that preliminary engineering studies and wind tunnel tests had proved satisfactory (and Conroy certainly knew what he was talking about in this area), and that the company had taken out options to buy two of the three aircraft. What he did not reveal was that Aero Spacelines had performed an earlier study (possibly contemporary with the Fairchild M-534, described later) utilising the wings and empennage of a B-36 bomber mated to a new fuselage with a cargo space 40ft (12.19m) in diameter.

With the Princess airframes becoming available, the original Conroy design was modified to incorporate the wings and empennage from that aircraft as the PG-2. The wing was enlarged to span an additional 40ft and the ten inadequate Proteus engines were replaced by six Roll-Royce Tynes. The cargo hold had a minimum diameter of 38ft (11.6m) and was 100ft (30.5m) long, and the maximum payload was claimed to be in excess of 200,000lb (104,600kg).

The Conroy design was revised again as the turbofan-powered PG-3. The eight turbofan engines, in four under-wing pods, were unspecified but likely to have been Pratt & Whitney TF33s in B-52H engine pods. Surprisingly, the PG-3 shrank in all dimensions, with the span being reduced to approximately that of the original Princess. While the dimensions were not stated, sizing the PG-3 cargo compartment to the Saturn S-II dimensions of 33ft (10m) diameter by 81ft 7in (24.87 m) length corresponds well with the overall reduction of aircraft size in comparison to the PG-2 design.

Although the proposal was both firm and clearly based on careful and knowledgeable study, the project never materialised. The problem was that upon inspection (having been in storage for ten years beside the sea), the airframes revealed too much corrosion and deterioration.

Convair Saturn S-II transport

Convair made two forays into the field of transporting outsize NASA loads, neither of which progressed beyond the design concept stage. One was an adaptation of the company's Model 990 airliner, the other a completely new aircraft adopting a unique approach to the problem.

BELOW The second iteration of the Princess Guppy saw the slightly smaller aircraft powered by eight turbofans in the TF33 class. It also had aerodynamic improvements in the landing gear fairings and the aft fuselage. It is shown loading an early configuration Saturn IV 'S-1(B)' First Stage. *Author collection*

Saunders-Roe and Aero Spacelines carriers compared

	Saunders-Roe SR.45 Princess	Aero Spacelines PG-2	Aero Spacelines PG-3
Powerplant	8 x Bristol Proteus 610 turboprops (coupled in pairs); 2 x Bristol Proteus 620 turboprops @ approx 2,820eshp (2,103kW)	6 x Rolls-Royce Tyne 12s @5,730eshp (4,273kW)	8 x turbofans @ 18,000lb (80.07kN) class (rating similar to P&W TF33)
Span	219ft 6in (66.93m)	259ft 6in (79.10m)	220ft (67.06m)
Length	148ft (45.11m)	200ft (60.96m)	185ft (56.39m)
Height	55ft 9in (16.99m)	86ft (26.21 m)	81ft (24.69m)
Cargo compartment	n/a	40ft (dia) x 100ft (12.19m x 30.48m)	n/a
Wing area	5,019sq ft (466.28m²)	6,328sqft (587.89m²)	n/a
Payload	137,000lb (62,142kg)	250,000lb (113,398kg)	greater than 200,000lb (90,718kg)
Max gross weight	330,000lb (149,685kg)	430,000lb (195,044kg)	460,000lb (208,652kg)

Convair's 'Composite Airplane' study made use of elements of several other aircraft. The front portion and tail-cone of the fuselage were taken from the Convair 880, the outer portion of the wings from the Canadair CL-44, and the T-tail from the Lockheed C-141. It was powered by the same Rolls-Royce Tynes as the CL-44, except that the Convair aircraft used six rather than four.

The most remarkable thing about this composite aircraft, however, was that it carried the Saturn S-II underneath the fuselage. This required the aircraft to have a fixed tailwheel landing gear, with the main wheels fitted at the end of non-retractable legs 44.25ft (22.50m) in length. To give the necessary ground clearance, the tailwheel was mounted at the base of a vertical fin (with rudder) extending beneath the aft fuselage, which was also required to give lateral stability. Sitting on the runway, the nose was around 55ft (16.8m) above the ground.

Convair 'Composite Airplane' Saturn S-II stage transport

Powerplant	6 x Rolls-Royce Tyne turboprops @ 5,500shp (4101kW)
Span	190.97ft (58.21m)
Length	192.5ft (58.67m)
Height	81.0ft (24.69m)
Wing area	3,311sq ft (289.0m²)

BELOW General arrangement (dated 28 January 1964) of the Convair 'Composite Airplane' to carry NASA outsize loads. *San Diego Air and Space Museum*

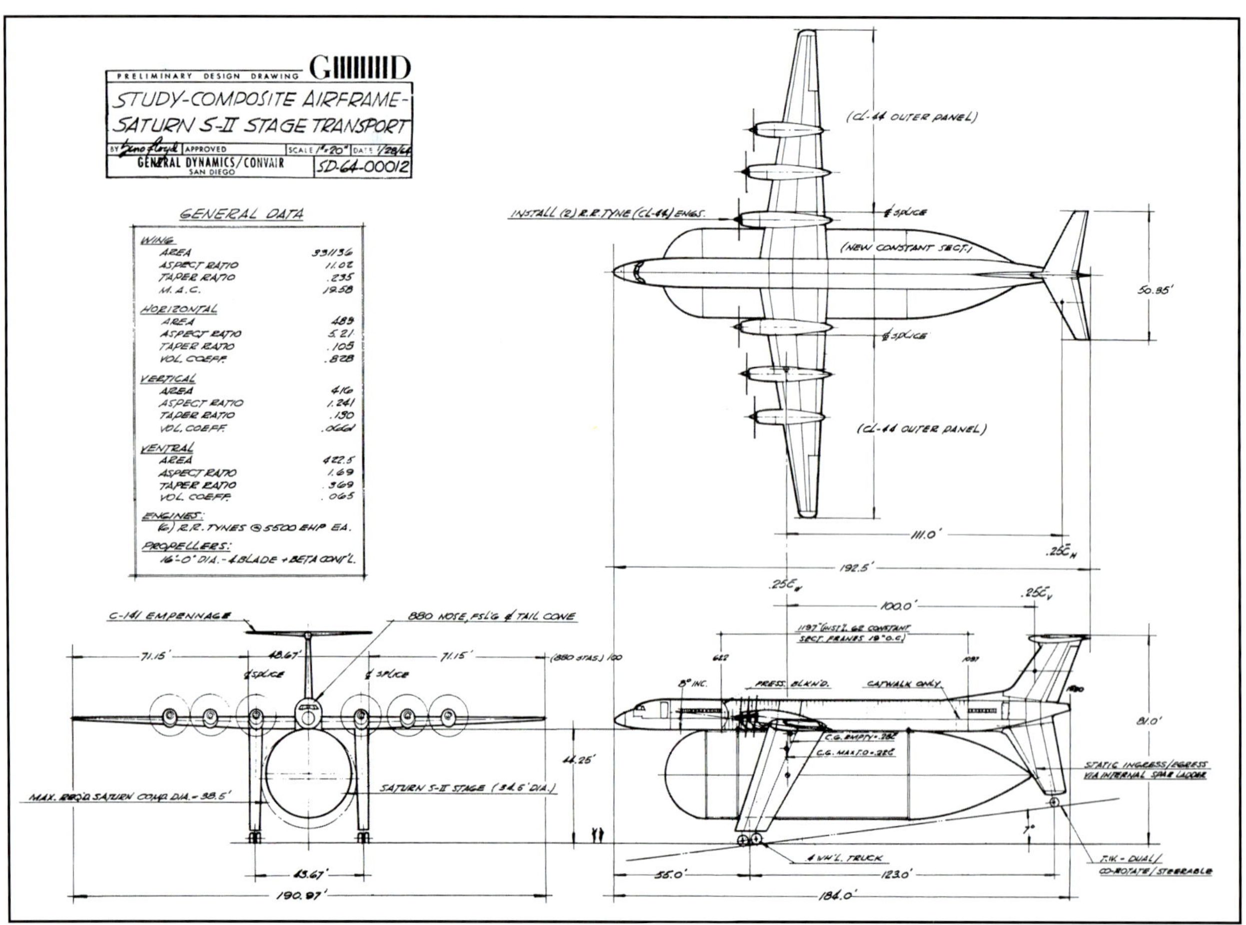

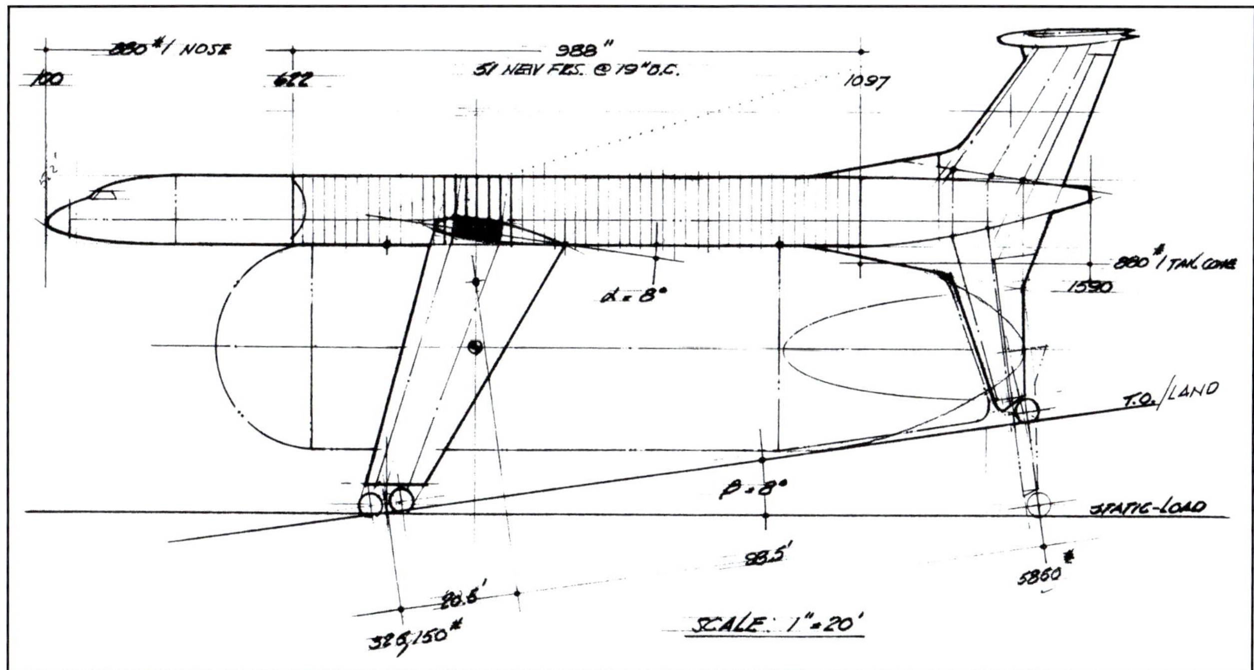

ABOVE The Convair 'Composite Airplane' proposed using the salvaged forward and aft fuselage from the first Convair 880 airliner, while the tail was from a C-141A Starlifter. The aft landing gear was extendable (translating downward) to provide a level loading attitude. *San Diego Air and Space Museum*

The Dee Howard Company: Howard 100 'DBA'

The Dee Howard Co of San Antonio, Texas, apparently designed the Howard 100 'DBA' (reputedly standing for Damn Big Airplane) to fulfil the NASA large booster transport requirement. The fuselage was remarkably similar to that of the Aero Spacelines PG-2 design. It incorporated wings salvaged from retired DC-7 airliners in a biplane configuration. This provided nearly the same wing area as the PG-2 with provision for enough engines to generate the necessary power. The upper wings carried six radial piston engines and the lower wings a further four.

The massive fuselage had an oval cross section squared at the bottom for the quadracycle landing gear, with an interior 40ft (12.19m) in diameter. The flight deck was (in comparison with the rest of the aircraft) a small protuberance, extending above a nose consisting of two huge side-hinged doors. The tail surfaces appeared to be adapted from a Boeing 367 or 377 and it is probably safe to assume that they planned to take many of the other components from existing aircraft as well. A surviving three-view drawing carries a date of August 1964, and photos show a model under test at the Vought wind tunnel in Texas.

The Dee Howard Co 'DBA'	
Powerplant	10 x radial pistons (believed to be R-3350)
Span	187ft (57m)
Length	200ft (61m)
Height	82ft 10in (25.25m) (estimated)
Wing area	5,450sq ft (506.32m²)

BELOW A 1/60th scale model of the Howard 'DBA' in the LTV/Vought wind tunnel. *Via Bill Spidle*

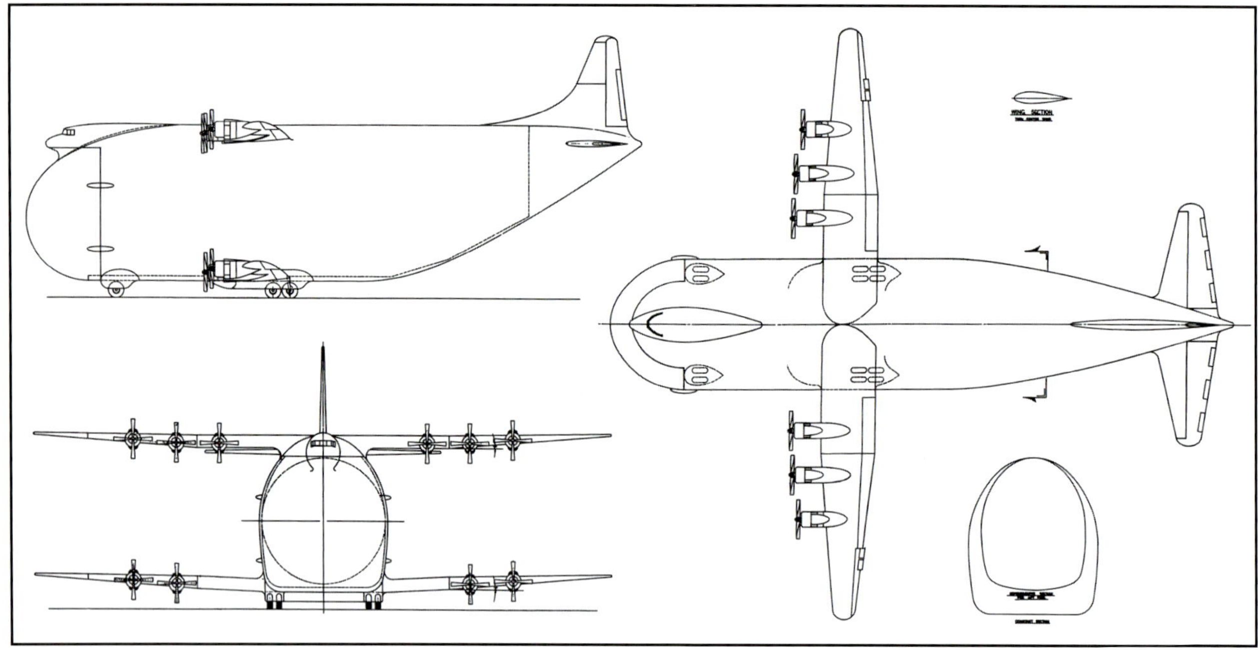

ABOVE General arrangement of the wind tunnel model of the Dee Howard Co 'DBA' outsize-load airlifter. *Greater St Louis Air and Space Museum via Mark Nankivil*

Fairchild Model M-534

Fairchild made a series of studies supporting the NASA transport requirements over four years. The M-534 resulted from the need to determine the best approach to air-transport the large Saturn S-II stage. After previous studies looked at a 'straddle' design and towed gliders, in 1963 Fairchild turned to the modification of an existing aircraft. This resulted in a concept mating the wings, engines and tail surfaces of a B-36 bomber to a completely new, purpose-designed fuselage under the 534 designation.

While audacious, the plan was hobbled by the fact that the last B-36 had been retired six years earlier and only six airframes remained (including the XC-99) – of which two (at the USAF Museum and the SAC Museum) were rated as being in 'good condition'

Fairchild Model M-534	
Powerplant	6 x P&W R-4360-53 radial pistons @ 3,800bhp (2,833.6kW); 4 x GE J47-GE-19 turbojets @ 5,200lb (23.13kN) thrust
Span	266.83ft (81.33m)
Length	220ft (67.06m)
Height	92.13ft (28.08m)
Wing area	6,093.17sq ft (566.1m²)
Normal payload	121,000lb (54,880kg)
Normal gross weight	385,000lb (174,630kg)
Alternative gross weight	410,000lb (185,970kg)

BELOW Studies performed by Fairchild for NASA outsize-load carriers. *NASM*

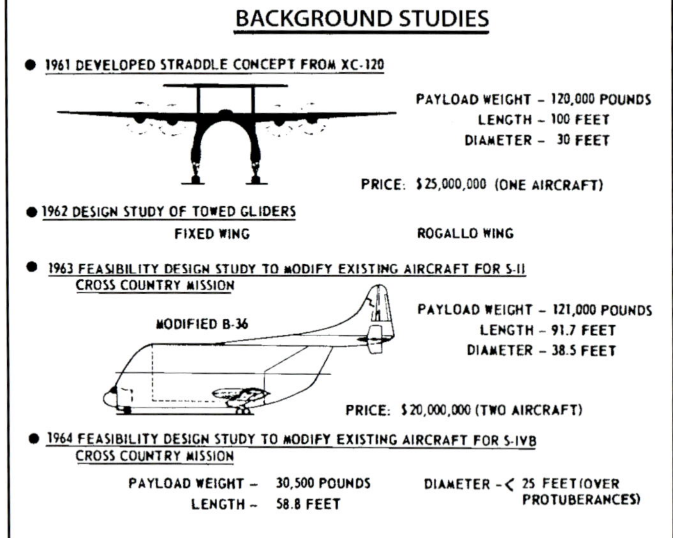

BELOW Six M-534 configurations were studied by Fairchild; drawbacks for each approach are listed. *NASM*

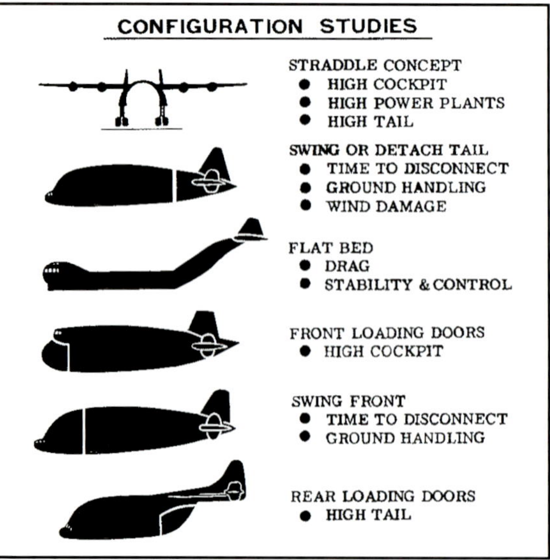

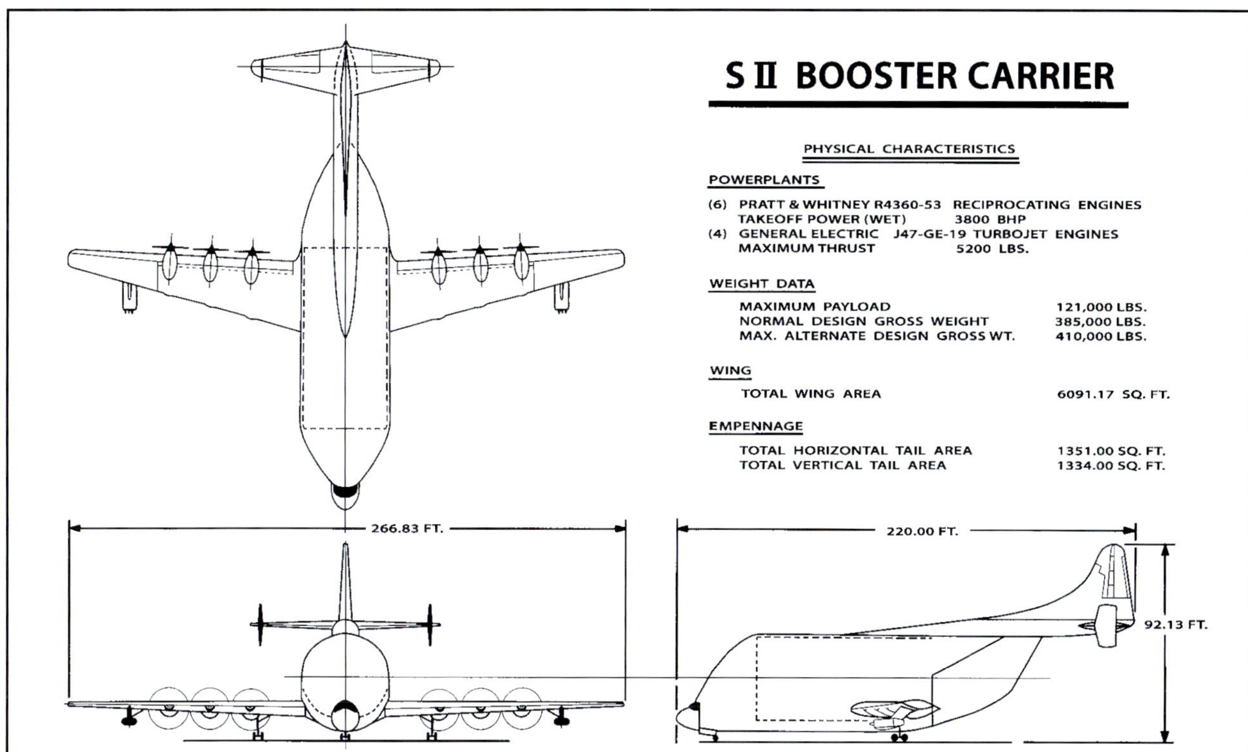

ABOVE Fairchild M-534 general arrangement. *NASM*

RIGHT Promotional artwork for the Fairchild M-534 NASA outsize-load carrier built around a B-36 bomber. *NASM*

and 'flyable'. This plan was overcome by events when NASA decided that the delays and risks of barge transport of the S-II from the North American facility at Seal Beach to the Kennedy Space Center were acceptable.

TEMCO (later LTV) Model 122 Air Trailer

The Model 122 Air Trailer concept was detailed in an unsolicited proposal submitted by the TEMCO Electronics & Missile Company (later the 'T' in LTV) to NASA in 1960. The concept outlined the use of the huge unpowered aircraft as a trailer glider, attached to a Lockheed C-130 tow plane using a rigid tow link rather than a tow line. The Air Trailer was intended to always be under tow but could be released as a glider in case of an emergency.

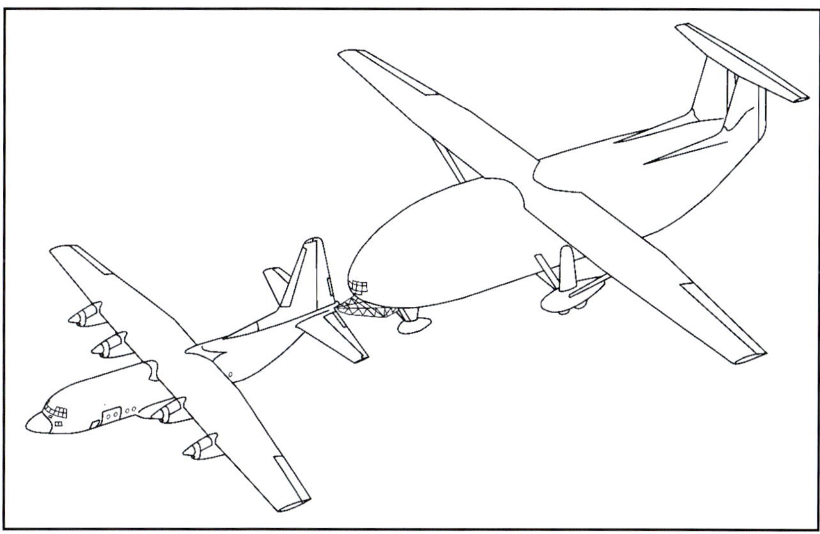

RIGHT Overview of the TEMCO Air Trailer and its C-130A tow aircraft. *LTV via Bill Spidle*

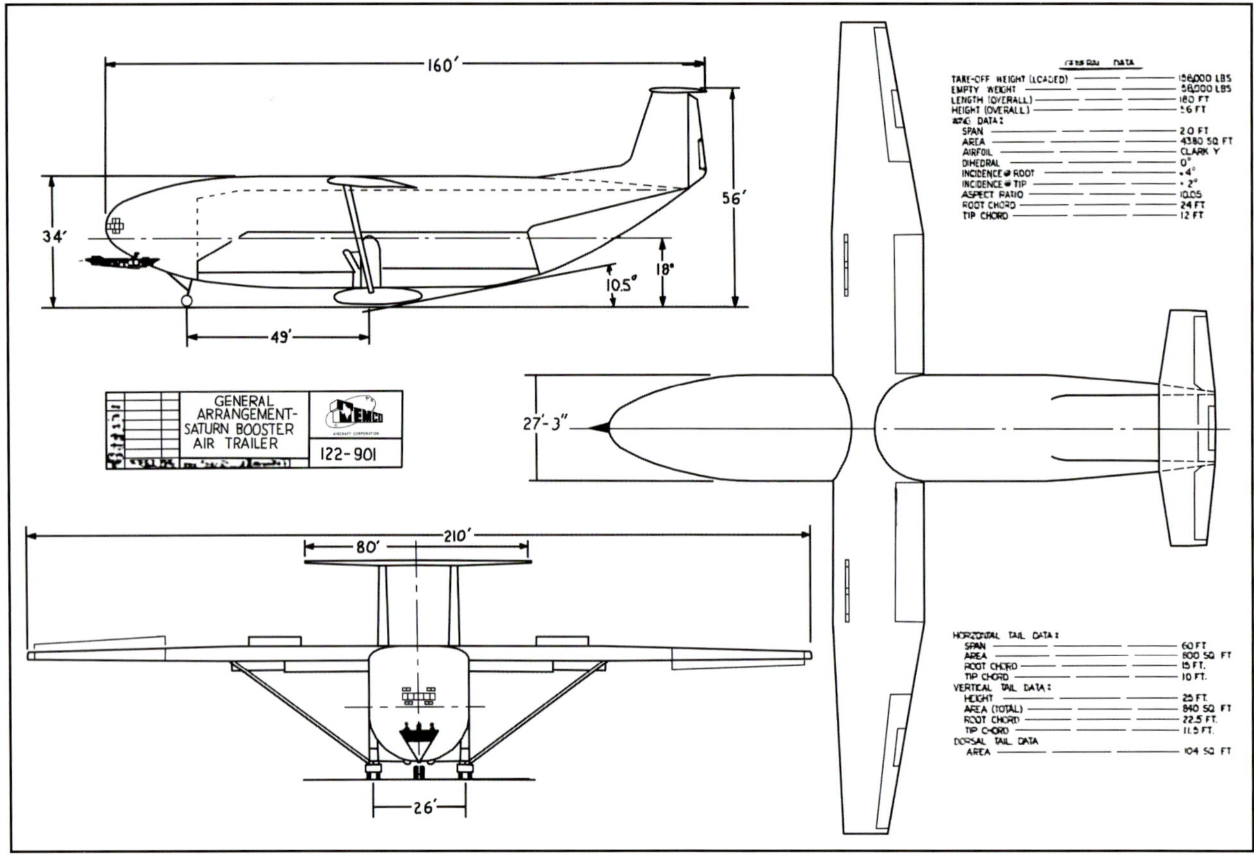

ABOVE TEMCO Model 122 Air Trailer general arrangement. *LTV via Bill Spidle*

BELOW An inboard profile of the Air Trailer is shown with the 24ft (7.32m)-diameter Saturn S-1 stage (as seen at the beginning of this chapter) securely loaded. A sphere containing the cockpit (capable of pressurisation) was placed in the front of the aircraft. *LTV via Bill Spidle*

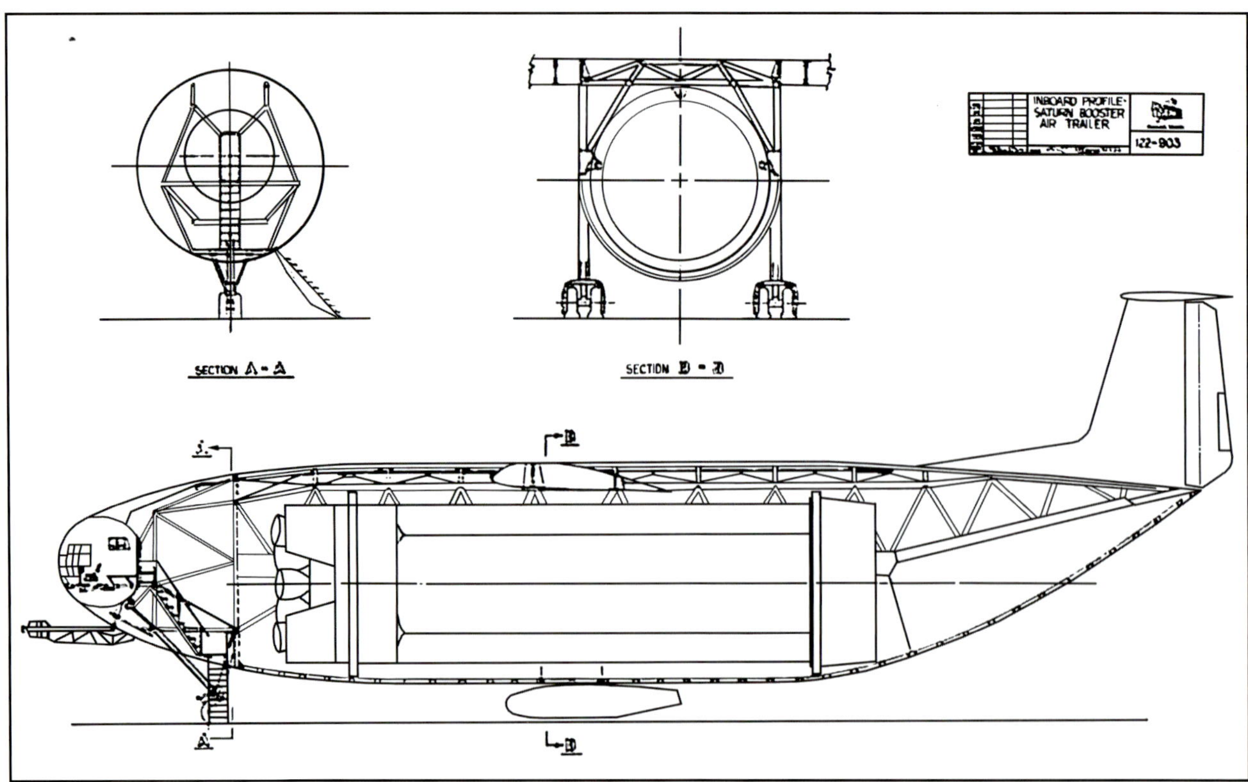

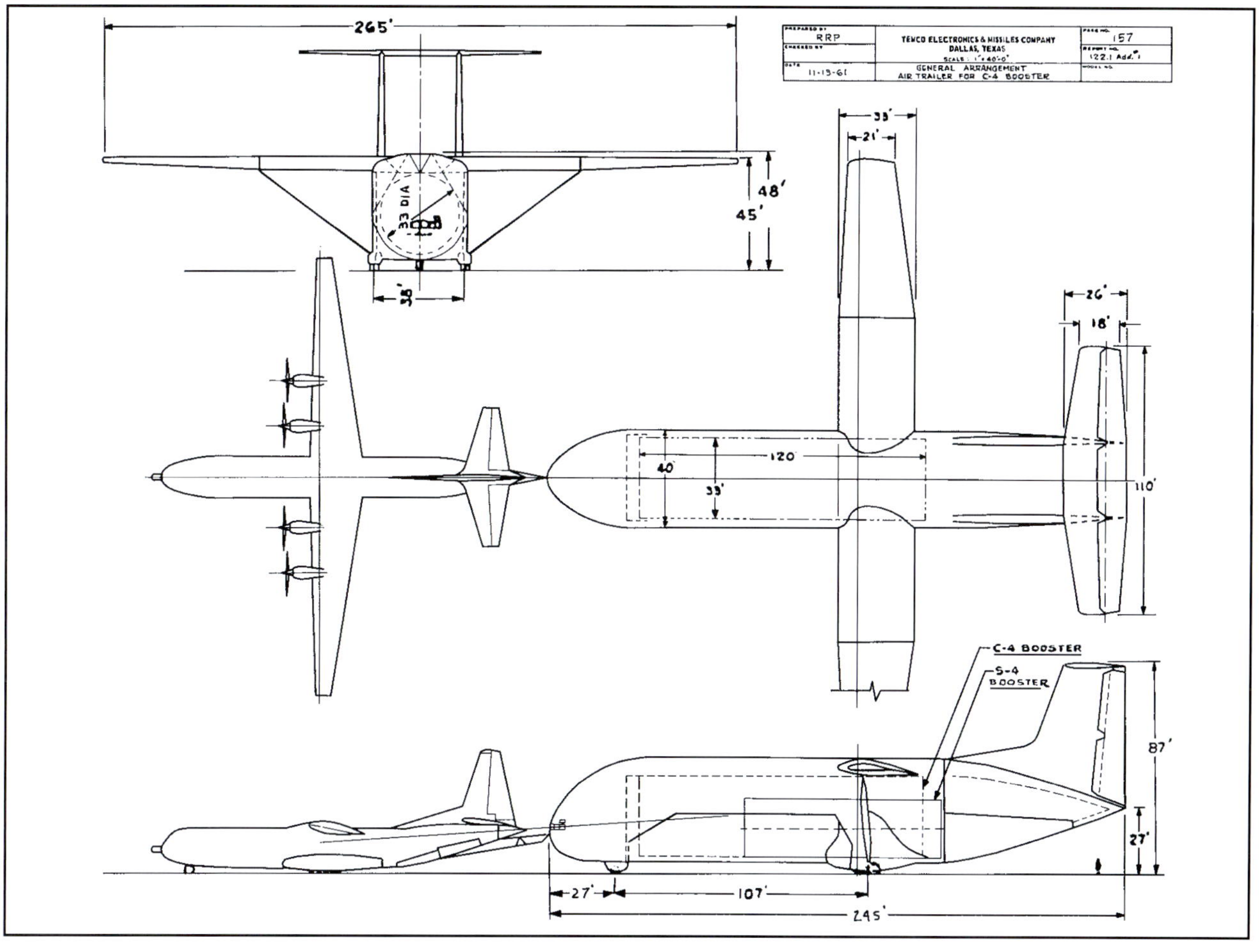

ABOVE **Identified as the 'C-4 Booster Carrier', this larger Air Trailer was to carry the 33ft (10.06m) diameter S-1B first stage for the Saturn C-4. It would have strained the capability of the standard C-133B tow plane; requiring it to have uprated engines.** *LTV via Bill Spidle*

BELOW **The revised TEMCO (LTV) 'C-4 Booster Carrier' was downsized to reduce profile drag and structural weight. This required that the aft fuselage tilt up to clear the S-1B stage.** *LTV via Bill Spidle*

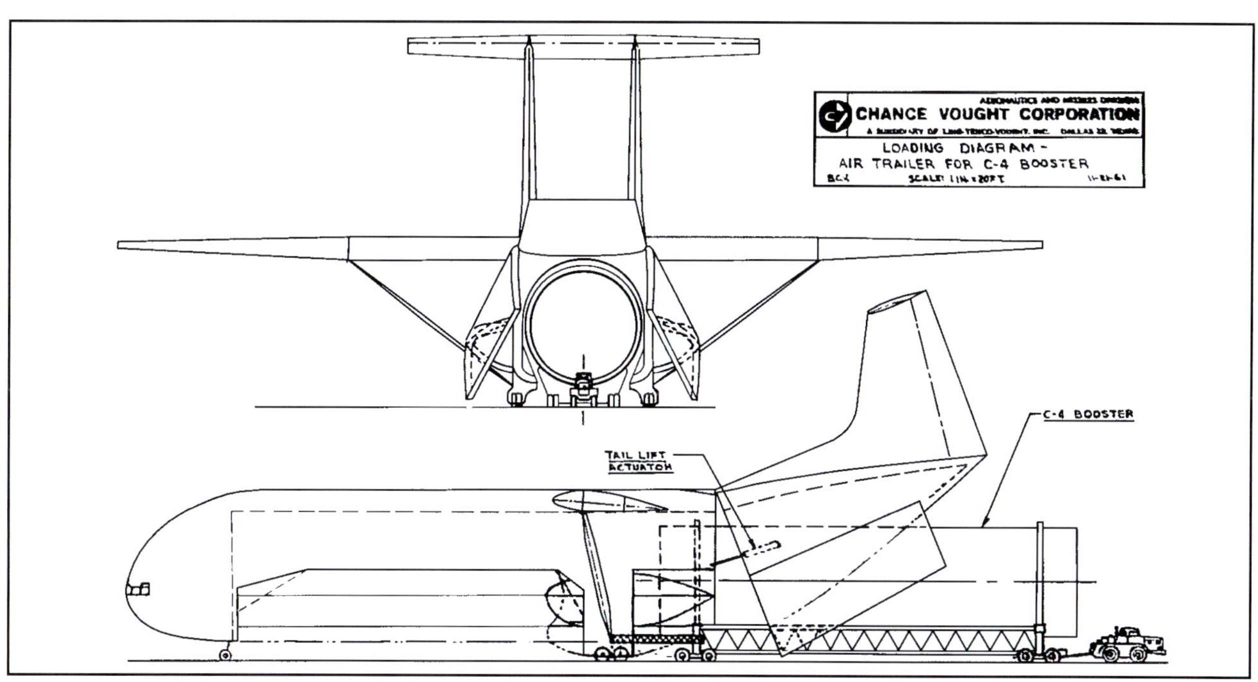

The operational concept was to open the aft and belly doors to load the S-IV; on its ground handling cradle, the S-IV stage was then towed under the Air Trailer and hoisted up by multiple cables to a stowed position, where it was bolted in place and the doors closed.

As designed, the upper fuselage consisted of a welded aluminium tubular truss structure that carried the loads, with a simple sheet metal skin. The Air Trailer wing was a simple 'Clark Y' airfoil for high lift at lower speeds. The outer wing panels were tapered to tailor the lift profile for an optimal span-wise lift curve and reduced structural weight. The wing was strut-reinforced to reduce bending loads as it was attached to the fuselage. A cross-member (detachable for cargo loading) linked the landing gear together under the fuselage to complete the load path.

TEMCO proposed to build five Air Trailers and modify two C-130As for a total programme cost of $21.49 million.

In a report addendum under the LTV name, the company outlined several growth versions of the Air Trailer to handle transport of the much larger and heavier Saturn S-I stage for the Saturn C-4 booster stack. Here the problem became more difficult. A notional 'C-4 Booster Carrier' was shortened by 30ft (9.14m) to reduce drag and weight; however, this then required a lift-up aft fuselage to provide full access to the cargo bay.

While the Air Trailer design was straightforward, there was a problem in terms of the total weight approaching, or even exceeding, standard runway limitations. Certainly, heavier boosters such as the 'Nova' would require runways to be rebuilt at a projected cost of $10 million per runway mile.

'Small Booster' airlifters

The second class of outsized airlifters was sized to carry the Saturn S-IV and later the S-IVB stage. Built by Douglas aircraft in Southern California, the stage required transportation to the test site near Sacramento, California, and Cape Canaveral (later Kennedy Space Center) in Florida. At least ten of the smaller S-IV and thirty-one of the larger S-IVB were built.

Convair 990 Apollo cargo carrier

In 1961 the company investigated the possibilities of carrying various elements of the Apollo programme in either a pod or a faired-in structure on the top of a Convair 990. To this end, the company adapted a 1:25 scale wind tunnel model and tested it with configurations to match a variety of Apollo components on 19-21 May 1962. With an outside diameter of 13ft 8.5in (4.13m), there was no possibility of transporting the S-IV, the smallest of the Apollo stages. There is no record of the project proceeding further.

Fairchild S-IVB carrier

In 1964 Fairchild carried out a study for an aircraft to carry the enlarged S-IVB, which encompassed the Boeing 377, Douglas DC-7 and Lockheed 1649A. This was done because successive redesigns of the Douglas S-IV to the S-IVA and S-IVB rendered the new booster too large to be carried in the Aero Spacelines 'Pregnant Guppy', first flown in 1962 (see below).

TEMCO Air Trailers	Model 122 Air Trailer	'C-4 Booster Carrier'	Revised 'C-4 Booster Carrier'
Powerplant	(1 x C-130A tow plane)	(1 x C-133B tow plane)	(1 x C-133B tow plane)
Span	210ft 0in (64.01m)	265ft 0in (80.77m)	265ft 0in (80.77m)
Length	160ft 0in (48.77m)	275ft 0in (83.82m)	245ft 0in (74.68m)
Height	56ft 0in (17.07m)	90ft 0in (27.43m)	87ft 0in (26.52m)
Cargo compartment	25ft (dia) x 92ft (7.62m x 28.04m)	40ft (dia) x 120ft (12.19m x 36.57m)	40ft (dia) x 120ft (12.19m x 36.57m)
Wing area	4,580sq ft (425.5m²)	n/a	n/a
Payload	100,000lb (45,359kg)	237,000lb (107,501kg)	237,000lb (107,501kg)
Empty weight	58,000lb (26,308kg)	133,000lb (60,328kg)	n/a
Max gross weight	158,000lb (71,668kg)	370,000lb (177,004kg)	n/a

BELOW A wind tunnel model drawing for testing an external pod adaptation of the Convair 990 to carry smaller outsize loads for NASA. *San Diego Air and Space Museum*

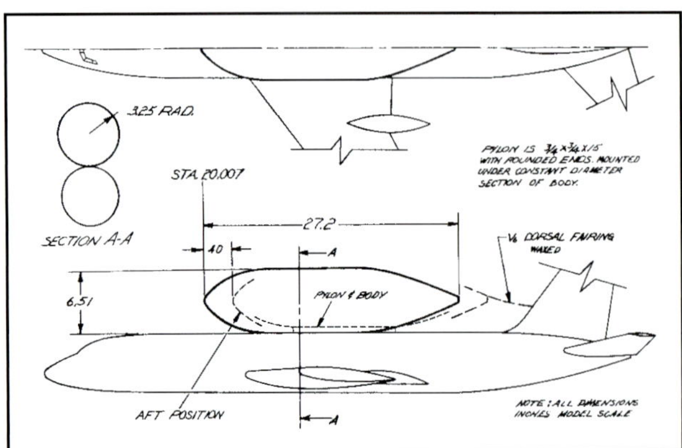

BELOW An alternative configuration had the cargo pod faired into the aircraft structure. *San Diego Air and Space Museum*

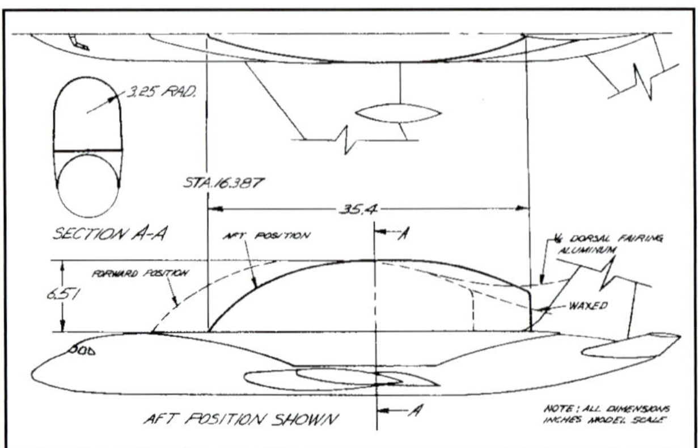

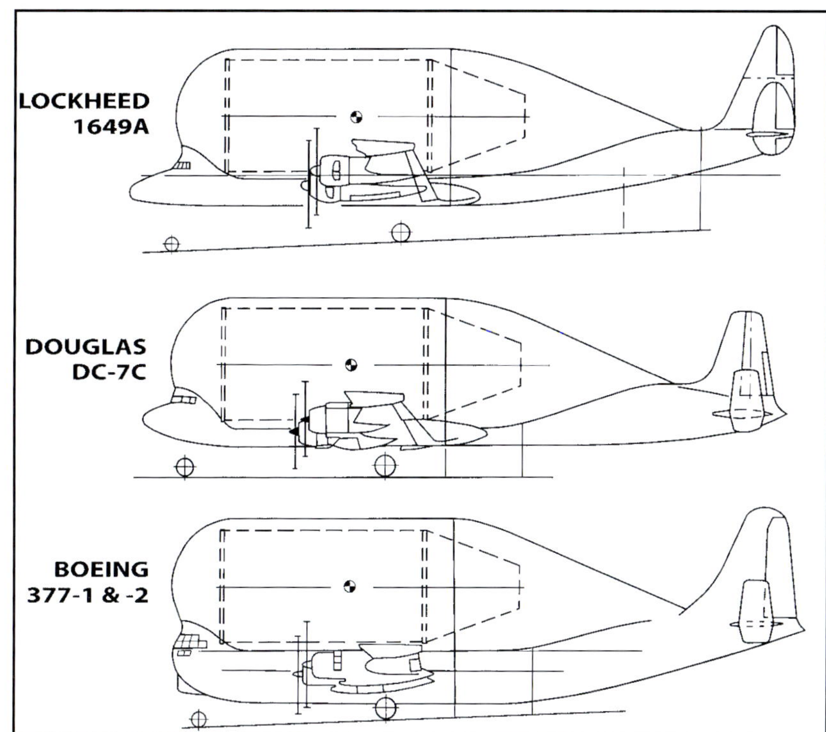

RIGHT Different options were considered by Fairchild for Saturn S-IVB transport conversions. Of the three, Fairchild selected the Lockheed Model 1649A Starliner as the basis for its proposed conversion. All three options had jet engines on the wingtips. *NASM*

Fairchild/Lockheed Model 1649A conversion	
Powerplant	4 x Wright 988TC18EA2 radial pistons @ 3,400hp (2535.4kW); 2 x GE CJ610 turbojets @ 2,850lb (12.7kN) thrust
Span	151ft (46.02m)
Length	136.2ft (41.51m)
Height	37ft (11.28m)
Wing area	1,872sq ft (173.9m²)
Gross weight	158,700lb (71,985kg)

Fairchild selected the final version of the Lockheed Constellation (the Model 1649A Starliner) for the basis of the conversion. Modifications included installing an upper lobe 26ft (7.92m) in diameter, stretching the aft fuselage by 20ft (6.10m), raising the centre tailfin by 10ft (3.05m) and adding GE CJ-610 (civil J85) jet engines on the wingtips.

Fairchild lost out to Aero Spacelines, which modified one of the two YC-97Js with private funding to meet NASA's requirements.

Lockheed Missiles and Space Division towed glider

Lockheed's newly formed Space Division (in Sunnyvale, California) also performed an early study for an S-I booster carrier glider. Much like the TEMCO design, it was meant to be towed by a C-133.

Lockheed Missiles and Space Division booster transport glider	
Powerplant	(1 x C-133 tow plane)
Span	211ft 0in (64.31m)
Length	158ft 4in (48.26m)
Height	65ft 7in (20.0m)
Payload	110,000lb (49,895kg)
Gross weight	153,000lb (69,400kg)
Payload size	24ft dia x 96ft (7.32m x 29.26m)

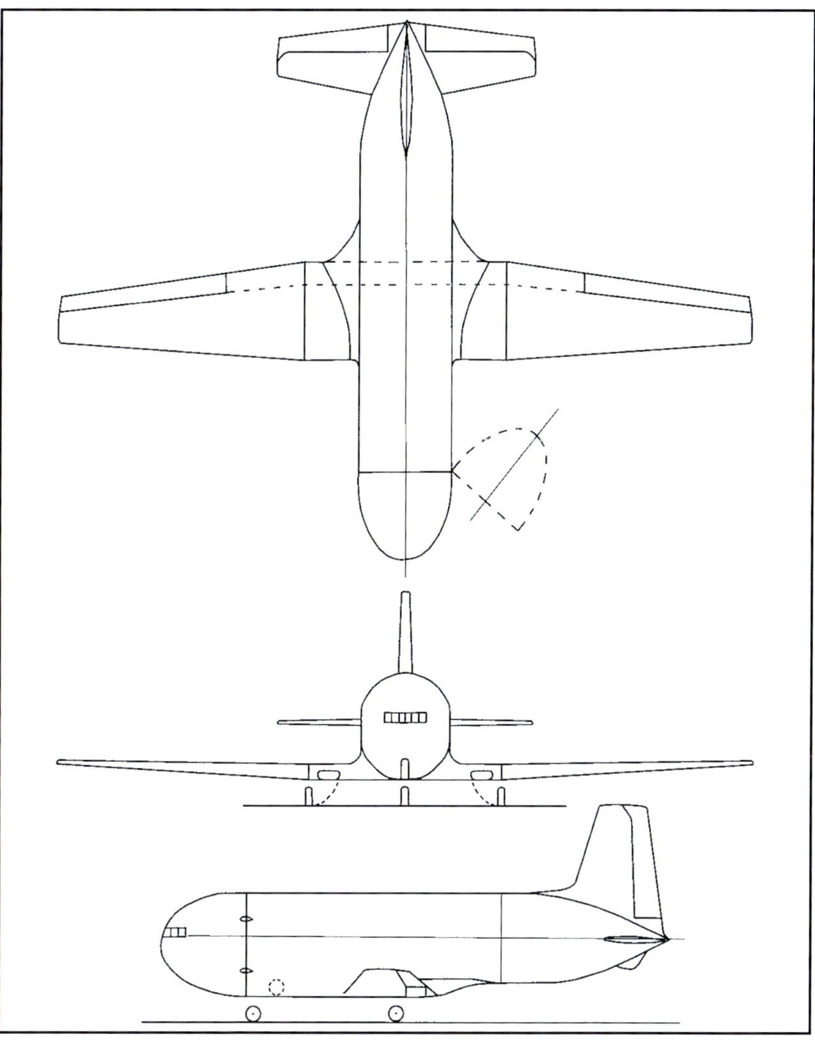

RIGHT In contrast to the TEMCO study, the Lockheed towed glider had a low-wing design, retractable landing gear, and was loaded through a swing-open nose. *Author collection*

Aero Spacelines 'Guppy' family

Aero Spacelines was incorporated on 15 November 1961 and headed by John M. 'Jack' Conroy. The company was formed to create a 'volumetric' transport for the space programme through conversion of a Boeing 377 Stratocruiser by greatly enlarging the upper lobe of the fuselage. Based on its bloated appearance, it was quickly named the 'Pregnant Guppy'. As such, it was the start of what became widely known as the 'Guppy' family of aircraft. These included:

B-377PG 'Pregnant Guppy'
(4 x R-4360 radial pistons) This was built to carry the 18ft (5.49m)-diameter Douglas S-IV stage in a cargo bay 19ft 9in (6.02m) high and 80ft (24.38m) long. The redesigned and larger S-IVB made the 'Pregnant Guppy' obsolete for its intended purpose. However, by creating this aircraft on a privately funded shoestring budget, Conroy outmanoeuvred Congress. NASA did not have to pay for the design and construction of a transport aircraft as one now existed; all NASA needed to do was rent it.

B-377SGT 'Super Guppy'
(4 x T34 turboprops) Originally cast as the 'Very Pregnant Guppy', the 'Super Guppy' was built with an expanded cargo bay (25ft x 94ft 6in – 7.62m x 28.80m) to carry the Douglas S-IVB, which had a 21ft 8in (6.60 m) diameter. It used the wings from the YC-97J and retained the powerful T34 turboprops of that aircraft.

B-377MG 'Mini Guppy'
(4 x R-4360 radial pistons) One piston-powered 'Mini Guppy', with a cargo bay 18ft 2in (5.54m) in diameter, was built for commercial use. The name was a bit of a misnomer, as the usable cargo bay diameter was only 19in (48.26cm) shy of that of the 'Pregnant Guppy'.

B-377MGT 'Mini Guppy' turbine/Guppy 101
(4 x 501D-22C turboprops) One aircraft, similar to the 'Mini Guppy', was built, but was destroyed in a crash less than two months after its first flight on 13 March 1970.

B-377SGT 'Guppy' 201
(4 x 501D-22C turboprops) This was the closest to a production aircraft, with four built over an eleven-year period. Although having lower-powered engines than the 'Super Guppy', the 'Guppy' 201 also had lower empty weights due to revised design and construction, with a greater payload. All were used by Airbus to transport A-300-series airliner fuselages for assembly. Three retired to museum display, while the last one built went to NASA to replace the 'Super Guppy'.

BELOW The Aero Spacelines 377PG 'Pregnant Guppy', with the aft fuselage detached for cargo loading. *Author collection*

ABOVE The 'Super Guppy' loading was simplified with the new swing-nose. The aircraft used major components from the Boeing YC-97J (and its T34 turboprops) and the Model 377 airliner. It featured an increased diameter fuselage tailored to the enlarged Douglas S-IVB third stage of the Saturn V. *Boeing*

BELOW As big as the 'Super Guppy' was, the Saturn S-IVB stage was a tight fit. Here S-IV-B-205 is loaded on 6 April 1968 for a flight from Mather AFB (near the McDonnell Douglas test facility adjacent to Sacramento, California) to Cape Canaveral AFS. Six months later it boosted the first manned Apollo mission, Apollo 7, into orbit. *Boeing*

ABOVE The last built and last flying, NASA's 'Guppy 201' No 4 was obtained from Airbus by NASA in 1991 and remains in service to this day. *NASA photo by Tony Landis*

Aero Spacelines 'Guppy' family

	B-337PG 'Pregnant Guppy'	B-377 SG 'Super Guppy'	SGT-201 'Super Guppy' turbine
Powerplant	4 x P&W R-4360-B6 radials @ 3,500hp (2610kW)	4 x P&W T34-P-7WA turboprops @ 7,000eshp (5,220kW)	4 x Allison 501-D22C turboprops @ 4,600shp (3,430kW)
Span	141ft 3in (40.05m)	156ft 3in (47.63m)	156ft 8in (47.80m)
Length	127ft 0in (38.71m)	141ft 3in (43.05m)	143ft 10in (43.84m)
Height	38ft 3in (11.66m)	46ft 5in (14.15m)	46ft 5in (14.15m)
Cargo compartment	19ft 9in (dia) x 80ft (6.02m x 24.38m)	25ft 0in (dia) x 108ft 10in (7.62m x 33.17m)	25ft 0in (dia) x 111ft 6in (7.72m x 33.99m)
Max payload	29,000lb (13,154kg)	41,000lb (18,589kg)	45,000 lb (20,4112kg)
Empty weight	n/a	105,000lb (47,627kg)	101,500 lb (46,039kg)
Max gross weight	133,000lb (60,328kg)	175,000lb (79,000kg)	170,000 lb (77,111kg)

Space Shuttle transporters

The Space Shuttle was the fastest manned winged aircraft ever flown. However, all the fuel for its main engines was carried in an external tank and this fuel was entirely expended during the ascent to orbit. The necessary pulses to slow the craft and leave orbit were provided solely by the orbital manoeuvring thrusters, with the Shuttle returning to earth as a pure glider. Although launched from Cape Canaveral in Florida, it could – in theory – land anywhere in the world. All that was required was a 9,800ft (3km) paved runway. In practice the prime landing site became the Kennedy Space Center in Florida, with Edwards AFB in California as the primary alternative (a solitary diversion was also made to Northrup Strip at White Sands, New Mexico, to avoid a flooded runway). As a contingency, however, seventy-nine sites – thirty-four in the USA and forty-five spread across twenty-six other countries – were identified as alternative locations.

This meant that NASA needed a plan to return the Shuttle to its launch site at the Cape from potentially any point on the globe. This was no easy task for a vehicle that had an empty weight of 172,000lb (78,020kg), a length of 122.17ft (37.24m) and a span of 78.06ft (23.79m), with large aerodynamic surfaces. Moreover, there was a further requirement: before it was launched into space, its atmospheric flying characteristics had to be tested just like any other aircraft, for which the standard rocket launch was impracticable.

The initial idea was to fit the Shuttle with removable jet engines, slinging five or six of them beneath the centre fuselage and wings. It is interesting to note that the Soviet shuttle, which never actually carried out a manned orbital flight, was flight tested with power provided by four turbofans, clustered around the rear fuselage. This idea, however, was quickly abandoned on the grounds of limited range (400mi or 644km) and the scar weight (the additional weight still carried once the engines were removed). In addition, the envisaged regular West

Coast to East Coast journey involved multiple stops and complex logistics.

Attention turned instead to the possibilities of airborne ferry, which became known as the SCA (Shuttle Carrier Aircraft). There were three basic options:

- A twin-hulled version of either the Boeing 747 or the Lockheed C-5
- A 747 or C-5 'piggy-back' carrier
- A basic, low-technology, purpose-built ferry

Both the first and third options easily permitted air-launch as well as ferry flights, but on a pure cost basis the piggy-back arrangement had a clear advantage.

A proposal fitting within the third option was put forward by engineers at NASA's Langley Research Center, who outlined a simple, purpose-built aircraft that carried the Shuttle Orbiter as an underslung payload. This concept was then further developed by Jack Conroy, with an already established reputation for conversions, but this time for a new aircraft (albeit one making extensive use of elements from existing ones).

ABOVE **A display model of a dual-fuselage Boeing 747-based SCA (Shuttle Carrier Aircraft).** *Author collection*

BELOW **General arrangement of an SCA utilizing two Boeing 747 fuselages.** *NASA*

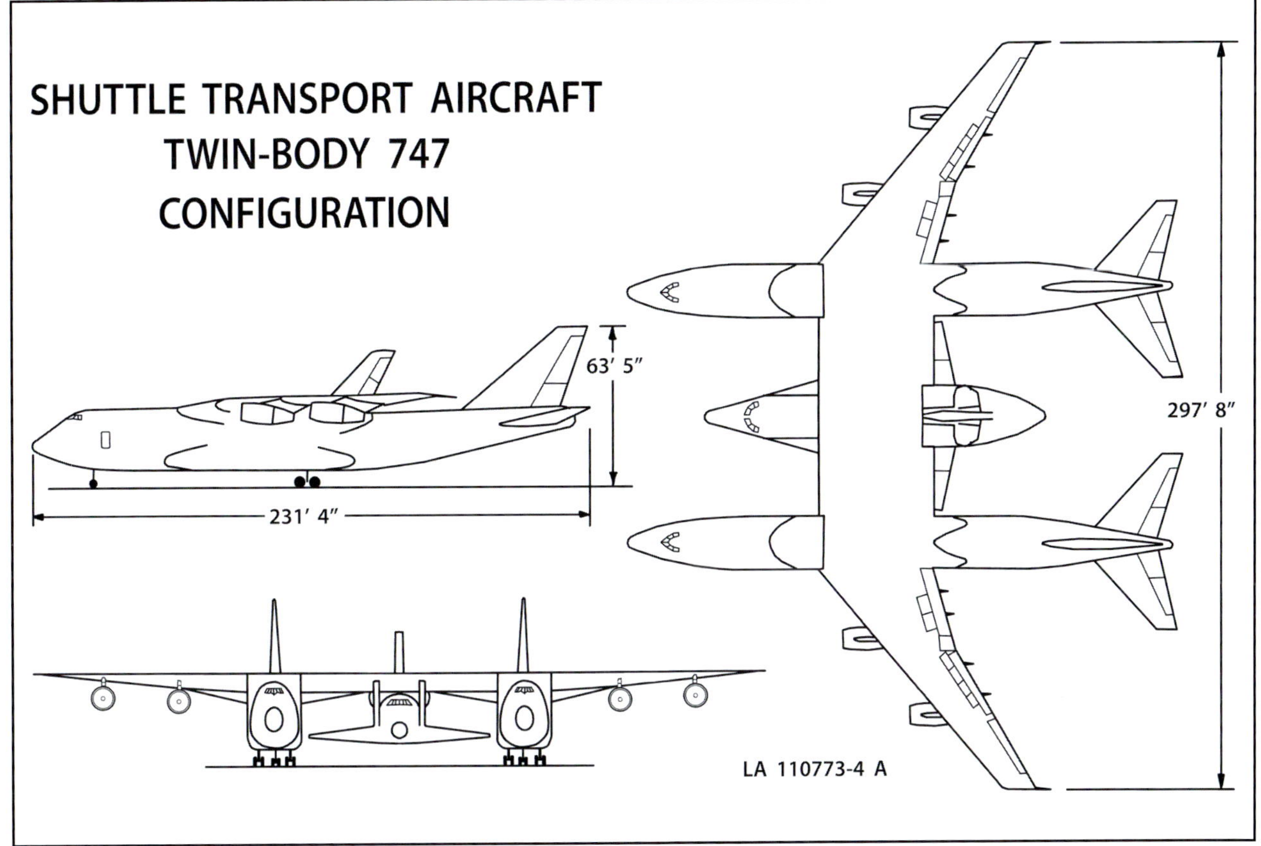

SHUTTLE TRANSPORT AIRCRAFT
TWIN FUSELAGE C-5
CONFIGURATION
LA 110773-5
65.2 FT
246.0 FT
111.39 FT
334.1 FT

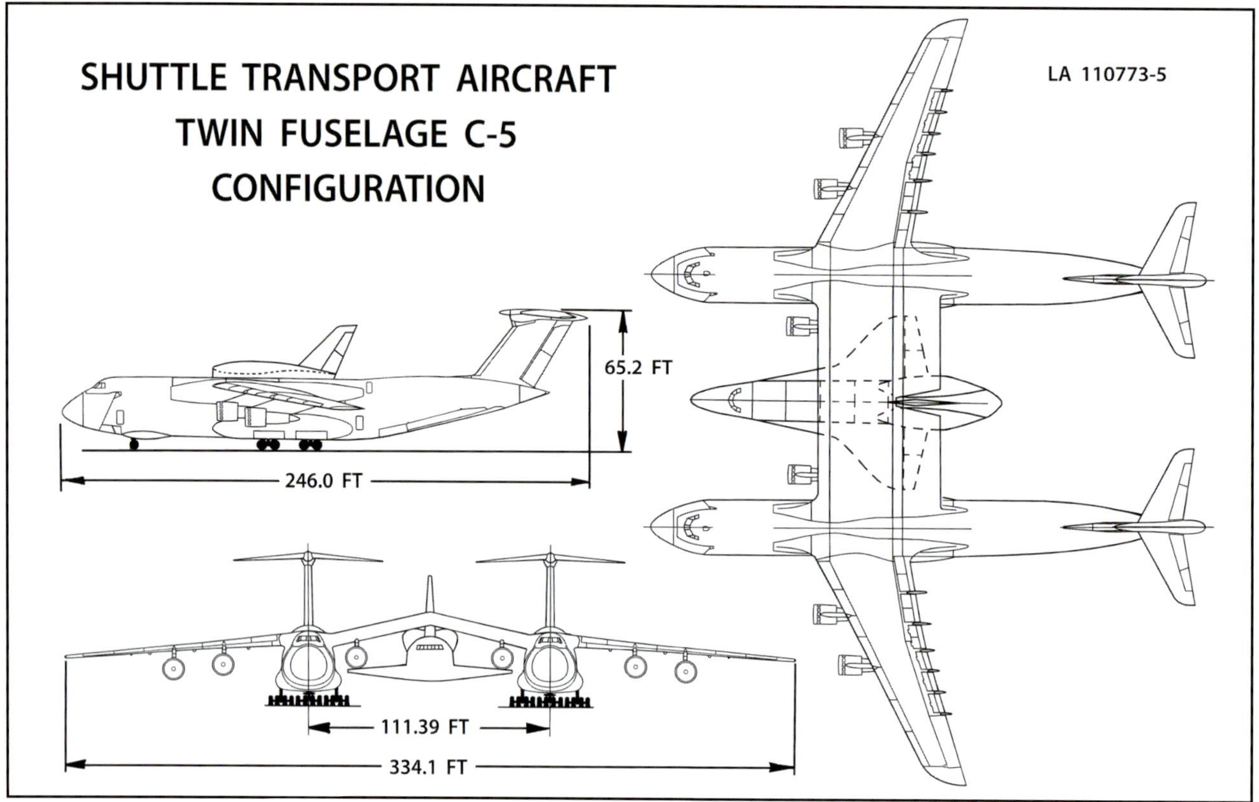

ABOVE General arrangement of an SCA using two Lockheed C-5 fuselages. *NASA*

BELOW General arrangement of a Lockheed C-5 piggyback Shuttle Carrier Aircraft. *NASA*

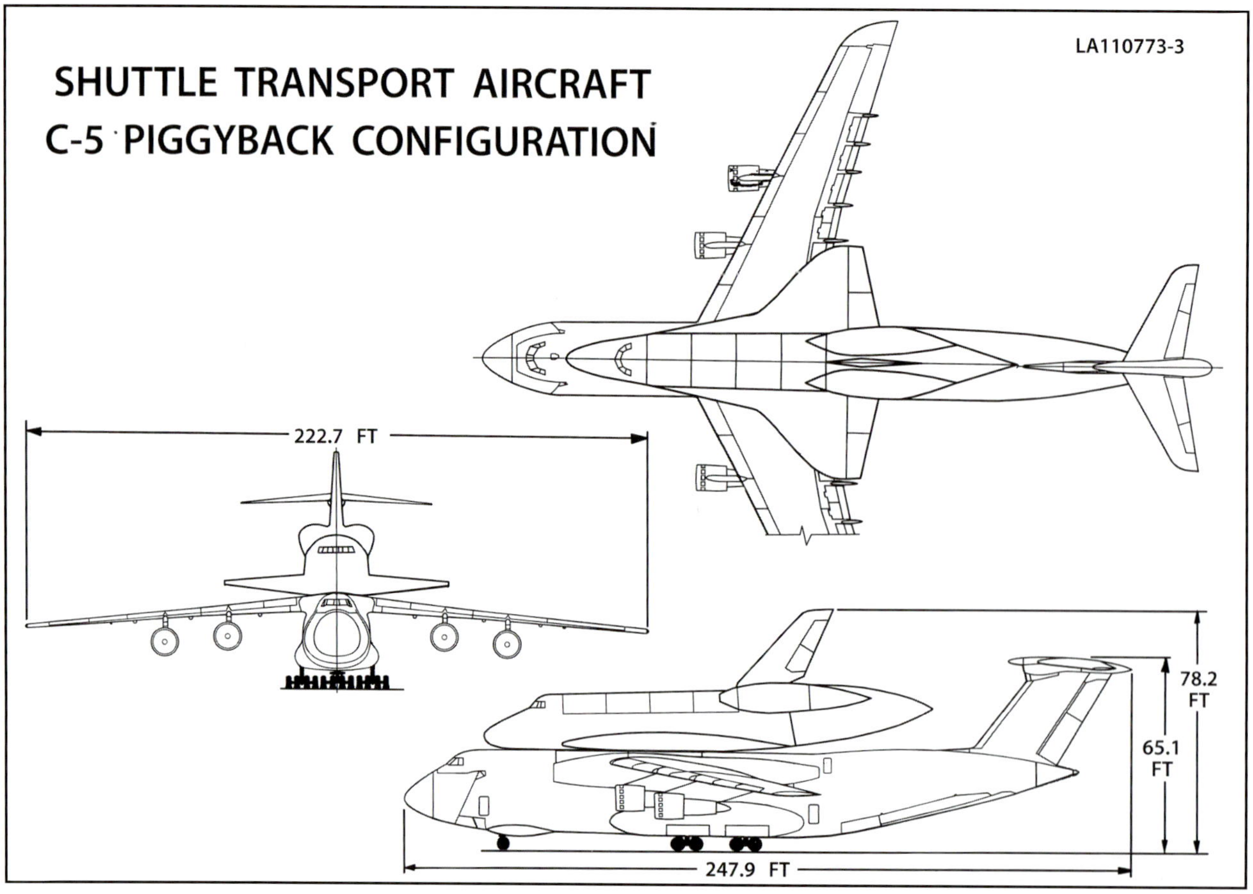

SHUTTLE TRANSPORT AIRCRAFT
C-5 PIGGYBACK CONFIGURATION
LA110773-3
222.7 FT
78.2 FT
65.1 FT
247.9 FT

ABOVE NASA finally selected the Boeing 747 as the piggyback SCA platform. Both aircraft used are seen here in flight near Edwards AFB before the end of the shuttle programme. *NASA*

By now Conroy had a new company named the Turbo-Three Corporation, based in Santa Barbara, California. Aware of the original NASA 'low-tech' design, his proposal embodied a combination of both a low-technology aircraft and the use of existing airframes.

Dubbed the Virtus, this proposal used two B-52 fuselages linked together by a common wing and a shared horizontal stabiliser. Since speed was not a critical aspect of performance (it was planned to cruise at 300mph/483km/h) none of the aerodynamic surfaces required sweepback. Power was provided by four P&W JT9D turbofans, each derated to 40,000lb (177.9kN) thrust. The Shuttle, or alternatively the Shuttle's external fuel tank, solid rocket boosters, or specially designed cargo pods, were slated for transport beneath the centre-wing section.

Given Conroy's record of development on the 'Pregnant Guppy' and 'Super Guppy', the proposal was taken very seriously, and a small contract was awarded for design and development work in conjunction with NASA.

The eventual choice of a Shuttle carrier came down to a matter of simplicity, cost and availability.

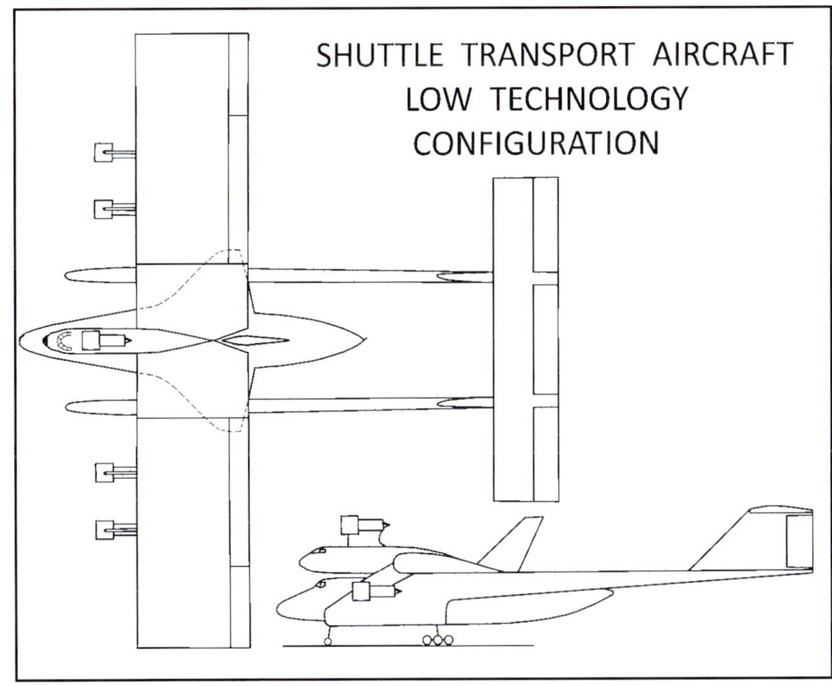

RIGHT General arrangement of a purpose-designed Shuttle Carrier Aircraft as initially laid out by engineers at NASA Langley. *NASA*

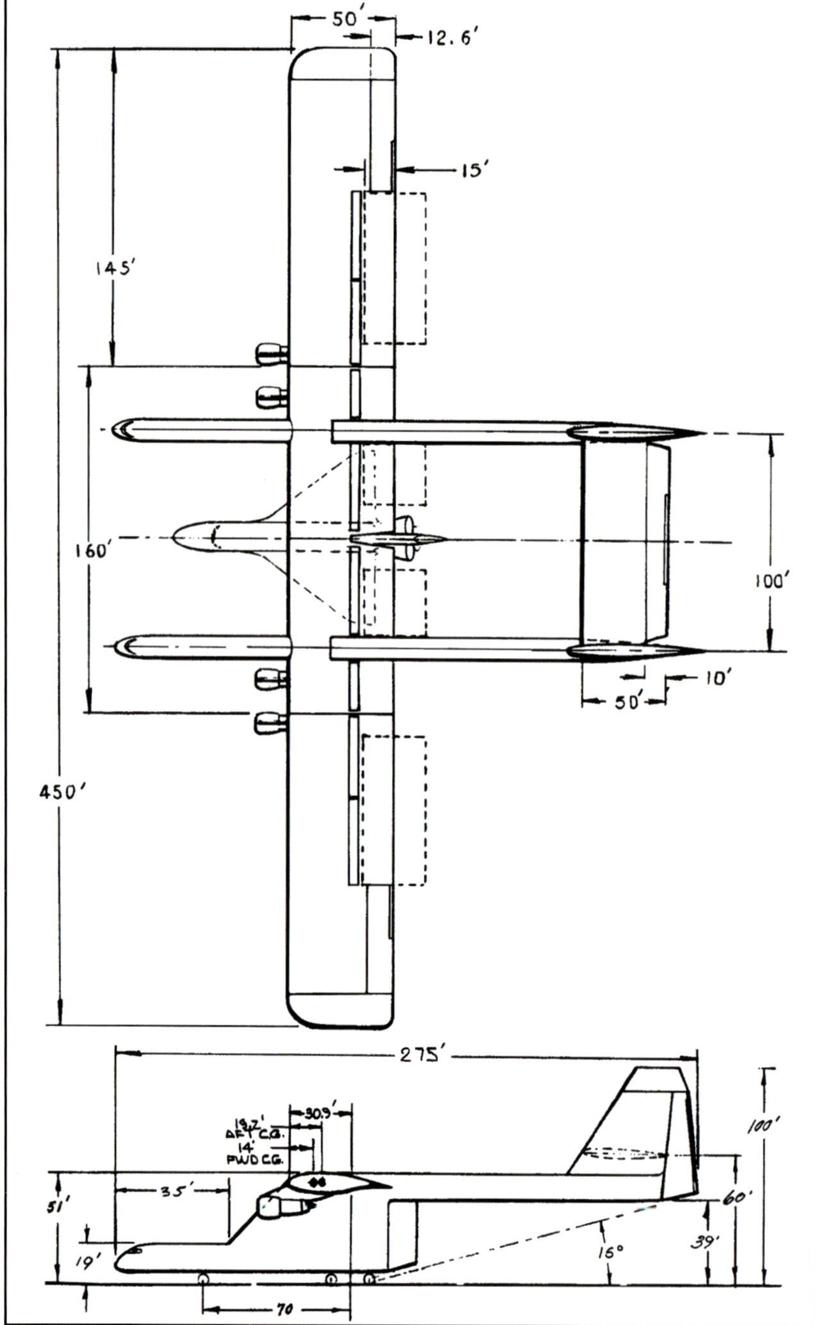

Turbo-Three Corporation Virtus	
Powerplant	4 x turbofans (JT9D, CF6 or TF39, derated to 40,000lb [177.93kN] thrust)
Span	450ft (137.16m)
Length	275ft (83.82m)
Height	100ft (30.48m)
Wing area	22,166sq ft (2,059.3m²)
Max TOW	850,000lb (385,550kg)
Cruise speed	261kt (483kph)
Payload	375,000lb (170,100kg)

LEFT General arrangement of the Turbo-Three Virtus. *Conroy*

Use of the single-fuselage option offered less engineering risk and cost, was less expensive, and utilised the existing belly mounting points employed to attach the Shuttle to its external fuel tank. Creating the new twin centre wing structure meant a new design and qualification effort. Converting the 747 to a twin also involved changing it from a low-wing to a high-wing aircraft.

The single-fuselage 747 offered better separation clearances from the Shuttle during drop tests. Using a single-fuselage C-5 meant obtaining a scarce aircraft from the Air Force, whereas second-hand 747s were becoming available on the market. In 1974 NASA obtained a Boeing 747-123 from American Airlines and used it for a series of tests before sending it to Boeing in 1976 for modification to the Shuttle-carrying role. It was subsequently designated the Shuttle Carrier Aircraft (SCA).

The modifications included adding removable vertical fins to the ends of the horizontal stabilisers to improve directional stability and upgrading the JT9D-3A engines to JT9D-7AH standard to increase the take-off thrust to 46,900lb (30.8kN). The air-launch procedure proved straightforward, with the SCA entering a shallow dive before release. For ferry flights the rear of the Shuttle was encased in a special aerodynamic fairing to reduce drag. In 1988 NASA procured

LEFT A model of the Turbo-Three Virtus, now with a single surplus Boeing Model 367 or 377 cockpit section on the port fuselage and dihedral added to the outer wing panels. *Turbo-Three Corporation*

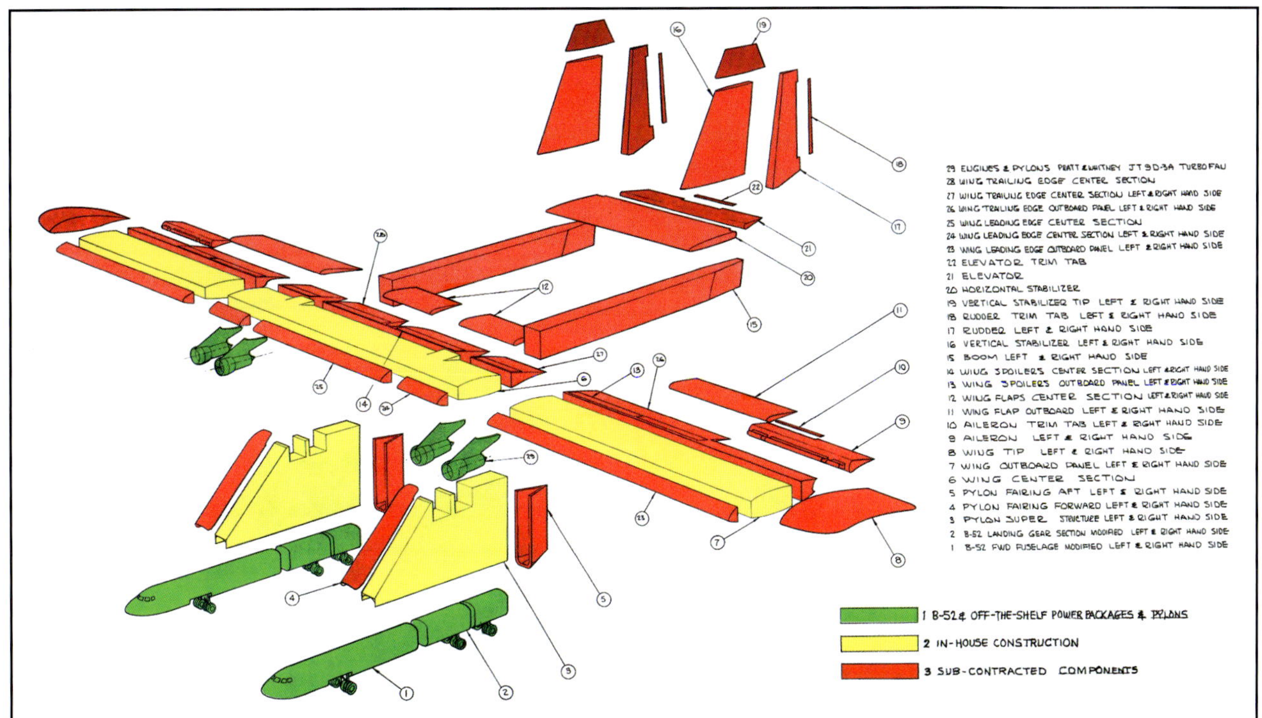

ABOVE Turbo-Three Virtus manufacturing breakdown. At least four B-52 airframes were needed as parts donors. *NASA*

RIGHT Artwork showing the Turbo-Three Virtus with dual B-52 fuselages releasing a Space Shuttle Orbiter for a glide test. *Tony Chong collection*

a surplus 747-100SR from Japan Air Lines, and it entered service with NASA in 1990 after undergoing modifications similar to those of the first aircraft. Between them, they carried every Space Shuttle from 1977 to 2012.

Spacecraft and satellite air launch

One possible mission for an airlifter adaptation not seriously considered in the early days of the space programme was that of air-launching spacecraft and satellites (a separate role from the air-launch of Intercontinental Ballistic Missiles, discussed in Chapter Seven). At the time it fitted none of the existing plans or priorities.

The NASA Shuttle Carrier proposals were aimed at the primary NASA mission of ferrying the Shuttle from one place to another, and with a secondary (initial) flight test role. They were not intended for air launching other than during the early glide test phase. The successful completion of the Shuttle Enterprise Approach and Landing Tests (ALT) in 1979 proved that upward deployment of an aerodynamic payload from the 747 was safe (within the well-controlled flight test environment).

By the 1980s, however, interest in the possibilities for adapting large aircraft to carry outsized loads above the dense lower atmosphere for air-launching of spacecraft became serious.

The Air Force impetus

This round of studies and concept exploration began in 1980 when the Air Force Rocket Propulsion Laboratory (AFRPL) outlined an 'Air Force Sortie Space System' (AFSSS) in a short document. The AFSSS had three major parts: a launch platform, drop tanks, and a Space Sortie Vehicle (SSV). The launch vehicle was to be a Boeing 747 with hydrogen-fuelled afterburners. To use the existing 747 as a basis for modification, the weight of the space vehicle, its drop tank(s) and the support equipment carried on-board could not exceed about 220,000lb (99,790kg). This eliminated the possibility of solid-fuelled rocket boosters.

The 747 carrier aircraft was to carry large Dewars (vacuum-insulated tanks) containing liquid hydrogen (LH_2) and liquid oxygen (LO_2). These were to be located in the mid-fuselage and would fill and replenish the orbiter's external and internal tanks before launch. They would also feed the 747's rocket engines or afterburners in those design variants.

The Air Force had been interested in a quick-reaction spacecraft (manned or not) since at least the early 1960s when the X-20 Dyna Soar was developed (and cancelled by Defense Secretary McNamara). As such, the SSV was recast as the Air Launch Sortie Vehicle (ALSV) and study contracts were issued by AFRPL to Pratt & Whitney and Rockwell. In 1981 the Air Force Flight Dynamics Laboratory (AFFDL) initiated an Advanced Military Spaceflight Capability (AMSC) Technology Identification Study as a broader study and survey of technologies and missions. The AMSC study preceded and ran concurrently with ALSV studies.

General Dynamics/ Convair concepts

After the initial Air Force concept became known, GD/Convair did a brief in-house study to determine the feasibility of the concept. The projected vehicle used an FDL-7 shape for the orbiter with two large external tanks. These were to be adapted from Atlas E missile tanks (approximately 60ft/18.2m long by 10ft/3.05m in diameter) and would be attached to the left and right sides of the orbiter.

The climb performance of the 747 launch aircraft was increased by fitting hydrogen-fuelled afterburners in the JT9D turbofans' bypass ducts. Thrust augmentation was projected to be up to 400% at altitude. The 747's vertical tail was removed and replaced by outrigger units mounted at the ends of the horizontal stabiliser (much like the ultimate C-133 external cargo carrier discussed earlier in this chapter).

Pratt & Whitney/Boeing concepts

In 1981 the Air Force Rocket Propulsion Laboratory (AFRPL) issued a contract to Pratt & Whitney to study the Air Launch Sortie Vehicle (ALSV), with P&W issuing a subcontract to Boeing for efforts that included designing a modified 747-200F as a launcher. The Pratt & Whitney study used a winged dart orbiter configuration powered by eight P&W RL-10 rocket motors as used on the Centaur upper stage, and the later McDonnell Douglas DC-X and DC-XA Single-Stage-To-Orbit (SSTO) conceptual test vehicles.

The Boeing 747 launch vehicle used a single RS-25 Space Shuttle Main Engine (SSME) mounted in the aft fuselage for added climb performance. Both engine types (RL-10 in the orbiter and RS-25) used common liquid hydrogen (LH_2) and liquid oxygen (LO_2 or LOX). The SSME on the 747 was later replaced by a cluster of five RL-10s, which were lighter, less expensive, offered greater throttling, and had far better pre-start conditioning times. The 747's projected climb angle was up to 60°.

BELOW Sponsored by the Air Force Rocket Propulsion Laboratory, this concept was developed by Pratt & Whitney with Boeing as subcontractor.
Via Scott Lowther/APR

Boeing 747 launch aircraft - rocket engine options

Installed Engine	Thrust rating	Thrust range	Weight	Comments
Pratt & Whitney RL-10 A-3	14,747lbf (65.60kN) (25,000lbf/111.21kN planned)	2,500lbf (11.12kN)* to 125,000lbf (556.03kN)**	664lb (301kg)	LR-10A-3 demonstrated throttling to about 10% of rated thrust
Rocketdyne RS-25	418,000lbf (1,860kN)	280,000lbf (1,245.5kN) to 418,000lbf (1859.36kN)	7,775lb (3,515kg)	Throttled to about 67% of rated thrust

* Minimum thrust: one engine of five in cluster operating at minimum throttle
** Maximum thrust: all five engines operating at maximum throttle
Both engines are classed as 'cryogenic engines' using LH_2 and LO_2

RIGHT Boeing's detailed air launch concept initially had the 747's performance boosted by a single RS-25 Space Shuttle Main Engine mounted in the aft fuselage. Only the two outboard ALSV engines would fire at launch to avoid damaging the 747's vertical tail. *Via Scott Lowther/APR*

Rockwell concepts

Inspired by the Minuteman air-launch tests in 1974, Rockwell engineers devised an air-launch system based on a Lockheed C-5. The orbiter used the FDL-5A shape and configuration developed by the Air Force Flight Dynamics Laboratory (AFFDL). However, Rockwell's use of the 747 for the Space Shuttle soon presented a much less confining launch solution allowing larger orbiters. Rockwell had multiple orbiter shapes under study, allowing for optimisation for differing missions and performance.

In general, the dart-like FDL-x orbiter shapes offered superior high-Mach re-entry performance (needed for some missions) at the cost of much greater structural heating. The lower internal volume of those designs also made fitting larger components inside the vehicles, such as the crew compartment and fuel tanks, much more difficult. Orbiters with Space Shuttle-like delta wing planforms and bulky rounded shapes offered better packaging for internal equipment, lower re-entry heating and better subsonic performance with more benign landing characteristics. As with most things in aerospace, form tended to follow function.

One of Rockwell's crewed orbiter designs used a forward-mounted external fuel tank. The 747 was fitted with a V-tail to avoid the exhaust plume from the orbiter's rocket engines. Rockwell also looked at an even more exotic idea involving an air-cushioned sled powered by jet engines. This approach allowed the spacccraft to have smaller wings and lighter landing gear than a more conventional take-off approach.

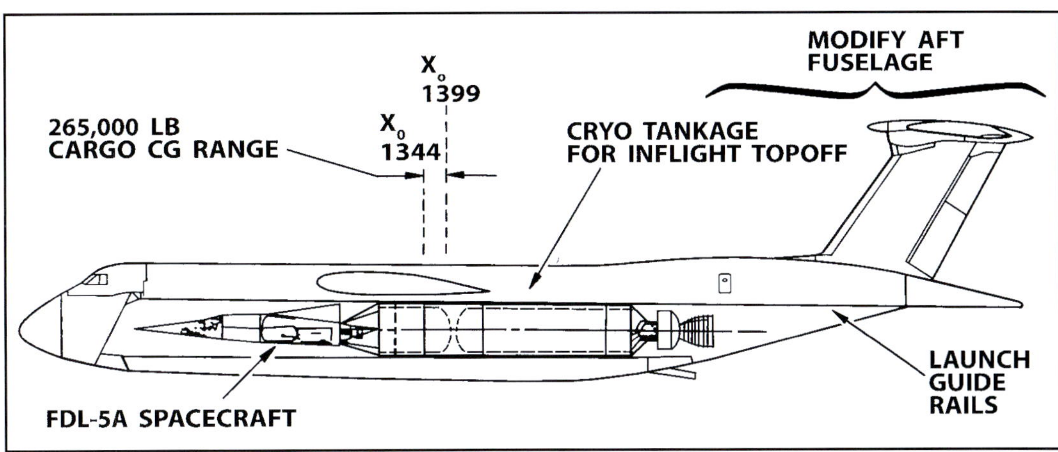

RIGHT The initial Rockwell spacecraft launch vehicle used a modified C-5A Galaxy. *Via Scott Lowther/APR*

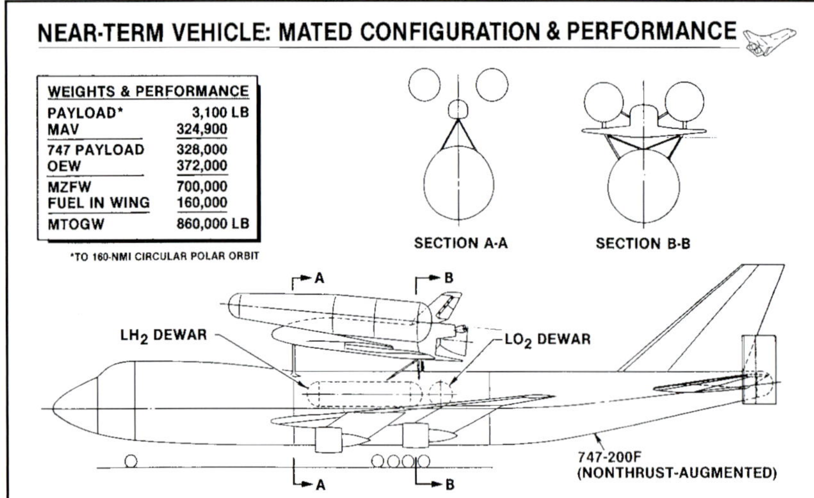

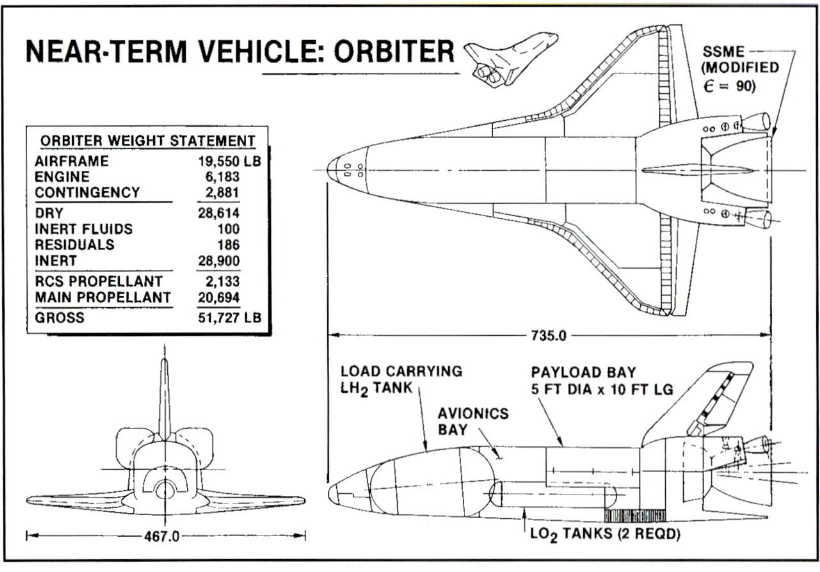

LEFT A later Rockwell launch concept was the 747 fitted with a V-tail to avoid damage from a twin tailed, crewed 'Near Term Vehicle', seen here with three main engines. *Via Scott Lowther/APR*

MIDDLE An early 1982 Rockwell concept (outlined in the AMSC study) proposed launching a small orbiter from an 'unaugmented' Boeing 747. Derived from the Space Shuttle planform and aerodynamics, this orbiter used a single modified Rocketdyne RS-25 Space Shuttle Main Engine (SSME). Two external fuel tanks flank the orbiter (as was also proposed by General Dynamics/Convair). *Author collection*

BOTTOM This uncrewed orbiter design was part of Rockwell's AMSC study of 1983. Eventually a smaller, much-modified design went into orbit as the Air Force's X-37B. Sized to fit in a Space Shuttle payload bay, the X-37B was carried aloft not by a 747 or a Shuttle, but by an expendable launch vehicle (five missions with the Atlas V, and one with the partially reusable Falcon 9). First launched in 2010, X-37B was now a Boeing product as that company purchased Rockwell's defence and aerospace units in 1996. *Author collection*

Orbital Sciences X-34 and L-1011 'Stargazer' (1999)

In 1992, Orbital Sciences (later Orbital ATK, then Northrop Grumman Innovation Systems) modified an airliner to launch its Pegasus XL rockets. The eighteen-year-old Lockheed L-1011-100 TriStar (named 'Stargazer') had been flown by Air Canada and Air Lanka, and was reconfigured by Marshall of Cambridge (Engineering) Ltd. A belly-mount configuration was used, as launch from the top of the fuselage would cause issues with the tail-mounted engine, and a 'drop' launch was more appropriate for the solid rocket-powered Pegasus XL. With numerous successful launches under its belt, the aircraft was adapted to launch NASA's X-34 winged research rocket, before that programme was cancelled in 2001. However, by the mid-1990s advances in technology allowed a much more ambitious approach.

ABOVE Orbital Science's converted Lockeed L-1011 'Stargazer' furthered the concept of using a modified airliner as a launch aircraft. It is seen here on 29 June 1999 taking NASA's X-34 aloft for its first captive flight at Edwards AFB. The aircraft is still in service today (after several corporate mergers) with Northrop Grumman Innovation Systems. *NASA photo by Tom Tschida*

The descendants of Virtus

The twin-hulled SCA proposals of the 1970s, such as the Boeing 747 or Lockheed C-5, and especially Conroy's Virtus, had configurations well suited to possible adaptation as launch platforms. Even so, that was not the mission under consideration at the time. Indeed, if it was, such a grandiose proposal might well be viewed as overly ambitious. Technological advances in the intervening decades, however, made the building of one-off (or limited production) large space vehicle launch aircraft technically feasible and economically viable. One factor was the reduction in the size of rockets capable of achieving orbital speeds. Another (and arguably the most important) was the introduction of new materials and construction techniques, together with advances in computational aerodynamics. The increased demand for satellite launch facilities, together with the growing commercial interest in private space flight, added further impetus for such a design.

The resulting projects – and flying aircraft – have made the proposals of yesterday seem comparatively mundane.

Scaled Composites/ Mojave Aerospace Ventures Model 318 'White Knight'

The first venture in terms of offering private space flight was a joint project between Burt Rutan's Scaled Composites and Microsoft co-founder Paul Allen's Mojave Aerospace Ventures. The carrier aircraft or 'mother ship' was known as 'White Knight' and the passenger-carrying spacecraft as 'SpaceShipOne'. It completed its first manned private spaceflight in 2004 and in that same year won the $10 million Ansari X Prize. While an impressive achievement, it should be recognised that the aircraft was only capable of a brief sub-orbital flight, reaching a speed of just over Mach 3 and an altitude of 367,360ft (112,000m).

BELOW Scaled Composite's Model 318 'White Knight' taxis in at Edwards AFB with a Northrop Grumman 'Natural Laminar Flow' test fixture under the fuselage. *Author photo*

ABOVE Scaled Composites' Model 348 'White Knight Two' was built for Virgin Galactic to launch 'SpaceShipTwo' into sub-orbital flight. *Photo © Chad Slattery*

Scaled Composites/Virgin Galactic Model 339 'White Knight Two'

Scaled Composites' successor to 'White Knight' is 'White Knight Two', built for Virgin Galactic, which first flew in December 2008. While primarily designed to carry 'SpaceShipTwo', a six-passenger sub-orbital manned vehicle, it is also intended as a multi-purpose high-altitude aircraft, including the capability to launch satellites. There is also the suggestion that in combination with 'SpaceShipTwo', it might provide a means of suborbital high-speed point-to-point travel. It is reported that the follow-up development will have orbital capability.

The first flights are all allocated to its launch customer, Virgin Galactic. The programme suffered a setback in 2014 when the high-drag re-entry configuration was reportedly selected out of sequence during flight, resulting in the loss of life of one of the two pilots. When the first commercial flights will take place is not clear, but there is apparently a long list of confirmed bookings.

Scaled Composites/ Stratolaunch Systems Model 351 'Roc'

Perhaps most significantly, a newly formed company named Stratolaunch rolled out its first carrier aircraft on 11 May 2017. With a configuration similar to the twin-fuselage proposals described above as potential shuttle carriers, it dwarfs those earlier designs. Indeed, in terms of span (385ft /117m) it is the largest aircraft ever flown. Powered by six P&W PW4056 turbofans, each with 56,750lb (252.44kN) thrust, it has a loaded weight of more than 1,300,000lb (589,670kg), including the fully fuelled launch vehicle, and requires a runway length of at least 12,000ft (3,700m). Some parts of the aircraft (notably the cockpits) have been repurposed from two Boeing 747s, but the primary structures have been built from composite materials.

The aircraft was the brainchild of Paul Allen (a co-founder of Microsoft), who sadly died before the project was completed. Dubbed the 'Roc,' the aircraft made its first flight on 13 April 2019 in honour of his vision. At the time of this writing the Paul G. Allen Trust is reorganising its operations,

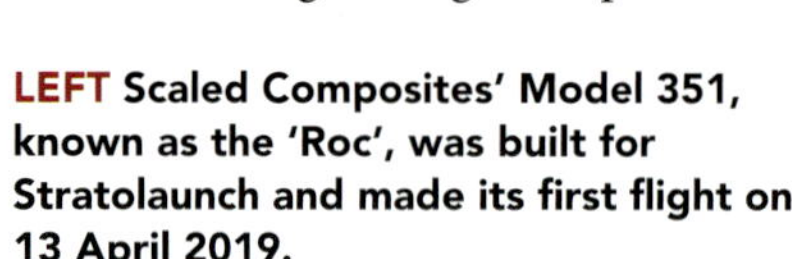

LEFT Scaled Composites' Model 351, known as the 'Roc', was built for Stratolaunch and made its first flight on 13 April 2019.
Photo by Kane Wickham – kanewickham.com

Scaled Composites models	Model 318 'White Knight'	Model 348 'White Knight Two'	Model 351 Stratolaunch 'Roc'
Powerplant	2 x GE J85-GE-5 turbojets @ 2,400lb (10.68kN) thrust, 3,600lb (16.01kN) afterburning	4 x P&W PW 308 turbofans @ 6,900lb (30.69kN) thrust	6 x P&W 4056 turbofans @ 56,750lb (252.44kN) thrust
Span	83ft (25.30m)	141ft 1in (43.0m)	385ft (117.35m)
Length	n/a	78ft 1in (23.8m)	238ft (72.54m)
Height	n/a	25ft 0in (7.62m)	50ft (50.24m)
Ceiling	53,000ft (16,154m)		
Max payload	7,000lb (3,175kg)	37,000lb (16,783kg)	500,000lb (226,796kg)
Empty weight	n/a	n/a	500,000lb (226,796kg)
Max gross weight	n/a	n/a	1,300,000lb (589,670kg)

making it likely that another entity will need to carry the project forward if it is to be an operational satellite launching service. As with so many other projects described in this book, operational success is determined by far more than just the soundness of the proposition or the execution of the design.

Conroy's legacy: 'Guppies' redux

Thc original Conroy 'Guppy' programme opened a whole new role for outsized cargo transportation that continues today. Airbus, in line with its international origins and structure, operates with a multinational manufacturing and assembly philosophy. This means transporting major components, such as wings or fuselages, between factories in different countries.

In the early 1970s Airbus acquired two 'Super Guppy' turbines to transport such parts to the final assembly facility in Toulouse. These proved highly effective in their role, and in 1982 and 1983 two additional aircraft were built by Union de Transports Aériens Industries (UTA) in France, after Airbus bought the rights to produce them. In the 1990s the company decided that it needed to replace the four 'Super Guppies' and looked at the potential for converting various airframes, including the Antonov An-124, Antonov An-225, Illyushin Il-86, Boeing 747, Boeing 767, and Lockheed C-5 and C-17.

Airbus eventually decided to construct a purpose-built aircraft based on the company's existing wide-body twin-engined A300-600R. The resulting vehicle became known as the Super Transporter, then Airbus Beluga, reflecting its whale-like appearance. Five such aircraft were built, the last being delivered in 1999. While its payload capacity is far below that of the C-5B (103,617lb/47,000kg as opposed to 281,001lb/127,460kg), the Beluga's enormous cargo hold volume gives it a unique advantage when it comes to transporting outsized cargo. Apart from their primary role within Airbus, the aircraft were also made available for charter, which involved transporting items like modules for the International Space Station, thus taking the concept back to its origins.

Faced with global transportation needs for manufacturing the 787 Dreamliner, Boeing commissioned the conversion of a total of three (later four) used 747-400s in October 2003. Formally named the 747-400LCF (Large Cargo Freighter), the Dreamlifter's fuselage was slightly lengthened, and the new upper fuselage was enlarged to 27ft 6in (8.38m) wide. Maximum take-off weight is 803,001lb (364,235kg), and cargo loading is through a swing-tail.

In 2013 Airbus decided to replace its five Belugas (based on the A300-600) with a new aircraft with even greater capacity. After studies it decided to base this on the larger A330-200 and -300. The first of five aircraft, known as the Beluga XL, flew on 19 July 2018. Maximum take-off weight is 500,449lb (227,000kg), and loading is via a lift-up 'visor' door above a repositioned and lowered cockpit.

The current giant Airbus and Boeing aircraft are a long way removed from Jack Conroy's first converted Stratocruiser, but the concept's line of development is a continuous one. There are surely further generations to come.

Adaptations of airlifters in perspective

The pressures of the American Space Programme inevitably looked at ways in which the newly developed large airlifters could be adapted to support it. The early possibilities of transporting outsized components produced some imaginative solutions, but none of the more radical proposals led anywhere. Instead, it was to be Conroy's conversion of the Stratocruiser – the first of the 'Guppies' – that was to open up a path of development that is still being extended today, not just for the original purpose of carrying large space vehicle components, but also for transporting aircraft subassemblies to facilitate multi-site manufacturing.

However, the most significant adaptation was not one of the early mission concepts, but a new possibility altogether: using airlifters as launch vehicles. Here was another area – as with many of those that have been described in this book – where ambition had to wait for technology to catch up.

BELOW Using a Boeing 747 as a space launch vehicle remained a concept until 2019 when Virgin Orbit released an inert launcher in a test. The climb angle of the 747 harkens back to the Boeing and Rockwell launch concepts of the 1980s. *Virgin Orbit*

Chapter Nine
The Once and Future Hercules
Capable variations on a theme

ABOVE As well as enlarging the Hercules, Lockheed planned a lightweight twin-engine version of the aircraft that was less expensive to operate. *Lockheed*

In 1951 the Lockheed C-130 emerged as the winner – by a narrow margin – of a competition for a new medium airlifter (a story told in *American Secret Projects 2*). When the prototype first flew on 23 April 1954, it looked like what it was: a solid, workmanlike response to a clearly specified requirement of the day. It was one of the first aircraft designed from the outset as a military transport, and as such took advantage of the lessons learned from the Second World War. It featured a high-wing configuration and a loading ramp, and had good rough-field capability. In short, nothing about its plain appearance indicated that it would become the most successful military transport in history.

Not only has the Hercules been in continuous production ever since (a record for any military aircraft) but its basic design has also undergone multiple developments to extend its capabilities. This history is well known; less familiar are the numerous paper proposals that never flew, or the various experiments in which the C-130 participated.

ABOVE The six-engined NC-130B is seen in slow flight over the NASA Ames Research Center. With Boundary Layer Control, the flaps are set at 90°, causing a characteristic nose-down flight attitude. Ailerons are drooped to the 30° positions as well. *NASA*

STOL C-130s: The NC-130B BLC/STOL test bed

In the late 1950s the Air Force issued a General Operational Requirement (GOR-130), specifying the need for an airlifter able to carry 20,000lb (9,072kg) for 1,000nmi (1852km) with a 500ft (152m) take-off and landing length at mid-mission. Lockheed design studies began in 1956 and resulted in an Air Force contract for an experimental aircraft in 1958. To this end engineers responded by adding two extra engines to the newly designated NC-130B, not to augment thrust but to provide bleed air for a Boundary Layer Control (BLC) system. The Air Force dropped the project in 1959 due to limited research and development funds, but Lockheed continued development with company funding, resulting in its C-130C STOL proposal.

Early designs for the BLC system used pairs of Fairchild J83-R-1 pod-mounted engines under each outer wing to produce the high-pressure air. After the cancellation of the J83 programme, Allison YT56-A-6 (Model 501-C5) prototype engines replaced them. These were a unique version of the T56 engine originally developed for the cancelled McDonnell XHCH-1 helicopter, with a standard T56 power section driving a Model 501-D2 compressor section instead of a propeller. The compressed air was then ducted to the flaps, ailerons, elevators and the extended-chord rudder. Designers predicted that the system would reduce the NC-130B's take-off and approach speeds from 80-100kt to 50-70kt (148-185km/h to 93-70km/h).

RIGHT Clamshell doors closed to cover the YT-56-A-6 BLC supply engine intakes in normal flight to reduce drag. Even so, top speed was reduced by about 10kt (18.5km/h). *NASA*

The NC-130B first flew on 8 February 1960 at the Lockheed factory at Marietta, Georgia, and after initial test flights operations moved to the Lockheed site at Palmdale, California. NASA's Ames Research Center for STOL Studies subsequently flew the test bed on additional research flights. After a successful and productive test programme, NASA restored its original configuration and in June 1968 took permanent possession of it as an Earth Resources Technology Satellite sensor test bed.

For the production C-130C, Lockheed proposed that the BLC air be supplied by a pair of much lighter Continental Model 365-17 (YJ69-T-35) engines, described as an 'air pump' variant of the J69 small turbojet. However, the Army and Air Force declined participation in the project, while the Air Force apparently chose to pursue true VTOL capability with the CX-6 programme.

Lockheed-Georgia Advanced Assault C-130J weights	
C-130E weight empty (pylon tanks removed)	67,729lb (30,721kg)
C-130J Assault/STOL additional weight	6,625lb (3,005kg)
C-130J weight empty (pylon tanks removed)	74,354lb (33,726kg)
Maximum take-off weight	155,000lb (70,300kg)
War emergency take-off weight	175,000lb (79,380kg)
Maximum landing weight, paved or rough fields	155,000lb (70,300kg)

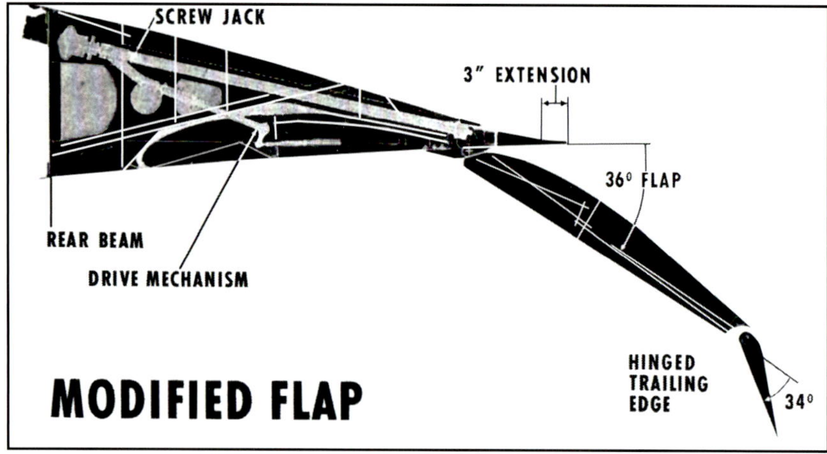

ABOVE A double-articulated flap, with a trailing edge that deflected a total of 70°, replaced the standard unit. *Lockheed*

C-130J Advanced Assault Hercules

In response to combat reports from Vietnam, Lockheed proposed the Advanced Assault/STOL C-130 Hercules in April 1966, provisionally called the C-130J. Derived from the C-130E, it was optimised for the rough-field assault mission.

To enhance STOL performance, engineers made significant changes to the basic design's flight control systems and instrumentation. They increased the aileron chord by 30%, providing great roll control, and enlarged the rudder chord by 40% for improved directional stability (the larger rudder having first flown on the NC-130B). The C-130 power-boosted system for aileron and rudder controls would be replaced by a fully powered system. Additionally, Lockheed re-indexed the elevator, increasing down travel by 5°.

BELOW The Lockheed C-130J Advanced Assault/STOL proposed in 1966 had high-capacity landing gear and oversized sponsons. *Lockheed*

The existing single-slotted flap added a new hinged trailing edge segment that provided a full aerodynamic 50° of flap for increased take-off lift, lower stall speeds, and more positive control on approach. Lockheed would reintroduce and improve on this double-slotted flap system for follow-on C-130 proposals through to the 1990s.

A new wide-stance landing gear with much larger wheels and tyres allowed the C-130J to land on unimproved fields strewn with 10in (25.4cm) rocks, stumps, holes, or gullies, at a sink rate of more than 540fpm (165m/min). New, double-acting, high-energy-absorbing shock struts provided up to 25in (63.5cm) of vertical wheel motion. The large tyres promised a major improvement in flotation characteristics; their 6ft (1.83m) increase in tread width improved ground roll and handling stability. New high-energy disc brakes were synchronised with the fully modulated anti-skid system to yield better braking under all conditions.

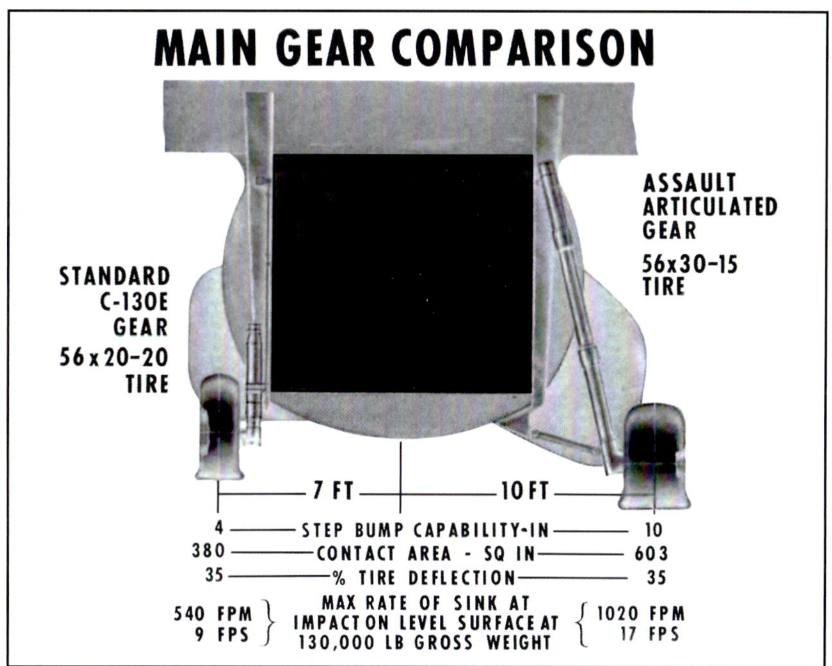

ABOVE A comparison of the C-130J's new main landing gear, which nearly doubled the maximum sink rate capability. *Lockheed*

BELOW A comparison of the first-generation Hercules stretches. The L-100-30 built on the 100in (254cm) stretch and added another 180in (457cm). *Lockheed*

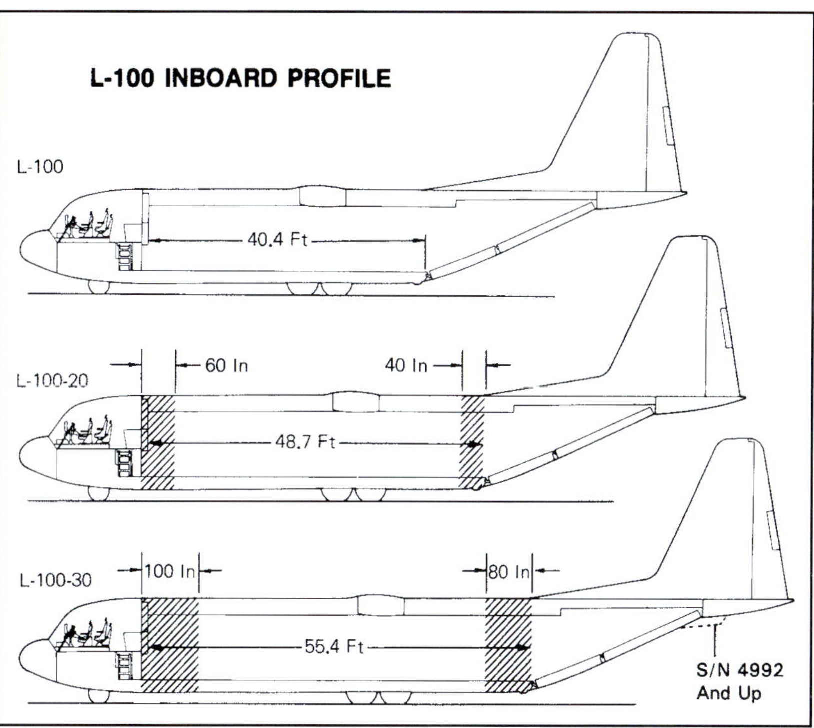

Commercial stretched C-130s

While never matching its success as a military airlifter (the C-130 was sold to around eighty air forces outside the US), the Hercules appealed far more to the commercial freight market than did any other airlifter. And ironically the variants aimed at civil operators often led to further versions of the military aircraft.

Lockheed's first approach to the civil market was the GL-207 'Super Hercules' (described in *American Secret Projects 2*). Provisional orders by Pan American and Slick Airways in 1959 seemed to promise a successful launch, but their subsequent cancellations kept the design from ever progressing beyond project stage. Lockheed bounced back with the L-100, a straightforward, freight-carrying commercial offering based on the C-130E. Without the need to meet military specs, Lockheed was able to increase the aircraft's maximum payload. The resulting design's rugged construction, good short-field performance, minimal ground handling requirements and easy loading/unloading facilities made it suitable for widespread global operations. The L-100 first took to the air on 20 April 1964.

Lockheed eventually built twenty-one L-100s. They proved effective in service, but carriers grappled with space limitations. Since commercial freight tends to be less dense than military cargo, loaders frequently filled up the available fuselage space before reaching the maximum possible take-off weight. Engineers responded by lengthening the fuselage by 100in (254cm), yielding a 20% increase in internal volume/floor space; they also incorporated Allison 500-D22A engines that produced an 11% power increase and a 6% increase in cruise speed. Designated the L100-20, the stretched aircraft entered service in 1968. Twenty-six were built, and nine L-100s were subsequently converted to the same standard. However, the main commercial version of the Hercules was the subsequent, further stretched Model L-100-30, which first flew in 1970. This added another 80in (203cm) in length, which gave it a 36% increase in cargo volume compared with the original L-100.

These stretched versions of the aircraft became the building blocks for future military development, with the C-130H becoming the lengthened C-130H-30. The modification reduced the maximum payload from 42,673lb to 38,900lb (19,373kg to 17,661kg), to compensate for the added fuselage weight, but substantially increased cargo volume by 37% from 3,675sq ft to 5,020sq ft (342m^2 to 526m^2). This increase allowed it to carry seven rather than five 463L pallets, or to accommodate ninety-two as opposed to sixty-four paratroops.

The Royal Air Force also modified twenty of its in-service C-130Ks, lengthening the fuselage by the same amount and designating the result the C-Mk3 Hercules.

When production of the L-100-30 ended in 1992, Lockheed had produced a total of 114 civil freighters. An updated civil variant of the C-130J-30 was proposed but put on hold in 2000. However, in February 2014 Lockheed Martin announced the relaunch of what had become the LM-100J programme with deliveries due to start in 2019, continuing the intertwined relationship between civil and military developments of this remarkably long-lived aeroplane.

HOW? The 'Hercules On Water' amphibian

Begun in 1964, the HOW concept explored the feasibility of developing a basic C-130E aircraft into an amphibian. It was further developed in 1968 by the Advanced Concepts Department of the Lockheed-Georgia Company under US Navy Contract N00019-68-C-0129, issued by the Naval Air Systems Command.

Modifying the C-130E to the HOW configuration included adding a hull to the underside of the aircraft and auxiliary floats beneath the wings, and relocating the engines to the top of the wing. However, its signature feature was a retractable single hydro-ski. Aeronautical engineers had investigated hydro-skis for the previous fifteen years with models and in Navy-sponsored full-scale tests with the Convair XF2Y Sea Dart. These tests had shown the following advantages:

On take-off:

- a Shorter run
- b Reduced wave impact
- c Hull lift-out (thereby reducing loads) at about 55 knots
- d Less time in spray
- e A positive nose-up force that reduced the tendency to 'porpoise'

On landing:

- a Reduced impact loads
- b Hull contact at slower speed
- c Minimised 'heave'
- d Reduced tendency to skip or porpoise

The C-130's high-wing design was particularly amenable to conversion as an amphibian. The major modification was adding a hull to the lower fuselage.

BELOW The 'Hercules On Water' (HOW) amphibian model form. *Lockheed*

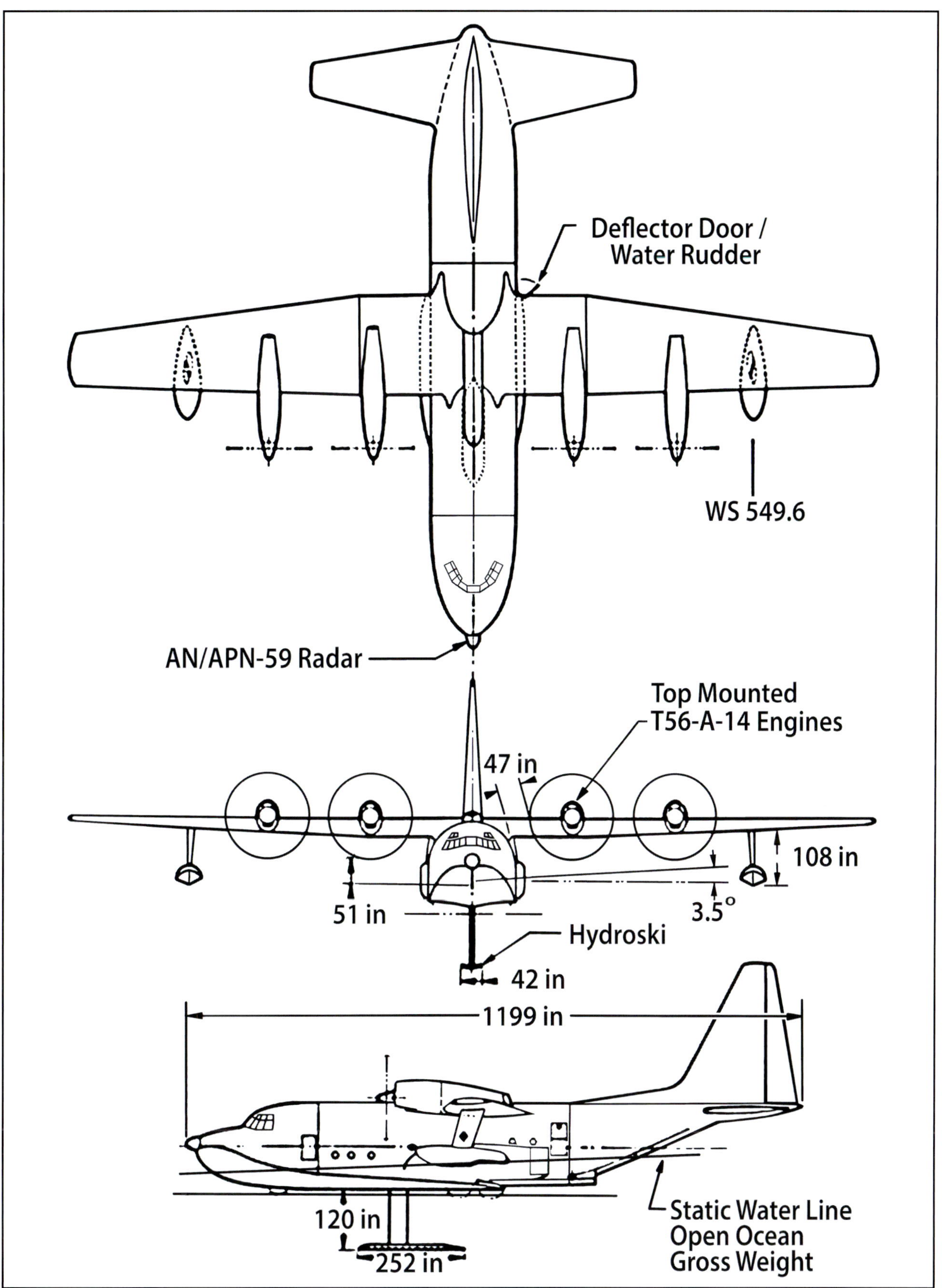

ABOVE General arrangement of the Hercules HOW, showing the revised powerplant installation that raised the engines and propellers out of the water spray pattern. *Lockheed*

Lockheed HOW ('Hercules On Water') amphibian	
Powerplant	4 x Allison T56-A-14 turboprops @ 4,591shp (3,424kW)
Wingspan	132ft 7in (40.41m)
Length	100ft 10in (30.75m)
Max TOW	155,000lb (70,307kg)
Max payload	36,250lb (16,443kg)
Cruise speed	345mph (555km/h)
Ferry range	3,736nmi (6,920km)

The Navy's interest in an amphibian may well have been driven by the retirement of the Martin P5M Marlin – the Navy's last patrol seaplane – at around that time. The C-130's proposed seagoing configuration certainly made it an attractive candidate. Lockheed was also promoting the HOW for commercial service; airlines operating it between New York and Boston, for example, could eliminate the delay incurred at out-of-town regional airports. Nonetheless, the proposed aircraft failed to secure any orders from either the military or commercial customers.

Lockheed C-130 alternatives to AMST

Shut out of the 1972 AMST competition, as described in Chapter Five, Lockheed-Georgia offered a series of unsolicited proposals to the Department of Defense while the AMST prototypes were being built and tested. These, the company claimed in 1979, could meet the bulk of the specified AMST requirements at lower cost than the Boeing and McDonnell Douglas aircraft. Lockheed reported that a full-scale development programme for either the VLS or the WBS could cost about $500 million.

Lockheed-Georgia C-130SS (Stretch STOL)

The first proposal, submitted in late 1975, pitched a stretched STOL version of the C-130H Hercules. Formally known as the C-130 Option IV, the 'C-130SS (Stretch/STOL)' modifications included lengthening the fuselage by 100in (254cm), identical to the L-100-20 commercial version of the C-130. Additionally, the new aircraft would feature a stronger wing; double-slotted Fowler flaps, larger ailerons and rudder; an enlarged dorsal fin; new horizontal fins ('horsals'); and spoilers to improve roll control at low speeds. Other refinements included a universal refuelling receptacle atop the crown of the fuselage, aft of the cockpit, and stronger landing gear to increase the touchdown sink rate from 9fps (2.74m/s) to 15fps (4.6m/s).

Both the Air Force and Boeing disputed Lockheed's claims that the aircraft could meet virtually all of the AMST demands, and there is no evidence that the proposal inclined the Air Force to change course. And when the service subsequently added the requirement that AMST be capable of accommodating the XM-1 (later M1A1) tank, it eliminated any chance that Lockheed could ever adapt the standard C-130; the company then moved on by developing the C-130 VLS and C-130 WBS.

About a year after pitching the unsuccessful C-130SS, Lockheed offered two radically modified versions of the Hercules: the VLS (Volume-Loadability-Speed) and the WBS (Wide-Body STOL). Each offered a different approach to upgrading the Hercules's capabilities.

Lockheed-Georgia C-130 VLS (Volume-Loadability-Speed)

The VLS version would create a faster, longer-range aircraft with an increased cargo volume. Much of the performance increase was due to the new Detroit Diesel Allison Model 501-M71 engine. This powerplant would develop 5,575eshp (4,159kW), an increase of 1,375shp (1,026kW) over the Allison T56-A-15 used on the C-130H then in production. The average cruising speed would increase from 351mph (565kph) to 414mph (666kph). In addition to being larger and faster than the C-130H, the VLS would provide a 21% improvement in fuel economy in high-speed cruise, and a 9% improvement in long-range cruise. Under certain conditions, this could have extended the unrefuelled range by as much as 33%.

BELOW The C-130SS (Stretch/STOL) was based on the L-100-20's stretch, with added features such as the inflight refuelling receptacle, and dorsal and 'horsal' tail extensions. Lockheed also marketed it as the C-130 Option IV. *Author collection*

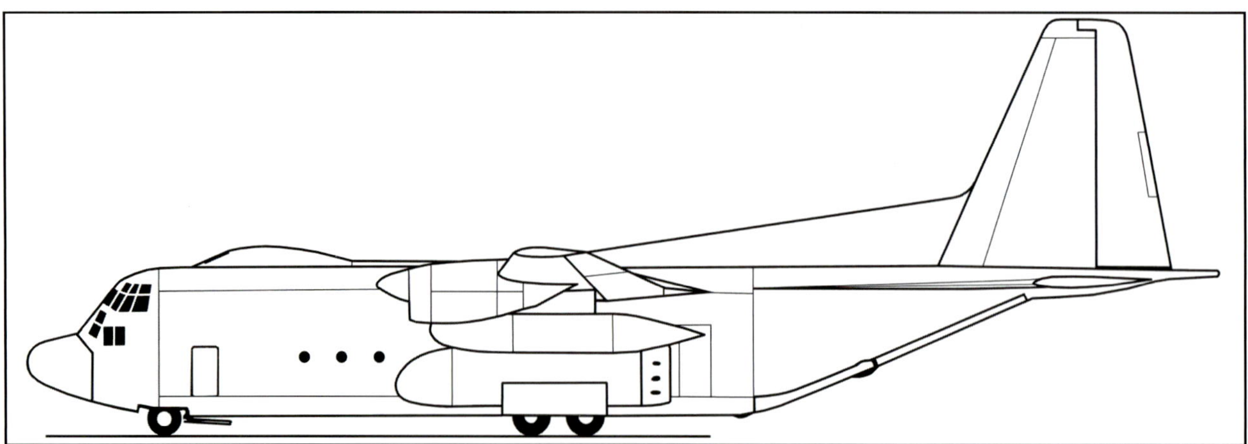

The VLS redesign increased the overall cargo box volume by 33%, compared with the baseline C-130H, by lengthening and widening the compartment. Drawing on the company's C-141 and C-5 experience, Lockheed designers reshaped the aft fuselage to reduce drag and gave the empennage a T-tail configuration that increased its effectiveness while further reducing drag. Finally, they made the cargo door/ramp opening 18in (45.7cm) wider for easier loading and unloading. Lockheed asserted that the C-130 VLS could accommodate 91% of the equipment of an Army Mechanised Infantry Brigade.

ABOVE The Lockheed C-130 VLS derivative. *Lockheed*

Lockheed-Georgia C-130 WBS (Wide-Body STOL)

The second development, the C-130 WBS, attempted to better align the C-130 with the AMST requirements. Although the requirements for the WBS were directed more towards rear area airfields, its design incorporated most of the VLS features associated with STOL and austere field operation.

Lockheed C-130 VLS (Volume-Loadability-Speed)

Powerplant	4 x Allison 501-M71 turboprops @ 5,575eshp (4,159kW)	
Cargo box	**C-130 VLS**	**Compared to C-130H**
Length	45.83ft (14.70m)	+180in (4.57m)
Width	10ft 8.75in (3.60m)	+4.75in (0.121m)
Height	9ft (3.27m)	No change
Max payload	68,000lb (30,840kg)	+23,000lb (10,430kg)
Max TOW	191,000lb (86,640kg)	

BELOW The enlarged C-130 WBS (Wide-Body STOL). *Lockheed*

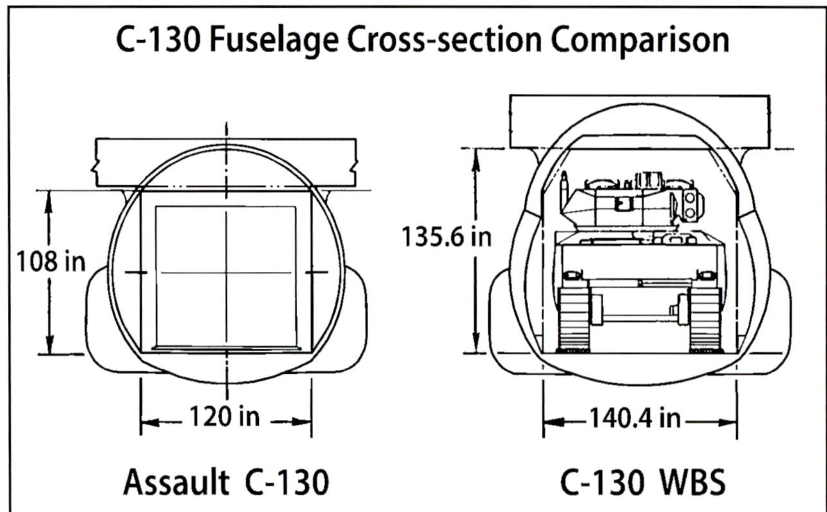

ABOVE Comparison of the C-130H and C-130 WBS fuselage cross sections. *Lockheed*

C-130 WBS (Wide-Body STOL)		
Powerplant	4 x Allison T56-A-15 turboprops @ 4,591eshp (3424kW)	
Cargo box	**C-130 WBS**	**Compared to C-130H**
Length	48.1ft (14.7m)	+200in (2.03m)
Width	11.7ft (3.6m)	+19in (0.48m)
Height	11.3ft (3.4 m)	+28in (0.71m)
Max payload	68,000lb (30,840kg)	+23,000lb (10,430kg)
Max TOW	191,000lb (86,640kg)	

Lockheed began the basic C-130's redesign by first lengthening the fuselage to incorporate a larger 'cargo box,' making its capacity generally equivalent to the civil model L-100-20. By splitting the fuselage horizontally and enlarging the lower lobe, the WBS would gain enough added height and width to carry 95% of an Army Mechanised Infantry Brigade's (MIB) equipment, excepting only the main battle tanks.

Lockheed's second group of modifications drew on the company's previous STOL experience with the C-130SS. Engineers added a larger-chord rudder, a larger dorsal fin, roll-control spoilers, compound double-slotted flaps to replace the single-piece Fowler flaps, landing gear improvements, and a flush-mounted aerial-refuelling receptacle above the cockpit. With a 27,000lb (12,250kg) payload at 3.0G load factor, the WBS could land in a distance of 1,810 feet (553m), bringing it into compliance with the AMST field-length requirements.

Despite Lockheed's design and marketing efforts, none of the C-130 proposals were accepted as an alternative to the AMST programme. The engineering effort was not wasted, however; as many of the product improvements were well defined and available for future customer requirements.

BELOW The Assault and WBS C-130 designs resurfaced in late 1984, promoted by Lockheed and General Electric. The aircraft would have been powered by four GE34 turboprops based on the compressor and hot section of the TF34 turbofan that powered the A-10 and S-3 aircraft. The powerplant was projected to be rated at 8,800shp (6,562kW). *Lockheed*

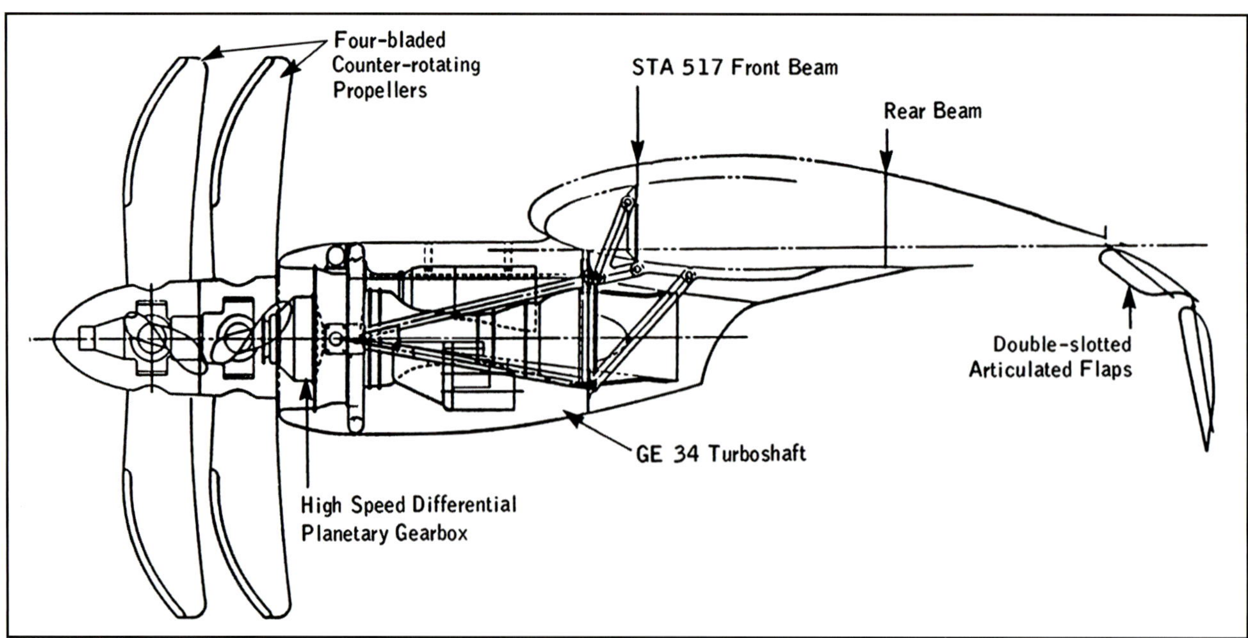

North American Rockwell (Columbus Division) NA-382 (C-130 conversion)

ABOVE Rockwell concept art of the NR-382 making a vertical landing to supply a forward operating base. Rockwell FV-12 fighter-attack aircraft are in the background. *Author collection*

Lockheed was not the only company interested in increasing the C-130's capabilities. One mid-1970s proposal came from North American Rockwell. Its V/STOL NA-382 incorporated the C-130 fuselage and tail, and looked to replace or supplement the existing Marine Corps C/KC-130F fleet by giving the Hercules a V/STOL performance compatible with the AV-8A Harrier V/STOL attack aircraft then entering service. The NA-382 would retain the C/KC-130 capabilities and use the existing KC-130F in-flight refuelling pods.

Much like the Bell and Lockheed AMST demonstrator test beds, the proposed vehicle retained the C-130 fuselage, possibly cannibalising existing USMC KC-130F aircraft as donors. A new structure with a 19% thick supercritical airfoil replaced the existing wing. VTOL performance relied on thrust augmentation generated by the exhaust flow from its GE F101 low-bypass turbofan engines. The exhaust exited through swing-out wing panels, where the static air would mix with the high-energy flow from the engines, amplifying the thrust. Using Navy funding, Rockwell International was also researching this concept with the company's ill-fated XFV-12A V/STOL fighter prototype.

Estimates for the two-prototype aircraft development programme ran to $100 million, covering only the retrofit of the augmenter propulsion system. Government-furnished airframes, engines and other equipment were not included in the cost. Programme plans called for building an additional twelve aircraft.

BELOW General arrangement of the NA-382, converted from the Lockheed C-130. *North American Rockwell*

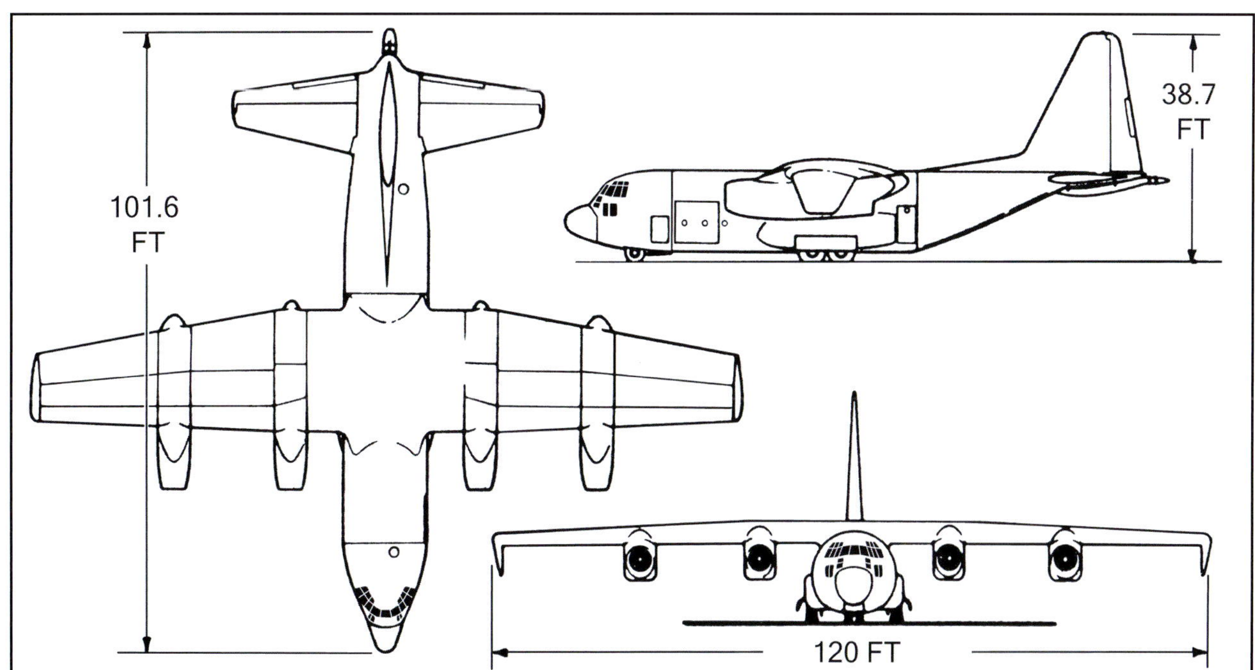

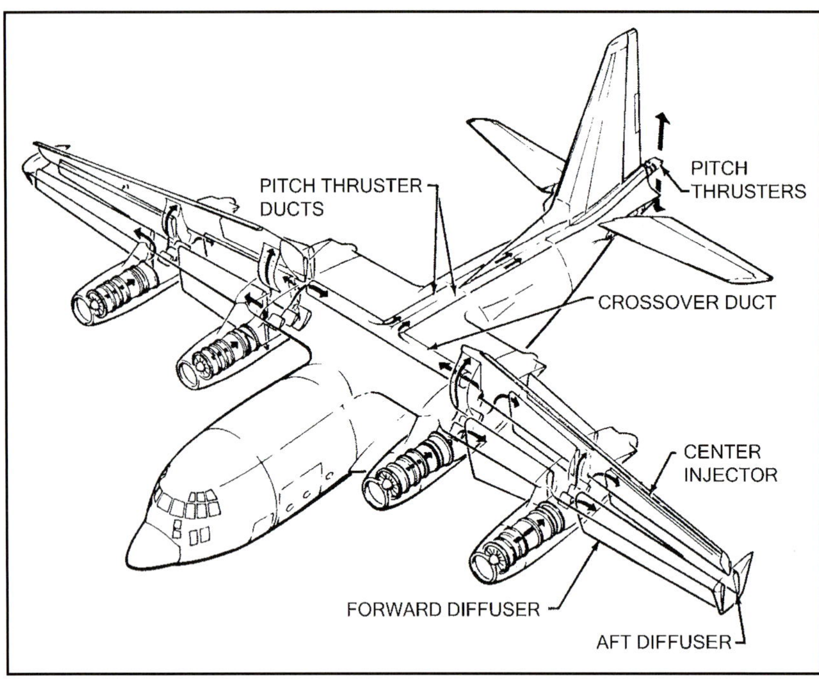

ABOVE An illustration of the jet flow into the thrust augmentation surfaces of the NA-382 wing, positioned for VTOL flight. *North American Rockwell*

North American Rockwell NA-382	
Powerplant	4 x GE F101-GE-100 'modified-afterburning' turbofans (alternatively P&W F401 turbofans)
Wingspan	120ft (36.58m)
Length	101.6ft (30.97m)
Height	38.7ft (11.80m)
Max TOW	175,000lb (79,400kg)
Max VTOL weight	113,130lb (51,310kg)
Normal VTOL load	30,260lb (13,730kg)
Ferry range	1,800nmi (3,330km) (with VTOL take-off and landing)

But when the XFV-12A's vertical lift implementation proved unsuccessful (it demonstrated thrust augmentation values of only 1.08 instead of the promised 1.48), the NA-382 proposal quietly faded from consideration.

Lockheed-Georgia KCX-130/ECX-130

By the mid-1970s the Marine Corps had begun to consider replacing its Hercules cargo/tanker fleet with the KCX programme. Lockheed-Georgia responded with a KCX-130/ECX-130 derivative. Ambitiously, the extensively redesigned aircraft had three CFM-56 turbofans to replace the C-130's four T56 turboprops, offering a cruise speed increase from 260kt (482kph) to 366kt (678kph), and a range improvement from 3,500nmi (6,480km) to 4,760nmi (8,816km). A new high-aspect-ratio wing with a supercritical airfoil would help extend the aircraft's range. Engineers also stretched the fuselage by 100in (254cm), increasing the available floor area in the cargo box by 30%. Other refinements included a redesign of the aft fuselage to include a T-tail, an improved cargo door, and a new low-profile nose radome to reduce drag.

Lockheed-Georgia proposed two versions: the KCX-130 for the Marine Corps to replace KC-130F cargo/tankers (competing with the Boeing and McDonnell Douglas AMST adaptations), and the ECX-130 for the Navy TACAMO (TAke Charge And Move Out) mission, replacing the Lockheed

LEFT Concept artwork for the Lockheed KCX-130. Without an AMST-class aircraft, Lockheed put this radically modified C-130 derivative forward as a KC-130F replacement (in competition with the Boeing KC-14 and McDonnell Douglas KC-15). *Lockheed*

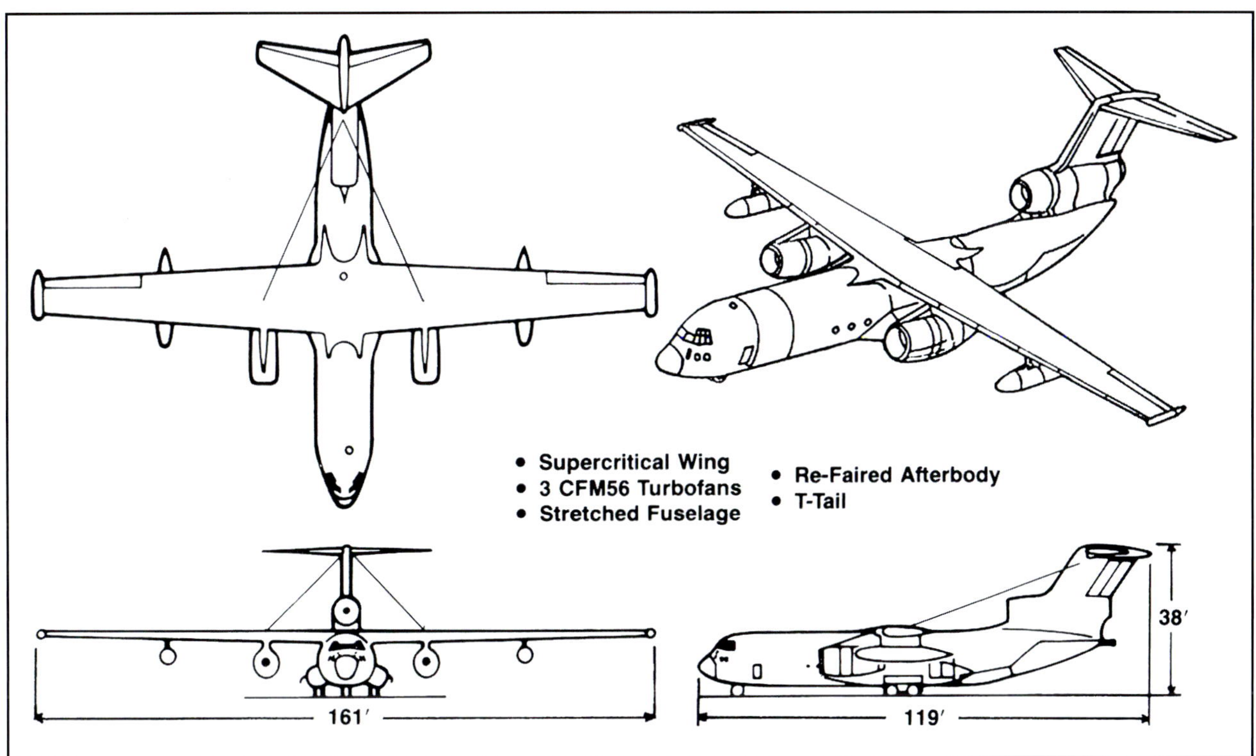

ABOVE Lockheed ECX-130 general arrangement. *Lockheed*

BELOW Lockheed ECX-130 antenna and internal arrangements. *Lockheed*

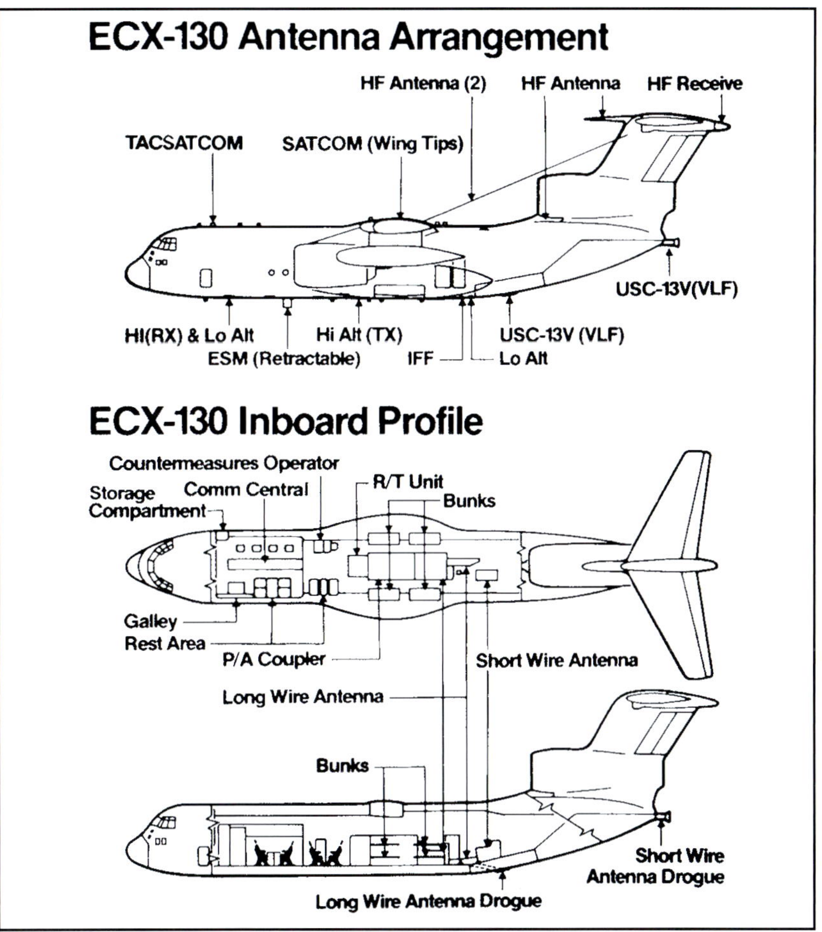

Lockheed KCX-130 and ECX-130	
Powerplant	3 x CFM-56 turbofans @ 24,000lb (106.76kN) thrust
Wingspan	161ft (49.1m)
Length	119ft (36.3m)
Height	38ft (11.6m)
Max TOW	250,000lb (113,400kg)

EC-130G/Q aircraft used by the Navy to communicate with its ICBM-carrying submarines.

Boeing submitted its own unsolicited proposal to the Navy for the TACAMO replacement, offering a 707-320 derivative powered by four CFM-56 engines, which was eventually selected. The Marine Corps eventually decided against the KCX-130, but there was much more mileage left in the C-130 design (indeed, far more than could have been foreseen at the time), and over the next decade Lockheed was selected to replace the 1960s-vintage C/KC-130F with KC-130R/T aircraft.

Despite the proven performance of the C-130 and the greatly enhanced capabilities of the proposed alternatives to the AMST, none appealed sufficiently to the Air Force, Navy or Marine Corps.

ABOVE Designated the YMC-130H, the surviving 'Credible Sport' aircraft was retained for test purposes after the second Iranian Hostage rescue effort was cancelled. Each of the four large fairings on the sides of the forward fuselage housed dual ASROC rockets for STOL performance, and the fairing atop the fuselage housed an air-refuelling receptacle. Additional rockets were mounted above the landing gear sponsons, and on the wing pylons normally occupied by external fuel tanks. Also visible are the dorsal and horsal strakes added to increase tail effectiveness at very low speeds. *Ray Leader/Flightleader*

Lockheed-Georgia 'XFC-130H' and YMC-130H 'Credible Sport'

One of the most ambitious modifications of the standard production C-130 was undertaken by Lockheed to execute a single, specific mission: a second US military attempt to end the Iranian Hostage Crisis. The crisis had begun when a mob stormed the US Embassy on 4 November 1979 and captured fifty-two US personnel in what was seen as a move to pressure the US to return the deposed Shah, Mohammad Reza Pahlavi, to Iran for trial. Frustrated by the failure of diplomatic efforts to release the hostages, President Jimmy Carter authorised covert military action. Coded Operation 'Eagle Claw', the rescue attempt began on 24 April 1980.

However, the mission was aborted during the insertion phase, when three of eight Navy RH-53D helicopters either experienced mechanical failures or failed to reach the initial 'Desert One' rendezvous point. During the recall, an RH-53D collided with a C-130, resulting in the deaths of eight servicemen. A firestorm of controversy erupted in the US, with critics labelling the 'Eagle Claw' plan as too complex and using too many aircraft (eight RH-53Ds, at least eight C-130s and several C-141s).

After the failure, planners scrambled to find a simpler rescue strategy. As before, they decided to land Special Forces rescuers inside the Amjadiyeh soccer stadium, just across the street from the US Embassy in Tehran. This time, though, the rescue aircraft would not be helicopters, but rather two heavily modified C-130 SSTOL (Super Short Take-off and Landing) aircraft. On 19 August 1980 Lockheed won a contract to modify three aircraft (two operational, plus a spare) to carry out the mission, under the programme name 'Credible Sport'.

Fortunately, given the situation's urgency, Lockheed was well prepared for the task. From years of earlier studies, it already had engineering data available for many of the planned modifications. These included the aerodynamic changes proposed in 1975 for the C-130H (Option IV) and the C-130WBS, with dorsal and horsal fins, spoilers, broad-chord ailerons and rudder, and revised double-slotted flaps. This particular mission, however, required even more radical alterations fully described in 'The Praetorian STARship' by Col Jerry L. Thigpen, which covers the history of Air Force 'Combat Talon' Special Operations:

> 'Five sets of rocket motors were required to create the super-STOL capability. Thirty rockets were mounted on the airframe, including eight antisubmarine rocket (ASROC) motors mounted on the fuselage and pointed forward to stop the aircraft during landing and eight AGM-45 Shrike rocket motors mounted above the wheel wells and pointed downward to break the aircraft's descent rate. In addition, for take-off, eight Mark 56 rocket motors were mounted

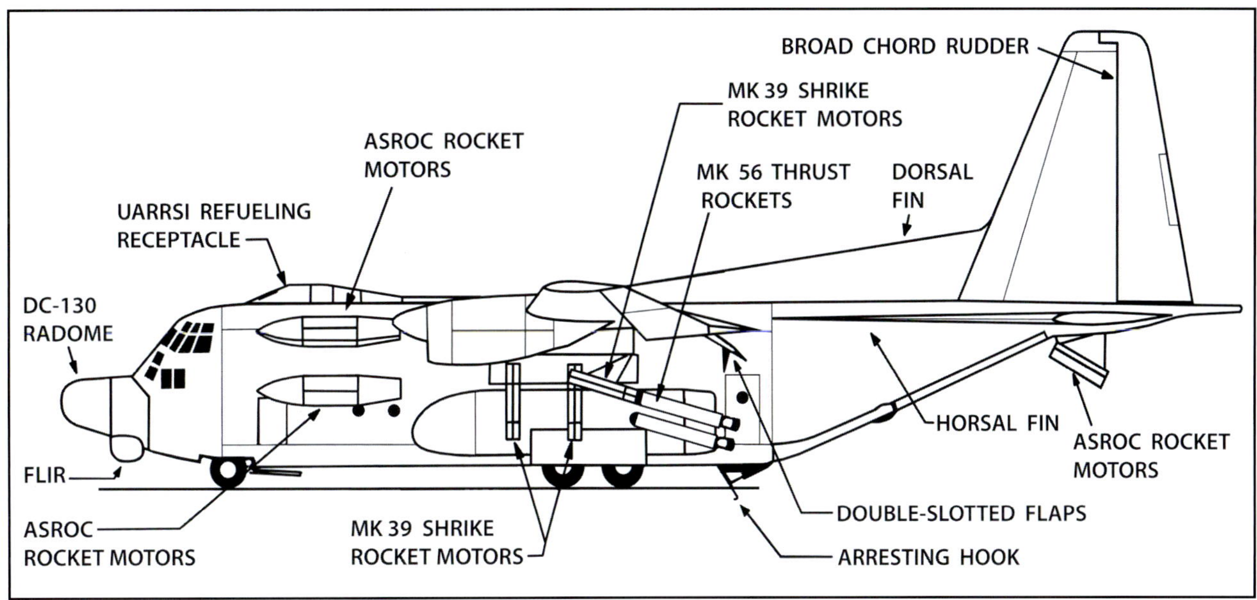

ABOVE A general diagram showing the modifications to the 'Credible Sport' 'XFC-130H' Hercules. *Via Chris Yasaki*

on the aft rear fuselage area on pylons and were pointed toward the rear of the aircraft and downward at approximately a 45-degree angle. To stabilise the aircraft during transition from take-off, two sets of Shrike rocket motors were mounted on each wing pylon. To prevent over-rotation during the take-off phase, two additional ASROC rocket motors were mounted on pylons in the rear fuselage area in front of the beavertail. An on-board computer had a manual backup should the computer fail to control the rockets.'

Other external modifications included a nose radome assembly from a DC-130 enclosing Terrain Following/Terrain Avoidance (TF/TA) radar, and a Forward-Looking Infra-Red (FLIR) turret. There was also a tail-hook for recovery by an aircraft carrier at the end of the mission.

The first fully modified 'XFC-130H' (a non-standard designation) aircraft (serial 74-1683) was delivered on 17 October 1979. Testing proceeded rapidly and on 29 October test pilots lifted off on a flight to demonstrate its full SSTOL capability. Take-off proved impressively successful. The nose gear lifted 6ft (1.8m) off the ground after 10ft (3.0m) of take-off roll, and with all eight Mark 56 rocket motors firing, the aircraft was airborne within 150ft (46m) and reached a 30ft (9.1m) altitude and a 115kt (213km/h) airspeed within the length of the soccer field. Landing was another matter. The deceleration rockets fired early, leaving the aircraft high above the ground with practically no forward speed. The Hercules fell to the ground, the right wing broke off, a fuel tank ruptured, and fire broke out. The aircraft was damaged beyond repair.

The entire 'Credible Sport' programme became redundant just two days later, when Tehran announced an Algerian-brokered plan to release the hostages. The second C-130H conversion, now designated the YMC-130H, became a test bed, supporting the MC-130H Combat Talon fleet for several years until retirement at the Robins Air Museum. In 2018, declared surplus by the Museum, it moved to the Empire State Aerosciences Museum in Glenville, New York, for extensive restoration and eventual display. The third airframe meant for conversion was never modified and returned to normal airlift operations.

Lockheed-Georgia L-100-40, -50 and -60 stretched Hercules

In the late 1970s and into the early '80s Lockheed explored three stretched L-100 designs for the civil airfreight market. Each version was successively lengthened to carry an additional standard cargo pallet/container (eight for the L-100-40, nine for the L-100-50 and ten for the L-100-60). After initial work there was little interest in the -40 variant and emphasis shifted to the more capable -50 and -60 models.

The L-100-50 was to have a 435.6in (11.06m) fuselage stretch compared with the original L-100, and the ultimate version, the L-100-60, was to have the fuselage lengthened by 556.6in (14.14m). At 143ft 2.4in (43.65m), the -60 version was in fact longer that the 'Ultimate Hercules' of the 1950s, the GL-207-25. As with the latter, the new variant required a new four-wheel bogie landing gear, stored in fairings outside the fuselage (similar to those on the C-141 and the GL-207-25). While this change permitted a wider cargo box, it also required the expensive design and qualification of a new fuselage centre section and landing gear. In contrast to the earlier big-stretch design, Lockheed proposed to keep basically the same wing as the standard

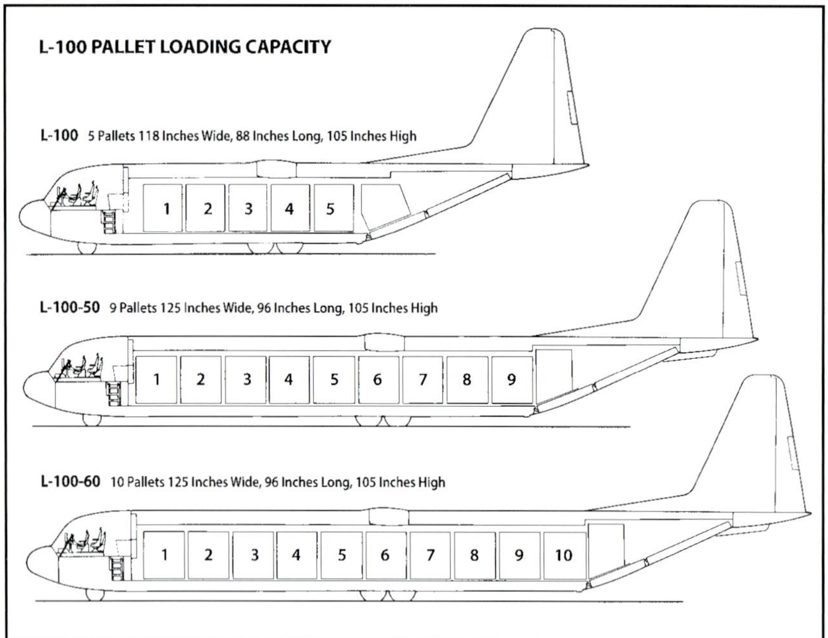

LEFT A comparison of the standard body length L-100/C-130 and the proposed L-100-50 and -60 stretches. *Authors*

Lockheed/Lockheed Martin Hercules models

	L-100	L-100-50	L-100-60
Powerplant	4 x Allison 501-D22 turboprops @ 4,050eshp (3020kW)	4 x Allison 501-D22E turboprops @ 4,910eshp (3,361kW)	4 x Allison 'T56-M71' turboprops @ 5,895eshp (4,396kW)
Span	132ft 7.2in (44.42m)	132ft 7.2 (44.42m)	132ft 7.2 (44.42m)
Length	97ft 9.6in (29.81m)	133ft 2.4in (40.60m)	143 ft 2.4in (43.65m)
Height	38ft (11.58m)	39ft 2.4in (11.94m)	39ft 2.4 (11.94m)
Wing area	1,492sq ft (138.6m²)	1,745sq ft (162.1m²)	1,745sq ft (162.1m²)
Design gross weight	155,800lb (70,700kg)	175,000lb (79,379kg)	n/a
Max payload	47,990lb (21,768kg)	67,000lb (30,391kg)	n/a
Design cruise speed	250kt (46.3km/h)	320kt (503km/h)	n/a
Range	3,000nmi (5,560km)*	1,000nmi (1,852km)**	n/a

* Maximum ferry
** At maximum normal payload

Hercules, albeit strengthened to accommodate the higher loads, weights and engine power.

The L-100-50 was to use the 4,910eshp (3,661kW) Detroit Diesel Allison 501-D22E engine. However, it could also accommodate Allison's 5,895eshp (4,396kW) T56-M71 engine that was in development for military applications such as an upgraded E-2C Hawkeye. (In comparison, the GL-207-25 would have used Allison's 5,500eshp/4,101kW T61 engines. The Air Force cancelled development of these engines in 1959, accelerating the demise of the GL-207-25.) Larger-diameter propellers were needed to absorb the extra power. Lockheed projected that the -50/60 would burn 34% less fuel than a DC-8-63F re-engined with the CFM-56 high-bypass turbofan.

Lockheed extensively marketed L-100 versions to airlines as ideally suited for hub-and-spoke cargo/freight operations, but found no launch customers.

BELOW An artist's illustration of the L-100-50F (Freighter) in flight. The large forward cargo door and low-profile radome are noticeable. *Lockheed*

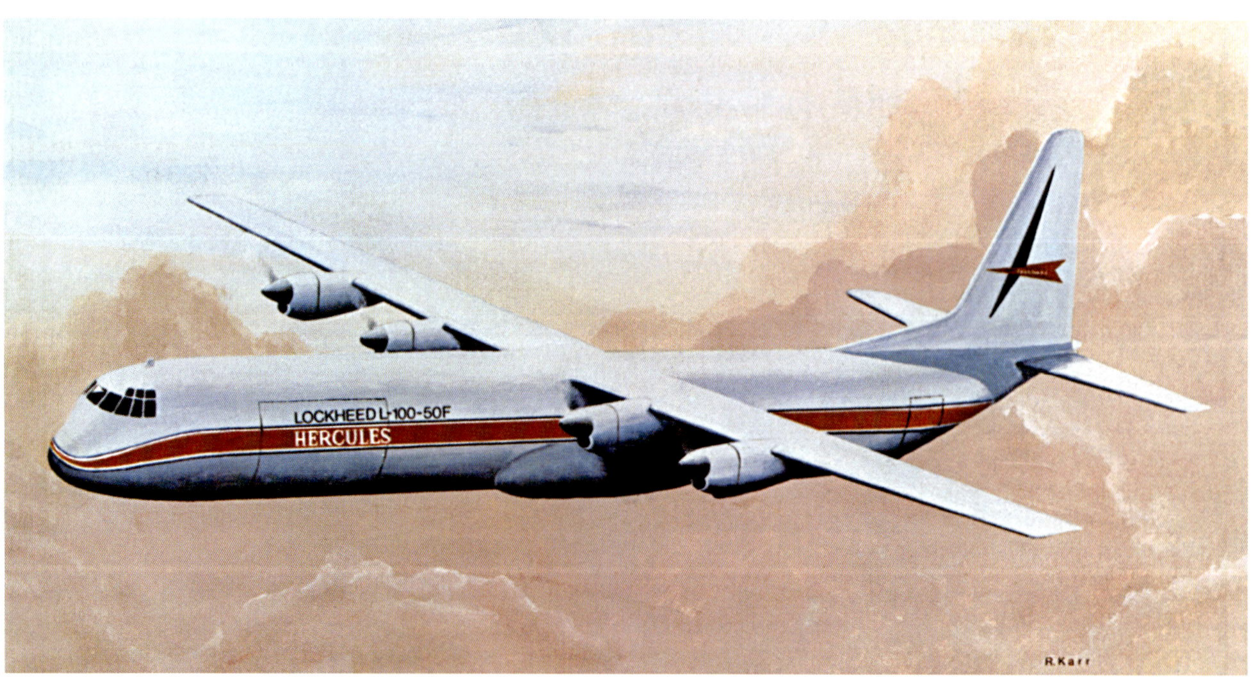

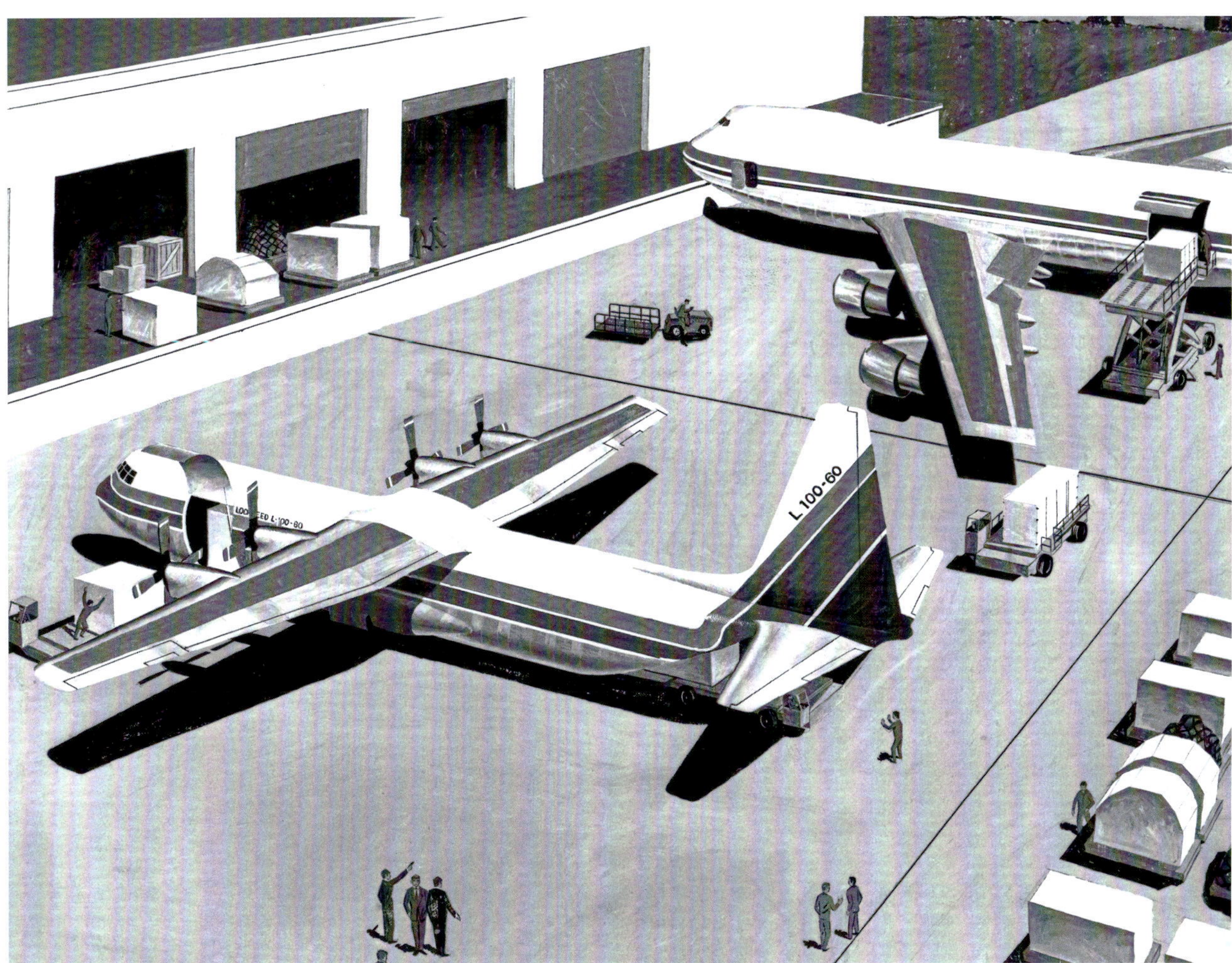

ABOVE An artist's concept depicting the L-100-60's reintroduction of the forward cargo-loading door. Sized at 114in by 108in (290cm by 274cm), the door was much larger than the 88in by 72in (224cm by 183cm) door in C-130A/B and the first sixteen C-130Es. *Lockheed*

Lockheed-Georgia L-400 Twin Hercules

At about the same time as the L-100-50/60 development effort, Lockheed had been studying a lighter-weight, twin-engined version of the Hercules, designated the L-400. The company began marketing the aircraft in 1977, seeing an opportunity for a smaller version of the C-130 in lower-payload market segments. This would give the company a product to compete with the Aérospatiale/MBB C-160NG and the Aeritalia G.222 (then being proposed for production) while offering a replacement for ageing C-47, C-119 and C-123 aircraft.

The design's primary airframe change was to the wing, eliminating the inboard engines and reducing the weight. Engineers retained the outer wing sections (complete with what had been the outboard engines), but reattached them to a new short-span wing centre section. Additionally, they grafted small constant-chord wing sections onto the wingtips. The fuselage was unmodified to the eye, but the main landing gear now needed only one wheel per side.

Lockheed announced the programme's launch via magazine advertisements in the early 1980s, promising that the first aircraft would be completed in 1981, followed by flight testing then customer deliveries by 1983. But there was no US military requirement or commercial support for the design, and the project languished for lack of a launch customer despite a price that was 75% of that of a standard Hercules. Lockheed also offered it to several overseas air forces (surviving promotional models show it in Greek and Israeli colours), but again without success. When the company began to divert resources to production of its new C-5B Galaxy in 1984, it quietly cancelled the L-400 programme.

Lockheed L-400 Twin Hercules	
Powerplant	2 x Allison 501-D22D turboprops @ 4,910eshp (3,661kW)
Wingspan	119ft 8.4in (36.48m)
Length	97ft 9.6in (39.81m)
Height	38ft (11.6m)
Empty weight	53,803kb (24,405kg)
Max TOW	84,000lb (38,102kg)
Max payload	25,100lb (11,385kg) @ 550nmi (1,019km)
Ferry range	3,000nmi (5,556km)

LEFT **A concept model of the Lockheed L-400 in US Navy colours. The L-400 fuselage would have remained the same length as the standard C-130.** *John Aldaz collection*

BELOW **Lockheed L-400 general arrangement. The aircraft used a new short-span wing centre section, existing outer wing panels and new constant-chord wingtip extensions. The main landing gear was reduced to single wheels on each side.** *Lockheed*

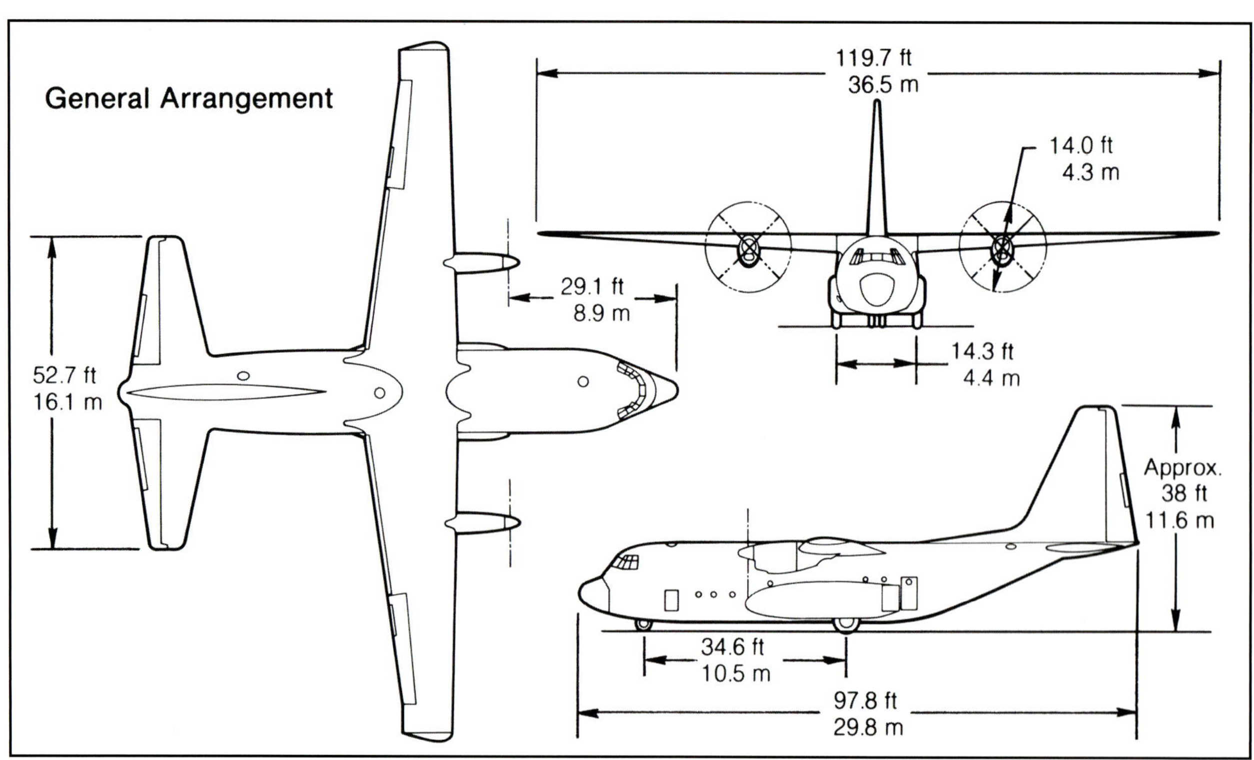

Competition for the Hercules Twin

Even as Lockheed was trying to market the L-400 as a replacement for piston powered C-47s and C-123s, upgraded versions of these aircraft were being developed for far lower costs.

ABOVE The introduction of the Mancro 'C-123T' conversion of the venerable C-123 (re-engined with two Allison T56-A-7Bs and nacelles from the C-130B/E) undermined the business case for the more expensive L-400. *Author collection*

Mancro C-123T

The Mancro C-123T conversion was the last in a long line of attempts to upgrade the C-123 design dating back to the Fairchild M-206 in 1954. The conversion was initially sponsored by the government of Thailand which operated a large fleet of ex-USAF C-123s and was facing greatly increased piston engine maintenance costs and the phase-out of high-octane aviation gasoline.

Mancro obtained a stored C-123B from MASDC which had previously served with the US Coast Guard and had a bulbous nose radome for the APN-158 weather radar. The airframe retained camouflage from subsequent service in the Air Force Reserve and after conversion, carried Thai Air Force roundels although it never saw service in that air force.

The prototype conversion (performed by Waco Airmotive) was limited to the replacement of the 2,500hp (1,864kW) Pratt & Whitney R-2800-99 engines with Allison T56-A-7B turboprops of 3,670shp (2,737kW), engine controls and instrumentation. With the deletion of the nacelle fuel tanks (the space being taken up by the T56 exhaust duct), fuel carriage was limited to the 856 gallons (3,240l) in the external tanks. Development began in September 1979 and the first flight was made on October 24, 1980.

The proposed fully configured aircraft would have had 'wet wing' fuel tanks in the outer wing panels (1,600 gallons/6,057l) with optional tanks in the left and right center wing section adding 800 gallons/3,028l. Alternately, the existing external tanks could be retained and 1,200 gallons 4,543l could be carried in an additional set of external tanks positioned between the fuselage and engine nacelles. A Gas Turbine Compressor (for self-starting) would replace the APU, and hydraulic boost for the ailerons, rudder and elevators, modern radios and anti-icing via bleed air from the engines would be added. Conversion workflow was projected to take 128 work days and conversion cost was estimated at about $3 million.

The project was ended after the Thai government ran into funding shortages, coincidentally having taken delivery of three C-130Hs from Lockheed in August 1980.

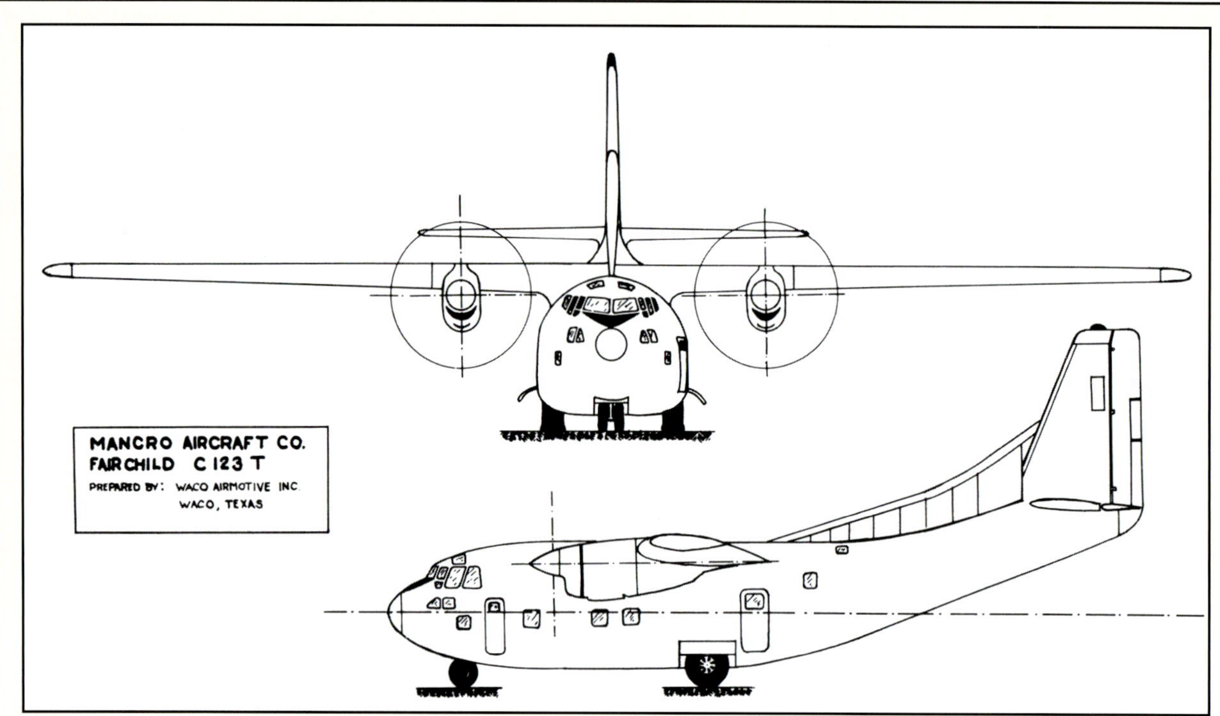

ABOVE Engineering for initial (and only) C-123T conversion was performed by Waco Airmotive for Mancro. *Author collection*

BELOW By 1978, Jack Conroy had new company, Specialized Aircraft and was promoting a trimotor DC-3/C-47 conversion (of his earlier Dart-powered DC-3 conversion). A further development was the swing-tail Tri-Turbo Three, seen here in military markings. *Specialized Aircraft*

Specialized Aircraft Tri Turbo-3

Jack Conroy's last aircraft project was a 1977 tri-motor conversion of his earlier Turbo-Three conversion, switching from two Rolls Royce Dart Mk 510 engines rated at 1,740 eshp/1,298 kW to three Pratt & Whitney Canada PT6A-41 rated at 850shp/634kW. While the PT6s had lower power than the Darts, they offered reduced fuel consumption and were one third the weight. In addition, the center engine could be shut down in flight to further conserve fuel.

A further development with a swing tail for military and civil use was offered at the 1978 Farnborough Airshow. Conroy's press release stated that the aircraft was suitable for commercial or military operations where in could carry three jeeps or other cargo. The sung tail was to be opened and closed hydraulically with the aircraft's weight supported by two hydraulic rams located forward of the swing tail.

The project was abandoned after Conroy's death on December 5, 1979. It took another decade for a viable DC-3/C-47 modernization/re-engining program to materialize in the form of the Basler BT-67. Using two PWC PT6A-67R engines rated at 1,294 eshp/965 kW, each airframe is remanufactured to essentially 'zero time'. Over sixty have been produced for civil and military customers.

de Havilland Canada C-130 PL (Powered Lift) demonstrator

In the late 1970s the de Havilland Canada (DHC) C-8 Buffalo Augmentor Wing test bed was the subject of a collaborative test programme with NASA and Boeing. This was a NASA investigation of a technology identified for possible use in the AMST programme (Chapter Five). DHC began studies for an application for the technology after the successful conclusion of the joint effort.

Their next step was to evaluate the concept on the C-130. The existing C-130 fuselage was retained but the wing was replaced with a new supercritical airfoil that had greater span, a higher aspect ratio and much increased thickness (partially to accommodate the bulky air ducting

ABOVE de Havilland Canada's proposed joint US/Canada C-130 jet flap demonstrator in Canadian Forces markings. *de Havilland Canada*

BELOW The unique Rolls-Royce RB 419 engine used a modified Spey 202 as a core engine (with the bypass airflow diverted to the jet flaps) to drive either an additional front fan or propeller. Later, de Havilland did a joint study with Pratt & Whitney to adapt the PW2037 for the role. *de Havilland Canada*

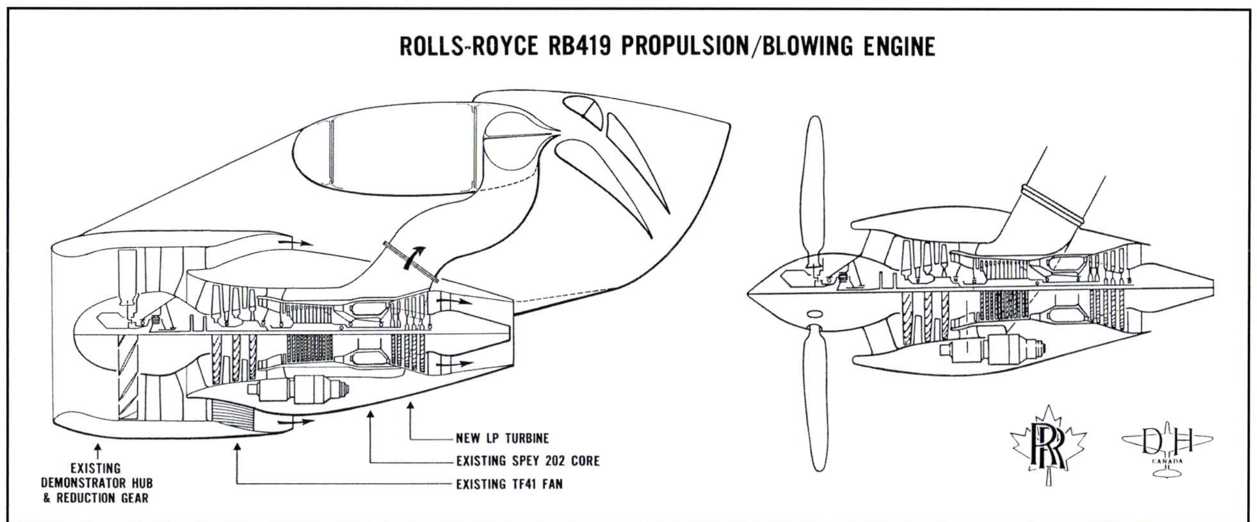

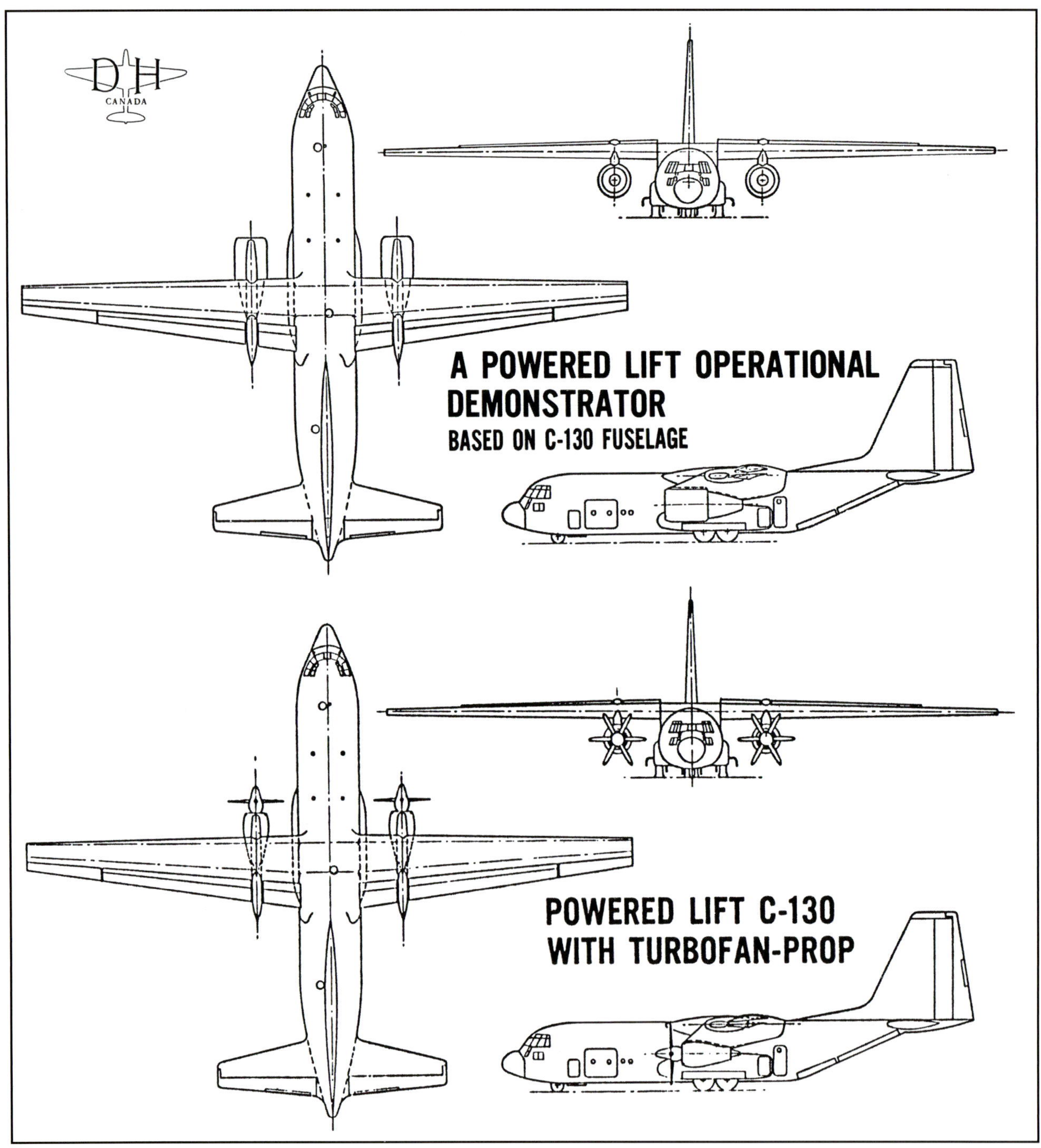

ABOVE C-130 PL variants with turbofan and turbofan-prop engines. *de Havilland Canada*

to the flaps). For the demonstration effort, Rolls-Royce Canada proposed modifying the existing Rolls-Royce Spey 202 turbofans to the RB.418 configuration. The entire Spey bypass flow (provided by the similar Rolls-Royce/Allison TF41 fan) would be ducted through the pylons to the flaps. A new low-pressure turbine would extract additional power from the core flow to drive a new, variable-pitch geared fan at the front of the engine for additional propulsive flow. Rolls-Royce also offered a turboprop version (with a six-bladed propeller) of its RB.419 with a lower cruise speed of approximately Mach 0.6.

DHC briefed the project to many offices in the US Air Force and even to Lockheed in August 1984. The programme was expected to cost about US$200 million; DHC reported that the Canadian Government would provide half of that amount (as Canada's C-130s would need replacement in the future). During discussions it was suggested that DHC might investigate a US engine derivative. Pratt & Whitney proposed a derivative of its PW2037 engine, which was already in airline service and under

de Havilland Canada C-130 PL (Powered Lift)	
Powerplant	2 x Rolls-Royce RB419 (Spey derivative) turbofans with Dowty/Rotol variable-pitch fan @ 24,000lb (106.76kN) thrust, or 2 x Pratt & Whitney PW2037 derivative 'three stream' turbofans @ 31,000lb (137.89kN) thrust
Wingspan	145ft (44.20m)
Wing area	1,745sq ft (162.12m²)
Wing aspect ratio	12
Wing thickness	to chord ratio 24
Length	119ft (36.3m)
Height	38ft (11.6m)
Empty weight	67,999lb (30,844kg)
Max TOW	168,310lb (76,344kg) (@ 2.25 G limit)
Dash speed	Mach 0.8
Range	4,000nmi (7,408km) (@ 36,000lb/16,329kg payload)

development for the C-17. P&W studies through 1986 resulted in what it called a 'three stream' engine. However, without US funding the proposed research and production programmes never took place.

Lockheed-Georgia L-100-20 High Technology Test Bed (HTTB)

The HTTB of 1983 capped three decades of company effort to develop and market an STOL version of the Hercules. Lockheed purchased a used L-100-20, serial number 4412, on the commercial market, and company-funded modifications began in 1984. When completed, the test bed was registered N130X and outwardly resembled the proposed C-130 (Option IV) from the 1970s.

The HTTB STOL performance goals were to:

- Fly an approach at 75-80kt (139-148km/h), using on-board-generated centreline and glide-path (up to 7°) guidance, in all weather conditions,
- Clear a standard 50ft (15m) obstacle and touch down on a soft field within 4ft (1.2m) laterally and 20ft (6.1m) longitudinally of a predetermined spot, with a descent rate of around 10ft (3.0m) per second,
- Have a landing distance not exceeding 1,500ft (457m) from the base of the 50ft (15m) obstacle
- Achieve this performance on a hot day at a gross weight of 140,000lb (63,500kg)

The difficulty of meeting such demanding performance requirements became tragically evident on 3 February 1993 when the HTTB crashed during a ground test run while evaluating the fly-by-wire rudder actuator at the ground minimum control speed. All seven Lockheed crew members were killed. The crash marked not only the end of the HTTB programme, but also Lockheed's hopes for an STOL C-130. Despite decades of expressed interest, no prospective customer had ever followed up the initial interest with a firm order.

With these programmes ended, C-130 development pivoted in new directions, towards a re-engined C-130 with more power and better fuel consumption, sporting new composite propellers and an expanded version of the digital avionics architecture.

BELOW The Lockheed HTTB at Pope AFB in April 1988. The aircraft exhibits the horsal and dorsal extensions for STOL performance, the fuselage stretch, and the low-profile nose radome as was first proposed in 1975 for the C-130(SS). *Author photo*

LEFT The fully realised double-slotted flap installed in the Lockheed HTTB. The design occupied the same space as the C-130's original single-slotted flap and had evolved through a series of configurations over the previous twenty-five years. The cambered and re-contoured outer-wing leading edge is also visible. *Author photo*

Lockheed/Lockheed Martin Hercules models

	L-400	L-382/C-130H	C-130J
Powerplant	4 x Allison 501 D-22F turboprops @ 4,662shp (3,476kW)	4 x Allison T56-A-15 turboprops @ 4508shp (derated) (3,361kW)	4 x RR AE-2100 D3 turboprops @ 4,637shp (3,458kW)
Span	119.7ft (36.48m)	132.6ft (40.42m)	132.6ft (40.42m)
Length	98.7ft (30.08m)	97.8ft (29.81m)	97.75ft (29.79m)
Height	38ft (11.58m)	38ft (11.58m)	38ft (11.58m)
Wing area	1,492sq ft (138.6m^2)	1,745sq ft (162.1m^2)	1,745sq ft (162.1m^2)
Design gross weight	84,000lb (38,100kg)	155,000lb (70,300kg)	164,000lb (74,400kg)
Payload	25,100lb (11,400kg)	42,673lb (19,356kg)	42,000lb (19,000kg)
Design cruise speed	250kt (46.3km/h)	320kt (503km/h)	348kt (644km/h)
Range	3,000nmi (5,560km)*	4,300nmi (7,960km)*	1,800nmi (3,330km)**

* Maximum ferry
** At maximum normal payload

Significantly, technology developed for the HTTB eliminated the need for a navigator on the flight deck. One observer noted that Lockheed had finally realised that its customers wanted a low-risk, low-cost replacement for the C-130s already in service in the 1990s, rather than high-risk STOL developments.

They got their wish with the C-130J Super Hercules (the third time a derivative aircraft had carried that name). Britain's Royal Air Force was the 1996 launch customer, with orders for twenty-five aircraft. After a number of worldwide sales, Lockheed finally sold the C-130J to the US military; the USAF bought both the standard-length C-130J and the stretched C-130J-30, the Marine Corps purchased the KC-130J, and the Coast Guard bought the C-130J.

The C-130's place in history

With the launch of the C-130J, Lockheed (now Lockheed Martin) had done what would have seemed unimaginable when the YC-130 first flew back in August 1954 – it had sustained an aircraft in production for more than sixty years. In doing so, it had continuously improved a design that, while often characterised as inadequate for new needs (much as the DC-3/C-47 was), had outlasted all its would-be replacements.

BELOW Despite years of effort and incremental improvement under the skin, the C-130J of the 21st century looks little different from that of the 20th. *USAF photo by A1C Rhett Isbell*

Chapter Ten
New Missions Emerge

1980 to the present day: A new combat role for the airlifter?

ABOVE The Boeing ATT (Advanced Theater Transport) super-STOL concept from October 2001. *John Aldaz collection*

By the mid-1980s most of the immediate US airlifter requirements had been met, with aircraft meeting those requirements either in service or on order. For the shorter range tactical mission, the C-130E/H was operational, and Lockheed had already begun marketing upgraded versions (demonstrated as the High Technology Test Bed – HTTB). The re-winged C-5A, together with the C-5B, met the need for long range and heavy lift, supplemented by dual-role KC-10 tankers.

At the time the highly capable C-17 remained slotted for the military's medium-range, wide-body missions, despite significant development issues and speculation that an alternative might be required. But the C-17 eventually overcame these problems, and is enjoying a highly successful service career with the USAF and eight other air forces worldwide. What the Air Force still needed, however, was a tanker replacement.

Meanwhile, an unforeseen requirement had emerged: providing close support for a new kind of warfare, one with fluid and ill-defined front lines. To meet the need, designers began tapping back into V/STOL and SSTOL (Super Short Take-off and Landing) research conducted many years earlier. They also investigated, for the first time in airlifters, applying low observable or 'stealth' technology.

The result was a slew of new initiatives over the last thirty years, with innovative concepts that explored ways to meet the Army's new mission requirement. While none of these has resulted in a flying aircraft to date (at least as far as is known), they may well have influenced future designs.

Special Operations airlift

The threat of conventional war receded during the later 1980s, but a new type of conflict began to emerge – one in which the enemy forces did not engage en masse but were far more elusive. The new tactics strained the Air Force's ability to support Special Operations Forces (SOF), and this weakness became painfully clear on 24 April 1980 when the air insertion mission Operation 'Eagle Claw' failed to rescue hostages being held in Iran.

The operation's failure reverberated for years, eventually resulting in the formation of a unified Command, the

Special Operations Command (USSOCOM or SOCOM) in April 1987 under the Goldwater-Nichols Act. Over the next several years the services reorganised their SOF units into subordinate commands reporting to the respective service and to SOCOM. On 22 May 1990 Air Force Chief of Staff General Larry D. Welch redesignated the 23rd AF as the Air Force Special Operations Command (AFSOC), with a primary mission of inserting, extracting and supporting Special Operations Forces.

By this time planners well understood the material shortcomings of Operation 'Eagle Claw'. The Sikorsky RH-53D helicopter (used by the Navy and assigned to the force), originally designed as a heavy lift (logistics) aircraft, lacked the reliability crucial for Special Operations; three of the original eight helicopters were unavailable or went unserviceable at the critical 'Desert One' staging site).

Consequently, two technologies would figure large in the quest for new aircraft – stealth (which had previously only been applied to bombers and fighters) and V/STOL. The latter technology had advanced considerably since the abortive attempts two decades earlier. Nonetheless, there was still a trade-off to be made between size and mission capability, just as the XC-142 had proved a more feasible proposition than the larger CX-6 (as discussed in Chapter Four).

These specialised and highly demanding requirements led to numerous imaginative proposals over the following decades.

1987: Scaled Composites Model 133 ATTT (Advanced Technology Tactical Transport – AT³)

Scaled Composites' Model 133 was an early example, exploiting the new technologies to produce a specialised Special Operations aircraft. This was a proof-of-concept, subscale prototype built under contract to the Defense Advanced Projects Agency (DARPA), funded by the Office of the Secretary of Defense (OSD). Scaled's intent was to blend promising technologies with an unusual STOL airlifter configuration tailored for SOF missions. Engineers would then upscale the prototype and optimise it for long-range, low-level infiltration and exfiltration of small forces deep behind enemy lines; it was planned to carry 8,500lb (3,860kg) at a range (with reserves) of about 2,400nmi (4,445km).

The programme's secondary goal was to determine if a development process could be shortened (and cost reduced) by producing a subscale prototype rather than going through traditional stages such as wind tunnel testing.

Following an initial feasibility study by Scaled Composites in 1984, and a short development effort, the Model 133-3.62 (Model 133, Version 3, 62% scale) made its first flight on 29 December 1987. Engineers intended the tandem-wing configuration, with the two wings linked by elongated engine nacelles, to permit as short a span as possible on high-aspect-ratio wings. It also made room for a large amount of fuel, carried well away from the cockpit area.

After it had flown fifty-one test flights between December 1987 and November 1988, technicians modified the empennage, installing a 'Pi' or Bronco twin-tail configuration to correct some persistent aerodynamic problems, particularly single-engine controllability at low speeds. The aircraft then resumed its test programme, successfully flying from April to July 1989 as the Model 133-4.62, before retirement into flyable storage.

BELOW The Scaled Composites Model 133-3.62 Advanced Technology Tactical Transport (ATTT or AT³) proof-of-concept demonstrator is seen here on the Mojave ramp on 7 August 1988 with the original cruciform tail. *Tim White photo*

ABOVE Scaled Composites Model 133-4.62 departs from the Mojave Airport on 15 May 1989 with the revised 'Bronco' tail. *Author collection*

BELOW General arrangement of the Scaled Composites Model 133-4.62 with the new tail configuration. A notional view of the projected full-sized vehicle is at lower right. *Author collection*

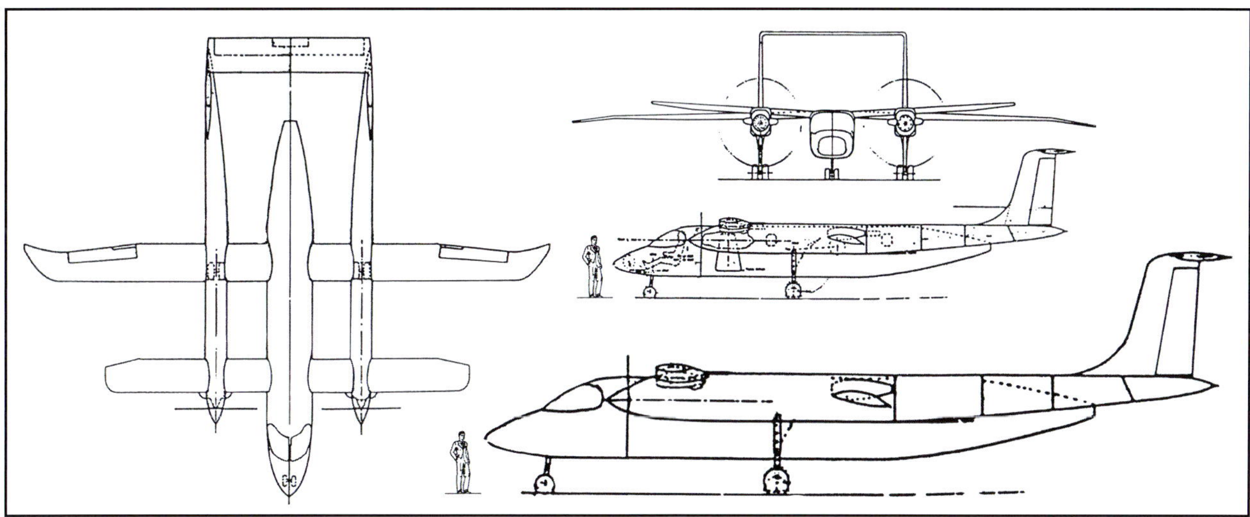

It later returned to flight in conjunction with the B-2 Spirit test programme, its aft fuselage fitted with a unique imaging radar to study deficiencies in the B-2's radar signature. Following innovative airborne diagnostics work, the B-2 issues were identified and corrected. An A-3 Skywarrior was fitted with an advanced capability for production flight testing of each B-2 and the AT[3] was again retired. That was the aircraft's last mission; it now resides at the Air Force Flight Test Museum at Edwards AFB. Although it never led to a similarly configured, full-size airlifter, the Model 133 proved an extremely productive test vehicle.

Scaled Composites Model 133-4

	133-4.62	**Notional full-scale aircraft**
Powerplant	2 x PWC PT6A-135A turboprops @ 787eshp (586kW)	2 x GE CT64-820-4 turboprops @ 3,133hp (2,336 kW)
Wingspan	53ft 2in (16.21m)	85ft 9in (26.15m)
Foreplane span	37ft 8in (11.48m)	60ft 9in (18.52m)
Length	44ft 10in (13.67m)	72ft 4in (22.05m)
Height	14ft 1in (4.29m)	22ft 8in (6.92m)
Wing area	179.4sq ft (16.67m²)	466.8sq ft (43.37m²)
Foreplane area	118.08sq ft (10.97m²)	307.2sq ft (28.54m²)
Gross weight	11,500 lb (5,216 kg)	n/a
Max speed	170kt (315 km/h)	n/a
Minimum control speed	63kt (117 km/h)	n/a

1988: ATTMA (Advanced Tactical Transport Mission Analysis)

By the late 1980s the US Army was promoting a new doctrine based on the predicted changes in future conflicts that it might be fighting. The Deputy for Development at the Air Force's Air Systems Command summarised it in this excerpt from a paper:

> 'The US Army's evolving AirLand Battle doctrine features the concept of a non-linear battlefield where versatile and highly manoeuvrable fighting units are operating autonomously with largely non-existent or indefensible ground lines of communication.'

This clearly had highly challenging consequences for air support. Supply aircraft would not only operate from unprepared airstrips without landing aids or handling equipment, but (quoting the same source) 'US Airlifters may be required to fly in harm's way more than they have ever done before.' Moreover, 'The theatre transport of the future … may be called upon to operate worldwide in a variety of climatic conditions ranging from the plains of Europe to the mountains of Southwest Asia to the jungles of Central America.'

This in turn influenced the airlifter that the Air Force would have to operate to meet the Army's requirements. The USAF began with a 1986/87 study entitled 'Advanced Tactical Transport Mission Analysis', or ATTMA, to determine precisely what these requirements implied, then issued a study to Boeing, Lockheed and Douglas. Each company was asked to examine a range of concepts for a future theatre airlifter, specifically examining STOL and V/STOL options and utilising low observable technology. The notional plan called for the Air Force to begin a process that would lead to acquiring replacements for the C-130E/Hs as they retired between 2011 and 2021.

The list of desired characteristics for the ATT was long.

Advanced Tactical Transport (ATT) desired characteristics

- Size of the C-130H with variants having payload capabilities from 25,000lb (11,360kg) to 60,000lb (27,270kg)
- Oversized/outsized cargo capability, advanced cargo-handling features, and articulated cargo ramp
- High-speed/low-level air-drop capability
- Super short take-off and landing capability
- High lift systems with externally blown flaps
- Fly-by-wire controls
- Off-the-shelf derivative engines and cross-shafted propellers and/or rotors
- Off-runway landing gear
- Advanced cockpit design with autonomous landing capability and on-board mission planning
- Survivability features including IR suppression, reconfigurable flight controls, and damage tolerance
- Enhanced reliability, maintainability, and availability

The ATT concept would allow delivery and extraction of medium-weight fighting systems and their support personnel at a much wider range of sites than was then available. The ATT would have both deployment and tactical missions.

For the deployment mission, the required range for a 60,000lb (30,480kg) payload was 1,300nmi (2,400km). The tactical mission was a 620mi (1,000km) radius and a High-Low-Low-High profile with SSTOL landing and take-off at mid-point, carrying a 60,000lb (30,480kg) payload both out and back. The ATT was required to have full 3.0G combat manoeuvrability and high dash speed at low altitude. The mid-point gross weight would include enough fuel to fly a 620mi (1,000km) return leg with sufficient fuel reserves. The runway length required when carrying a full payload was just over 750ft (229m), which meant that the total airstrip length required was just over 1,250ft (381m).

Given such a demanding set of requirements – and such an open brief as to how they might be met – the three companies came up with a wide variety of solutions; some proposals actually exceeded the specified requirements. For example, among the designs considered were tilt-rotor and tilt-wing concepts that would theoretically transport 60,000lb-plus (30,480kg-plus) loads in and out of runways as short as 500ft (152m). Although not intended as a Special Operations platform, the ATT would clearly have a majority of its capabilities tailored to this use. At this time, low observability, or stealth, also became a design driver.

Boeing ATT/ATTMA

Boeing conducted its study, which lasted sixteen months, in two phases. The first looked at an aircraft with the same cargo box size as the C-130, the second at one where the box size was determined by operational needs analysis. For each of these cases, Boeing investigated three categories of aircraft: V/STOL, STOL and SSTOL. This resulted in eight different concept configurations.

Starting with an analysis of the worldwide threat scenarios likely to be faced by the US and the missions likely to be required of the Air Force, the study concluded that a significant number of requirements could not be met by the C-130 or C-17. Two significant deficiencies were their inability to land in fields less than 2,000ft (610m) in length, or to operate in medium- or high-threat environments. Moreover, the C-130's cargo box size could not accommodate the key weaponry required by early-deploying forces like the Army's Light Infantry or Airborne Divisions. The new aircraft would also require the capability to operate from open fields and roadways.

The study's purpose was to identify and evaluate options rather than result in a single proposed design. Significant findings were:

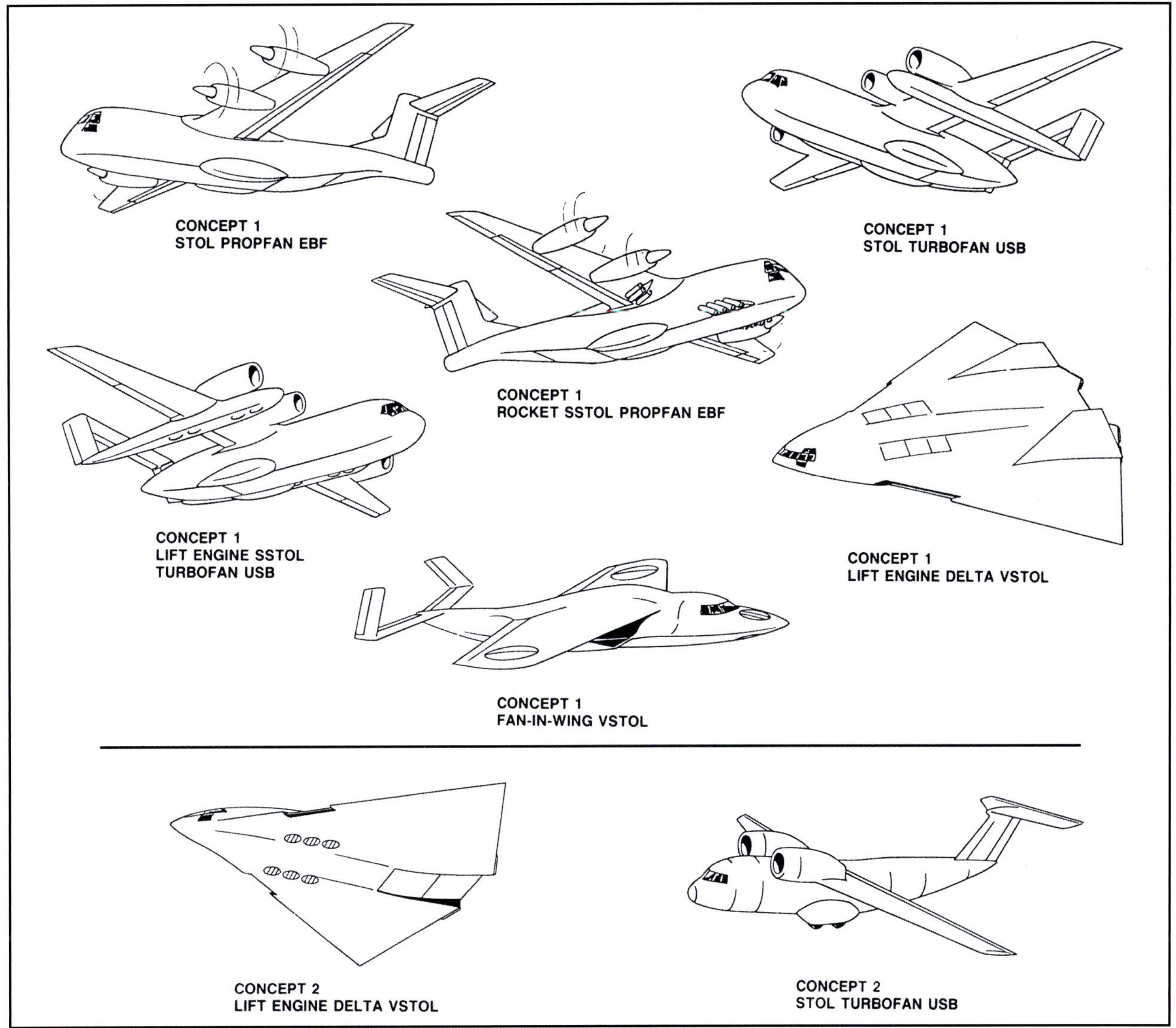

ABOVE Boeing ATT configurations. The 'Concept 1' aircraft were sized for larger volumetric payloads. *Boeing*

- MAC's role was changing and the existing resources could not meet the future needs
- Survivability was a key requirement, with threat avoidance and terrain masking being the best countermeasures
- The ATT's ability to use roads and open fields was a great asset
- The introduction of the ATT would improve theatre force effectiveness
- V/STOL would offer additional flexibility to the air and ground commanders and increase survivability
- A single airlifter might not be the best solution to future needs

Boeing placed strong emphasis on the advantages of V/STOL, but acknowledged that technology efforts needed to focus on the development of new and more capable lift systems that minimised both foreign object damage (FOD) and ground erosion when delivering large loads to unprepared landing sites. The study also concluded that the delta versions of the concept aircraft offered significant advantages in terms of survivability but offered much poorer ride quality, which became significant at altitudes below 150ft (45m) travelling at speeds above 0.7 Mach.

Selected Boeing ATTMA concepts	Concept 1 'Small Delta'	Concept 1 upper surface blowing Super STOL
Powerplant	2 x cruise turbofans @ 13,510lb (60.10kN) thrust; 6 x lift turbofans @ 20,940lb (93.15kN) thrust	2 x cruise turbofans, thrust n/a; 8 x lift turbofans, thrust n/a
Span	85.5ft (26.1m)	134.3ft (40.94m)
Length	108.0ft (32.92m)	112.5(34.29m)
Height	22.8ft (6.95m)	40.9ft (4.67m)
Gross weight	127,300lb (57,740kg)	n/a
Range with max payload	1,850nmi (3,426km)	n/a

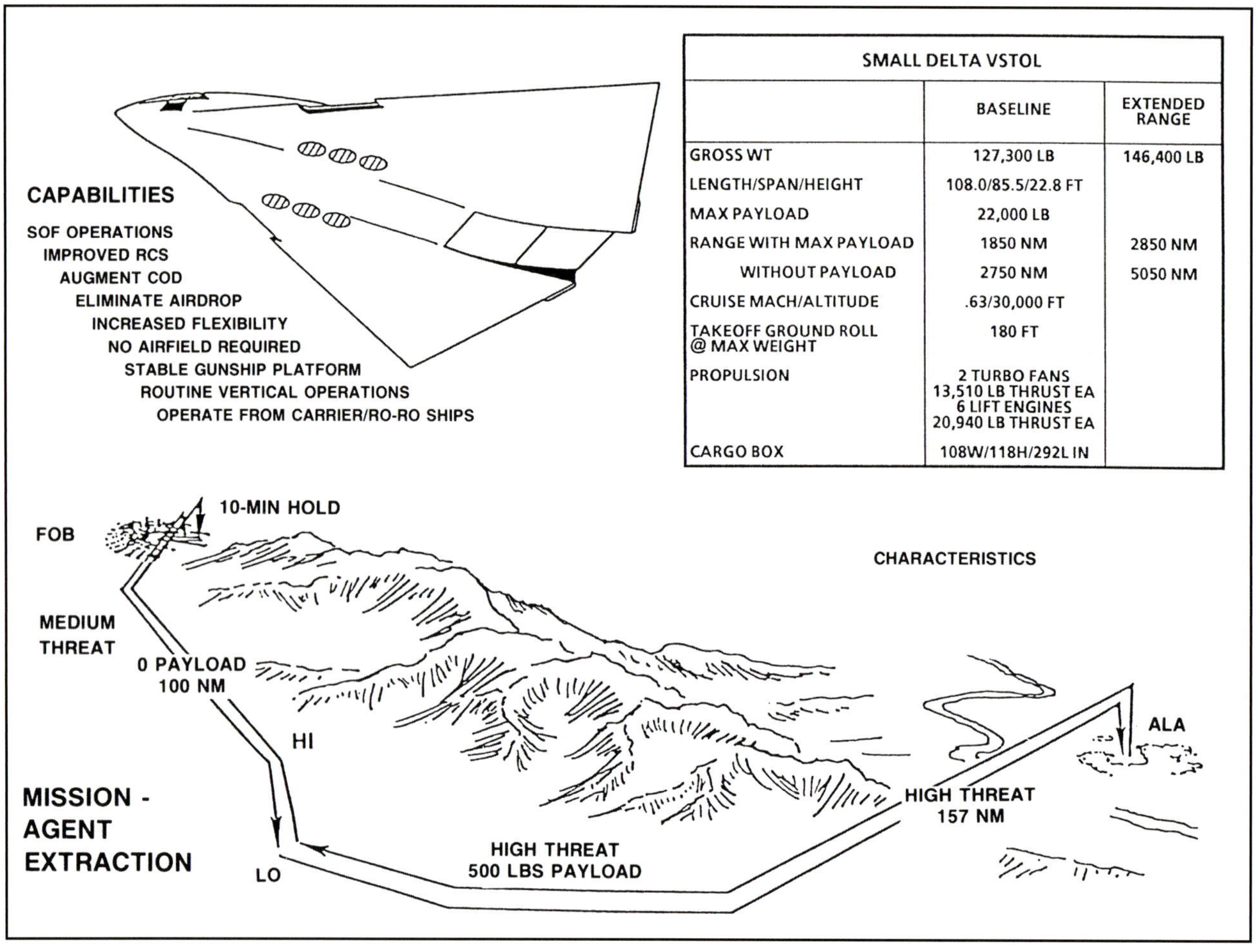

SMALL DELTA VSTOL		
	BASELINE	EXTENDED RANGE
GROSS WT	127,300 LB	146,400 LB
LENGTH/SPAN/HEIGHT	108.0/85.5/22.8 FT	
MAX PAYLOAD	22,000 LB	
RANGE WITH MAX PAYLOAD	1850 NM	2850 NM
WITHOUT PAYLOAD	2750 NM	5050 NM
CRUISE MACH/ALTITUDE	.63/30,000 FT	
TAKEOFF GROUND ROLL @ MAX WEIGHT	180 FT	
PROPULSION	2 TURBO FANS 13,510 LB THRUST EA 6 LIFT ENGINES 20,940 LB THRUST EA	
CARGO BOX	108W/118H/292L IN	

CAPABILITIES

SOF OPERATIONS
IMPROVED RCS
AUGMENT COD
ELIMINATE AIRDROP
INCREASED FLEXIBILITY
NO AIRFIELD REQUIRED
STABLE GUNSHIP PLATFORM
ROUTINE VERTICAL OPERATIONS
OPERATE FROM CARRIER/RO-RO SHIPS

CHARACTERISTICS

MISSION - AGENT EXTRACTION

FOB
10-MIN HOLD
MEDIUM THREAT
0 PAYLOAD
100 NM
HI
LO
HIGH THREAT
500 LBS PAYLOAD
HIGH THREAT
157 NM
ALA

ABOVE Conceptual mission employment for the Boeing 'Concept 2' 'Small Delta V/STOL' configuration. Improved RCS (Radar Cross Section) was a key consideration for this design. *Boeing*

BELOW A Boeing 'Small Delta V/STOL' ATT proposal employing six lift engines. *Boeing*

BELOW This Boeing Super STOL 'Concept 1' ATT design employs upper surface blowing, much like the YC-14. *Boeing*

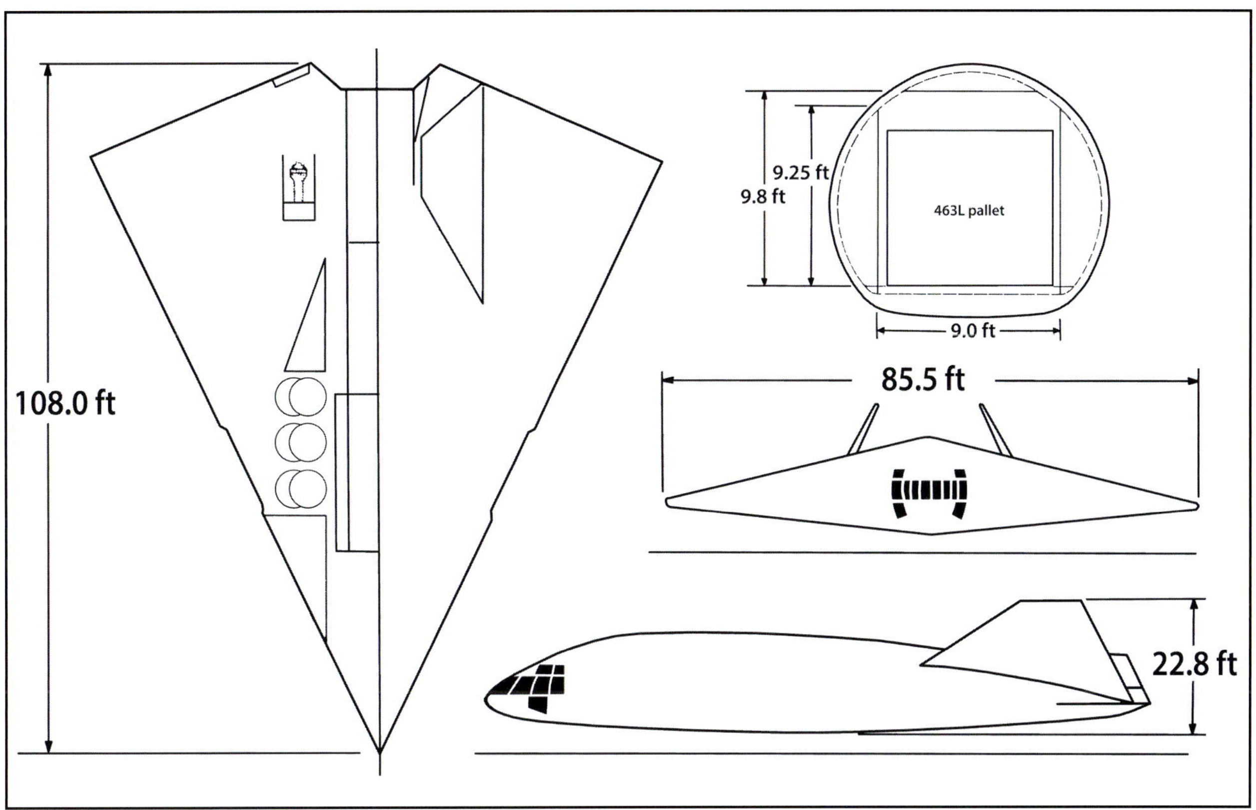

ABOVE **Boeing 'Small Delta' ATT V/STOL aircraft general arrangement.** *Boeing*

BELOW **Boeing ATT general arrangement, showing the four upper-surface blowing engines together with eight lift engines (in the booms) needed for Super STOL performance.** *Boeing*

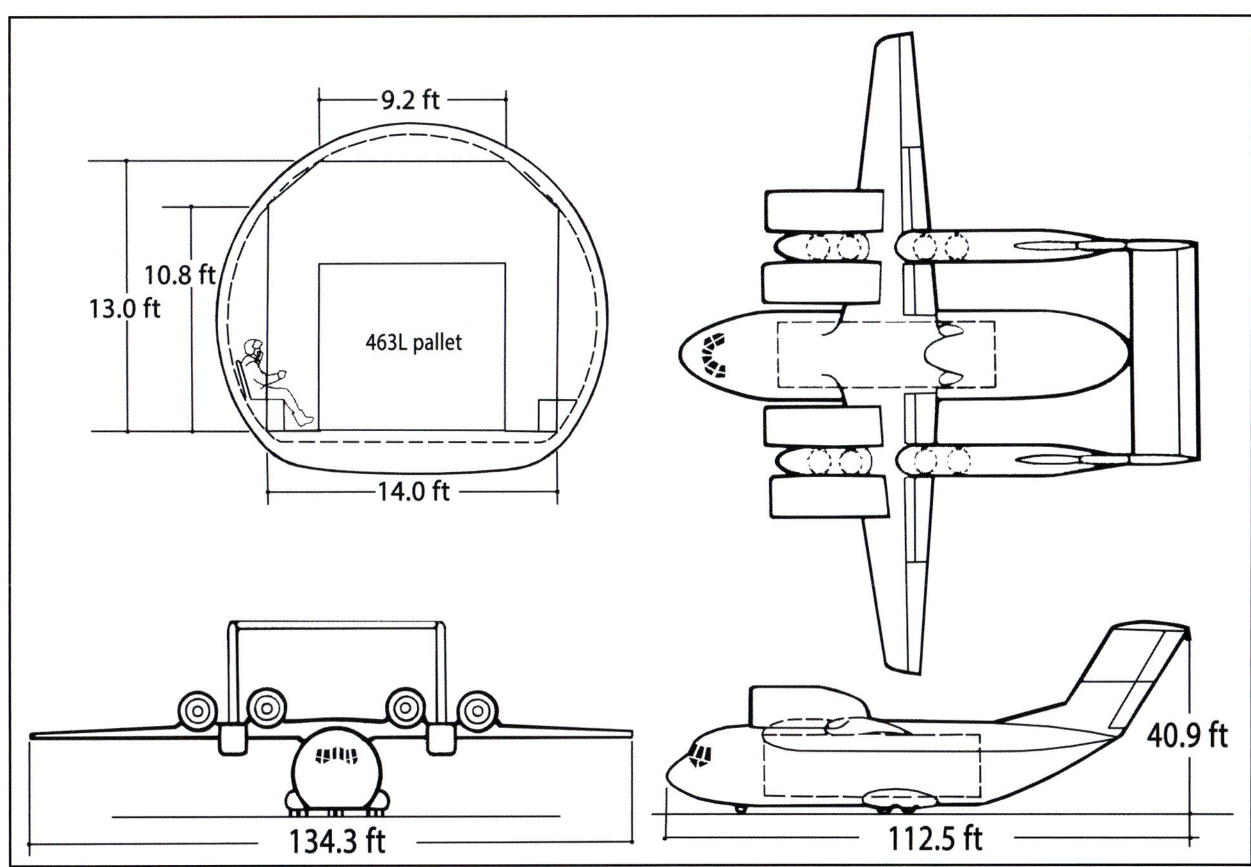

Lockheed ATT/ATTMA

Like the Boeing and Douglas studies, Lockheed began by analysing the necessary changes required in strategic airlift capability to match the changing military threat. Instead of nuclear confrontation with the Soviet Union, the United States now faced quickly developing, large-scale conventional conflicts together with an increase in low- and mid-intensity conflicts. As the study report noted, 'while we are quite familiar with what the role of tactical airlift has been and is today, the myriad factors currently impacting on the future tactical airlift environment preclude our simply projecting the past into the future.'

The airlift aircraft would have to operate in a far more hostile environment than in the past, facing anti-aircraft fire, surface-to-air missiles and fighters in the air, as well as artillery fire while on the ground. Survivability would require the ability to get in and out quickly, to fly low and fast, to hug the terrain, and possibly to incorporate low observable technology.

Lockheed concluded that the ATT would need to simultaneously satisfy four requirements:

- Deliver Army manoeuvre units and fire support systems in a combat configuration, including the M-198 howitzer, 5-ton truck and multiple-launch rocket system
- Operate day or night, in bad weather, from unpaved runways less than 2,000ft (610m) long at elevations above 4,000ft (1,220m)
- Operate routinely within 20nmi (37km) of, and occasionally cross, the front line, with survivability features to diminish the threat of missiles, anti-aircraft fire, helicopters or fighters
- Carry out multiple unrefuelled missions with a total distance up to 1,520nmi (2,810km)

The study focussed on six designs, STOL, ASTOL (Alternative STOL – a lower payload variant) and V/STOL, in both conventional and low observable formats, and evaluated within the context of four expected-threat scenarios: NATO, Southwest Asia, Central America and Korea.

Lockheed concluded that the low observable aircraft had the advantage of much lower attrition rates, but the disadvantages of higher gross weight, increased production costs, and higher operation and support expenses. The benefits of V/STOL included higher flight-hour utilisation rates, less unscheduled ground time, and higher fleet effectiveness; the penalties were higher gross weight, much higher fuel consumption, and substantially higher costs.

The conventional STOL emerged as the best choice, followed by the low observable STOL. But factoring in the assumed en route attrition rates changed the ranking: the low observable STOL came first and the low observable VTOL second. Thus, the overall assessment depended primarily on the scenario parameters, particularly when survivability was emphasised. The studies also reached some interesting conclusions, including the following:

- Ground-based threat was the design driver for a survivable aircraft
- For the early days of hostilities in the NATO, Southwest Asia and Korean scenarios, the high attrition rate of the conventional aircraft, whether STOL or V/STOL, actually precluded their use other than for very high-risk operations involving just one or two aircraft
- Sustained terminal area operations severely reduced the otherwise high level of mission survivability enjoyed by low observable aircraft
- Infrared detection rather than radar posed a greater threat to all six aircraft designs
- Low observable aircraft essentially eluded fighters and had better en route survivability
- Low-altitude flight, ideally 200ft (61m), was essential for a survivable transport mission

McDonnell Douglas ATT/ATTMA

McDonnell Douglas studied fifteen different types of propulsive lift systems as potentially suitable for the ATT. This resulted in twenty-four concepts, from which engineers selected eleven for further development. Five were designed for STOL operations, capable of operating within a 1,500ft (458m) field length; four were V/STOL aircraft requiring less than 300ft (92m); and two were categorized as SSTOL – defined in this case as an STOL aircraft capable of near VTOL operations when additional lift devices were attached.

Designers examined each of the eleven selected concepts with three different cargo box sizes, including both conventional and low observable designs, as well as different propulsion systems.

The outcome of ATT/ATTMA

The independent studies by Boeing, McDonnell Douglas and Lockheed confirmed both the Army and Air Force beliefs that only a new type of airlift capability could meet the changing shape of global threats to US interests.

McDonnell Douglas ATTMA concepts	Small box	Baseline	Larger box	Low observable
Powerplant	2 x cruise turbofans; 4 x lift turbofans	4 x turboprops @ 17,427shp (12,995kW)	4 x turbofans	2 x cruise turbofans; 6 x lift turbofans
Span	86.3ft (26.30m)	93.6ft (28.53m)	109.8ft (33.47m)	98.3ft (29.96m)
Length	92.9ft (28.32m)	117.8ft (35.91m)	124ft (37.80m)	114.8ft (34.99m)
Height	23.6ft (7.19m)	33.0ft (10.06m)	41.4ft (12.62m)	27.3ft (9.32m)
Gross weight	146,700lb (66,542kg)	155,000lb (70,307kg)	158,100lb (71,713kg)	192,400lb (87,271kg)

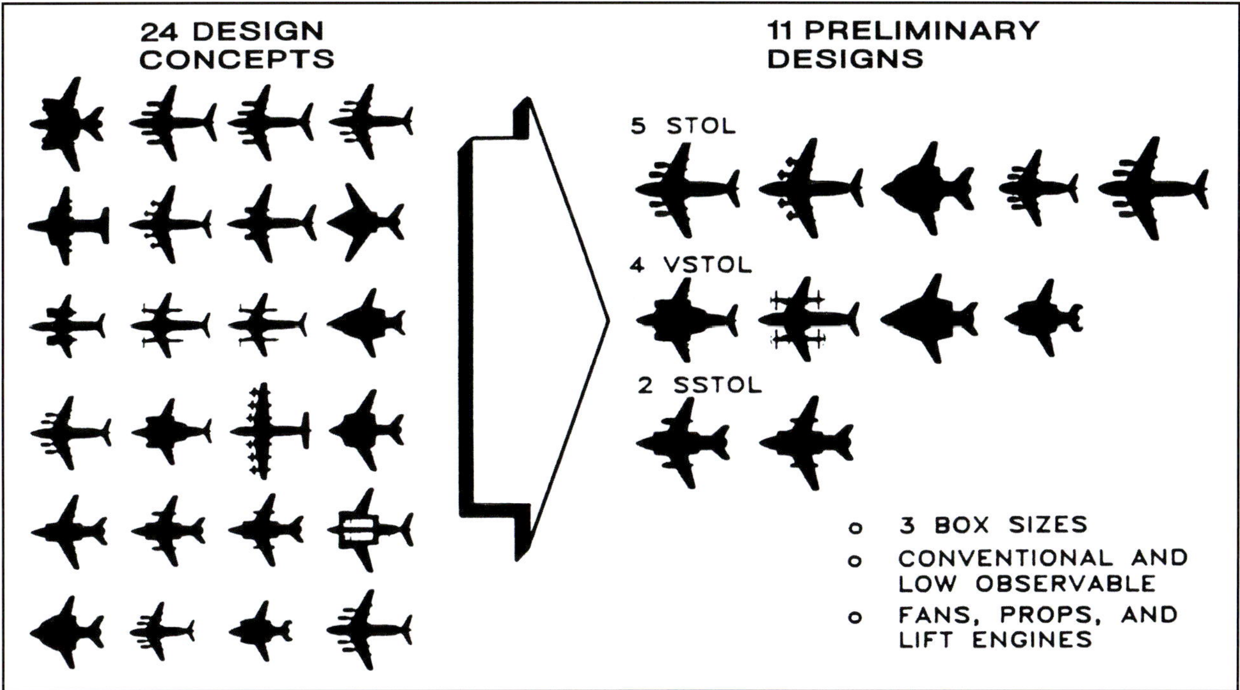

ABOVE A McDonnell Douglas illustration of the ATT design concept down-selection. *Boeing*

BELOW This 'small cargo box' configuration was adaptable to both the STOL and V/STOL configuration. *Boeing*

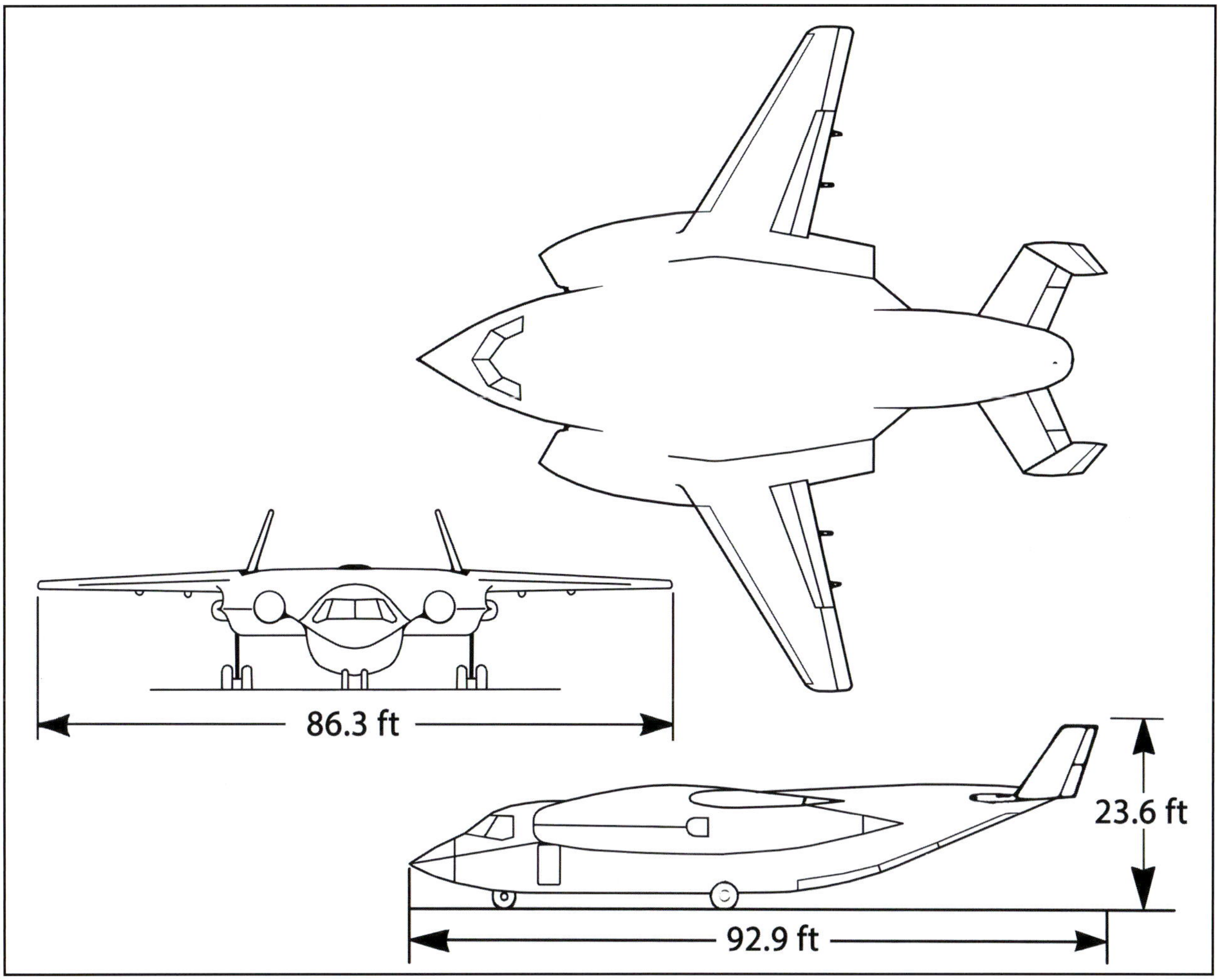

86.3 ft
23.6 ft
92.9 ft

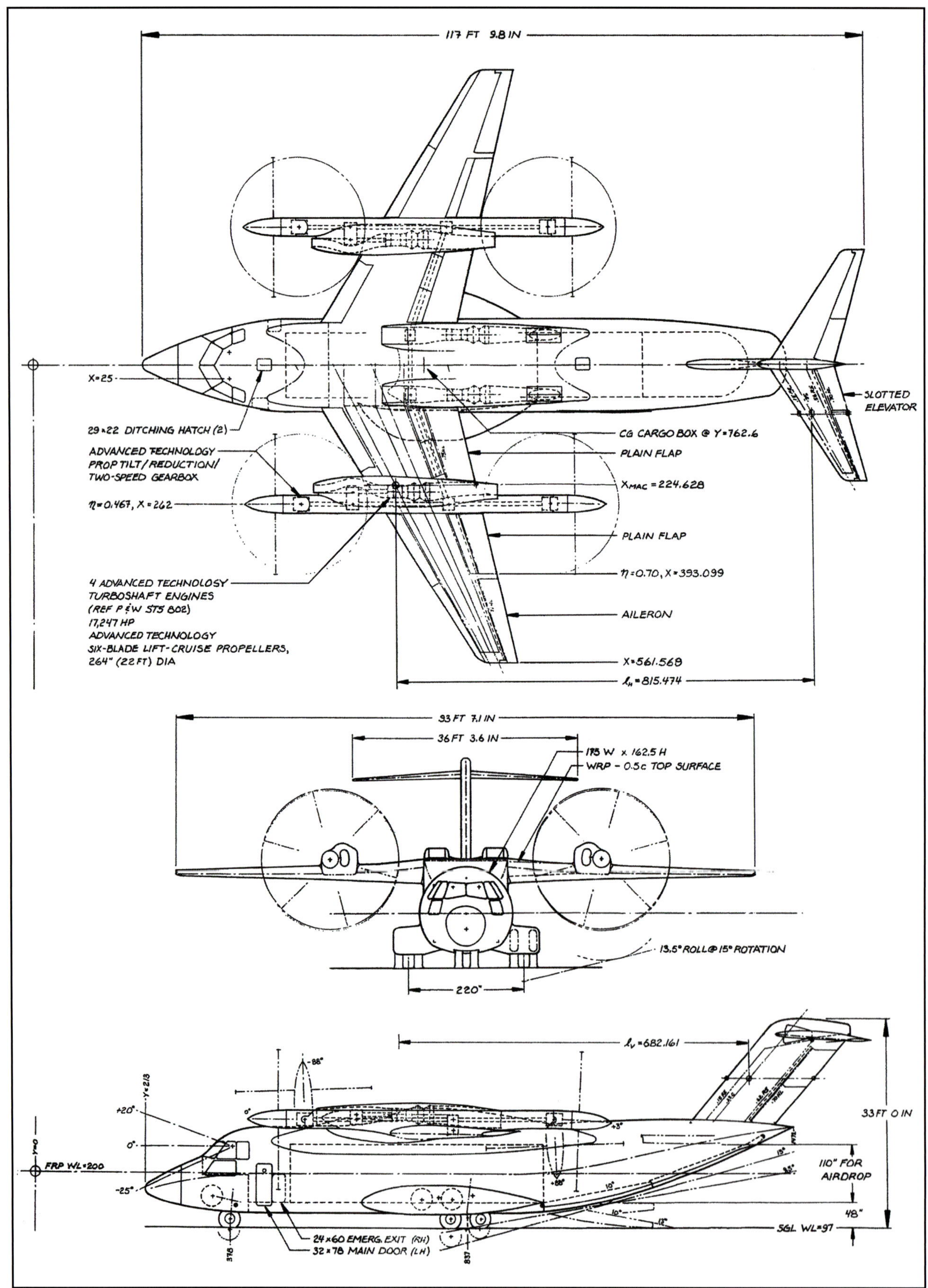

ABOVE **The McDonnell Douglas Model D-3132-43 tilt-prop ATT concept.** *Boeing*

ABOVE A McDonnell Douglas ATT proposal employing deflected thrust and lift-jets for VTOL 'small cargo box'. *Boeing*

ABOVE The McDonnell Douglas ATT Model D-3132-43 VTOL 'medium cargo box/baseline' proposal employed tilt-prop technology. *Boeing*

BELOW The McDonnell Douglas ATT STOL 'large cargo box' proposal featured blown-flap technology that drew deeply on the YC-15 design. *Boeing*

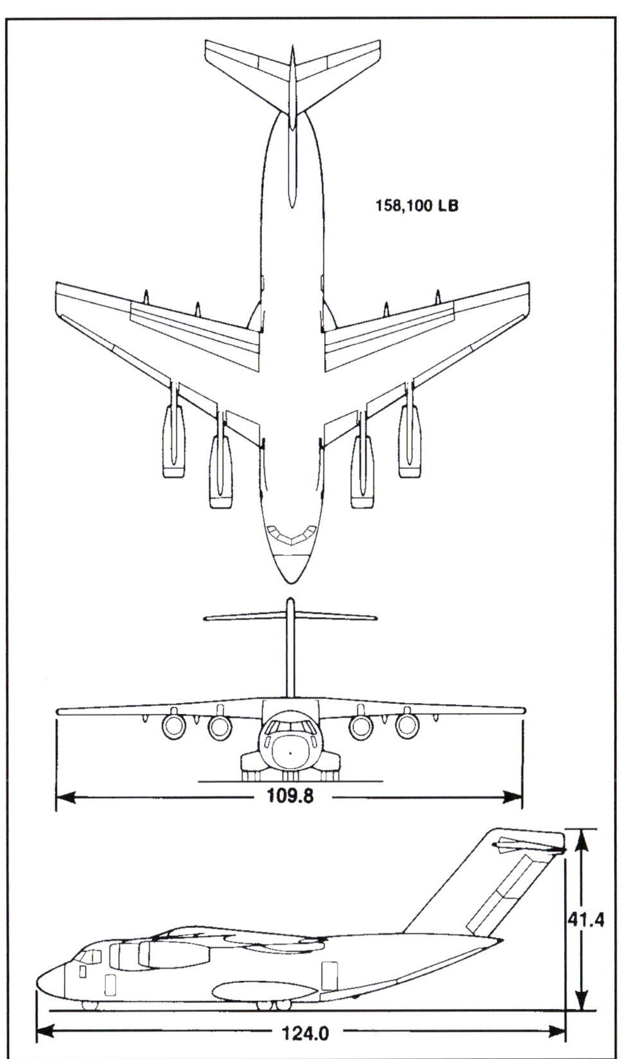

BELOW The McDonnell Douglas low observable ATT design featured six lift engines and two cruise engines. *Boeing*

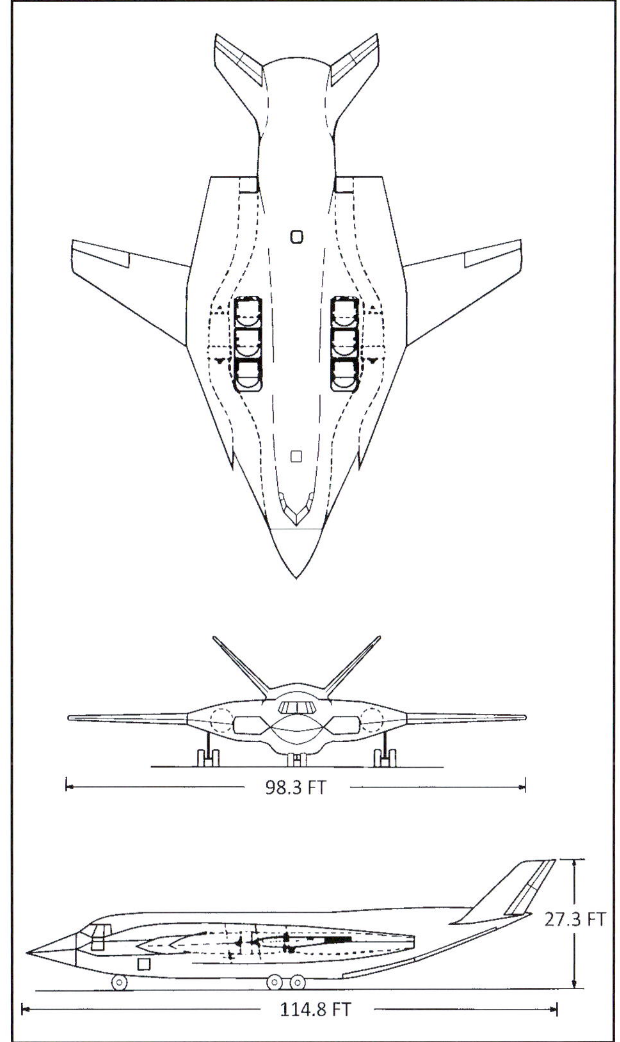

ABOVE This low observable ATT design displays an alternative circular intake design. *Boeing*

It would require aircraft better suited to operating in the combat zone: flying low and fast, with greater manoeuvrability and able to withstand higher G-loads; capable of using roads or unprepared landing sites; able to undertake rapid turnarounds; and incorporating threat avoidance (possibly 'stealth') technology.

One would have expected this to result in a specification and formalised requirement for a new aircraft, or perhaps two different types of aircraft. But it did not – the world had changed while the studies were in progress. By 1991 the peaceful collapse of the Soviet Union had brought about a sea change in US military spending and emphasis. Major top-line programmes were stretched out (such as the Advanced Tactical Fighter, or ATF), curtailed (B-2), or cancelled outright (SRAM II, A-12). Nonetheless, the ATT/ATTMA investigations informed the future thinking of the Army and Air Force, as well as that of the aircraft.

DARPA, SO/LIC, and Northrop's SMOCA

In January 1990 the Defense Advanced Research Projects Agency (DARPA) issued a 'Broad Agency Announcement' soliciting 'Research in Technologies Supporting Special Operations/Low Intensity Conflict (SO/LIC)'. In its April response, Northrop submitted a proposal to study a 'SMOCA' – a 'SO/LIC Mission Oriented Combat Aircraft' – described as a multi-purpose midsized aircraft with a 15,000lb (6804kg) payload.

Created at Northrop's Aircraft Division, the initial design concept proposed a vehicle resembling Northrop's earlier Tacit Blue radar surveillance test bed aircraft; it featured a high-volume fuselage, an internal cargo bay, a high-mounted, highly tapered straight wing and a V-tail. Engineers adapted Northrop's patented transverse-thrust lift augmentation (TTLA – essentially span-wise blowing of engine bleed air across the flaps and control surfaces to re-energise the detached airflow) to help achieve Super-STOL (SSTOL) performance.

Northrop SOTAC concept	
Powerplant	2 x turbofans
Span	75ft (22.86m)
Length	65ft 3in (19.89m)
Height	19ft (5.79m)
Payload	15,000lb (6,804kg)
Mission radius	1,500nmi (2,778km)

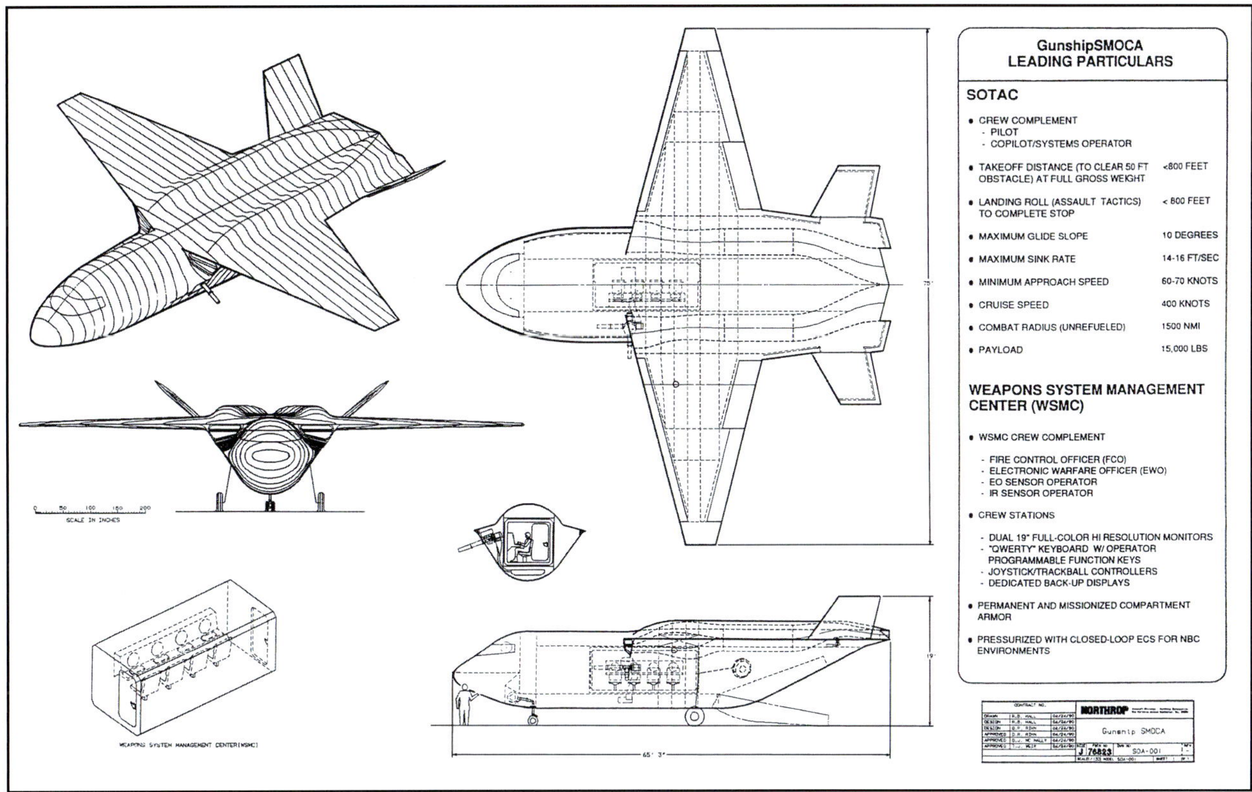

ABOVE **This early Gunship/SMOCA design appears to have drawn its planform from the earlier Northrop Tacit Blue demonstrator. In this design, the air vehicle itself was called the Special Operations Tactical Air Carrier (SOTAC) and the crew capsule was the SMOCA Air Vehicle Enclosure (SAVE).** *Courtesy of Northrop Grumman Corporation*

BELOW **An alternative design drew on the more rigorous edge alignment design seen on the B-2 bomber. Engine exhaust was discharged through thin, rectangular ducts ahead of the inboard flaps.** *Courtesy of Northrop Grumman Corporation*

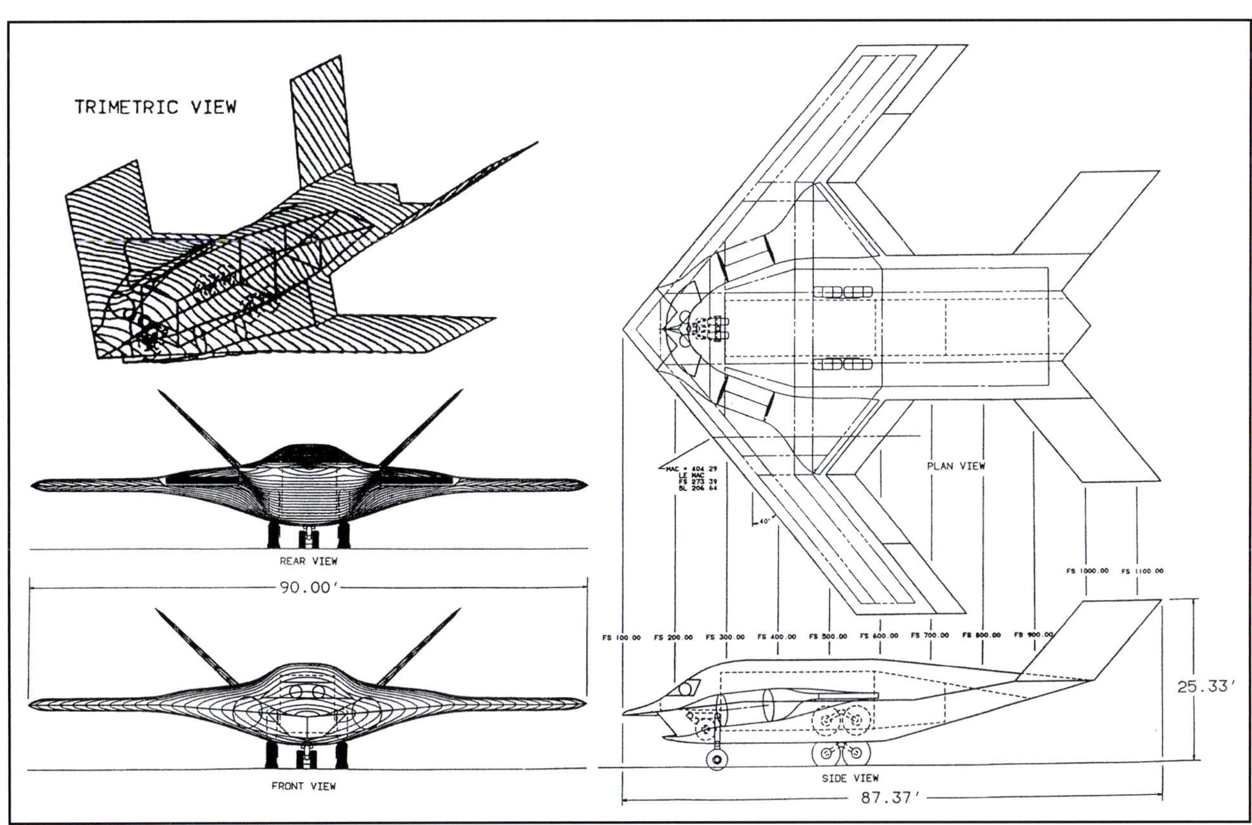

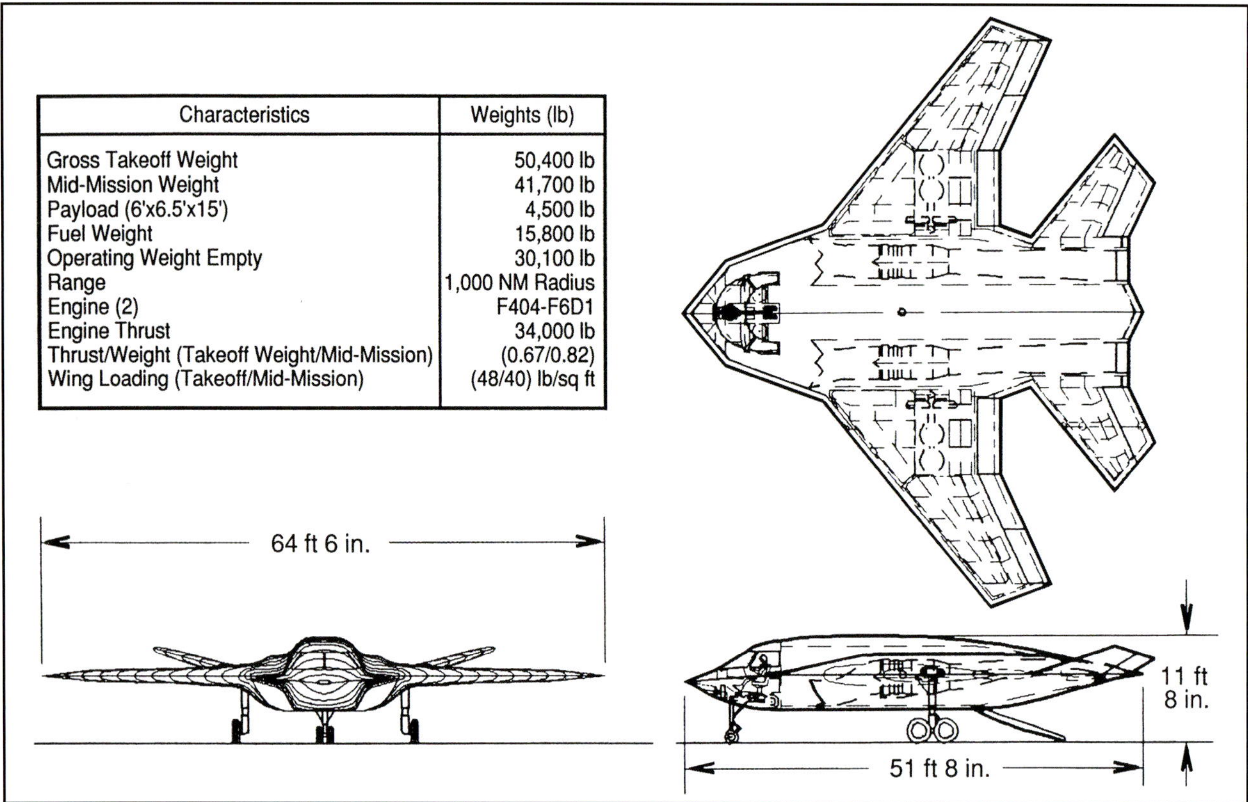

Characteristics	Weights (lb)
Gross Takeoff Weight	50,400 lb
Mid-Mission Weight	41,700 lb
Payload (6'x6.5'x15')	4,500 lb
Fuel Weight	15,800 lb
Operating Weight Empty	30,100 lb
Range	1,000 NM Radius
Engine (2)	F404-F6D1
Engine Thrust	34,000 lb
Thrust/Weight (Takeoff Weight/Mid-Mission)	(0.67/0.82)
Wing Loading (Takeoff/Mid-Mission)	(48/40) lb/sq ft

ABOVE The final Northrop SMOCA design combined elements of the previous studies into a form that balanced low observability with other mission requirements. *Courtesy of Northrop Grumman Corporation*

BELOW These views show a SMOCA being 'missionised' at a forward operating location, with the installation of mission-specific conformal under-wing sponsons and a crew enclosure ready to be rolled into the cargo bay. *Courtesy of Northrop Grumman Corporation, art by Aldo Spadoni*

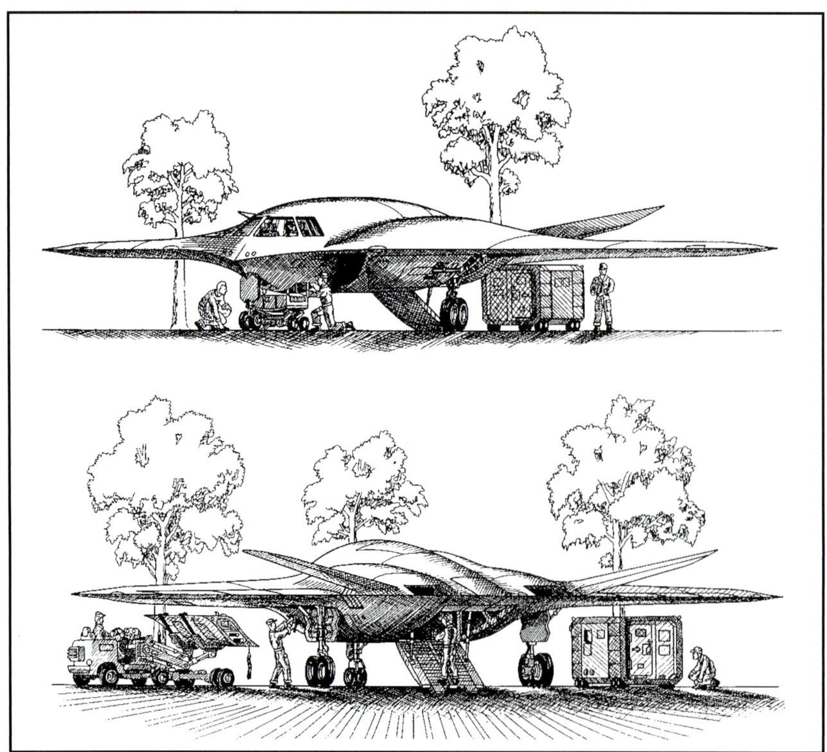

By the initial study's completion in November 1990, the SMOCA design had evolved considerably. It now had a full perimeter chine, and from the side looked similar to the B-2, although with low-mounted intakes. Two fixed horizontal stabilisers with elevators controlled pitch. Its twin F404-GE-F6D1 turbofans were buried in the fuselage on either side of the cargo bay. Its wingspan of just 64ft 6in (19.66m) made it compatible with carrier stowage without the need for wing folding.

Four missions were planned: basic airlifter, gunship, covert infiltration/exfiltration, and special mission platform. To accomplish these missions, the aircraft would use basic stealth technology and have nominal cargo capability. If missions required additional capabilities, aircrews would optionally add tailored avionics, under-wing conformal sponsons (to contain side-firing guns or drogue refuelling gear), or a cargo bay capsule carrying any extra crew needed to perform a particular mission.

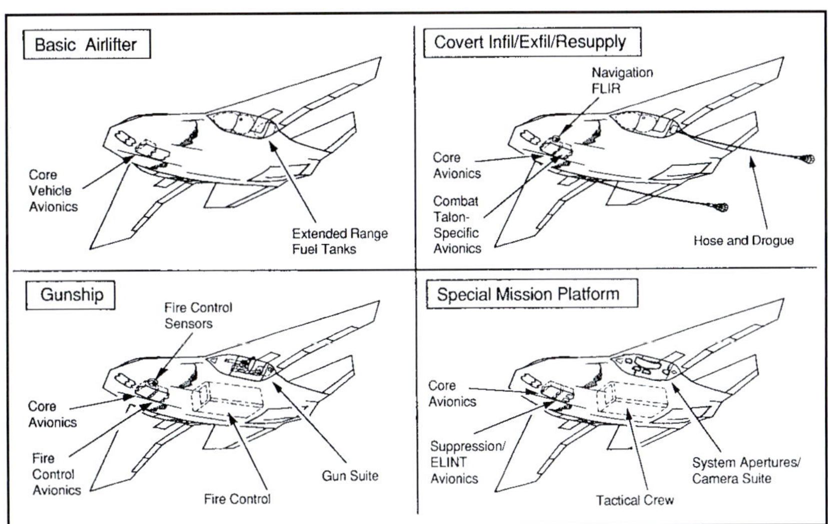

RIGHT Northrop's SMOCA was to have a multi-mission capability with add-on conformal under-wing sponsons and palletised avionics. *Courtesy of Northrop Grumman Corporation*

Northrop SMOCA proof-of-concept design	
Powerplant	2 x GE F404-F6D2 turbofans @ 17,000lb (78.62kN) thrust
Span	64ft 6in (19.66m)
Length	51ft 8in (15.75m)
Height	11ft 1in (3.38m)
Wing area	2,123sq ft (197.3m²)
Gross weight	50,400lb (22,961kg)
Payload	4,500lb (2,041kg)
Radius	1,000nmi (1,852km)

BELOW Comparative sizes of the SMOCA and other aircraft in USAF service at the time. The SMOCA is shown with an alternative higher-aspect-ratio wing and tail for longer range. *Courtesy of Northrop Grumman Corporation*

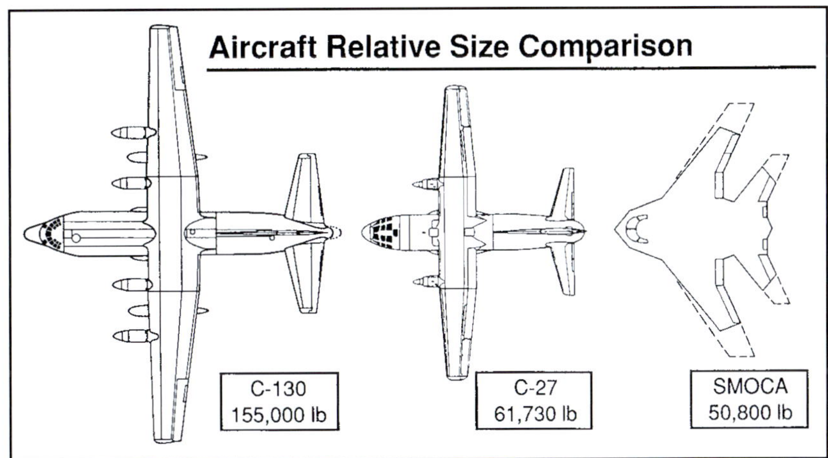

1990: Special Operations Forces Transport Aircraft (SOFTA)

From October 1988 to May 1989 the Air Force sponsored Special Operations transport studies by Boeing Military Airplanes and McDonnell Douglas. Northrop followed with a study in the second half of 1990 and Rockwell International's North American Aircraft Operations continued work on similar designs. All of the VTOL studies focused on using lift-fans, apparently responding to the Air Force's belief that no other VTOL propulsion method (such as tilt-rotor) was compatible with stealth technology.

Boeing and Lockheed SOFTA designs

Few details have emerged of the Boeing and Lockheed Martin SOFTA designs. However, one Lockheed illustration from the period shows a design that matches SOFTA requirements, with fan-driven vertical lift and low observability, and compact enough for shipboard operations.

RIGHT The Lockheed STOVL SOFTA concept used two large fans embedded in the wing for vertical lift. *Lockheed*

ABOVE The Northrop fan-in-wing SOFTA concept. *Courtesy of Northrop Grumman Corporation*

Northrop SOFTA

Northrop's SOFTA study was a six-month effort carried out in 1990 at Northrop's Advanced Technology Development Center (ATDC), based at the B-2 Division, Pico Rivera, California. It drew on the company's unique experience of designing and building the large, stealthy B-2 Advanced Technology Bomber.

The Northrop Special Operations Aircraft (SOA) design study requirements were:

- STOL/VTOL capability
- 1,000nmi (1,850km) unrefuelled mission radius, flown at low altitude
- 2,400nmi (4,440km) deployment range at 0.7 Mach
- 300kt (555km/h) cruise speed
- 4,500lb (2,040kg) payload
- 9ft x 9ft x 30ft (2.75m x 2.75m x 9.15m) cargo volume
- Five-minute hover, mid-mission
- Aircraft carrier compatible
- In-flight refuellable
- Engine-out capable

Northrop's study recommended four concepts – three VTOL and one STOL design for comparison – with the potential to carry out SOFTA missions:

- The 'preferred' design was a 100ft (30.5m) span, multi-engine, edge-aligned trapezoidal flying-wing planform with no vertical stabiliser. The wingtips were capable of being folded upwards for carrier storage. The four tip-driven lift-fans, covered by doors during horizontal cruise, used the same basic technology as demonstrated during the Ryan XV-5A programme in the 1960s.
- The 'baseline' was the same size and externally very similar to the 'preferred' design, but used a different propulsion arrangement featuring fixed inlets below the chine.
- The 'alternative' design was a scaled version of the 'baseline' with the payload bay volume reduced from 9ft x 9ft x 30ft (2.75m x 2.75m x 9.15m) in the 'preferred' and 'baseline' designs to 6ft x 6.5ft x 15ft (1.83m x 1.98m x 4.78m). It used a unique but complex propulsion system that combined four F404 Growth II engines, four lift-fans, and two turbine-driven aft-fans.
- The 'STOL' design from the previous SMOCA effort was included for comparison.

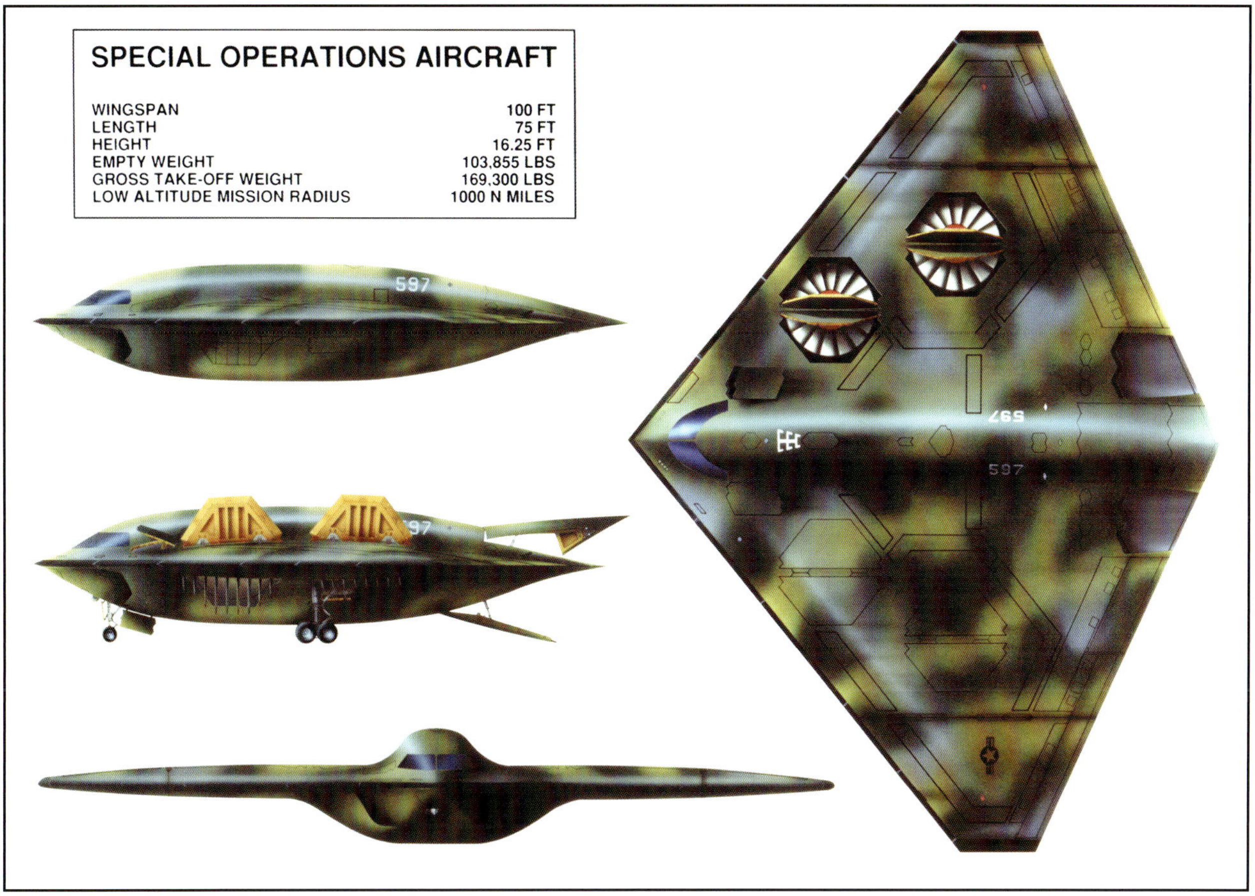

SPECIAL OPERATIONS AIRCRAFT

WINGSPAN	100 FT
LENGTH	75 FT
HEIGHT	16.25 FT
EMPTY WEIGHT	103,855 LBS
GROSS TAKE-OFF WEIGHT	169,300 LBS
LOW ALTITUDE MISSION RADIUS	1000 N MILES

ABOVE Northrop's 'baseline' SOFTA design drew heavily on B-2 design strategies including edge alignment for low radar observability. Primary engine inlets were positioned below the chine, and auxiliary inlets above. *Courtesy of Northrop Grumman Corporation, art by Aldo Spadoni*

The 'preferred' SOFTA design won for its overall simplicity, and its ability to complete the mission (including the hovering phase) with one engine inoperative. Moreover, Northrop anticipated that advanced materials and improved dynamics would yield substantial improvements in both performance and efficiencies of the lift-fans over the technologies in the 1960s-vintage fans demonstrated by General Electric in the Ryan XV-5A/B.

The upper and lower rear doors allowed wide access to the cargo bay and opened in flight for air-dropping. Special Forces could rapidly deploy while the aircraft was hovering (as was sometimes the case with helicopter operations), although jet velocities beneath the aircraft presented a difficult challenge to overcome.

Northrop concluded that the design, when fully developed, could meet all of the specified requirements, but needed engineering refinements to optimise the tip-driven fans' location and performance.

BELOW Northrop's SOFTA 'preferred' design had an alternative inlet arrangement, repositioning them all above the chine. *Courtesy of Northrop Grumman Corporation*

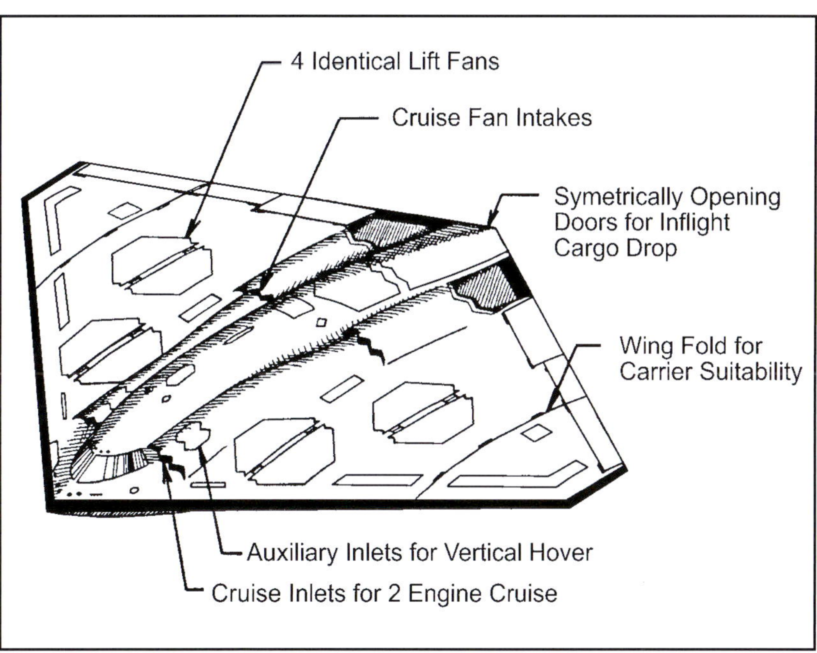

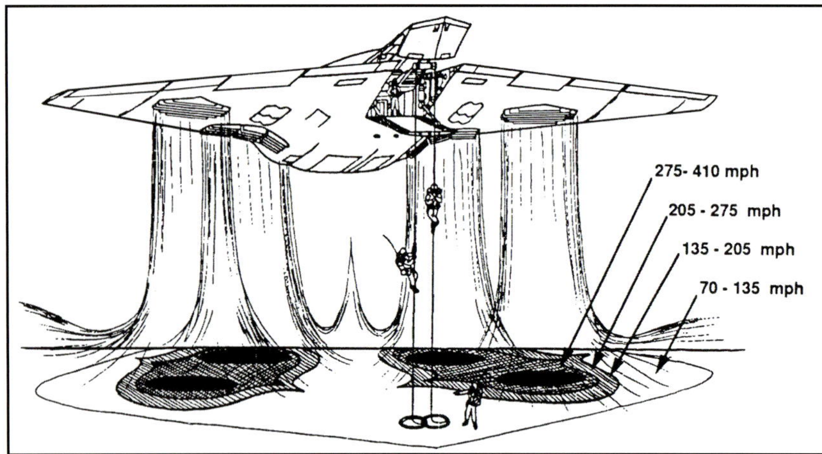

ABOVE Northrop's 'preferred' SOFTA design is seen in hover mode as Special Forces soldiers rappel down to the ground, illustrating a major operational challenge: rocks and other debris were turned into lethal projectiles by the powerful downward fan exhaust. *Courtesy of Northrop Grumman Corporation*

BELOW Aircraft carrier elevator and hangar deck door compatibility for two of Northrop's SOFTA design options and the STOL alternative, recognisable as the earlier SMOCA design. The designs were capable of taking off from the carrier without the use of the catapult. *Courtesy of Northrop Grumman Corporation*

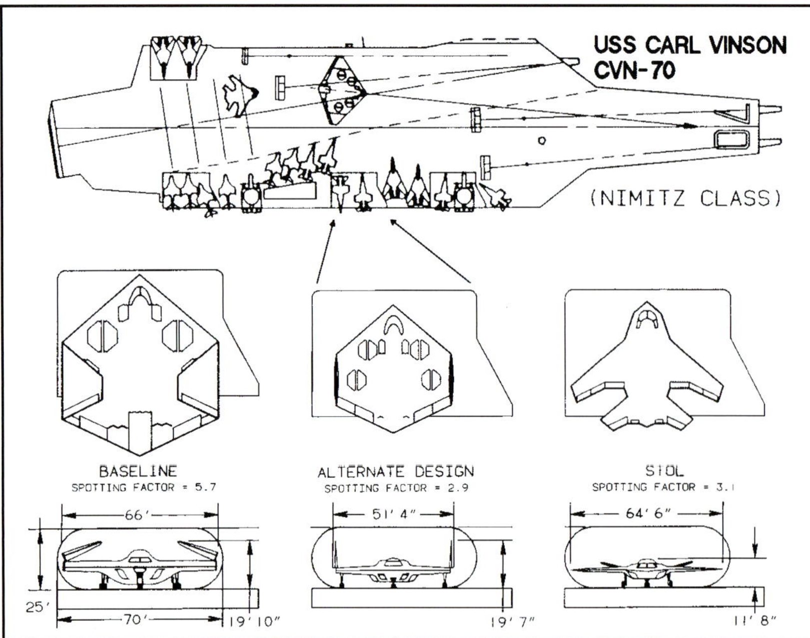

Northrop SOFTA concepts	Baseline	Preferred	Alternative
Powerplant	4 x cruise turbofans; 4 x tip-driven lift-fans	4 x cruise turbofans; 4 x tip-driven lift-fans	2 x GE F404 Growth II cruise turbofans @ 18,000lb (80.07kN) thrust; 4 x tip-driven lift-fans
Span	100ft (30.48m)	100ft (30.48m)	71ft (21.64m)
Length	75ft (22.86m)	75ft (22.86m)	53ft (16.15m)
Height	16ft 3in (4.96m)	16ft 3in (4.96m)	12ft 2in (3.71m)
Wing area	4,130sq ft (383.7m²)	4,130sq ft (383.7m²)	2,123sq ft (197.2m²)
Gross weight	169,300lb (kg)	173,650(kg)	130,300lb (kg)
Payload	4,500lb (2,041kg)	4,500lb (2,041kg)	4,500lb (2,041kg)
Cruise speed	300kt (556m/h)	300kt (556m/h)	300kt (556km/h)
Range	2,400nmi (4,440km)	2,400nmi (4,400km)	2,400nmi (4,400km)

Rockwell (North American Aircraft Operations)

Little is known about Rockwell's submission for the SOFTA study, other than drawings showing a VTOL aircraft with fan-in-wing lift, an unusual low-aspect-ratio wing shaped like a trapezoid, and a butterfly tail.

Late 1990s: Boeing (former McDonnell Douglas) 'Super Frog' and ATT

As discussed in Chapter Four, companies had proposed numerous tilt-wing STOL aircraft during the late 1960s, during the development of the Light Intra-Theatre Transport (LIT). At the time these came to nothing. However, by the 1990s computing and material technologies had advanced tremendously, and Boeing began to comb through those earlier LIT studies for new possibilities. The result was an updated tilt-wing design affectionately dubbed 'Super Frog'. The initial aircraft's straight wing planform quickly evolved into a dramatic forward-swept wing development, now renamed the 'Advanced Theater Transport' or ATT (not to be confused with the ATT/ATTMA of the early 1980s).

Boeing unveiled the design in May 2000. It was a tail-less, four-engine aircraft with eight-bladed propellers. The tilt wing rotated to a 45° angle and incorporated externally blown flaps that generated lift under all conditions. Although this ruled out VTOL (which would have required far greater engine power or much reduced gross weight), it enabled landing and taking-off from strips as short as 600ft (183m), as well as very steep approaches and take-offs – critical capabilities in forward war zones. It also permitted the aircraft to fly as slowly as 36kt (67km/h).

Boeing (McDonnell Douglas) D3132-187 ATT	
Powerplant	4 x turboshafts
Span	134.8ft (41.09m)
Length	107.6ft (32.80m)
Wing area	2,942sq ft (m²)

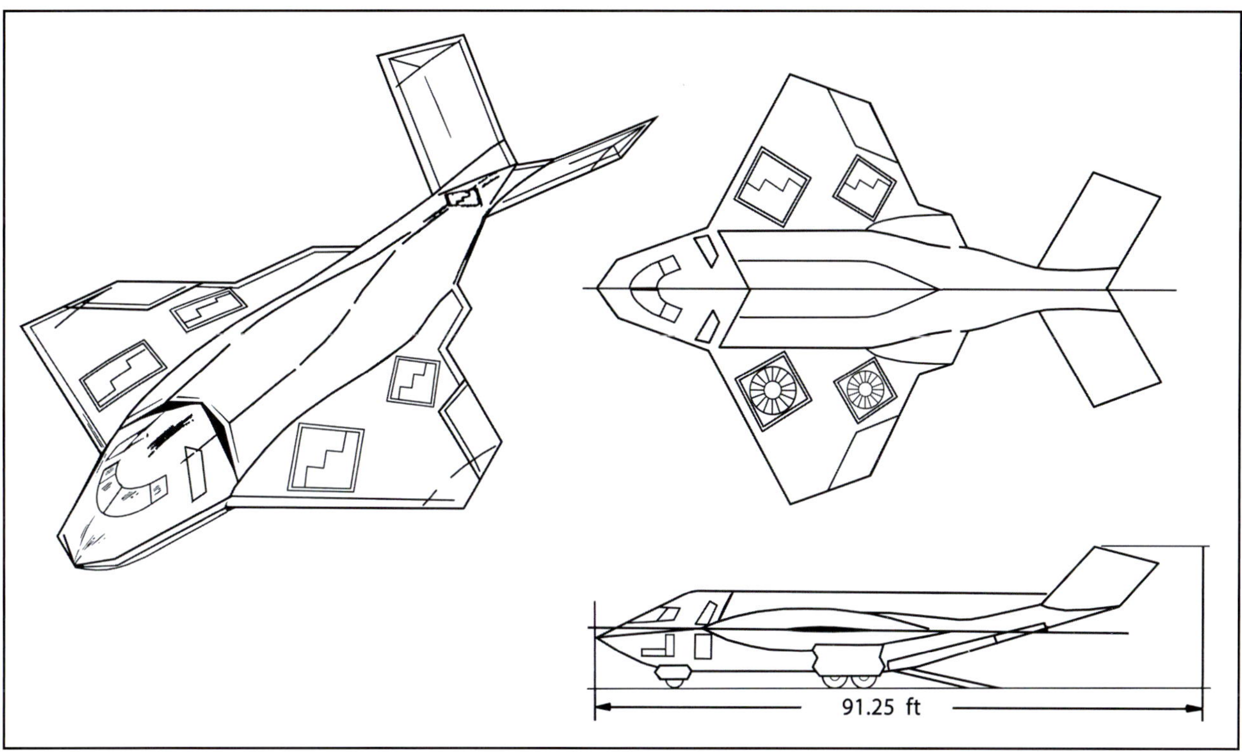

ABOVE The North American Aircraft Operations SOFTA concept. *Boeing*

BELOW Boeing's 'Advanced Theater Transport' continuation of the SSTOL studies, dated October 2001. The Model D3132-187 was designed at the former Douglas/McDonnell Douglas site in Long Beach and kept the Douglas design numbering sequence. After the heritage Douglas Long Beach plant was closed, the Advanced Design group relocated to what was originally the Douglas Space and Missiles campus in Huntington Beach and continued its focus on military airlifters. *Boeing*

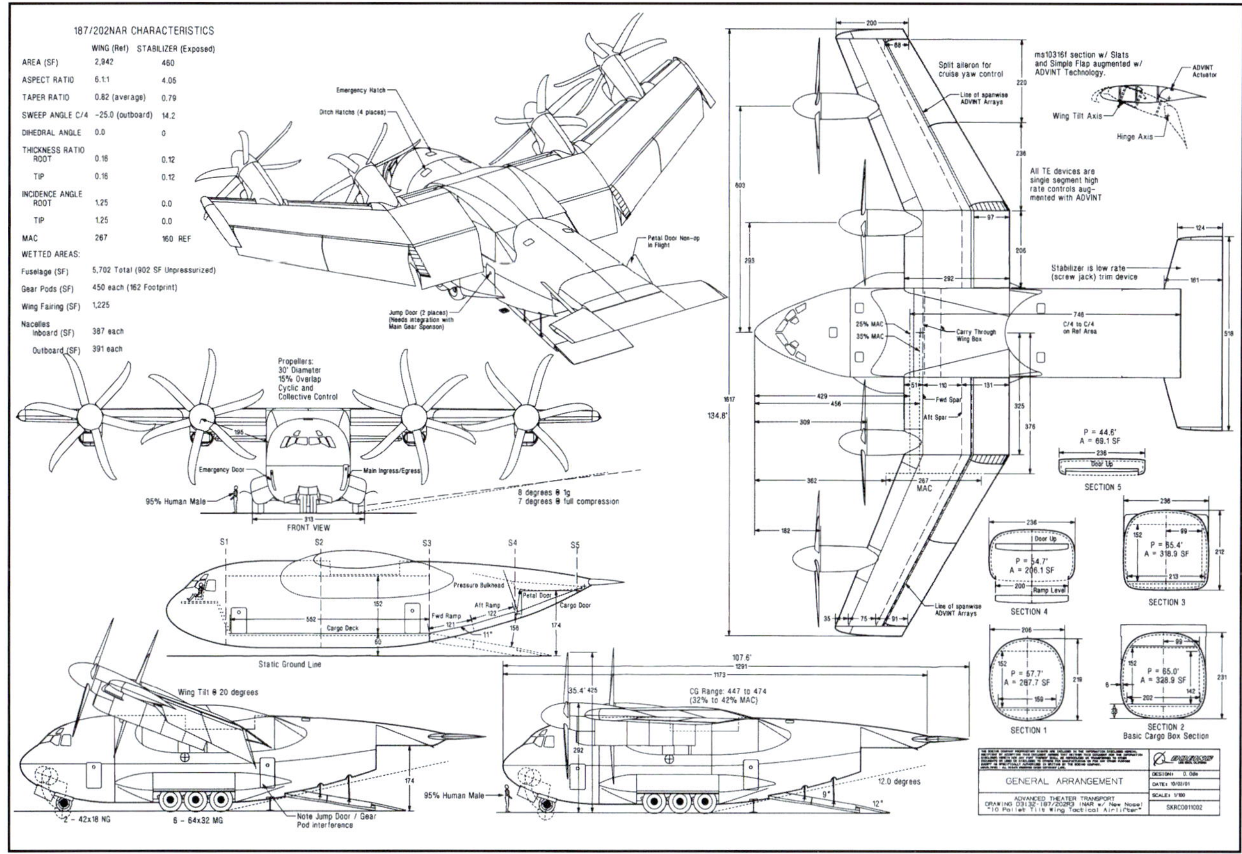

ABOVE **The Boeing 'Advanced Theater Transport' as developed from the early McDonnell Douglas 'Super Frog'.** *John Aldaz collection*

BELOW **This Boeing ATT variation has a fuselage 216in (6.46m) wide, sized to carry a partially disassembled MH-47 and twenty-seven soldiers.** *Boeing*

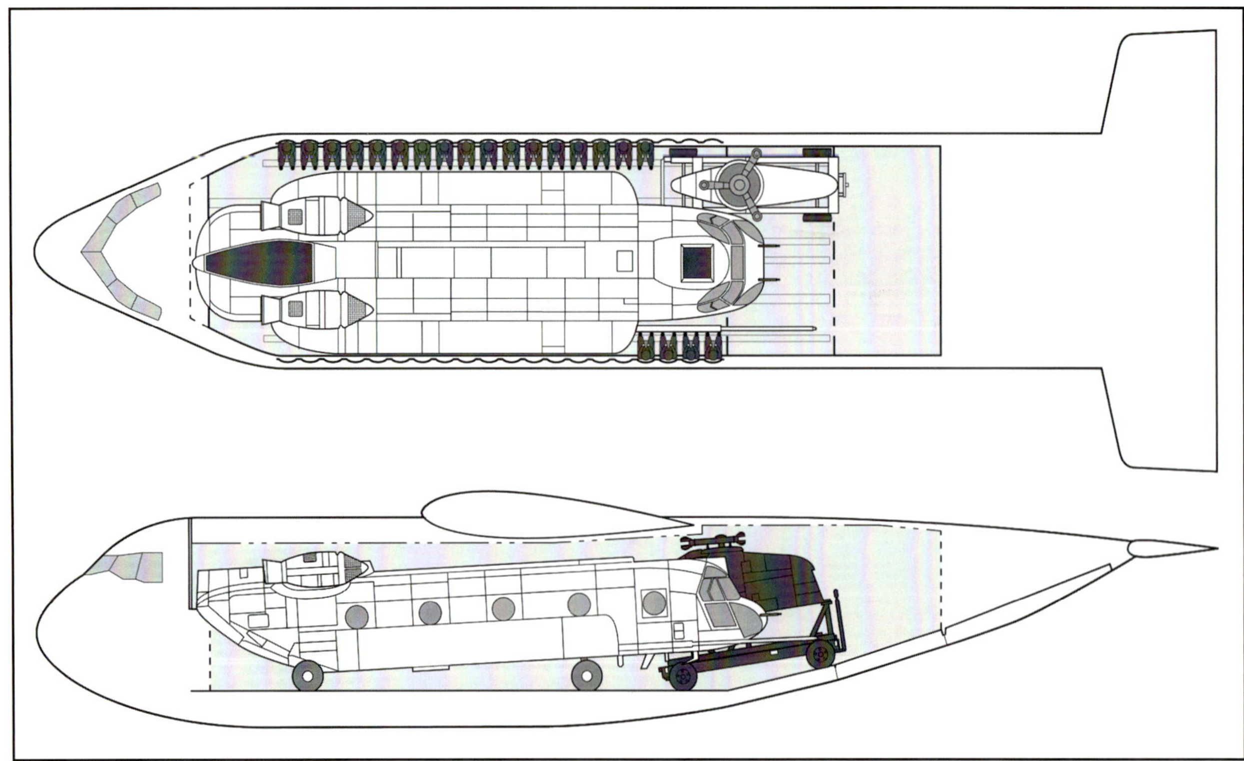

The outboard section of the wing was swept forward to enable pitch control through engine/propeller modulation when the wing was tilted. This feature minimised the aft stabiliser area. The swept-forward design also increased ground clearance in case there was a sudden roll input from a wind gust during take-off or landing. The wingspan and length of the aircraft were less than that of a C-130, while the fuselage was almost twice as wide, and Boeing claimed that its ATT could carry a 100,000lb (45,360kg) payload – twice that of the C-130J.

Special Operations airlifters: The status to date

For decades engineers have wrestled with the unique challenges thrown at them for a viable Special Operations airlifter. Designers have responded with a tremendous range of imaginative and extremely innovative proposals, but as yet none has ever flown – at least as far as is known. Of those special operations aircraft operated openly, the Air Force CV-22B Osprey comes closest to meeting the capabilities sought over the past thirty years. It is an impressive aircraft, with VTOL capability, but comes nowhere near the performance specification and low observability characteristics sought in the programmes described above.

While the existence of a small number of highly classified craft cannot be ruled out (such as the highly modified UH-60 Blackhawk helicopters used in the 2011 Bin Laden raid), the Special Ops forces have turned in the meantime to a mixed fleet of C-130 derivatives and smaller aircraft that maintain their 'stealth' nature, not by employing low observability technology, but by simply not attracting much attention. These are commercial aircraft that exist in plain sight but blend into the background through their sheer banality.

In drafting this chapter, the authors have taken care to cover only those concepts supported by credible, supportable documentation. Many more 'secret projects' undoubtedly remain to be revealed – and will stay that way until declassification allows their discussion in public.

BELOW Despite the decades of study and effort, the only acknowledged SOF V/STOL (non-helicopter) platform today is the CV-22B Osprey, leveraged from the Marine Corps V-22 programme. Here, viewed through night vision equipment, an AFSOC CV-22B conducts a covert refuelling operation in darkness off of the coast of San Diego, California, during the 'Emerald Trident' exercise on 24 January 2019. *USAF photo by SRA Erin Piazza*

Chapter Eleven
Exploring New Technologies

1980 to a future that could look very different

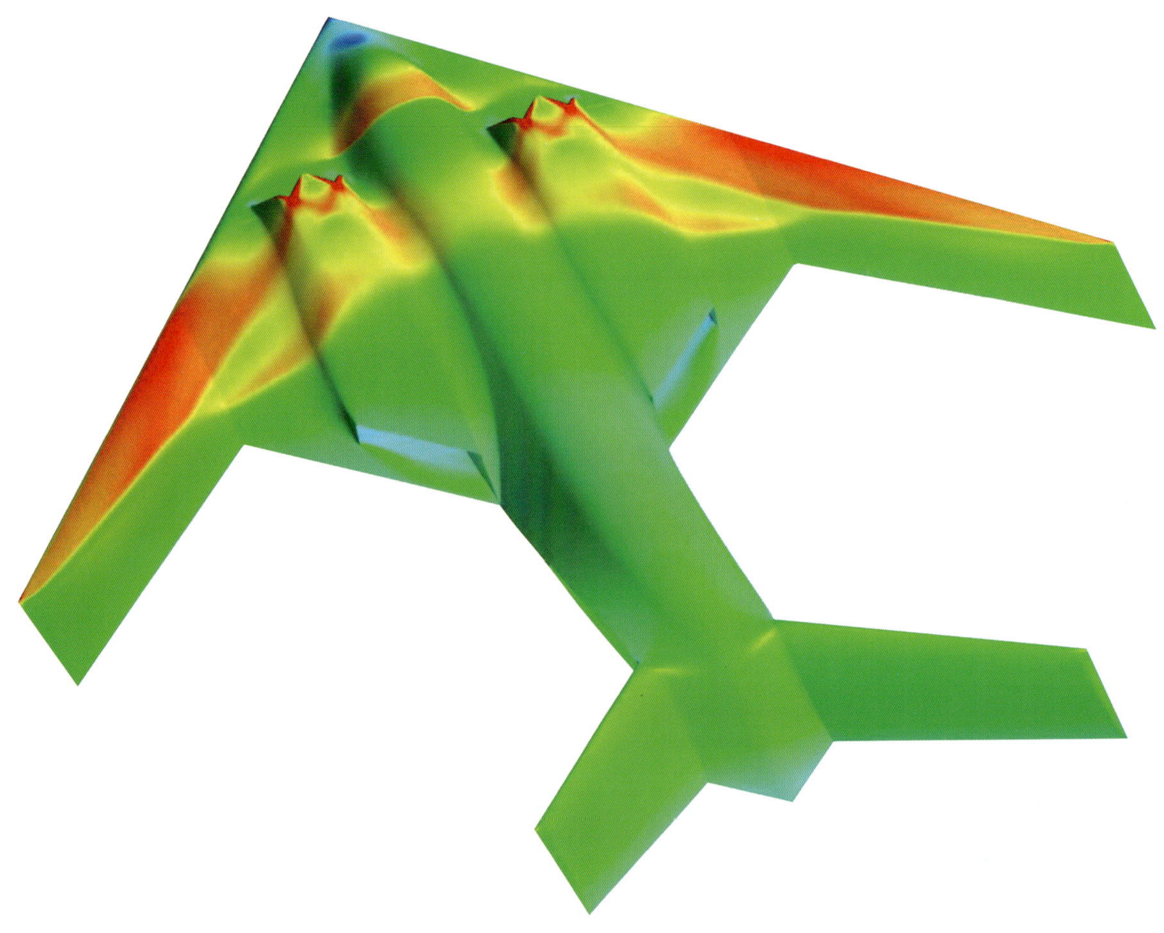

ABOVE A computational fluid dynamics (CFD) diagram of pressures on the Boeing's proposed Speed Agile Concept Demonstrator (SACD) – blue is the highest pressure and red denotes the lowest pressure areas. *Boeing*

This book and its companion volume, *American Secret Projects 2: Airlifters from the Second World War to 1961*, chart the development of US military air transport design from its inception to the present day. It is a path that has been shaped by the changing face of conflict and ever-advancing technology.

Entering the 21st century, the Air Force finally had a highly capable airlifter fleet developed for its specific needs over many years, with a long service life ahead. Nonetheless, it felt pressured to expand and enhance this capability; its future fleet would not only be larger and smarter, but also integrate entirely new technologies. Continuing global tensions make it inevitable that future transports will incorporate stealth; will use modern structures and materials to enable previously impossible configurations; and will probably integrate new tilt-rotor technologies developed following the CV-22 Osprey's introduction. This chapter describes recent projects that may well point to the next generation of airlifter design.

Even as Special Operations transport studies ramped up, tactical long-range airlift capability continued to present problems. By 1994 Congress was alarmed by the C-17's escalating costs and schedule slippage during the Engineering and Manufacturing Development (EMD) phase. It temporarily capped the

ABOVE By the early 1990s it seemed that the pieces of the heavy airlifter fleet were finally in place: the C-17A (left), the C-5A/B (middle) and the dual-role KC-10 tanker-transport. However, the C-17's development problems and cost overruns led to Congressional support for the Non-Developmental Airlift Aircraft (NDAA). *US Air Force photo by Heide Couch*

programme at forty aircraft and began a complete evaluation of the airlifter's cost and performance.

1994: Non-Development Airlift Aircraft (NDAA)

In March 1994, the DoD responded to Congressional pressures with a study of alternatives to acquiring the remaining eighty C-17s on order. Labelled the Non-Developmental Airlift Aircraft (NDAA) programme, it examined the viability of substituting a commercial freighter, including even out-of-production types like the DC-10-30, Lockheed L-1011 and Boeing 747 variants, as an 'off-the-shelf' solution.

Eight companies or consortia expressed initial interest in the requirement, but only Boeing responded to the Request for Proposal (RFP). It proposed two variations of its 747-400F. The first was the standard 747-400F commercial aircraft; the second was a modified version with a strengthened floor and enlarged cargo door. The Air Force gave it the C-33 designation. This was not the first USAF transport designation assigned to the 747; in 1988 the designation C-19 had been reserved for the 747-100 if modified for CRAF use. While considering Boeing's submission, the DoD also requested Lockheed to submit costs for an upgraded C-5, designating the new design as the C-5D.

BELOW A display model of the Boeing C-33/747-400F. *John Aldaz collection*

ABOVE Despite fifty years of strenuous sales efforts, Boeing sold only one 747 cargo variant to the Air Force, a Model 747-400F subsequently converted to the YAL-1 Airborne Laser test bed. It is trailed here by the NC-135 that served as a surrogate missile target. *US Air Force*

But on 3 November 1995, convinced that the development problems were solved, the DoD announced its decision to reinstate its original order for a total of 120 C-17s. It also announced that no other aircraft would be bought either to replace or to supplement the C-17. As a side note, despite submitting numerous 747 proposals to the Air Force over a period of fifty years, Boeing sold just nine aircraft to the service during those five decades: one YAL-1A Laser test bed, four E-4 Command Posts, two VC-25A presidential transports, and two 747-8Fs as VC-25A replacements.

The 2000s: The KC-X tanker-transport battle

By 2000 the Air Force was recognising that its fleet of KC-135 Stratotankers – the oldest type in its inventory – desperately needed replacements. Yet despite the clear requirement, easily met by simply adapting an existing airframe, the process proved to be lengthy, difficult, and highly controversial.

The service initially explored replacing nearly a hundred of its oldest KC-135Es with the Boeing KC-767, an adaptation of the Boeing 767 civil airliner/freighter that had first flown some twenty years earlier. In 2002 the DoD gave the substantially modified aircraft the designation KC-767A. Unusually, the cash-strapped Pentagon considered leasing rather than purchasing the fleet from Boeing, in an effort to offload the aircraft's development and manufacturing costs. The proposal met with opposition in Washington, led by Senator John McCain, who decried it as out of step with established practice (at least in the US) and poor long-term value for the taxpayer.

Under pressure, the Air Force offered instead to purchase eighty of the KC-767s and lease only the additional twenty. That compromise fell apart just two months later, in December 2003, amid allegations of corrupt practices (which later resulted in a criminal prosecution); the contract was cancelled in January 2006.

But pressure to replace the KC-135 fleet continued to increase. In 2006 the Air Force launched a more time-honoured approach to satisfying it by issuing an RFP for a new aircraft temporarily designated the KC-X. KC-X would be the service's first step in a three-stage programme (the other airframes tentatively designated the KC-Y and KC-Z) to dramatically enhance its refuelling capability by replacing its entire tanker fleet.

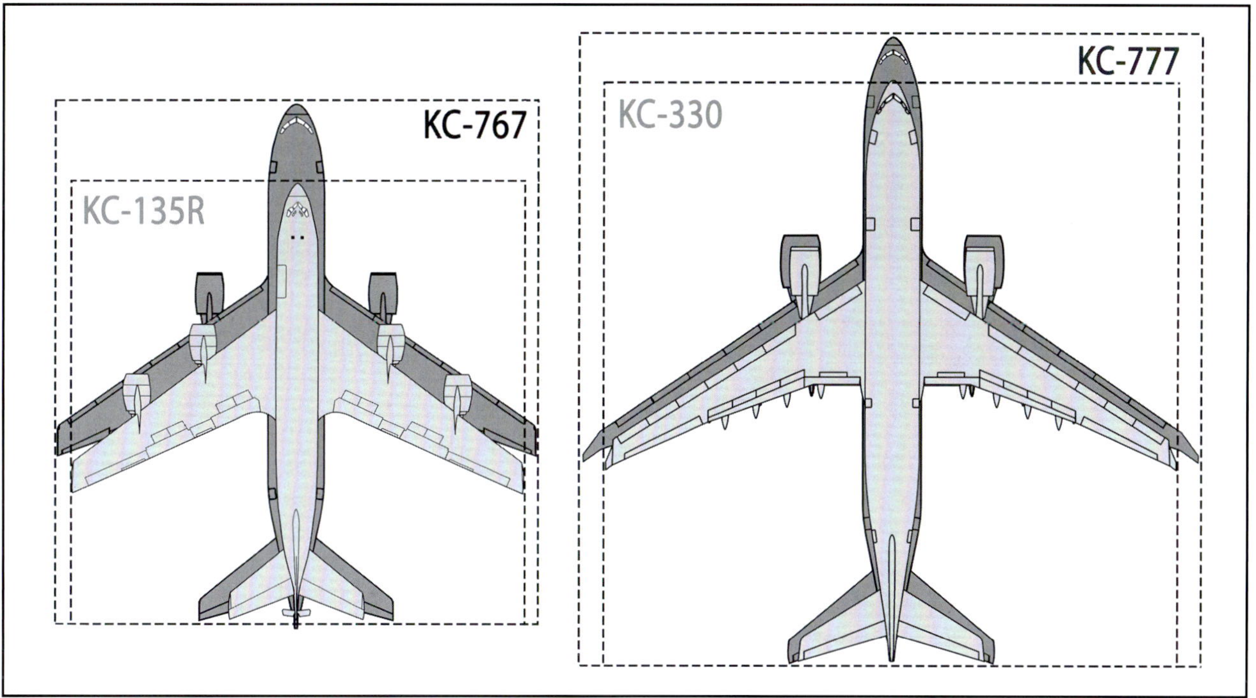

ABOVE Size comparisons between the KC-135 and KC-767 (left) and the larger A330 and 777 (right). Airbus's only competitive airframe was the A330, which forced Boeing to match it in that size class with the KC-777. *Author collection*

Manufacturers quickly realised that the impossibly short KC-X timeline made a new design impossible. As a result, the only two organisations capable of adapting an existing design were the only two that responded: Boeing with the 767, and Northrop Grumman/EADS in a joint bid based on the Airbus A330 MRTT (Multi-Role Tanker Transport). Boeing, concerned that the Air Force might want the larger A-330, quickly modified its proposal by swapping in a tanker version of its 777.

In January 2007 the USAF revised its RFP, stating that it would now need 179 aircraft, including an initial four for development and testing. Boeing responded with a proposal based on its 767-200LRF, believing that it best matched the new requirements. The A330 was a bigger aircraft with more capability, but also more expensive and needed greater ramp space and larger hangars. After evaluating the two submissions, in February 2008 the Air Force selected the A330 (or KC-30 as it was known within EADS) and designated it the KC-45A. But the matter was far from over. The political reality was that awarding the tanker contract for an aircraft not designed in the US was certain to be challenged.

BELOW Photographed during certification testing near Edwards AFB, this RAAF KC-30 version of the A330-MRTT provides an idea of what the KC-45A would have looked like in action. *US Air Force photo by Christian Turner*

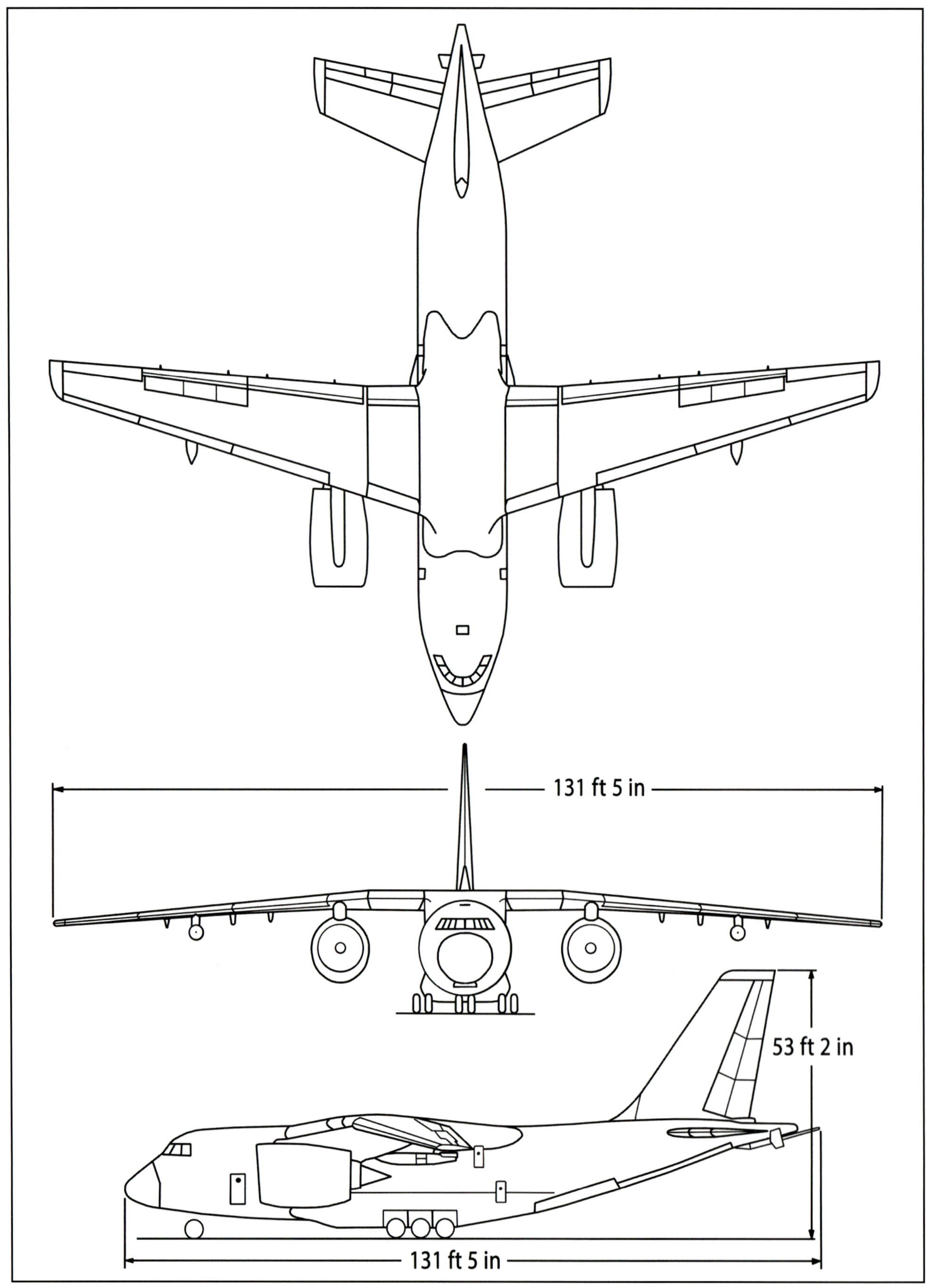

ABOVE **Antonov and US Aerospace teamed up to bid a variant of the AN-70 called the AN-112KC.** *Author collection*

KC-X submissions	Boeing KC-135R	Boeing KC-767 Advanced Tanker	Northrop Grumman EADS A-330 MRTT	US Aerospace/Antonov An-112KC
Engines	4 x CFMI CFM-56 turbofans @ 21,634lb (96.2kN) thrust	2 x P&W PW4062 turbofans @ 63,500lb (282kN) thrust	2 x RR Trent 700 or GE CF6-80 turbofans @ 72,000lb (320kN) thrust	2 x GE GEnx-1B74/75, Engine Alliance GP7277s or P&W PW4074/74Ds @ 74,100lb (330kN) thrust
Length	136ft 3in (41.5m)	159ft 2in (48.5m)	192ft 11in (58.8m)	131ft 5in (40.1m)
Height	41ft 8in (12.7m)	52ft (15.8m)	57ft 1in (17.4m)	53ft 2in (16.2m)
Wingspan	130ft 10in (39.9m)	156ft 1in (47.6m)	197ft 10in (60.3m)	166ft 2in (50.6m)
Passengers	80	190	226-280	300
Cargo	6 x 463L pallets	19 x 463L pallets	32 x 463L pallets	8 pallets
Maximum fuel	200,000lb (90,700kg)	Greater than 202,000lb (91,600kg)	250,000lb (113,000kg)	139,000lb (63,000kg)
Range	11,015nmi (20,400km)	6,590nmi (12,200km)	6,750nmi (12,500km)	6,800nmi (12,590km)
Cruise speed	Mach 0.79 (853km/h)	Mach 0.80 (853km/h)	Mach 0.82 (859km/h)	n/a
Maximum speed	Mach 0.90 (966km/h)	Mach 0.86 (917km/h)	Mach 0.86 (917km/h)	n/a
Max take-off weight	322,500lb (146,300kg)	Greater than 400,000lb (180,000kg)	507,000lb (230,000kg)	364,000lb (165,000kg)

And, of course, it was. Boeing filed a formal protest to the US Government Accountability Office (GAO), which subsequently upheld the objection, finding that the Air Force had not completely followed the rules that it had set up for evaluating the proposals. The GAO recommended that the bid process be reopened. The Defense Secretary supported that decision, and cancelled the initial contract with Northrop Grumman for the eighty KC-45As.

Just over a year later, on 24 September 2009, the Air Force issued a revised set of KC-X requirements projecting an order for 373 aircraft. Boeing again bid the KC-767 and EADS (without Northrop Grumman this round) bid the A330 MRTT. A surprise late entrant was the virtually unknown US Aerospace Inc, which teamed with Ukrainian manufacturer Antonov to offer a twin-jet version of the prop-fan AN-70, designated the AN-112KC. This proposal was disqualified without Air Force evaluation when it was formally submitted five minutes after the official deadline; the GAO denied the company's subsequent protests.

The Air Force announced its selection on 24 February 2011, and to nobody's surprise Boeing won. The development programme did not go smoothly, suffering from cost overruns and delays. The first aircraft, now known as the KC-46A Pegasus, was not delivered to the USAF until 2018, at least fifteen years after the Air Force had first sought to acquire a 767-based tanker/transport.

BELOW The first KC-46A is pictured in the Benefield Anechoic Chamber at Edwards Air Force Base where it underwent electromagnetic compatibility and interference testing. *US Air Force photo by Christopher Okula*

ABOVE Three generations of tankers are caught in flight: the KC-10A (left), KC-135R (middle) and KC-46A (right). *US Air Force photo by Christopher Okula*

BELOW The Air Force Research Laboratory displayed this model of a notional KC-Z 'stealth' tanker in 2018 and 2019. *Tony Chong*

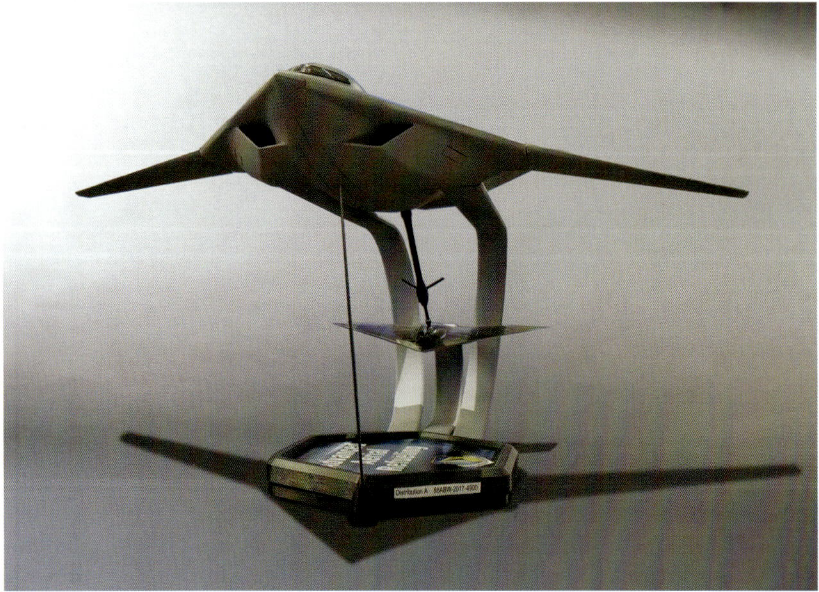

The KC-46A is equipped with flying boom as well as probe-and-drogue refuelling systems, and can carry 212,99lb (96,300kg) of fuel.

The follow-on KC-Y and KC-Z tanker-transports

While the KC-X saga was unfolding, resulting in the KC-46A, the Air Force was already taking a longer-term look at its tanker requirements. The planned aircraft, designated KC-Y and KC-Z, would (eventually) replace the KC-10 and KC-135R respectively. Given the time taken to resolve the KC-X requirement and bring the KC-46A into operational service, it seems unlikely that the KC-Y will ever fly. That leaves, as a possible KC-10 replacement, a mixed fleet of additional KC-46As and whatever emerges as the KC-Z.

To put the replacement issue in perspective, planners do not foresee the KC-Z entering service until 2048. By then, the oldest KC-135R airframes, although still within their lifetime flying hours limitation, will be ten years short of a century old.

The KC-Z is likely to be totally different from previous tankers. Many of the aircraft that it will refuel will have stealth technology, and operate in otherwise denied airspace. So tankers too will need low observable features that reduce their radar and infrared signatures. Many of the projects currently under study are clearly cloaked in secrecy, but in 2018 the Air Force Research Laboratory displayed a notional design concept for such a penetrating tanker. It had a hybrid wing body configuration with a butterfly tail, clearly borrowing from work done on the Boeing and Lockheed Martin Speed Agile Concept Demonstrators (SACD) described later in this chapter.

LEFT The AFRL KC-Z 'stealth' tanker concept would have sufficient internal volume for an alternative mission as an airlifter. *Tony Chong photo*

2004/2008: AMC-X and AJACS Air Force programmes

In 2004, again seeking a replacement for the ageing C-130E/H fleet, the Air Force launched a programme known as the Advanced Mobility Concept – Experimental (AMC-X). It envisaged an aircraft having SSTOL abilities, able to carry an 80,000lb (36,320kg) payload. Planners expected that with only a slightly lesser payload, it would also be compatible with shipboard operation. That level of flexible airlift capability would make the aircraft theoretically suitable for additional surveillance, radio relay and ground fire support missions.

AMC-X did not win enough DoD support (or funding) to become a 'programme of record,' which would have launched a formal competition with requests for proposals. Manufacturers were nonetheless eager to submit proposals, capitalising on their earlier ATT efforts. In 2008 the programme was succeeded by the Advanced Joint Air Combat System (AJACS), given that name to imply that it reflected a 'joint' effort between the Army (as the 'customer' for the transportation services) and the Air Force. But again, the effort failed to win support and faded away.

During this period the Air Force Research Laboratory was funding five projects to mature technologies that would likely be useful to the AMC-X or AJACS programmes:

- ACCA – Advanced Composite Cargo Aircraft (manufacturing/aircraft project)
- HIBRID – Higher Bypass Ratio Inlet Development (engine technology project)
- HEETE – Highly Efficient Embedded Turbine Engine (engine technology project)
- INVENT – Integrated energy management (engine technology project)
- Speed Agile – Wind-tunnel demonstration of a Mach 0.8 STOL transport (aircraft design project)

Despite the many efforts to create a new aircraft, none ever won enough support to advance to a fully funded 'top-line' Air Force programme. The reasons were many:

- The 2008 economic recession, leading to a difficult federal budget environment, with funding resolutions that made it legally impossible to implement a 'new start' programme
- Competing funds requirements for two ongoing wars (Afghanistan and Iraq)
- Tepid (at best) support from the Army, which saw this sort of airlifter as unable to meet its battlefield delivery and mobility requirements
- Continuing Congressional budget 'add-ons' for the Lockheed C-130J, which undermined the need for a 'new start' C-130E/H replacement

2007-2011: X-55A Advanced Composite Cargo Aircraft (ACCA)

In 2007 the Air Force Research Laboratory launched a competition to produce an experimental aircraft that would explore potential uses for advanced composite materials, together with new techniques to quickly fabricate them. Funding constraints limited the programme's scope; the Air Force stated that its main goal was simply to try and replace a conventional metal fuselage with a composite structure that used low-temperature bonding techniques, thereby avoiding the use of autoclaves.

Nine companies expressed interest in the project, and the Air Force selected bids from Aurora Flight Sciences and Lockheed Martin's Skunk Works for the Phase 1 design effort. Aurora based its proposal on the Antonov An-72, while Lockheed Martin chose a Fairchild Dornier 328JET passenger jet. The Skunk Works won the Phase 2 construction contract and began to convert the airliner to an airlifter. Engineers eventually replaced the entire fuselage aft of the cockpit, including the vertical stabiliser, with new composite structures. Fabrication issues delayed the first flight from the winter of 2008/2009 to 2 June 2009, and that October the ACCA received the coveted X-55A designation.

The jet made relatively few flights before retirement. Its purpose had centred not on aerodynamic research, like most X-planes, but rather the manufacturing feasibility of laying up and curing large composite structures at room temperature. It currently sits on public display near the Skunk Works in Palmdale, California.

Lockheed Martin X-55A ACCA (converted Dornier DO-328JET)	
Powerplant	2 x P&W 306B turbofans @ 6,050lbf (26.9kN) thrust each
Span	68ft 10in (20.98m)
Length	69ft 10in (21.28m)
Height	23ft 9in (7.24m)

BELOW The X-55A Advanced Composite Cargo Aircraft (ACCA) during its first flight on 2 June 2009. *Lockheed Martin via US Air Force*

2007: Speed Agile Concept Demonstrator (SACD)

In late 2011 Air Force researchers at Wright-Patterson AFB completed a series of experiments exploring a new STOL transport aircraft concept. Termed the 'Speed Agile Concept Demonstrator', it was a four-engine, multi-mission aircraft using what they called a 'Hybrid Powered Lift System' (HPLS). It would feature simple mechanics together with a low-drag profile, yielding an aircraft with high speed yet able to operate from short, improvised airstrips. The term 'Speed Agile' derived from its unusual ability to fly at speeds from a slow 90kt (167km/h) up to Mach 0.8.

The full-scale aircraft modelled in the SACD effort would carry a 65,000lb (29,480kg) payload 500nmi (926km), landing on a 2,000ft (610m) site with a specified measure of ground firmness, taking off with the same payload and returning 500nmi (926km). Additionally, the design offered a ferry (self-deployment) range of 3,300nmi (6,111km) with a 5,000lb (2,270kg) payload at cruise speeds greater than Mach 0.8. The cargo bay would have held seven 463L pallets.

The SACD's goal was to increase the Technology Readiness Level (TRL) on a number of airlifter fronts, including the HPLS. SACD wind tunnel testing ended in 2011, and in 2013 the government/industry team won *Aviation Week & Space Technology* magazine's 2013 prestigious Laureate Award in Aeronautics and Propulsion.

Boeing SACD

Boeing's concept evolved from its earlier TEMPO (Transonic Efficient Mobility Platform Optimisation) effort. It had the appearance of a B-2 bomber trailing an extended fuselage that ended in a butterfly tail. The deep fuselage section accommodated its large cargo box, while the rear extension provided room for a loading ramp; the butterfly tail provided increased pitch authority and allowed a greater CG range.

Boeing's powered lift system consisted of upper surface blowing on the inner wing section (similar in concept to that of the YC-14), and circulation control/internally blown flaps on the outboard wing. Wind tunnel testing started in July 2007 and ended in October 2009.

Lockheed Martin SACD

Lockheed's SACD concept superficially looked similar to its Boeing equivalent, with a sharp chine marking the horizontal periphery of the fuselage, which blended into the wings and horizontal tail. However, it differed in several significant aspects. The engines sat on the sides of the forward fuselage, with the air intakes on either side of the nose, and its empennage showed a horizontal tail surface with canted vertical fins mounted at the tips.

Lockheed tested a 23% scale model in the National Full Scale Aerodynamic Complex wind tunnel at NASA Ames, operated by the Arnold Engineering and Development Center (AEDC).

BELOW The Boeing SACD model undergoing wind tunnel tests. *Boeing*

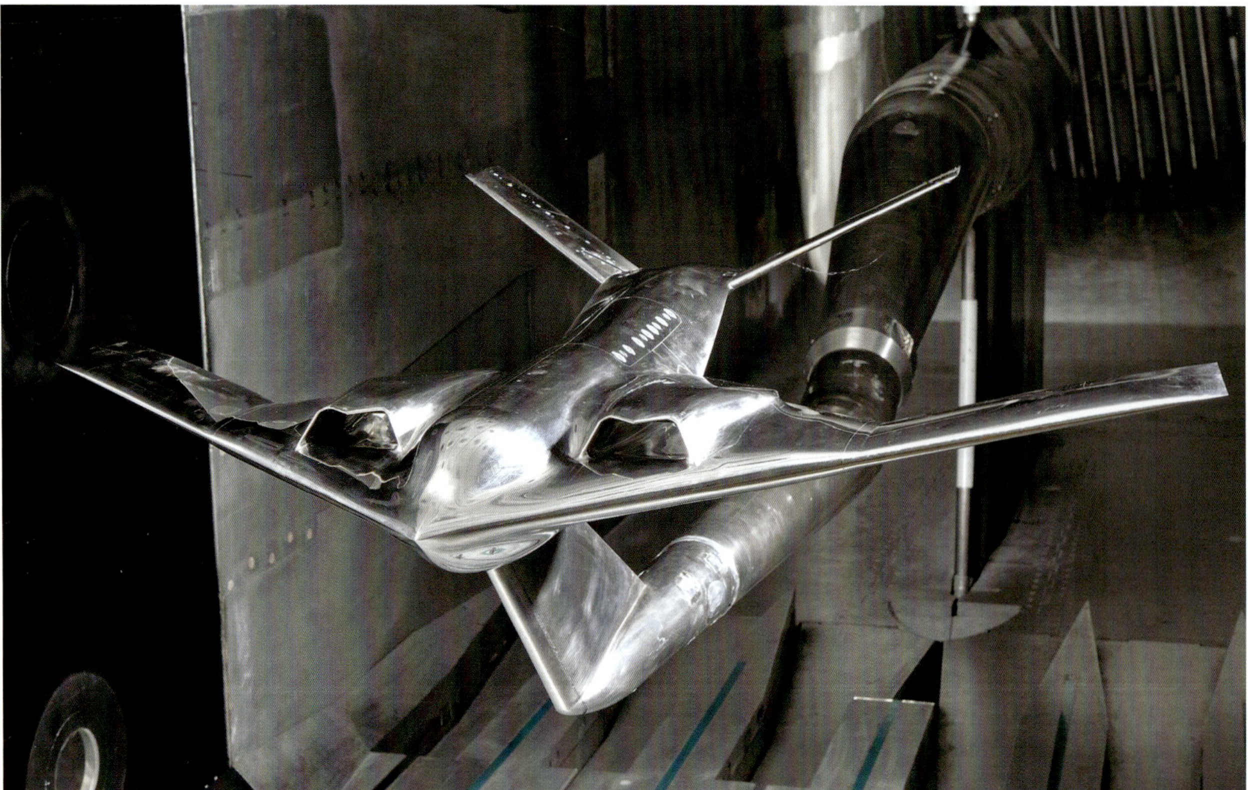

ABOVE The Lockheed Martin SACD concept. *Lockheed Martin*

Unusually for wind tunnel testing, the model was fully powered, with two flightworthy Williams FJ44 turbofans. Engineers needed them in order to accurately simulate the effects of both the circulation control wing (CCW) and the Reversing Ejector Nozzle (REN), which added a thrust reverser to its two-dimensional ejector exhaust nozzle. To accommodate the FJ44s, technicians configured the model with oversized nacelle fairings and large circular air intakes – resulting in a somewhat bizarre appearance for what was intended to be a low observable airframe design. By late 2011 the programme had been completed.

ABOVE The Lockheed Martin SACD concept undergoing wind tunnel tests. The engine inlet design was peculiar to the wind tunnel model and accommodated the turbofan engines to provide the exhaust airflow necessary for the high lift systems. *US Air Force*

2007 Northrop Grumman 'cranked kite' modular aircraft

During the mid-to-late-2000s, Northrop Grumman was working on developing another concept – the 'cranked kite' airframe. This configuration represented an aerodynamic compromise. A pure diamond-shaped planform provided a very low radar signature, but its poor lift characteristics limited long-range flight. By adding edge-aligned outer wing panels, engineers increased the aspect ratio for lower drag, but could still minimise the aircraft's radar cross section. (Northrop Grumman took this exact route when it later grew the diamond-shaped X-47A UAV into the X-47B carrier-based UCAV demonstrator.)

A strong advantage to the cranked-kite design was its suitability for a broad range of missionised modular aircraft. In this case, the During 2007, designers at Northrop Grumman's Engineering Visualization Resource group created several design/illustrations for public release. These depicted a notional low observable airframe was sized for a useful cargo volume. This was then adapted into air-refuelling tanker and medium bomber variants that shared common structural elements. While

ABOVE Northrop Grumman Airlift version of the 'Modular' aircraft concept. Created by the Engineering Visualization Resource group, this illustration showed general features of the modular cranked kit rather than depicting any specific point design under development. *Courtesy of Northrop Grumman Corporation*

broadly representative of Northrop's thinking at the time, these images did not reveal specific design details under development by the Engineering organization.

Northrop Grumman HAWSTOL

The Northrop Grumman 'High-speed All Wing STOL' (HAWSTOL) was a further refinement of the cranked-kite wing. It was developed in response to a study requests for the 'Multi-Role Transport' issued by the Air Force Research Laboratory (AFRL) dating from at least 2005. Northrop Grumman and NASA tested one variant, featuring a flattened upper centre fuselage and other refinements, at the Langley Research Center's large subsonic wind tunnel between April and June 2007. Engineers were seeking data to assess the feasibility of building an all-wing STOL airlifter that carried heavy loads but cruised efficiently.

To enhance STOL performance, designers turned to a lift-generating centre body that, combined with steady flap blowing across much of the wingspan, yielded high lift coefficients. The very low wing loading meant that STOL performance would require minimal additional power. Additionally, thanks to the blown air diverted from the fan stage of the aircraft's engines instead of the core, the impact of an engine-out situation would be less critical. A retractable, high aspect ratio canard surface was planned, with an innovative boundary-layer control system that eliminated the need for

BELOW The Northrop Grumman HAWSTOL wind tunnel model. *NASA*

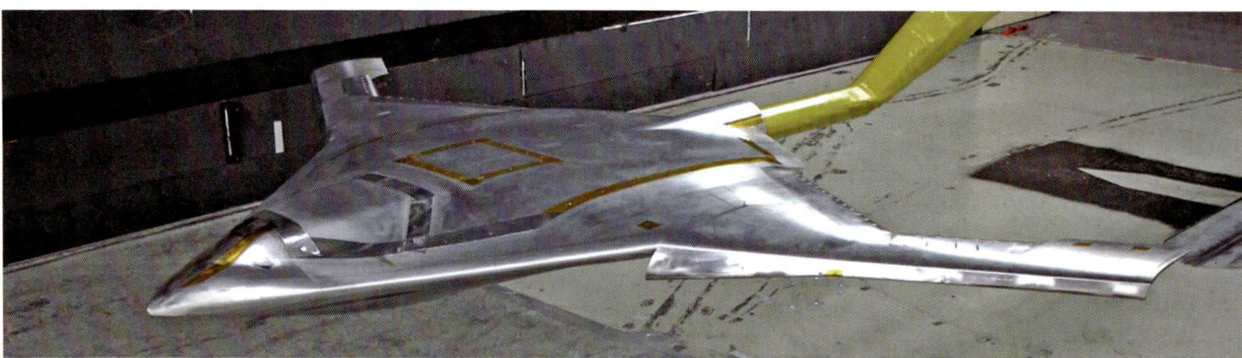

RIGHT Labelled 'C-X/PK-X' (Cargo Experimental/Penetrating Tanker Experimental), this art depicts a full size design with HAWSTOL features. *Courtesy of Northrop Grumman Corporation*

canard trailing-edge flaps. The tests accumulated extensive data, much of it supporting the configuration's many advantages, but never led to a flying proof-of-concept vehicle.

During the same timeframe, Northrop Grumman was developing the Advanced Composite Aircraft Structures Demonstrator (ACASTD). Utilising the developed cranked kite planform, it may have been an early competitor to what became Lockheed Martin's winning X-55A ACCA. To minimise costs the design would have adapted four engine nacelle assemblies from the RQ-4A Global Hawk as 'off-the-shelf' structural assemblies.

BELOW Northrop Grumman's proposed Advanced Composite Aircraft Structures Demonstrator (ACASTD). Engine nacelles were to be adapted from the RQ-4A Global Hawk. *Courtesy of Northrop Grumman Corporation, Tony Chong photo*

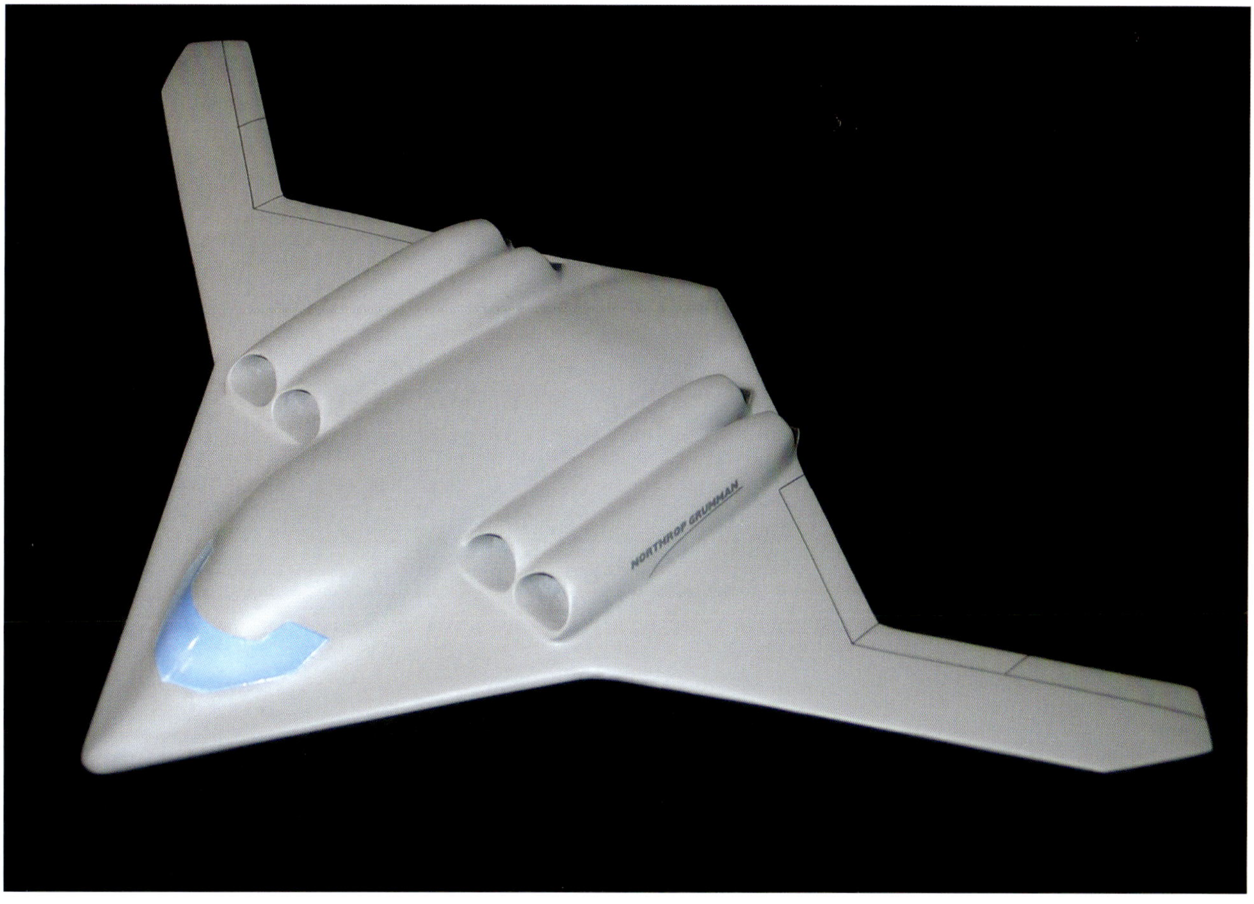

ABOVE An underside view of the ACASTD showing the rear cargo loading ramp.
Courtesy of Northrop Grumman Corporation, Tony Chong photo

2007: Joint Heavy Lift (JHL)

While able to meet the Army's strategic airlift requirements, the Air Force's ability to support that service's front-line needs were lagging. Army planners clamoured for specific aircraft able to take off and land vertically but, following the 1948 'Key West' agreement, the Air Force is barred from operating rotary aircraft (with the exception of rescue helicopters). The only remaining USAF option was to develop fixed-wing VTOL transport aircraft and, as seen in Chapter Eight, this proved prohibitively difficult. The Army therefore had no choice but to commission a number of advanced rotorcraft studies, and for the last twenty years it has done exactly that.

While rotorcraft are generally outside of the scope of this book, one programme merits mention: the Army-led Joint Heavy Lift (JHL) programme, which was conducted in parallel with the Air Force-led AMC-X and AJACS effort. The Joint Heavy Lift design process began in January 2005, when the Defense Undersecretary for Acquisition, Technology and Logistics (AT&L) established a joint investigation of capability gaps in heavy vertical lift requirements and technology. The Army, based on its interest and experience, was tasked to lead a joint service body that would define operational requirements and define technology issues and expectations.

Also in 2005, at the beginning of the DoD JHL study process, five contracts totalling $30 million were awarded to airframe manufacturers for Conceptual Design and Analysis (CDA). Issued by the Army's Aviation Applied Technology Directorate (AATD) at Fort Eustis, Virginia, recipients would create concepts to meet the emerging JHL requirements.

Unfortunately, after several years of effort, the programme began to experience an insidious problem known as 'requirements creep'. Small but steady increases in the size and weight of Army Future Combat Systems (FCS) vehicles pushed the payload requirement from 20 tons (18,140kg) and a C-130-size cargo box closer to 30 tons (27,220kg) and an A400M-size cargo box.

In July 2010, after five years of extensive DoD and industry studies, the Acting Assistant Secretary of the Air Force for Acquisitions halted plans for an Overarching Integrated Product Team (OIPT) as preparation for a Material Development Decision (MDD). Instead, he directed the Air Force to conduct a study 'other than an Analysis of Alternatives (AoA)', the legally mandated study required before a weapon system can proceed into development. However, the Air Force would not support the AoA study, and in August 2010 it reached an agreement with Army Vice-Chiefs of Staff to perform an AoA-like study called the JFTL Technology Study (JTS) using the existing AoA Study Team structure. That effort was completed in 2012, and although JHL was a DoD 'programme of record' (indicating high-level DoD support and formal budget planning, unlike the Air Force-promoted AMC-X or AJACS), the programme stalled.

Mission requirements and inter-service disagreements had proved insurmountable, but the JHL programme played out during an era when US military resources and funding were stretched by the 'Global War on Terror', the wars in Afghanistan and Iraq, and budgetary constraints such as sequestration. This made it very difficult to launch new development programmes.

The most significant proposals are described below. While a new advanced rotorcraft has yet to emerge from these studies, they will undoubtedly influenced future rotorcraft designs.

Boeing Advanced Tandem Rotor Helicopter

Boeing's Phantom Works based its 2005 Advanced Tandem Rotor Helicopter (ATRH) concept on the company's well-proven Marine Corps CH-46 and Army CH-47 aircraft. The ATRH incorporated internal carriage with a split-ramp door, and the tandem-rotor configuration eliminated the need for a tail rotor. Boeing proposed it to fill the need for lower-speed JHL aircraft flying between 160 and 200kt (300 and 370km/h).

Bell-Boeing Quad Tiltrotor

The Bell-Boeing joint venture won a contract in 2005 to develop a Quad Tiltrotor (QTR) concept with a top speed of 275kt (510km/h). The QTR was a four-rotor configuration drawing on the successful joint development of the V-22, a twin-engine tilt-rotor. Both front and rear wings would provide lift in forward flight. The QTR represented Bell Boeing's proposal for the high-

ABOVE The most conventional Joint Heavy Lift (JHL) concept was the Boeing Advanced Tandem Rotor Helicopter, which followed the general CH-47 layout. *Boeing*

BELOW The Bell-Boeing Quad Tiltrotor drew on technology developed for the Bell-Boeing V-22 Osprey. *Boeing*

speed category of JHL – vehicles flying at 250kt (460km/h) or faster. During the initial baseline design study, Bell's engineers were responsible for designing the wing, engine and rotor, while the Boeing team focused on the fuselage and internal systems.

Karem Aircraft Optimum Speed Tilt Rotor (OSTR)

The smallest company to receive a development contract was Karem Aircraft (which had also received technology development contracts from DARPA). It proposed an Optimum Speed Tilt Rotor, predicting a top speed of 310kt (574km/h). A key design feature allowed adjustment of rotor speeds between 40% and 100% of maximum, optimising flight for either low fuel consumption or high-speed flight. The outer section of the wing tilted with the nacelle to reduce the large wing's rotor downwash in hover.

Sikorsky X2 Technology Crane and High Speed Lifter

In September 2005 the US Army's Applied Aviation Technology Directorate (AATD) awarded two contracts to Sikorsky. The first was to study a coaxial rotor-powered vehicle called the X2 Technology Crane (XTC), needing no tail rotor and able to fly at 165kt (305km/h). It would carry heavy loads externally; the only internal payload would be contained in a fourteen-seat cabin with sliding doors.

The second contract was for an advancing-blade compound concept called the X2 Technology High Speed Lifter (HSL). The HSL featured a coaxial configuration with hingeless rotors and auxiliary propulsion that gave it a very fast 245kt (453km/h) in forward flight. The helicopter would have been slightly longer than a C-130 Hercules, with a cargo bay able to carry seven standard 463L pallets, a loaded HEMTT truck, a fully equipped armoured gun system, or two combat-ready Light Armoured Vehicles (LAVs). The design provided for 'straight in' loading for internal carriage. Belly-mounted single, dual and triple cargo hooks permitted external cargo carriage in slings.

Both XTC and HSL were powered by the X2 coaxial rotor system developed by Sikorsky Aircraft. Both could take off and land vertically, hover, manoeuvre at low speeds, and transition seamlessly to forward flight like a helicopter. In a high-speed configuration, one or more 'pusher props' in an integrated auxiliary propulsion system would have enabled high speed with no need to reconfigure the aircraft in flight.

As with the other rotary-winged projects described above, neither project led to a flying aircraft.

BELOW Karem Aircraft's Optimum Speed Tilt Rotor reduced rotor speed in horizontal flight for greater fuel efficiency. *Author collection*

ABOVE The 'C-17B' was to have added a centerline main landing gear for higher gross weights or lower ground pressures, triple slotted flaps for additional lift and uprated engines. *Boeing*

BELOW A comparison of the standard C-17A with the narrower body 'C-17FE'. *Boeing*

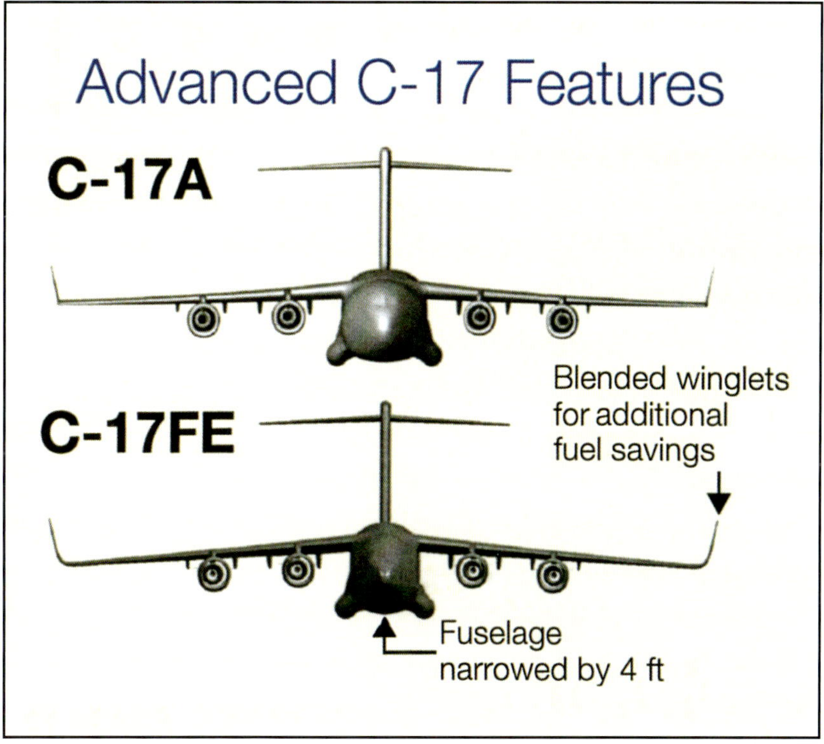

C-17 military derivatives: C-17B and C-17FE

C-17 production ended in 2015, with 279 aircraft built. In the early 2010s, with the production line slowing down, Boeing proposed several C-17 variants as AJACS alternatives. One was known within the company as the C-17B, with an increased gross weight to carry heavier payloads. It would need upgraded engines, an additional centreline main landing gear and triple-slotted flaps that gave it near-STOL capabilities. Boeing estimated that a two-year demonstration and test programme would cost $250 million. It found no customers.

Boeing subsequently proposed another variant, the C-17FE (Fuel Efficient). It was to have a new fuselage, 4ft (1.22m) narrower than the original aircraft and constructed from composites. It also incorporated blended winglets, reflecting the twenty years of aerodynamic refinement since the C-17's original design in 1990. However, like the C-17B, the performance improvements were not sufficient to persuade the Air Force or other potential customers to proceed further.

Sales forces also offered the C-17 to civilian markets, initially as the MD-17 and subsequently (after the merger of McDonnell Douglas and Boeing) as the BC-17X, but attracted no commercial customers. Thus – somewhat surprisingly for what proved to be an extremely capable aircraft, enjoying a successful service life with nine air forces – C-17 production finally ended.

Future heavy airlifters: Blended Wing Body (BWB) development

Aerodynamicists have recognised the advantages of a Blended Wing Body (BWB) aircraft for decades. The configuration is structurally well suited to both freight and tanker applications, although arguably less so for passenger transportation. As described in *American Secret Projects 2*, there have been several proposals for airlifters using this configuration, dating back to the Kaiser and Northrop 'flying wings' and Burnelli's 'lifting fuselage' designs in the 1940s.

The BWB configuration offers a much higher lift/drag ratio than conventional aircraft layouts. But three barriers have prevented its adoption. The first centres on issues of aerodynamic stability. The second challenge involves the industry's reluctance to accept a radical new concept, with its very different approach to ground handling. In recent years the stability issue has been largely resolved, thanks to advances in computational aerodynamics and computer-driven flight control. New developments in materials and construction techniques have also made more sophisticated wing-body shapes possible.

The third obstacle to a BWB cargo aircraft is the impact of its shape on airframe sizing. For an airlifter, the height of the cargo bay is as significant as its total capacity; for a BWB aircraft, it is this factor that determines the required height of the centre wing box – which in turn dictates the overall aircraft size. The result for airlifters is that the BWB configuration works best for very large aircraft, and that is where the most significant efforts have focused.

Modern BWB development began in 1988, led by McDonnell Douglas's Robert Liebeck, spurred by conversations with Dennis Bushnell of NASA's Langley Research Center. The initial work was focused on creating a more efficient airliner, but designers soon began to study applications for military airlifter missions.

In the 1990s McDonnell Douglas initiated design studies for a large BWB transport aircraft, with high-aspect-ratio outer wing sections terminating in winglets, and turbofans mounted on pylons above the centre section of the trailing edge. The resulting planform was surprisingly elegant – a rare occurrence among airlifters.

The development and refinement of the BWB design continued after the

BELOW **Initial BWB designs semi-submerged the engines to reduce the wetted area and drag and to ingest the turbulent and drag-inducing boundary layer airflow. The drag penalty for moving the engines above the wing turned out to be minimal.** *Author photo*

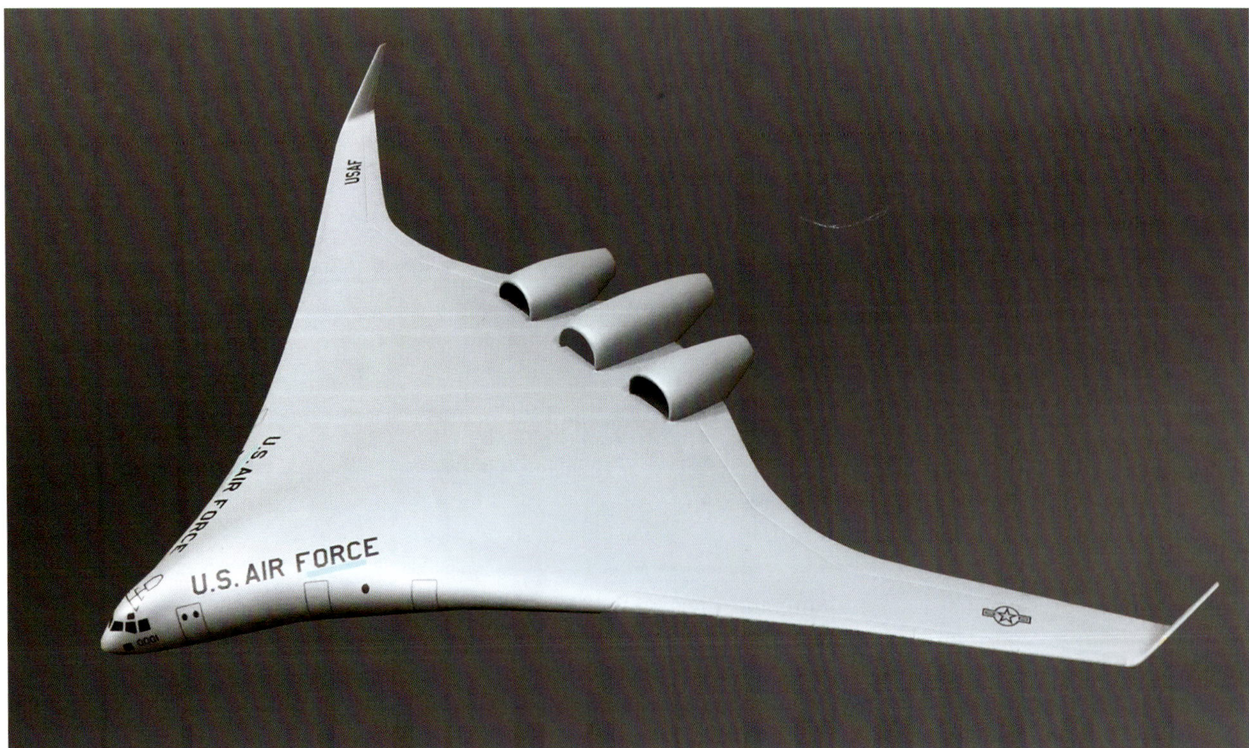

ABOVE This later military BWB design was configured for bulk cargo carriage. Cargo loading doors are in the leading edge of the wing, aft of the crew door. *John Aldaz photo*

BELOW This aft-loading Boeing BWB airlifter concept featured an elongated aft deck and a revised engine mounting installation with shorter stub pylons. *Author photo*

BELOW The extended BWB upper aft deck serves both as a 'reflexed' part of the airfoil and provides the vertical clearance needed to access the cargo bay through the rear loading ramp. *Author photo*

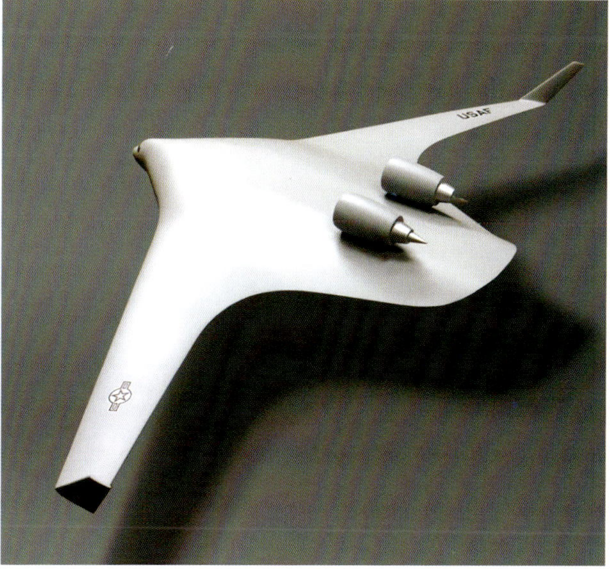

Boeing and McDonnell Douglas merger, supported by company funds and NASA.

During the following decade, Boeing's Phantom Works partnered with NASA's Langley Research Center to produce two remotely piloted flying models. NASA assigned a high priority to the project, reflected in its coveted designation as an X-series aircraft. After the X-48A with its large 30ft (9.1m) span was cancelled, two smaller X-48B test beds with a 22ft 7in (6.9m) span were built, powered by three Jetcat P200 turbojets with 52lb (231N) thrust. Constructed at Cranfield Aerospace (part of Cranfield University) in the UK, the first unit was used for wind tunnel testing and the second made its initial flight on 20 July 2007. Flight trials continued until 2010.

ABOVE The X-48B parked on Rogers Dry Lake at Edwards AFB. The large 'stinger' at the rear of the aircraft is the deployment boom for the emergency spin parachute system. *NASA photo by Tony Landis*

LEFT The X-48C subscale model in flight. The wingtip fins have been moved inboard to an extended aft deck. This configuration had the advantage (for an airliner) of reducing engine noise. *NASA photo by Carla Thomas*

ABOVE Coated in fluorescent oil and bathed in ultraviolet light, this NASA BWB wind tunnel model from 2013 shows the complex airflow and vortex patterns that a full-sized aircraft would encounter. *NASA photo by Preston Martin*

The second X-48B was modified to the X-48C. The three engines were replaced by two more powerful AMT turbojets with 89lb (396N) thrust. The aircraft took to the air on 7 August 2012 and testing continued until April 2013, by which time thirty test flights had been completed.

A full-size aircraft with a similar configuration would have fitted the profile of what the Air Force had dubbed the Global Range Transport (GRT) – an aircraft capable of carrying 459,000lb (208,400kg) with a range of 3,860nmi (7,150km), or 157,150lb (71,350kg) with a range of 10,840nmi (20,000 km) flying at 489kt (905 km/h).

If built, it would have been the largest US aircraft flown up to that time, with a maximum take-off weight of 1,357,000lb (616,000kg). By contrast, the C-5 has a maximum take-off weight of 920,000lb (417,700kg) and the Russian An-225 1,420,958lb (644,536kg). It would also have required a runway length of at least 7,000ft (2,135m), constraining its global deployment options.

Lockheed Martin Hybrid Wing Body (HWB) development

Since the early 2000s the term BWB (if not the concept) has fallen into disfavour, and has been replaced by 'Hybrid Wing Body' (HWB). Lockheed Martin has put a different twist on the Boeing BWB for its HWB designs, mating the smoothly blended nose and wing of the now-familiar BWB with a conventional T-tail and aft fuselage. This retains much of the BWB's aerodynamic efficiency while making the aircraft better suited for airlift missions, including air-drop. Large engines project aft over the trailing edge of the wing.

Developed under the sponsorship of the Air Force Research Laboratory's (AFRL) Revolutionary Configurations for Energy Efficiency (RCEE), Phase 1 of design refinement ran from 2009 to 2011. It defined a next-generation mobility fleet that would use 90% less fuel than today's military transports and tankers. Lockheed Martin reports that it studied a wide range of configurations and technologies in this phase in search of the 90% goal, and concluded that a hybrid wing body (HWB) offered the most potential. Under Phase 2, which began in 2011 and ran until 2015, specific configurations were developed. Phase 2 identified three potential powerplants: General Electric's GEnx, Rolls-Royce's conceptual Ultra Fan, and a GE open rotor (prop-fan) that could be available after 2025.

The twin-engine HWB is designed to take off in less than 6,500ft (1,980m) and fly 3,200nmi (5,926km) carrying 220,000lb (99,790kg), including all the outsize cargo now airlifted by the C-5M. Lockheed estimates that the aircraft is 65% more aerodynamically efficient than the C-17, which it states is penalised by its 1980s design, and meets

ABOVE An artist's concept of a sub-scale demonstrator for Lockheed Martin's HWB. *NASA*

the requirement for STOL capability. Fuel burn is projected to be 70% less than the Boeing C-17 through a combination of better aerodynamics, newer engines and lighter structures.

Recent decades in perspective

As the second decade of the millennium draws to a close – eighty years after air transportation started to play an essential part in military strategy – the United States has built up an impressive strategic and tactical airlift capability. Today's fleet of airlifters is destined to serve for some time. Despite extensive studies carried out over recent decades, no hardware has yet been built, nor has the US military ordered into production any new transport designs to replace or supplement the existing fleet of C-130Js, C-17s and C-5s (other than the KC-46A, which has a primary tanker role). Since 2015 versions of the C-130J have successively replaced their aged counterparts, which were based on vintage 1970s and 1980s C-130H airframes.

The airlifters' longevity is due partly to their less intensive use compared with commercial equivalents; during intervals of peace, military aircraft fly fewer hours and cycles. An additional factor is simply the quality of their basic design, aided by lengthy development cycles that smoothed out initial shortcomings. But the primary reason is that these aircraft simply do the job very well, and their development cost has long since been amortised. This is particularly relevant given the continued funding demand for other types of aircraft like the F-35, KC-46, B-21 and, in time, replacements for the F-15 and F-22.

Some may argue that there will never again be a future strategic airlifter designed for military use alone; the development cost for such a massive aircraft would be unrealistically high when set against the prospect of a limited production run. As discussed in Chapter Seven, Lockheed won the competition to build the C-5 and subsequently produced 131 aircraft, whereas Boeing lost the competition, turned its efforts to a commercial airliner/freighter of a similar size, and to date has built more than 1,500 747s.

As a consequence, it is possible that the cost of a future large, global-range transport might be feasible only by creating a hybrid commercial/military airlifter. But arguing against this scenario is the complete absence of civilian sales for the C-141 (L-300), C-5 (L-500) and C-17 (MD/BC-17). Airlines have no tolerance for the cost inefficiencies of an adapted military transport (unless accompanied by government subsidies as with the CRAF programme), and the US military has the distinction of always wanting things done its way. The US Government has usually found the budget to accommodate the military's requests, particularly in times of international tension. Time will tell.

Meanwhile, there are other requirements to fill. One is front-line support for the Army, since for forty years the Air Force has failed to develop a fixed-wing airlifter that could meet that service's expressed needs. It would require VTOL capability, something that, as described in this book, has still not been achieved in an operational fixed-wing airlifter. The technology is there, but the cost of developing and operating such an aircraft has to be viewed against other priorities.

Over the last fifteen years both the Air Force and the Army have struggled to meet the operational demands of two simultaneous regional conflicts. This is in addition to directing adequate funding to the Air Force's primary goal of air dominance (achieved through strike, refuelling tankers and ISR aircraft) as well as completing C-17 procurement. Funding sequestration hit the Air Force hard, which negated some of the gains of the early 2000s by retiring the C-5A fleet. Some of those airlifters went to museums, but most to the scrapyard. They were becoming expensive and unreliable to operate, with most coming to the end of their service lives of 30,000 flight hours.

The Army similarly has made hard decisions in order to meet budget restrictions. Only now have some long-in-the-making technical developments and budget commitments enabled development of its new rotor-borne light and medium transports. One might suggest that the Marines' CH-53K heavy lift helicopter would fill the need, but observers note that the Army cannot match the Marines' ability to muster the Congressional support to pay a unit price that exceeds that of an F-35 fighter.

In the meantime, the Army continues to upgrade the CH-47, a tandem-rotor design that first flew more than fifty-five years ago. And due to the 'role and missions' issue, first delineated in the 'Key West' Agreement imposed on the Air Force and Army some sixty years ago, the only path for the Army to autonomously develop an airlifter that meets its operational requirements is to pursue a non-fixed-wing solution.

One possibility is that the necessary technology – and development funding – will flow over from another, currently unfulfilled requirement: stealthy Special Operations support. Despite the large number of studies carried out during the 1980s and 1990s, no bespoke SOF airlifters have been publically revealed. In fact, the Air Force does have a V/STOL Special Operations support capability, filled by the CV-22B version of the tilt-rotor V-22 Osprey. Neither, however, possesses the stealth features essential for airspace dominance.

The future will undoubtedly introduce radically new designs: stealthy, V/STOL, small or medium-size transports, each specifically intended for combat. Recent decades have seen many proposals for such aircraft, as discussed in this final chapter. Many more are currently shrouded in secrecy and may well already be in an advanced stage of development.

Over the past eight decades airlifters have continuously adapted to the changing pattern of military conflict. This has resulted in a plethora of imaginative designs. The research behind this book has revealed the inventiveness of generations of engineers, producing imaginative concepts to meet ever-advancing demands. Collectively, their aircraft and proposals demonstrate a remarkable history of ingenuity: a history that can only be appreciated by looking at the hundreds of designs that lie behind a handful of successful aircraft.

It is clearly a story that hasn't ended.

BELOW The priority procurement of a stealthy KC-Z tanker (as seen in the 2004 Northrop Grumman concept) may enable the development and fielding of a closely related airlifter. Every strategic tanker operated by the Air Force has had a secondary airlift capability. *Courtesy of Northrop Grumman Corporation*

Glossary, terms and units

Abbreviations

AATD	[Army] Aviation Advanced Technology Directorate
AAW	Anti-Air-Warfare
ABLE	Advanced Blown Lift Enhancement
ACASTD	Advanced Composite Aircraft Structures Demonstrator (Northrop Grumman)
ACCA	Advanced Composite Cargo Aircraft
ACEE	AirCraft Energy Efficiency
ACFC	Air Corps Ferrying Command
ACMA	Advanced Civil/Military Aircraft (successor to the C-XX)
ADAM	Air Deflection and Modulation
ADC	Air Defense Command
ADO	Advanced Development Objective
AEDC	Arnold Engineering and Development Center
AEW	Airborne Early Warning
AEW&C	Airborne Early Warning and Control
AFB	Air Force Base
AFFDL	Air Force Flight Dynamics Laboratory
AFRL	Air Force Research Laboratory
AFRPL	Air Force Rocket Propulsion Laboratory
AFSOC	Air Force Systems Command
AFSSS	Air Force Sortie Space System
AJACS	Advanced Joint Air Combat System
ALBM	Air Launched Ballistic Missile
ALCS	Airborne Launch Control System
ALT	[Space Shuttle] Approach and Landing Test
AMC	Air Materiel Command (USAF, 1947-61)
AMC	Air Mobility Command (USAF, name from 1 July 1992)
AMC-X	Advanced Mobility Concept – Experimental
AMMX	Air Mobile Missile System
AMP	[C-5A/B] Avionics Modernization Program
AMSC	Advanced Military Spaceflight Capability
AMRAAM	Advanced Medium Range Air-to-Air Missile (AIM-120)
AMSA	Advanced Manned Strike Aircraft (or America's Most Studied Airplane)
AMSS	Advanced Multi-Sensor System
AMST	Advanced Medium Short Take-off and Landing Transport
ANP	Aircraft Nuclear Power
AoA	Analysis of Alternatives
APU	Auxiliary Power Unit
ARDC	Air Research and Development Command
ARPV	Advanced Remotely Piloted Vehicle
ASAS	[Boeing] Advanced Strategic Aircraft Study
ASD	Aeronautical Systems Division
ASLV	Air Launch Sortie Vehicle (spacecraft)
ASR	Army Study Requirement
ASTOL	Alternative STOL
ASW	Anti-Submarine Warfare
ATA	Advanced Transport Aircraft (Lockheed programme)
ATC	Air Transport Command
ATCA	Advanced Tanker/Cargo Aircraft
ATF	Advanced Tactical Fighter
ATOCA	Advanced Tanker/Outsized Cargo Aircraft
ATCD	Advanced Technology Development Center (Northrop)
ATF	Advanced Tactical Fighter
ATMR	Advanced Technology Medium Range (McDonnell Douglas proposed airliner)
ATRH	Advanced Tandem Rotor Helicopter (Boeing)
ATT	Advanced Tactical Transport
ATT	Advanced Theatre Transport
ATTMA	Advanced Tactical Transport Mission Analysis
ATTT	Advanced Technology Tactical Transport (also AT^3)
bhp	Brake horsepower
BLC	Boundary Layer Control
BuAer	Bureau of Aeronautics
BWB	Blended Wing Body
C^3	Command, Communication, Control
CALAC	California Lockheed Aircraft Company
CARA	Combat Aircrew Recovery Aircraft
CCW	Circulation Control Wing
CFD	Computational Fluid Dynamics
CFP	Concept Formulation Phase
CIC	Combat Information Center (alternatively Communication & Information Center)
CILOP	Conversion In-Lieu-Of Procurement
CL	California Lockheed (Lockheed California Company design prefix)
CLASS	Cargo Logistics Airlift Systems Study
CMCA	Cruise Missile Carrier Aircraft
CNO	Chief of Naval Operations
COD	Carrier On-board Delivery or Cargo On Deck

CRAF	Civil Reserve Air Fleet
CSA	Common Support Aircraft
CTA	Cold Thrust Augmentation
CTC	Contractor's Technical Compliance [Inspection]
CTOL	Conventional Take-Off and Landing
CVE	Aircraft Carrier, Escort (type)
CX-4	Cargo Experimental 4
CX-6	Cargo Experimental 6
CX-HLC	Cargo Experimental – Heavy Logistics Carrier
CX-HLS	Cargo Experimental – Heavy Logistics System
CX-L	[Navy] Cargo Experimental – Light
CX-X	Technologically advanced version of the CX-HLC
C-XX	Programme designation of a concept for a 1970s common civil/military transport aircraft
DARPA	Defense Advanced Projects Research Agency
DDR&E	Director of Defense Research & Engineering
DEI	Development Engineering Inspection
DEW	Distant Early Warning
DHC	de Havilland Canada
DoD	Department of Defense
DOS	Design Options Study
DS	Design Specification (Douglas Aircraft Company usage)
DTS	Detailed Type Specification (Douglas Aircraft Company usage)
EBF	Externally Blown Flap
ECMO	Electronic Counter Measures Officer
ECP	Engineering Change Proposal
EET	Energy Efficient Transports
EMALS	Electromagnetic Aircraft Launch System
EMD	Engineering and Manufacturing Development (term replaces 'FSD')
eshp	Equivalent shaft horse power
ESM	Electronic Support Measures
EW	Electronic Warfare
FAA	Federal Aviation Administration
FOD	Foreign Object Damage
fpm	Feet per minute
fps	Feet per second
FSD	Full Scale Development
FY	Fiscal Year
GDP	Gross Domestic Product
GE	General Electric
GL	Georgia Lockheed (Lockheed Georgia Company design prefix)
GOR	General Operational Requirement
GS	General Specification (Douglas Aircraft Company usage)
GTOW	Gross Take-Off Weight
GT	Global Transport
GRT	Global Range Transport
HAWSTOL	High-Speed All Wing STOL (Northrop Grumman)
HEETE	Highly Efficient Embedded Turbine Engine
HIBRID	Higher Bypass Ratio Inlet Development
HOW	'Hercules On Water'
HS	Hawker Siddeley Ltd
HSL	High Speed Lifter (Sikorsky)
HTTB	High Technology Test Bed (Lockheed C-130 project)
HWB	Hybrid Wing Body
IADS	Innovative Aircraft Design Studies
IAV	Inter-theatre Air Vehicle
ICBM	Intercontinental Ballistic Missile
INVENT	Integrated Energy Management (engineering technology project)
IOC	Initial Operating Capability
INVENT	Integrated Energy Management
IR	Infrared
IRBM	Intermediate Range Ballistic Missile
JATO	Jet Assisted Take-Off
JHL	Joint Heavy Lift
JMENS	Joint Mission Element Need Statement
JVX	Joint Vertical, Experimental (programme that became MV-22 Osprey tilt-rotor)
kN	KiloNewton
kW	Kilowatt
LG	Lockheed Georgia (Lockheed Georgia Company design prefix)
LAAD	(Rockwell International) Los Angeles Aircraft Division
LEA	Long Endurance Aircraft
LFC	Laminar Flow Control
LG	Lockheed Georgia (design designation prefix)
LIT	Light Intra-Theatre Transport
LST	Light STOL Transport
LTV	Ling-Temco-Vought [Corporation]
LWF	Light Weight Fighter
MAC	Military Airlift Command
MAPS	Multiple Application Prop-fan Studies
MATS	Military Air Transport Service
MDC	McDonnell Douglas Corporation
MDD	Material Development Decision
MENS	Mission Element Needs Statement

MI	Mock-up Inspection
MIB	[Army] Mechanised Infantry Brigade
MMVX	Multi Mission Heavier Than Air Experimental (Navy)
mph	Miles per hour
MOL	Manned Orbital Laboratory
MOU	Memorandum of Understanding
MPLE	Multi-Purpose Long Endurance
MPLEA	Multi-purpose Long Endurance Aircraft
MPSNA	Multi-Purpose Subsonic Naval Aircraft
MR	Mission Requirements
MRSA	Multi-Role Strategic Aircraft (Lockheed C-5 derivative)
MRTT	Multi-Role Tanker Transport (Airbus A330 derivative)
MSFC	Marshall Space Flight Center
MST	Medium STOL Transport
MX	Missile-X (later the LGM-118 Peacekeeper)
N	Newton
NAA	North American Aviation
NaK	Sodium/Potassium (nuclear reactor working fluid)
NAR	North American Rockwell (successor corporation to NAA)
NACA	National Advisory Committee for Aeronautics
NADC	Naval Air Development Center
NAS	Naval Air Station
NASA	National Aeronautics and Space Administration
NATC	Naval Air Test Centre
NATO	North Atlantic Treaty Organisation
NATS	Naval Air Transport Service
NDAA	Non-Development Airlift Aircraft
NEPA	Nuclear Energy for the Propulsion of Aircraft
nmi	Nautical mile
NuERA	Nuclear [power] for Extended Range Aircraft (Westinghouse reactor programme)
OEI	One Engine Inoperative
OIPT	Overarching Integrated Product Team
ONR	Office of Naval Research
OPEC	Organisation of Petroleum Exporting Countries
OWE	Operating Weight Empty
OSD	Office of the Secretary of Defense
OSTR	Optimum Speed Tilt Rotor (Karem)
P&W	Pratt & Whitney
PACCS	Post-Attack Command and Control System
PDP	Project Definition Phase
PL	Powered Lift
psi	Pounds per square inch
QEC	Quick Engine Change
QMR	Qualitative Material Requirement
QOR	Qualitative Operating Requirement
QTR	Quad Tilt Rotor (Bell-Boeing)
QUESTOL	Quiet STOL [aircraft]
RCEE	Revolutionary Configurations for Energy Efficiency
RCS	Radar Cross Section
REN	Reversing Ejector Nozzle
RERP	[C-5] Reliability and Re-engining Program
RFI	Request For Information
RFP	Request For Proposal
RFQ	Request For Quote
RI	Rockwell International (Successor corporation to NAR)
ROC	Required Operational Capability
RPV	Remotely Piloted Vehicle
rpm	Revolutions per minute
SAC	Strategic Air Command
SACD	Speed Agile Concept Demonstrator
Saro	Saunders Roe Ltd
SAVE	SMOCA Air Vehicle Enclosure
SCA	Shuttle Carrier Aircraft
SCS	Sea Control Ship
SL	Sea level
SLBM	Submarine Launched Ballistic Missile
SLEP	Service Life Extension Program
SMOCA	SO/LIC Mission Oriented Combat Aircraft
SNECMA	Société Nationale d'Études et de Construction de Moteurs d'Aviation (National Company for the Research and Construction of Aviation Engines, now Safran Engines)
SOCOM	Special Operations Command
SOF	Special Operations Forces
SOFTA	Special Operations Forces Transport Aircraft
SO/LIC	Special Operations Low-Intensity Conflict
SOR	Specific Operational Requirement
SOTAC	Special Operations Tactical Air Carrier
SPO	System Program Office
SR	Study Requirement
SRAM	Short-Range Attack Missile
STOL	Short Take-Off and Landing
SSBN	Submarine, Ballistic Missile, Nuclear-powered
SSD	Systems Study Directive
SSME	Space Shuttle Main Engine

SST	Supersonic Transport
SSTOL	Super Short Take-Off and Landing
STOVL	Short Take-Off and Vertical Landing
TAC	Tactical Air Command
TACCO	Tactical Coordinator
TACAMO	TAke Charge And Move Out [Navy]
TDN	Temporary Design Number (Lockheed)
TEMPO	Transonic Efficiency Mobility Platform Optimization
TOW	Take-off Weight
TTLA	Transverse Thrust Lift Augmentation
UHB	Ultra High Bypass
UHF	Ultra High Frequency
ULD	Unit Load Device (standard airline cargo container)
UNREP	Underway REPlenishment
USA	United States Army
USAAC	United States Army Air Corps
USAAF	United States Army Air Force
USAF	United States Air Force
USB	Upper Surface Blowing
USCG	United States Coast Guard
USMC	United States Marine Corps
USN	United States Navy
USSOCOM	Special Operations Command
VERTREP	VERTical REPlenishment
VHF	Very High Frequency
VHR	Vought Hiller Ryan (Consortium)
VLF	Very Low Frequency
VLS	Volume-Loadability-Speed [C-130 Version]
VOD	Vertical On-board Delivery
VRC	[Navy] Fixed Wing Cargo Composite [Squadron]
VSS	V/STOL Support Ship
VTOL	Vertical Take-Off and Landing
V/STOL	Vertical/Short Take-Off and Landing
WADC	Wright Air Development Center
WBS	Wide-Body STOL [C-130 Version]
WOD	Wind-over-deck
WS	Weapon System
WWABNCP	World-Wide Airborne Command Post
X	Experimental
XTF	X^2 Technology Crane (Sikorsky)

Terms

Ailerons	Hinged surfaces on the outer trailing sections of the wing, used to control the aircraft in roll
Airfoil or aerofoil	The cross-sectional shape of a wing or other flying surface
Arrester gear	A mechanism for stopping aircraft after landing on an aircraft carrier. It normally consists of three restraining wires, any one of which can be caught by a hook lowered from beneath the rear fuselage of the aircraft
Aspect ratio	The ratio between the span of the wings and their average chord. A high-aspect-ratio aircraft will have long slender wings; a low aspect ratio will have shorter stubbier ones
Boundary Layer	The thin layer of air next to the surface of the aircraft
Boundary Layer Control	A system of forcing high-pressure air over the wing to keep the airflow following the contour of the airfoil, rather than breaking away to cause drag
Canard	An aircraft configuration in which the horizontal stabiliser is placed ahead of the wings rather than in the normal aft position
Catapult	A launching mechanism employed on aircraft carriers, whereby the aircraft's take-off acceleration is greatly boosted by means a high-pressure steam-driven piston or electromagnetic shuttle, located immediately beneath the forward deck
Chord	The distance between the leading and training edges of the wing
Elevator	A hinged surface on the rear of the horizontal stabiliser (tailplane), used to control the pitch of the aircraft
Empennage	The aft end of the aircraft, consisting of the vertical stabiliser (fin), horizontal stabiliser (tailplane) and their supporting structure
Fairing	An aerodynamically shaped non-load-bearing addition to the aircraft's structure, covering protuberances or linking parts of the airframe to maintain the intended lines of airflow and reduce drag
Flap	A hinged surface on the rear edge of the wing, lowered to increase lift at slow speeds, normally used during take-off and landing
Fowler Flap	An advanced flap arrangement, whereby the flap extends (sliding out from within the wing structure) as well as hinging downwards

Fin	Vertical stabiliser
Fuselage	The body of the aircraft, excluding wings and tail surfaces
Gross weight	The designed maximum weight of the aircraft including fuel, crew and cargo
Horizontal stabiliser	The horizontal surfaces at the rear of the aircraft designed to provide stability in pitch, to which the elevators are normally attached
Nacelle	A non-load-bearing part of the aircraft structure designed to accommodate the engines and their support equipment in a streamlined housing
Payload	The weight of the useful load – cargo or passengers – that can be carried, excluding crew and fuel
Pitch	Rotation of the aircraft about a horizontal axis between the wingtips (i.e. with the nose either rising or falling), normally controlled by deflection of the elevator
Pylon	A streamlined part of the structure carrying or supporting an engine nacelle
Radial engine	A piston engine in which the cylinders are arranged around the crankshaft, like the spokes of a wheel
Roll	Rotation of the aircraft about a horizontal axis between its nose and the tail, normally controlled by differential movement of the ailerons
Rudder	A hinged surface at the rear of the vertical stabiliser, used to control yaw
Tailplane	Another term for the horizontal stabiliser
Turbofan	A jet (gas turbine) engine in which all of the air goes through a fan at the front of the engine but part of the flow then bypasses the compressor, fuel injection/ignition and turbine. Thrust is a combination of both the exhaust from the latter and the fan
Turbojet	A jet (gas turbine) engine in which all of the air passes the compressor, fuel injection/ignition system and turbine, with the thrust being created by the exhaust gases
Turboprop	A gas turbine engine in which the turbine is linked by a driveshaft to a propeller, with only a small amount of residual thrust being provided by the exhaust gases
Undercarriage	Landing gear
Wind-over-deck	The combination of wind speed and ship speed when an aircraft carrier is heading into the wind
Vertical Stabiliser	The vertical surface at the rear of the aircraft designed to provide lateral (weathercock) stability, of which the rudder normally forms part
Yaw	Lateral rotation of the aircraft about a vertical axis through its centre of gravity (i.e. with the nose swinging left or right), normally controlled by the rudder

Units

The units used throughout this book are given in the form in which they originally appeared in the source material. The metric equivalent is also given in each case.

1 inch	= 2.54cm
1 ft	= 0.305cm
1sq ft	= 0.093m^2
1cu ft	= 0.0284m^3
1 mile	= 1.609km
1nmi	= 1.851km
1mph	= 1.609km/h
1kt	= 1.851km/h
1lb	= 0.454kg
1lb/sq ft	= 4.84kg/m^2
1lb thrust	= 4.45N
1hp	=0.746kW

Reference sources and Bibliography

Archives

Air Force Materiel Command History Office, Wright Patterson AFB, Ohio
Air Force Historical Research Agency, Maxwell AFB, AL
American Aviation Historical Society (AAHS), Huntington Beach, CA
Avro Heritage Centre, Manchester, UK
Boeing Company Archives (Boeing content), Bellevue, WA
Boeing Company Archives (Douglas content), Huntington Beach, CA
Glenn L. Martin Maryland Aviation Museum, Middle River, MD
Greater St Louis Air and Space Museum, St Louis, MO
Grumman History Center, Bethpage, NY
Jane and Winfield Arata papers (now accessioned into The Huntington Library, San Marino, CA), courtesy of Martha and Allen Arata
Northrop Grumman Aerospace Sector Archives, Redondo Beach, CA
National Air and Space Museum (NASM), Washington DC
National Archives and Records Administration, College Park, MD (NARA II)
San Diego Air and Space Museum, San Diego, CA
Wright State University Libraries, Special Collections and Archives, Dayton, OH

Bibliography

Anderton, David and Miller, Jay *Boeing Helicopters CH-47 Chinook* (Aerofax)

Andrade, John M. *US Military Aircraft Designations and Serials – 1909 to 1979* (Midland Counties Publications)

Bowers, Peter M. *Boeing Aircraft since 1916: Volume 1* (Putnam)

Bowers, Ray L. *The United States Air Force in Southeast Asia – Tactical Airlift* (Office of Air Force History)

Bradley, Robert E. *Convair Advanced Designs, Secret Projects from San Diego 1923-1962* (Specialty Press)

Breihan, John R., Piet, Stan and Mason, Roger S. *Martin Aircraft 1909-1960* (Narkiewicz // Thompson)

Brown, David A. *The Bell Helicopter Textron Story* (Aerofax)

Cenker, August Jr *Aerospace Technologies of Bell Aircraft Company: A Pictorial History 1935-1985* (AuthorHouse)

Chambers, Joseph R. and Chambers, Mark A. *Radical Wings & Wind Tunnels – Advanced Concepts Tested at NASA Langley* (Specialty Press)

Chong, Tony *Flying Wings & Radical Things: Northrop's Secret Aerospace Projects & Concepts 1939-1994* (Specialty Press)

Converse III, Elliott V. *Rearming for the Cold War 1945-1960 (History of Acquisition in the Department of Defense, Vol I)* (Office of the Secretary of Defense, Historical Office)

Dean, William Patrick, *Ultra-Large Aircraft, 1940-1970 – The Development of Guppy and Expanded Fuselage Transports* (McFarland & Co)

Fails, Lt Col William R., USMC *Marines and Helicopters 1962-1973*, History And Museums Division, (Headquarters, US Marine Corps/US Government Printing Office – GPO)

Fitzgerald, A. Ernest, *The High Priests of Waste*, (W. W. Norton & Company)

Francillon, René J. *Grumman Aircraft since 1929* (Putnam)
— *McDonnell Douglas Aircraft since 1920: Volume 1* (Putnam)
— *McDonnell Douglas Aircraft since 1920: Volume 2* (Putnam)
— *Lockheed Aircraft since 1913* (Putnam)

Futrell, Robert Frank *Ideas, Concept, Doctrine Volume I – Basic Thinking in the United States Air Force 1907-1960* (Air University Press)
— *Volume II – Basic Thinking in the United States Air Force 1907-1960* (Air University Press)

General Electric Company *Eight Decades of Progress – A Heritage of Aircraft Turbine Technology* (GE Aircraft Engines)

Gibson, Chris *On Atlas' Shoulders – RAF Transport Projects since 1945* (Hikoki Publications)

Gorn, Michael H. *Harnessing the Genie: Science and Technology Forecasting for the Air Force 1944-1986 (Air Staff Historical Study)* (Office of Air Force History)

Gunston, Bill *World Encyclopaedia of Aero Engines* (Patrick Stephens Limited)
— *The Development of Jet Turbine Aero Engines, 4th edition* (Haynes North America)

Hager, Roy D. and Vrabel, Deborah *Advanced Turboprop Project*, NASA SP-495 (NASA)

Harding, Stephen *US Army Aircraft since 1947* (Specialty Press)

Holder, Bill and Vadnais, Scott *The 'C' Planes* (Schiffer)

Holley Jr, Irving Benton *Buying Aircraft: Materiel Procurement for the Army Air Forces* (Office of the Chief of Military History, Department of the Army)

Head, Dr William *Reworking the Workhorse – The C-141B Stretch Modification Program – Volume I: Narrative and Appendices*, Office of History WR-ALC/HO (US Air Force)

Hopkins III, Robert S. *Boeing KC-135 Stratotanker – More than just a Tanker* (Midland Publishing)

Hurturk, Kivane *Individual Aircraft History of the 707* (BUCHair) (USA)

Johnson, E. R. *American Military Transport Aircraft Since 1925* (McFarland & Company)

Launius, Roger & Dvorscak, B. J. *The C-5 Galaxy History, Crushing Setbacks and Decisive Achievements*, (Turner Publishing)

Leonard, John M. *The Allison Engine Catalog 1915-2007* (Rolls-Royce Heritage Trust – Allison Branch)

London, Peter *Saunders and Saro Aircraft since 1917* (Putnam)

Miller, Jay *Lockheed Martin's Skunkworks, The Official History (updated edition)* (Midland Publishing)
— *The X-Planes: X-1 to X-45* (Midland Publishing)

Mitchell, Kent A. *Fairchild Aircraft 1926-1987* (Narkiewicz // Thompson)

Newhouse, John *The Sporty Game – The High-Risk Competitive Business of Making and Selling Commercial Airliners* (Alfred A. Knoff)

Norton, Bill (William) *Boeing C-17A Globemaster III (Warbird Tech Series Vol 30)* (Specialty Press)
— *Lockheed Martin C-5 Galaxy (Warbird Tech Series Vol 36)* (Specialty Press)
— *STOL Progenitors: The Technology Path to a Large STOL Aircraft and the C-17A* (American Institute of Aeronautics and Astronautics)
— *Vought/Hiller/Ryan XC-142A Tiltwing VSTOL Transport (Air Force Legends Number 213)* (Ginter Publishing)

Owen, Robert C. *Air Mobility – A Brief History of the American Experience* (Potomac Books, 2013)

Paszek, Lawrence J. *A Guide to Documentary Sources* (Office of Air Force History)

Pearcy, Arthur *Flying the Frontiers – NACA and NASA Experimental Aircraft* (Naval Institute Press)

St Peter, James *The History of Gas Turbine Engine Development in the United States: A Tradition of Excellence* (The International Gas Turbine Institute of the American Society of Mechanical Engineers)

Pomeroy, Steven A. *An Untaken Road – Strategy, Technology, and the Hidden History of America's Mobile ICBMs* (Naval Institute Press)

Rice, Berkeley *The C-5A Scandal: An Inside Story of the Military-Industrial Complex* (Houghton Mifflin)

Rose, Bill *Secret Projects: Military Space Technology* (Midland)

Staszak, Richard and Staehr, Nancy *Military Transports In Detail, Volume 1* (Air Transport Publications)

Steoffen, Arthur A. C. *McDonnell Douglas DC-10 and KC10 Extender, Widebody Workhorses* (Aerofax)

Sterling, Robert *Boeing: Legend & Legacy* (St Martins)

Thigpen, Jerry L. *The Praetorian STARship* (Air University Press)

Thum, Marcell and Thum, Gladys *Airlift: The Story of the Military Airlift Command* (Dodd, Mead & Company)

United States Congress, Senate Committee on Armed Services *Authorization for Military Procurement, Research and Development, Fiscal Year 1970, and Reserve Strength – Hearings on S. 1192, S. 2407 and S. 2546*, 91st Congress, 1st Session, Part 2 (of 2 parts) (US Government Printing Office – GPO)

Weinert, Richard P. Jr *A History Of Army Aviation – 1950-1962* (Office of the Command Historian, United States Army Training and Doctrine Command)

Williams, Nicholas M. *Aircraft of the United States Military Air Transport Service* (Midland)
The Jet Engine: Rolls-Royce (Wiley)

Winpress, John K. and Newberry, Conrad F, *The YC-14 STOL Prototype: Its Design, Development, and Flight Test* (American Institute of Aeronautics and Astronautics (AIAA)

Reports and Papers (in chronological order)

Studies of Fourteen Nuclear-Powered Airplanes, Hutton, J. L. et al, Fairchild Airplane and Engine Company, NEPA-1639, 1 September 1952

Results of Design Preliminary Study of ANP Logistic Carrier Aircraft, Douglas Aircraft Company, Report SM-19106, 15 May 1955

Model 1875 Interim Report Chart Presentation, Douglas Aircraft Company, Report SM-19233, 1 August 1955

The Fairchild M-216 Flying Lighter for Adequate Carrier-On-Board Delivery, Fairchild Aircraft Division, MSR-1, 1 March 1956

Ducted Propeller Assault Transport Summary Report, Bell Aircraft Company, D181-945-001, 15 May 1956

Ducted Propeller Assault Transport, Bell Aircraft Company, D181-945-002, 15 May 1956

Final Summary Report, Propelloplane Transport Study, Hiller Helicopters, 15 May 1956

Carrier On Board Utility Assault Aircraft Operations Analysis, Douglas Aircraft Company, Report SM-22652, 19 November 1956

Carrier-On-Board Utility Assault Aircraft Technical Data and Summary Report, Douglas Aircraft Company, Report SM-22646, 19 November 1956

The Fairchild 'Provider' in Fleet Supply, Fairchild Aircraft Division, OER-1102, 1 December 1956

Model 1940 Short and Medium Range Transport Airplane, Douglas Aircraft Company, Report SM-22672, 1 February 1957

Model 1940-A Short and Medium Range Utility Transport, Douglas Aircraft Company, Report SM-22673, 1 February 1957

The Model 1906 for the F.E.A.F. Combat Cargo Command 315th Air Division, Douglas Aircraft Company, Report SM-22722, 12 February 1957

Proposal - Model 1906C-1 AEW Aircraft, Douglas Aircraft Company, Report SM-22760, 26 July 1957

Model 2007 Carrier On-Board Delivery Aircraft, Douglas Aircraft Company, Report SM-22927, 20 September 1957

Study, Model 1906A ASW Application, Douglas Aircraft Company, Report SM-22761, 15 November 1957

Douglas Model 1906 Series Aircraft, Model 1906B Utility Transport, Douglas Aircraft Company, Report SM-23106, 15 March 1958

Model 820 Long Range Military Air-Logistics Systems Progress Report from April 1 to July 1 1958, Boeing Aircraft Company, D2-2895, 1 July 1958

Boeing Cargo Jets - 735 - Cargo Version of the 707, Boeing Aircraft Company Transport Division, D6-1863, July 1958

Model 2042 Army Assault Aircraft and Carrier On-Board Delivery, Douglas Aircraft Company, Report SM-23249, 14 August 1958

Development Program for a Long-Range Military Air-Logistics System, Boeing Aircraft Company, D2-3022, 22 August 1958

Presentation Results of Aircraft for the Supply, Assault and Support Mission, Douglas Aircraft Company, Report SM-23313, 1 October 1958

Boeing Transport and Wichita Divisions Joint Presentation - VSTOL Summary, Boeing Airplane Company, D3-2768, 9 December 1959

SR175 VTOL STOL Study Final Report (to Study Requirement 175), Boeing Transport Division and Wichita Division, Report D6-5280, 25 February 1960

Preliminary Feasibility Study of the Transportation of the Saturn S-IV Stage by C-133 Airplane, Douglas Aircraft Company, Report SM-30380, 26 August 1960

BLC 741-6, Boeing Transport Division, Report D6-5690, 1 September 1960

Multi-Purpose Long Endurance Aircraft - Program Plan and Cost, Boeing Airplane Company, Aero-Space Division, D2-7102, September 1960

Multi-Purpose Long Endurance Aircraft - Technical Report SSD 7993-17531, Boeing Airplane Company, Wichita Division, D2-7102-2, September 1960

NASA Conference on V/STOL Aircraft - Compilation of Papers, NASA Langley Research Center, 17 November 1960

Verticraft, enclosure to letter VC-3101, Verticraft Corporation, 30 March 1961

Standard Aircraft Characteristics Model D-828 VTOL Transport, Douglas Aircraft Company, 31 March 1961

Standard Aircraft Characteristics Model D-829 VTOL Transport, Douglas Aircraft Company, 31 March 1961

Summary Report Tri-Service VTOL Transport Vanguard Model 30, Schneider, J. J., Vanguard Air and Marine Corporation, Report 30-X-1, 31 March 1961

Proposal for a Peripheral-Jet VTOL Aircraft, The House of Kraft Nuclear & Consulting Engineers, 1 April 1961

Tri-Service VTOL Transport Aircraft Technical Summary Report, North American Aviation, Columbus Division, NA61H-102, 1 April 1961

Tri-Service VTOL Transport Proposal Summary, North American Aviation, Columbus Division, NA-61H-101, 1 April 1961

Proposal for a Tri-Service VTOL Prototype Transport Aircraft, Boeing Wichita, D3-3900-1, 3 April 1961

M-351 Proposed Low Speed Control System Investigation for Tri-Service VTOL Assault Transport, Copeland, J. and Harkleroad, E., Fairchild Aircraft and Missiles Division, R351-001, 3 April 1961

Grumman Design 242 Tri-Service VTOL Transport - Part 1 - Proposal Summary, Grumman Aircraft Engineering Company, PDR-242-1, 3 April 1961

VTOL Tri-Service Transport Model 175, McDonnell/Canadair, Report 8070, 3 April 1961

Tri-Service VTOL Prototype Transport - Engineering Proposal Part 1, Sikorsky Aircraft, SER 50145, 3 April 1961

Proposal for the Development of a Vertical Take-off and Landing Aircraft, Prewitt Plastics Company; Atlantic Research Corporation, 4 April 1961

Breguet 941 VSTOL (sic) Transport Detail Specification for Tri-Service VTOL Prototype Transport Aircraft, Fowler, Harlan D., 9 April 1961

Boeing Vertol Model-137 Detail Specification PR-378-2, 10 April 1961

D252 Tri-Service VTOL Aircraft, Bell Helicopter Company, D252-099-001, 14 April 1961

Proposal for Tri-Service VTOL Prototype Transport Aircraft - The Concept/The Plan/The Capability, Boeing Wichita, D3-3900-16, 19 April 1961

Studies of a C-123 Replacement Aircraft, Douglas Aircraft Company, Report LB-30579, 28 April 1961

Study of Air Transportation for Saturn S-I and S-IV Stages by C-133 Aircraft, Douglas Aircraft Company, Report LB-30589, 15 May 1961

A Flight Examination of Operating Problems of V/STOL Aircraft in STOL-Type Landing and Approach, Innis, Robert C. and Quigley, Hervey C., NASA, D-862, 1 June 1961

Summary Report Saturn Air Trailer, Vought Aeronautics – Division of Chance Vought Corporation, Report 122.1, 16 June 1961, revised 4 December 1961

Advanced C-135, Boeing, Report D6-8513, September 1961

D2064A Extended Range Tri-Service VTOL Transport, Bell Aerosystems Company, D2064A-953002, September 1961

Advanced STOL Assault & Logistics Transport Model 2217, Douglas Aircraft Company, Report LB-30684, 12 October 1961

C-133 Replacement Studies, Douglas Aircraft Company, Report LB-30759, 28 December 1961

V/STOL C-142, Hiller/Vought/Ryan, Report B-53, April 1962

Aircraft Nuclear Propulsion Application Studies, Comasser, S., General Electric Nuclear Materials and Propulsion Operation, APEX-910, 30 April 1962

STOL Turboprop Assault Transport Model 2252, Douglas Aircraft Company, Report LB-30959, 20 July 1962

Model 743 10-Ton V/STOL Assault Transport, Boeing, Report D6-(), 1 December 1962

Review of Manned Aircraft Nuclear Propulsion Program, Comptroller General of the United States, B-146759, 1 February 1963

Parametric Aircraft Design Study CX-4 (Model 748), The Boeing Company, Transport Division, Report D6-4853, 20 February 1963

Breguet S.T.O.L. Transport 941, S. A. Des Ateliers D'Aviation Louis Breguet, Notice 941-2A, May 1963

VTOL Assault Transport Models 743-100-81 and -85, Boeing Airplane Division, Report D6-8571, May 1963

History [of the C-141] Vol III Supporting Documents, Tab III-4, Historical Summary of the C-141 (SOR-182), USAF, AFHRA Reel K3076, 16 May 1963

Loading Demonstration – CX-4 Mockup (Douglas Model D-902) Heavy Logistics Support Aircraft, Douglas Aircraft Company, Report LB-44271, 8 July 1963

Carrier Suitability of Model 188E, McDonnell Aircraft Company, Report B029, 21 September 1964

Mac Prototype Tour Of The United States From 12 June Through 8 July 1964, McDonnell Aircraft Company, Report A952, 22 July 1964

Global Transport Development Status Report – CX-HLS Supportability, The Boeing Company/Airplane Division, Report D6-1103-1, October 1964

Design Feasibility Study of a Large Logistic Transport, Tuttle, C. R., General Dynamics/Convair, ERR SD-89-024, December 1964

System 410A Heavy Logistic Support System C-5A, Project Definition Phase Final Report, Part I – Summary Report Vol 1, Technical and Management, Douglas Aircraft Group, C-5 Division, Report 50000, 24 April 1965

CX-6 Final Report V/STOL Assault Transport Support System Study, Boeing, Report D6-16159-23, 1 August 1965

CX6 V/STOL Assault Transport System – Support System Study – Technical Report, Boeing, Report D6-16294, 1 June 1966

C-5 Logistic Support, The Boeing Company, Airplane Division, Report D6-11111, 18 June 1966

C-5A Program History, The Boeing Company, Airplane Division, Report D6-14011-1, 28 June 1966

SAC Refuelling Tankers for the 1970 Requirements, The Boeing Company, Commercial Airplane Division, Report D6-58246, 1 May 1967

The Lockheed C-5 – Case Study in Aircraft Design, Garrard, Wilford C., American Institute of Aeronautics and Astronautics, AIAA Professional Study Series, 1970

STOL Tactical Aircraft Investigation, The Boeing Company, Military Airplane Systems Division, D162-10050-1, 1 March 1971

Proposal For AMST Prototype Aircraft With Cold Thrust Augmentation Vol I Technical and Tradeoffs, Bell Aerospace Company, Division of Textron, D7436-953001, 1 March 1972

Proposal – Advanced Medium STOL Transport Prototype, Vol I, Technical Approach and Tradeoff Analysis, McDonnell Douglas, MDC J5363-1, 31 March 1972

Carrier Onboard Delivery C-9 (COD) Technical Data and Development Plan, McDonnell Douglas, Proposal 72D-37ST, 30 August 1972

General Accounting Office Staff Study – C-5 Aircraft, GAO Staff, US General Accounting Office, Report 713058, 1 February 1973

DC-10 Rivet Joint Program Flight Crew Training, McDonnell Douglas, MDC, J4375, 30 March 1973

STOL Tactical Aircraft Investigation Externally Blown Flap, Vol I, Configuration Definition, Owens, Herschel et al, Air Force Flight Dynamics Laboratory, AD-772 738, 1 April 1973

STOL Tactical Aircraft Investigation Volume 1, Configuration Definition, Herbert, J. Jr et al, Convair Aerospace Division of General Dynamics Corporation, Air Force Flight Dynamics Laboratory, Air Force Systems Command, AFFDL-TR-73-21-Vol 1, 1 May 1973

YC-14 Configuration Description, Rev D, The Boeing Company, D748-10028-1, 3 December 1973

Space Shuttle, Space Tug, Apollo-Soyuz Test Project -1974, Status Report for the Committee on Science and Astronautics, US House of Representatives, 1 February 1974

Multimission Large Freighter Airplanes – Visit of the House Appropriations Committee Surveys and Investigations Staff, Bower, George N., The Boeing Company, 28 March 1974

Feasibility Study to Consider an Aircraft for the Air Launch and Air Transportation of the Space Shuttle Orbiter, Turbo-Three Corporation, April 1974

C-15 Advanced Medium STOL Transport of the Imperial Iranian Air Force Tactical Airlift Modernization, McDonnell Douglas, 1 August 1974

Large Freighter Aircraft Presentation, The Boeing Company, Commercial Airplane Division, Report D6-22410, 22 August 1974

Design Concepts for Future Cargo Aircraft, Lange, R. H., Lockheed-Georgia Company, AIAA Paper 95-306, February 1975

C-15 SASH STOL Airborne Surgical Hospital, McDonnell Douglas, MDC J4490, 24 February 1975

Design Definition Study of a Lift/Cruise Fan Technology V/STOL Aircraft, Volume II, Technology Aircraft, Cavage, Robert L. et al, NASA, June 1975

Design Definition Study of NASA/Navy Cruise Fan V/STOL Aircraft Vol I – Summary of Navy Multimission Aircraft, Cavage, Robert et al, NASA, CR 137695, July 1975

Design Definition Study of NASA/Navy Cruise Fan V/STOL Aircraft Vol. II – Summary Report of Technology Aircraft, Cavage, Robert et al, NASA, CR 137696, July 1975

Aerodynamic Characteristics of a Large Aircraft to Transport Space Shuttle Orbiter or Other External Payloads, Paulson, John W. Jr, NASA, TN-D-7962, August 1975

747 Advanced Military Applications – Summary, Boeing Aerospace Company, D180-19033-1R1, November 1975

Three-Engine Two-Fan Navy Multimission V/STOL Aircraft Considerations, Ford, J. C., Society of Automotive Engineers (SAE), 751104, November 1975

Airborne Minuteman, Kolega, Daniel J. and Leger, James E., American Institute of Aeronautics and Astronautics, AIAA, 75-1388, November 1975

Technical and Economic Assessment of Span-Distributed Loading Cargo Aircraft Concepts Final Report, Boeing/NASA, CR-144963, June 1976

Technical and Economic Assessment of Span-Distributed Loading Cargo Aircraft Concepts, Johnson, William M. et al, Lockheed/NASA, CR-145034, August 1976

The United States Marine Corps KC-15 Aerial Tanker, McDonnell Douglas, B6-1270, 1 September 1976

Executive Summary to C-15 AMST – Key to Tactical and Strategic Airlift Modernization Cost Savings, McDonnell Douglas, MDCJ 4545 Rev A, 1 November 1976

Preliminary Feasibility Analysis C-XX Concept, The Boeing Company, 1 November 1976

Advanced Strategic Airlift Systems (Progress Report), Boeing Commercial Airplane Company, Report D6-45132, November 1976

Follow-On Studies for Design Definition of a Lift/Cruise Fan Technology V/STOL Airplane, Boeing Military V/STOL Group Final Report Vol I, NASA, CR-137976, January 1977

Innovative Aircraft Design Study, Task II – Nuclear Aircraft Concepts, Craven, Eugene P. et al, Aeronautical Systems Division, USAF, LG77ER0008, 11 April 1977

YC-15 USAF/McDonnell Douglas Worldwide Airlifter for Peace, McDonnell Douglas, B7-622, 1 May 1977

2 for 1 – The Boeing Advanced Tanker/Cargo Aircraft, Boeing Aerospace Company, D180-20626-1, 1 May 1977

Low Speed Aerodynamic Characteristics of Vectored Thrust V/STOL Transport with Two Lift/Cruise Fans, Renselaer, Dirk J., NASA, CR 152029, 1 July 1977

Parametric Study of Advanced Long-Range Military/Commercial Cargo Transports, Lange, R. H., Lockheed-Georgia Co, AIAA 77-1221, August, 1977

Technical and Economic Assessment of Swept Wingspan-Distributed Load Concepts for Civil and Military Air Cargo Transports, Boeing/NASA, CR-145229, October 1977

YC-15 Development and Test Highlights, Lane, John P., McDonnell Douglas, Paper 6665, 14 October 1977

Nuclear Bi-Brayton System for Aircraft Nuclear Propulsion Study, Thompson, R. E. et al, Westinghouse Electric Corporation, Advanced Energy Systems Divisions, WAES-TNR-234, March 1978

Tactical Airlift Study, Boeing, D745-10115-1, The Boeing Company, 13 April 1975

Studies of Advanced Transport Aircraft, Nagel, A. J., NASA, TM, 78697, May 1978

Innovative Aircraft Design Study – 1977 – Volume 1, Barber, E. A. et al, The Boeing Aerospace Company, D-180-24713-1, July 1978

Cargo Logistics Airlift Systems Study (CLASS) Vol 1, Burby, R. J. and Kuhlman, W. H., NASA, CR-158912, 1 October 1978

Cargo Logistics Airlift Systems Study (CLASS) Vol 2, Burby, R. J. and Kuhlman, W. H., NASA, CR-158913, 1 October 1978

Cargo Logistics Airlift Systems Study (CLASS) Vol 5 (Summary), Burby, R. J. and Kuhlman, W. H., NASA, CR-158951, 1 October 1978

Type A V/STOL Propulsion System Development, Glasgow, E. R. and Skarshaug, R. E., American Institute of Aeronautics and Astronautics, AIAA, 79-1287, June 1979

Identifying Desirable Design Features for the C-XX Aircraft: A Systems Approach, Mikolowsky, W. T. et al, American Institute of Aeronautics and Astronautics, AIAA, 79-1796, 1 August 1979

Application of Powered High Lift Systems to STOL Aircraft Design, Frederick Donald Ameel,

Lieutenant Commander, United States Navy, Naval Postgraduate School, September 1979

Technology Options for an Enhanced Air Cargo System, Winston, Mathew M., NASA, TM, 80173, 1 October 1979

Final Report of the Defense Science Board Task Force on V/STOL Aircraft, Office of the Under Secretary of Defense for Research and Engineering, AD-A201049, November 1979

Future Multi-Mission Transport Aircraft: Requirements and Design Possibilities, Lange, R. H. and Mikolowsky, W. T., Society of Automotive Engineers (SAE), 791097, 1 December 1979

Design Options Study – Final Report, The Boeing Company, The Boeing Military Airplane Company, Advanced Airplane Branch, D180-24258-3, 29 February 1980

EC-X PACCS Replacement Aircraft, McDonnell Douglas, S-80-1275, 1 May 1980

Design Options Study Final Report: Volume IV, Detailed Analysis Supporting Appendices, Lockheed-Georgia Company, LG80ER0009, September 1980

Study of an Advanced Transport Airplane Design Concept Known as FLATBED, Smethers, R. G. et al, Lockheed-Georgia Company, NASA Contractor Report 159337, October 1980

Design Options Study Vol I: Executive Summary, Lange, R. H., Lockheed Georgia Company, Report LG8ER0006, 1 September 1980

Design Features of a Sea Based Multipurpose V/STOL, STOVL and STOL Aircraft in a Support Role for the US Navy, Bradfield, G. W., American Institute of Aeronautics and Astronautics, AIAA-81-2650, December 1981

Advanced Military Spaceflight Capability (AMSC) Earth-To-Orbit Vehicle Overview, Rockwell International Space Transportation & Systems Group, SSV82-85, 1982

KC-135 Winglet Program Review, Symposium Proceedings, NASA, NASA Conference Publication 2211, 1982

Aerodynamic Development for Efficient Military Cargo Transports, Webber, G. W., American Institute of Aeronautics and Astronautics, AIAA, 83-1822, 1 July 1983

A Split Fan Concept for a Medium Speed V/STOL, Waller, J. D. and Yackle, A. R., Society of Automotive Engineers, SAE, 831548, 1 October 1983

V/STOL Concepts in the United States – Past Present, and Future, Neims, W. P. and Anderson, S. B., NASA, TM, 85938, 1 April 1984

The United States Air Force in Southeast Asia – Tactical Airlift, Bowers, Ray, L., Office of Air Force History, USAF, 1984

Tasks of Hercules, Moss, R. A., Lockheed-Georgia Company, MER, 418E, 1 June 1984

EC-17 Study for Worldwide Airborne Command Post Aircraft, McDonnell Douglas, MDC, J9589, 12 November 1984

Near-Term Application of Modern Propulsion Technology to a Tactical Transport, Ryle, D. M. Jr (Lockheed-Georgia Co), Perkins, F. W. (United Technologies Corp) and Eddy, J. L. (General Electric Co) AIAA-84-2506, October 1984

EC-17 Worldwide Command Post, McDonnell Douglas, MDC-K0232, 1 February 1985

Augmentor Wing Powered Lift Technology Affordable Alternatives To Enhance Tactical Airlift Capability, Mcgee, Lt Col John E., Canadian AF, USAF Air War College, Air University AU-AWC-86-143, 1986

Multiple-Purpose Subsonic Naval Aircraft (MPSNA) Multiple Application Prop-fan Study (MAPS), Winkeljohn, D. M. and Mayrand, C. H., NASA, CR-175096, 1 March 1986

Multiple-Purpose Subsonic Naval Aircraft (MPSNA) – Multiple Application Prop-fan Study (MAPS), Engelbeck, R. M. et al, NASA, CR-175104, 1 September 1986

AMSS Progress in Design and System Definition, Northrop Corporation, NB-86-245, October 1986

VSTOL Design Implications for Tactical Transports, Wollaston, James W. and Brown, Derrell L., Society of Automotive Engineers, 872338, 1987

'The 21st Century Tactical Airlifter', Meese, J. R. and Millett, M. L. Jr, Boeing Wichita, 1987

Advanced Turboprop Project, Hager, Roy D. and Vrabel, Deborah, NASA, SP-495, 1988

Advanced Technology Tactical Transport (ATTT), SRS Technologies, AD-A227 498, 1988

History of the KC-10A Aircraft Acquisition, Holubin, Thomas E., Air Command and Staff College, 88-1260, 1 April 1988

Multiple Purpose Subsonic Naval Aircraft (MPSNA) Multiple Application Prop-fan Study (MAPS), Dannenhoffer, N. et al, NASA, CR-179252, November 1988

Evolutionary Aspects of Large Sweptwing Aircraft, Steiner, John E., Boeing Commercial Airplanes, 26 October 1989

Special Operations Aircraft Design Study – Technical Report, Weir, Thomas J., Northrop Corporation, NOR 90-37, 1 April 1990

The Study Approach and Perceived Needs for an Advanced Theater Transport', Vukmir, Vladimir, Air Force Systems Command, 1 May 1990

SMOCA – SO/LIC Mission Oriented Combat Aircraft, Northrop Corporation, NB 90-95, 1 November 1990

Special Operation Aircraft Design Study Technical Report, Final Report for Period July 1990 to December 1991, Weir, Thomas J., Northrop Corporation, NOR 91-37, February 1991

Crew Escape Technologies (CREST) Mission Area Requirements Study, Current and Future Crew Escape Requirements, North American Aircraft, Rockwell International Corporation, Air Force Systems Command, AL-TR-1992-0183 (NA-92-42), 1 February 1992

C-17 Globemaster III Technical Description and Planning Guide, McDonnell Douglas, MDC, 96K0018, 1 August 1996

Design And Development History Of The Canadair CL-84 V/STOL Tilt-Wing Aircraft, Upton, Bill, Canadian Aviation Museum, 1994

Expanding the National Airlift Fleet: The Quest for a Civil-Military Transport, Zadalis, Timothy M., School of Advanced Airpower, Air University, USAF, 1 May 1997

Military Aircraft and Aircraft Procurement: The Case of the C-5, Knaack, Marcelle Size, Air Force History & Museums Program, AFD-120916-007, 1 August 1998

The Chronological History of the C-5 Galaxy, Leland, Dr John W. and Wilcoxan, Kathryn A., Office of History Air Mobility Command, USAF, 1 May 2003

UK V/STOL Transport Aircraft Concepts of the 20th Century, Hirschberg, Michael J and Pryce, Michael J, American Helicopter Society, presented April 2008

Flow-Field Measurement of a Hybrid Wing Body Model with Blown Flaps, Lin, John C, Jones, Gregory S, and Allan, Brian G; Westra, Bryan W and Collins, Scott W and Zeune, Cale H, American Institute of Aeronautics and Astronautics, AIAA 2008-6718, August 2008

An Overview of the Air Force's Speed Agile Concept Demonstration Program, Zuene, Cale, January 2013

Low Speed Powered Lift Testing of a Transonic Cruise Efficient STOL Military Transport, Barberie, Fred et al, American Institute of Aeronautics and Astronautics, AIAA 2013-1099, January 2013

Lockheed Super Hercules, Lockheed Aircraft Corporation Georgia Division, Marietta, Georgia, GELAC-MSHB-AF-5901, undated

747F Near Term Airlifter, Boeing Airplane Company, undated

Boeing Model Numbers (abridged), Boeing Airplane Company, D-337, undated

Boeing Model Records Models 485 -700, Boeing, D-4500 Book 18, undated

990 Apollo [Wind Tunnel Report], General Dynamics Convair, CVAL 340, undated

Model 738 [tri-fold brochure, marked as C-135C], Boeing, D6-8510, undated

747 Air Launched Cruise Missile System Concept, The Boeing Aerospace Company, D180-17990-2, undated

Advanced Tactical Transport, Boeing Military Airplanes [Wichita], [brochure] 2885K3549, undated

"A" V/STOL Integrated Weapon System – Grumman Design 698, Grumman, undated

High-Speed-Ratio STOL Aircraft Design Study – Model 221 Summary Report, Fairchild Engine and Airplane Company – Aircraft Division R221-001, undated

Lockheed C-141 Versatility, Lockheed Georgia Company, undated

Tilt-Wing Applications, Parkin, Blaine (General Dynamics-Convair) and Bernstein, Saul (Canadair Limited), undated

Journals (as referenced in the text)

Air and Space Smithsonian Magazine

Aviation Week and Space Technology

Flight and *Flight International*

Journal of the American Aviation Historical Society

Naval Institute Proceedings

Websites (addresses current at time of writing)

Aerospace Projects Review: http://www.aerospaceprojectsreview.com/

Aerospace Projects Review Patreon: https://www.patreon.com/user?u=197906

Designation Systems: http://www.designation-systems.net

The Secret Projects Forum: https://www.secretprojects.co.uk

The Space Review: http://www.thespacereview.com/index.html*

Of special note are four articles on The Space Review by Dwayne Day, entitled *Fire in the Sky: the Air Launched Sortie Vehicle*

Part One: http://www.thespacereview.com/article/1569/1

Part Two: http://www.thespacereview.com/article/1580/1

Part Three: http://www.thespacereview.com/article/1591/1

Part Four: http://www.thespacereview.com/article/1608/1

Index

General index

Aircraft and design proposals index (arranged by manufacturer)